Frontier Illinois

A History of the Trans-Appalachian Frontier

Walter Nugent and Malcolm Rohrbough, general editors

Andrew L. Cayton. *Frontier Indiana*

R. Douglas Hurt. *The Ohio Frontier: Crucible of the Old Northwest, 1720–1830*

Mark Wyman. *The Wisconsin Frontier*

Frontier
Illinois

JAMES E. DAVIS

INDIANA UNIVERSITY PRESS   BLOOMINGTON & INDIANAPOLIS

This book is a publication of

Indiana University Press
601 N. Morton Street
Bloomington, Indiana 47404-3797 USA

www.indiana.edu/~iupress

Telephone orders   800-842-6796
Fax orders   812-855-7931
Orders by e-mail   iuporder@indiana.edu

© 1998 by James E. Davis

The paper used in this publication meets the minimum
requirements of American National Standard for
Information Sciences—Permanence of Paper for Printed
Library Materials, ANSI Z39.48–1984.

Manufactured in the United States of America

Library of Congress Cataloging-in-Publication Data
Davis, James Edward, date.
Frontier Illinois / James E. Davis.
p.   cm. — (A history of the trans-Appalachian
frontier)
Includes bibliographical references and index.
ISBN 0-253-33423-3 (alk. paper)
1. Illinois—History—1778–1865. 2. Illinois—History—to
1778. 3. Frontier and pioneer life—Illinois. I. Title II.
Series.
F545.D38 1998
977.3'03—dc21   98-8070

ISBN 0-253-21406-8 (pbk : alk. paper)

2   3   4   5   6   05   04   03   02   01   00

☙ Contents

☙ Illustrations

☙ List of Maps

Foreword

For most Americans, the phrase "the American West" conjures up the western half of the nation. From the Great Plains across the Rockies and the Intermontane Plateaus to the Pacific Ocean came a flood of popular images, from trappers, cowboys, miners, and homesteading families to the "Marlboro Man" and country-western music. This has been "the West" since the California Gold Rush and the migration of '49ers propelled this region into the national consciousness.

But it was not always so. There was an earlier American West, no less vivid and dramatic. Here the fabled figures were not John Charles Frémont but Daniel Boone, not Geronimo but Tecumseh, not Calamity Jane but Rachel Jackson, not "Buffalo Bill" Cody but Davy Crockett. This earlier West ran, geographically, from the crest of the Appalachian Mountains to the Mississippi River, from the border with Canada to the Gulf of Mexico. It was the West of Euro-American expansion from before the American Revolution until the middle of the nineteenth century, when the line of frontier settlement moved through it toward that next, farther West.

In its initial terms, the story of the First American West involved two basic sets of characters: first, the white people of European origin (and south of the Ohio River, many African American slaves), who spread relentlessly westward; second, the original settlers, the Native Americans, who retreated grudgingly before this flood. These first Europeans, French and Spanish, appeared on this landscape in the 1600s and early 1700s, where their interactions with the original native peoples involved both cooperation and conflict. The English arrived a half-century later. In numbers, the Europeans were almost always a minority, and so both sides sought not conquest or annihilation but mutual accommodation, a joint occupation of the land and joint use of its resources, a system of contact allowing both sides to survive and even to benefit from one another's presence. Trade developed and intermarriage followed; so did misunderstandings and violence. But a delicate balance, supported by mutual interests, often characterized relations among Europeans and native peoples.

When Anglo-Americans began moving through the Cumberland Gap from Virginia into what hunters called the Kentucky country in the 1750s, they soon tilted the balance between the two cultures, occupying large portions of Kentucky and pressing against native groups from Ohio south to Georgia. By 1780, the Anglo-Americans had also occupied the former French settlements of Cahokia in Illinois and Vincennes in Indiana. Despite strong resistance by several native groups, the seemingly unending reinforcements of white families made their gradual occupation of the trans-Appalachian frontier inevitable.

In the 1780s the infant American government issued ordinances spelling out how the land between the Great Lakes and the Ohio River was to be acquired, subdivided, and sold to the citizens of the new republic, and how a form of government organization would lead to statehood and equal membership in the Union. A parallel process was soon set up for Kentucky, Tennessee, and the lands south to the Gulf.

In the 1830s and 1840s, the remaining native groups east of the Mississippi were removed to the West. The expansion of settlement into the trans-Appalachian frontier now continued unchecked into Illinois, Wisconsin, Michigan, and the great cotton lands and hill country of Alabama, Mississippi, and Florida. The frontier period had been completed—as early as the 1820s in Kentucky, and within the next twenty years over much of the Old Northwest and in the Old Southwest.

In brief terms, this is the story of the trans-Appalachian frontier. Over scarcely three generations, the trickle of settler families across the mountains had become more than four million, both white and black. Beginning with Kentucky in 1792 and running through Florida in 1845 and Wisconsin in 1848, a dozen new states had entered the American Union. Each territory/state had its own story, and it is appropriate that each should have a separate volume in this series. The variations are large. Florida's first European arrived in 1513, and this future state had both Spanish and American frontier experiences over 350 years. Missouri had a long French and Spanish history before the arrival of American settlers. Kentucky and Ohio did not, and Americans in large numbers came there quickly through the Cumberland Gap.

The opening and closing of the settlement frontier is the subject of each of these volumes. Each begins with the world that existed when Europeans made contact with native peoples. Each describes and analyzes the themes associated with the special circumstances of the individual territories/states. And each concludes with the closing of the frontier.

The editors have selected these authors because of their reputations as scholars and interpreters of their individual territories/states. We believe that you will find this history informative and lively, and we are confident that you will enjoy this and other volumes in the Trans-Appalachian Frontier series.

James E. Davis begins his volume on the frontier period in Illinois history with three eye-witness accounts of the settlement process during its highest tide, the 1830s. We hear Sarah Aiken of northern New York, David Henshaw of Massachusetts, and Charles Watts, an Englishman, describe what Illinois life was really like in those days, and why Sarah wrote to a friend back home, "O, this is a delightful country!"

Professor Davis then looks far back into the Illinois of the glaciers, and the series of Indian civilizations that changed the land. These included the villages around Cahokia, where 20,000 people lived in the year 1100 C.E., more than in any city in Europe. The French explorers La Salle and Jolliet appear next, the precursors of other French men and women who created stable settlements like Kaskaskia and the rest of the old French colonial zone, in uneasy accommodation with the Indians. The brief history of British Illinois, and the Revolutionary War which assured Illinois' American future, then follow. Davis then traces the complex settlement process, first from Kentucky to the south, and later from New York, Pennsylvania, and Ohio to the east, bringing distinct cultural traditions to Illinois.

One of his most important findings, and a major theme of this book, is the relative absence of violence—at least after the Black Hawk War of 1832 which removed the last substantial Indian presence from the state. Among whites, however, whether they came from the upland South or from Yankee roots, struggles over land, courthouses, county seats, railroads, markets, and even the explosive fugitive slave question were resolved with a minimum of bloodshed. Davis explains all of these events in Illinois' early history and many more. Railroads started crisscrossing the state in the 1840s; Chicago began its role as the gateway between East and West; and in the 1850s, on the eve of the Civil War, Illinois passed beyond its frontier period.

Throughout the book, James E. Davis keeps the reader mindful of what happened to Illinois' ordinary people. This will not surprise those familiar with his best-known previous work, *Frontier America, 1800–1840*, a path-breaking synopsis of the early demographic history of Trans-Appalachia. For many years a professor of history at Illinois College in Jacksonville (the oldest continuing higher-educational institution in the state), and a renowned teacher there, Davis brings to life in this book the frontier period of Illinois history.

WALTER NUGENT
University of Notre Dame

MALCOLM J. ROHRBOUGH
University of Iowa

Preface

This is a story of frontier Illinois. It is largely the story of three sets of forces that shaped it: the natural environment; people who inhabited the region that became the State of Illinois; and people who never inhabited Illinois, but who influenced its history. Various relationships and interactions, including much cooperation and conflict, among and between these sets of forces shaped Illinois.

Although this story necessarily recounts actions of prominent leaders, it stresses ordinary people pursuing daily life in commonplace frontier settings. Through their letters and other sources they speak to us from frontier Illinois, often with eloquent dignity, intelligence, and charm. Frequently studded with delightful misspellings and unusual grammar, their letters sparkle with hopes, fears, plans, endeavors, and frustrations—and much good sense, quiet bravery, and empathy. These letters and other sources reveal ordinary people's roles in laying foundations for today's Illinois.

But the history of frontier Illinois and modern Illinois could have been different. Glaciers retreated from Illinois late in geological time, only some twelve thousand years ago. Had retreating glaciers functioned somewhat differently, Illinois' soils, vegetation, drainage patterns, and other significant features would be markedly different. Similarly, had a short, sharp battle at faraway Quebec City in 1759 gone the other way, France might have retained Illinois after 1763. Had seemingly small incidents involving George Rogers Clark occurred differently in 1778 and 1779, Iilinois today might be part of Canada. Had political maneuvering accompanying statehood in 1818 taken different courses, Illinois would have entered the Union later and without its northern counties and Chicago, and its crucial ties with the South would have persisted much longer. Early inhabitants and others faced many forks in the road, many contingencies. Fundamental developments hinged on contingencies, which involved choices, capabilities, and actions. Because few people inhabited Illinois even into the 1820s, handfuls of people—even just individuals—acting decisively often heavily influenced its history. Clearly, perceptions, choices, and actions during Illinois' frontier era were important.

Of the five states carved from the Old Northwest, Illinois extended farthest south and its ties to the South were strongest. More than any other state, Illinois and its rivers, canals, and railroads connected the Mississippi River system and the South to the St. Lawrence and Great Lakes system. Of the five states, Illinois gave Abraham Lincoln the thinnest majority in the election of 1860 and contained the largest numbers of blacks and French. Unlike other Old Northwestern states, Illinois is home to very few Indians, and it has no Indian reservation. It is the most populous of the five states, and Chicago is the region's largest city. These realities and other significant features of Illinois' history sprang from the frontier era.

Acknowledgments

Many talented people cheerfully helped me with this work. Cheryl Schnirring, Curator of Manuscripts at the Illinois State Historical Library, once again provided valuable manuscripts and sound advice about sources and evidence. Elsewhere in the library Kathryn Harris, George Heerman, Connie Holbers, Linda Oelheim, Cheryl Pence, Janice Petterchak, and Ellen Whitney rendered valuable assistance. In Schewe Library at Illinois College, Michael Westbrook and Patricia Schildman provided accurate answers to innumerable questions concerning frontier Illinois, and Laura Sweatman hauled in countless sources via interlibrary loan. Thanks, too, to personnel at the American Antiquarian Society, the Chicago Historical Society, the Henry Pfeiffer Library at MacMurray College, the Illinois Survey at the University of Illinois, the Sangamon Collection in the Lincoln Library in Springfield, and the Jacksonville Public Library. My understandings of issues, sources, and interpretations were strengthened by discussions, lengthy and brief, with various specialists: William Beard, Cullom Davis, Rodney Davis, Raymond Hauser, John Hoffman, Mark Johnson, Thomas Schwartz, Keith Sculle, Richard Taylor, and Ellen Whitney. William I. Woods, professor of geography at Southern Illinois University at Edwardsville, provided valuable evidence concerning Indian life and decline at Cahokia. Stacy Pratt McDermott, Daniel W. Stowell, and Dennis S. Suttles—all of the Lincoln Legal Papers, Illinois Historic Preservation Agency—kindly provided copies of papers they presented at the Eighteenth Annual Illinois History Symposium in December, 1997. These papers brim with valuable insights into nineteenth-century social history. Bernd Estabrook drafted the maps. He also skillfully overcame problems with computers, word processors, and printers, as did Chris Wherley, Don P. Filson, and Martin Dickey. Other colleagues at Illinois College and other institutions also displayed lively and supportive interest in this project. Special thanks to Jeff Abernathy, Jose Arce, Bernd Estabrook, Wallace Jamison, Royce Jones, Ann McEntee, Jeffrey Mueller, Alvin Schmidt, Paul Spalding, Donald Tracey, and Iver Yeager, and to members of my department. Faculty Development Grants, travel grants, various awards, and a sabbatical enhanced this work and my professional life. Current and former students volunteered valuable assistance: Raymond Gillmore, Jim Fanning, Dan Keller, Stephen Gibson, Alice Grady, Rachel Thebus, Jason Schoolfield, Kevin Kampanowski, Jacob Ballard, Jacob Palmatier, Becky Richards, and Anthony Del Giorno. My sincere thanks to these people for their help, enthusiasm, and good cheer. Hearty thanks to Walter Nugent and Malcolm Rohrbough, series editors, whose keen attention to detail, vast range of knowledge, and wisdom grace this work.

As always, my best friend and wife, Joanna, critiqued the work and steered me away from ambiguous wording, questionable conclusions, and errors. Our daughters, Kathleen and Mary, maintained lively, supportive interest from their homes in Michigan. I treasure the loving, steady enthusiasm of all three.

A Note on Quotations, Citations, and Sources

Quotations from manuscript sources are accompanied by dates of the quotations. Quotations from manuscripts are reproduced in original form, except on rare occasions when clarity demanded slight changes in punctuation. All cited manuscript sources appear in Works Cited. Quotations and other material pertaining to specific counties are from the pertinent county histories in Works Cited. Occasionally, specific citations are provided for quotations from county histories

Frontier Illinois

PROLOGUE:
THREE OBSERVERS

New Year's Day of 1833 found fifteen-year-old Sarah Aiken far from dear friends. She and her parents had recently left their home in Keeseville, New York, and traveled seven weeks to a new home, a farm about fourteen miles east of Peoria. She had not wanted to move, and separation from childhood friends, the trek to frontier Illinois, and settlement among strangers weighed heavily on her.

On January 1, 1833, she wrote to Julia Keese, a close friend back in Keeseville, "We have at length taken up winter quarters in Illinois, that far distant country." Her reference to Illinois as "that far distant country" reflected views of many settlers in Illinois and people elsewhere. She correctly assumed that "a short detail of our journey might not be altogether uninteresting." News from settlers fascinated people back east and in Europe, and news from close friends and relatives was usually deemed reliable.

Sarah Aiken's New Year's Day letter stressed nature's abundance: "The land is extremely rich and produces from 30 to 40 bushels of wheat per acre." Her brother, Joshua, she observed, "has killed one prairie hen. Ma drest it and we had it on the table." Nature's bounty beckoned many. At the same time, however, abundance posed problems: "We are living in a small frame house, and just opposite the window where I now sit are two stacks of wheat not thrashed, that have been standing all summer, and are now going to waste." She added, "And three fields of corn are in sight not gathered. This will go to show how abundantly things will grow here and how indolent and unconcerned the inhabitants are about getting a living." Indolence marred Illinois, settlers and visitors agreed, but Sarah Aiken's conclusions may have been flawed.

Perhaps rotting crops indicated other conditions, such as chronic labor shortages and high wages. Malaria and other maladies debilitated workers. Inadequate storage facilities, wobbly market conditions, and poor transportation all led to ungathered crops. In short, various frontier conditions—not just indolence— allowed nature's bounty to rot.

Sarah Aiken claimed the Illinois frontier "is entirely a new place." Reactions to new and unfolding frontier conditions varied. Some people saw unfinished and evolving conditions in Illinois as golden opportunities to wipe the slate clean, put past failure and woe behind, and start life anew. For others, though, frontier Illinois was essentially unfamiliar, capricious, and dangerous, an uncivilized setting where calamity threatened hourly. These people longed for conditions they had enjoyed elsewhere and hoped to replicate much of what they had previously enjoyed. Cherished values were threatened, and sustaining institutions were either absent or weak. From pristine conditions, these settlers feared, barbarism would spring. For still others, the Indians, the frontier offered mixed possibilities. Via the frontier Indians tapped resources of a technologically superior culture, but such contact altered and crippled Indian culture and evolving mixed white-Indian culture.

Sarah Aiken's letter lamented qualities of frontier life, but it also expressed hope. She wrote, "The society to be sure is not *first rate*, but a new place must grow, and probably another year we shall [be] nearly as good as in Keeseville, for it is rappidly increasing." This belief in the future—this sense of tomorrow and desire to be anticipatory in expectations—typified settlers. Hope focused settlers' attention on tomorrow, helped them to endure present tribulations, and gave meaning to suffering. Very likely, hope was the settlers' greatest resource.

Another concern burdened Sarah Aiken: her ability to depict pioneer life accurately. She cautioned Julia Keese, "You must bear in mind that I have not seen it all in its primitive glory." Unlike some observers of the frontier, she was aware of her limitations, and this awareness lends veracity to her letters.

On April 30, 1834, she again wrote to Julia, "There are two or three families here and they are a low set of people, from Kentucky, Tennessee & thereabouts. You see we are not favored with good society as in K[eeseville]." Although men sometimes expressed concern about the quality of frontier society—especially if they were clergymen, teachers, or members of social elites— Sarah Aiken's frequent references to social conditions reflect women's great concern about the quality of frontier life. As was true of others after 1832, she expressed great interest in Indians and much sympathy for them, but no fear.

The reference to "a low set of people, from Kentucky, Tennessee & thereabouts" suggests another dimension of frontier Illinois. Even before statehood in 1818, tensions surfaced between people with southern roots and people from the North, especially New Englanders. By the 1830s, following failed attempts to introduce full-scale slavery to Illinois, northern reformers heaped abuse on people from slave states, which stirred resentment. Hostility directed against immigrants compounded social tensions. To the end of the Illinois frontier by 1860, social spats and cultural clashes flickered across the state.

Sarah Aiken was hardly alone in comparing life in frontier Illinois to life in her childhood home. She and others, in making comparisons, placed new experiences into previously known contexts, which gave these experiences diverse meanings.

Sarah Aiken had not wanted to come to Illinois. Like many women and children, she emigrated involuntarily. Her letters reveal loneliness and general discontent. She tried to adjust to uneven conditions, with mixed results, but her thoughts drifted back to the friends she had left behind. On January 24, 1835, she again wrote to Julia Keese: "I suppose you would like to hear whether I have become more contented. Well, I think on the whole I have, yet I must confess it seems rather strange not to have any more society. O, for *one* friend, Julia." Her adjustment to fresh lands and embryonic society took time, as was true of countless others over decades, some never adjusting fully and well. In expressing her unhappiness, Aiken provided valuable glimpses of frontier Illinois. By January 24, for example, labor shortages were a worry: "The truth is there is no such thing as getting hired help here which is a great inconvenience." Such scarcities benefitted laborers, enabling them to command top wages, which was impossible in the East or in Europe, where plentiful labor depressed wages. High wages affected social relationships. Sarah's letter continued, "Every one feels as good and as well off as his neighbor which is a fact." Feelings of equality and fairness shaped and undergirded frontier society, providing crucial invisible social "glue" that held frontier society together. Such "glue" was rare in European countries, and was relatively scarce in locales on the East Coast.

Aiken's letter of August 26, 1836, reflected soaring spirits amid unfolding society: "I confess I take a deep interest in the prosperity of our 'beloved Illinois.' And who would not, who has seen the old adage of 'great oaks from little acorns grow' fulfilled to perfection, in innumerable instances." Clearly, improving frontier life brightened her outlook, for she added, "Our society in general is all that I could ask. O, this is a delightful country. Nothing would induce me to return to New York to remain." Memories of childhood home and society in New York became dim, replaced by kaleidoscopic events, images, and changes in "that far distant country" of frontier Illinois.

During the next three years, Sarah Aiken continued to correspond with Julia Keese. Her letters reveal her hopes and fears, joys and sorrows, aspirations and disappointments, and other thoughts and feelings about an emerging society far from her childhood home and friends.

Despite her successful adjustment, however, Sarah Aiken still cherished friends back in New York. Like many others who settled in Illinois, she worried she would never again see loved ones who remained behind: "It is hard to think we may not meet again on this earth. But oh, Julia, let us live so that in another world we may be where there is no separation and where all sorrow and sighing are done away." Sarah Aiken hoped for a good life in

Illinois, but she anticipated a better life in "another world." Many settlers shared these sentiments.

Sarah Aiken died of tuberculosis on January 28, 1839, at the age of twenty-one. Perhaps some of her final thoughts wandered back to "our happy home in dear Sweet Keeseville" and her initial reluctance to come to Illinois. And perhaps she recalled Illinois prairie country "in all of its primitive glory" and anticipated a better life in "another world."

The state's physical beauty captivated Sarah Aiken and countless others. Her motives in describing physical and social features of Illinois were pure: she wanted to inform friends and relatives back east about her new home. New lands and settlement processes keenly interested Julia Keese, Sarah Aiken's friend back in New York, and many others far removed from Illinois, sometimes because they contemplated trekking to Illinois themselves.

Frontier conditions in Illinois impressed many eastern observers. David Henshaw wrote an article for the *Boston Post*, which appeared in the January 31, 1839, issue of the *Pittsfield Sun* of Pittsfield, Massachusetts. The article discussed construction of the Illinois & Michigan Canal, which in 1848 finally linked Lake Michigan to the Illinois River. Henshaw accurately foresaw the canal's importance. He also told of plans for railroad construction in Illinois.

Henshaw wanted to impress readers with persuasive evidence of frontier growth, writing, "These gigantic works would startle the citizens of the east; but any judicious person, in examining the nature and extent of this great State, would say they evince great energy and sagacity. This state is large enough to form eight States the size of Massachusetts." He then advised Massachusetts to construct a railroad to Albany, New York, to siphon commercial traffic flowing from Illinois via the Erie Canal and the Hudson River to New York City. He warned Massachusetts that Illinois and other western regions would soon be "as well peopled as they are vast—abounding in mineral resources and blessed with a soil of unrivaled fertility." Finally, Henshaw chided Massachusetts for seeking unlikely overseas markets while ignoring the potentials of Illinois and other western domains. Henshaw wrote during racking financial crisis. Work on the Illinois & Michigan Canal sputtered, and the state's ambitious railroad plans folded. Even so, Henshaw's basic points had merit: Illinois' growth was vastly impressive, a fact Massachusetts dare not ignore.

Perhaps physical, tangible progress impressed male settlers more than female settlers. Many males embraced education and other social undertakings, to be sure, but most measured success via economic, political, and even military activities. Women's talents found outlets in religion, managing households, sustaining others, and spearheading reforms and education. Men sometimes dispelled doubts and fears by succeeding in physical and economic realms.

For example, Charles Watts migrated from England to America in late 1835, a boom time for frontier Illinois. On December 26, 1847, he wrote from Bureau County to his brother in London, recalling, "Twelve years ago today I was riding on the bosom of the great Atlantic within soundings of the Newfoundland banks enveloped in a thick fog, while the spray was freezing on the head of the ship & rigging, full of hopes, doubts, and fears with a boundless uncertainty before me." And then Watts added, "I can see before me a good little farm containing some of the best land under heaven, a neat little house, and a comfortable fire side, and industrious, frugal wife, & another little fellow that will help to amuse and keep us busy, and enough of the necessaries that nature requires, inalienable and secure while life shall last, the produce of my own toil and economy." For people who were essentially landless, obtaining "a good little farm" was supremely important. Moreover, countless settlers joined Charles Watts in boasting of "the produce of my own toil and economy." Settlers, perhaps especially men, placed great value on economic independence. His "inalienable and secure" property indicates low taxes, a condition unknown in Britain. For innumerable pioneers, buoyant feelings of success, independence, and security displaced fears and doubts amidst "boundless uncertainty."

Glimpses of frontier Illinois provided by Sarah Aiken, David Henshaw, and Charles Watts span nearly fifteen years. During these years, surging settlement, brisk land sales, nascent railroads, progress on the Illinois & Michigan Canal, and myriad other developments heralded the waning of frontier conditions.

These writings reflect widely held ideas about the frontier: isolation, loneliness, nature's bounty, sloth, labor shortages, exhilaration and worry in establishing new homes, evolving society, feelings of equality and equity, sectional and class tensions, self-governance, republicanism, meanings of frontier life, sickness and death, optimism, security, desire to begin anew, desire to replicate previous conditions, diligence, markets for crops, adjustments to crude conditions, thoughts about returning home, Illinois as potential threat, upward mobility, feeling of accomplishment and independence, and visions of the future. These conditions formed much of the thematic fabric of frontier Illinois. From them sprang both cooperation and conflict.

These accounts brim with references to pristine freshness, belief in possibilities, eagerness to embrace tomorrow, gratitude for new beginnings, and awareness of significant aspects of frontier life. Yet at the same time they caution about social loss, incipient barbarism, simmering strife, and personal and collective failure. In short, innumerable opportunities and lurking dangers abounded.

Although dangers lurked and tensions flared, frontier Illinois was amazingly tranquil, a highly significant fact. Settlers and visitors—people on the scene—rarely wrote about conflict, violence, and homicide. Some writers mentioned threats, only to admit to false alarms. Infrequent references to mayhem indicate that violence shocked Illinoisans precisely because it was so infrequent. Evidence strongly indicates three realities: settlers craved tranquility, they strove to preserve order and justice, and they believed the frontier was peaceful. One startling fact attests to frontier tranquility: the Federal Census for 1850 indicates the state's northern thirty-two counties—which in 1850 still witnessed boisterous frontier activities and which attracted assorted people from diverse places—contained more than 317,000 people in that year. During the twelve months prior to June 1, 1850, the thirty-two counties experienced just one murder—exactly one—the victim a young boy.[1] Even allowing for undercounting, homicides disguised as accidents, and deliberate killings masked as justifiable homicides, just one recorded murder among 317,000 people in a twelve-month period is compelling. Ingredients for ghastly frontier violence abounded, but persuasive evidence reveals tranquil frontier conditions. This tranquility is central to understanding frontier Illinois.

PART I

VAST LANDS AND CONTENDING PEOPLES

I.

THE SHAPING OF SETTLEMENT

Three basic factors shaped frontier Illinois: the natural environment; settlers and others in Illinois; and outsiders—people who never lived in Illinois. Over time these factors and relationships among them changed, altering the frontier, making it distinct, and providing national and international context.

These three fundamental factors—the natural environment, the settlers, and outsiders—spawned tension and conflict. Some conflict was indigenous to the frontier. Emerging from the hubbub of rapid growth and competing subcultures, most conflict was spontaneous and non-ideological. Some conflict originated in Europe and other faraway places. Some conflict, such as abolitionism, sprouted elsewhere, but found fertile soil in Illinois. Much frontier drama bubbled from competing personalities, values, and institutions.

Illinois is 211 miles wide and 381 miles long. Nearly all of it was glaciated within the last 100,000 years, some of it a scant 12,000 years ago. Patches escaping glaciation include the southern tip, most of the American Bottom,[1] Calhoun County, southern Pike County, and Jo Daviess County. The *quality* of glaciation is significant. Although glaciers scoured Illinois, as they retreated they laid down thick deposits, covering nearly all bedrock. In Canada and the northern United States, by contrast, vast stretches of bedrock have skimpy glacial deposits. Moreover, Illinois' glaciers pulverized, transported, and deposited limestone, thereby greatly enriching soil. Illinoisans farmed finely pulverized glacial deposits, topped with thick soil, rocks interfering with farming largely in northern counties. Consequently, they escaped New Englanders' annual drudgery of building stone walls around fields.

Glacially created landforms altered settlement. Avoiding soggy places, trails followed sinuous eskers and recessional and terminal moraines. Farm buildings perched on drumlins. In northern Illinois kettle ponds provided water for man and beast. Glaciers greatly eroded mountain barriers south of Lake Superior, allowing winter's polar blasts to rake Illinois. Freezing winters, however, help soils retain vital nutrients, unlike leached reddish-yellow soils of southeastern states.

Other factors influence climate. No mountain barrier blocks warm, moist winds from the south. The Gulf of Mexico provides huge amounts of warming, moderating moisture, usually giving the southernmost counties 240 frost-free days annually—long enough to grow cotton and tobacco—and the northern counties up to 180. Although annual precipitation in the northern quarter of the state is generally at least thirty-three inches, compared to between forty and forty-six inches in Illinois' southern fringes, the evaporation rate in the north is relatively low. Precipitation in Illinois, moreover, usually peaks during the growing season, tapering off during harvest, and generally sustains shipping on waterways. Without moisture-laden Gulf winds, Illinois would have parched growing seasons and colder and drier winters. The claim, "No Gulf of Mexico, no Illinois as we know it," hardly exaggerates the Gulf's significance.

Glaciers graced Illinois with fine drainage. Unlike eastern Canada and northern United States, where swamps dot exposed bedrock, Illinois enjoys mature drainage systems. Traversing Illinois, rivers slice across thick glacial deposits. Poor drainage in eastern Illinois and elsewhere hampered settlement, but this was the exception. Significantly, glaciers produced the Great Lakes and the Great Lakes drainage basin. The Great Lakes–St. Lawrence River system played vital roles in Illinois' history.

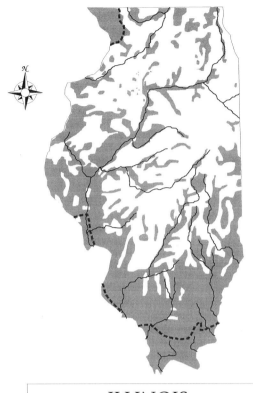

ILLINOIS

0   25   50   100 MI.

Maximum Glacial Extent	··················
Woodland	
Prairie	
Rivers	

The state's topography suggests poor drainage. The state's average elevation is just over 600 feet, the highest point only 1,235 feet. Illinois lies in a vast shallow depression formed by higher elevations to the west, north, and east. From these directions rivers flow toward Illinois. The state's drainage systems, however, generally handle these rivers and Illinois' precipitation runoff, with only sporadic local flooding. Retreating glaciers and glacial melt heavily influenced river location. Rich alluvial floodplains produced bumper harvests for centuries. The fertile

American Bottom floodplain stretches over 100 miles, from Wood River down to points opposite Ste. Genevieve, Missouri.

Rivers serve Illinois very well. The Illinois River and its tributaries, alone, drain half of the state's 56,400 square miles. People long desired to connect the Illinois-Mississippi river route to the Great Lakes–St. Lawrence system, which was done in 1848. The tiny Chicago River and the Kaskaskia, Rock, Fox, and Sangamon rivers also loom large in history.

Two features of Illinois' waterways conferred advantages to navigators. Rivers connect Illinois to both the Atlantic Coast and the Gulf of Mexico; Illinois' rivers generally flow south. Other factors affected settlement: short portages connect navigable rivers; few falls or rapids block vessels; watercourses traversing prairies sustain timber.

Navigable waters tugged Illinois toward the Gulf and toward the Atlantic. This tugging produced much of Illinois' history. East-west and north-south communication axes competed for dominance. The scarcity of falls or rapids precluded a "fall line," a line connecting points on rivers where rough water and rocks obstruct navigation and where towns consequently developed. In Illinois, as a result, towns sprang up almost anywhere along rivers, in marked contrast to settlement along the Atlantic seaboard, where major towns such as Richmond and Raleigh developed along the fall line. Furthermore, in Illinois shipping is ice-free longer than in other Lower Great Lakes states. Moreover, the headwaters of Illinois' rivers, lying northward, freeze before the main channels farther south, and stay frozen longer, enabling water to continue to flow into lower reaches of river systems after headwaters freeze. This prevents disastrous spring and fall floods, which inundate lower portions of northward-flowing rivers. It also lengthens the shipping season.

Watercourses snaking across prairies sustained trees, creating lengthy peninsulas of timber. Settlers valued timber resources, particularly before railroads provided lumber from distant sources. Timber yielded game, mast for livestock, syrup and sugar, other foods, and wood for building, fencing, heating, cooking, furniture, wagons, and tools. It also comforted settlers accustomed to wooded life. Cabins dotted edges of peninsulas of tim-

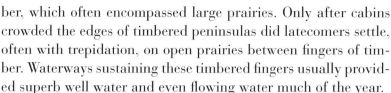
ber, which often encompassed large prairies. Only after cabins crowded the edges of timbered peninsulas did latecomers settle, often with trepidation, on open prairies between fingers of timber. Waterways sustaining these timbered fingers usually provided superb well water and even flowing water much of the year.

Water transportation gave Illinois a central position in the region east of the Rockies. Railroads connected Chicago to the Great Plains, accentuating this central location and extending the city's hinterland. Lake Michigan funneled land transportation around its southern edge, benefitting northern Illinois.

***

Frontier Illinois had unique features. It differed significantly from frontier Alabama and even frontier Indiana, and these three frontiers differed from frontiers in Russia, Argentina, Australia, Canada and elsewhere. Variations in climate, soils, and other natural features produced some differences, but variations in peoples and culture produced the most significant ones.[2]

Specifically, characteristics of the settlers themselves heavily influenced society in frontier Illinois: their origins; motives for migrating and for settling in Illinois; sequence of arrival; relative numbers; modes of arriving and settling; age and gender compositions; racial makeup; basic values and assumptions; significant institutions; lingering ties with former homes; and technologies available at the time of settlement and afterwards. Moreover, interactions among settlers altered these traits and changed their relative importance. Countless interrelated social, economic, and political experiments graced frontier Illinois for decades, new ingredients constantly changing and new cultures constantly evolving. Hybrid societies flourished.

Nature and people clashed. Some disputes sprang from settlers' ambiguities and contradictions in viewing nature. For example, nature both pleased the eye and tormented the flesh. For some, nature's fount regenerated individuals, groups, and larger society. Nature was bountiful and beautiful. For others, though, untamed nature unleashed capricious forces, sweeping off the able and the weak alike. It sometimes lured or shoved even the virtuous into barbarism and abject destruction. Some believed nature had to be wooed and won. Others saw nature as primeval seductress, a dark force bringing moral and physical destruction. Some settlers and others strove to replicate treasured values, institutions, restraints, and overall culture they had enjoyed elsewhere, while others used embryonic and unsettled frontier conditions to wipe the slate clean, build anew from scratch. Most tried to do both. Many feared unfinished frontier society provided limitless opportunities to enemies. Some hoped the frontier was a Garden, a place free from foibles and sin. Others saw no Garden, only a cultural desert, devoid of refinement. Many believed nature was a blank slate, on which they sketched airy plans for improved—even utopian—life, plans leading believers via lofty ideas and strictures toward perfection. But such plans foundered on sickness, vanity, quarrelsomeness, faulty assumptions about human nature, life in Illinois, and other realities. In short, some people cherished frontier Illinois' beneficent features, others feared its destructive capabilities, and others—probably the overwhelming majority—balanced its beneficent and dangerous aspects.

In relentless strife between nature and people, however, humans were not flotsam, tossed and turned by primeval forces. Settlers tempered, thwarted, harnessed, and even overcame nature, impressing themselves and others. Individuals, communities, and institutions resisted and assaulted nature, mitigating its forces and even overcoming some. Sometimes settlers sidestepped formidable natural forces, avoiding head-on conflict. For example, they skirted poorly drained regions of eastern Illinois until drainage technology appeared and railroads crossed them. Drained lakes yielded rich, gently sloping alluvial material. Settlers initially avoided prairies, worrying about grass fires, winter's blasts, water, problems of plowing and raising a crop, and related concerns. Their worries, though, were overcome by steel plows, better knowledge of soils, enhanced drainage techniques, improved ability to sink wells, and better transportation, so settlers trod into these billowing seas of grass and farmed. Railroads dramatically facilitated prairie settlement, bringing distant pine to fence boundless prairies, supplying farmers with manufactured goods, and whisking to distant markets livestock, wheat, and countless other prairie products.

Simple technology altered the stalemated struggle between wooded regions and prairie grass. Axes decimated virgin forests, providing settlers with building materials, tools, furniture, fuel, fencing, wagons and boats, and myriad other useful objects. Steel plows sliced through tangled roots of prairie grasses, opening rich prairie soil to cultivation. Cultivation of prairies created effective firebreaks in oceans of prairie grass, making spectacular, wind-driven prairie fires of late summer and autumn only memories. Grass-munching livestock soon consumed and matted down much grass, inhibiting grass fires. Sometimes settlers in given locales checked prairie fires within three or four years. Occasional fires by 1860 were nothing like early infernos, shimmering orange walls of fire swirling over undulating prairie, which awed so many settlers and visitors.[3] Consequently, saplings soon encroached on virgin prairie land. Settlers accelerated biological changes by bringing or importing seeds, bulbs, and saplings, and new species of animals. Treelines grew, sheltering both game and pests, and clumps of trees and bushes bordered houses.

Rivers played huge roles in settlers' lives. Most settlers in early Illinois hailed from states south of the Ohio. Most migrated to Illinois via rivers, settled in wooded areas reminiscent of home, and tapped waterways for transportation, water, power, and food. Water from wells, some believed, was inferior to flowing water, so they sought springs tumbling from hillsides, which inhibited prairie settlement.

As soon as population reached certain thresholds in different locales, water-powered mills began to hum along rivers. Impounded water in mill ponds supplemented rushing water, enabling millers to overcome nature's droughts, at least temporarily, and extended milling operations. By the 1820s, steam power further freed millers and customers from nature's grip. Steam power allowed mills to operate almost anywhere and encouraged settlement and towns to spring up in areas remote from waterways.

Improved means of transportation surmounted nature's obstacles. Bridges and ferries, however rickety, enabled travelers

to mock unfordable rivers, saving lives and stimulating commerce. Dredging saved crews and passengers of vessels from
watery deaths and stimulated commerce. Late in the frontier era,
plank roads—expensive, difficult to maintain, and quickly impractical—brought limited relief. Railroads quickly aborted this
plank-road craze, bringing far better transportation.

Steam power overcame other handicaps imposed by nature.
The greatest bottleneck in river transportation was upstream shipping: it was expensive, time-consuming, arduous, and uncertain.
Consequently, Illinois sent vast quantities of farm produce,
hides, and other goods downstream to Louisiana, but basically
only luxury goods and other low-bulk, high-value goods withstood the return voyage. Steam power changed this. After the
War of 1812, steamboats plowed upstream almost as quickly as
they sped downstream. Costs, dangers, and uncertainties plummeted as steamboats raced upstream swiftly and surely on the
Mississippi and then the Illinois, Wabash, and other waterways.
This changed trade patterns.

The first railroad experiment in Illinois, in the 1830s, was premature and unimpressive. But once track laced Illinois, by 1855,
the impact was tremendous. Steam-powered locomotives pulled
trains over tracks laid, in many instances, far from rivers. Speeds
of thirty and forty miles per hour thrilled passengers and bystanders alike, who saw this technology conquer space and free
farmers, merchants, and the public from nature's vicissitudes and
from reliance on meandering river routes. Now railroads cut across
open prairies, giving birth to towns at intervals along the tracks.
Where tracks crossed, towns gained promise of prosperity, particularly if they also garnered county seats. Towns with dependable supplies of water and fuel attracted railroads, especially if
sizeable subsidies tempted the railroads. Trains coursing through
seas of prairie grass in bad weather impressed people, including
those contemplating taking up prairie farming. Trains greatly
facilitated mail delivery, a crucial fact following drastic reductions in postal rates by 1851.

Even before railroad track sliced through billowing prairie,
telegraph wires overcame distance. Telegraphs greatly facilitated railroad traffic and prevented collisions, and they also coordi-

nated wholesale and retail activities. Local, regional and national economies were stimulated as wires sped orders, inventory data, and other vital information among major commercial interests. Frontiersfolk in Illinois communicated virtually instantaneously with associates on the East Coast.

* * *

So over many decades people partially overcame nature. As they did so, however, they fought each other. Illinois' relative location, constantly changing, influenced struggles among people. Indian residents enjoyed advantages of central location, maintaining contacts with other Indians in all directions. Yet central location also exposed Illinois' Indians to attack from every direction. France initially regarded Illinois as a shadowy region, a land brimming with mystery and promise. By the 1720s, though, France constructed a chain of forts, posts, and missions strung from eastern Quebec to the Gulf of Mexico, making Illinois the arc's keystone. (Ominously, French brought slaves into Illinois about 1720.) By the 1750s France enhanced the region's centrality by reconstructing on a grand scale in the American Bottom Fort de Chartres, inland North America's most impressive fort. France also established posts eastward to Pennsylvania to blunt British probes westward. After Britain ousted France from North America in 1763, it regarded Illinois as a remote, largely unknown, and potentially destabilizing region, not the keystone of a vast imperial arc. British control was troubled, tenuous, and brief—but important. During the American Revolution, Illinois was a distant sideshow, one warranting few resources from either side. And yet, stakes were high, and relatively few combatants in the region accomplished much. Settlers flocking into this region placed the United States on a collision course with Indians, again changing Illinois' relative location. With British authorities equipping and encouraging desperate Indians, lands north of the Ohio saw jarring battles. Britain and Indians tried to stem American expansion and deflect it as far south as possible, thereby protecting Canada from grasping Americans. For British authorities, Illinois was a buffer. For advancing Americans, frontier Illinois was irresistibly attractive. For Indians, strife in frontier Illinois was part of a larger struggle to determine their fate. As late as 1814, Indians, Americans, and British contested frontier Illinois, Americans emerging triumphant. The War of 1812 severely sapped Indian power north of the Ohio and terminated overt British intervention there, changing Illinois' relative location yet again. Soon Illinois became the center of complex battles between Southerners and Northerners, proslavery forces and abolitionists. No state north of the Ohio had so many slaves or came closer to providing constitutional protection for slavery. None had such a high percentage of its borders adjacent to slave states. But when frontier Illinois faded by the late 1850s, slavery there was extinct. Several factors created northern dominance in frontier Illinois and signalled slavery's demise. One was transportation revolutions inexorably loosening riverine ties to the South and reinforcing ties to the East. With each struggle, Illinois' relative location changed.

Other people struggled in frontier Illinois. Yeomen farmers tussled with nonresident speculators. Nativists tried to corral and suppress immigrants, particularly Catholic immigrants. Residents suppressed lawbreakers. Towns vied to obtain and keep county seats. Craving order and certainty amid raw conditions, some sought to replicate conditions they had enjoyed elsewhere, and those wanting to wipe the slate clean and start anew opposed them. Almost certainly, most settlers wanted both; they replicated the best of what they had known elsewhere, but wiped the slate clean and started over in other spheres of life. Both shaped frontier Illinois.

Migration involved many decisions, two of them basic: the decision to migrate; the selection of a destination. Many voluntarily left comfortable homes for no apparent reason, other than wanderlust or zest for adventure. Nevertheless, economic dislocations, wars, and other pressures pushed or nudged people from homes in Europe, the East, or elsewhere. Millions of settlers flocked to frontiers in different countries: Canada, Australia, Argentina, Russia, and North Africa, among others. Indiana, Missouri, California, and other fresh lands in America attracted others. Migrants did not simply plop into frontier Illinois. Pushed or lured, people pondered and then *chose* to settle there, a highly significant fact. Unless invasion, revolution or other convulsion abruptly expelled migrants, scattering them willy-nilly, forces tended to lure them to one destination instead of another. Sometimes relatives or friends, usually trustworthy people with some resources, guided migrants to frontier Illinois. Most Illinois settlers probably responded to both forces, push and pull.

The third basic factor shaping frontier Illinois consisted of outsiders, people who never settled in Illinois. From outside Illinois, Indians, French, Spanish, British, Americans, and others—kings, generals, chiefs, diplomats, financiers, speculators and countless ordinary nonresidents—influenced political, economic, social, diplomatic, and military features of frontier life and indelibly shaped emerging culture. For example, Virginian officials sponsored George Rogers Clark, who wrestled Illinois away from Britain. American and British diplomats in Paris in 1782 ratified his conquest. British authorities in Canada stiffened Indian resistance to American westward expansion. War declared in faraway Washington, D.C., in 1812 triggered massacre in Illinois. In addition, countless ordinary outsiders, including Julia Keese and David Henshaw, indelibly influenced frontier Illinois. Keese's friendship and concern helped sustain the Aiken household, and Henshaw focused attention on growing Illinois.

Frontier Illinois differed markedly from nearby American frontiers. In northern Indiana, for example, nonresident speculators stymied settlement, a rare occurrence in Illinois. In Michigan and Wisconsin, settlers occupied the southern three or four tiers of counties and some points on water to the north, and then the frontier stalled, something that never happened in Illinois. Much of Michigan and Wisconsin was settled well after the Civil War, and mining camps, logging, and port activities comprised major frontier activities, yeoman farms and agricultural villages and towns playing comparatively minor roles. In Kentucky, warfare killed many hundreds of Indians and whites over decades, making Kentucky "the Dark and Bloody Ground."[4] Much the same was true of Ohio and Michigan. Except for the Fort Dearborn Massacre, frontier Illinois escaped such bloodletting. Unlike Illinois, Kentucky and Missouri had slavery that thrived into the Civil War and relatively many free blacks. (At the same time,

though, numerous slaves and free blacks into the 1830s made
frontier Illinois qualitatively different from other frontiers north
of the Ohio.) Kentucky and Missouri, steeped in southern culture, supplied organized military units to Confederate armies.
Individual Illinoisans joined southern armies, but no organized
unit. Illinois helped settle Iowa's frontier, helping make frontier
Iowa similar to frontier Illinois. But aridity in western Iowa produced unique frontier experiences. Moreover, urban growth made
frontier Illinois unique: compared to other towns in Illinois in
1835, Chicago was minuscule, but soon it was the state's largest
city and becoming the region's metropolis. In short, frontier Illinois was significantly different from nearby frontiers.

* * *

Environmental factors, settlers, and nonresidents *influenced*
developments in the Illinois frontier, but they did not *determine*
them. Human actions had immense leeway. For example, George
Rogers Clark, leading his men to invade Illinois, stumbled across
an individual who guided his men, thus helping to defeat the
British. British defeat altered geopolitical realities for America,
Britain, and Indians. Similarly, Nathaniel Pope, representing the
Territory of Illinois in Congress, added to Illinois the region that
later formed the state's northern fourteen counties. This gave
Illinois many northern features before 1860, altering state and
even national history. Clearly, some hinges of history—contingencies in human activities—sprang from small incidents or just
one person's actions. Such contingencies shaped much early history. Each major turning point—each contingency—sprang from
specific, unique blends of events and conditions. Moreover, each
blend existed only briefly.

Not every influence was equal. Only a few thousand Indians
inhabited Illinois during historic times, and their removal was so
thorough that today not one reservation exists in Illinois. Accordingly, their influences may be underestimated. Similarly, it
is easy to underestimate roles played by the few hundred French
residents, the Americans trickling into Illinois by the 1790s, and
the foreign colonists at statehood in 1818. They generated rela-

tively few records and artifacts, and their roles may seem limited and transitory.

But Indians, French, early Americans, and early foreign colonists shaped frontier life all out of proportion to their numbers. Their imprints became pilings upon which later layers of civilization rested. They gave place names to sites, blazed trails, located villages, introduced plants and animals, experimented in countless ways, and molded early understandings about the region. Their choices and actions, in short, greatly influenced frontier life.

Finally, although frontier Illinois was unique, its context was similar to the contexts of other frontiers. Many features of frontier Illinois—available bountiful land, a sparse Indian population, friction between settlers and Indians, energetic diplomacy, controversies among settlers, shared values that included republicanism and sanctity of private property, adaptive technology, and modes of settlement—were also present throughout much of North America. The Illinois frontier was only part of a continental frontier, which included Canadians pushing west under British auspices, Spaniards entering the Southwest from what is now Mexico, and Russians poking down the West Coast. Furthermore, North America's frontiers fit into vastly larger expansionist endeavors, which began in Europe in the late 1400s and splashed into Australia, New Zealand, Russia, Latin America, southern Asia, Africa, and Oceania. It lasted over four centuries. Additional understanding is gained by comparing North American settlement to Chinese expansion into Tibet and settlement in Southeast Asia, Zulu migration and other African migratory movements, frontiers in ancient Indochina and Indonesia, waves of migration into the Indian subcontinent, sweeping movements largely within Eurasia's interior, and similar vast episodes of humanity. Properly understood, frontier Illinois is part of a global story that unfolded over millennia and still continues to unfold. It is part of the human story.

2.

COMMINGLING CULTURES

About 8000 B.C., early Archaic Indians filtered into Illinois. Inching northward, they tracked animals, fished, and foraged for seeds, roots, berries, and nuts. Archaic Indians lived in the American Bottom, in caves in bluffs along the Illinois River Valley, and at several other sites. Even rudimentary agriculture was unknown to them. About 1000 B.C. they and newcomers commingled, producing Late Archaic Culture. They developed snares, spears, spear-throwers, woven baskets, refined stone axes, awls and drills, hoes, and pottery. Not having bows and arrows, they probably fired prairies to stampede game over cliffs. Their trade involved inhabitants of Michigan, Missouri, Kentucky, and other places.

Early Woodland culture emerged around 600 B.C. Climate changes had enhanced food supplies. Gardens made life more certain and sedentary, population increased, village life developed, and elaborate burial practices emerged. Members fashioned refined flint tools and pottery. Trade flourished, adding to abundance. Middle Woodland Culture arose around 2,000 years ago, and by A.D. 300 it evolved into Late Woodland culture, which lasted until approximately A.D. 800. Woodland people cultivated, stored, and traded corn, beans, pumpkins, and squash. Bows and arrows supplied protein. Some mounds were used for ceremonies and housing the dead.

Around A.D. 500, Mississippian Indians, other mound-building Woodland people, appeared, probably from the southeastern United States. Developing floodplain agriculture and using rivers for trade, they established villages near waterways. Their mainstay was corn, which appeared in the Illinois Valley by A.D. 650. Earthworks, moats, and palisades protected villages from marauding enemies. They traded with Plains Indians, inhabitants of the Northeast, and kin in the Southeast, and had ties with Mexico.

Boasting the most sophisticated society north of Mexico, villages around Cahokia housed some 20,000 people and featured houses in rows and plazas. Ceremony and ritual, possibly including fire and sun worship, flourished. Leisure time, love of ceremony, and stability fostered construction of about one hundred mounds around Cahokia. Monks Mound, the largest prehistoric earthen structure in North America, covered fourteen acres and towered 100 feet. Completed around A.D. 1100, with minor modifications afterwards, it was topped by a building 105 by 48 feet. Sacrificed individuals and others were buried in conical mounds and a few ridgetop mounds. The latter also served as boundary markers. Buildings topped numerous platform mounds.

Mississippians tapped resources of two broad ecosystems: rivers and their floodplains, and bluffs and regions beyond the bluffs. Ponds, sloughs, marshes, floodplains, streams, woods, bluffs, prairies, and forests presented complementary resource options. Ecosystems complemented each other, one system supplying necessities when another failed. Resources that were complementary encouraged settlement along the boundaries of two or more ecosystems, a rational means of gaining resources from each. This settlement pattern continued into historic times; pioneers settled on the fringes of timber within yards of prairies, tapping resources of both.

Mississippian bows and arrows felled deer, waterfowl, turkey, and raccoon, and rivers and marshes yielded fish and turtles and other sources of protein. Indians continued to gather berries, roots, nuts, and other wild food. Fertile, well-watered, rock-free alluvial soils in floodplains delivered abundant harvests: squash, sunflowers, corn, gourds, and beans. The society was corn-based, and stored surplus harvests cushioned against catastrophe. No draft animals assisted cultivation, and farming resembled European neolithic farming. Leisure time yielded ornaments, ceremonial pipes, pottery, and other items. Trade reached the Rockies and the St. Lawrence River. At its peak, the Cahokia site boasted perhaps 25,000 inhabitants, but estimates vary widely.

After Mississippian civilization flourished for about 500 years, decline began by perhaps 1050, accelerated by 1150, and produced rapid collapse. Population plummeted, with only sporadic and low-density settlement persisting into the 1500s. Mystery shrouds this decline. Perhaps environmental degradation, especially forest depletion, occurred. Woodland depletion on bluffs triggered floods from streams and soil erosion, burying fertile alluvial soils with inferior slope materials. By A.D. 1250 cooler and drier summers may have decreased corn output. Perhaps leadership faltered, possibly sparking strife. By the late 1400s external enemies preyed on weakened descendants. Whatever caused the catastrophe, in 1673 Father Jacques Marquette and Louis Jolliet, the first whites to visit Illinois, found few Indians along the Mississippi and Illinois rivers. Nine years later Robert Cavalier, sieur de La Salle, saw few Indians around Cahokia or elsewhere on the Mississippi's left bank. He found mounds overgrown with vegetation, abandoned villages in ashes, and a handful of Indians, people of the Oneota culture.

A group of tribes, the Illinois Confederacy, lived in Illinois by the early 1600s, occupying Cahokia by mid-century. Never numerous, they nevertheless had at least sixty-five villages throughout much of Illinois, parts of Iowa and Missouri, and along Lake Michigan in southern Wisconsin. Tribes comprising the Illinois Confederacy—Cahokia, Kaskaskia, Michigamea, Moingwene, Peoria, and Tamaroa—were of the Algonkian family. Related to them were Shawnee to the south, Miami to the east, and Fox and Sauk to the north. The confederacy was a defensive league, their operative mechanism being kinship ties, not formal political obligations.

Illinois villages clustered along the American Bottom and the

Illinois River. The American Bottom's deep alluvial soils stretched from near Wood River down to where the Kaskaskia River entered the Mississippi. Paralleling the Mississippi, rocky bluffs a few miles away demarcated its eastern boundary. The American Bottom's loamy, fertile soils and those of the Illinois River, renourished by floods, supplied maize, squash, beans, sunflowers, pumpkins, gourds, and other crops. Valleys teemed with roots, nuts, berries, fruit, and other plant life. Rivers and river valleys also yielded wide varieties of fish and game. In summer and especially in winter, hunting parties ventured for days from river bottoms and bluffs, returning with hides, bone for tools, and meat. Typically, perhaps 80 percent of food consumed during warm months came from collecting, fishing, and hunting, with collecting providing over half of this total. Most of the rest came from stored food. In winter months, however, hunting was the mainstay, accounting for over half of all food consumed. Most of the rest came from stored supplies, with collecting and fishing providing little. Indians hunted deer, elk, and such smaller animals as turkey, squirrel, and raccoon. Observing Indians in 1673, Father Marquette wrote, "They live by hunting, game being plentiful in that country, and on Indian corn, of which they always have a good crop; consequently, they have never suffered from famine."[1] He also referred to buffalo, which then ranged over the eastern United States. Before disappearing from Illinois around 1800, buffalo provided Indians with food, clothing, bones for tools, and other resources.

Clans and tribes provided structure, but individuals enjoyed much personal freedom. There was no priesthood, fixed set of rules, or imposed belief system. Illinois governance, Father Marquette observed, was informal, light, and most energetic at the local level. Families made decisions affecting families, clans made decisions affecting clans, and clan leaders addressed tribal matters. Individual discretion guided participation in war and religion. Someone deciding to wage war collected like-minded men, and then that party fought; those choosing not to participate sat on the sidelines. Renowned warriors commanded loyal followings. When individuals tired of war—perhaps agreeing by informal, almost unspoken consensus—they quit fighting. As a result, personal, desultory, seasonal warfare was traditional; large-scale warfare was virtually unknown. Well into the 1630s, Illinois Indians waged traditional small-scale war on six or seven traditional enemies, including the Sauk, Fox, and Sioux. One authority on Illinois Indians concluded, "The cultural importance of martial activity in the Upper Mississippi Valley dictated that a continuous state of war exist between the Illinois and one or another of the neighboring tribes. War was a 'normal' element in intertribal relations, and peace could only obtain a temporary armistice, a mutually agreeable period of recovery during which antagonists prepared for the resumption of hostilities." He added, "The male role in Illinois society emphasized war and the hunt first, and then such activities as religious ceremonies, athletic contests, and gambling."[2] Father Marquette encountered Illinois Indians who were kind to him but fierce in conducting raids to procure slaves.

He also noted that individuals often prevented warfare, regulated it, and even stopped it altogether by using a calumet, a stone pipe about two feet long. Its power was virtually absolute among most Indians. Individuals showed it to enemies, who then laid down their weapons and allowed them to pass unmolested. This impressed Father Marquette: "There is nothing more mysterious or more respected among them. Less honor is paid to the Crowns and scepters of Kings than the Savages bestow upon this. It seems to be the God of peace and of War, the Arbiter of life and death."[3] Father Marquette learned this first-hand; a calumet the Illinois gave him averted trouble during his journey down the Mississippi. Unfortunately, the calumet was not always honored; some Indians presenting it to foes were slain.

Between 1655 and 1674 events shook the Illinois Confederacy. It reeled under Sioux (especially Winnebago) onslaughts and then slashing Iroquois raids. The Iroquois Confederacy consisted of Cayuga, Mohawk, Oneida, Onondaga, and Seneca in New York and adjacent regions. Forming a league by about 1570, Iroquois became a deadly fighting machine. By the 1620s firearms obtained from Dutch in Albany upgraded their offensive power. Instilling stark terror in enemies, hegemonic Iroquois drove the Fox, Kickapoo, Mascoutens, and Sauk from lower Michigan into Wisconsin. (These tribes later played significant roles in Illinois' history.) Destroying or scattering tribes in the eastern Great Lakes, Iroquois then assaulted the Illinois by 1655.

* * *

Compounding matters as far away as Illinois, England by 1664 displaced the Dutch in New York and adjacent places. England eventually pushed westward, rattling French authorities, sparking war, and dragging Indians into the fray on both sides.

Officials in Paris and Canada committed France to explore, settle, and hold the Mississippi River Valley. Influential French longed for a water route to the Orient, a quest fueled by Indian claims of such a route. Members of the Society of Jesus, the Jesuits, sought converts. Fur traders wanted western furs. Unbridled nationalism and love of adventure spurred others westward.

Nevertheless, French arrival in Illinois was tardy. Freed from the Thirty Years' War, decision makers in Paris and Quebec City finally planned posts farther west. Iroquois, however, blocked Lake Ontario, deflecting the French up the Ottawa River, over portages, into Georgian Bay. Consequently, French authorities founded Sault Ste. Marie in 1668, thirty-three years before founding Detroit. When French explorers finally entered Illinois, they met Illinois Indians reeling from pummeling by Sioux and then Iroquois. This embattled condition defined their relationships with French officials.

Repeatedly, in sum, people outside Illinois imperiled Illinois Indians. The region became contested territory, with struggles lasting approximately 175 years, until Black Hawk's defeat in 1832.

Technological and social shock waves preceded advancing French culture, affecting Indians even before Frenchmen set foot in Illinois. Although Indian proficiency with bows and arrows impressed visiting Father Marquette in 1673, he wrote, "They also use guns, which they buy from our savage allies who trade with our french. They use them especially to inspire, through noise and smoke, terror in their Enemies; the latter do not use guns, and have never seen any, since they live too far toward the West."[4] Similarly, kettles, beads, and knives appeared in Illinois before French explorers showed up. One scholar suggests, "European trade goods induced the tribe to alter profoundly their martial practices *before* the first Europeans arrived in the Illinois country."⁵ For example, the scale of warfare changed. Indians abandoned traditional small-scale warfare by raiding parties and adopted full-scale communal warfare, warping lines of authority and other social arrangements. Moreover, Indians in Missouri obtained horses by the 1680s. Such changes conditioned Indians to accept additional trappings of French culture.

French-Indian relations were generally good, much better in general than British-Indian relations. French goals and way of life generally complemented Indian culture. The fur trade, for example, bound French and Indians together. Indians usually did the trapping, and French handled the collecting, transporting, and marketing of furs and pelts. Moreover, French men readily married Indian women. A middle ground society developed, a society in which French, Indians, and their offspring lived, mingled freely, borrowed from each other, got along, occasionally spatted, and fashioned a hybrid world. Although many French adopted Indian food, clothing, and other Indian features, Indian religion, warfare, economics, and culture changed greatly. Conversions among Indian girls and women were frequent, often leading to conversions of men. Sometimes Indian converts quickly rose far in French society. For example, the daughter of Chief Rouensa of the Kaskaskia, Marie, who resided at Peoria, was converted in 1694 by Father Jacques Gravier and married Michael Accault, a French trader. She embraced French culture, moved to Cahokia, and prospered, her descendants scaling the social ladder in Louisiana society.⁶ Despite significant troubles with Iroquois, Fox (who were also known as Mesquakie, which means "People of the Red Earth"), and Chickasaw, French and Indians generally got along.⁷

Middle ground culture spawned no battles of extermination and cultural annihilation. Instead, French, Indians, and their mixed offspring borrowed from both cultures and the evolving hybrid, mediating culture. The middle ground—this borderland world—endured clashes among colorful and strong-willed personalities, but it also produced intermarriage, much cooperation, and true friendships.[8] These cemented ties and mutual respect between French and Indians.

French attitudes toward nature sustained this harmony. Although some French tilled farms along rivers, many hiked and paddled vast distances, often living off the land. Indians realized that French civilization threatened them less than English civilization. The exclusive use of land for farming by growing English colonists worried Indians. Moreover, relatively few Britons married Indians, often dismissing them as irredeemably savage, heathen, or both. Consequently, the numerically inferior French, fitting into the middle ground and blending with Indian cultures, earned Indian support in fighting Britons, their outdoor skills serving them well in combat.

In 1669 Father Claude Jean Allouez planted a mission on Green Bay's shores. The next year Robert Cavelier, sieur de La Salle, attempted to explore south of the Great Lakes. Such contacts with Indians in the western Great Lakes whetted French appetites for more, and impressed the Indians with French religion, technology, and other capabilities.

Making impressions, though, was a two-way street, and Indians impressed French long before any Frenchmen trod across Illinois, teaching them about the Illinois region. For example, Father Claude Allouez and Father Claude Dablon arrived in Wisconsin, met visiting Illinois Indians, and learned about the Mississippi River. Father Dablon wrote, "Some Savages have assured us that this is so noble a river that, at more than three hundred leagues' distance from its mouth, it is larger than the one flowing before Quebec." He added, "They also state that all this vast stretch of country consists of nothing but treeless prairies,—so that its inhabitants are all obliged to burn peat and animal excrement dried in the Sun." The Illinois Indians impressed Father Dablon: "These people showed us much politeness, caresses, and evidence of affection as will scarcely be credited; and this is especially true of the chief of that Illinois nation, who is respected in his Cabin as a Prince would be in his Palace."[9]

Jesuits sought conversions, which involved teaching. Nevertheless, they also learned, aided by their acute powers of observation and reason. At Sault Ste. Marie on June 14, 1671, French officials formally claimed western lands, including the Illinois country, and then formed an expedition to explore the river called "Great Water" or "Missipi" by Indians. The leader was Louis Jolliet, an experienced explorer and proven leader. Born in Quebec in 1645, he excelled at map making and surveying and brimmed with courage, knowledge, and appreciation of Indians, knowing several dialects. He also maintained close ties with Jesuits. Father Jacques Marquette, a Jesuit, was the expedition's chaplain. French-born, the thirty-six-year-old Marquette displayed personal courage and focused zeal in proselytizing Indians.

After spending the winter of 1672–1673 at Mackinac, Jolliet, Marquette, and five others paddled two canoes westward on May 17, 1673. Using the Fox and Wisconsin rivers, they reached the Mississippi on June 17 and paddled downstream, Father Marquette recording Indian customs along the way. Pushing beyond the confluence of the Mississippi and the Ohio, they began to doubt the Mississippi led to the Orient. Provisions ran low and worry mounted about Spanish officials and Indians further downstream, so the party turned back in mid-July, a decision hastened by sultry weather and voracious mosquitoes.

An incident on this journey illustrates a common cause of friction between whites and Indians. On the Mississippi, Father Marquette wrote, "We perceived on land some savages armed with guns, who awaited us. I at once offered them my plumed calumet, while our frenchmen prepared for defense, but delayed firing, that the savages might be the first to discharge their guns. I spoke to them in huron, but they answered me by a word which seemed to me to be a declaration of war against us." And then he added something highly important: "However, they were as frightened as we were; and what we took for a signal for battle was an Invitation that they gave to us to draw near, that they might give us food." Violence was avoided, and Father Marquette and his party ate well. The incident ended peacefully, but mutual fears often generated misunderstandings, sometimes sparking trouble. Other troubles arose over concepts of ownership. Illinois Indians believed land belonged to the tribe, not to individuals. Owning land

Kaskaskia Indian with
some evidence of middle
ground influences. From
Victor Collet, *A Journey
in North America*. Paris:
Arthur Bertrand, 1826.
COURTESY OF ILLINOIS
HISTORICAL SURVEY,
UNIVERSITY OF ILLINOIS
LIBRARY, URBANA-CHAMPAIGN.

and selling it was alien to their understanding. Furthermore, Indians held the idea of fixed value of commodities. In this view one fish, for example, was always worth one measure of corn, regardless of supply and demand. These ideas of ownership and value clashed with European ideas.

After backtracking northward, the exploring party entered the Illinois River and paddled toward Lake Michigan. Forests, prairies, soil, elk, deer, ducks, swans, and other natural splendors captivated the French, the river's first European visitors. The party came across a village of Kaskaskia Indians, who greeted the French warmly and extracted from Father Marquette a promise to return and teach them.

After the party reached Green Bay, Jolliet proceeded to Montreal. Sickness kept Father Marquette at Green Bay until late 1674, when he and companions headed southward to keep his promise to return, wintering at the Chicago Portage. Local Indians there assisted them. They then proceeded to the village of Kaskaskia, near present-day Ottawa.

Father Dablon recorded Kaskaskia's reception of Father Marquette: "On at last arriving at the village, he was received as an angel from Heaven." Father Marquette, he added, preached to 2,000 men, including 500 elders and chiefs, as well as numerous women and children.

Father Marquette established the first mission in Illinois, the mission of the Immaculate Conception of the Blessed Virgin, then started for St. Ignace. He never arrived, dying on May 18 in western Michigan, probably near the mouth of the river named for him. His writings during his first journey to Illinois reflected his commitment to his calling and to Indians: "Had this voyage resulted in the Salvation of even one soul, I would consider all my troubles well rewarded."[10] Father Claude Allouez, another Jesuit, replaced Father Marquette at the Kaskaskia mission, serving well for twenty-four years.

Disputes in New France affected exploration south of the Great Lakes. Jesuits tried in vain to shield Indians from coureurs de bois, backwoodsmen who traded weapons, kettles, axes, other utensils, and other goods with Indians for furs, especially beaver. Unfortunately, they also furnished Indians with brandy. Accompanied by voyageurs, who manned the canoes, coureurs de bois plied innumerable small rivers into remote regions, trading with Indians. Indians turned to alcohol, becoming dependent on trade and craving French-made products. This injection of European wares into Indian culture altered society, eroding Indian self-sufficiency.

Disputes in New France and Paris hampered French influence south of the Great Lakes. Into this scene of uncertainty stepped Louis de Buade, conte de Frontenac. Made governor of New France in 1672, Frontenac exuded talent, energy, and ambition. A veteran of campaigns from Flanders to Crete, he was tough and direct. Ousted from office after incurring disfavor, he was reappointed governor just in time to wage eight years of war against Britain and the Iroquois.

Over time, France planned to hem in English influence to the east by creating an arc of forts, posts, and missions from the Gulf of Mexico to eastern Quebec, with Illinois as the keystone. Frontenac's reappointment was part of this vast undertaking, and he faced great odds. The French population in all New France was only 6,700 in 1674, a figure far below the approximately 120,000 in English colonies at that time. French colonial policy excluded from New France Huguenots and Jews, highly talented subjects. Moreover, absolutist French officials in Paris fine-tuned even mundane matters in New France, generally stifling initiative and reinforcing deference. Unlike English colonies, New France developed little self-government, toleration, or healthy individual initiative. Even so, Frontenac had assets, including Indian allies. Jolliet and Marquette's contacts with Indians along the Illinois were strong, as were French ties with other Indians in the Great Lakes–Mississippi Valley region, continuing troubles with dreaded Iroquois being anomalous. Clearly, France was serious about Illinois and neighboring regions.

One of Frontenac's assets was Robert Cavelier, sieur de La Salle. Arriving in New France in 1666, when he was twenty-three, La Salle quickly learned to know the forests, waterways, and Indians. Frontenac tasked him with establishing French power south of the Great Lakes. La Salle dreamed of empire, profits for himself, and glory. Courageous, arrogant, headstrong, and needlessly offensive, he ultimately undid himself.

La Salle's right-hand man was Henri de Tonti, who mirrored some traits of his mentor. Having lost his right hand in combat, Tonti impressed Indians with his "iron hand," a metal hook, and with his forceful personality. Aided by Tonti, supported by Frontenac, and backed by financial interests, La Salle soon monopolized fur trade south of the Great Lakes. This helped project French power westward.

La Salle needed sailing ships to service lands south of the Great Lakes. Canoes were labor-intensive and slow. Accordingly, on the Niagara River's banks, he supervised construction of *Griffon*, the first ship of sail on the western lakes. In the summer of 1679, *Griffon* slipped into Lake Erie, with La Salle aboard, sailed to Green Bay, and loaded a cargo of pelts. La Salle stayed at Green

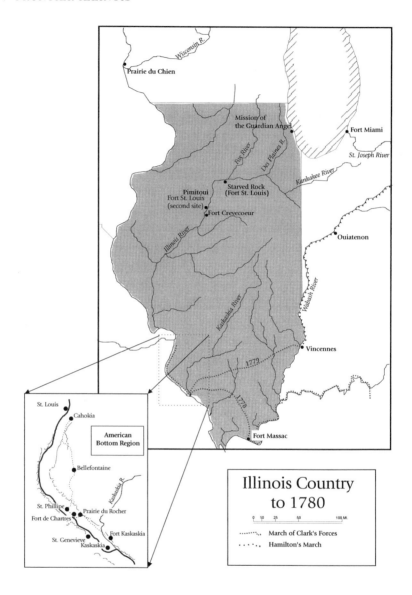

Bay, and *Griffon* sailed toward Niagara, hit a raking storm in
Lake Michigan, and vanished with all hands, a loss unknown to
La Salle for some time.

After a wretched trip down the Wisconsin coast, a party including La Salle, Father Louis Hennepin, and three Recollect

friars of the Franciscan Order arrived at the St. Joseph River in southwestern Michigan. Tonti joined them there in late November from Mackinac. In early December 1679, they entered icy St. Joseph River, seeking the portage to the Kankakee River, a headwater of the Illinois River. Trudging through wintry storms, they blazed the St. Joseph–Kankakee river route, arriving at present-day Peoria in early January.

There they built Fort Crevecoeur, Illinois' first European structure. It stood on a low hill, enhanced by ravines on two sides, a marsh on the third side, and a man-made ditch connecting the two ravines. An earthen embankment surrounded the fort. Impressive walls, palisades twenty-five feet high, contained a building inside each corner, lodging personnel, friars, the magazine, and a forge.

Undaunted by incessant desertion, La Salle set men to work on a vessel to ply the Mississippi and advance his fortunes and the French empire. In addition, La Salle in late February dispatched from Fort Crevecoeur the voluble Father Hennepin to explore the lower Illinois River. Sioux captured him, spirited him up the Mississippi, and released him. Never fastidious about accuracy, he returned from this odyssey with grist for fantastic tales, which he later spun for the unwary.

Learning of the loss of *Griffon*, La Salle realized he had lost equipment vital to outfitting his vessel. Hounded by numerous problems, he returned to New France to address them. In the autumn of 1680, Iroquois attacked Illinois Indians with whom Tonti lived, nearly killing Tonti. After an arduous flight to Green Bay, he rejoined La Salle. In February 1682, La Salle and Tonti led a party of fifty-four French and Indians down the Mississippi, reached its mouth, and on April 9 La Salle claimed the entire Mississippi Valley for the King of France, naming it Louisiana, after King Louis XIV.

Its brimming potential excited La Salle's ambitions, but he knew it needed development. He wished to develop a major port in lower Louisiana, one eclipsing Quebec City and Montreal, ports that iced up in winter. Piling ambition upon ambition, he wanted to colonize Louisiana, mobilize French power, command the region's Indians, and then challenge Spanish authority along the Gulf.

But other concerns riveted his attention. Hearing rumors that Iroquois were massing to invade Illinois, he and Tonti raced northward to counter the threat. He hoped Illinois would channel furs and other products from the lower Great Lakes and upper Mississippi downriver to ports on the Gulf. Accordingly, he sought to protect the crucial Illinois River corridor through French-Indian alliances. He and Tonti in December fortified Starved Rock, naming the palisaded stockade Fort St. Louis. Perched in this fort 125 feet above the Illinois River, La Salle watched as perhaps 4,000 Indian warriors and thousands of non-combatants settled nearby, mostly across the river. Knowing he still needed supplies from New France and Frontenac's support, La Salle dispatched two men to establish a post at the Chicago Portage. La Salle was forging important links in his empire.

Then everything collapsed. His enemies recalled Frontenac to France, and La Salle failed to sway the new governor of New France, Governor Antoine le Febvre de la Barre. La Salle's arrogance, lust for power, and anti-Jesuit stance were anathema to the new governor. De la Barre canceled La Salle's fur monopolies, diminished his power, and actually acceded to Iroquois demands concerning La Salle and his Indian allies. De la Barre feared antagonizing Iroquois, and he realized their distaste for La Salle's activities coincided with his own dislike of La Salle.

Fighting back, La Salle sped to France, spoke to Louis XIV, rekindled support for empire, and in 1684 led a large expedition to the Gulf. Landing on coastal Texas, he vainly tried to locate the Mississippi, but was assassinated in March 1687. Intrepid, adamant, and visionary, he accomplished much and failed enormously. Several survivors of his expedition struck northeast, showing up at Starved Rock on September 14. Disease along with angry Indians and Spaniards decimated those who stayed on the Gulf.

Tonti carried on. More diplomatic and socially adept than La Salle, Tonti worked with tact and boundless enthusiasm. Wanting Illinois to be the keystone in France's empire, he tried to increase its French population, parry Iroquois power, get along with Jesuits, and forestall English expansion. At war with England in the 1690s, France worried about English probes westward.

Tonti also dealt with problems at Fort St. Louis. He realized that Starved Rock's defenders, 125 feet above the Illinois River, could not obtain water. The region's thronging Indians, moreover, placed immense pressure on local supplies of food and wood. Weighing these realities, Tonti during the winter of 1691–1692 selected a new site for Fort St. Louis, a point eighty miles downstream. This move was significant.

The new fort was at an Indian village, Pimitoui, on the Illinois River's right bank about a mile and a half from the outlet of the wide place in the river commonly called "Lake" Peoria. Tonti named the post Fort St. Louis, but most called it Fort Pimitoui. Commodious, it boasted four buildings inside a palisade, including quarters for soldiers. The fort became a trading center, prospered, and under Father Jacques Gravier's leadership a mission to local Indians. Frenchmen, their Indian wives, offspring, and Indians clustered in nearby hamlets, lending a semblance of permanency. The complex symbolized French presence along the Illinois River until Britain took over in 1765.

However, events soon undermined much of Tonti's work. Gaining influence at the royal court, anti-imperialist elements in Paris and New France throttled Tonti. Fur trading unglued Indian culture, making Indians increasingly dependent upon the French. Jesuits anguished over alcoholism and other debilitating influences visited on Indians by coureurs de bois, wanting to restrict fur trading. Practical considerations also eroded Tonti's labors. For example, pelts from south of the Great Lakes were inferior to northern pelts. And pelts shipped southward in summer's heat deteriorated. Finally, unregulated traders aggravated sensitive situations, recklessly irking Iroquois and others.

As a result, on May 26, 1696, Paris withdrew most garrisons from the West and ordered fur traders to desist. Officials exempted Tonti to some degree, and some stubborn coureurs de bois continued traveling clandestinely, but the overall result was chilling.

Enterprise and initiative shriveled, respect for French law waned as coureurs de bois flouted restrictions. Relations between French authorities and those Indians who continued previous trading patterns became strained. Furthermore, Tonti's declining influence sent fur traders scrambling to establish new trade arrangements, some trading illegally with English colonists to the east. Indians in the Ohio valley did the same, and trade began to run along east-west lines to English colonies. This enticed some English colonists farther west, a worrisome occurrence.

French strategic thinking now focused on the Gulf. And so did Tonti's. When France and Britain made peace in 1697, France resumed imperial activities. Instead of relying on fur trading, though, France struggled to colonize and build forts. Biloxi was founded in 1699, Detroit in 1701. Louisiana became a royal colony in 1699. Tonti failed to receive permission to build a fort just below the mouth of the Ohio, so he turned southward, visited Mobile, and died there of yellow fever in 1704.

Things started to unravel before he died. Although Iroquois threats to Illinois tapered off, threats from the Fox to the north mounted. Yielding to Fox pressure, in 1700 Jesuits abandoned the mission started at Chicago Portage in 1696, and in the same year Kaskaskia Indians evacuated the Fort Pimitoui region, the fort then being abandoned. Missionaries, Kaskaskia, settlers, traders, and soldiers moved downstream to the American Bottom. Until about 1740, troublesome Fox kept Illinois, Wisconsin, and nearby regions in an uproar.

In 1698 Bishop de St. Vallier of Quebec authorized priests of the Seminary of Foreign Missions to plant a mission on the American Bottom. Accompanied by Tonti, the Very Reverend Jolliet de Montigny, the Reverend Antoine Davion, and the Reverend Jean Francois Buisson de St. Cosme ventured from Quebec City in late 1698. In March 1699, Father Montigny, who served as vicar-general, and Father St. Cosme founded at Cahokia the Mission of the Holy Family, soon constructing a house and then a chapel. During the third week in May, some two thousand Cahokia, Michigamea, Peoria, Tamaroa, and other Indians attended the ceremony of raising the cross.[11]

Jesuits vied with the Seminary of Foreign Missions to establish missions among western Indians. Once the Mission of the Holy Family at Cahokia was under construction, Jesuits dispatched three priests to Cahokia to found a competing mission. Mission rights in the vast Mississippi Valley were at stake in this turf war. Although restraint and civility marked the dispute, quiet passion bubbled. Each side appealed to civil and religious authorities in France, and in 1701 French bishops ceded the region to the Seminarians, with the proviso that Jesuits have opportunities to minister to other Illinois Indians. Jesuits capitalized on this proviso. After abandoning Fort Pimitoui to be with Kaskaskia Indians, Jesuits accompanied them across the Mississippi, to present-day St. Louis. Then they all recrossed the river and entered the southern end of the American Bottom, where French traders lived along the Kaskaskia River.

The mission of the Immaculate Conception of the Blessed Virgin, founded by Father Marquette in 1674 and then transferred to Fort Pimitoui, was now established at Kaskaskia. By 1711 Jesuits owned one windmill and two horsemills near Kaskaskia. Milling indicates regular sizeable surpluses and trade. The narrow floodplain between Cahokia and Kaskaskia now housed two missions and was soon the center of French influence in the middle Mississippi. As the keystone in a thin arc of settlement from eastern Quebec to the Gulf, Illinois helped sustain other French possessions. It linked French settlements in the Great Lakes–St. Lawrence region to French settlements planned for along the Gulf and lower Mississippi. In addition, Illinois soon sent foodstuffs and other products to faraway French posts.

Other changes followed the shift from the Illinois River to the American Bottom. Coureurs de bois, trapper-traders, voyageurs, and explorers began to yield to farmers and merchants. Some French were *traiteurs*, men who traded directly with Indians. They relied on voyageurs, the men who crewed the vessels. These two groups of individuals sometimes carried goods of *negociants*, itinerant businessmen who usually farmed and did business on the side. Some were also *habitants*, settlers who raised crops, livestock, and performed other agrarian work. Some dabbled in all these undertakings, engaging in farming and trapping, providing goods for trade, and transporting goods. Nevertheless, as more French settled and became productive, a complex tapestry of production and distribution evolved, helping to sink the taproot of French culture deeply into Illinois.

Facing threats from Iroquois, Illinois Indians and French made common cause in the late 1600s. By 1763 defeated France ceded North America to Britain. Some Illinois Indians then threw their lot in with Britain, only to see Britain lose everything east of the Mississippi to the nascent United States. As their political fortunes sagged, their numbers shrank. Illinois Indians in present-day Illinois possibly numbered 33,000 in 1660. Just twenty years later only 10,500 were left, excluding the Michigamea. This number plummeted to around 6,000 by 1700, and 2,500 by 1736. Fewer than 500 survived in 1763, fewer than 100 by 1783, and no more than eighty in 1800, clustering in just one village in Illinois. Lethal diseases, warfare, and social and economic dislocations took their toll. (Some Illinois found refuge west of the Mississippi.) In addition, dependency on whites made Indians vulnerable, precipitating overall decline.[12] Dependency on whites and on the United States Government also earned them enmity from other Indians.

Obviously, contingencies changed Illinois' history: Deadly Iroquois expanded, targeting the French, Illinois tribes, and other Indians. Illinois tribes, furthermore, suffered as allies of France in wars against England. And then, as if to make amends, the region's Indians generally allied themselves with Britain, another mistake. In the end, forlorn fragments of the region's Indian tribes stood alone, facing advancing Americans.

3.

TIES SOUTH AND WAR FOR EMPIRE

Relatively few French in Illinois brought great changes. French society in Illinois, moreover, differed significantly from French society elsewhere in North America. In some ways, in fact, it more closely resembled English colonial society than French society in Canada or around the Gulf.

French society was riverine, a crucial fact. Virtually all towns, missions, forts, posts, and early farms abutted navigable water. River junctures and portages sprouted strategic settlements, and bluffs overlooking waterways caught the attention of military officers. The long-lot system of land division, imported from France, spread along the St. Lawrence River, in the Great Lakes, and elsewhere. Some long-lot farms were a quarter of a mile or more long and just thirty or forty feet wide. These long, narrow farms—dubbed "ribbon farms" or "strip farms"—gave owners water frontage. Ribbon farms maximized the number of owners enjoying water transportation. Furthermore, they increased variations in soil, vegetation, and topography. One long-lot farm, for example, might enjoy fertile soil, sandy soil, rocks, timber, scrub vegetation, meadows, swamp, bluff, and other features. Ribbon farms facilitated plowing. Turning oxen at the end of furrows was time-consuming, inefficient, and even dangerous, reducing crop yield there. Long-lot furrows required relatively few turnings.

Social benefits also accrued from this system. Although some French farmers in French Canada and Louisiana lived in farming villages like Europeans and walked to their long-lot fields, most lived on farmsteads. Their homes dotted river banks at intervals or clustered in small groups. Connecting paths and then roads ran along the far ends of their ribbon farms. In northern regions, winter witnessed sleds hauling bulky loads on frozen waterways. Shortened winter workdays encouraged evening socializing, with people visiting via frozen waterways and roads. Communication was relatively easy and frequent, fostering community, cohesion, and safety.

Illinois' long-lot system, however, differed significantly from Canada's. For unclear reasons—perhaps related to perceived security needs—very few Illinoisan farmers lived on isolated farmsteads. Instead, they lived in villages and hamlets, walking to fields daily.

The long-lot system also had common fields, a practice which was widespread in Europe and English colonies. Commons in Illinois and Canada, sometimes a thousand acres in size, were often just behind lots adjacent to rivers. Commons provided firewood, timber, and grass, as well as game, fruit, berries, nuts, and other necessities.

* * *

The Treaty of Utrecht in 1713 ended war with Britain, allowing France again to focus on North America, triggering dreams, schemes, and projects. In 1713 France restructured Louisiana, a royal colony since 1699, giving it civil government, and the next year France made its first permanent settlement there. In 1717 John Law, a Scot, obtained a trading monopoly in Louisiana. He planned to retire France's national debt by promoting agriculture, cities, and mines in the Mississippi Valley. Law dazzled the public with novel possibilities and fantastic schemes. In 1717 Illinois fell under Louisiana's jurisdiction, becoming Upper Louisiana, further diluting Quebec's influence on Illinois. Law's Company of the Indies enjoyed impressive powers in Upper and Lower Louisiana: trade monopoly, appointment of officials, and control of forts and posts. In late 1718 soldiers, officials, mining engineers, and workers arrived at Kaskaskia from newly founded New Orleans to bolster French power, constructing Fort de Chartres in 1720. A natural north-south economic, social, political, and military axis linked Illinois to the lower Mississippi. In 1720 goofy gold mining schemes brought black slaves from Santo Domingo to Illinois, Jesuits owning many. The same year, though, saw the collapse of John Law's financial empire, a "bubble."

Other designs were less fanciful and fraught with dire consequences. By the early 1700s France took a serious interest in the continent's interior. Perhaps this reflected mounting interest in furs, perhaps it reflected France's efforts to deflect Britain from French possessions in the West Indies, and perhaps it was part of a complex geopolitical and economic undertaking. Driven by mercantile notions, France tried to control and develop four distinct regions: the Atlantic maritime, later called Acadia; New France, which consisted of the St. Lawrence River system and the Great Lakes; the lower Mississippi region and the Gulf Coast; and the West Indies.

Fort de Chartres' construction in 1720 strengthened ties with the lower Mississippi and Gulf Coast, signaled France's unequivocal intention to amass power in Illinois, and reflected John Law's soaring ambitions. Located some eighteen miles upriver from Kaskaskia, it comforted waning Indian allies and possibly impressed troublesome Fox.

The first of three Fort de Chartres had log walls, a dry moat, a blockhouse at each corner, enabling enfilading fire to rake attackers. It also had a storehouse, troops' quarters, a countinghouse, and other structures. But by 1725 flood damage necessitated a new fort, farther from the Mississippi. This fort had log walls some 160 feet square, a blockhouse at each corner. Providing enfilading opportunities, the blockhouses also housed a magazine, stable, and jail. Buildings soon cropped up outside the walls, including a chapel and some houses.

Decisive struggles accompanied the second fort's establishment. Since 1712 Fox (Mesquakie) Indians from Detroit to Green Bay sporadically harassed French, the conflict turning ominous in the 1720s, when Fox pounced on French and Indians in Illinois. Despite a truce in 1726, relations worsened as French established ties with Sioux via central Wisconsin, the Fox heartland. Resisting this incursion with raids, the Fox became targeted for French retribution. Fearing retaliation, some 950 Fox men, women, and children streaked eastward toward protective Iroquois. About 1,400 French and Indian allies intercepted this band in August 1730, besieged its fortified position for perhaps twenty-three days, and in September mauled fleeing remnants. This campaign and subsequent actions virtually wiped out the Fox, quickened French military activity around Illinois, and brought relative tranquility from Detroit to central Wisconsin and regions to the south.

Inept commanders at Fort de Chartres, collapse of the Company of the Indies, and deferred maintenance at the fort produced rotting walls and other troubles. By 1748 the garrison moved to Kaskaskia.

Although both forts crumbled, they accomplished much. They augmented and symbolized French power and stability, encouraged economic growth, and produced a nearby satellite hamlet. They reflected seriousness of purpose. By the 1720s the American Bottom became a huge cereal grain producer for all of French North America. In addition, discoveries of lead deposits across the Mississippi lent impetus to France's securing the region, accentuating Illinois' keystone role between Quebec and the lower Mississippi. The two Fort de Chartres, however rickety, underscored France's role as the major player in interior North America. Moreover, from Illinois France planned to project power as far as Pennsylvania via forts and Indian alliances.

Weighing possible locations for a new fort, authorities chose a site near the old fort, not near Kaskaskia. Ignoring costs, French officials used limestone for the walls and buildings. Quarried from bluffs north of Prairie du Rocher, it was rafted and then hauled by oxen to the site. Work started in 1753, just one year before the French-Indian War. Despite desertions of skilled personnel and

French dwelling in eighteenth-century Illinois. Of *poteaux en terre* (posts set into the ground) or *poteaux en solle* (posts set on a wooden sill) construction, with *bousillage* (clay mixed with straw) wedged between the posts, these houses often had one or two chimneys and a *galerie* (porch) on two, three, or four sides. From Victor Collet, *A Journey in North America*. Paris: Arthur Bertrand, 1826. COURTESY OF ILLINOIS HISTORICAL SURVEY, UNIVERSITY OF ILLINOIS LIBRARY, URBANA-CHAMPAIGN.

marginal support from France, most work was completed by 1754. Glistening cream-colored stone walls replaced decaying wooden walls, symbolizing Illinois' growing importance.

The fort was square, with large bastions and sentry towers at each corner. The limestone walls—two feet thick, seventeen feet high, and 490 feet long—and a massive gate tower impressed visitors, as did two limestone barracks, government buildings, a commandant's house, and a solid magazine. The magazine is possibly the oldest extant structure in Illinois. A guardhouse quartered troops, a priest, a chapel, and storage rooms.

The fort had religious as well as military functions. The parish of Ste. Anne, which centered on the fort's chapel, was founded in 1721. It served the fort and St. Philippe, a hamlet just north of the fort. It also sponsored the mission chapel of St. Joseph in nearby Prairie du Rocher, a village founded in 1722 and named for nearby bluffs.

* * *

Life was good. Bountiful harvests, neat houses, and general prosperity graced the region. Villages associated with Fort de Chartres, especially, prospered: "The villagers flourished; the documents suggest the life in the Illinois offered many amenities, in sharp contrast to modern stereotypes of frontier existence." During halcyon years before the French-Indian War, trade flourished along the Illinois–Gulf of Mexico axis, Illinois serving as the granary of Louisiana.[1] Illinois' products reached the Caribbean and even France. Hams, bacon, venison, poultry, buffalo meat, cheese, corn, wheat, flour, nuts, honey, port, deerskins, hides, some pelts, tallow, leather, timber, lead, and copper slipped down the Mississippi, as did wheat, hops, barley, corn, buckwheat, rye, and oats. Wheat was the mainstay. Cattle, chickens, turkeys, and fish supplied protein, and well-tended gardens enriched diets. Hemp and some tobacco were raised. Oxen were the main draft animals, hauling wagons, turning mills, and pulling plows with iron-plated shares. Impressive manufactured goods, European utensils, clothing, fabrics, as well as sugar, indigo, and rice, reached Illinois. Ordinary residents in the 1720s used napkins from Rouen, tin-lined kettles, candlesticks, bottles and flasks, stockings, and numerous other items from France, and enjoyed houses of frame timbers with stone chimneys. Significantly, "Their standard of living was good, far higher than that of the pioneers who grappled with the Illinois prairies a hundred years later; no wonder many of the soldiers settled here after their service rather than returning to France."[2]

Because heat spoiled pelts, French shipped few downriver to New Orleans; rather, they shipped them to Quebec, maintaining Illinois' ties to the St. Lawrence. These durable ties attracted to Illinois steady trickles of Canadiens, some leaving Quebec to escape brutal, lengthy winters.

Prospering, French communities in Illinois generated far more
self-government than Quebec, Louisiana, or France. Unlike their
habitually deferring kith and kin in Quebec and Louisiana, Illinois residents stood on their hind legs and bucked unfair, capricious maladministration. For example, in 1725 the commander
at Fort de Chartres, Sieur de Pradel, arrested a fellow for alleged
insolence. Led by one La Plune, settlers became unruly, getting
Pradel arrested and exiled to New Orleans. Illinois villagers generated incipient self-government: "Their significance lies, above
all, in their representing possibly the only example in continental North America of French settlers establishing themselves independently of official or metropolitan elite guidance and control—the very opposite of French settlement in Canada." This
may overstate the case, but French residents in Illinois behaved
much like New Englanders. They voted for clergymen and militia officers. Town meetings sprang up, at which residents vented
concerns. Both societies enjoyed fee-simple land holdings and
only traces of feudalism. Clearly, "What the New Englanders did,
the Illinois French, with some obvious Gallic variations, did too."[3]
Republican sentiment welled up in both societies, long before
Lexington and Concord or the French Revolution. French subjects in Illinois, it appears, moved toward becoming French citizens. In sum, Illinois' culture differed markedly from French societies elsewhere.

Several factors distinguished society in Illinois. Widespread
ownership of land, substantial social mobility, and freedom from
feudal restrictions generated self-worth and assertiveness. The
dearth of feudal institutions and mentality helped residents establish "themselves independently of official or metropolitan elite
guidance and control" and avoid habitual, demeaning deference.
Unlike Canada, Illinois witnessed no seigniorial grant, no seigniorial system of land holding. Large holdings did exist, fostering
understandable deference, but a conditional and tenuous deference. Property in Illinois was nearly always granted *en franc alleu*,
owners getting land outright, unencumbered by feudal taxes, fees,
or other obligations. For example, Illinoisans, unlike Canadians,
enjoyed fishing and hunting rights, the usual prerogatives of sei-
gniors. Moreover, enforcement of arcane restrictions and vesti-

gial dues was feeble and sporadic, most such annoyances laps-
ing altogether. Essentially, Illinois escaped stultifying feudal restrictions saddling other North American French communities.

A related social development was significant. In Ste. Genevieve,
a settlement founded around 1750 on the Mississippi River opposite Kaskaskia, women acquired economic, social, and even political power. They "did in fact decide, or strongly influence, decisions affecting themselves, their families and their community."
Legal contracts mitigated inheritance customs, enhancing wom-
en's status. Husbands taking extended trips gave wives "additional power and ample opportunity to function as deputy husbands, protecting their own interests and those of their families."
Women's property was protected, and "possession of wealth gave
women greater opportunity to control their lives."[4] The fact that
comparatively few women lived in Ste. Genevieve increased their
value and helped secure them rights not enjoyed by women in
Quebec. Similar developments probably occurred in adjacent Illinois.

* * *

British colonists, far more numerous in North America than
French, looked westward across the Appalachians. For decades
British traders and explorers salivated over western lands.
Infiltrating the Mississippi Valley during the 1730s, British personnel helped the Chickasaws crush a French-Indian campaign
in 1736.[5] British officials wooed tribes, and merchants plied them
with inexpensive trading goods. By the late 1740s, Delaware, Iroquois, Miami, and Shawnee succumbed to these blandishments,
tentatively adhering to Britain. Worse yet for the French, Britain
in 1749 granted to the Ohio Company lands on both sides of the
Ohio, lands claimed by France. France stirred in response to this
unabashed encroachment.

As France sought solutions to its brewing Indian and British
problems, in June of 1752 a huge Fox-led Indian raid by northern tribes jolted Cahokia and Michigamea Indians—Illinois Indians—encamped near Fort de Chartres. A year earlier some Cahokia had bested the Fox in a raid and then killed seven prisoners.
Fearing retaliation, Cahokia moved southward to just north of

Fort de Chartres, to the summer camp of the Michigamea, who welcomed them. Using stealth and skill, hundreds of Fox-led raiders soon attacked and mauled these Illinois Indians. Illinois anguish over slain and captured members was heightened when they learned that the French—their defenders and patrons—had deliberately betrayed them and exposed them to the raid. This betrayal was a free-lance operation by a rogue French commander, Macarty, who knew the Illinois Indians were enticed by superior goods sold at cheaper prices by British traders and were considering abandoning the French and joining the British. Macarty believed a sharp Fox raid would force the Illinois to stick with the French, and his machinations paid off. Although some Illinois left the region, most admitted their dependency on the French. By 1765 many surviving Illinois moved west of the Mississippi.[6]

Hoping to blunt British encroachment, France projected power to the headwaters of the Ohio. In 1749 the governor of Canada sent an expedition through much of western Pennsylvania and Ohio to claim the region by planting inscribed lead plates. Constantly stumbling across evidence of British influence, it demonstrated that France was projecting power eastward none too early. Seeing ominous omens, France was rolling the dice in one supreme effort to stem the Anglo tide.

In 1752 Canada's new, vigorous governor parried British encroachment, throwing up three forts in western Pennsylvania and assiduously courting the region's Indians. Built where the Allegheny and the Monongahela form the Ohio, Fort Duquesne was impressive. Tensions between French and British parties sputtered in 1752, and erupted into open warfare in 1754. Called the French and Indian War in America and the Seven Years' War in Europe, it quickly escalated into a global duel between France and Britain, the last such duel in North America.[7]

At the outset of the war, the British North American colonial population probably topped 1,300,000, while the French colonial population was under 100,000, about one-fifteenth that of the British. During the early 1760s as fighting turned against France and refugees fled fighting in the upper Ohio and elsewhere, Illinois probably gained population.

Illinois and Fort de Chartres played secondary roles in this struggle, but the fort was a "central supply center," shipping grain and other provisions to French forts up the Ohio and along the Mississippi. In September 1755, for example, a convoy of flour and pork reached Fort Duquesne from Illinois. In the same year, the government moved from Kaskaskia to the protection of Fort de Chartres, spawning the nearby village of New Chartres, home to about forty families. By 1756 the fort housed British prisoners.

To thwart a British drive via the Tennessee against Mississippi towns, French forces in the spring of 1757 hurried south and constructed a fort on the Ohio, as close to the mouth of the Tennessee River as possible. Variously known as Fort Ascension, Fort Massiac, and under the Americans as Fort Massac, this fort was constructed of earth and timber. It repulsed a major Cherokee assault in late 1757 and later witnessed several sharp skirmishes, but after France evacuated the fort in 1764 Chickasaw burned it.

Units from Fort de Chartres reached Fort Duquesne in early 1758 and helped repel British threats. But fortunes of war changed abruptly. Burning Fort Duquesne and abandoning the upper Ohio Valley, French soldiers lugged cannon back to Illinois. In 1759 a force of 400 from Illinois tried to reverse these setbacks, attacking Fort Presq 'Isle on Lake Erie and Fort Niagara. It was trounced, the commander taken prisoner. The same year Kaskaskia's residents, jittery about security, erected earthworks on overlooking bluffs. But relative isolation limited Illinois' military roles. French fortunes plunged with stunning defeats in 1759 at Quebec City and elsewhere.

British and colonial forces in 1760 and 1761 inched across the lower Great Lakes and the Ohio River Valley, occupying St. Joseph, Miami, Ouiatenon, and other posts. By late 1761 French power north of the Ohio existed only around Illinois. Since Illinois was under Louisiana's jurisdiction, however, it was not surrendered. Authorities in Illinois, in fact, assumed the war was still on and attack might be imminent, a belief shared by authorities in Louisiana, who dispatched troops to Illinois. Supplementing this force, 132 soldiers showed up at Fort de Chartres after slipping away from Mackinac. Authorities in Illinois abandoned vulnerable Peoria, its small garrison heading south, and beefed up Fort Massiac. These measures, though, were too little too late, unable to undo catastrophic French defeats elsewhere. In late 1765 French authorities ceremoniously surrendered Fort de Chartres to arriving British occupation forces.

Ironically, Fort de Chartres, the most formidable military structure in interior North America, played marginal roles in the war. It was simply too far from the theaters of war. And to man the fort adequately required well over 300 men, more than were ever present. The fort hosted British prisoners and launched forays eastward, but its cannon never fired in anger. Illinois' isolation spared residents from war's horrors. Practically no casualties occurred within Illinois.

* * *

In peace and then war, French accomplished much. Amazing prosperity, vibrant women's roles, and robust political activity adorned the American Bottom and Ste. Genevieve. French authorities never planned these accomplishments; they just happened, and they happened essentially peacefully. France busied itself in protecting its empire, not in sustaining unintended achievements, however impressive.

Outnumbered French and Indian allies performed military miracles against British forces, but France tried to do too much across too great a distance with insufficient resources. France's thin and stretched population base in North America had hobbled imperial designs. France overextended itself, undermining impressive achievements. With military defeat in Canada, life in Illinois unraveled.

Illinois' sparse French population reflected overall weakness. In June 1723, Kaskaskia contained just 196 whites, the village near Fort de Chartres only 126, and Cahokia just twelve—for a total of 334 whites. By January of 1732, a census enumerated 190 children for the whole region, suggesting about 400 to 600 whites. The 1752 census counted 768 French subjects, including some Indian wives, consisting of 284 men, 132 women, and 352 children. Fort de Chartres housed an abnormally large contingent of soldiers, some 300. In 1767, two years after British occupation and some French flight across the Mississippi to avoid British rule, a census listed some 600 white men, women, and children in Kaskaskia. Cahokia had sixty families, Prairie du Rocher twenty-five, the settlement associated with Fort de Chartres just three families, and St. Philippe three. In 1767 these places had 1,055 permanent residents. If soldiers and transients are included, then whites topped 1,500.

By 1726 a census revealed that blacks constituted 24 percent of Illinois' recorded population. The census of 1732 recorded black slaves: Kaskaskia, 102; Chartres village, 37; St. Philippe, 22; Cahokia, 4—for a total of 165, or possibly nearly 30 percent of the total population. Mid-century population figures for Illinois settlements are revealing: 768 French, 445 black slaves, and 147 Indian slaves. Black slaves constituted over 32 percent of Illinois' population. They toiled alongside Indian slaves. Indian slavery eventually faded, but black slavery grew,[8] and it strengthened powerful links between Illinois and southern culture and economy, links lasting into statehood and sparking heated debate.

Although most blacks originally arrived in Illinois as slaves in mining schemes and related work, masters soon employed them in agriculture and other pursuits. From the beginning, at least a few free blacks lived among the French, their numbers augmented by manumission. Records indicated fifteen slaves gained their freedom at Kaskaskia. Free blacks had rights, including the right to buy and sell, bear arms, and make contracts. One, Jacques Duverger, bought a house in Kaskaskia, hired a Frenchman to go on a winter hunt and to New Orleans, contracted to ship cargoes to and from New Orleans, and received payment for work as a surgeon.[9]

Just as sparse population crippled France's military efforts, it also weakened vestiges of French culture. Over decades, waves of Anglo settlers and others washed into Illinois, altered customs, language, and even religion, and eroded and distorted French society. (The last native French-speaking resident died after World War II.) Only in Quebec and other tight, cohesive population clusters did language, religion, and other vital cultural traits thrive.

At the close of the war in 1763 the Treaty of Paris gave Britain everything east of the Mississippi and everything in Canada to the Rockies. Spain got everything west of the Mississippi, a reward for entering the war, however belatedly. Ninety years after Louis Jolliet and Father Marquette canoed the Illinois River, France's North American empire vanished.

4. LIGHT BRITISH RULE

Obtaining Illinois by treaty was one thing; projecting British power to Illinois, occupying it, and administering it were other matters. In the end, British authorities reached Illinois, but they never really occupied or administered it.[1] Moreover, Britain's acquisition of French North America put it on a collision course with British colonists, who increasingly regarded themselves as Americans. Hearing stories of natural wealth west of the Appalachians, they believed opportunity lay there. Looking longingly at these lands, Americans assumed France's departure insured ready access to the region. They were wrong. British ideas concerning these lands differed sharply from Americans' ideas. Therein lay the rub.

Two and one-half years elapsed between the Treaty of Paris and British occupancy of Fort de Chartres. The chief obstacle was a bold, deadly plot simmering in Chief Pontiac's mind to annihilate British power in the West. An Ottawa chief and leader of other Indians, Pontiac planned audacious, coordinated attacks against a dozen British posts north of the Ohio River. Although British traders paid Indians well for furs and other products, some merchants mistreated Indians. Indians, moreover, lamented

France's withdrawal, worrying about westward American migration.

Pontiac coordinated numerous Ottawas, Potawatomis, Ojibwas, Wyandots, Chippewas, Delawares, and Shawnees, and he also attracted Seneca, the only Iroquois adhering to this conspiracy. With one major exception, tight security kept Pontiac's conspiracy secret, a reflection of Pontiac's standing among diverse Indian tribes. The twelve targeted posts lay within a triangular region from Fort Ligonier east of Pittsburgh, to Fort Michilimackinac on the straits of Mackinac, to Fort Ouiatanon on the Wabash. By spring 1763, major Indian contingents were poised to strike.

Beginning on May 7, attacks rippled across the region, picking off posts, ambushing relief columns, and besieging forts that withstood being taken by storm. The first objective, Detroit, escaped destruction on May 7 through timely warning. Other forts were not so fortunate, falling by combinations of onslaught, deception, or siege. By mid-June British forts in the western part of the vast triangular region lay in ashes, most of their garrisons dead or in grim captivity. Only forts in the triangle's eastern fringes— Pitt, Ligonier, Niagara, and Detroit—withstood the attacks, enduring sieges of varying intensities. In just six weeks Indians had hurled British power eastward hundreds of miles.

But the effort failed. Detroit's resistance caused defections among Indians, Fort de Chartres' commander informed Pontiac to expect no assistance from French authorities, General Jeffrey Amherst soon seized the strategic initiative, and Pontiac lifted the siege of Detroit. Spanish takeover of trans-Mississippi lands denied Pontiac a strategic hinterland from which to draw support. British victories in 1764, moreover, led Pontiac to sue for peace, an admission of defeat.

Illinois witnessed Pontiac's final, tragic activities. In April of 1769, he visited Cahokia, imbibed, and was murdered by either a Peoria or a Kaskaskia, inciting vengeful Potawatomi, who in 1770 at Starved Rock nearly annihilated remnant Illinois Indians. Nearly half a century later Tecumseh picked up Pontiac's mantle and crusaded to halt westward expansion north of the

Ohio. Only this time the crusade was against Americans, and it had British support. And about twenty years after Tecumseh's effort, Black Hawk fought to preserve a semblance of Indian life in northwestern Illinois.

* * *

Peaceful efforts paralleled Pontiac's onslaught. In Britain in the early 1760s several factions jockeyed to formulate policy for lands acquired from France. The futures of Indians, British, Americans and Illinois hung in the balance. For various reasons, influential British hoped to stop, channel, or at least retard movement beyond the Appalachian divide, leaving the region north of the Ohio to just French and Indians. The region would become, at least temporarily, an Indian preserve containing only Indians, licensed traders, and some trappers. Others sought speedy removal of Indians and swift occupation and settlement by British. British policy, such as it was, vacillated between these two incompatible positions, and nothing consistent was ever devised and enforced. In the meantime, though, Britain wanted no settlement in the region, which irked prospective settlers and speculators.[2]

The Proclamation of 1763 forbade settlement west of the Appalachian divide—for the time being. It sought time, a breathing spell, in which to solve the entire Indian question, without having to worry about settler-Indian troubles. Villages in Illinois were on their own, and French civil and military officials continued functioning. But rude reality quickly undermined the Proclamation; fresh lands lured settlers and traders westward. The Treaty of Fort Stanwix of November 5, 1768, further eroded the Proclamation. The floodgates were opening.

Pontiac's onslaughts in 1763 and vacillating British trans-Appalachian policy stalled British arrival in Illinois. Authorities simply had difficulty getting there. Within two and a half years after the Treaty of Paris in 1763, Britain launched two major military expeditions and seven less formidable ones to establish a presence in Illinois. Beginning in early 1765, British parties trickled into Illinois from Mobile, West Florida, and Fort Pitt.

On August 24, 1765, Captain Thomas Stirling led about 100 men from the Forty-Second (Black Watch) Regiment from Fort

Pitt toward Illinois. They arrived on October 9, and the next day a formal ceremony surrendered Fort de Chartres to Captain Stirling. This terminated French authority in Illinois.

Having waged successful warfare against the French, Britain clearly indicated it would not destroy French culture. Captain Stirling carried with him a magnanimous proclamation from General Thomas Gage, British commander in North America. It granted to French inhabitants "the liberty of the Catholic religion." French residents, the proclamation added, "may exercise the worship of their religion." Moreover, they were free to sell property, leave, and take belongings with them. (Only debtors and parties to criminal proceedings were not free to leave.) If inhabitants stayed, they could own lands and personal properties, and would "enjoy the same rights and privileges, the same security for their persons and effects and liberty of trade, as the old subjects of the King." At least 1,055 permanent residents still lived in villages in the American Bottom in 1767, perhaps persuaded to stay put by this proclamation.

Yet despite British efforts to allay French anxiety, some French worried. Concerned about the impact of British occupation on their religion and on their slaves, some believed life in Spanish Louisiana across the Mississippi offered greater promise, and by 1770 fairly large numbers crossed, siphoning off people of means and talent. By 1770, in fact, most civil and military authorities in Spanish Louisiana were French.[3] Some had served in the West before 1763, gone to France, and then returned to North America. Their presence encouraged French in Illinois to pull up stakes. Even so, many French who left Illinois for Spanish Louisiana moved back once conditions settled down.[4]

Pierre La Clede, trapper and entrepreneur, adjusted to fluid conditions. Crossing the Mississippi to Spanish Louisiana, he assumed responsibility in 1764 for constructing a village and a river depot on the west bank, just south of the Missouri-Mississippi confluence. He named it St. Louis. This new village attracted some French from Illinois, as did Ste. Genevieve. A few Illinoisans went to New Orleans.

The French exodus included talented, energetic, and prosperous people, a real loss of human capital. Moreover, some took slaves with them. Since French Illinois suffered chronic labor shortages, the exodus was painful. Among those staying in Illinois were comparatively many elderly, sick, and discouraged.

Loss occurred in other ways. Institutional and cultural life declined. The church of Ste. Anne, for example, was abandoned, its records transferred to St. Joseph's in Prairie du Rocher. Adding to Illinois' woes, the Jesuits fell victim to court intrigue, being expelled from the province of Louisiana to which Illinois belonged. In late 1763, the order was executed, confiscating all Jesuit property and selling it by early November. About a year later, France outlawed the Jesuit order in France and all its colonies, which had monumental repercussions. This was a catalyst for Father Forget Duverger, who headed the Seminarian mission at Cahokia. Troubled by unsettled conditions, including British influence, he hurriedly sold the mission's lands, buildings, and slaves, then departed for New Orleans. At a critical time, Illinois was without the regular services of a priest.

Father Sebastien Louis Meurin left with his fellow Jesuits. At New Orleans, though, he tried to return to Illinois. Failing, he went to Ste. Genevieve, from where he ministered to Indians and French in Illinois. Faltering health and other factors kept him from ministering to faraway Vincennes, but he served the faithful in Illinois. The bishop of Quebec helped out, making Father Meurin his vicar-general in the West, an office which gave him authority to carry out specific functions. Two events in 1768 changed things. Meurin spatted with Ste. Genevieve's commandant, who tried to arrest him. The aging, feeble priest escaped across the river to Illinois and swore allegiance to the British Crown. In the same year, the indomitable Father Pierre Gibault arrived to assist Father Meurin. In his mid-thirties and bursting with energy and talent, he threw himself into his duties, even ministering to distant Vincennes. In 1770 he was appointed vicar-general in the West, relieving the failing Father Meurin. Despite herculean labors of Father Meurin and Father Gibault, French folk and institutions languished and chaffed under British rule.

Spain's takeover of enormous Louisiana compounded loss. Spain now owned virtually everything west of the Mississippi.

Although Spanish rule for French people was better than British rule, it nevertheless degraded French society. Old trade patterns, for example, established by French over decades decayed. Capricious Spain controlled the lower Mississippi, including New Orleans, crippling French economic interests upstream. Prosperous and vibrant participatory French village life in Illinois, Ste. Genevieve, and elsewhere degenerated, replaced by subsistence production, barter, and lethargy. Demoralization and general decline set in, conditions apparent to Americans trickling in following British occupation.

Old French patterns changed in another way. For decades English colonists traded with Indians and French west of the Appalachians, and now they sought quick profit in western lands. Ignoring the Proclamation of 1763 and scoffing at draconian penalties enacted by Pennsylvania, they pushed beyond the Appalachian divide and contacted French and Indians. Eastern merchants, moreover, wanted lucrative contracts to provision British soldiers in western posts. Merchants in Philadelphia extended lines of credit to traders operating north of the Ohio. Speculators in Virginia, Connecticut, and Pennsylvania conjured schemes to colonize Illinois. Although many undertakings were unprofitable or premature, they nevertheless focused American attention on Illinois, at a time when Spanish occupation of Louisiana loosened ties southward. British influence in Illinois was thin and transitory, but this influence and Spanish control of Louisiana reoriented life in Illinois. Talented French quitting Illinois accelerated this reorientation.

Nature obliterated traces of French presence in Illinois. The meandering Mississippi threatened Fort de Chartres, renamed Fort Cavendish by Britain. The river cut to within 250 feet of the fort by 1765, about 30 feet in 1770, and cut into fort's south wall and bastion in 1772, when Britain abandoned it. Nature brought flooding, rampant sickness among garrison troops, and crop disease. The flight of able-bodied men across the Mississippi crimped efforts to fight nature's assaults. Checkered British leadership aggravated matters. Captain Thomas Stirling, who had occupied Fort de Chartres in October 1765, was replaced within two months and died a month later. Stirling's numerous successors—there were eight—varied in quality, but most were bad. Colonel John Wilkins of the Black Watch Regiment had the longest tenure, arriving on September 5, 1768, and serving over three years. High turnover of commanders and uneven quality retarded civil government. Colonel Wilkins did establish a court system, but its existence was troubled and brief. Favoritism and corruption were rife. Britain lacked direction and resolution concerning the West, which hurt Illinois. Britain's vacillating policies toward the seaboard colonies worsened matters.

Moreover, some British subjects who entered Illinois antagonized French residents. Although few British subjects ventured to Illinois, "the influx of opportunistic, conniving, and often arrogant Anglos . . . did not help relations between the two elements of the [European] Illinois population."[5] The change of governance from French to British systems—involving different judicial procedures, contracts, language, land titles, and other crucial matters—was inherently difficult. Newly arrived British riffraff worsened an already ticklish situation. Many French contemplated alternatives, an important fact once the American Revolution broke out.

Goods from Spanish Louisiana went down the Mississippi more cheaply than British goods went from Illinois to the East Coast, which gave Spain power and gave St. Louis brisk business in Illinois. One historian noted, "The overriding problem was that New Orleans was in Spanish hands. Even if the fur trade flourished, its profits seemed likely to go to the Spanish, not the British."[6] Illinois' economy became a satellite of Louisiana's. Illinois' French population now pestered British authorities with requests for civil government and some measure of self-rule.

Their pleas brought sympathetic responses from General Thomas Gage, the British commander for North America. As early as 1768 he proposed abandoning Fort de Chartres, concentrating all the French in just one village in the American Bottom, allowing them to organize militia, and granting local civil government. But shifting political fortunes and intrigue in London throttled Gage's efforts to improve conditions. Uncertainty over the course

of empire, vacillation in executing policy, bickering among officials, and reinterpretations of policy muddled the scene. Gage
trimmed his sails accordingly. He enjoyed limited success, and
Illinois suffered as a result.

Lord Shelburne and Lord Hillsborough, policy makers in Britain, wanted the West to be a vast Indian preserve, a lightly administered region closed to general settlement. They wanted to
tightly restrict traders, trappers, and other British subjects in the
region. They hoped to avoid unrest and more widespread con-
spiracies and bloodbaths. Minimal contacts between whites and
Indians would insure tranquility, they assumed. Furthermore,
they knew low administrative costs would gladden hearts in tax-
weary Britain. Making the Proclamation of 1763 permanent appealed to British officials, including those wanting to squelch
commercial competition from Americans.

In 1774 Parliament passed the Quebec Act, a measure righting
wrongs in Quebec and soothing French sensibilities. It shored up
French religion, language, laws, and customs. But it did more,
much more. It extended Quebec's boundaries southward to the
Ohio River, making Illinois part of Quebec. Significantly, the
Quebec Act essentially obliterated claims in colonial charters to
trans-Appalachian lands, destroying at a stroke long-held assumptions. It throttled American movement and activity north
of the Ohio, hamstringing two land companies planning speculation in the West, the Illinois Land Company and the Wabash
Land Company. To prevent needless Anglo-Indian tension, it
placed regulations on the region's fur trade and alcohol trade.
These regulations, however, pleased British trappers and traders
in Quebec and elsewhere, who feared settlement's impact on trapping and fur trade. Settlement, they knew, would sap vital relationships between themselves and Indians, relationships necessary for fur traffic. In short, extending Quebec's boundaries to
the Ohio would assuage Indian concerns, dispel French fears,
and cushion British fur traders. Furthermore, Britons worried
that Americans would trade with Spanish Louisiana, which annoyed them for three reasons: it would benefit Spain, hoist administrative costs to Britain, and settlers trading with Spaniards

might gravitate toward Spain, forsaking their ties to the Crown. The Quebec Act, authorities hoped, would stifle this trade by keeping Americans away from the Mississippi.[7]

These hopes were dashed. Despite the Proclamation of 1763 and the Quebec Act eleven years later, Americans seeped westward and spilled into Kentucky and Tennessee, creating permanent settlements, enjoying much self-governance, and irking Indians, which worried Britain. Furthermore, by protecting French religion and culture, the Quebec Act infuriated English colonists, who harbored anti-Catholic sentiment. In short, the Quebec Act, while humanely protecting French culture, angered Americans, who saw in western lands opportunities for future generations. The act thrust loathsome French culture squarely athwart westward migration, and inflamed Americans, who lumped it with the hated Intolerable Acts and saw it as the last straw.

Anger soon boiled into action, sweeping aside the Quebec Act. Americans organized for war, gathered arms and supplies, and waited for trouble. In April of 1775 fighting crackled across Massachusetts and then seared the entire seaboard. Illinois and the whole region took backstage to larger upheavals in the East.

PART II

AN AMERICAN
PRESENCE

5.

A Tenuous Conquest

The American Revolution was several wars rolled into one: war for independence, invasions of Canada, civil war, struggles involving Indians, contests for western lands, and world war. Americans sought independence and control of much of the continent. The war tested Britain's frail grip on Illinois and adjacent regions. French allegiance to the Crown was unproven, Spanish intentions across the Mississippi murky, and Indian ties uncertain. The region was up for grabs.

Following Pontiac's Rebellion in 1763, Britain consciously wooed Indians. As their memory of France dimmed and as they heard insurrectionary violence crackling from Boston to Savannah, Indians concluded British rule was preferable to American. Britain, in turn, understood three facts about Indians: they were desperate, they had nowhere to turn, and they could buffer Canada from Americans.

The conjoining of British and Indian causes produced unintended consequences. Slashing Indian attacks during the Revolution, harsh punitive campaigns into 1794, smoldering troubles, and horrors of the War of 1812 embittered Americans for generations. The Declaration of Independence, in fact, referred to Britain's siccing "merciless Indian Savages" on frontier folk, a charge calculated to inflame. Frontier strife, coupled with British willingness to defend Canada to the last Indian, exacerbated hard feelings for decades.

However, Americans too courted Indians, an uphill task. Months before the Declaration of Independence, the Continental Congress plied Indians with revolutionary thoughts. Congress divided the West into three Indian districts, Illinois constituting the middle district, and tasked commissioners and an agent to each district to sway Indians or at least insure neutrality. George Morgan, agent for Illinois, had ties with Kaskaskia and circulated easily among Indians and French, with sparse results.

British agents had advantages. They splashed money and presents at Indians, touted existing trade structures, and stressed threats to Indian life, suggesting staid, predictable British were preferable to raucous Americans. Most Indians either stuck with Britain or stayed neutral.

Still, Americans exploited latent anti-British sentiment among French residents in the American Bottom, Vincennes, and elsewhere, winning over many. But French along the Great Lakes and St. Lawrence Valley were less tractable, comparatively few welcoming American invaders in 1775.

Henry Hamilton, Britain's lieutenant governor of Detroit, toiled to maintain Indian and French loyalty. Lacking social graces and dubbed "the hair buyer" by Americans for paying Indians for scalps, he was nonetheless formidable. From Detroit he defended British positions to the south and attacked Kentucky and other places. Americans parried these thrusts and launched attacks from Pittsburgh, their western headquarters. This duel between Detroit and Pittsburgh saw antagonists in Kentucky, Pennsylvania, and elsewhere chop each other up in nasty, personal warfare.

Talented Captain Hugh Lord, British commander of Kaskaskia after Fort de Chartres was abandoned in 1772, soothed French residents and converted the sturdy house formerly owned by Jesuits into a strongpoint, outfitting it with cannon from Fort de Chartres and naming it Fort Gage. Unforeseen contingencies, though, undid his formidable efforts.

After thrashing invading Americans in 1775–1776, British authorities strengthened Canada, ordering Captain Lord to Detroit in early 1776. Lord authorized Philippe-François de Rastel de Rocheblave to manage British interests. Rocheblave had served France at Fort de Chartres until 1763, served Spain at Ste. Genevieve, and then returned and became a British subject. Energetic and talented, he was also mercurial and obnoxious. Although Lord's departure hobbled British power in Illinois, British presence persisted; French and Indians knew existing economic structures and arrangements were beneficial—and in British hands. Some traders, to be sure, flitted away by 1776, others tried to stay neutral, and still others joined the Revolution. But some remained loyal, their presence bolstering Rocheblave.

At this point, though, a contingency brought abrupt change: Thomas Bentley showed up. He and Rocheblave were foreign born, had French wives, bubbled with ambition, intrigued incessantly, and melded personal aspirations into prevailing realities. Months before fighting spilled into Illinois, they clashed, partly because Rocheblave fined Bentley for selling liquor to Indians. Bentley, furthermore, favored the Revolution.

But Rocheblave alienated St. Louis' commandant, while Bentley got along with him. In addition, Bentley influenced some recently settled British traders and colonists. Commercial ties with Kentucky, moreover, cemented some French to the American cause. Sensing spongy support for Britain, Rocheblave exhorted British authorities to rush troops and civil administrators to Illinois. Ultimately, the power each side projected into Illinois, along with extraneous factors, decided the issue.[1]

* * *

Meanwhile, Americans agonized about defending Kentucky's fledgling settlements. Kentuckians appealed to Virginia, which made Kentucky a county, put its defense in George Rogers Clark's hands, and sent tepid and sporadic assistance. The choice of Clark was superb.

Indians mauled Kentucky in 1777, toppling station after station and penning settlers in just three fortified posts. Never lacking audacity or vision, Clark ignored advice to abandon Kentucky, which would have conceded to Britain lands north of the Ohio. Instead, he chose to defend it via preemptive attack. Clark knew attacks against Kentucky were orchestrated in Detroit, not Illinois, but he also appreciated three facts: Illinois was far from concentrations of British power; its French residents' loyalty to the Crown was untested; American attacks into Illinois offered much gain at minimal risk. Accordingly, he and Governor Patrick Henry of Virginia targeted Illinois.

In spring of 1778 spies which Clark dispatched to Kaskaskia and Vincennes reported languid French loyalty to Britain. Clark convinced Patrick Henry of his daring plan, and secured from Virginia supplies and a commission as lieutenant colonel. After assembling forces at the Falls of the Ohio, today's Louisville, he and his 175 men slipped downriver on June 24. For Illinois' French, Clark carried exhilarating news: France was about to fight Britain. En route Clark met John Saunders, who knew Illinois and agreed to guide Clark's force. Landing near abandoned Fort Massiac, Clark's men trudged toward Kaskaskia, unencumbered by wagons, horses, artillery, or surplus supplies. At one point John Saunders suffered memory lapses concerning local landmarks, but Clark refreshed his memory by threatening to kill him.[2]

Rocheblave, sensing danger, prodded the supine French to act, in vain. He requested reinforcements from Vincennes, also in vain. Rocheblave finally requested to be relieved of his command, but no successor showed up.

Approaching Kaskaskia late on July 4, Clark's men slipped across the Kaskaskia River, fanned out, and captured the village, rounding up Rocheblave. Keeping the jittery French guessing concerning his intentions, Clark conferred with Father Pierre Gibault. He announced France's war against Britain, and assuaged French apprehensions concerning religion. He noted that his assurances worked: "This seem'd to compleat their happiness. They returned to their families, and in a few Minutes the scean of mourning and distress was turned to an excess of Joy, nothing else seen or heard—Addorning the streets with flowers & pavilians of different colours, compleating their happiness by singing &c." At Clark's suggestion, French swore hearty allegiance to Virginia. In a twinkling, torpid British subjects became radiant republican citizens. Cahokia and other villages followed suit.

Clark protected private property, arranged for elections, created
judicial machinery, and kept his soldiers on a short leash.

Vincennes' residents, spies informed him, were ready to tumble
into the American camp. Father Gibault knew Vincennes—it was
part of his parish—so he volunteered to go there to arrange the
transfer of power. On July 14 Clark named him and Dr. Jean
Baptiste Laffont, whose medical practice encompassed Vincennes,
to lead a delegation there. The delegation sent back glad tidings:
Vincennes longed to avoid trouble and join the American cause,
and local Indians were skittish. Clark dispatched Captain Leonard Helm, who occupied Vincennes and its fort, Fort Sackville.

The overall situation brightened. British power recoiled northward, Frenchmen in Illinois and at Vincennes voluntarily organized militia companies, and merchants like Gabriel Cerre of Kaskaskia plied Clark's men with food and clothing.[3] The Spanish
commandant at St. Louis, Fernando de Leyba, lent his support,
and supplies came up the Mississippi to Illinois. Clark, furthermore, used French connections to assemble at Cahokia many Indians from the lower Great Lakes, impressing chiefs and securing pledges of peace. This augured well for Kentucky. With Indian
loyalty to Britain tottering, the way to Detroit and even Mackinac looked open.

American success, though, was wobbly and even illusionary.
It assumed solid French support for Clark and inert British authorities. Neither was true. In addition, Clark's invasion force
melted away, enlistments having expired. French volunteers and
others filled vacant ranks, but overall quality slumped. With supplies running short, Clark plunged into debt to buy some. (Debt
dogged Clark to his dying day.) Clark's treaties with Indian tribes
were fragile, many Indians still sympathized with Britain, and
tiffs between Americans and local French surfaced. Although
Britain had initially showed scant interest in the West, on August 6 news of Clark's force slicing into Illinois reached Lieutenant Governor Hamilton in Detroit, quickening British interest.

Hamilton concocted ambitious plans: retake Illinois; regain
use of the Mississippi; throttle American movements by constructing fortifications where the Mississippi and Ohio join; control the

Missouri's mouth, thereby squeezing Spanish trade with Indians and pushing Indians toward British traders. Clearly, Britain sought complete control of the West. Hamilton's personal objective: escape Detroit's vexing petty politics. All signs pointed to a campaign against Vincennes.

Hamilton marched from Detroit on October 7 with only 175 white troops, almost exactly the number in Clark's force the previous June. Two-thirds were French, and only sixty Indians accompanied him. But Hamilton's agents had cultivated the Miami, Ottawa, Wabash, Chippewa, and Shawnee; as Hamilton pushed up the Maumee River and down the Wabash, his Indian contingent swelled to over 500.

Hearing rumors, Captain Leonard Helm, commanding Vincennes, dispatched scouts to locate Hamilton's force, which they did, getting captured in the process. And British patrols snapped up couriers Helm dispatched to Clark. Then, suddenly, Hamilton's force appeared three miles from Vincennes. Helm's French militia scampered, leaving him in the lurch with just one soldier to defend Fort Sackville. Concluding that he and his companion were unlikely to prevail, Captain Helm surrendered.

Hamilton entered Vincennes on December 17, taking over the fort. Fickle local French took a new oath, this time to the Crown. Ensconced in Fort Sackville, Hamilton contemplated attacking Kentucky, sent couriers to Illinois urging Indians to either flee or join him, and learned that British forces at Pensacola had been dispatched to assist him. News that Clark's force had dwindled to only eighty men gladdened him.

Hearing on January 29 about Vincennes' fall, Clark huffed that British control of Vincennes was intolerable. He knew that Hamilton, with good weather, could slice southward, devastate Kentucky, and isolate Illinois from Virginia. A dearth of reinforcements, supplies, payment, and even communication from Virginia crowned Clark's woes. Gnawing uncertainty generated "more uneasiness than when I was certain of immediate attack, as I had more time to reflect."[4]

Hamilton also stewed. Weather postponed any attack until spring, most Indians drifted away, and French returned to Detroit, leaving just ninety soldiers and some Indians. Until his forces reassembled for upcoming attacks, Hamilton assumed, life would be monotonous.

Not if Clark had his way. He devised ways to enliven Hamilton's life. In retaking Vincennes on December 17, Hamilton had captured François Vigo, a pro-American St. Louis entrepreneur. In captivity, Vigo soaked up important intelligence. Freed after pledging not to harm British interests as he returned home to St. Louis, he raced home, doing nothing to injure British interests. Having kept his word, he darted to Kaskaskia by late January to inform Clark of Hamilton's meager force. He insisted listless French residents were not wedded to Britain, despite their alacrity in switching sides in December. Vigo's report, an ebullient Clark reported, "gave me every Intiligence that I would wish to have." Trusting this volunteered information, Clark acted, risking everything in an audacious preemptive attack against Vincennes. Clark explained this gamble: "I saw the only probability of our maintaining the [Illinois] Country was to take advantage of his [Hamilton's] present weakness. . . . I considered the Inclemency of the season, the badness of the Roads &c.—as an advantage to us, as they would be more off their Guard on all Quarters." His indomitable spirit inspired officers and men.

Local French became enthused. Clark wrote, "The Ladies began also to be spirited and interest themselves in the Expedition, which had great Effect on the Young men." Men joined Clark's force, others scraped up supplies, and soon all was ready. Clark bought a Mississippi flatboat, festooned it with six cannon, christened it the *Willing*, and assembled a forty-man crew. Its tasks: reach Vincennes via the Wabash, soften up Fort Sackville, suppress hostile fire, and block British escape routes downriver.

The *Willing* cast off for the Wabash on February 4. The next morning Clark and about 130 men—at least half of them French volunteers—sloshed from Kaskaskia in cold rain, sustained by Father Gibault's blessing. Their 180-mile route included icy, swollen streams. Forty men shook with chills and fever. Makeshift rafts ferried those unable to walk. Clark, barely twenty-four years old, humored, cajoled, and prodded his men through clinging mud, chest-deep water, and sleepless nights. Clark wrote, "This would have been enough to have stop'ed any set of men that was

not in the same temper of that we was. But in three days we contrived to cross by building a large Canoe, ferried across the two
Channels, the rest of the way we waded." Additional trials lay
near the end of the trek. On February 17 they reached the Em-
barras River, near its confluence with the Wabash. Unable to ford
it at a point nine miles from Vincennes, they shivered all night
in freezing drizzle. Provisions dwindled, morale sagged, and the
force huddled two days in rain waiting for the *Willing*. Ever agile, however, Clark snared five hunters from Vincennes, who revealed Hamilton suspected nothing and French residents eagerly
awaited Americans.

Building crude rafts, Clark's men crossed the Wabash. On early
February 23, with ice a half inch thick covering floodwaters, Clark
lunged into the water and waded toward Vincennes, six miles
away, his men following. To enliven those with sagging spirits,
he had twenty-five men bring up the rear of the column, with
orders to shoot stragglers. Most soldiers, though, needed no such
encouragement; having overcome ordeals, Clark observed, his
soldiers felt confident.

Late on February 23, Clark's men emerged from the ordeal
onto relatively dry ground, about a mile and a half from Fort
Sackville. Here they rested, dried clothes in the sun, and geared
up for battle. Snagging a French hunter, Clark sent him into
Vincennes with a letter extending glad tidings and announcing
that Americans were about to descend upon the town. He admonished those loyal to Britain to fly to Fort Sackville and fight
like men; everyone else should stay indoors. Individuals caught
with weapons, he warned, would be considered enemies.

The letter worked. Frenchmen wavered, none tattled on the
hovering Americans, and Indians either vanished or rallied to
Clark. Clark's men then filed through town toward the fort. British soldiers learned of imminent danger only when rifle fire
crumpled one. Now Hamilton knew desperation. Sickness and
desertions had trimmed his force to just thirty-three effectives,
which Clark's men further whittled by firing through gaps between the logs of the palisades. The fort's cannons thundered
through the night, but they could not be depressed enough to
rake the attackers. Some artillerists, furthermore, found life ex-

citing but brief, as accurate rifle fire thinned their ranks. As cannon fell silent, Britons became morose.

Trapped, Hamilton stalled for time. Knowing this, Clark demanded unconditional surrender. At this point, pro-British Indians and French bumbled into town, mistaking Clark's men for pro-British French. They towed two American prisoners behind them and displayed scalps of Kentuckians, bad moves. Americans, pretending to be British, cheerily escorted them through town. Clark, relishing the event in memory, wrote, "The poor Devils never discovered their mistake until it was too late for many of them to escape." Six were tomahawked in front of the British garrison. The effect was salutary, and Hamilton asked for terms, got none, and then surrendered unconditionally. The next day, February 26, the *Willing* pulled into view.

Fort Sackville yielded plentiful supplies of clothes, traders' goods, military equipment, and small cannon. Clark, moreover, learned Hamilton expected supplies from Ouiatenon, a post 120 miles upstream, so he dispatched Captain Helm and fifty men to seize it. They did, capturing forty men, seven bulging supply boats, and other spoils. Clark's men divided the booty in accordance with republican ideals, the officers getting little.

Clark's victories at Vincennes and Ouiatenon produced dividends. For example, a British expedition heading down the Mississippi reached Rock River, heard of his victories, and turned back. Sitting on as many prisoners as he had men in his command, Clark packed Hamilton off to prison in Virginia. He treated French militia from Detroit humanely, accepting oaths of allegiance from those desiring to join his command and sending the rest back to Detroit with provisions, boats, and even some arms. This magnanimous behavior probably gave Clark sources of intelligence in Detroit. Clark appreciated Detroit's strategic importance, knew French there were lukewarm to Britain, and knew his victories impressed Indians. Detroit's capture would cripple Indian resistance in the lower Great Lakes, partially isolate British posts to the west, and give America trump cards in claiming the entire region. Correctly assessing the situation, Clark opined in late 1779 Detroit's fall would "bring them to my feet," and would establish "a profound peace on the Fronteers." The same year found Clark assembling resources to attack Detroit, heartened by French residents there who toasted American victories. Knowing this, British commanders scurried to stave off catastrophe, urgently pleading for reinforcements.

Attacks against Detroit, however, never materialized. Sickness among Clark's men, bickering between Clark and Pittsburgh's commander, and skimpy supplies stymied offensive action. An impulsive foray against Shawnee villages at present-day Chillicothe siphoned nearly 300 Kentuckians from Clark's force, further hobbling attacks against Detroit. Realizing that striking northward was futile, he scattered units to posts from Vincennes to the American Bottom, at least securing the region. To war's end, Clark pined to march on Detroit, but lacked the wherewithal. Staying on the strategic defensive galled him.

This stalemate had profound effects. Britain's control of Detroit until 1796 (and again in 1812–1813) stiffened Indian resolve against Americans. Although Illinois was spared major battles before 1812, raids and rumors kept residents edgy. British in Detroit and elsewhere kept advising, outfitting, and covertly leading Indians, postponing the departure of Indians from Illinois.

Even so, Clark realized his conquests' significance. Following crises in 1780, fighting tapered off, and in late 1781 Clark mused: "However foreign it may be to most people in power, it is beyond all doubt, that our possessions in the Illinois [Country] and Kentucky have been the salvation of all our frontiers since the commencement of the war, and have enabled them to give that assistance against the British armies they have done." This claim contains truth. Although authorities slighted his achievements and allowed debts to pester him, pioneers appreciated Clark's deeds, welcoming breathing spells from war.

Amidst war's disruptions, settlers in Illinois craved stability, certainty, and effective, restrained government. Most wanted few laws, but enforced. They wanted orderly land sales, roads, protection from Indians and brigands, justice, and few other services. They desired safe political, economic, and civic arenas in which to function. Remembering British abuses, however, they feared excessive, arbitrary, and remote power. Britain's light grip on Illinois was replaced by Virginia's even lighter grip. Virginia formed the County of Illinois in late 1778, created government offices, and held elections, and people took office. Illinois had a government, on paper.

Establishing government was one thing, but making it function even minimally was another. For one thing, some people broke laws. For another, the distance from Virginia inhibited effective government. Highly irregular mail service and similar uncertainties undercut governance. There was desultory fighting. Illinois' population mix compounded problems of governance. Clark's men and other Americans mingled with Indians, a few residual British, resident French, newly arrived French, some blacks, and French-Indians. Governing such heterogeneous people was difficult under good conditions. The war and the next fifteen years were hardly good times.

Finally, Americans knew little of Illinois. It was shrouded in mystery, even dread. But the unknown was also an asset, a resource. It allowed, even demanded, agility, flexibility, and imagination. It encouraged people to see beyond daily challenges and peer decades into the future. Amid uncertainties, undaunted minds and spirits approached the future with hope, expectation, and vision.

A sense of unknown laid Illinois' foundations. Since the early 1600s Virginia claimed vast western tracts, including everything north of the Ohio. Wedged between the Ohio and Mississippi, the County of Illinois ran north to some undetermined boundary, a boundary made fuzzy by British and Indian power. Despite Virginia's population base and the fabled Virginia Dynasty leaders, Illinois was weak. Unknown features, in fact, drove Illinois history for decades. In determining the northern boundary, creating new counties, locating county seats, and providing local government, Illinoisans immersed themselves in unknowns.

Political as well as physical unknowns abounded amidst turmoil. The top political authority was the county lieutenant, also known as the commandant. Wielding executive powers, he commanded the militia, appointed its officers, deputy commandants, and commissioners. He could stay executions until Virginia's governor or assembly rendered opinion.

In late 1778 Governor Patrick Henry of Virginia made Colonel John Todd of Kentucky county lieutenant. A veteran Indian fighter, twenty-eight years old, and well-educated, Todd arrived at Kaskaskia in May 1779. He commissioned as deputy commandants Francois Trottier at Cahokia, Jean Ste. Barbeau at Prairie du Rocher, and Richard Winston at Kaskaskia. As commander of militia, he appointed Nicholas Janis and Joseph Duplassy captains. With the top executive and military posts filled, Todd turned to elections.

Elections reflected effervescent republicanism, affirming that sovereignty rested with the people, not the Crown. The Revolutionary experience reinforced republicanism. And rambunctious colonial French in Illinois had defended their interests, unlike quiescent kin in Quebec, checking abusive officials and sometimes getting odious practices rescinded. Even so, they knew nothing of regularly scheduled elections.

American courts, at Kaskaskia and Cahokia, required elections. Kaskaskia elected Richard Winston, deputy commandant at Kaskaskia, its sheriff. All other elected officials in Kaskaskia and Cahokia were French. Others held two positions simultaneously. Nicholas Janis and Joseph Duplassy commanded militia and served on Kaskaskia's court. Cahokia's deputy commandant, Francois Trottier, also served on court.

Electing officials was one thing; making government work was another, as Colonel Todd quickly learned. While he was away, court officials—mostly French—convened, concluded they disliked alien Virginian jurisprudence, and then adjourned the court indefinitely. Returning, Todd admonished the officials, convened the court, and requested cooperation. Illinois survived this crisis, and all subsequent crises.

Legislation creating the County of Illinois respected French culture. Virginia retained existing French legal code, somewhat modified. French basked in unencumbered religious freedom and ancient customs. Significantly, Todd created local offices similar to French offices, local revenues financing them. Virginian revenues financed offices unknown to French. Not unexpectedly, Virginians respected slavery. The month Virginia established the County of Illinois, December 1778, George Rogers Clark proclaimed specific prohibitions involving slaves: selling alcohol to black and Indian slaves, renting dwellings to them, allowing their going about after tattoo, and buying indiscriminately from them. Clark's proclamation stipulated fines for violations. Of course, Clark's proclamation implied these banned activities were, in fact, occurring. In other words, French slavery was lax, slaves enjoying considerable latitude. Clark wanted slavery tightened up, and his proclamation signaled contests over slavery and social roles of blacks, contests persisting well into statehood.

* * *

By the 1780s several population groups graced Illinois: American soldiers, mostly Virginians, choosing to stay after serving in Illinois; British soldiers who served and stayed; French residents, not permanently defecting to Spanish Louisiana; small numbers from Quebec and France; Indians, slaves, free blacks; a sprinkling of Spanish; and people of mixed ancestry. Stark religious, linguistic, political, social, and other differences abounded, differences capable of igniting strife.

Overt conflict, when it occurred, sprang largely from two types of sources. One type was ordinary: misunderstandings, petty disputes, spats over interpretation, and similar mundane problems.[5] In diverse frontier Illinois, ingredients for such low-grade friction were manifestly great. The other type was profound: irreconcilable concepts of land, ownership, use; ideas concerning just prices; judicial foundations and procedures; and other deep, complex cultural differences, including language and religion.

Another factor complicated matters. For decades French settlers enjoyed tranquility, which arriving Americans rudely jolted. French men and Clark's soldiers, nominally allied, sometimes disagreed over religion, treatment of slaves, language, and similar traits, producing misunderstandings, suspicions, and even violence. Indians' modes of warfare and treatment of prisoners often disgusted and enraged whites.

For decades French subjects lived harmoniously with most Indians, intermarriage and children of mixed ancestry tangible proof of close relations. French and Indians forged symbiotic arrangements, often involving trapping and related activities. Americans, on the other hand, devoured stories of Indian atrocities and regarded Indians as savages and British stooges. Settlers and Indians realized, almost instinctively, that their ways of life, cultures, and approaches to nature were incompatible.

Most Americans met relatively few French residents. Much land, they saw, was uncultivated, its ownership often tangled. British bungling and war's chaos muddied ownership, encouraging some Americans to farm without worrying about ownership. Such carefree farming attitudes and American sensitivity about continuing French-Indian coziness generated friction.

Religious animosity worsened matters. Few Americans were Roman Catholic. Many, in fact, were ardent Calvinists, for whom Catholicism was anathema. The Quebec Act, joining Illinois to Quebec and strengthening French institutions, had rankled Americans. Americans and French smarted over cleavages in language, religion, work ethic, Indian connections, and even dress, foods, and methods of farming. Though these inflamed passions, most quarrels were petty, sporadic, and non-violent.

French residents were generally inoffensive, deferential to authority, appreciative of music and dance, and not ostentatious in house maintenance. Vibrant prosperity into the 1760s had yielded to social and economic distortions, malaise, and decline, partly owing to the departure of many French and their relocation in Spanish Louisiana. Despite Britain's honorable intentions and marginal control, defeat and occupation afflicted French life, smothering confidence, work ethic, and commercial interactions. The Revolutionary War further battered French culture, institutions, and morale. Consequently, residual French residents, often unkempt and apparently enervated, appeared indolent and cowed by priests and authorities. Also, some French during the Revolution switched sides with unseemly alacrity. Lackluster French loyalty to both the Crown and Americans was perhaps understandable, but this fickleness dismayed Americans. Although time softened perceptions, few French truly impressed early Americans favorably.[6]

Americans, by contrast, reveled in rough-and-tumble, spirited ways. They brimmed with assertive republicanism and boisterous anti-monarchism. Testy, somewhat cocky Americans

descending onto somnolent French society triggered sparks, misunderstandings, and some conflict.

Glaring differences sometimes threatened to produce mayhem,
but rarely did so. Still, they did encourage folk to cluster in distinct, separate communities, limiting and channeling contacts,
minimizing conflict. Abundant space abetted peace.

Rather quickly, however, diverse people mingled under broad
consensus, rubbed elbows, and tolerated one another. Business
dealings, true friendships, and even marriage soon blurred and
softened salient ethnic, religious, and linguistic lines. Fluid, amorphous, transitory middle grounds of diverse peoples replaced the
Indian-white middle ground. These mediating middle grounds
lessened friction and militated against mayhem.

These middle grounds, though, were asymmetrical and therefore transitory. Only Americans received sizeable infusions of
reinforcements. Some French dribbled in from Quebec and
France, handfuls of Indians entered Illinois, some Britons settled
before statehood, and a few blacks arrived, largely at others'
behest. Eventually, Northerners produced middle grounds, involving Southerners, immigrants, and themselves. By then Anglo
swells swamped French culture, demoralized Indians departed,
and northern culture ascended.

* * *

American settlers, discharged soldiers, and visitors penned
glowing letters about Illinois, which generated considerable interest. Many communications sang praises of soil, navigable rivers, game, and verdant forests. George Rogers Clark, for example,
lauded Illinois to Virginians in late 1779:

> This you may take for granted that its more Beautiful than any
> Idea I could have formed of a Country almost in a state of Nature,
> every thing you behold is an Additional Beauty. On the [Mississippi]
> River You'll find the finest Lands the Sun ever shone on; in the High
> Country You'll find a variety of poor and Rich Lands with large
> Meadows extending beyond the reach of your Eyes Varigated with
> groves of Trees appearing like Islands in the Seas covered with Buf-
> faloes and other Game; in many Places with a good Glass You may

see al those that is on their feet in half a Million Acres; so level is the
Country which some future day will excell in Cattle.[7]

Although buffalo faded from Illinois around 1800, game remained abundant. Like Clark, later writers described fertile soils
and island groves set in prairie seas. Significantly, Clark and others
believed in "some future day." Visions of future progress—thriving on hope, on tomorrow—were vital in shaping Illinois.

Clark's letter embodied his personality's motivating power,
luring Virginians to Illinois. His takeover of Cahokia, July 1778,
found recently arrived Thomas Brady and Richard McCarty living there, possibly the only Americans. But this quickly changed,
households and small parties soon filtering in. An American contingent alighted in 1779 midway between Cahokia and Prairie du
Rocher, at a spring adjacent to today's Waterloo. Appropriately
named Bellefontaine, this community was the first permanent
settlement of English-speaking Americans north of the Ohio.

Other settlers ventured in as fighting tapered off. In 1781, James
Moore led talented Marylanders into Illinois, nearly all veterans
from Clark's command. They included Shadrach Bond, Sr., the
uncle of the state's first governor, and Robert Kidd, James Piggott,
and Larkin Rutherford. Kidd farmed near Fort de Chartres, Rutherford in St. Clair County. Robert Whitehead and John Doyle
had helped Clark secure the American Bottom and he later settled
there. Other veterans saw Illinois, liked it, retrieved their families, and settled north of Kaskaskia. Very possibly, it was they
who coined the term "American Bottom." As warfare sputtered
in 1782, others from Clark's outfit settled down, some founding
New Design, a community perched on the fringes of settlement
on a lovely elevation four miles south of Bellefontaine. (For decades—indeed, through World War II—soldiers serving in Illinois formed favorable impressions of the region, which tugged
veterans and their families to Illinois.) Almost simultaneously,
dozens of other American households settled from Cahokia to
Kaskaskia. Some households came straight to Illinois. Others
waited either back East or en route while advance parties prepared the way.

Americans arriving in the 1780s had few settlement options.

Uncertain titles and surveys inhibited them from buying land directly from the French. A few settled in marshy places, but those alighting in the fertile American Bottom encountered poor drainage. Imperfectly understanding disease, settlers nevertheless correctly assumed that stagnant water, sultry weather, and fetid vegetation were unhealthy. Escaping soggy conditions, many built houses either on slopes adjacent to the bluffs or on conical Indian mounds towering sixty feet above the bottom. Some became merchants and artisans in villages. A handful entered Spanish Louisiana, completely leaving U.S. jurisdiction.

Most, though, moved into fringe regions, even into lands still contested or controlled by Indians. They "boldly intruded on Indian soil, founding settlements at New Design, Bellefontaine (Waterloo), and Grand Ruisseau (Columbia)—foolishly believing that grants awarded them by officials in the name of Virginia would protect them against Indian efforts to prevent encroachment of their lands."[8] Virginia tried to support settlers. In its land cession to the United States in 1784, it inserted wording to protect settlers' claims. Three years later this wording appeared almost verbatim in the Northwest Ordinance, reassuring settlers and worrying Indians.

Whatever their motivation for migrating, Americans and foreigners chose Illinois. Fertile land enticed them to Illinois through the 1850s, but so did opportunities in retail stores, mills, pulpits, schools, and elective and appointed offices. Illinois offered other attractions: relative tranquility, improving markets, little destructive speculation, receding slavery, declining and departing Indians, virtual absence of taxes, and very low thresholds for most occupations. No other free state was closer to the Deep South or had such fine transportation to it, and yet Illinois constantly strengthened ties with the East. For those weighing options, Illinois' attractions were strong.

Chain migration lured and assisted many settlers. It occurred when one or more settlers got established, liked the locale, convinced others to migrate, and helped them move and settle. Personal correspondence and visits prompted most chain migration. Letters written back home by relatives or close friends, people whose word and judgment were trusted, convinced others to come west. It was especially helpful in ushering to this frontier elderly, infirm, toddlers, and other dependent individuals.

But it was nothing new. English colonists settling America used it, as did Americans breaching the Appalachians. Then and in frontier Illinois it smoothed transitions from known, settled conditions to relatively alien, fluid situations. It bolstered courage, knowledge, and other vital resources. It fostered clusters and networks of relatives, co-religionists, or friends, who perpetuated religious practices, farming techniques, cookery, and other familiar cultural traits.[9] Chain migration promoted certainty in chaotic times.

* * *

Sometimes settlement outran effective law, especially during the 1780s. The Revolution brought into question assumptions concerning governance, uses of power, human nature, social arrangements, and right and wrong. Social and physical fluidity abounded, structural vacuums loosened restraints, and power was exercised without authority. Well into statehood Illinoisans debated problems arising from settlement outstripping law.

During the Revolution, furthermore, Britons and Americans employed Indian and French allies, further dissolving traditional law and authority. Complicating geopolitical dynamics, Spain pounced on Britain in 1779, Spaniards from Louisiana traversing Illinois' soil and claiming southern Michigan. For Britain, the violence erupting in Massachusetts in 1775 turned into a world war, with combat raging in both Americas, Africa, the Mediterranean, Europe, and even Asia.

Turbulent times attracted rambunctious men and some despicable characters, often men either away from home—and home's restraining influences—for the first time, or eager to jettison social restraints. War encouraged actions not normally allowed, weakening existing norms and laws.

Before war's end, even officials tacitly sanctioned lawbreaking. For example, Virginia law forbade Americans settling north of the Ohio, the region temporarily reserved for French and Indians. But realities negated law. Clark's men wanted conquered lands, law or no law. In addition, Clark and John Todd, the county lieutenant, knew stalwart yeomen would ferociously defend loved ones, thereby helping secure the land. Accordingly, Clark and Todd winked at some lawbreakers, the reality of settlement overriding laws fabricated by strangers in distant places. Faraway Virginia, furthermore, beset by financial woes and British attacks, lacked coercive means. Consequently, pioneers crossed the Ohio, airily violating Virginian law, and took up land.

Desultory warfare sputtered into the early 1780s, compounding military, political, and social problems in Illinois. For strategic reasons, Britain concentrated on the South, targeting Virginia. Spain's entering the war in 1779 bolstered America's western efforts, but this advantage was offset when Virginia virtually abandoned the West. Additionally, like France, Spain had ulterior motives, some inimical to Illinois and America.

Worse, British commanders devised ambitious plans: a two-pronged offensive to roll up the Spanish posts between New Orleans and Illinois. One prong, slated to drive from Pensacola up the Mississippi, was to meet another prong descending from the north. The northern prong consisted of British, Indians, and French, cobbled together in early 1780 at Mackinac under Captain Patrick Sinclair. Its goals: drive from Mackinac and snap up St. Louis, Cahokia, Kaskaskia, and Ste. Genevieve; levy tribute on Illinois; seize Missouri's lead mines; and enroll Indians into the British cause. If both prongs succeeded, Britain would interdict Spanish support to Illinoisans, control the northern Mississippi and the Missouri River fur trade, and possibly regain the Ohio Valley.

But beginning in September of 1779, preemptive attacks from energized Spanish forces from New Orleans hit British posts at Baton Rouge and elsewhere, Mobile falling in February. British posts toppled and communications snapped, immobilizing the southern prong and crippling the entire offensive.

Even so, Captain Sinclair's northern prong jumped off, pushed southward, and appeared outside St. Louis on May 26, 1780. It flailed about, murdered some cattle, scalped hapless local folk, incensed Spanish residents, and stalled. Its Indian contingents grew skittish and cohesion unraveled. This frazzled force then beat a retreat northward, hurried along by Colonel John Montgomery's pursuing force of some 350 men. Montgomery hounded Sinclair's men up the Mississippi, dallying at Rock Island to pillage Sauk and Fox villages and crops. Thus ended the last major threat to the American Bottom.

Clark parried threats against central Kentucky, sacking some villages north of the Ohio and thumping Indians near Piqua in 1780, which discouraged future forays against Kentucky. Locally, Kaskaskia beat off raiding Indians on July 17. In August Spanish soldiers and French citizens at Cahokia frustrated another Indian probe.

American allies also launched forays. A shadowy French officer, Augustin Mottin de la Balme, sponsored one fiasco, learning in the process that war is grim business. Appearing at Kaskaskia in July of 1780, he led French and Indians to attack Detroit. After destroying Indian facilities near the Maumee's headwaters, he and many companions were slain by irate Miami. Another force, from Cahokia, pushed to the British post at St. Joseph, at present-day Niles, Michigan. It seized the post briefly and started home, but Potawatomi and British pounced on the group near Chicago, routing it. Stung, Cahokians sought revenge. Spanish officials supported them, including Eugenio Pierra, a militia captain. Organizing and leading a force of Spanish, Indians, and possibly twenty Cahokians, Captain Pierra started for St. Joseph on January 2, 1781. There this hybrid band found only a few British traders, so his men looted the place and scooted for St. Louis and safety.

These allied expeditions failed to tip the region's balance of power, but did sustain American toeholds in Illinois. Significantly, Americans did not have to conquer to win; all they had to do was hang on.

The expeditions, however, strained relationships between Americans and their allies. Stalemated conditions, aggravated by meager support from Virginia, drove wedges between Americans and their allies. For example, when Captain Pierra seized St. Joseph, he claimed the region and the Illinois River for Spain. Although his force scurried back to St. Louis, not bothering to garrison anything for Spain, Pierra's claim surfaced next year during peace negotiations in Paris. This claim was unabashed trolling—casting a claim to snag something for Spain—and American negotiators easily dumped it.

After Pierra's expedition, fighting in Illinois faded, allowing ethnic tensions to well up. Some French in the American Bottom writhed under American rule. They petitioned Virginia's governor, stating they wanted French troops stationed in their villages, not Americans. This complaint became moot, though, for beleaguered Virginia withdrew its soldiers from Illinois by late 1781. The only American presence was a small force at Kaskaskia commanded by Captain John Rogers.

At this point several problems erupted, including petty clashes among leaders. John Todd, the county lieutenant, who had arrived in May of 1779, quickly requested permission to resign, appointed Richard Winston his deputy, and left Illinois in November. Richard Winston needlessly antagonized French residents, and Connecticut-born John Dodge challenged him. Dodge's performance during war caught the attention of George Washington, who recommended him to Thomas Jefferson, Virginia's governor. Jefferson tapped Dodge to serve Virginia as Indian agent for Illinois. Once in Illinois, though, Dodge and cronies, supported by Americans at Bellefontaine, confounded Winston and abused Kaskaskians. Unfortunately, gullible Captain John Rogers, commander at Kaskaskia, assisted Dodge's clique. Humiliated, Winston skulked away.

Dodge tyrannically squelched local French, who petitioned Virginia for redress. The petition never reached Virginia. British personnel killed the courier, read the petition and related documents, and learned of Kaskaskian misery. Had British forces marched decisively on Illinois, French residents would have hailed their arrival. Only overall exhaustion kept British authorities from exploiting this wretched condition.

Adding to troubles, the statute creating the County of Illinois expired on January 5, 1782. The war was almost over, to be sure, but civil government barely functioned. (Ironically, John Dodge's harsh rule and a few soldiers provided stability and order, such as they were.) Groaning under occupation, the war, and Dodge's clutches, French residents winged petitions to Congress, in vain. Smarting, some slipped over to Spanish Louisiana. Confusion, arbitrary rule, and uncertainty reigned.

With troubles brewing and Dodge holding sway, peace negotiations could have given Britain the lower Great Lakes region, including Illinois. Unreliable, conflicting maps added ambiguity to American claims for the present U.S.-Canadian boundary. Moreover, although both sides held chunks of the region, they still contested other areas. Other factors complicated matters. For example, neither side could ignore Indians' claims, Spain's impressive victories east of the Lower Mississippi, or legitimate interests of residual French, even with their elastic loyalties. Clearly, major players vexed negotiators.

Despite limited capabilities, Spain tried to protect vast Spanish Louisiana, twenty years old in 1783. Although Spanish Louisiana benefitted from disgruntled French quitting Illinois, Spanish officials nervously peered eastward and saw expanding and energetic Americans, people impatient with European imperial designs. Consequently, in peace negotiations Spain advocated a permanent Indian preserve—a permanent barrier—south of the Ohio, with Britain getting everything north of the river. (In addition, Spain sought exclusive control of the lower Mississippi.) In short, it sought Indian and British buffers between its string of settlements along the Mississippi's right bank and expanding America.

Remarkably, however, by late 1782 British and American diplomats negotiated a framework for peace giving the lower Great Lakes to the United States. After Lord North and other British officials who prosecuted the war left office in early 1782, the Earl of Shelburne became prime minister. He took a long view concerning British interests. His old friend, Benjamin Franklin, negotiated for America, with skills undiminished by age. Actually, American negotiators wanted via treaty what American arms had failed to obtain—namely, Canada, or valuable portions of it— but Franklin knew Britain would rebuff such demands; Canada had expelled invading Americans, something Britain helped make stick. Even so, Franklin emphasized the goodwill a generous peace would give Britain. In the end, Franklin's friendship and Shelburne's fondness for America likely led him to concede everything north of the Ohio. Britain retained southern Ontario and joint control of four Great Lakes.

In yielding, Shelburne sought to weaken Britain's enemies.[10] Pragmatism tempering his idealism, he hoped to placate nascent America. In addition, Britain occupied forts north of the Ohio, from which ensconced British authorities exerted considerable leverage until 1796. Also, desperate Indians were in Britain's corner, having no alternative. Signed on September 3, 1783, the peace treaty gave the United States everything north of the Ohio. Lord Shelburne hoped the treaty established "a strong foundation laid for eternal amity between England and America."[11] At the same time, though, it gave Florida to Spain, as well as lands south of the Thirty-first Parallel east of the Mississippi, rankling Americans and requiring remedy.

Agile, talented British agents operated from posts in the lower Great Lakes. They prowled waterways as trappers and traders, cultivating ties with Indians via trade, gifts, and personal friendships—ties cemented by the common need to encumber American control of the lower Great Lakes. This fundamental need provides a framework, a scaffolding, for understanding much Illinois, regional, and national history through 1814. Facing threats from expanding Americans, British authorities and Indians embraced each other, Indian survival north of the Ohio being at stake. Although Britain sought improved Anglo-American relations, it prepared for a day when reactivated British-Indian power would again defend mutual interests. And that day was not far off.

6.

FIRM FOUNDATIONS

The United States acquired by treaty the region wedged between the Ohio, the Mississippi, and Canada. Its potential excited Americans. One historian noted, "The vision of the British empire extending into the American West . . . [was] merely transferred to the vision of an American empire."[1] Three advantages Britain never enjoyed suggested Americans would succeed: time, numbers, and proximity. Over decades scores of thousands of settlers engulfed Indians, French, British, and others. The weight of numbers was a telling factor, and each year American power inched westward. Moreover, trans-Appalachia never fully excited Britons, but it definitely caught America's attention.

Problems persisted, however. Some were cosmic, requiring acts of Congress and international treaties. Others were local and mundane, often petty, sometimes stemming from personal vanities and irrationalities. In the end, increased settlement and improved communication solved most local and mundane problems and larger, complicated problems. Each settler's arrival, each acre plowed, every road and bridge built, every institution planted, and every other success eliminated problems.

Americans had mixed, contradictory thoughts about the region. On the one hand, exercising sovereignty there, governing it, and settling it were difficult. The United States in 1783 projected even less power into the region than Britain did in 1765. Home to doubting French, simmering Indians, and comparatively few Americans, the immense region was also rife with complexities. On the other hand, some opined, rampant settlement meant either chaos or economic and political growth that would overshadow the East. Others feared Virginia would make its land claims stick, dominate the region, and create an empire for slavery.

Concerned about Virginia's land claims, Maryland balked at ratifying the Articles of Confederation, holding out until 1781. Other states shared Maryland's concern. In 1783 Virginia finally ceded claims north of the Ohio and elsewhere, keeping Kentucky. Other states followed suit. Very significantly, ceded lands became *national* lands, generating public domain, a treasure of inestimable value.[2]

Virginia's Act of Cession promised the French inhabitants in Illinois and along the Wabash "shall have their possessions and titles confirmed to them and be protected in the enjoyment of their rights and liberties." This protected slavery, creating festering sores in Illinois for decades.[3] Virginia, furthermore, stipulated that states carved from the region be small in geographical size; worried Easterners envisioned swarms of sparsely populated little states hatching to their west, each having one vote in Congress under the Articles of Confederation and outvoting the original states.

Virginia formally turned over the lands on March 1, 1784. To facilitate governance in regions soon called the Old Northwest and the Old Southwest, Congress established a commission, chaired by Thomas Jefferson. Reporting to Congress on the day Virginia relinquished the lands, it recommended sixteen basically rectangular states, ten north of the Ohio. Jefferson's classical training and interest in Indians begat delightful state names. Illinois, for example, would contain parts of three states: Assenisipia, Illinoia, and Polypotamia. Congress referred the plan back to committee for revision.

Under Jefferson's revised plan, a region's free males, including propertyless, received congressional permission to form a provi-

sional government. Bubbling with democracy, Jefferson's plan
authorized settlers, not Congress, to choose a governor and judges,
and it sought to ban slavery after 1800. Moreover, the road to
statehood was smooth and simple. Congress approved the plan
in April 1784.

This law, however, lay dormant. Congressional impotence, lingering Indian and British power, and anarchy punctuated by John
Dodge's tyranny burdened Illinois. General economic depression
afflicted Illinois, the region, and the country. Few migrants entered Illinois. Also, diplomatic assignments spirited Thomas Jefferson to Europe.

Seeking to resolve the impasse, Congress dusted off Jefferson's
plan, added its own imprint, and drew upon two traditions of
land sales. One tradition thrived from Pennsylvania southward.
There, people claimed authorized quantities of land with un-
designated locations. Property descriptions included locations of
trees, rivers, rocks and other ephemeral markers, producing odd-
shaped fields and irregular boundaries. Surveying came later.
This topographic system, the metes-and-bounds system, produced
flexibility and minimal initial costs, but it generated crazy-quilt
patterns of land claims, often conflicting. Trees died, rivers me-
andered, and rocks moved, sparking uncertainties and disputes.
Roads conformed to these boundaries, rarely going in straight
lines. In addition, settlers quickly snapped up prized properties,
undesirable parcels remaining unsold for decades. The second
tradition, New England's, advanced regularity. There, "towns"
—corresponding roughly to townships in today's Midwest—contained a leading village with meeting house and commons. Surveyors there plotted lots within townships before sale and settlement and used straight lines whenever possible, creating certainty
and minimizing disputes. Except for squatters, settlers waited
until surveying was completed in a given region before investing
labor in a parcel of land.

Borrowing New England's passion for order, the Land Ordinance of 1785 established the township and range rectangular
survey system, dividing land into townships six miles square according to cardinal directions, fields assuming rectangular
shapes. (The French long-lot system, though, still persisted along

waterways.) Townships contained thirty-six sections, each one
mile square and consisting of 640 acres. Significantly, this ordinance specified systematic surveying before sales.[4] The range
system, pre-sale surveys, and generally level terrain fostered
checkerboard patterns. Roads hugged section lines and crossed
each other at right angles. (Towns and cities adopted analogous
gridiron street patterns.) Used across U.S. public domain lands,
this system led to orderly land sales, settlement, and social harmony and helped Illinois escape the chaos, squabbling, and bit-
terness over sales that marred Kentucky and other states. After
authorities untangled colonial land records, few boundary disputes rocked Illinois. Troubles over titles persisted, but certitude
of boundaries abetted tranquility. Orderly people who operated
within structures appreciated packaged land and harmonious
sales. And Kentuckians and others weary of debilitating land
feuds also valued it.

Unfortunately, it was the buyers in Illinois who bore surveying
costs, not promoters of colonies or the public, as in New England. Also, in New England, town meetings and village congregations promoted community, and rural dwellers identified with
villages or towns, something less common in Illinois. Of course,
Ilinoisans had feelings of community, but often as offshoots of
ordinary rural voluntary associations, not as the planned feature
of some grand undertaking. Illinois did contain towns founded
to promote shared values and mission, New Englanders founding many, but usually original impetus slackened, vision dimmed,
shared sentiment withered, and outside attractions diluted their
sense of mission. Ironically, this weakened commitment, along
with influxes of outsiders, often generated unintended feelings of
community by allowing for spontaneous joining together to solve
pressing problems.

Squatters dogged Illinois.[5] They occupied public land before
survey or sale, sometimes never filing claim. Perhaps because
squatting abetted disorder, New England resisted it, preventing
squatters from obtaining lands they occupied. In Illinois, over
time customs and laws expanded squatters' rights, especially for
those intending to settle.

Clamoring petitions to Congress during the early 1780s testify to ineffective government north of the Ohio. In early 1786 talented, well-connected, and energetic New Englanders and New Yorkers organized the Ohio Company of Associates to invest in the Old Northwest and encourage settlement. Congress approved, with stipulations. Speculating in southeastern Ohio and sponsoring settlement there in early 1788, the company forged east-west links back to the Northeast, perhaps soothing northeastern concerns about potential competition from the region. Its crowning accomplishment: helping craft the Northwest Ordinance, adopted on July 13, 1787. This created framework and provisions for governance, strengthening ties to the Northeast, and giving hope.

Although the Northwest Ordinance was somewhat contradictory and vague in provisions and operation, it carried revolutionary implications and put forth guarantees and precise procedures.[6] It was visionary and practical, daring in assumptions and cautious and methodical in structuring power, radical in understanding pressing problems and conservative in devising solutions, and democratic in grand design and paternalistic in details. Of uncertain authorship, it clearly bore James Monroe's skeptical imprint. He made abbreviated fact-finding trips to the region in 1784 and 1785, the latter into northern Illinois. Unimpressed, he predicted stagnation or slow development. He therefore favored carving just three to five states from the Old Northwest. Replacing Jefferson's optimism of 1784, he prescribed orderly, guided, systematic development.

The ordinance contained property qualifications for political involvement and allowed limited self-governance during the first stage of government. With second stage government came a territorial legislature, but the governor could check it. The ordinance, moreover, countenanced existing slavery among the French. Even so, Jefferson's vision of 1784 was present: the ordinance of 1787 laid foundations for self-rule, statehood on an equal basis, and republicanism. By providing orderly, pragmatic, and essentially conservative government, and by succeeding—something Jefferson's plan might not have done—it resuscitated the spirit of Jefferson's plan. The Northwest Ordinance of 1787, furthermore, worked in tandem with the Land Ordinance of 1785, nourishing

Jefferson's "belief that America and the world would be best
served if self-governing, republican communities were empow-
ered to shape their own destinies as America's population spread
westward across the continent."7

First stage government consisted of three appointed officials:
a governor, a secretary, and three judges. They constituted a legislature, with authority to adopt civil and criminal laws from
existing states "as necessary and best suited to the circumstances
of the district." The laws were to be published and reported to
Congress. When "there shall be five thousand free male inhabitants of full age" in a district, that region could form a general
assembly, achieving the second stage. Voters elected the lower
house, the House of Representatives. This house sent Congress a
list of men meeting property qualifications, and from it Congress
selected five to form the upper house, the legislative Council.
Property, citizenship, and residency requirements for members
of the general assembly were reasonable, as they were for suffrage. Bills required majorities in both houses, and the governor
had absolute veto. In selecting a non-voting delegate to Congress, the houses met jointly.

The governor's term was three years, the secretary's four, and
judges' terms subject only to good behavior. The governor commanded the militia. Prior to second stage government, the governor appointed sheriffs and other county and township magistrates; after the general assembly was organized, it defined and
regulated such magistrates, the governor keeping power of appointment. Political power in relatively few hands fostered patronage, which led to political personality-driven factions and
wrangling.

In July of 1787, when the Northwest Ordinance was issued,
delegates in Philadelphia were crafting the current federal Constitution. Not surprisingly, the ordinance reflected fundamental
constitutional principles: the people are sovereign; legitimate
governmental powers spring from the people; self-government is
preferred; government should be limited. Both documents
reflected continuing tensions between liberty and order.

Both documents guaranteed republican government. The ordinance required new states' constitutions to "be republican,"

bolstering self-government and republican spirit and even affecting later trans-Mississippi settlement. Furthermore, the ordinance provided protections found in the Bill of Rights: religious rights, habeas corpus, and trial by jury, as well as sanctity of contract, and related protections. It addressed Indians, noting, "The utmost good faith shall always be observed towards the Indians; their lands and property shall never be taken from them without their consent." It added, "laws founded in justice and humanity, shall from time to time be made for preventing wrongs being done to them, and for preserving peace and friendship with them." Protecting nonresident owners, including speculators, the ordinance decreed, "in no case, shall nonresident proprietors be taxed higher than residents." Provisions were occasionally bent or violated outright, but they provided a workable framework— an arena—in which political, social, and economic life evolved.

The ordinance stipulated three, four, or five states could be carved from the region. A region attaining territorial status and containing 60,000 free inhabitants could seek statehood. New states, significantly, would be "on an equal footing with the original States in all respects whatever." Under certain unspecified conditions, the ordinance added, "such admission shall be allowed at an earlier period, and when there may be a less number of free inhabitants in the State than sixty thousand."

Article 6 cheered abolitionists: "There shall be neither slavery nor involuntary servitude in the said territory," except for incarcerated convicts. But another provision noted that residents around Kaskaskia and Vincennes who had sworn allegiance to Virginia enjoyed different laws "relative to descent and conveyance of property." This exemption for "French and Canadian inhabitants, and other settlers" brewed trouble.

Finally, the ordinance delineated boundaries. The Mississippi, Ohio, and Wabash bounded Illinois, as did a line running straight north from Vincennes. It stipulated that Congress "shall have the authority to form one or two States in that part of the said territory which lies north of an east and west line drawn through the Southerly bend or extreme of Lake Michigan." The line "drawn through the Southerly bend or extreme of Lake Michigan" produced friction. Approaching statehood, Indiana and then Illinois finessed this provision, nettling Wisconsin for decades.

The ordinance, furthermore, was a "compact between the Original States and the People and States in said Territory." Its guarantees and republican sentiment were radical in a crucial way: the Old Northwest would never contain formal colonies. No colonizers, colonized, and—of paramount importance—no servile colonial mentality would infest the region. Instead, for perhaps the first time in history settlers in lands adjacent to a Mother Country would receive from the beginning protections, freedoms, and predicable processes in attaining full self-government and political equality; Westerners would never have to wage a war for independence. The Articles of Confederation, furthermore, gave each state one vote in Congress, regardless of population size. This meant that new, sparsely populated states had the same voting power in Congress as older, much larger states. Republicanism, the ban against colonization, and hefty voting power enhanced the West's attractions.

By 1787 Virginia and the national government laid foundations for success. Illinois ultimately attracted scores of thousands of settlers, became a laboratory in which principles and practices of governance and orderly land sales were repeatedly tested. Over decades the laboratory's successes replicated themselves across America. Migrants entered Illinois without degenerating into colonial people with debilitating colonial mentality. People contemplating leaving seaboard states and settling north of the Ohio need not fear losing rights as citizens. Rather, they migrated, confident about retaining full civil and political liberties. Moreover, western states craved newcomers, courting them with low suffrage hurdles.

Low suffrage requirements in the Old Northwest and the absence of religious requirements, unlike those in such states as Connecticut and North Carolina, enticed people. Although first stage government was hardly democratic and the second stage's steep property requirements screened out most voters from the Council, undemocratic features diminished after statehood. The Northwest Ordinance's basic process was so successful and appealing that thirty-one states used the ordinance's basic mechanisms in attaining statehood. Judged in terms of maintenance of order, protection of liberties and properties, transmittal of republican values and government, and attainment of full equality between new and old states, the Northwest Ordinance was immensely successful. It and the Land Ordinance of 1785 succeeded brilliantly, shaping frontier Illinois and much of the country. It set high standards and raised expectations for future territorial expansion.

* * *

The Northwest Ordinance provided blueprints for governance and statehood, but providing effective governance was another matter. Similarly, Britain had agreed to evacuate the region, but ousting them and dissolving their Indian connections were other matters. Finally, surveying, clearing titles, and opening land to sale were planned, but enticing people into Illinois was something else. Settling and planting social taproots took time.

Several factors aggravated the situation. The numbers of Illinois Indians dwindled over time, creating a vacuum filled by Potawatomi, Miami, and others, who harassed French residents. Far worse, in August 1787 the army commander in the Old Northwest, Colonel Josiah Harmar, visited—and promptly plopped into John Dodge's camp, shoring up Dodge's sagging fortunes. French petitioners had helped to bring Harmar to Illinois, but he merely offered them the sunny advice to be good citizens and obey authorities. John Dodge's heavy, corrupt hand triggered further westward flight. Finally, riling stormy opposition and sparring with George Rogers Clark, Dodge in 1787 saw the writing on the wall and crossed the Mississippi. From his new home, however, he kept meddling.

Franco-American relations posed another problem. With peace in 1783, French residents hoped for justice and tranquility, but events dashed these hopes. Some Americans disliked the French and their culture, one source observing, "Not a few of the American settlers who arrived came with a distinct dislike for Catholics; the French thus found themselves doubly tarred, as foreigners and as Catholics." Chaos in the late 1780s undermined French

Kaskaskia, sending additional residents to Spanish Louisiana, further compounding matters. Ethnic scrapes, endless litigation over boundaries and titles, costs of surveys, and implications of Article 6 in the Northwest Ordinance burdened many French. Slave owners read between the lines, comprehended Article 6's antislavery spirit, and worried. Some hustled their slaves and themselves to Spanish Louisiana.

Statistics of this exodus are spongy, but census figures suggest a hefty drain. Kaskaskia in 1778 contained about 500 white inhabitants, virtually all French. In 1783 it had some 155 French-speaking heads of families, along with thirty-nine heads of recently arrived families; perhaps American rule initially brought population increase, including influxes of Anglos. In 1787, though, only 191 French and Anglo males resided in Kaskaskia, and by 1790 only forty-four French heads of families lived there. Other small villages and hamlets were virtually depopulated.[8]

Frosts, floods, John Dodge's tyranny, economic malaise, worthless pay certificates from Virginia, Franco-American tensions, a talent drain to Spanish Louisiana, and general depression reigned. Father Pierre Gibault and eighty-seven others petitioned Governor St. Clair on July 9, 1790, poignantly expressing grievances:

> . . . by an act of Congress of June 20, 1788, it was declared that the lands heretofore possessed by the said inhabitants should be surveyed at their expense; and that this cause appears to them neither necessary nor adapted to quiet the minds of the people. It does not appear necessary, because from the establishment of the colony to this day, they have enjoyed their property and possessions without disputes or lawsuits on the subject or their limits . . . and each of them knew what belonged to him without attempting to encroachment on his neighbor, or fearing that his neighbor would encroach on him. . . . Your Excellency is an eye witness of the poverty to which the inhabitants are reduced, and of the total want of provision to subsist on. Not knowing where to find a morsel of bread to nourish their families, by which means can they support the expense of a survey which has not been sought for on their parts, and for which, it is conceived by them, there is no necessity. Loaded with misery and groaning under the weight of misfortune accumulated since the Virginia troops entered their country, the

unhappy inhabitants throw themselves under the protection of your Excellency, and take the liberty to solicit you to lay their deplorable situation before the Congress.

Without doubt, the inhabitants were unhappy. Equally clear, according to Father Gibault, Virginia's troops arriving in 1778 had brought misfortune. (Ironically, Father Gibault had helped Clark conquer Illinois.) Other misery sprang from disrupted trade patterns, aggravated by British control of the St. Lawrence River and Spanish control of the Mississippi, two water arteries historically vital to French in Illinois.[9]

Cahokia, however, weathered storms well, witnessing slight American intrusion, limited influence by Dodge's henchmen, and minor social friction. Consequently, some French gravitated to Cahokia, there enjoying unsullied French culture, as well as order and justice.

Furthermore, rivulets of French-speaking newcomers, many talented and energetic, partially offset French flight. Some fled turbulent France, some hailed from Switzerland, and some were like Pierre Menard, a venturesome Canadien. Menard settled in Kaskaskia in 1790, opened a store, and entered politics. Humanely generous and merciful to debtors, he served in Indiana's territorial legislature, Illinois' territorial legislature, and in 1818 became the state's first lieutenant governor. He and other Canadiens displayed little despondency, unlike disillusioned French Illinoisans suffering from vagaries of British and American administrations. Under British rule, Quebec's society had stayed cohesive and durable. Migration to Illinois, furthermore, was probably self-selecting, attracting energetic and confident Canadiens.

French Canadiens entered Illinois, settled, and led productive lives. They consciously migrated to Illinois, finding life there attractive, even among boisterous Americans. Significantly, they passed up opportunities to settle in Detroit and other established French settlements. These opportunities along the way—intervening opportunities—failed to impede their migration to Illinois. In addition, Canadiens lie buried in Illinois, their adopted home, not Quebec. Clearly, French Canadiens functioned well among incoming Anglos, language and religious differences and other cultural cleavages notwithstanding. Fleeing the excesses of the French Revolution, some French even arrived directly from France, bypassing either Quebec or New Orleans altogether.

* * *

In late 1787 General Arthur St. Clair became governor of the Northwest Territory, boosted there by Ohio Company officials. He visited Kaskaskia only in early March of 1790. Never unseemly modest, St. Clair initiated government by creating Illinois' first county, St. Clair County, appointed his cousin county clerk, and filled county positions with twenty-eight men, twenty his friends. Aggravating matters, he gratuitously interpreted Article 6 of the Northwest Ordinance, indicating it was merely prospective, not retrospective, which ran counter to previous understanding. Although this probably pleased French slaveowners, it confused the situation. He tarried in Illinois until June 11 and then departed, not returning for five years.

Governor St. Clair, his secretary, and three judges constituted the first government. St. Clair and the judges borrowed civil and criminal laws from other states. The laws provided for several things: the establishment of courts, a militia, and the office of coroner; capital punishment for treason, murder, and lethal arson; whipping, fines, and imprisonment for burglary and robbery; fines, whipping, the pillory, or disenfranchisement for minor crimes. Criminals could avoid fines by being sold by the sheriff for specified periods of time, depending on the offense. Laws threatened saucy servants and mulish children with stays in houses of correction. Laws curtailed work on Sunday, charitable activity on Sunday, and "idle, vain and obscene conversation [or] profane cursing and swearing." Other laws regulated marriage.

Government had its hands full. Sensing abandonment by the British and encroachment by Americans, Indians girded for war. To squelch Indians along the Maumee, General Josiah Harmar in late 1790 led nearly 1,500 men northward, blundered into an ambush, suffered over 180 killed, and barely limped back to Fort Washington. Seeking revenge, St. Clair led 3,000 men northward, and on November 4, 1791, stepped into disaster. Survivors bolted southward, forsaking about 630 dead and nearly 285 wounded, America's greatest military defeat by Indians. Emboldened, Indians swept to the Ohio, impressing British authorities and lending credence to the idea of an Indian barrier.

Two years later General "Mad Anthony" Wayne tried his hand at subduing Indians. Belying his reputation for rashness, he inched northward, methodically consolidating power. A peace treaty he made with Indians in northern Illinois split Indian ranks. Wintering at Fort Greenville, Wayne crept further north, to the Maumee River. On August 20, 1794, along the river, vicious fighting erupted at Fallen Timbers. Although shaken, Wayne's forces won decisively. This led to a telling incident. Britain still occupied forts in the Old Northwest. One was near the mouth of the Maumee, and defeated Indians streaked to it from Fallen Timbers, sought protection, and found the gates closed. The British were inhospitable, but wise. Americans would not have been amused by defeated Indians scooting into a British fort on American soil.

Fallen Timbers led to a meeting at Fort Greenville the following August, where U.S. authorities met over 1,100 chiefs and warriors. Kickapoo, Potawatomi, Kaskaskia, and other Indians attended, and some signed the Treaty of Greenville, ceding most of southern and eastern Ohio. Indians also ceded land in Illinois: a six-mile square tract at the mouth of the Chicago River, where in 1803 authorities built Fort Dearborn to control the portage of the Des Plaines River; a six-mile-square tract at Peoria, which later housed Fort Clark; and Fort Massac and its hinterland. The treaty, moreover, confirmed squatters' rights. Indians retained the remainder of Illinois, for awhile. In return, various tribes received annual payments in goods. About fifteen years of relative peace followed, marred only occasionally by isolated incidents.

Fallen Timbers and the subsequent Treaty of Greenville notified Indians that time was running out. This downward trajectory accelerated. The Jay Treaty, ratified in 1795, finally pried Britain from the Northwest Territory. Relinquishing Detroit and Mackinac in 1796, Britain shifted Indian-trading operations to Fort Malden, near Detroit, and to St. Joseph's Island, between Lake Superior and Lake Huron. From these and other Canadian posts, British authorities continued communing with Indians across the border.

British agents ranged far south, sustaining trading arrangements. In 1793, before Fallen Timbers, Mackinac's commander assessed British influence in Illinois: "Traders descend with facility to the American settlements at the Illinois who are affected to the British Government. The trade to that County is much in our power, as they consume a great quantity of British Manufactures, particularly Cottons, and not having a sufficiency of Peltries to give in return, the balance is paid in Cash which they receive from their neighbors the Spaniards."[10] Despite Fallen Timbers and the withdrawal of British forces from American soil, Britain's roaming agents still labored mightily, cementing ties with gifts and other signs of friendship. The shared Anglo-Indian goal of blocking American expansion undergirded this relationship.

As the British commandant in Mackinac implied, neighboring Spaniards influenced Americans in Illinois. Spanish officials in New Orleans controlled vital choke points of American commerce, a fact driven home whenever Spaniards arbitrarily throttled Mississippi river traffic, sometimes by goading local Indians to launch nuisance raids. Economic realities convinced some Westerners that their interests lay with Spain, not with the United States. Dismemberment of trans-Appalachian America by foreigners and disaffected Americans was not farfetched.

Many Americans seethed over disrupted river commerce and Spanish-Indian intrigue. Seeking a way out, in 1795 they had Spain sign the Pinckney Treaty, giving Americans unimpeded navigation rights on the Mississippi and right of deposit at New Orleans. The Pinckney Treaty and the Jay Treaty, just months apart, resolved potentially mortal problems confronting Illinois.

Malfunctioning courts afflicted residents. Governor St. Clair divided St. Clair County, Illinois' sole county until late 1795, into three judicial districts, centered in Kaskaskia, Cahokia, and Prairie du Rocher. Each district had courts of common pleas, general quarter sessions, justices of the peace, and probate. Each district's court of quarter sessions exercised overall administrative authority. This court also handled cases involving capital punishment, lengthy imprisonment, and forfeiture of property. The court of common pleas, meeting quarterly, heard appeals in civil suits. The judicial machinery was fine, on paper. But it worked badly.

Inept men staffed the courts, except at Cahokia, where William St. Clair, the governor's cousin, performed well. Courts at Kaskaskia and Prairie du Rocher malfunctioned, rarely meeting and keeping sloppy records. Governor St. Clair sent Judge George Turner to clean up Kaskaskia.

Arriving in Kaskaskia in October of 1794, Turner opined that Kaskaskia, not Cahokia, was the county seat, requesting William St. Clair to send court records to Kaskaskia. St. Clair balked, then resigned. Meddlesome Judge Turner stirred up more local folk, who promptly petitioned Congress for redress. Cowed by congressional investigations and possible indictment, he resigned. Kaskaskia and Cahokia kept feuding, prompting Governor St. Clair to establish the County of Randolph in October of 1795, Kaskaskia becoming the county seat. This county, the second in Illinois, covered southern Illinois. Struggles over county-seat location and possession of records erupted, the first such disputes; over decades, some counties experienced five or more county-seat battles. As was true with this fight, virtually all ended peacefully.

Slipshod militia posed another problem. French militia, established in the 1720s, defended communities, built docks, repaired roads, performed other useful tasks, and celebrated at festivals. Reduced Indian troubles after 1795 created sluggishness among American militia. Men avoided muster, officers shirked duties, and militia structure decayed.

* * *

Difficult, expensive, and uncertain pre-steam transportation combined with sparse population to hobble Illinois. Upstream transportation, especially, was prohibitively expensive for most cargo. Floodwater, occasional icing, low water, shifting bars, snags, planters, sawyers, pirates, Indians, long journeys back home with no cargo, and other vicissitudes wreaked havoc among canoes, pirogues, skiffs, flatboats, and keelboats and their crews.[11] Thugs murdered those lured ashore at such places as Cave-in-Rock on the Ohio River. Men crewing craft to New Orleans and hiking home by way of the infamous Natchez Trace fell prey to nefarious individuals. Some simply vanished.

Travelers afoot or on horseback found the going rough. Mud
clung to feet and hooves like heavy glue, dust choked, flies and
mosquitoes tormented travelers and horses, dangerous fords
snatched lives, rickety bridges dumped victims into swollen creeks,
trackless paths disoriented travelers, and carts and wagons brav-
ing trails suffered broken axles and wheels. Guests in over-night
accommodations confronted weird food, spooky bed mates, ver-
min, and occasional murderous hosts. (Some sparkling exceptions delighted jaded travelers.) Dirks and pistols now and then
snuffed the lives of unwary travelers. Transportation costs restricted distances farmers traveled to mill grain, market produce,
or buy necessities. Accordingly, surpluses not marketable locally
either rotted or became whiskey, brandy, or other high-value items
capable of withstanding transportation costs.

Vast distances through wilderness between river landing and
consumer escalated shipping costs. Moreover, sparse settlement
precluded good roads, bridges, and ferries, and crimped construction of mills, ferries, inns, and even small manufactories.
Good money was scarce. Bartering and informal systems of credit lubricated local commerce. Road traffic consisted largely of local folk, irregular mail, migrants, itinerant clergy, peddlers, animals going to market, and a few high-value products.

Sparse population and inexpensive land produced other problems: shortages of hired hands—"helps," as they were called—
and high wages. Land-labor ratios persisting for centuries in
Europe and decades in eastern states were radically different in
frontier Illinois. In the East and especially in Europe, land was
scarce and expensive, labor was plentiful and inexpensive. The
opposite was true in Illinois, making profound differences in ordinary people's lives. Scarce labor, high wages, and ready alternatives generated saucy servants and workers. Some, for example, insisted on eating with employers' households, and if stung
by even a trifling hurt they quit in a huff. Significantly, they addressed employers as "boss," which indicated subordination to
employers only at work, not social or moral subordination. Just
as American farmers never regarded themselves as peasants, so
frontier workers saw themselves not as common laborers, but as
people temporarily in the employ of others. Some gender lines

were blurred. Women, for example, planted corn, ran taverns, and engaged in other work normally reserved for men back east. Similarly, men sometimes did "women's" work. Amelia Roberts wrote from near Tremont on June 18, 1835, "Help is very hard to be had, [and] it is amusing to see how assiduous the husbands &c are to wives and sisters &c. It is not an uncommon occurrence for them (the men) . . . to do all the washing . . . bring in the wood & water, make fires, being useful generally," apparently with no objection from either gender. Labor's value also manifested itself in spirited political and social republicanism. With statehood, laborers voted, campaigned, ran for office, and engaged in civic affairs, many for the first time in their lives.[12] Workers gleefully flaunted feelings of self-worth.

* * *

Scarce labor led to softened laws. For example, lengthy prison incarcerations were expensive, and denied frontier society labor's fruits. In 1795 imprisonment for debt was virtually abolished: "No person shall be kept in prison, for debt or fines, longer than the second day of the sessions next after his or her commitment; unless the plaintiff shall make it appear, that the person imprisoned hath some estate that he will not disclose." Furthermore, debtors were to "make satisfaction, by personal and reasonable servitude, according to the judgment of the court where such action is tried (but only if the plaintiff require it) not exceeding seven years, where such debtor is unmarried, and under the age of forty years."[13] Servitude was preferable to prison. These progressive laws were far more humane than Europe's debtor laws and those of eastern states. No concept of "debtor class," or "vicious stratum" saddled Illinois' frontier society. Society deemed most debtors worthy people who experienced temporary misfortune, much like young Abraham Lincoln.

Other laws reveal much. Exuberant social behavior triggered restraints during the 1790s. Laws enjoining innkeepers from harboring or entertaining servants indicate that servants had sufficient cash, free time, and social latitude to frequent inns, and innkeepers welcomed them. Clearly, servants commanded resources and bent laws with some impunity. On the other hand, predators and other career criminals courted disaster. Murder, treason, forgery, counterfeiting, and lethal arson were capital offenses, labor shortages notwithstanding. Even so, by contemporary standards Illinois had few capital offenses. Thirty-nine lashes across the back penalized thieves.

Suffrage laws also reveal much. By 1799 suffrage included "every free male inhabitant of the age of twenty-one years, resident in the territory, and hath been a citizen of any state in the union, or who hath been two years resident in this territory" who either held a freehold in fifty acres of land within any county in Illinois or held fewer acres worth one hundred dollars, including improvements. These were amazingly low suffrage requirements for the era. With statehood, moreover, virtually all white males could vote, something unknown in eastern states and Europe. Non-citizens also voted in Illinois. Widespread universal suffrage energized frontier society, conferring on pioneers a vital stake in politics and society.

Lawmakers addressed disorderly, harmful Indian-settler contacts. A law adopted in 1791 regulated liquor sales, fining offenders five dollars for every quart sold to Indians. The law's rationale: "Many abuses dangerous to the lives, peace, and property of the good people of this territory, and derogatory to the dignity of the United States have arisen by reason of traders and other persons furnishing spirituous and other intoxicating liquors to the Indian inhabiting, or coming into the said territory." Settlers valued order in the middle ground and elsewhere.

Wild animals preyed on livestock, prompting bounty laws. One law in 1795 stated: "For every grown dog or bitch-wolf, two dollars: for every wolf-puppy, or whelp, one dollar: for every grown fox, or wild-cat, twenty-five cents: for every young fox, or young wild-cat, twelve and a half cents."

Increased settlement brought increased bounty payments. This probably reflected two conditions: more predators, and more kills. Settlers decimated forests, suppressed predators, and spread tree growth by planting trees on prairies and by checking prairie fires here and there by plowing. These altered the environment. Migrants brought with them animals, crops, and trees and bushes alien to Illinois. These provided food for small animals, which in turn sustained wolves and other predators. Well after the Civil War, consequently, to protect livestock neighbors conducted massive, day-long sweeps against wolves.

Laws in the 1790s focused on chaotic transportation. For example, ferry operators were licensed, and laws prescribed rates, hours of operation, and penalties for gouging. Laws approved Sunday operation and exempted operators from militia duty, jury duty, and road duty. To facilitate governance, judges, other court officials, and couriers on public rounds received free ferry service. The law noted, "If any person or persons, other than ferry-keepers, licensed as aforesaid, shall, for reward, set any person over any river or creek, whereon public ferries are appointed or established, at any place within five miles of any such public ferry, he, she, or they, so offending, shall forfeit and pay a sum not exceeding twenty, nor less than five dollars, for every such offense." These heavy fines penalized unauthorized ferry operations, highlighting ferry service's importance to society. Ferry service was, in effect, a quasi-public utility, ferry-keepers having virtual monopolies and close regulation. Curbing laissez faire capitalism, these laws were precursors to public utility laws.

Shortages of mills posed problems, discouraging potential settlement, and thus laws regulating mills were viewed as a priority. Farmers carried grain, often in bags slung over horseback, great distances to mills, often finding others waiting in line or an inoperative mill. Milling therefore sometimes involved costly overnight stays. Worse, the decline and flight of many French led to disrepair and abandonment of some mills. Some American settlers, furthermore, avoided the French and their mills.

Although early mills were usually either hand-powered or horse- (or oxen-) powered, many substantial mills were water-powered. Americans around the 1790s switched from undershot to overshot mills, in which water cascaded onto wheels from above. Lack of mills curtailed flour and meal output, negating bumper harvests and relegating unmilled grain to animal feed or to waste. Droughts stymied milling, and floods and fire destroyed mills. When capacity increased and transportation to mill and market improved, commercial farming thrived, boosting collateral economic and social development and enhancing land values.

People creatively addressed milling deficiencies. For example,
settlers used graters, perforated tin sheets. Ears of corn rubbed
against the perforated side yielded coarse meal, the basis of many
dishes. Mortars, more complicated and efficient, consisted of a
butt of a thick log, one end hollowed to take a peck or two of
grain, which hand-held pestles ground into meal. Heavy pestles
were suspended from logs or tree branches, with counterweights
balancing them.

Mill evolution entailed increasing cost and complexity. For
example, animals walking on circular inclines replaced hand-
operated mills. Windmills, then water-powered mills, and eventually steam-powered mills appeared, usually replacing animal-
powered mills. Increased grain production, regions undergoing
swift population growth, and access to markets triggered improvements in mills, which required substantial capital and technical
investments.

Milling laws of the 1790s were analogous to laws regulating
ferries. They promoted mill construction, predictable operation,
and public confidence. They enjoined millers to provide accurate
measures of one-quart, two-quart, half-peck, one-peck, and half-
bushel sizes. Millers who kept inaccurate measures, lost entrusted
grain, or overcharged faced fines or jail. Mills were quasi-utili-
ties, like ferries. Laws shelved competition, supply and demand
dynamics, and other market mechanisms, in exchange for responsible behavior by millers. These laws were on the books for
decades.

Under law, operators of water and wind mills received in payment one-tenth of the wheat and rye they ground; one-seventh
of Indian corn, oats, barley, and buckwheat, if bolted; one-eighth,
if bolting was not requested; and one-twelfth for grinding malt
and chopping rye. Farmers providing their own horses at horse
mills paid the rates charged at water or wind mills. Millers providing horsepower kept the following fractions: wheat, one-fifth;
rye, Indian corn, oats, barley, and buckwheat, one-fourth; malt
and rye, one-sixth.

* * *

For decades laws reflected problems of fencing and stray animals. As late as May 7, 1830, for example, the *Illinois Intelligencer*

ran stray animal notices. One noted, "Taken Up. By James Gray, living in the County of Marion, and State of Illinois, on the head waters of the East Fork, one bay mare, supposed to be 13 or 14 years old, having a 75 cent bell on, a saddle spot, and a small star in her forehead, no brands perceivable." Despite laws holding owners responsible for damages perpetrated by strays, only with improved fencing in the 1850s did farmers maintain purebreds.

Laws addressed militia problems, including the need to protect officers and enlisted men from abuse heaped on them by insensitive bystanders. Since all military-age males were militia members, perhaps abuse originated from society's fringe elements, possibly reflecting incipient class tension.

Some laws in the 1790s focused on destructive fires. Nature, Indians, and settlers regularly fired prairies in late summer and autumn, promoting dynamic environmental balance. Sometimes, though, people firing prairies destroyed crops, fences, outbuildings, houses, animals, and human life. Stiff fines awaited "persons in the habit of setting fire the leaves and herbage in the woods, prairies, and other grounds, thereby producing a configuration [*sic*] prejudicial to the soil, destructive to the timber and the improvements within this territory." Significantly, this law referred to "the improvements" in Illinois.

During 1795 Governor St. Clair and his judges finished the legal code of the Northwest Territory. This code summarized existing laws, added some family laws, and explicitly adopted common law. Strengthened by subsequent legislation, common law linked the Old Northwest back to Kentucky, Virginia and other English colonies, and to English common law. Governance proved itself flexible, able to adapt, decentralized, alert to local needs, and eventually efficient. This was Governor St. Clair's crowning achievement, the one which compensated for his many deficiencies.[14]

* * *

French decline continued. Andre Michaux, an observant French scientist, reported from Kaskaskia on August 30, 1795, that it "is inhabited by former Frenchmen under the American Government. The number of families is about forty five." He then added, "It is agreeably situated but the number of inhabitants has decreased; nothing is to be seen but houses in ruins and abandoned because the French of the Illinois country, having been brought up in and accustomed to the Fur Trade with the savages, have become the laziest and most ignorant of all men. They live and the majority of them are clothed in the manner of the Savages." On September 5 he "started for the village called Prairie du Rocher about 15 miles distant from Kaskaskia. Passed by the village of St. Philippe abandoned by the French and inhabited by three families of Americans." Finally, on September 20, he wrote, "Kaskaskia 45 families; Prairie du Rocher 22 to 24 families. St. Philippe 3 American families. Fort de Chartres in ruins." He reported 120 families living in "Casks," a garbled spelling of Cahokia, and some 35 American families living in Corns de Serf and Bellefontaine.[15]

Society's decrepit state impressed Michaux. Abandoned settlements suggest group migration or the consolidation of settlements—or both. Americans living in St. Philippe and other hamlets suggest a reluctance of people to mix.

Andre Michaux counted fewer people in 1795 than were gleaned five years later. Very likely uncertainties during the early 1790s both dissuaded American settlement and encouraged French departure. Most remaining French residents were residual folk, people not leaving for Spanish Louisiana. Many had lived in Illinois for years, assisted the Revolution, raised families, and buried loved ones. Despite bruising dislocations, they had a stake in Illinois. As young French couples left, births sagged, contributing to overall population decline in the 1790s, despite newcomers trickling in from Quebec and France.

The mid-1790s witnessed American influxes, which further eroded French culture. New Design, founded by Virginians in 1782 south of Bellefontaine, became by 1795 Illinois' largest English-speaking settlement. It spurted in 1797 when the Rev. David Badgley, a Baptist minister, arrived with 154 newcomers. Stepping off flatboats at Fort Massac, Badgley's party slogged for weeks through swamps and mud before reaching New Design. Scorching heat and wretched food and shelter triggered sickness, half dying before winter, many survivors dispersing.[16] The Rev.

Badgley had organized New Design's Baptist Church, Illinois' first Protestant church. This probably disquieted some French residents.

Although a Baptist elder had preached as early as 1787, Badgley was very likely Illinois' first Protestant clergyman. Arriving from Kentucky in 1793, the Rev. Joseph Lillard was Illinois' first Methodist clergyman, the first circuit rider making rounds in 1803.

Despite incoming Americans, population grew slowly. In 1750 Illinois contained about 2,500 French subjects. Fifty years later non-Indians still numbered around 2,500. Deaths and French exodus to Spanish Louisiana offset live births, a trickle of Canadiens, residual British, and Americans arriving after 1778. Between 1750 and 1800 the non-Indian population remained basically static, although its ethnic composition changed.

By 1800 Illinois contained some 800 to 1,000 English-speaking people, nearly all Americans. (Perhaps only 150 had arrived before 1787.) Many huddled in three clusters: some 186 in Bellefontaine; about 250 at Eagle in southern St. Clair County; and 90 down at Massac. In addition, about 334 lived in scattered settlements and farms, mostly in modern Monroe County. A few score lived in or near Kaskaskia, Cahokia, and other French communities. The French population in 1800 also clustered: Cahokia boasted 719 inhabitants, Kaskaskia 467, and Prairie du Rocher 212. Peoria contained about 100. Kaskaskia's figure included 47 Indian and black slaves, Prairie du Rocher's some 60 Indian and black slaves.

Population shifts brought changes. As the French left, aged, declined in vitality, or died, religious life waned. Even Father Pierre Gibault, redoubtable patriot priest, packed up and crossed the Mississippi to New Madrid. Churches fell into disrepair, masses were said infrequently, and few priests ministered to parishioners from Spanish Louisiana. French culture, implanted over a century earlier, wilted. Apparently, the mid-1790s saw Illinois' demographic nadir. But with influxes of American settlers, many of whom were young, the American star began to rise.

7.

Rumblings Across
the Land

Between approximately 1800 and 1815, interplay among outsiders, settlers, and natural forces brought sweeping changes.
However haltingly, American culture, values, and institutions ascended in Illinois, spearheaded by vanguards of households and
federal commitment and energy. Docile residual French and continuing French flight probably gladdened incoming Americans.
American and French land holdings commingled by 1809, when
Illinois attained territorial status. In addition, fruitful existing
treaties and ongoing diplomatic and military activities largely
negated previous military defeats, British meddling, and crippling commercial restrictions.

Non-Indian population jumped from 2,458 in 1800 to 12,282
ten years later. Population growth helped overcome vulnerability, poor transportation, weak markets, and related difficulties,
but knotty problems festered, some worsening. Lingering international scrapes, ethnic and religious spats, slavery issues, shoddy
land records and tangled claims, predators, ominous squatter-
Indian troubles, British intervention, misinformation and rumor,
and nature's whims all marred progress. Although the likes of
Micajah and Wiley Harpe, murderous brothers who infested Cave-
in-Rock on the Ohio, were eradicated by 1799, occasional atroci-

ties still horrified residents. Certain problems retarding settlement budged only with population growth and the weight of numbers.

Sparring with Spain, federal authorities ordered Fort Massiac, the dilapidated French installation near Illinois' southern extremity, to be rebuilt.[1] Quickly dubbed Fort Massac, it housed Regular Army forces until 1812, its cannon lending credence. Becoming a port-of-entry in 1799, it collected duties and presided over quickening commerce. Just before Fortescue Cuming, an intelligent and intrepid English visitor, landed at Fort Massac in May 1808, a corporal from the fort "came on board, and took a memorandum of our destination, &c. We landed, and approaching the fort, we were met by Lieutenant Johnston, who very politely shewed us the barracks, and his own quarters within the fort, in front of which is a beautiful esplanade, with a row of Lombardy poplars in front." He added,

> The fort is formed of pickets, and is a square, with a small bastion at each angle. The surrounding plain is cleared to an extent of about sixty acres, to serve for exercising the garrison in military evolutions, and also to prevent surprise from an enemy. On the esplanade is a small brass howitzer, and a brass carronade two pounder, both mounted on field carriages, and a centinel is always kept here on guard. The garrison consists of about fifty men.

Although the fort lost port-of-entry functions in 1808, its presence symbolized federal commitment to the region. Cuming noted, "There is no kind of society out of the garrison, and there are only a few settlements in the neighbourhood, which supply it with fresh stock." Impressing Spain and river pirates, the fort also stimulated local trade.

Leaving Fort Massac, Cuming sailed downstream seventeen miles, stepped ashore in Illinois, and "purchased some fowls, eggs, and milk, at a solitary but pleasant settlement on the right just below Cash island. It is occupied by one Petit with his family, who stopped here to make a crop or two previous to his descending the Mississippi, according to his intention on some future day."[2] Isolated houses temporarily inhabited by westward-wending folk demonstrated confidence.

Governor Arthur St. Clair and the territory's three judges and secretary had enacted appropriate laws, generating additional confidence. Mirroring earlier laws, these laws regulated mills and ferries, contacts with Indians, militia, fires, and squatters. Laws or no laws, Indians obtained liquor, squatters filtered into lands, and prairies burned.

In 1798 St. Clair claimed the Northwest Territory contained over 5,000 white adult males, the threshold for second stage government. He slated elections to the general assembly, the country's first territorial legislature. Of its twenty-three members, two represented Illinois. Shadrach Bond, Sr., represented St. Clair County, and John Edgar, Randolph County.

The body sat at Cincinnati in early 1799, compiled names from which President John Adams selected the legislative council, and adjourned. After Adams made his choices, the entire legislature convened at Cincinnati on September 16. Sparkling with talent, the first legislative session met until December, producing forty-eight bills, eleven of which the aristocratic governor vetoed. St. Clair's vetoing of legislation slated to create new counties affronted settlers. (Eventually ousted from office and pitched into political oblivion, he died penniless.) This legislative session of the Northwest Territory was the only one that affected Illinois; on May 7, 1800, before another session met, Congress created the Indiana Territory. This newly created territory included Illinois.

William Henry Harrison helped create the Indiana Territory. The son of a three-term governor of Virginia and a veteran of Fallen Timbers, he advocated liberal land policies to settle lands gained via warfare. In 1798 he became territorial secretary, and the next year the territorial legislature elected him non-voting delegate to Congress, edging out Arthur St. Clair, Jr., the governor's son. As he labored tirelessly in Congress, his brilliant career soared.

The Indiana Territory included everything lying west of a line drawn north from the mouth of the Kentucky River to Fort Recovery and then due north to Canada. East of the line lay the present state of Ohio, a sliver of southeastern Indiana between the mouth of the Kentucky and the Great Miami rivers, the eastern half of the lower peninsula of Michigan, and the eastern tip of the upper peninsula. It contained 4,875 whites, 135 black slaves, and perhaps 100,000 Indians. Nearly all non-Indians inhabited the southern fringes, mostly in the American Bottom and along other rivers. Vincennes was the capital.

The Indiana Territory faced many challenges. Wilderness tracts hindered governance, especially in St. Clair and Randolph counties. Courts functioned sporadically, bizarrely, or both. At Prairie du Rocher, for example, a man who slew a hog stood trial for murder. Another court paraded a recently convicted individual through town with his horse's tail tied to his face, the horse led by his wife. Erratic justice emboldened miscreants, while laws promoting secure land titles, which settlers craved, went unenforced. On the other hand, even zany judicial activities reflected genuine efforts to solve intractable problems.

A federal law which Harrison advocated reduced to 320 acres the smallest tract of public land available for sale. It stipulated cash down payment of 25 percent, the balance in three yearly installments. Still inadequate for some settlers, partly because of the cost of $2 per acre, the law nevertheless bolstered Harrison's standing, as did his battles with congressional Federalists. The law, furthermore, "set a trend toward family-sized farms, stimulated migration," and "generally met frontier needs."[3] On May 13, 1800, just months after becoming delegate to Congress, twenty-seven year-old Harrison was appointed governor of the Indiana Territory.

Harrison's twelve-year stint as governor was rocky. In 1800 Illinois contained fewer than 2,500 non-Indian inhabitants, including about 1,000 Americans. The rest consisted of French, French-Indians, and a few dozen blacks. Illinoisans complained about Vincennes' remoteness. Citing labor shortages and noting slavery across the Mississippi, French slave owners in Illinois sought to shore up slavery. Article 6 of the Northwest Ordinance still worried French masters, some shunting their slaves across the Mississippi. Petitioning Congress in 1800, some 268 French and others sought repeal of Article 6. Similar petitions inundated Congress until 1809. Some requested a ten-year suspension of that article, insisting that slave owners avoided Illinois. Others proposed manumitting slaves at a specific age, and some opined that slave competition could lower Illinois' high labor rates. Hoping to elect a proslavery delegate to Congress, they agitated for second stage government. Others sought secure land titles, speculative opportunities, broader suffrage, more laborers, improved transportation, justice, and law and order. Scathing charges of favoritism assailed Harrison. Recently arrived American settlers and entrenched French residents sometimes quarreled, and there was agitation to detach Illinois from the Indiana Territory. Governor Harrison resisted these pressures.

Adding to political complexity, John Edgar and William Morrison spearheaded proslavery forces. John Edgar, a former British naval officer, had settled in Kaskaskia in 1784, served in the Northwest Territory's legislature at Cincinnati, and made fortunes in land, mills, and river shipping. He was a major-general of militia. William Morrison, settling in Kaskaskia in 1790, was one of six brothers forsaking Philadelphia for Illinois. Receiving capital from Philadelphia, he ran businesses throughout the Mississippi Valley, joining Edgar in speculation and empire building.

By 1803 Governor Harrison adjusted his views somewhat. He, the territory's three judges, and the secretary—the legislature—legalized indentured servants, a subterfuge for slavery. Slaves made their marks on indentures, documents binding them for up to ninety-nine years of service. Late, in 1814, territorial legislators approved importing slaves for hire for twelve-month terms, renewable indefinitely. Renewed terms were hardly necessary, however, since employers or owners working slaves beyond their terms rarely faced prosecution. Indentured servitude and other thinly veiled forms of slavery persisted into statehood.[4]

Although Harrison helped create the indentured servitude subterfuge, his proslavery foes grumbled. They claimed Harrison, the judges, and the secretary lacked authority to adopt such laws, maintaining that only elected bodies could enact legitimate laws. Whereupon, Harrison in 1804 quickly ordered a referendum on granting Indiana second stage territorial government, the stage that would have a legislature, according to the Northwest Ordinance of 1787. His maneuver confounded his opponents, leaving them sputtering about Harrison's unseemly haste.

The referendum, held in September of 1804, carried by 269 to

131. Elections in January of 1805 for the Indiana Territorial legislature gave Harrison's followers all three seats from Illinois. Shadrach Bond, Sr., and William Biggs represented St. Clair County, and Dr. George Fisher represented Randolph County. After Bond was appointed to the legislative council, his nephew was elected to fill the vacancy.

* * *

Federal diplomatic activities also affected Illinois. After France muscled vast Spanish Louisiana from Spain in 1800, it sold it in 1803 to the United States, radically changing Illinois, national, and international history. Significantly, the Louisiana Purchase solved vexing commercial problems, giving Westerners unimpeded navigation to the Gulf. The Purchase lifted Illinois from the country's western fringes and placed it nearer the geographic center. Illinois was no longer a marginal region adjacent to European-held territory. Frontier lands now lay westward. Soon Illinois became a staging point, a jumping off place for explorers, trappers, and settlers crossing the Mississippi. Among the first to jump off were William Clark and Meriwether Lewis. After wintering in 1803–1804 at the mouth of Wood River, they headed up the Missouri for the Pacific, returning victoriously to St. Louis in late 1806.

Although the purchase of Louisiana tightened America's grip on the Old Northwest, control of the Chicago Portage was vital. This portage crossed the six-mile-square parcel which had been ceded at Greenville in 1795. To establish tangible presence and impress Indians and British, Captain James Whistler arrived there by sloop in 1803, met Regular Army troops marching from Detroit, and then built Fort Dearborn just south of where modern Michigan Avenue crosses the Chicago River.

Very likely, though, federal trading factories impressed Indians and British authorities more than forts. Such factories had several functions: to provide Indians with reasonably priced goods, promote friendship with them, lure them into American culture, and thwart Britain's influence in general. In 1805 Fort Dearborn housed a factory, one of twelve in the West by 1808. It operated successfully until 1812. John Kenzie, arriving in 1804, augmented these efforts. Dynamic and creative, he traded, befriended Indians, boosted civic undertakings, and became a driving economic and social force in fledgling Chicago.

The Treaty of Greenville had established American property rights in the Old Northwest, but in it the United States relinquished all claims north of the Ohio and east of the Mississippi, except for such portions as the six-mile-square tract at the Chicago Portage. Significantly, however, the treaty added, "but when those tribes, or any of them, shall be disposed to sell their lands, or any part of them, they are to be sold only to the United States." This was vastly important. Declining fur trade prompted some Indians to sell land, and before land offices offered parcels for sale squatters pushed into tribal lands.

Governor Harrison unabashedly wanted Indian lands for settlers. He arranged and signed many treaties, not being excessively fastidious about whether signing Indians had authority to sign. In June 1803, at Fort Wayne, representatives from five tribes sold over 2 million acres west and southwest of Vincennes, including the valuable salt springs west of Shawneetown.[5] Weeks later, in August, enfeebled Kaskaskia Indians at Vincennes relinquished nearly 9 million acres in southern Illinois, virtually extinguishing Indian claims there. In St. Louis in November of 1804, Foxes and Sauk yielded lands lying west of the Illinois and the Fox rivers to the Mississippi, some 14,800,000 acres. One prominent Sauk, Black Hawk, refused to sign. The next year Harrison returned to Vincennes, where Piankashaws sold more than 2.5 million acres between the lower Wabash and its western watershed. By 1807 most of Illinois had been ceded.

From Greenville in 1795 to St. Louis in late 1833, eighteen treaties signed by representatives from at least seventeen distinct tribes sold nearly 88,600,000 acres, some 40 million by 1809, and some 17,863,000 acres in 1818 alone. By statehood, remaining Indian lands in Illinois lay largely in the northern quarter of Illinois and poorly drained regions in eastern Illinois. Harrison zealously obtained lands through 1809, as did Governor Ninian Edwards, Pierre Menard, and other territorial authorities.

These transactions usually brought Indians a few thousand dollars in goods, services, or promises. Moreover, prominent chiefs sometimes refused to sign, calling the treaties into question. Finally, tribal territorial disputes sometimes necessitated several treaties to extinguish all claims in some tracts.

In 1804 federal law authorized public domain sales in the Indiana Territory. That same year Kaskaskia, Vincennes, and Detroit obtained land offices, each having a register and receiver as land commissioners. Favorable treaties and Kaskaskia's office spurred development: "Immigration was further stimulated in consequence of the conclusion of the treaties with the Indians in 1803–4–5, and the establishment of the land-office at Kaskaskia in 1804."[6] Treaties and offices signified federal support for settlement. Ignoring snarled land claims and stymied sales, pioneers arrived.

Nevertheless, prior to 1804 no public land was sold west of a line running north from the mouth of the Kentucky River. Three obstacles hampered the sale of public domain lands in Illinois: continuing Indian claims, which took decades to extinguish; survey stipulations of the Ordinance of 1785, which also took decades; and nearly three thousand conflicting claims, which stemmed from sales Indians had made to individuals and land grants by France, Britain, Virginia, and the United States.

British officials had gleefully showered cronies with titles, ignoring earlier French claims and transactions. Poor records further muddled matters, as did wartime instability from 1778 to 1783 and tangled land claims and titles spanning decades. Old claims, however dubious, suddenly appreciated, triggering rabid speculation. Shady deals were rife, conniving and lying rampant. Soon a "class of professional witnesses with elastic memories sprang up and did a thriving business" of swearing to falsehoods.[7] In 1807 Vincennes' land office finally sold public domain land. Kaskaskia's land office took ten years to sort through and adjudicate French and British land grants, belatedly selling land only in 1814.

Governor Harrison's faction and opponents clashed over land sales. Unfortunately for Harrison, speculative mania splashed into territorial politics and beyond. Land commissioners heard sworn testimony concerning claims, adjudicated, and reported their findings to Congress for approval or rejection. In 1804 Harrison named able, honest Michael Jones as register at Kaskaskia. He and the receiver at Kaskaskia quickly uncovered gross impropriety, fraud, and corruption. This led to the formation of the Edgar-Morrison political clique, which clamored to fire Jones.

Furthermore, some of Harrison's allies, hip deep in questionable land deals, defected. Ordinary people, as well, shuddered over investigations of irregularities. Consequently, Edgar-Morrison candidates scored victories in legislative elections. Moreover, some proslavery voters backed Edgar-Morrison candidates, who generally supported slavery but who also wanted territorial status for Illinois. The bubbling land scandal quickly became enmeshed in efforts to achieve territorial status.

* * *

Jesse Burgess Thomas, residing in eastern Indiana, arose to champion the creation of the Territory of Illinois. Born in Maryland in 1777, Thomas grew up in Lawrenceburg, Indiana Territory, entered politics, and became Speaker of the Territorial House of Representatives. Proponents of securing territorial status knew the process hinged on the delegate to Congress. After the incumbent delegate resigned, proponents extracted from Jesse Thomas a written pledge to press the matter in Congress. Formidable interests opposed Thomas: Hoosiers around Vincennes, who realized that slicing Illinois from Indiana would cause the territorial capital of Indiana to leave Vincennes and gravitate to a more central location; Thomas's constituency in eastern Indiana; Harrison forces, which enlisted the Edgar-Morrison clique's nemesis, Michael Jones.

Violence in Vincennes marred the delegate-selection process, and some constituents burned Thomas in effigy, denouncing him as a traitor. Nevertheless, the legislature again met in Vincennes in late 1808 and narrowly selected Thomas as delegate. Thomas chaired the congressional committee considering separation, working tirelessly for separation.

On February 3, 1809, Congress established the Territory of Illinois as of March 1. Kaskaskia was the territorial capital. Territorial Illinois included all of modern Illinois, Wisconsin, western upper peninsula of Michigan, and northeastern Minnesota. Thomas's committee estimated some 11,000 people lived west of the Wabash in Illinois, a reasonably accurate figure.[8]

Illinois Territory continued to have problems, however, including poor transportation, inefficient land office operations, slavery matters, and petty sniping. Of greater importance, British agents huddling with Indians generated chronic instability, treaties notwithstanding. Some problems became solvable only after Americans and British thrashed out disputes via war. In fact, from 1809 to early 1815, British-American struggles dominated life, soaking up resources and retarding growth. Inexorably involved, Indians flung themselves against Americans in last-ditch efforts to stem the tide.

Debilitating political bickering marred government in Territorial Illinois. The formidable Edgar-Morrison faction guided political appointments and economic policy. This faction blocked Nathaniel Pope, the first Secretary of the Territory of Illinois and a relative of Michael Jones, from becoming territorial governor. But Nathaniel Pope's brother, Senator John Pope, helped select the governor. Following Senator Pope's advice, President Madison tapped Ninian Edwards, the Pope brothers' cousin from Kentucky.

Edwards had impressive credentials. Born in Maryland in 1775, he was educated at Dickinson College. As a teenager he moved to Kentucky, flaunted dissolute behavior, reformed himself, studied law, became a legislator, and rose to Chief Justice of the Court of Appeals, Kentucky's highest court. Charged with aristocratic tendencies, he nonetheless espoused Jeffersonian principles as Illinois' territorial governor, and served until statehood. Appointing county and militia officers was his prerogative, but he courted public input via petitions, letters, and recommendations. Fretting over simmering Indian problems, he organized Rangers and urged blockhouse construction. These beefed-up defenses blunted Indian-British attacks before and during the War of 1812. Large and handsome, Edwards was also intelligent, energetic, courtly, a bit stuffy and verbose, and magnanimous. He died assisting cholera victims in 1833.

Although a few newcomers filtered into Illinois from the Northeast, Canada, and even Europe, most were Southerners, with

Kentucky the chief donor state. The territory's political core, cen-
tering on Governor Edwards, was southern. Jesse Thomas, one
of three territorial judges, hailed from Maryland. Another, William Sprigg, was born and raised in Maryland, where his brother
was governor. A Virginia native, Alexander Stuart, was the third
judge. Nathaniel Pope, coming from powerful circles in Kentucky,
became territorial secretary. Other highly active political figures
included Maryland-born Shadrach Bond and tubercular but
adroit Daniel Pope Cook, a Kentuckian. John McLean, a North
Carolinian raised in Kentucky, coalesced with Thomas and others to block Edwards. Joseph Phillips, a Tennessee native, was
territorial secretary just before statehood. Robert McLaughlin, a
powerful legislator, moved from Virginia to Kentucky as a young
man. A few prominent politicians, including Elias Kent Kane
and Samuel D. Lockwood, were non-Southerners, but deferred
to southern colleagues on important questions. Pierre Menard
presided over the territorial legislature, but few French gained
political prominence. Clearly, southern imprints were obvious and
profound.

Territorial laws, moreover, were to be selected from laws of
existing states, giving framers wide latitude. From the outset,
Illinoisans selected southern laws. Kentucky supplied five laws,
Georgia three, Virginia two, and South Carolina and Pennsylvania one each.

Southerners left other imprints on Illinois. They settled in or
near woods in southern Illinois. Settlers derived much from wood:
fuel, cabins, furniture, wagons, utensils, yokes, tools, fences, barrels, and other necessities. Nuts, acorns, fruit, berries, roots, bark,
and other forest products provided food, mast for animals, dyes,
medicines, and other useful items. Also, southern Illinois was
heavily forested, partially settled, close to the South, and distant
from most British-Indian threats.

Much like the French, Southerners were riverine people, and
river valleys were wooded. Kentuckians, Virginians, and others
reached Illinois by rivercraft, settled along rivers, hunted and
fished, raised crops in rich, rock-free alluvial soils, traveled on
rivers, and used water power for mills, saws, and trip hammers.
Ice, furthermore, rarely clogged rivers of southern Illinois.

They regarded prairies as desolate unknowns. Dreadful rumors retarded prairie settlement: prairies floated on bodies of water and swallowed unwary travelers; scarce timber indicated insufficient water and poor soil; grasslands fostered lethal cold snaps and diseases. In reality, spectacular, wind-whipped prairie fires deterred people from even traversing grasslands. Voracious flies and other prairie tormentors drove humans and livestock berserk. Prairie grasses' dense roots defied plowing until the 1830s.

Conversely, early settlers believed, woodlands implied water, fertile soil, as well as protection from icy blasts, roaring conflagrations, and summer's ferocious pests. Furthermore, pioneers along prairie-timber margins tapped both forest and prairie resources.

So Southern Illinois acquired a distinctly southern cast, which was strongly contrasted following statehood by infusions into northern Illinois of Northerners and others. (Illinois' central region spawned cultural mixtures of Southerners, Northerners, and others.) Cultural differences sparked prolonged shrill clashes, reaching crescendo levels by the late 1830s.

* * *

Prior to the War of 1812, newcomers used various methods and means to migrate, select homesteads, and settle down. No steamboats or trains sped them westward, no canals glided bulky possessions to Illinois, no Great Lakes shipping insured regular passage to Illinois, no telegraph fired messages eastward, and no safe and speedy conveyance carried discouraged people back home. Leaving home and heading to Illinois were momentous events, often resulting in permanent separation from family and friends.

Once ideas of migrating sprouted, the next phase involved learning about alternative destinations. The learning process varied. Practically no guidebooks or geographies existed to assist aspiring settlers. Sometimes soldiers served in Illinois, liked it, and returned to settle, often convincing others to come with them. In other instances, young businessmen arrived with goods from Pittsburgh, Cincinnati, or other commercial centers upstream, liked southern Illinois, and returned. Some rivermen crewing flatboats gazed longingly at Illinois' lush riverbanks. Moreover, by early 1804 St. Louis was American, no longer a foreign river port. Visitors to St. Louis slipped into Illinois and settled, forming a prong of settlement stretching up the Illinois River.

Facing dangers and uncertainties, prospective settlers sent out scouting parties. Many parties—often a father, older male offspring, a nephew, and perhaps other young men—arrived, scouted locally, obtained use of some land, threw together a three-sided lean-to, planted corn, scratched out other improvements, and then either returned home for winter or holed up at or near the site, sometimes with pioneer friends or relatives. Usually, at least one returned home, helped relatives prepare to migrate, then escorted them—typically females, the very young, and occasionally the elderly and infirm—back to the site, often doing so after spring rains slackened and swollen streams subsided. Household members wintering near the site emerged in early spring, improved their dwellings, prepared land for crops, and took steps to purchase the land. Wintering members often discovered something unfavorable about their chosen site or something favorable about a nearby site, and this led to small adjustment moves. Chain migration operated, original settlers assisting relatives and friends with shelter or employment, sufficient inducements to attract newcomers. James Stockton and Abraham Pruitt came from Knox County, Tennessee, and settled near the mouth of Wood River. Within a few years, a sizeable number from Knox County and adjacent regions joined them. Sometimes households and groups of households and others migrated as a single unit directly to a specific site via chain migration.

Canadiens filtered into Illinois in the early 1800s, almost certainly by chain migration. For example, in 1798 three young brothers named Pensoneau—Louison, Etienne, and Louis—from the Trois Rivières region settled in Cahokia and soon married. Louison traded with Kickapoo along the Illinois River. Etienne bought and sold land in modern Belleville and built a water mill on Richland Creek. Louis for many years provided ferry service at St. Louis. The energies and talents of these brothers enlivened early Illinois' commercial and social scene. About the time the Pensoneau brothers arrived at Cahokia, two other Pensoneaus (Augustine and Francois), their second or third cousins, moved to

Cahokia. Very likely, the success or one or more of the Pensoneau brothers enticed others to migrate, knowing that nearby kin would render needed assistance.[9]

Sometimes, large groups migrated westward without the assistance of either scouts or chain migration. This, however, was more common well after statehood, when guidebooks and newspapers regaled readers with enticing accounts of life in Illinois. Despite notable failures, group migration and settlement had distinct advantages: economies of scale, pooled capital, division of labor, shared risk, increased protection, collective wisdom, and institutional memory. Individual initiative, responsibility, and acceptance of consequences for one's acts magnified advantages of group migration. Advantages usually outweighed tendencies for groups to smother creative nonconformists and bicker and fragment. (Large groups, though, often overloaded local environments, depleting pasturage, wood resources, water supply, game, wild fruits, and other resources.)

Religious and humanitarian impulses produced group efforts, sometimes involving a charismatic figure whose vision and personality guided and energized the project. Some of these group migrations ended with grief. For example, Father Urbain Guillet, a leader of Trappist monks, left France for America, settling in Kentucky in 1805. Governor Ninian Edwards and Nicholas Jarrot, a respected French resident, persuaded the monks to settle in 1809 at Cahokia. About this time Catholicism's activities and influence in Illinois had ebbed. No regular masses were said and many faithful were demoralized or scattered. The vegetarian monks laid out gardens, opened a free school, comforted the afflicted, observed strict silence and other obligations, and suffered greatly. Abetted by meager harvests and inadequate diets, disease thinned their ranks. Further discouraged by sour land transactions, the colony returned east in 1813, reaching France after Napoleon's downfall. The monks, however, did leave a legacy: the huge Indian mound on which they lived, Monks' Mound, was named after them.

Group settlement was common among New Englanders and Europeans. New Englanders, especially, still throbbed with impulses of community and mission. Some highly organized groups

settled, remained intact for months or longer, and fulfilled tran-
scendent goals. Some were commercial ventures, which often had
eastern or foreign financial backing that profited from transplanted groups. Many enjoyed limited, and usually brief, success. Quarrelsome personalities, undercapitalization, imperfect
understandings of human nature, and nearby competitive opportunities weakened cohesion. So did success. The group's advantages were no longer needed. Individuals and households could
largely function on their own, banding together now and then to
achieve some specific goal.

Most groups were merely collections of people who coalesced
to go to Illinois. They had no grand mission, other than to arrive
uneventfully. Other groups formed along the way. For example,
a migratory party started west, ran across interested households
and individuals, and amalgamated them into the larger party.
Group migration's heyday, following statehood, insured varied
demographics through the twilight of frontier Illinois, since they
helped the very young, old, and disabled migrate as well as ordinary settlers.

Generally speaking, groups which were not highly planned,
rigidly organized, narrowly focused, and tightly operated were
successful.

Tight groups led by strong personalities often foundered, splin-
tering into factions, disintegrating after the leaders' deaths, or
needlessly alienating neighbors. Fortunately, most groups were
ad hoc and had few ideological constraints. These groups ushered people into Illinois, sank taproots of community, and then
dissolved. Before they did, they made lasting contributions. Stepping into uncertainty, venturing into fog, and encountering unforeseen contingencies, members soon expected the unexpected
and even welcomed the unknown—highly valuable traits. Opportunity, they knew, lay on the edge of the unknown. Loose,
open, ad hoc groups taught members to be pragmatic, flexible,
and open to ideas expressed by strangers.

* * *

In 1810 only 12,282 whites lived in Illinois. A fivefold increase
since 1800, it nevertheless starkly underscored Illinois' sparse

population. Prospective settlers often went elsewhere. For some Southerners concentrations of slaves in Mississippi, Louisiana, Alabama, western Kentucky and Tennessee, and central Missouri beckoned. New Englanders rushed to northern Ohio, and for decades their descendants and others flooded southern Michigan and southern Wisconsin.

Normally, few elderly people entered the American frontier.[10] In the nineteenth century, very many elderly were poor, in marginal health, and dependent upon others, factors which often curtailed their movement westward. Death en route and shortly after reaching the West decimated elderly settlers, and misfortune compelled others to return east. Even so, frontier Illinois' census figures are anomalous, requiring explanation. In 1810 among white males throughout the entire northern frontier only about 5 percent were forty-five or over, and among white females only about 4 percent were that age. In 1810 among white males throughout northern settled portions of the county, some 7 percent of both white males and white females were forty-five or over, and among both genders throughout the southern settled regions 6 percent were that age. Still, a portion of the federal census for 1810 counted 3,665 free males in Illinois, of whom 285 were forty-five years of age or older. These constituted 7.8 percent of the free male population. In the same year Illinois contained 2,973 free females, of whom 210 were forty-five or older and constituted nearly 7.1 percent of the free female population. Cursory examination of census data suggests some residents over forty-five were French folk who stayed put as younger kin crossed to Spanish Louisiana. Others were Southerners, their journey to Illinois facilitated by strong kinship ties.

* * *

Although unable to buy land, even marginal people settled, often finding land on fringes of populated regions. Some simply moved in, or squatted, built shelter, and scraped out a living by tapping local resources. Disputed land claims and vague laws helped them do this. Squatters who improved land and intended to settle permanently received sympathy. Time benefitted many of them; laws eventually gave them opportunity to buy lands they occupied. Only as the frontier faded, in the 1850s, did laws really restrict squatters.

Many squatters and others regarded timber stands as commons, regardless of ownership. Owners moaned and grumbled about timber losses, observing how wooden fences, sheds, and other improvements appeared like apparitions on neighboring prairie lands. Pilferers plundered timber owned by absentee landlords, including the federal government. Frustrated owners warned unknown timber poachers. For example, on April 11, 1816, Isaiah Levens and Caldwell Carnes ran the following notice in the *Illinois Herald:* "CAUTION. This is to forewarn any person or persons what ever from cutting timber or hauling any that may be cut, or tresspassing [*sic*] in any way whatever on the south west fractional quarter of Section no. 1 and the north west fraction quarter of the section no. 1 of township no. 5 . . . As the law will be in force against any persons offending." Over decades frequent notices decrying unauthorized cutting suggest laws were ineffective.

Thick timber in southern Illinois and groves and timbered watercourses elsewhere provided mast for hogs. Providing food, bristles, bones, hides, and fat for numerous household purposes, hogs were vitally important. They were also hardy, usually withstanding daily vicissitudes. For example, rattlesnake bites barely fazed them, and after being bitten they devoured the offending reptiles. Hogs were a versatile, durable mainstay in pioneer society, and a dozen or two graced typical farms.

Not fastidious about timber ownership, settlers were often equally nonchalant about where their swine dined, many turning them loose in autumn to munch on acorns and other mast. Some settlers then stuffed them with corn, just before butchering them. Cold weeks following harvesting encouraged butchering by retarding spoilage, sharply reducing flies and other annoyances, and providing some slack time. Neighbors shared tools, males performed specialized tasks, and reciprocal obligations multiplied. Along with log-rolling, house-raising, harvesting, and constructing block houses and schools, butchering fostered community ties.[11]

One or more households announced a "hog kill" on an upcoming cool morning. Early dawn saw large vats of boiling water greet arriving participants and their hogs. The neighborhood's best shot initiated the grisly work, trying to dispatch each hog with just one bullet, ridicule awaiting shooters who either "made the hog squeal" or required two shots. Men then slit each victim's throat, wrestled the carcass into a scalding kettle, swished it around, hauled it out, scraped off the bristles, and hoisted the steaming carcass on a pole wedged in a nearby tree. Workers removed entrails and hacked off hams, shoulders, sides, and other cuts for smoking. Unsmoked parts were sliced up, fried, slathered with lard, and preserved in jars. This meat—"fried down meat"—and smoked meat, if processed properly, remained palatable for months.

In winter and early spring pork surpluses found ready markets, often a nearby village or a river port. Merchants accepted properly preserved pork as payment. Some merchants traded it and even offered it as change. Others accumulated sizeable quantities of pork in special rooms and shipped it, often employing cutters, coopers, packagers, teamsters or draymen, and river vessels. The pork industry was huge and had many linkages.

For years, hog drives to and from markets in Vandalia, Vincennes, Peoria, St. Louis, and later Chicago took several days or even weeks, involved a dozen or more men and boys, and engendered cooperation among households. Some drives ushered hogs to Cincinnati, the Queen City, nicknamed "Porkopolis." Packing houses there slaughtered hogs, made soaps and lotions from fats and oils, and shipped processed pork to distant markets.

But some hogs evaded cold-weather butchering. After enjoying autumnal mast, some fugitives hid in forest recesses, often turning ferocious and eluding detection. Tusks terrorized hapless passersby, prompting settlers to band together and purge neighborhoods of belligerent swine. Hogs posed other problems, too. Although owners marked them and registered the marks with county clerks, disputes over ownership arose. Some were honest differences of opinion, usually settled amicably. But other troubles involved hog rustlers, arrests, prosecutions, fines, and occasionally physical violence. Well into the 1800s counties tried to regulate swine. Laws stipulated the times of the year for mast feeding, the locations, and other facets of feeding. As with most unpopular laws, these were often ignored or loosely enforced.

* * *

Nature's daily and seasonal rhythms circumscribed many activities. Lighting interiors of houses was a formidable challenge. Candles were expensive and provided only fair lighting, and making them took time and skill. Tallow lamps were poor substitutes. Consequently, households capitalized on good weather and did chores outside, often shaded by a porch or tree. Deep shadows and dusk curtailed most work. Spring plowing, planting, cultivating, constructing and repairing, cleaning and burning, and other tasks were arduous and subject to the whims of nature. Fall harvests, especially those involving fragile and perishable fruits and vegetables, fatigued settlers. Harvesting corn and other crops took weeks, but certain fruit and vegetables required extraordinary harvest and preservation efforts. Usually, work slackened only during late summer and winter.

Social gatherings accompanied busy times, helping to ease pressing work. Neighbors voluntarily raised houses for newcomers, tasks often taking one day, with owners finishing the house later. Meals, music, dances, and drinking accompanied school, church, bridge, and road construction and repair, as well as hog kills, weddings, militia musters, trials, political rallies, and other public or quasi-public activities. Typically, cheering, hilarity, and whisky accompanied bombastic speeches during day-long Fourth of July celebrations. Fun punctuated daily toil and tedium.

Neighbors also banded together to harvest, assist injured and infirm neighbors, conduct day-long wolf drives, and track lawbreakers. Such undertakings were voluntary, and loners sometimes excluded themselves. Yet to exclude oneself for no apparent reason broke unspoken, powerful understandings concerning neighborliness, mutual obligations, and other social interactions. People generally freely participated, perhaps more for social benefit than for the sake of the common project.

Social life also buzzed during slack times. Dinners, story telling, wrestling matches, fist fights, races, shooting contests, mu-

Early American cabin in Illinois. Heavy dependence on local timber supplies for construction, utensils, cooking, heating, and other needs encouraged many early settlers to locate in or near woods or groves. From Grace Humphrey, *Illinois: The Story of the Prairie State.* COURTESY OF ILLINOIS HISTORICAL SURVEY, UNIVERSITY OF ILLINOIS LIBRARY, URBANA-CHAMPAIGN.

sic, and dances (where not prohibited by religious sentiments) entertained folk. Pie and cake raffles financed school and church construction. School activities attracting families included spell-downs, skits, picnics, and special ceremonies.

Forests, prairies, bottom lands, and waterways teemed with seasonal edibles, many of which could be stored almost indefinitely. "Bee trees" supplied honey, a food and cash commodity which stored indefinitely and withstood shipment costs to distant markets. Maple syrup and sugar also withstood marketing costs and provided another source of income. Both served as preservatives for fruit. Generally, coffee and tea were expensive and available, if at all, only for special occasions. Wild grapes, roots, berries, crab apples, wild plums, persimmons, and mushrooms graced frontier tables. Nuts, fish, deer, fowl, and other animals provided protein and fats.

Numerous predators made poultry-raising chancy. Similarly, sheep and cattle required great initial investment and sustained care. Poultry and livestock flourished as settlement increased, predators diminished, feed became more assured, and markets developed.

* * *

In southern Illinois and in other wooded regions log cabins were the norm for settlers. These pioneers ate at rough tables, some fashioned from bottom and side boards of discarded wagons. Benches and stools persisted for years. Chairs appeared only over time, and were reserved for esteemed household members and guests. Eating utensils were wooden or, at most, pewter. Few early households had silver or plate. Window glass, metal door hinges and locks, and even nails were expensive and rare. Weapons, axes, and fireplace implements were the most common metallic objects.

Settlers arrived with few clothes and imported even fewer, unlike eighteenth-century French Illinoisans, who enjoyed imported European clothes and fabrics. Hunting and trapping yielded hides, pelts, and skins for moccasins, boots, gloves, and hats. Locally produced flax and cotton appeared in caps, shirts, britches, dresses, and other garments, much production occurring during winter's slack hours. Predators, though, continued to suppress wool production for decades after statehood.

Settlers made most tools, furniture, and other common household items. Some items, such as cooking implements, were either made locally or brought westward in wagons and boats. Settlers purchased from afar a few items, scarce goods that withstood transportation costs. Manufacturers in Pittsburgh, Wheeling, Cincinnati, and Louisville shipped goods downstream to eager consumers. Even so, glass and other fragile products rarely graced early frontier homes. Upstream traffic was limited to few products. To sail, paddle, row, pole, warp, cordel, or bushwhack a vessel upstream took at least three times longer than to go the same distance downstream. It was labor intensive and prohibitively expensive for most products. Low-value goods, bulky items, and perishable products rarely went upstream. Goods sent upstream to Illinois or from Illinois to such places as Pittsburgh were either high value, low bulk, or both. For example, tea cost $15 per pound in Illinois when many pioneer laborers earned only a dollar or two a day. Consequently, settlers purchased tea in small quantities, for special occasions. Sassafras bark served as a substitute. Illinoisans enjoyed tea and other luxuries only after steamboats became common.

Poor transportation also restricted Illinois' exports. Grains, apples, cider, pork, hides, honey, and pelts rode downstream on flatboats, some provisioning regional centers like St. Louis and others reaching New Orleans and beyond. Some goods moved upstream eastward, such as honey, but they usually moved relatively short distances.

* * *

Between 1811 and 1813, events originating outside Illinois jolted everyday frontier life. Despite British withdrawal by 1797 from American posts in the Northwest, British influence persisted. Protecting territory and lucrative fur trade, British and Indians combined to block encroaching Americans, who depleted forests of furs. British agents west of Lake Michigan, near Detroit, and elsewhere plied Indians with impressive gifts, weapons, and advice, facts Americans knew by 1809. Extensive networks of fur trade, friendship, and marriage cemented Anglo-Indian ties. For example, British traders at Prairie du Chien annually cultivated ties with thousands of visiting Indians. Operating with impunity there, the British agent and trader Robert Dickson and nearly one hundred nearby families largely monopolized the region's brisk fur trade, shutting out Americans.[12] The talented Dickson ran far-flung networks among Indians.

It made sound geopolitical sense for Indians and British to embrace each other. Both faced a showdown with Americans, inflamed by Great Lakes tensions, bruised American honor, American economic misery, and navigation problems. Britain's huge, deadly struggle with Napoleonic France, moreover, greatly exacerbated such problems.

Needing little prodding, by 1811 Indians of Illinois, Wisconsin, and Indiana spearheaded onslaughts against the lapping tide of settlement. Their raids scorched southern Illinois. Indians were still powerful and settler encroachment still marginal, but construction of American forts and the recent Louisiana Purchase posed threats. Tecumseh brilliantly mobilized Indian opposition against Americans, gaining influence even among southern tribes. His brother, Lalawethika, a lowly drunkard, underwent regeneration in 1805 and led Indian spiritual renewal. Reborn "Tenskwatawa," the Prophet, he railed against expanding Americans, proposing solutions. Tecumseh and Tenskwatawa's message about imperiled Indian culture resonated among young Indians. Tenskwatawa urged Indians to divest themselves of American utensils, clothing, spouses, alcohol, values, and similar influences. He demonized Americans, claiming they were the invading Serpent who stripped humanity from Indians. Regeneration and return to ancestral ways, he intoned, would gird them for the final battle, upon which the fate of Indian culture east of the Mississippi depended. Tecumseh and his reborn brother knew that only unified Indian power, stiffened by British support, could stem American expansion.

Meeting with other Indian leaders in August 1810, Tecumseh urged unity in explicitly repudiating recent land cessions at Fort Wayne. He wanted intertribal effort to replace piecemeal raids. But in Illinois followers of Main Poc, a powerful Potawatomi whose influence extended to the Kickapoos, Sauks, and Fox, picked off isolated settlers and unwary travelers across Illinois. On June 2, 1811, on Shoal Creek, the Cox household suffered one dead and one severely wounded. Indians murdered a young man and wounded another near modern Alton. The mounting toll through the summer dissuaded some from settling and caused some settlers to flee.[13]

American response was prompt and vigorous. To protect the frontier, Congress in 1811 authorized the organization of ten companies of Rangers, a regiment commanded by Col. William Russell. Samuel Whiteside, William B. Whiteside, James B. Moore, and Jacob Short commanded the four companies charged with protecting Illinois. These Rangers, residents of Illinois, furnished their own equipment and horses. They ranged between settlements, spotting danger and mounting spoiling attacks. They kept Indians off balance, hit hostiles before they struck, and pursued those who had attacked. Raised locally, Rangers realized they protected loved ones from destruction. Also, remuneration of one dollar per day was not inconsiderable.

Augmenting the Rangers, five companies of cavalry watched the lower Wabash. They patrolled stretches between settlements, checked on isolated households, and instilled fear of pursuit. Rangers and cavalry kept most threats at bay, but the regions entrusted to them were so large that some attackers slipped through, bringing death and destruction to isolated places.

Hoping to magnify Chief Pontiac's great feat in mobilizing Indian power, Tecumseh wooed Chickasaws, Choctaws, and Creeks in the South. Like their northern cousins, southern Indians foresaw a gloomy future from unchecked settlement. Tecumseh left Tenskwatawa, the Prophet, in charge while he went south to enroll tribes into a mighty bloc, one that just might halt migration before it was too late. Still, chances for success were slim. Everything hinged on British support and gaining time for the alliance to work.

While Tecumseh visited southern tribes, Governor William Henry Harrison struck, marching in late 1811 from Vincennes with some 700 men. Arriving at Tippecanoe near Prophetstown by November 6, he was met by emissaries from the Prophet and agreed to talks the next day. Harrison kept his men on the alert, a sound decision; at night Indians massed for a pre-dawn attack.

The attack was driven home furiously. Absorbing the initial shock of onslaught, Harrison's forces rallied and repulsed additional attacks. Both sides suffered severely. Harrison's losses totaled over sixty killed and 125 wounded, including Captain Isaac White and Major Joe Daviess, each having a county in Illinois named after him. Nevertheless, Harrison's force prevailed and destroyed Prophetstown before withdrawing. This showdown crippled Tenskwatawa's influence.

All pretense for peace negotiations shattered, people girded for war. British and Indians huddled over war plans. Galvanized by defeat at Tippecanoe, Indians marshaled impressive power, targeting inhabitants across southern Illinois and elsewhere. Authorities in Illinois threw up additional strongpoints, dispatched Rangers, and summoned militia. Lacking public funds, Governor Edwards used personal resources to buy weapons and supplies.

Nature heralded the impending collision. From December 11, 1811, into the following February, three massive earthquakes along the New Madrid fault rocked the middle Mississippi River region, the most destructive tectonic activity in Illinois' recorded history. Houses disintegrated, chimneys toppled, and the Mississippi actually flowed northward. River banks collapsed, landslides occurred, and water spouts and sand plumes erupted from fields. White sand gushed from a fissure beneath the Kaskaskia River below New Athens. Shock waves clanged church bells in faraway Boston and Washington, D.C. Hundreds of additional tremors rumbled for weeks, repeatedly jolting Kentucky and Indiana. Falling objects and agitated waterways claimed lives. Some people simply disappeared, though sparse western population limited casualties.

Amid terrestrial rumblings, human strife escalated. Indian raids struck the middle fork of the Big Muddy, near Galena's lead mines, four miles from Fort Dearborn, and elsewhere. Indians waylaid careless travelers and stormed farmsteads. The approximately twelve thousand whites in Illinois occupied a great U-shaped region extending from the Alton area, down through the American Bottom, southward toward the southern tip of the territory, and then northeast up the Wabash to the Vincennes area. Galena, Chicago, and a few other settlements dotted northern regions. Between the two arms of the U-shaped region, settlers were few, widely scattered, and vulnerable. Recoiling from attacks, some fled by early 1812, distressing territorial officials.

Settlers fell back on themselves for local protection. In southern Illinois they fortified existing sturdy houses and built solid blockhouses and stockaded forts. Strongpoints soon stretched from the Mississippi River, over to the lower Illinois River, down the Kaskaskia, across to the salines near Equality, along portions of the Ohio, and up the Wabash. When troubles brewed, settlers drove livestock into strongpoints, augmenting food supplies for a siege. After war burst in 1812, blockhouses and forts complemented Rangers and cavalry in protecting settlers from marauding Indians.

Some blockhouses were just fortified log houses, but even these were formidable. Most were two stories high, or at least a story and a half, with the second floor sometimes projecting three or four feet over the first and having gunports in the overhang to rake Indians rushing the ground floor. Gunports dotted the log walls on both the first and second stories. Trimmed logs denied grips and footings to attackers who tried to climb to the roof. The door—and usually there was just one—contained strong puncheons, and two or three horizontal bars inside prevented attackers from bashing it in. Single households sometimes occupied such structures, but in perilous times several households huddled in or near these strongpoints.

Stockade forts protected more people for greater periods of time. The walls, forming squares or rectangles, consisted of logs or timbers stuck endwise into the ground, rising twelve to fifteen feet above ground level. Usually two walls had wide, securely barred gates to admit wagons. Riflemen standing on firing platforms along the walls raked attackers with rifle fire through gunports located six feet or more above the ground. Indians reaching the walls could not easily fire through the gunports unless they dragged something to the wall on which to stand. Some gunports, moreover, were closed by small barred doors. Gunports in the sides of two-story blockhouses at each corner allowed defenders to pour enfilading fire on attackers who darted to the wall. In short, attackers rushing the walls had an exciting and uncertain time of it.

Within the walls, defenders kept cattle, horses, oxen, provisions, and other necessities. Some stockades, furthermore, had wells. Defenders often cleared thick grass, small trees, brush, and other combustibles around forts, reducing fire hazards and providing clear fields of fire in which to cut down attackers.

Fort Russell was the largest, strongest, and most impressive fort. Governor Ninian Edwards ordered its construction in 1812, just in time for war, and soon serviceable cannon from Fort de Chartres festooned its walls. Located on the northwest side of present Edwardsville, it became a base for militia and Rangers, serving as the staging point for forays northward. It was also the main military supply depot in Illinois. Headquarters for Governor Edwards, Fort Russell attracted talented and energetic people from throughout the territory.

Forming Ranger and cavalry units, constructing the strong-points, and amassing supplies and provisions proved beneficial. A storm was about to break, one that would involve Tecumseh and Indians, governors of the territories of Indiana and Illinois, and the United States and Britain.

In March of 1812, Governor Edwards fielded Ranger companies, promoted fort construction, and urged tribal chiefs in Illinois to talk. Weakened, Piankashaws and remnants of the Illinois were no problem. On the other hand, Potawatomi, Kickapoo, Winnebago, Ottawa, Sauk, and Fox were numerous, powerful, and arrayed against settlers. Fielding over 3,000 combatants, their total populations probably topped 15,000, exceeding Illinois' white population. In April Edwards met important chiefs at Cahokia. He underscored his peaceful intentions, upbraided tribal leaders for exhorting followers toward destruction, denied covetous intentions of the federal government, demanded surrender of Indians accused of outrages, castigated Britain, touted American strength, and warned he would shield settlers and punish Indian troublemakers. Edwards was impressive, but his words had limited impact.

Time ran out. Agitated Indians in Illinois and nearby regions would not back down. Tecumseh's message and British coaching had worked. Indians realized the status quo was untenable. Continued settlement in Illinois spelled disaster for Indian life. There was no turning back.

Just before and after war erupted Illinois took important political steps. Following Edwards's lead, a referendum in April produced overwhelming approval for second stage territorial government, which Illinois attained less than a month before war was declared. Although this step probably influenced the war only slightly, it boosted public confidence.

Governor Edwards now consulted Congress on a sticky mat-

ter. The Ordinance of 1787 restricted voting rights to freeholders, people who owned land in fee simple. The tedious process of
validating land titles kept most potential voters from becoming
freeholders. Technically, they owned no land. In fact, only about
220 settlers met suffrage property requirements. Furthermore,
the ordinance specified an unelected upper house, the Council,
chosen by the President from a list of names submitted by the
territorial House of Representatives. Finally, the delegate to Congress was not elected popularly.

A Congressional Act of May 20, 1812, swept aside these shortcomings by sidestepping tangled land claims, conferring suffrage
on adult males who paid even token county or territorial tax and
had resided in Illinois for a year. Furthermore, now voters selected territorial representatives, the territorial council, and the
delegate to Congress. Even squatters could vote. This act made
the Territory of Illinois the country's most democratic territory,
reinforcing democratic institutions and republican spirit.

Continued settlement and government inadequacies during
Indian troubles spurred county creation in mid-September, and
Gallatin, Johnson, and Madison counties joined St. Clair and
Randolph. Elections that October chose five council members
(one from each county), seven representatives, and the delegate
to Congress. St. Clair and Gallatin counties each elected two rep-
resentatives, the other three counties one each. The delegate to
Congress was elected at large.

The election illustrated three salient facts. Dispirited French
residents were by and large inactive. Newcomers, especially from
southern and border states, did well. Quarreling factions fared
poorly, suggesting that sleazy politics repelled voters.

Voters elected to the council the respected Pierre Menard, a
native of Quebec. Gracing the Council with dedication and pleasing manners, he became that body's president. Two sons of Maryland, Samuel Judy and William Biggs, represented Madison
County and St. Clair County, respectively. Dr. George Fisher, a
physician from Virginia, represented Randolph County, wielding
considerable influence. Natives of slave states dominated the
House of Representatives.

Shadrach Bond, Jr., was elected delegate to Congress. Born in
1773 in Maryland, in 1794 he sought success on the frontier,

acquiring substantial lands near New Design. A good judge of people, congenial, honest, and generous, he was possibly the territory's most popular politician. The congressional suffrage act of May 20 and resulting elections cultivated democracy. They were tempered, though, by the absence of preemption law. Accordingly, Shadrach Bond, Jr., made the passage of a preemption act his cardinal responsibility.

Legislators met in November at Kaskaskia, the territorial capital. Ignoring wretched accommodations, lawmakers performed admirably, responding to searing attacks against Illinoisans following war's outbreak in June. But they did much more. Enhancing order and continuity, ingredients for security, in December legislators reenacted germane Indiana territorial laws in force on March 1, 1809, and all laws passed by the first stage territorial government.

Lawmakers quickly addressed taxation, placing land into three categories: first rate (Mississippi and Ohio river bottom land), second rate, and third rate. Tax on first rate land was one dollar per hundred acres, on second rate seventy-five cents, and on third rate thirty-seven and a half cents. Legislators, furthermore, authorized counties to tax personal property, including productive slaves and indentured servants. Finally, they taxed houses and lots in towns, rural mansions and other real property, and even billiard tables, horses and cattle, and gave towns taxing authority. They enacted a poll tax, required licenses for ferries, mills, retail stores, and similar enterprises. They minutely regulated mills, ferries, medicine, surgery, and many other activities. Laws addressed public safety, transportation, and other matters impinging upon daily life. Some laws, significantly, regulated local medical societies, the playing of billiards, and other matters not normally associated with frontier conditions. These acts largely replicated the regulated, ordered, and channeled economic and social order of colonial America and the young Republic. Unrestrained laissez faire or entrepreneurship had not yet blossomed in Illinois.

Authorities grappled with inadequate courts. Federally appointed judges often shirked duties by avoiding courts, despite a substantial salary of $100 per month. Although travel was difficult, especially with fighting, judges absenting themselves from courts irked people, kindling efforts to compel them to be responsible. Now, territorial legislators offered remedies, some of them controversial. Federal judges, for example, fumed that territorial legislators lacked jurisdiction over them, that territorial measures infringed on federal prerogative. To resolve matters, lawmakers in 1814 created circuit courts. Federal judges howled, speeding the controversy to Congress. Congress disappointed the judges by approving the courts, backing legislative authority over federally appointed officials. Each judge was assigned two counties, required to travel the circuit twice a year and actually hold court. The judges, moreover, were to hold a Court of Appeals twice a year in Kaskaskia. This fight had political overtones, pitting Governor Edwards and his allies against Judge Jesse B. Thomas and Judge William Sprigg and their followers. The feud festered for years. Some pressing problems sprang largely from American weakness north of the Ohio, and territorial legislators addressed them. But only the results of the War of 1812 solved some.

Questionable land titles, preemption, unsurveyed lands, and sluggish land office operations required redress. Congress forbade land sales until uncertain claims were resolved. Kaskaskia's land commissioners, wishing to be completely aboveboard, worked diligently and methodically, uncovering deceit, perjury, and forgery in previous land transactions. Speculation in dubious land titles flourished, lying became an art, and suborning witnesses a profession. Via painstaking work, commissioners rejected hundreds of claims. Starting in 1810, surveying teams crisscrossed southern Illinois, dragging chains, driving stakes, noting potential mill sites and salt licks, and shooting lines at one-mile intervals. Surveyors' maps featured neat township and section lines, hinting that the logjam would break and sales would begin. Still, few surveyed and secure properties reached market. Secure land titles were still not available when Illinois attained second stage territorial government in 1812. In 1812 at Shawneetown another land office opened, no more ready to sell land than Kaskaskia's office. Unable to get secure titles, frustrated settlers squatted, igniting disputes and further testing territorial and federal government. Squatters clamored for a preemption law to enable them to bid first on lands they had improved.[14] Such law, they insisted, was both fair and necessary.

Shadrach Bond, Jr., delegate to Congress, sympathized. He helped craft a monumentally important preemption law, passed in February 1813. For over twenty-five years, settlers had risked losing their improvements because they could not purchase lands they occupied; the preemption law changed this, and more.[15] It allowed each squatter to preempt a quarter section—160 acres—of land they occupied. Upon paying one-twentieth of the purchase price, a squatter initiated the purchase and entered the land. Squatter anxiety dissipated, triggering a land rush. Even during turbulent times from 1810 to 1815, when casualties and flight thinned ranks, Illinois gained some 3,000 people. Some gain occurred prior to the war, and some reflected high birth rates, but even during 1812–1814 settlers slipped into Illinois. Those deterred by war formed a pent-up backlog, waiting for tranquil times before pushing west. Their wait was short.

* * *

Illinois had made impressive strides between 1800 and 1812: it became part of the Indiana territory; the Louisiana Purchase changed its relative location and solved navigation problems; new federal land offices anticipated surging sales and preemption law; treaties transferred Indian land to the federal government; in 1809 the Illinois Territory was formed; suffrage was expanded; Illinois' non-Indian population more than quadrupled. Federal agencies played crucial roles in these strides.

Clearly, numerical strength, time, and proximity strengthened America's hand and bolstered Illinois. Nevertheless, many thousands of determined Indian inhabitants, backed by Britain, resented and feared American intrusion and settlement. Before surveyors finished their work, before veterans earned bounty lands, and before settlers bought lands, a showdown with Anglo-Indian power occurred. The War of 1812 was fought and not lost.

A catharsis for many, the war surprised no one. It unfolded

against a backdrop of Napoleonic upheavals in Europe and American desire for expansion. Canada appeared ripe for the taking. British and Indian leaders intrigued to construct a permanent barrier to American expansion, but many Indians were now willing to go it alone if necessary, so great was their desperation. American War Hawks believed a showdown would thrash recalcitrant Indians and gain new lands, humiliating Britain in the process. Outsiders, inhabitants in the region, and geographic conditions slated the lower Great Lakes as a theater of war.

For Britain the war was annoying, threatening, and yet promising. France was Britain's mortal enemy, not America. Nevertheless, the war posed at least four threats: loss of Canada; destruction of the Great Lakes Indian bloc; loss of merchant shipping; and tipping the world-wide balance of power against Britain. On the other hand, war might accomplish two things: strengthen the Great Lakes Indian barrier, and severely cripple or even dismember the aggressive American Republic. In sum, the war's global nature and its contending players around the Great Lakes showered on all parties grim dangers and splendid opportunities. Finally, complexities and uncertainties abounded, producing unexpected turning points and contingencies.

Illinoisans faced uncertain prospects in early 1812. Harrison's preemptive strike at Tippecanoe in late 1811 and desultory conflict that winter both degraded Indian power and stirred them to action. The American declaration of war in June confirmed this slide toward war.

With formal hostilities, American fortunes north of the Ohio soared. Governor Edwards's tireless war preparations paid dividends. Ranger units prowled regions between settlements, and fortified places sheltered Illinois' residents. Spirits ran high. Americans confidently eyed Canada.

After lunging briefly into Canada, however, American General William Henry Hull withdrew to Detroit, allowed himself to be penned up there, and on August 15 he surrendered. Hull, however, had dispatched a Potawatomi runner, Winnemeg, to Captain Nathan Heald, the commander of Fort Dearborn at Chicago, with orders to abandon the fort "if practicable" and withdraw to Fort Wayne. With evacuation, the orders stipulated, federal supplies at the fort were to be distributed to Indians. The orders, received on August 8, unleashed unintended consequences.

Captain Heald commanded three officers, including a surgeon, fifty-four regulars, and twelve militia. Civilians clustered around Fort Dearborn, awaiting evacuation. Heald's officers feared seething Indians would interpret evacuation as weakness, triggering trouble. Winnemeg, the Potawatomi runner, knew local Indians and concurred. Unable to convince Captain Heald to hole up in the fort and withstand siege, Winnemeg urged immediate evacuation of Fort Dearborn. John Kenzie, for eight years a prominent local trader, also counseled speedy departure. Heald dithered.

On August 12 he announced the fort's evacuation, and pleased local Indians by suggesting that they provide an escort to Fort Wayne. The next day blankets, cloth, paint, and other goods were distributed. But this failed to assuage Indians, and some became incensed when soldiers destroyed surplus arms and ammunition and casks of whiskey. The following day, August 14, Captain William Wells rode in from Fort Wayne, leading thirty Miami Indians, escorts for the return journey. Captain Wells's odyssey included youthful Indian captivity, marriage to an Indian, leading Indians against General St. Clair in 1791, return to white society, and then combat against Indians. His current assignment: lead the withdrawal to Fort Wayne.

The next day, August 15, was hot and windless. Troops and households formed up, Captain Wells and his Miami contingent in the vanguard. Sensing death, Wells blackened his face in the style of Indians who faced certain death.[16] The column consisted of militia, regulars, and wagons containing twenty-seven women and children and some sick men. Some additional Miami formed the rearguard. As the column moved southward, perhaps five hundred mounted Potawatomi, Winnebago, Kickapoo, Chippewa, and others paralleled it, hovering close to the right.

With Lake Michigan to the left and low sand dunes to the right, the procession traveled about a mile and a half. Captain Wells, seeing Indians wheeling to attack, shouted warnings. Rifle fire sputtered from the low dunes, soldiers charged, sustained losses by flanking fire, and fell back. With just one exception, the escorting Miami Indians vanished.

Attackers entered the wagons, their tomahawks hacking children. Twelve died in one wagon. Captain Wells fought well before being cut down. Leading the regulars, Captain Heald was wounded and captured. Soon nearly half the regulars died, along with all twelve militia. Indians spared Heald's wife and another officer's wife, two other women died, and five were captured. Surviving children disappeared into captivity. Indians confined John Kenzie and his wife to their home near the fort. Deaths among Americans at this time totaled at least fifty-three. Indians later killed some American wounded, and that night they tortured to death five captured regulars. By the end of the slaughter, at least seventy-five people had died, including perhaps fifteen attackers, the largest toll via combat in Illinois in historic times. Celebrating Indians sacked and burned Fort Dearborn, parceled out surviving prisoners, and went home.

* * *

The fall of Mackinac, Detroit, and Fort Dearborn crippled American operations in the Great Lakes. Tenuous links between Illinois and the East snapped at key points. A powerful Indian barrier was in place, and Illinoisans recoiled southward. Along the broad U-shaped region of settlement in southern Illinois, authorities and private citizens built blockhouses and forts, havens for fleeing settlers. Most strongpoints were near timber supplies and near most exposed people. Although war sent inhabitants fleeing across the Ohio, some intrepid souls entered Illinois, nestling near protective strongpoints. Whenever danger arose, they grabbed prized possessions and scurried to the fortified structures, some doing so several times. Authorities offered imperfect protection, and as Illinois became a war zone ordinary settlers were thrown back on themselves again and again.

Following Fort Dearborn's sacking and other setbacks, Governor Edwards used limited resources imaginatively, launching two expeditions to forestall anticipated follow-up attacks against Illinoisans. He learned that Potawatomi, Kickapoo, and some Miami were assembling near Peoria. Many Potawatomi, who harassed isolated settlements, were only lukewarm allies of Britain. Some leaders, in fact, counseled neutrality, and a few advocated friendship with Americans. Nevertheless, such distinctions were largely lost on Americans, who feared Indians at Peoria and wanted to oust them. Realizing this, Governor Edwards sought political advantage by pummeling Indians.

Fort Russell became the staging point for attacks. On October 18, Governor Edwards led a foray from Fort Russell, commanding nearly 400 men, but some promised mounted Kentuckian riflemen never showed up. Edwards's unit skirted the west side of Cahokia Creek, reached Macoupin Creek, crossing near today's Carlinville, then sliced in a northeasterly direction, crossing the Sangamon River just downstream from the juncture of the north and south forks, to the east of modern Springfield. It filed east of Elkhart Grove, crossed Salt Creek near present-day Lincoln, and came upon an abandoned Kickapoo village, which featured wigwams with designs showing whites being scalped. Not amused, soldiers reduced the village to ashes, then pushed toward Peoria.

The primary objective was a village at the upper end of Lake Peoria on the east side of the river. Approaching the village, scouts spotted an Indian and his wife. The couple may have tried to surrender, but he was shot and his wife taken prisoner. The soldiers then rushed the village, found it empty, and plundered and burned it. They clashed with lurking Indians, suffering a few wounded and killing several Indians. Realizing the Kentuckian riflemen would not arrive, Edwards beat a retreat. As John Reynolds, a scout on the expedition and later governor of Illinois, wrote years later, the little army "returned home with all convenient speed."

The thirteen-day hike accomplished little of immediate value. Even so, such forays served notice that Illinoisans would venture far from the security of fortified places in search of a fight. Although the expedition failed to draw Indians into pitched battle, which was just as well, Americans had marched into Indian country, inflicted damage, destroyed or seized provisions, rattled Indians, and returned home virtually unscathed. (Such spoiling raids in the Northwest kept Indians off balance and had a cumulative effect: Indians suffered unsustainable losses.) Speeches greeted the returning men, lauding the largely uneventful foray. Following recent disasters, puffery and self-congratulations were understandable. American morale soared.

Another thrust northward in 1812 yielded little. Captain Thomas E. Craig led a force upriver from Shawneetown to Peoria, appropriated private possessions from a largely vacated village, took fire from an unknown person, and then sacked and burned the village. They dragooned seventy-seven local French, French-Indians, Indians, and Americans of all ages and shunted this assortment of humanity down the Illinois River, abandoning them on a dreary November day south of modern Alton. Rankled and embarrassed, Governor Edwards arranged compensation for the marooned folk. Craig received opprobrium. Although the raid accomplished little of direct value, Americans again had mounted an offensive, traversed hostile territory, and returned safely. The real test, though, came when Americans projected power north of Peoria.

Piecemeal measures and poor coordination undermined American campaigns throughout the Northwest. Territorial governors in Indiana, Illinois, and Missouri oversaw war efforts within their jurisdictions, giving little thought to adjacent regions.[17] A major military reorganization on May 1, 1813, addressed this defect, dividing the United States into nine military districts. Ohio and Kentucky and the territories of Michigan, Indiana, Illinois, and Missouri constituted the eighth military district, Major General William Henry Harrison commanding. Illinois and Missouri formed a subdistrict, St. Louis its headquarters. A former governor of the Territory of Missouri, Brigadier General Benjamin Howard, commanded. Redoubtable Governor Edwards, having prepared Illinois for war and launched expeditions northward, was passed over. Miffed, he visited kin in Kentucky, returning in early winter. Nathaniel Pope, territorial secretary, served as acting governor.

In June General William Clark led two hundred men northward, taking Prairie du Chien. (Thirteen months later British-led forces snapped up Prairie du Chien's small garrison.) Hoping to boot British-Indian influence from the upper Mississippi, General Benjamin Howard in August dispatched forces to Peoria, this time to stay. They built Fort Clark there, garrisoning it until war's end. These accomplishments heralded more strenuous projections of power.

* * *

Outside military leaders heavily influenced Illinois. Specifically, in September of 1813, Oliver Hazard Perry captured the British fleet on Lake Erie, prying British forces from the Detroit region. General Harrison's forces harried withdrawing British-Indian forces, smashing them in Canada along the Thames River on October 5, the legendary Tecumseh dying in the fighting. Jolted, mauled British forces now tried to save Canada, not seize American territory.

This sharp reversal should have assisted Illinois, but it did not. Ironically, defeats on Lake Erie and the Thames sent many dispirited Indians westward to the upper Mississippi River region, where they pressured Illinois and surrounding regions.

Responding to Illinois' peril, in early summer of 1814, Lieutenant John Campbell and about 110 Regulars left St. Louis in keelboats to reinforce Prairie du Chien's garrison. Violent weather and Sauk and Fox under Black Hawk's command stopped them at Rock Island, inflicting heavy casualties. In late August, another American force moved upstream against Rock Island. Captain Zachary Taylor, whose Mexican War exploits later catapulted him into the White House, led forty Regulars. Captain Nelson Rector and Captain Samuel Whiteside led nearly 300 Rangers and volunteers. Numerically superior British and Indians, backed by artillery, pounded them. Following heavy fighting and mixed results, the battered force limped downriver, halting opposite the mouth of the Des Moines River to construct Fort Edwards, near modern Warsaw. Other losses compounded these twin defeats. In July 1814 Prairie du Chien's garrison surrendered. Worse, dwindling provisions and enemy harassment forced Fort Edwards's garrison to retire downriver.

Fortunately, Illinois had other defenses. Between Alton and Kaskaskia alone, at least twenty-two household strongpoints sprang up, products of local efforts, and forts were repaired. New

Ranger companies prowled stretches between forts, intercepting raiders. These fortified places and scouring Rangers kept American casualties down. Authorities encouraged vulnerable, isolated households to evacuate to secure places.

To Indians, households settling in their region were every bit as threatening to their way of life as Regulars, Rangers, and other soldiers. Every household sinking taproots into frontier soil undermined traditional Indian life. Despite good intentions and many kind acts between Indians and settlers, irreconcilable cultural chasms between them meant that dense settlement doomed Indian culture.

Scattered raids still rippled across Illinois, pin-pricks terrorizing combatants and non-combatants alike. Near the mouth of Cash River in early 1813, Indians slew two families. Pursuers chased the killers clear to Kentucky, but lost the trail there. Then Indians attacked two travelers near modern Carlyle, killing one, the other barely escaping. Four miles southeast of today's Covington, Indians killed and mutilated four members of the Lively family, including two women and a young boy. Along Wood River, east of present-day Alton, on July 10, 1814, a Mrs. Reagan and six children lost their lives. Henry Cox and a son died in mid-1814, near Hill's Fort along Shoal's Creek. In autumn of 1814 Jesse Bayles and his wife, searching for stray hogs near modern Aveston, encountered Indians, who killed Mrs. Bayles. Although relatively few civilians died, Illinoisans were few and every loss stung. Such desultory, low-grade, nasty raids enraged settlers, and pursuers sometimes administered blistering retribution.

By late 1814 raids slackened. A calm descended on the territory and region, though neither side had gained a decisive advantage. Americans had failed to oust the British from the upper Mississippi and crush Indian power. Securing Peoria and garrisoning adjacent Fort Clark there were the major territorial gains in Illinois. Late 1814 found settlement largely confined to the same broad U-shaped region stretching from near Alton to modern Franklin County and then northeast to the Wabash north of Vincennes. On the other hand, British designs had failed. No Indian barrier existed, Indian offensive power was broken, and British influence had withdrawn to Canada. Unlike American losses, moreover, these losses were irreparable. Illinoisans suffered nothing like the massacres, sieges, raids, and pitched battles that seared New York, Pennsylvania, Ohio, Michigan, Kentucky, and even Indiana. The worst calamity, the Fort Dearborn massacre, killed perhaps sixty-five Americans, only some of whom were Illinoisans. Furthermore, pent-up Illinoisans and other Americans itched to flood westward once peace arrived; no countervailing wave of Indians waited to surge eastward. Time and the growing demographic imbalance favored settlers. This was reflected after 1815 in fewer migratory groups forming for protection. Increasingly, groups fostered social mission, economic gain, or antidotes to loneliness. This change helped make the war a watershed.

Enormous fatigue from Napoleonic wars, coupled with British reversals on Lake Champlain and at Baltimore, prodded British peace negotiators in Ghent. But one last ominous threat to the West reared up: Britain's plan to capture New Orleans and seize the former Louisiana Territory. Britain's huge invasion force included civil administrators to govern the huge region, and heavy reinforcements were dispatched from Europe *after* peace was signed at Ghent on Christmas eve. Clearly, Britain hoped via one massive campaign to recoup its losses in the Northwest by stopping Americans at the Mississippi and blocking American expansion.

Negotiators at Ghent ignored the war's true causes—Napoleon's defeat dispelled them—and addressed the Great Lakes region and related border problems. Holding western Great Lakes territory and the upper Mississippi, Britain negotiated from strength. Some British fur trading interests and others advocated incorporating recently captured territory into Canada. Others, less ambitious, favored constructing the Indian barrier. Furthermore, some wanted to allow only British naval forces on the Great Lakes, negating America's victory on Lake Erie and consigning America to inferiority.

American negotiators fumed against British naval proposals and the Indian barrier. In the end, Article Nine of the Treaty of Ghent simply called upon *both* sides "to restore to such Tribes or Nations respectively, all of the possessions, rights, and privileges which they may have enjoyed or been entitled to in 1811, previous to" the war, which let Americans off the hook. Although Britain had serious designs on Louisiana, its negotiators abandoned long-standing Indian allies and ideas of an Indian barrier. To be sure, America pledged to abide by conditions existing in 1811, but this was a convention, a cover allowing Britain to save face. American gains via negotiations outstripped battlefield achievements, as was true in 1783. Indians north of the Ohio now stood alone, facing impending migratory surges. To cushion reality, Britain gave Indians refuge in Canada, pensioning them off. British military disaster at New Orleans on January 8, 1815 sealed the terms of the Treaty of Ghent. This dashed Indian hopes.

Indians knew others controlled their fate. Tecumseh lay dead, his confederacy in ruin, Indian settlements anemic or abandoned, economic and social structures broken, and morale devastated. Indians faced pent-up settlers alone, many of whom nursed grisly memories of Indian raids and whose attitudes toward Indians had hardened. Indians never again seriously vied with Americans for control of Illinois, despite alarm generated eighteen years later by Black Hawk's incursion into Illinois. Ironically although the Illinois Indians had not allied themselves with the British, the few who were still around by 1814 were endangered by settlers, who did not discriminate between pro-British Indians and others. The War of 1812 essentially settled Illinois' Indian question.

PART III

STATEHOOD AND TROUBLES

8.

SHAPING A STATE

Illinois changed greatly between 1815 and 1832. As it rushed toward statehood, waning Indian offensive power and dismantled British influence heartened settlers and prospective settlers. Coincidentally, steamboats plied western waters, shriveling upstream shipping costs. Work commenced on the Erie Canal in 1817, launching canal projects elsewhere which eventually bound Illinois to northeast markets and suppliers and loosened ties with the lower Mississippi.

Postwar population growth was impressive. Territorial Illinois boasted 12,282 white inhabitants in 1810, but in 1820 the new state contained 55,211 white residents, an increase of about 450 percent. Since the war had slowed migration into Illinois and since some Illinoisans had fled the fighting, nearly all the increase occurred after 1814.

Soldiers campaigning in Illinois had marveled at the state's beauty and potential. Veterans who had marched to Peoria, for example, sang the region's praises "far and near, and caused a large inflow of population from the south, as rapidly as the Indian title could be extinguished."[1] John Reynolds, later governor of Illinois, traversed Illinois during his service in the war. He recalled, "The soldiers from the adjacent States as well as those from Illinois itself, saw the country and never rested in peace until they located themselves and families in it."

Congress in 1817 helped veterans by designating the triangle of land between the Mississippi and Illinois rivers as bounty land, each veteran receiving title to 160 acres. This region, the Military Tract, contained 3,500,000 acres. Veterans also received back pay, which assisted settlement. Moreover, the preemption law of 1813 encouraged general settlement, and Edwardsville's new land office facilitated distribution by 1816. Treaties with Indians added vast tracts to the public domain.

In mid-1815, downstream from Alton, Governor Ninian Edwards and Governor William Clark of Missouri met representatives of most Northwest tribes. Having little choice, Indians signed a peace treaty. It and subsequent treaties over the next eighteen years reflected stark geopolitical realities of weakened, abandoned Indians facing restless, determined Americans. In August of 1816, in St. Louis, discouraged Potawatomi, Ottawa, and Chippewa signed away land south of a line connecting the southern tip of Lake Michigan to the Mississippi River. They also ceded lands along the Illinois River and the Des Plaines for a canal route. Federal authorities rebuilt Fort Dearborn in 1816 and erected Fort Armstrong at Rock Island, signaling federal commitment to exercise sovereignty over the region and further eroding vestiges of Indian life. To wean Indians away from Britain, federal authorities built trading factories at Chicago, Fort Edwards, and Prairie du Chien. Authorities, moreover, eager to preclude resurrected British-Indian power, excluded from American territory British traders with close Indian ties. Britain ceased its meddling. These federal actions pleased Illinoisans and prospective settlers elsewhere.

Federal law in 1817 reduced the minimum purchase of public domain land by half, to eighty acres. Although the price of two dollars per acre discouraged eastern laborers who toiled fourteen hours a day for eighty cents, terms were reasonable: a 5-percent down payment held land for forty days, when another 20 percent was due. The remaining 75 percent was due, interest-free, in three equal annual payments. Land reverted to the federal government only after five years' delinquency. By 1817 prospective

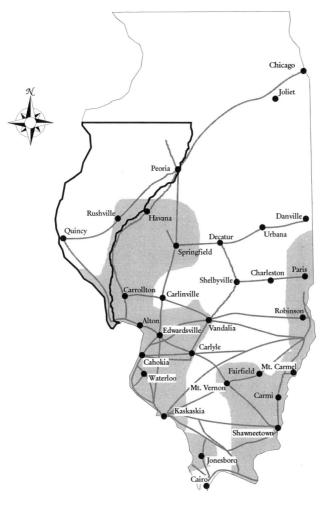

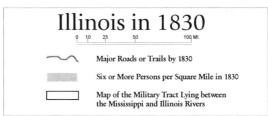

Illinois in 1830

0 10 25   50   100 MI.

〜〜〜   Major Roads or Trails by 1830

▒▒▒   Six or More Persons per Square Mile in 1830

▭   Map of the Military Tract Lying between
     the Mississippi and Illinois Rivers

settlers waited anxiously as surveyors traipsed Illinois and packaged land for orderly sale.

International treaties promoting tranquility encouraged westward movement. In 1817 and 1818 Britain and America sharply reduced naval forces on the Great Lakes and Lake Champlain and established an unfortified Canadian-U.S. border, remarkable achievements for countries that for decades had clawed at each other.

Although peace with Britain and Indians and such federal activities as reconstructing Fort Dearborn generated confidence, northern Illinois initially saw little settlement. Chicago, for example, remained a hamlet into the 1830s. By 1818 only small parties from Missouri and elsewhere worked Galena's lead deposits. Next year, Richard M. Johnson, who in 1813 had probably killed Tecumseh, brought about 100 free men to Galena's lead mines, where about 100 slaves already labored. This premature effort failed, however, as did others involving northern Illinois. Even so, with Indians weakened, treaties with Britain holding, Chicago again on the map, and the western Great Lakes under federal control, northern Illinois' rolling lands soon attracted settlers.

Freakish dry, very cool weather in 1816 produced a "year without summer" nationally and boosted settlement in Illinois. Crop failures afflicted the East, breeding speculation, hoarding, and economic dislocation. Seeking relief, people prayed, restricted grain sales to distilleries, and inflicted that fall "the greatest defeat on incumbent congressmen in American political history." One source noted, "New England in particular lost many of its farmers to the West."[2] Between 1815 and late 1818 Illinois' population increased by about 160 percent.

In addition, the war and then abrupt peace produced economic dislocations. High taxes burdened New Englanders, farm productivity tumbled, farmland became inexplicably expensive, and social and economic constraints frustrated many, especially young people. Although thousands streamed to northeastern urban centers, some reached Illinois, especially central Illinois. Analogous woes saddled the South. There was dizzying land speculation in Kentucky, for example, as moneyed interests snapped up smaller land holdings, and litigation over land titles expelled people from western Kentucky.

Dislocations from postwar cotton booms spawned additional exoduses. National cotton production rose from 75 million pounds in 1808 and again in 1812 to over 124 million pounds in 1816, topping 210 million pounds in 1822. Upland cotton, worth $.15 per pound in New York in 1814, brought $.34 in 1818. Cotton plantations encroached onto new lands of southern upland regions, worrying southern yeomen, some of whom resisted raising cotton for distant markets.[3] Some questioned slavery's morality, others feared grasping new elites and stratified society, and still others dreaded living near numerous blacks, slave or free. Slave labor, some insisted, stigmatized and devalued yeoman labor and culture. Many sold out and moved, taking distaste for slavery with them and resolving to settle where slaves would not follow. Abraham Lincoln's father was one of these. He left Kentucky for Indiana. Although few championed racial equality, many vehemently opposed slavery. Their resolve helped smash attempts to introduce full-scale slavery to Illinois.

In 1824 the Rev. Peter Cartwright, a Methodist minister, fled the upland South for Illinois. He and his family had eked out a living from 150 acres in Kentucky, but high land prices precluded his six offspring from owning land. Disliking class distinctions and loathing slavery, he feared his daughters would marry into slave-owning families. Finally, he knew frontier regions needed preachers. Clearly, economic, social, and moral impulses persuaded Cartwright to lead his family to Illinois.

Illinoisans varied in origins, but most had southern roots. In 1818 perhaps 15,000 Indians lived in Illinois, nearly all in the northern half, and at least 35,000 non-Indians. Some 38 percent were born in southeastern states, over one-third of whom hailed from Virginia and slightly fewer from North Carolina. Western states contributed 37 percent, over half from Kentucky and sizeable numbers from Tennessee. (Not surprisingly, Kentucky was Illinois' largest single donor state.) Furthermore, many Illinoisans born in Indiana and Ohio had Virginian and Kentuckian roots. The Middle Atlantic states contributed just 13 percent, half from Pennsylvania. New England's contribution was slim, only 3 percent, two-thirds from Massachusetts and Vermont. Europe, adjusting to peace, donated 9 percent, about four-fifths from the British Isles. Only one in every 237 Illinoisans was born in Illinois, and less than half the state's population had resided in Illinois three years. The most salient fact: 71 percent of Illinois' population hailed from below the Mason-Dixon Line and the Ohio River.[4]

Southern influence dominated the state in its formative years. Of Illinois' first seven governors, for example, six hailed from slave states, three from Kentucky alone. Although Governor Edward Coles and others opposed slavery, they imbibed many southern values. Moreover, all governors to 1857 were Democratic. Even such rising Whigs as Abraham Lincoln had southern roots, mentors, partners, or spouses. Finally, northern settlers who became prominent by the 1820s, like Elias Kent Kane, adopted southern stances on key issues. Absorbing southern culture by living in Tennessee before arriving in Illinois in 1814, Yale-educated Kane defended slavery and other southern interests.

Talented, energetic, and well-connected Southerners and others spearheaded statehood. A Kentuckian, Daniel Pope Cook, settled in 1815 to practice law. Governor Edwards appointed him the territory's first auditor of public accounts. Cook quickly bought part interest in the *Illinois Herald*, Illinois' first newspaper, founded at Kaskaskia in 1814. The *Herald* soon became the *Western Intelligencer* and then the *Illinois Intelligencer*. By November of 1817, this political organ began advocating statehood. Statehood, it trumpeted, would accomplish much: attract settlers, foster development and raise land prices, strengthen republicanism by ending absolute gubernatorial veto over territorial legislation, sweep away corrosive legislation, improve the judiciary by placing it within the State Constitution and state laws, give Illinois congressional representation, free Congress to address pressing national problems, and meet the public's needs and desires. Cook contended that the territory, currently groaning under semi-monarchial administration, had 40,000 inhabitants and was politically mature enough for statehood.[5]

Three problems, however, clouded the statehood question: uncertainties about the northern border; sparse population, hardly half of the 60,000 threshold cited by the Northwest Ordinance; slavery and quasi-slavery, anomalies both protected by the Northwest Ordinance and violating its spirit. Although southern settlers divided over slavery, they basically reinforced existing slavery and quasi-slavery, even if they opposed extending them.

Initially surprised by pro-statehood activity, Nathaniel Pope, delegate to Congress and former secretary of the Illinois Territory, borrowed Daniel Pope Cook's arguments in striving for statehood. Politically astute, focused, and tireless, Pope served on a five-man congressional select committee formed to weigh statehood for Illinois and propose suitable legislation. The committee met on January 18, 1818, to formulate plans for statehood, plans patterned after acts admitting Indiana and, to a lesser extent, Mississippi. After recalling that Ohio had achieved statehood with fewer than 40,000 residents, he convinced Congress to lay aside the requirement of 60,000 inhabitants and accept just 40,000. Agreeing, the House stipulated a census to count the inhabitants.

But the devil is in the details, and Pope's lobbying allowed Illinois authorities—not federal authorities—to count heads, a crucial fact. Governor Edwards appointed census commissioners. Additionally, the territorial legislature moved the census date from June 1 to December 1, allowing late arrivals to be counted. Even so, this boost failed to conjure up 40,000 inhabitants. The situation called for creative counting, and census takers rose to the challenge: they counted travelers passing through Illinois, sometimes several times; they liberally estimated remote communities; valiantly ignoring the amorphous northern border, they counted people at Prairie du Chien, adding about 600 to the tally; some Illinoisans, displaying unbridled civic enthusiasm, allowed themselves to be counted more than once. Creative counting succeeded, tallying 40,258, a tad over the lowered threshold. With a wink and a nod, Illinois slipped into the Union with perhaps 36,000 bona fide residents, making it the smallest state ever admitted.[6]

Machinations involving the northern border matched finagled head counting. The Northwest Ordinance stated the border should run westward from Lake Michigan's southern tip to the Mississippi. But Nathaniel Pope wanted it thrust north to put Chicago in Illinois, not Wisconsin, and he advocated this without the support or suggestion of the territorial legislature. Envisioning a canal connecting Lake Michigan to the Illinois River, he wanted it entirely within Illinois. As Pope explained to congressmen, shoving the border northward would "afford additional security to the perpetuity of the Union, inasmuch as the State would thereby be connected with the States of Indiana, Ohio, Pennsylvania, and New York, through the Lakes."[7] Furthermore, Galena's lead deposits, although currently unprofitable, intrigued those anticipating thriving mines, collateral activities, and surging land values. Finally, Pope knew northern Illinois would attract people.

Attaining statehood in 1816, Indiana illuminated Illinois' path. Indiana's enabling legislation ignored the Northwest Ordinance's stipulation that its northern border run eastward from Lake Michigan's southern tip. Legislation hoisted the border ten miles northward, giving Indiana forty-five miles of lake frontage. Originally, Pope simply wanted to follow Indiana's example and raise the border ten miles. As statehood approached, though, he raised his sights. He urged Congress to fix the border at 42 degrees 30 minutes north latitude, forty-one miles above the lake's southern extremity, not ten. Congress readily agreed.

Thanks to Pope's land grab, Illinois gained about 8,000 square miles, one-seventh its present area, and sixty-three valuable miles of lake frontage. About the size of Massachusetts, this region became highly populous, prosperous, and politically important. It included Galena's lead mines, which boomed for decades, and valuable dairy lands along the Rock River. Chicago, Rockford, Dekalb, Aurora, the Illinois & Michigan Canal, ten counties, and portions of four others lie within the region. Although Wisconsians wailed about the border for decades and even abetted secessionist movements among northern Illinoisans, Pope's handiwork stuck.

Had he failed, both Illinois and Wisconsin would have had markedly different histories. For one thing, the northern region attracted mostly New Englanders, New Yorkers, and Europeans, who provided most of the region's values, institutions, speech patterns, and even architectural forms, making it distinctly dif-

ferent from downstate. It largely balanced downstate Illinois'
southern orientation.

Illinois' enabling legislation contained other important provisions. It made military bounty lands tax-exempt for three years,
encouraging settlement. To discourage nonresident speculation,
nonresident land owners paid taxes at the same rate as resident
land owners. Nathaniel Pope earmarked proceeds from Illinois'
federal land sales to benefit society. Indiana designated 5 percent
of its proceeds from federal land sales for canals and roads.
Through Pope, Illinois also earmarked 5 percent, but three-fifths
of it was to support education. (Of this total, one-sixth was to
support a college or a university.) The federal government was to
use the other two-fifths to construct roads leading westward to
Illinois, strengthening ties with other states. Pope opposed using
the two-fifths for roads *inside* Illinois. Other states, he knew, doled
out road funds to counties in driblets, producing crazy-quilts of
roads, not rational state networks. Furthermore, he claimed nature in Illinois left "little to be done" to improve surface transportation, which he knew was a patently hollow claim. (He made
the claim to avoid needless fighting over internal improvements,
a contentious issue not immediately germane to statehood; Pope
was agile in sidestepping obstacles.) Interestingly, no funds were
earmarked to improve river transportation. The enabling act also
dedicated profits from Illinois' salines to education. Finally, income from each township's Section 16 would support education.

President Monroe signed enabling legislation for Illinois on
April 18, 1818. Voters in July chose thirty-three delegates to a
constitutional convention. Twelve of Illinois' counties each had
two delegates, and the three most populous (St. Clair, Madison,
and Gallatin) each had three. Delegates assembled at Kaskaskia
in early August, organized themselves, and chose Jesse B. Thomas president of the convention and William C. Greenup secretary. Most delegates were farmers with limited education, but
their judgment, intelligence, and experience compensated for educational deficiencies. Only five were lawyers. None was of French
extraction.

Elias Kent Kane, representing Randolph County, was a talented, focused powerhouse in the convention. He framed the

constitution's basic features, allayed concerns, and marshaled support. The constitution contained just eight articles. Although Illinois was overwhelmingly southern, the constitutions of New York, Ohio, and Kentucky supplied nearly all the articles. Finishing on August 26, the convention submitted the constitution to Congress for approval. Though Illinoisans had no direct vote on the proposed constitution before it went to Congress, electing delegates to constitutional conventions and drafting constitutions were radical democratic experiments, confined then to very few countries.

Under the constitution, voters elected the governor, legislators, and county sheriffs and coroners. The General Assembly appointed judges, prosecutors, justices of the peace, circuit clerks, and recorders, which propelled office-seekers to the capital to flatter, cajole, and pressure, not unlike what occurred in other states. A constitutional defect—one later causing much grief— authorized Illinois to borrow massively to finance virtually any public or private undertaking. Similarly, the constitution authorized virtually unlimited state loans.

Still, the constitution was impressive. Broadly humane and inclusive, it sustained robust republicanism. It was the first state constitution to abolish imprisonment for debtors. It conferred suffrage on virtually all white males of age—not just *citizens*— who resided in Illinois for just six months. Indiana and Mississippi, recently admitted to the Union, both required a year's residence. British, Germans, French Canadians, and others voted, most for the first time. (Constitutions and laws in some eastern states delayed suffrage for foreigners and established other restrictions.) The constitution denied the governor veto powers, but via an exotic constitutional provision he and four supreme court judges constituted a council of revision. They determined the constitutionality of bills, expressing their findings in writing, but the General Assembly could override their opinions with a simple majority, allowing bills to become law. This Byzantine process blended executive and judicial functions, weakening the judiciary and vitiating judicial review. Nevertheless, by subordinating judicial and executive branches, the constitution reflected republican faith in the legislature, the branch closest to the people.

Controversy over slavery threatened Illinois' march toward statehood. Illinois had nearly a century of robust slavery, and by 1818 most slaves north of the Ohio lived in Illinois, the American Bottom and salines near Shawneetown home to most. Slavery heated races for delegates to the constitutional convention. Elias Kent Kane, himself a slaveowner, hoped to minimize the furor, knowing Congress would reject a blatant proslavery constitution.

A compromise was worked out, one offering something for everyone. Virginia's act of cession protected ownership of "French slaves" present when Americans arrived in 1778. French-owned slaves remained slaves. Furthermore, an indentured servant system, by which blacks "contracted" to work for decades, grafted quasi-slavery onto the State of Illinois. Freedom nevertheless awaited indentured servants' male offspring who became twenty-one years old and female offspring who turned eighteen. Slaves could be brought into Illinois only to work salines near Shawneetown, and only until 1825.

This compromise garnered votes from proslavery delegates, who knew not to push slavery too stridently, while it avoided antagonizing moderate and antislavery congressmen. Perhaps it was the best deal proslavery forces could get in 1818. It glossed over sensitive matters and left much unaddressed, postponing decisive battles. Although it assured current slave owners, it mortally wounded slavery masked as indentured servitude, heralded slavery's eventual death, and ratified true indentured servants. Slaves working as indentured servants reflected a beleaguered institution. The compromise certainly eased statehood for Illinois. Elections occurred in mid-September. All white adult males residing in Illinois when the constitution was framed, less than a month earlier, could vote. Shadrach Bond, Jr., former delegate to Congress, ran unopposed for governor. Three men, including Pierre Menard, ran for lieutenant governor. Menard, moderate and unsullied by self-serving factionalism, handily won a four-year term. Ironically, in the congressional race, John McLean,

Elias Kent Kane's young ally from Kentucky, narrowly edged Daniel Pope Cook, an early statehood proponent. The First General Assembly met on October 5, and Bond was inaugurated the next day. Bond nominated Elias Kent Kane as first secretary of state. Ninian Edwards and Jesse B. Thomas were chosen U.S. senators.

Steering statehood through Congress required talent.[8] On November 16 Henry Clay, Speaker of the House, presented the constitution to the House, where some New Englanders and other Northeasterners moaned about slavery and cast thirty-four votes against statehood. But 117 affirmative votes swamped them, and the Senate approved without dissent. President Monroe signed the statehood resolution on December 3, admitting Illinois as the twenty-first state. Senators-elect Edwards and Thomas and Congressman-elect McLean took office. On December 16 Governor Bond summoned the legislature to meet in January. The State of Illinois was functioning. Nathaniel Pope had succeeded.

* * *

Statehood saw slavery tottering. Notices for runaways suggest tenuous control. For example, Robert Collet, of Milton on Wood River, advertised in the June 23, 1819, issue of the *Illinois Intelligencer*, that Harry, a newly purchased slave "about 23 years, about five feet eleven inches high, very stout built, uncommonly large feet, carries his head unusually erect" had run away and was probably heading toward Vincennes. Advertisements offered slaves for rent, adding that those not renting out would be sold in Missouri. Basically, only the salines near Shawneetown offered hope for masters. Furthermore, French-owned slaves, people generally assumed, were anomalies, historical anachronisms with little future.

The Missouri Compromise of 1820 defused national confrontation, but it complicated slavery in Illinois. Slavery in Missouri grew, especially along the Missouri River. Perhaps Missouri's lengthy border with Illinois cheered Illinois' proslavery folk, but Missouri also siphoned some masters and slaves from Illinois.

At the same time, Illinois attracted Northeasterners and Europeans, most of whom disliked slavery. Some southern settlers, moreover, including Virginia-born Edward Coles, assailed slavery. Coles freed his slaves in 1819 in a ceremony on flatboats on the Ohio River, ran for governor in 1822, and defeated three opponents, including two who backed slavery. He quickly embroiled himself in antislavery fights, using personal funds to print blistering antislavery tracts.[9] Other southern natives thrashed slavery on pragmatic grounds. They argued it depressed wages of whites, crippled such social institutions as schools, and threatened yeoman society. One source notes that Southerners "who came to the Midwest were deeply suspicious of planter society. They feared its aristocratic, unrepublican aspects, its tendency toward luxury, its devaluation of white free labor. They also feared that whites would be debased and enslaved politically just as blacks were physically."[10]

Responding to attacks, proslavery residents slated a referendum over whether to call a constitutional convention to revise Illinois' constitution to allow outright slavery. Following spirited campaigning, this crucial referendum, held on August 2, 1824, stung proslavery people. On the question of whether or not to call a convention, some 6,640 voted no and only 4,972 voted yes. Obviously, even many southern settlers voted no. Reflecting this sentiment, eleven of the eighteen antislavery men in the legislature hailed from the South.[11]

As a general rule, older and more southern counties favored calling a convention, while newer and more northern counties opposed it. Exceptions to this rule (Fayette, Johnson, Marion, and Union) had close elections. As a percentage of the votes cast, the counties strongest in favoring a convention were Gallatin (596 for, 133 against) and Madison (351 for, 58 against). The counties strongest against were Edgar (3 for, 234 against), Fulton (5 for, 60 against), Morgan (43 for, 555 against), Pike (23 for, 261 against), and Sangamon (153 for, 722 against).[12]

Victory for proslavery forces would have vitiated the Northwest Ordinance, sabotaged the intent of Illinois' constitution, allied Illinois with other slave states, and put it on a collision course with the North.[13] Sparring over the Missouri Compromise had raised specters of civil war, and adoption of full-scale slavery in Illinois might have ignited armed conflict. Antislavery citizens and immigrants might have either avoided Illinois or flocked to it to resist violently, as happened in Kansas thirty years later. Finally, Illinois' northern regions might have tried to secede. Significantly, this crucial referendum sparked angry words and veiled threats, but practically no violence.

Ironically, Coles's referendum victory was pyrrhic. It reflected his opponents' divisions, apathy, and perhaps arrogance, not his own strengths. From the beginning, Coles stumbled. His humane inaugural speech, urging justice for blacks, was politically stupid. After the referendum, vindictive opponents scuttled his cherished projects, including substantial tax support for education. His own lieutenant governor, a semiliterate oaf, undermined him. Backing William H. Crawford's presidential aspirations against Andrew Jackson's, Coles bucked rising democracy, a bad political move, and voters trounced Coles's allies. These stinging reversals illustrate roles personality played as the Second Party System emerged. His political career in shambles, Coles left office in late 1826, performed dismally in a congressional race in 1830, and in 1832 moved to Philadelphia, from which he continued to lash slavery. He outlived slavery, dying in 1868. Ironically, a son died fighting for the Confederacy.

* * *

New migration to Illinois was now assisted by technological breakthroughs. In 1811 the first steamboat on the Ohio and the Mississippi rivers, the *New Orleans*, chugged from Pittsburgh to New Orleans. Unfortunately, the war quickly crimped commercial traffic on the Mississippi. (The *New Orleans* never left the lower Mississippi Valley.) With peace, however, steamboats multiplied and upstream traffic surged. In August 1817 St. Louis saw its first steamboat. The next year Great Lakes steamboats appeared, *Walk-in-the-Water* churning waters between Buffalo and Detroit, sails supplementing its steam engine. Nevertheless, steamboating's great boom occurred on western rivers, not on Lake Michigan. Chicago, for example, obtained steamboat service in 1832, fifteen years after St. Louis.

Steamboats serving the Mississippi and its tributaries increased from twenty-three in 1818 to eighty-nine in 1822, 198 in 1831, and

640 in 1843, reaching some 1,300 in 1848.[4] These vessels were constructed everywhere, not just on western rivers.

Road developments were impressive. The National Road pushed from Cumberland, Maryland, to Wheeling by 1818 and then to Columbus, Ohio, in 1833. As it and other roads opened up Ohio and Indiana, Easterners and Europeans trekked on them toward Illinois. Well before the National Road reached Illinois, people used it to reach the Prairie State.

Beginning in 1825, the year the Erie Canal opened, freight rates between Illinois and New York City fell to as low as one-twentieth the rates prevailing in 1818. Decreases in storage and insurance costs followed. Transportation breakthroughs extended markets radically, bringing eastern manufactured goods to Illinois and whisking Illinois farm and forest products eastward. Steamboats, canal barges, sailing vessels, and then Great Lakes steamers further oriented Illinois eastward. Moreover, steamboats plying the Missouri River extended the frontier and markets westward.

Radically reducing upstream freight and passenger costs, steamboats doomed western keelboats, the early handlers of upstream commerce, but they invigorated flatboating. Illinois' men, including Abraham Lincoln, crewed flatboats down the Mississippi. Steamboats sped many home safely, sparing them the dangers of the Natchez Trace, and began towing some flatboats back upstream for reuse, saving them from being discarded or becoming scrap. Steamboat interests, moreover, lobbied state and federal authorities to rid waterways of sawyers, planters, bars, and other dangerous obstacles, thereby enhancing nighttime flatboat navigation. Furthermore, flatboats supplied steamboats with copious quantities of firewood, some engines devouring a cord an hour. Western flatboating peaked between 1846 and 1861, just when frontier Illinois faded. Flatboats grew in size to 100 feet, carried an average of 150 tons, transported coal and other new cargoes, navigated very shallow water, sported cabins and other conveniences, and were towed upstream by steamboats, enabling them to make several round trips a year.

Steamboats sculpted western town life and town formation. They serviced riverine towns and even hamlets, and packet lines

soon touted regular visits. They radically restructured existing
regional economic systems, collapsing prices of such goods as
sugar, tea, glass, and manufactured items. Shucking shady reputations, spirited river towns became more cultured. Even flatboat
crews drank in lectures, music, theater, circuses, bowling, and
similar social activities previously unavailable to Illinoisans.[15]

Into the 1830s most Illinoisans hugged southern waterways,
developing local and regional economies and social fabric. Although rickety bridges, uncertain ferries, and marginal roads
brought goods inland, overland transportation was still expensive and undependable. Early steam-powered craft quickened
existing river towns and reoriented commerce, and wooding stations dotted waterways.[16] Steamboats reshaped existing communities and economic and social arrangements, linking Illinois
upstream to Cincinnati and Pittsburgh. Steam power linked
southern settlers to the outside world. It affected northern Illinois differently. Northern communities, farms, institutions, and
economic structures grew from infancy alongside of steam power.
In fact, steamboat traffic outstripped settlement, whisking settlers along uninhabited riverbanks to new homes. Pioneers happily embraced this unfolding technology and the changes it
brought. And steam power brought other significant changes.

Steam-powered mills escaped nature's vicissitudes of drought,
ice, and flooding. They also eliminated problems of fatigue among
horses and oxen used to power mills by treading on circular inclines. They could locate almost anywhere, market demand and
the availability of fuel being the only major constraints. Some
operated by the 1820s, the engines sometimes coming from
wrecked steamboats. The *Hampshire Gazette* on April 13, 1831,
contained a letter written by P. R. Bryant to his brother in Cum-
mington, Massachusetts. The letter was written in Jacksonville
the previous December 30 and observed, "Mill seats are rare: the
want of water mills is supplied by those which are propelled by
horse or steam power. There are seven or eight water mills in this
County. It is said that mill seats are more common further north."
Asa and George Thomas built a stream-powered flour mill in the
late 1830s near Sugar Creek. Henderson County's first steam mill
operated in 1840, and nearby counties acquired steam mills at

about the same time. Randolph County got its first steam flour mill in 1840. Even when towns lacked water power, they sometimes became milling centers, thanks to steam-powered mills, which usually located on the outskirts of town. During the 1850s major steam-powered mills located close to railroad depots, trains whisking flour to distant consumers. Steam-powered mills killed off some older water-powered and animal-powered mills, although some earlier water mills converted to steam.

Most settlers craved permanency and certainty. Although pioneers hunted, gathered, fished, and in other ways supplemented their income, most aspired to become commercial farmers or businessmen, eager to relegate hunting and fishing to sporting or recreational pastimes. They welcomed transportation breakthroughs to speed their farm produce to distant markets and receive manufactured goods from remote sources, and they championed improved wholesale and retail distribution systems and enhanced credit arrangements. This implicitly meant town growth.

Following the War of 1812 villages and towns popped up, often promoted by individuals or groups. On the western tongue of settlement, Belleville, Edwardsville, Harrisonville, Brownsville, Collinsville, Jonesville, and Alton joined Kaskaskia and Cahokia. The eastern tongue of habitation, along the Wabash and Ohio rivers, boasted of Shawneetown, Colconda, Carmi, Palestine, Palmyra, and Albion. Perrysville, Salem, and Covington—and a few other communities—had already graced the southern interior of Illinois, but Greenville, Carlyle, and Vandalia soon sprouted there, too. By 1830 Jacksonville, Springfield, Fairfield and many small villages sprang into existence. Except for Springfield, Albion, Jacksonville and several others, virtually all were on navigable water and near timber. Intersections of two or more trails sponsored many communities, especially when the intersection was near a ford or ferry.

* * *

Educational development was sporadic, uneven, and private. In late 1824, Senator Joseph Duncan from Jackson County introduced a bill similar to the plan pushed by Thomas Jefferson when he was governor of Virginia. Essentially, Duncan's plan called for free, universal education. His "Free School Law" authorized the raising of local taxes for education, local control, and popularly elected school officers. Governor Coles signed the bill into law in January of 1825. Unfortunately, within two years the law's taxation feature fomented opposition, and during this fight Coles's influence vanished and Duncan was in Congress. A law in 1827 gutted the Free School Law by authorizing taxation in local districts only after every taxpayer in the district agreed in writing to be taxed. Although education's advocates persisted in the state legislature, only in 1855 did the state create free, universal education, complete with a State Superintendent and a common school fund.[17]

A few towns championed decent education. The Reverend Desmoulin of Kaskaskia, for example, taught Latin and French. A woman from New England ran a school at Salu. Aratus Kent offered Latin and Greek at Galena in 1829, as did a school at Ebenezer, which also offered mathematics. An endowment of one hundred lots helped Alton provide religion and free public education. By 1830 girls' schools offered painting, needlework, and related subjects deemed appropriate. The Monticello Seminary for Girls adorned Godfrey, just north of Alton. Numerous individuals, operating with various motives and abilities, endeavored to make a living by teaching. They opened subscription schools here and there, some of which lasted for a few weeks or months and some of which enjoyed greater longevity. The school masters running these establishments advertised for students, stated the terms of the school, and charged each student a fixed tuition, one that usually ranged from $3.50 to $7 per quarter per pupil. Typically, these teachers accepted room and board at the pupils' homes as a form of payment, generally moving from family to family every few weeks. At the age of twenty, Stephen A. Douglas arrived in the fall of 1833 at the town of Winchester. After searching for students, he found himself teaching a class of forty, each of whose parents paid him $3 per quarter. Reflecting popular sentiment, Douglas regarded teaching as just a stopgap measure to put food on his table as he prepared himself for other undertakings. He read law while teaching, and by March of 1834 he was admitted to the bar and terminated his teaching career. Other subscription teachers were farmers, who managed to teach a term now and then. In general, formal education fared poorly.

* * *

Typically, at this time, a village of a hundred or more souls contained a mill, general stores, a tavern, an inn, a couple of coopers, a church or two, a school, one or more blacksmiths, a wagon maker, and often a wheelwright, gunsmith, cabinet maker, a pork-packing operation, a tanner, a physician, carpenters, and even a printer. Milliners, watchmakers, hatters, and others catering to people of means served some settlements. Hamlets and villages served not only their residents, but also hinterlands that often extended several miles and contained hundreds of people.

Towns that were also county seats enjoyed distinct advantages. They sported lawyers, sheriffs, jailors, surveyors, a post office, several inns and taverns—including the region's finest—bankers, and a newspaper. County residents trekked to them to transact business involving county, state, or federal government. Federal land offices blessed some county seats. With such solid underpinnings, county seats usually withstood economic downturns.

From territorial days until the early 1820s, Shawneetown was Illinois' financial hub, possibly the busiest place west of Pittsburgh. One of two banks operating in Illinois in 1818, the Bank of Illinois, functioned in Shawneetown. (The other, the Bank of Edwardsville, operated in Edwardsville.) Designated a port of entry, Shawneetown received innumerable settlers, who then pushed toward St. Louis on the connecting road. By 1820 another road connected Shawneetown to Kaskaskia, Illinois' other port of entry. Settlers commonly used these towns as bases while searching for land. Shawneetown, moreover, transshipped salt from impressive salt works on Saline Creek. Home to an early land office, it transacted in 1820 about 35 percent of public acreage sold in Illinois. Boasting a jewelry store, it attracted people seeking luxury goods. Nevertheless, it was primitive and its advantages tenuous. Rains transformed streets into quagmires, smells offended sensibilities, and smoke cloaked it, conditions common in urban places. Urban centers to the north soon eclipsed Shawneetown.

Only one economic mainstay sustained some towns, creating boom-or-bust realities. Early Galena, for example, depended almost solely on lead deposits. Home to few residents in 1824, it contained over four hundred two years later, and some two thousand by 1829. Lead's fluctuating prices propelled Galena through nerve-wracking cycles.[18] Some single-resource communities, though, developed alternative functions, acquiring stability through diversification. Original functions sometimes disappeared entirely.

Illinois' constitution virtually named Vandalia the new capital, fixing its location for twenty years. Vandalia's boosters trumpeted this advantage. On June 23, 1819, the *Illinois Intelligencer* announced the sale of 150 lots in Vandalia, assuring readers, "The situation is high, dry, and commanding—there are several springs of excellent water, and no part of the state is better timbered; the country for many miles around is beautiful, delightfully watered and timbered, interspersed with some excellent prairies; the river is navigable for many miles above, and passes through an extensive tract of the finest lands in the state." The notice continued, emphasizing, "The practicability of making excellent roads in every direction, the navigation of the river, the excellence of soil, timber and water," and the belief that Vandalia "will remain the permanent seat" of government for the state.[19] Though Vandalia longed to become vitally important, its dream was unfulfilled. Such boosterism flourished in hundreds of towns, newspapers regaling readers with supposed advantages, both existing and proposed. These claims reflected bubbly speculation, on the one hand, and confidence in Illinois, on the other hand. They also reflected efforts to convince others of incipient prosperity and importance.

* * *

The reference to "some excellent prairies" is significant. By the 1820s, people began to be convinced about virtues of prairies,[20] as facts began to displace inaccuracies and myths. For example, on July 28, 1819, the *Illinois Intelligencer* featured im-

pressions formed by "An Agriculturalist" during a three-week
sojourn along the Sangamon River. The region, he noted, had
"the advantage in many respects to any other water course in the
state of Illinois, or any other country west of the Ohio. The prairies are too large, but they are the richest and best kinds of prairie, the uplands as well as bottoms. The timber is very large and
lofty . . . without underwood or barrens. The country is well
watered with large and small springs." Admitting that prairies
"are too large" reflects lingering concern about grasslands. Even
so, this admission was buried in the paragraph and surrounded
with inducements to settle—slick marketing. Pure water from
prairie springs and wells and access to groves and valley timber
dissipated anti-prairie prejudices. Pioneers building cabins on
fringes of grasslands tapped woodland and prairie ecosystems.
Soon, others located hundreds of yards into prairies, and farther.[21] By the 1830s the major impediment to grassland settlement was tough prairie roots, a cohesive matted obstacle impervious to most plows.

Improved transportation affected the movement of Illinoisan
settlers to either new frontiers beyond the Mississippi or back
home. Into the mid-1830s, once settlers were established, they
did not usually travel far from the Illinois frontier. But with ad-
vancements in railroads and large numbers of vessels on western waterways, the Great Lakes, and canals, travel became
much easier. Settlers could return East for visits, or even to retire. Many Easterners, at the same time, visited Illinois, often for
a few weeks. And Illinoisans and others plunged into new frontiers in Iowa, Minnesota, and elsewhere. Wherever they went,
people traveled quickly and at relatively slight cost, danger, or
discomfort.

Although many settled in frontier Illinois to escape difficult or
impossible conditions elsewhere, most tried to bring with them
the best of what they had known earlier in their lives, whether
these were a love of learning and collections of books, business
connections, church affiliations, or close family ties. They were
usually keenly interested in sinking roots in their new neighborhoods and replicating valued features of their earlier lives as well
as they could.

For these reasons and others, these later pioneers often set-

tled near relatives, friends, or at least people from similar backgrounds. Unlike some of the first arrivals, they valued institutional life and the stabilizing effect of institutions. Schools and
churches were valued by most, even by those with few books
and by those who never formally joined a church. They differed
from the footloose people who preceded them in wanting to overcome, or at least tame, nature's rough and ragged features. These
folk plowed fields, girdled trees, decimated game, bridged and
dammed rivers, turned trails into roads, checked prairie fires by
plowing the land and introducing grass-eating livestock, planted
orchards and stands of special trees, introduced new animal and
plant species, drained swamps, mined and quarried, improved
their houses and built additions, and sought ways to get surplus
production to market and obtain from remote sources manufactured goods and luxury items. In short, they entered the frontier,
not to live harmoniously with nature, but to subdue its wilder
features and harness its productive elements for economic and
social gain.

By the late 1820s southern culture in Illinois was giving way to
cultural influences from Middle Atlantic states, Quebec, New
England, and Europe. New England's values and institutions,
often undergirded by strong feelings of mission, were especially
dynamic and durable, compensating for Illinois' relative paucity
of New Englanders before the 1840s. And by mid-century New
Englanders, other Northeasterners, and the foreign-born were
attaining great cultural and economic influence.

* * *

A close reading of letters, diaries and other accounts from the
Illinois frontier reveals a significant fact. None of these accounts
indicate any feeling of helplessness in the face of lawlessness;
quite the contrary.[22] The few mentions of illegal activity generally encompass swift and sure punishment for miscreants. Some
petty crime is cited, and outlaw bands may have operated here
and there with impunity for a time, but these were the exceptions. Accounts tell, instead, of severe—even brutal—treatment
meted out to those who chose to break the law. Especially harsh

punishment was reserved for those who jeopardized the lives
and livelihood of settlers.

Occasionally, law enforcement and courts failed to subdue stubborn defiance by especially brutal and well-organized lawbreakers. When this happened, settlers were thrown back on themselves for protection, and some extralegal activities often resulted in whippings or hangings. Consensual silence usually protected the leaders and members of extralegal organizations that suppressed lawlessness, as did winks and nods from authorities. Unfortunately, some of those who took it upon themselves to suppress lawbreakers sometimes themselves became true criminals, making it difficult to distinguish between the original criminals and those who became criminals in the fight against crime. Some contemporary accounts compared crime on the Illinois frontier to crime in the more settled sections of the country and crime in Europe. In such comparisons, the frontier of Illinois came off well.

9.

MIGRATION, TRIALS, AND TRAGEDY

Many letters and other accounts of Illinois brimmed with depictions of pristine land, an exhilarating and bewildering land, one generating both liberating hope and gnawing fear and anxiety. Associated with feelings of fresh, vibrant life was awareness that migration and settlement were facets of larger, glorious national undertakings. The nation was on the move, on a momentous westward surge that swept Americans over the Great Plains and established settlements on the Pacific Coast. In this surge was a buoyant sense of tomorrow, a sense of eternal renewal, of hope. Sometimes this sense of hope and expectation focused on embryonic society's potential, and sometimes it emphasized hope for life in the hereafter. In various ways, settlers sweeping into virginal Illinois were future-oriented folk.

One factor allowing and encouraging pioneers to be expectant and gaze hopefully into the future was Illinois' remoteness. It was separated from relatively congealed societies of Europe and the East Coast. Even after the Erie Canal and regularly scheduled Great Lakes steamship traffic linked Illinois to New York, Illinois was still to Sarah Aiken "a far distant country." Though for decades in Illinois people tried to replicate features of societies they had known elsewhere, they also reveled in its inviting newness. Anything was possible. A powerful key to success in Illinois, many knew, was sustained exertion by individuals and voluntary associations.

Nevertheless, the stark reality of "a far distant country" affected people differently. Some Illinoisans suffered a sense of loss, a sense of being isolated. Evidence of loneliness cropped up in letters. On May 26, 1836, for example, Eleanor Robbins wrote from Rushville back to relatives in eastern Ohio, hoping "you will not forget us in this distant land." She added, "Hard it is to be separated from parents, brothers, and sisters, never more to meet till we meet in eternity. I often think can it be possible that I can live and die in this distant land far from all that is near to me." Alma Stevens, in 1836, wrote to a friend in Connecticut, "Now let us try to live if we meet no more on earth that we may meet in heaven and part no more. Life is uncertain and we must soon enter into an untried state of existence." Women held no monopoly on expressions of loneliness. John Garner and his wife, who lived in Waddams Grove in 1836, longed to see their grandchildren. On December 11, John wrote to his children:

> I and your Mother takes many a Cry about you and them Dear little Grand Children and . . . oftimes wishes I could see the boy. We are now getting old and perhaps not long for this world, and to be near you and them Darling Babes would make our Declining years a Blessin. For when those names are mentioned, which is very often, our hearts are afflicted and at this moment my Eyes are Dropping fast with Tears. May God bless you all. Adieu. Let us hear from you soon, for God sake.

Relatively few defeated early settlers took the costly, lengthy, and sometimes dangerous trip back home. Well into the 1830s settlers assumed that leaving home for frontier Illinois meant permanent physical separation.

Moreover, pioneers expected to see loved ones again only if they, too, migrated to Illinois. Sarah Aiken understood this. In innumerable instances, pioneers encouraged and even begged relatives and friends to come to Illinois. Their motives varied, but earnest pleas often lured friends and relatives to Illinois. This, of course, was a form of chain migration.

Though chain migration promised support at the end of the trip, the travel itself was difficult, especially for households containing numerous children. The journey to Illinois was a grim slog, a lengthy, tedious, expensive, and often dangerous undertaking. Before railroads, travel from the East Coast to Illinois often took at least six weeks, occasionally three months. Accommodations en route usually ranged from uncertain to wretched, food was often positively weird, and travel companions could be untrustworthy.

Even so, nature's bounty vastly impressed people in frontier Illinois. The rich, deep soil was fertile—incredibly fertile to those from rocky New England and sandy stretches of northern Europe—and the growing season was long. In addition, the frontier teemed with game, enjoyed both sufficient precipitation and good drainage, and sported many navigable streams. Stands of fine timber graced Illinois, especially in southern Illinois and along waterways. Inexpensive land awaited ordinary people.

* * *

Not only was land plentiful, but labor commanded top wages and perks well into the nineteenth century. These facts led some to worry about the likelihood of indolence. Richard Powel traveled through central Illinois in 1838 and claimed, "The first year a man worked here he was astonished at his crops & next year did not do so much and by the 3rd year was as lazy as an old settler."[1] Some settlers did revel in indolence, but far more drank of the frontier's regenerating qualities. Readily available land, bountiful harvests, opportunities for bracing self-sufficiency and independence, pride in achievement, and perceived fluid social conditions and narrow gaps between rich and poor collaborated to nourish republicanism.

Liberating feelings of independence were probably stronger among foreigners than among native-born. For example, in early 1829 John and Elizabeth Killam left Hull, England, reached Morgan County on July 21, purchased public land west of Jacksonville, and settled on it. On February 11, 1831, the Killams wrote to English relatives. After noting bountiful game, they exclaimed, "There is no tithe nor tax on land till it has been bought five years; there is a small tax on cattle and farming utensils, but no other things. Our tax is $.87." Significantly, they added, "We can make our own soap or candles, and grow tobacco or anything else without duty; we have no exisemen nor any inspecting officer."[2] The Killams stressed, "All we grow is our own, we have no tax nor poor-rates but what I have mentioned. I never see any beggars here, almost every man owns a piece of ground, more or less." After noting that tradesmen were in demand—especially tinners, wire-workers, brickmakers, tailors, blacksmiths, basket makers, riddle makers, millwrights, and stone masons—John Killam lamented, "As soon as those that come can buy land, they turn farmers." This eagerness to abandon trades and "turn farmers" reflected a hunger for land and the assumption that its ownership produced true independence.

New Englanders noticed western expressions of independence and upward mobility. One wrote, "the free air they breathe, far away from the restraints of religious teaching and well organized society, modifies essentially their temper and habits." This modified behavior was readily apparent: "Men who in the circles where they had their origin, would have ever stood back, relying upon others' opinions, are not unfrequently, in a new settlement, thrown upon their own resources, and compelled to think and act. They are forced to read, observe, and resort to all available sources for information." Consequently, they became new people, and "the West abounds with what are sometimes called self-made men—men who have fitted themselves for the emergencies into which they are thrown." This often produced worldly success: "It frequently occurs that those, who in the land of their birth were in the lowest conditions of society, suddenly find themselves standing at its head."[3] Success and belief in it, girded by strong feelings of worth, impressed observers.

Buoyed by feelings of independence, people wanted a hand in shaping public affairs. Ordinary settlers often ran for office, were elected, and governed. Plunging into public arenas, people shook off habitual deference and chronic social subordination. Observers wrote about manifestations of independence, about people feeling free for the first time in their lives.[4] Feelings of self-worth, eagerness to participate in public matters, and civic virtue were vital for republics' well-being. People truly assumed that government was the public's servant, not its master.

Republican spirit surfaced in other ways. Elections in territorial Illinois and the state were frequent, many offices were elective, and voting qualifications were amazingly low. The unfinished, embryonic quality of frontier life attracted many people to early Illinois, including many who previously were excluded from political processes and who longed to participate.[5] The frontier's unfinished and dynamic nature promoted, perhaps even required, participation in political processes.

* * *

But frontier fluidity and newness also produced problems. People nervously pondered the direction and quality of future social developments. The future, in short, was up for grabs, which motivated individuals, groups, and organizations to try to shape young Illinois according to specific values. Settlers trying to transplant treasured values and institutions feared the transplants would either wither and die, or undergo severe mutation because of inhospitable frontier forces. Even shortly after statehood, the Illinois frontier—perhaps more so than other state frontiers—contained a diverse population, settlers hailing from many states and foreign countries. Compared to Kentucky, Ohio, Indiana, Missouri, Wisconsin, and Iowa, frontier Illinois was home to relatively large numbers of blacks and French. Although this mixture piqued the curiosity of some settlers and visitors, others shuddered over competing values and institutions; some resented or feared strange accents and customs, odd forms of worship, and what they perceived as bizarre notions.

Competing ideas about the nature of the good life generated friction and even clashes, some occasionally becoming violent. By 1818 Illinois had seen squabbles and fights between Indians, French, British, Americans from various places, immigrants, and others. Furthermore, within each ethnic group factions bickered. Settlers from southern states wrangled with people from elsewhere, slavery sometimes sparking contention. Southerners, themselves, argued about extending slavery to Illinois. Racial attitudes generally consigned blacks, free and slave, to the lowest rungs of the social ladder. Occasionally there were religious tensions, mostly between Catholic and non-Catholics and Mormons and non-Mormons. Lusting to reform themselves, their neighbors, and everyone else, Yankees, particularly those from southern New England, could be annoying. Despite basic economic and social equity, class conflict flared now and then. Finally, especially near the end of the frontier era, foreign immigrants were persecuted by native-born residents. Conflict's most striking feature was not that it occurred—the heterogeneous population practically guaranteed some troubles would brew up—but rather that it was so limited, spontaneous, and mild. Of course, for victims of mayhem and those traumatized by it, even sporadic and limited conflict was horrendous.

Beginning in the 1780s with independence from Great Britain, the United States frontier pushed westward for over a century. During this century or so, throughout the entire United States perhaps only 10,000 whites and fewer Indians died in open conflict. Only a few score died in Illinois, but the killing of even two or three people sent shockwaves across the state and beyond. This was significant: if violence had been large scale or chronic, a few deaths now and then would have gone virtually unnoticed. It is precisely because the Illinois frontier was so tranquil that the occasional murder or skirmish evoked such shock, outrage, and alarm.

Accompanying social turmoil was social change. Settlers and visitors to Illinois noticed, for example, that relationships between men and women were different than in the East. The new relationships did not include suffrage for women or other radical changes, but they did include many changes in daily life, including a blurring of gender lines concerning traditional work roles. Several frontier factors influenced gender relationships and roles: shortages of labor; scarcity of women; desire by men to make women feel appreciated; surging republicanism. In any case, along with traditional roles, some new gender roles evolved. For example, in Jefferson County women affixed their names to the charter document of the "Mount Vernon Temperance Society," founded in 1832. They pitched in to provide food for various community activities, such as house raisings and slaughtering. When prairie fires approached, both women and men cleared the ground of combustible material, started backfires, snuffed out fires started by flying embers, and suppressed fire with wet sacks. Women also served as midwives and rendered general medical assistance. Moreover, since female servants were rare, women did their own work, a novel experience for some.[6]

New roles also evolved for other elements of society who flocked to Illinois. For example, new relationships were forged between employee and employer, politician and voter, leaders of social experiments and followers, and between other segments of society. Many of these new relationships resulted from the fact that relatively large amounts of land were available to ordinary people.

* * *

In addition to the great opportunities Illinois had to offer, another major theme surfaces repeatedly in the writings of settlers and visitors: their health. Opinion was sharply divided on whether or not Illinois was a healthy place. Some people wrote back home about how much their health had improved since arriving in the new lands. The frontier attracted relatively many young folk, people in the prime of life. The sickly, the uncertain, and the very poor generally did not even attempt migration. Once people arrived, bountiful and varied food supplies generally awaited them, doing much to fortify them for pioneer life. A heightened sense of expectation, the thrill of making a new home, and improved morale upon arriving in an emerging society lifted spirits for many. For a large number of people, it appears, Illinois was a place where the healthy became stronger.

For others, though, Illinois was a place of sickness, chronic woe, and death. Accounts are nearly unanimous in indicating that river bottoms and other low-lying, damp places were sources of sickness and death, especially during summer. This was thought to be especially true after rains on hot summer days, and some blamed it on decaying vegetable matter. The sickly time began in August and ran into October; often half to two-thirds of annual deaths occurred during these three months. Children under five years of age and older folk were especially vulnerable. Chronic sickness, including ever-present malaria, also known as ague, was noticed by many travelers. Many people were laid up for weeks at a time by fevers and general sickness, which often weakened them sufficiently that some other disease could kill them.[7] Two massive outbreaks of cholera, one beginning in 1832 and the other in 1849, swept frontiersfolk off to graves by the thousands.

* * *

Illinois' emerging society was malleable, and some settlers sought to shape it according to carefully prepared agendas; they wanted to block slavery in Illinois, for example, or to found utopian communities. Whether they hoped to influence Illinois' development or even alter national life, they founded institutions and urgently labored to promote their undertakings, hoping it was not too late. Competing interests in the 1820s and later underscored urgency. Slaveowners and opponents, for example, swiftly marshaled forces. Similarly, Roman Catholics and Protestants abhorred and ardently undercut each other. Other contentious interests also contested for dominance.

Seeking to remake Illinois in their own image, some Yankee settlers were cultural imperialists, promoting pet causes and striving to save the Mississippi Valley—the "Valley"—from horrid consequences. Many were clergy, teachers, physicians, and social reformers, but many ordinary Yankees also avidly supported Yankee ways. For instance, they assailed ignorance, indolence, slavery and slaveholders, drinking, and Roman Catholicism, and even endured privation and downward mobility to combat forces hostile to values and institutions they cherished.[8] These cultural missionaries gleefully waded into the Valley's cultural frays.

The 1820s witnessed Yankee organizations launching business ventures, churches, colonies, and the state's first college. These often maintained ties with eastern sponsoring organizations. This was true, for example, of Illinois College, founded in 1829 by the Yale Band, an organization of seven young men associated with Yale College who covenanted in New Haven to found and support in Illinois an institution of higher learning. Two basic motives motivated them: they fervently wanted to combat barbarism, ignorance, and related dark forces; they also strove to save the Valley from Roman Catholicism, firmly entrenched in St. Louis and other strategic points through such institutions as St. Louis University.[9] To Yankees, ongoing moral and cultural battles were determining the Valley's future and even that of the Republic. Stakes were immense.

Shortly after opening in 1829, Illinois College appeared to espouse abolition, rankling folk with southern ties. Its connections to New England aroused suspicions. Similarly, Yankee churches often maintained ties with eastern sponsoring organizations, unlike typical southern churches. Under the Plan of Union, adopted in 1801, Congregationalists and Presbyterians cooperated in the West, with Presbyterians apparently dominating and enjoying organizing rights in the West. Consequently, no Congregational congregation was created in Illinois until 1833, but Illinois Congregationalists wielded considerable influence under the rubric of the Plan of Union. Congregationalist doctrines, forms of worship, and social messages clashed with those of most Baptists, Methodists, and Presbyterians, most of whom were southern. The cohesion, zeal, and eastern support enjoyed by northern churches and other institutions smacked of conspiracy and imperialism to southern settlers.

Some southern settlers spoke out against slavery, while others pounced on drunkenness and other social evils. Still, few Southerners strode forth as cultural warriors, cloaked with righteousness and bolstered by southern organizations to do battle for the Lord. To be sure, most hoped to replicate certain social features, but they spawned few institutions, other than decentralized churches. Few swung ideological axes, launched moral campaigns, or harbored desire to refashion others. Quiet traditionalists, most treasured kin, a few friends, custom, and stability. Noisy slavery advocates were not typical, and most of those fell silent after failing on the referendum issue in 1824. Uncompromising abolitionism, however, shook the country in 1831, punctuated by Nat Turner's rebellion in Virginia. The South closed up, silenced or expelled outspoken opponents, and girded for siege. Reverberations rumbled across Illinois, pitting neighbor against neighbor and poisoning rhetoric. Such intense feelings, though, rarely triggered mayhem in Illinois, unlike elsewhere.

Slavery, nevertheless, was only one flashpoint. Southern settlers saw Northerners as imperialists, hypocrites, and grasping
people, who saddled others with norms while laying up worldly
treasure. In short, people believed Yankees started out doing good
and ended up doing well. Northern emphasis on education sometimes reinforced this view. Yankees and others struggled against
deplorable deficiencies in Illinois' educational opportunities, but
Southerners often looked upon these efforts with suspicion, especially if those pushing education were also crusaders for certain social causes.

For example, the Rev. Peter Cartwright in 1824 fled Kentucky's
slavery, settled in central Illinois, and energized Methodism. Feeling threatened by college-educated clergy who intellectualized
sermons and who lacked fiery conviction, he boasted about never
attending college, reflecting rampant anti-intellectualism, which
especially afflicted southern Illinois.

Although Illinois held out numerous inducements to settle, it
also repelled some people. Some who came with high hopes found
it not to their liking, and returned home in disappointment. Others, accounts indicate, returned east for another reason. These
people had succeeded on the frontier, piled up earthly treasure,
and returned to their childhood homes to enjoy the fruits of their
successes. They were returning in triumph, not unlike many
people today who return to their native land to retire after a
career in another county.

By at least the 1830s, some people pushed farther west, carving out homes and new lives in Iowa, Minnesota, Missouri, on the
Pacific coast, and elsewhere. By the late 1840s people left Illinois
for such places as Utah and California.

Many people became dissatisfied with life in the new lands of
Illinois, but it appears that among them were people who had
not experienced failure. These people simply saw opportunity
farther to the west. For a number of reasons, it is possible that
those who pushed farther west were quite different in important
ways from those who returned to the East.

Finally, defeated individuals did not always return home and
stay defeated. Perhaps the days of the Gold Rush are instructive
here. The vast majority of the people who went to California

beginning in 1849 failed to strike it rich in gold or do well in other undertakings. Great numbers returned home, many of whom succeeded after returning. In fact, it is not too much to say that the trek overland, including the defeat in California, was good for them, helping to prepare them in various ways for life's challenges.

* * *

Significantly, ordinary settlers' letters and diaries mentioned another subject relatively rarely: the roles of blacks in frontier society. With the exception of some accounts from key turning points in controversies over blacks and slavery, most whites wrote relatively little about blacks. Few people at the time regarded blacks to be citizens, members of the body politic, or legitimate elements of society. They were not deemed to be second class citizens; they were not deemed to be citizens, period. A few notable exceptions do nothing to undermine this basic fact. Moreover, despite widespread antagonism against blacks in general, in Illinois the relatively few blacks were rarely seen as true threats. Although the heating up of the abolitionist movement during the 1830s and later did focus attention on the problems of slavery, blacks—free and slave—were usually seen largely within the confines of the larger questions of slavery.

Another group of non-citizens, however, occasionally elicited sharp comment in letters written by settlers—Indians. When the Black Hawk War brewed up in the spring of 1832, settlers wrote a great deal about Indians, much of it negative. A few concerned people, including some college students and residents of Jacksonville, tried to mitigate conflict by forming a peace society in 1832.

Some accounts, especially those generated by visitors to the frontier, lamented the shabby treatment the Indians had often received at the hands of whites. Others, especially those written long after the frontier vanished in Illinois, contained nostalgic comments about Indians and their way of life. Relationships between whites and Indians were very complex, full of nuances, and ever-changing, and brimmed with contradictions and surprises. Some settlers remembered downcast clusters of Indians leaving their burial grounds for the last time as they headed across the Mississippi River. Others called the readers' attention to artifacts, mounds, and other physical evidence of the Indian past.

Settlers and visitors regarded Indians as objects of interest, even sympathy, and references to Indians were certainly more frequent and more favorable than references to blacks. Even so, the plight of the Indians, and threats posed by Indians, received relatively little attention, if the daily accounts written by ordinary settlers are any indication. Relatively few white settlers came into contact with Indians after 1832 or had much reason to think, much less write, about them.

Nevertheless, frontier Illinois was a hybrid society. Two basic forces shaped society: the cultural baggage—values, institutions, customs, and overall culture—settlers brought to Illinois; and, fluid, evolving conditions in frontier lands. These forces varied over time, as did their ingredients, so societies springing from them also varied.

Well into statehood, cultures from slave states dominated frontier Illinois. But migration filtered southern culture, making the Illinois strains different from home cultures in the South, so that southern cultures in Illinois were not simply transplants. Rather, migration mutated cultures, then in frontier Illinois mutating cultures blended, and then frontier conditions changed the hybrids.[10]

Although black culture was subordinated, some blacks played remarkable roles, especially in the amorphous, fluid society that preceded full settlement. This society included Indians, residual French inhabitants, adventuresome whites, some blacks, and many people of mixed ancestry. These people—mostly men— were regarded as shiftless and indolent, and they usually disappeared as soon as yeoman households settled nearby. Their society connected cultures, including elements of a transitory Indian society reeling from onrushing whites. It also manifested lingering French traits, tempered by blacks, descendants of slaves brought to Illinois decades previously. Other blacks arrived from the South with American masters. This culture also included Americans, a boisterous fringe element that preceded settlement by yeoman households.

Changing frontier conditions tempered diverse and blended cultures: Specifically, the abundance of land, a sparse population and scarce labor, costly and uncertain transportation, difficulties in obtaining shelter and clothing and other necessities, and the likelihood of war with Indians and possibly Britain.

* * *

Southern dominance of the political and cultural machinery in the state was challenged by shifts in the composition of the state's population. In the first fifteen years or so of statehood, while the slave question and other weighty matters were thrashed out, an important shift in demographics occurred. Increasingly, large numbers of people came to Illinois from the Northeast. Migration from the South did not dry up, but each year saw larger and larger contingents of people arriving from states to the east of Illinois. Mixed in with the rising tide of newcomers from the Northeast were settlers from such foreign places as Britain and the German states. The pace of migration from places to the east, including locations in Europe, picked up with the opening of the Erie Canal in 1825 and spurted again with the arrival of Great Lakes steamships at Chicago in 1832. Easterners and foreigners began to constitute an increasingly hefty percentage of settlers.

The defeat of proslavery forces in the referendum of 1824 certainly discouraged some people from trekking from the South and settling in Illinois. Nevertheless, those who were deterred from settling in Illinois by the defeat were probably more than offset by the number of Southerners who came to Illinois to escape slavery's baneful effects. As in earlier years, most southern settlers were not friends of either blacks or, especially, abolitionists, but many detested and feared slavery.

The movement northward of the frontier in Illinois affected the flow of migration from the South. The distance between Southerners and the frontier increased yearly. Much the opposite was true for Northerners. Not only were the frontier lands closer to people in Ohio, New York, and New England, for example, but such technological breakthroughs as the Erie Canal and steam-powered vessels made the trip to northern Illinois faster, cheaper, and smoother than ever before. The prairie lands of northern Illinois by the mid-1830s were much more accessible to people along the eastern end of the Great Lakes than they were for people in most of the South.

Through the 1820s and beyond, individuals, parts of households, households, groups of households and their friends, as well as organized colonies arrived from England, the German states, and later from such places as Sweden, Norway, and France. They came to Illinois for a variety of reasons, some of which were social, some religious. Some fled war or threats of war, and some wished to avoid the draft or political persecution. Almost certainly, the majority came for economic opportunity and personal advancement. Some of the early foreign settlers, including colonies of foreigners, settled in southern Illinois in such places as Edwards, Madison, and St. Clair counties. They usually had southern settlers for neighbors. As time passed, though, increasing numbers settled in the northern half of the state and moved in alongside Yankees, New Yorkers, Pennsylvanians, Ohioians, and others from the Northeast. This was apparent in Morgan County in 1829, when a colony from Yorkshire, England, settled at Lynnville. They had some Southerners for neighbors as well as a growing number of Northerners.

Generally speaking, foreign colonies can be grouped into two broad categories. One category consisted of people who wanted to use group support to migrate to Illinois and get established in the new society. Highly pragmatic in nature, they lacked shared ideological commitment and a sense of higher mission. In fact, once settlement was accomplished and members of the group began to prosper and become independent, the group began to dissolve. Individuals broke off from these groups and went about the business of making it in frontier society, becoming thoroughly American. Since they often settled not far from where the original group had alighted, there were often little offshoot colonies from Yorkshire, Baden, Quebec, The Frisian Islands, or other specific places. Over time, English (as spoken in Illinois) became the mother tongue of nearly all the offspring, and many adults learned to function via English. Ethnic customs, clothing styles, and food preparations either faded completely or were adapted to the ways of the larger society. Only religion was somewhat stable, but by the second or third generation many Illinoisans did not share the religion of the homelands of their ancestors. Even in religion, there was blending and blurring.

The other basic category of people arriving in groups consisted of those whose group membership was far more than utilitarian. These people identified with the values, institutions, and goals of the group, often bringing these to Illinois and continuing to nurture them once they settled. A strong sense of group identity, purpose, and even discipline pervaded some groups. Groups from New England and certain groups from Europe typified this category. They often migrated westward with religious or social motives. Settling together, they assisted each other and exhorted one another. Those groups which did not give grievous offense to neighbors by weird practices or calculated aloofness often maintained the goal and zeal of the founders of the organization—but only for a generation or two in most instances. Such organizations usually dissolved, disintegrated, or moved on after a generation or two, the original leaders having fallen into disfavor, rifts having split the group, or other calamity having sapped the zeal and fiber of the organization. In many instances, such groups simply took on the coloration of their environment, intermarriage greatly facilitating the process. If the group arrived with a particular language as part of its cultural foundation, it usually began to fade within the first few years as youngsters borrowed English, and within a generation or two maintaining the language was accomplished only with great effort and even expense. In innumerable instances, such colonies melted into the fabric of the larger society. Place names, names on mailboxes, and distinctive churches are often the only major indications that the group ever tried to maintain a separate existence and carry out a mission. This process of peaceful assimilation was a very large part of the history of frontier Illinois.

In 1830 Illinois was still a raw, partially settled state. Most of its fifty-one counties lay south of nascent Springfield, and most Illinoisans lived south of Vandalia, the capital, and had roots in slave states. Central Illinois still contained hybrid middle ground culture. A few isolated farmsteads and communities dot- ted northern Illinois, where vibrant Indian culture and power persevered, and Chicago was a few jumbled huts and stores. Steamboats served major rivers, but none had visited Chicago, and erratic transportation severely hampered northern regions.[11]

* * *

The Winnebago War of 1827 foretold an ominous change in Indian-white relations. Indian anger over sexual liberties taken by white men against Winnebago women, the movement of Indians, and spates of violence sent settlers and soldiers scurrying about. This frenetic activity convinced Chief Red Bird, the Winnebago leader, to yield and sign treaties. Between August 1828 and August 1829, Winnebago and other Indians signed three treaties, which yielded 4,500,000 acres in northern Illinois in return for annual cash payments, salt, tobacco, blacksmithing and other services, and promises. Pierre Menard helped negotiate these treaties.

In 1831, Fox, Sauk, and Kickapoo followers of chief Black Hawk simmered. A Sauk veteran of the War of 1812, Black Hawk rose by dint of ability to lead the so-called British Band. He and his followers resented encroaching squatters, seething at wanton destruction of crops and homes near Rock Island. They crossed the Mississippi to Iowa, hoping treaty terms would be honored, including the right to farm in northern Illinois.

Malnutrition and sickness in Iowa necessitated returning to northern Illinois to plant corn. Black Hawk ordered whites to vacate the Rock Island region, punctuating his demand by torching some settlers' homes, acts which stirred state officials to mobilize volunteers. The arrival of nearly 2,000 Army Regulars stiffened volunteer forces and impressed Black Hawk. He and his followers backed down by late June and withdrew to Iowa. The severe winter in 1831–1832, dwindling food supplies, and disease in Iowa decimated his followers. Desperate, Black Hawk planned to cross the Mississippi, push fifty miles up the Rock River to Prophetstown, join remaining Winnebago and possibly other Indians, and grow corn there. Further, he hoped to forge Winne-

bago and other regional tribes into a bloc to resist future encroachment, perhaps with British support.

Black Hawk may have seen himself as Tecumseh's successor.
So-called "British Indians" still trekked to Canada to receive
annual gifts and rekindle ties. But Britain had virtually abandoned the Indians of the lower Great Lakes.[12] Illinois, now a state,
had its own coercive instruments, and its population was fourteen times greater than in Tecumseh's heyday. In 1812 Indians
and British had truly hoped to arrest American advance across
the lower Great Lakes, but by 1832 such hope was unrealistic.

On April 5, 1832, Black Hawk and his followers crossed the
Mississippi near Oquawka, Illinois. They were driven by necessity, but among them were at least 500 warriors, which incited
frantic responses among whites. Even so, for perhaps three weeks
after crossing, Black Hawk hoped to resettle and farm in peace.
Governor John Reynolds, an ardent Indian fighter during the War
of 1812, summoned militia. Volunteers assembling at Beardstown
included Abraham Lincoln, who derived great satisfaction from
being elected Captain by his company. The volunteers from
Beardstown and various other places marched to Fort Armstrong
at Rock Island, where they met ten companies of Regulars. General Henry Atkinson commanded.

By late April, Black Hawk realized his band's foray into Illinois had ignited massive opposition. Worse, he received chilly
responses from Winnebago and Potawatomi and absolutely no
support from British authorities, so he decided to beat a retreat
back to Iowa, a decision clinched by the presence of numerous
women, children, and other noncombatants among his followers. Given the band's vulnerability, retreat made good sense. First,
however, they had to cross the Mississippi.

As Black Hawk's group pushed up the Rock River to avoid
confrontation, the first violence erupted on May 10. Volunteers
under General Samuel Whiteside sauntered into abandoned
Prophetstown and gleefully sacked it. To them and junior officers
they had elected, war was a lark. Emboldened by destroying
Prophetstown, they marched to Dixon's Ferry and beyond, into
eastern Ogle County.

General Whiteside's force linked up with mounted volunteers,

men hot for combat commanded by Major Isaiah Stillman.
Whiteside dispatched Stillman's force farther up the Rock River
to locate the withdrawing Indians. May 14 found Stillman's force,
now numbering some 275 men, encamped about three miles east
of the Rock River in northeastern Ogle County. Flabby discipline
and alcohol degraded the unit, transforming it essentially into
an armed mob. Black Hawk and followers, including some recent arrivals, camped some eight miles away, where he received
reports of tepid support from the region's Indians and silence
from British authorities. Facing reality, he determined to end the
fiasco and seek peace terms, dispatching three men under a flag
of truce to Stillman's camp for talks. He also sent five warriors to
observe the party carrying the flag and their dealings with Stillman's force.

Itchy trigger fingers and possibly fear and loathing of Indian
warriors produced disaster. Volunteers shot and killed two of the
five warriors sent to observe. Hearing firing, volunteers in camp
shot at the three carrying the flag, killing one. Surviving Indians
fled for their lives. Volunteers, having shed blood, lusted for more.
Abandoning all restraint, they sprinted to their horses and gal-
loped pell-mell toward Black Hawk's band, which possibly numbered only forty.

As mounted volunteers bore down on them, Black Hawk's party
determined to die fighting. They hurriedly concealed themselves,
waited as the volunteers drew near, unleashed a withering volley,
and then pounced at those who toppled from saddles. The shock
of downed comrades panicked mounted volunteers arriving on
the scene, triggering a stampede. Although some volunteers fought
bravely and died fighting, most bolted and streaked clear to
Dixon's Ferry. Stillman's incompetency compounded the debacle.

Although only about a dozen volunteers died in the rout, news
of mutilated bodies rippled across the countryside, conjuring
images of marauding Indians and blood-drenched soil. Six days
after Stillman's rout, disaster struck La Salle County, where some
settlers ignored warnings from a concerned Indian and stayed
put. Potawatomi and possibly other Indians, not part of Black
Hawk's force, capitalized on chaos for personal gain and vengeance and fell upon the La Salle County residents, killing fif-

teen men, women, and children and carrying Rachael and Sylvia Hall into captivity, from which they were later ransomed. Additional sporadic attacks claimed several others, generating wild rumors and sending settlers scurrying for safety.[13] During the night of June 4 someone fired Galena's alarm gun, signaling imminent attack. On June 6 a resident, Dr. Horatio Newhall, described the resulting pandemonium:

"The Indian war assumed an alarming character. On Monday night last we had an alarm, at midnight, that the town was attacked. The scene was horrid beyond description. Men, women & children flying to the stockade. I calculated seven hundred women & children were there within fifteen minutes after the alarm gun was fired. Some with dresses on, and some with none; some with shoes and some barefoot. Sick persons being transported on others' shoulders. Women & children were screaming from one end of the town to the other."

Newhall then added, "It was a false alarm."

With hindsight, Dr. Newhall's account contains humor. But for those present—both whites and Indians—war's terror was real, war's results ghastly. Mrs. Caroline Strong lived about four miles from today's Naperville. On July 12, 1832, she wrote that Indians had killed a soldier sent with others to construct a fort at Naperville. She wrote of Indians, "Where they find two or three men alone with horses they are sure to kill them in the most horrid manner. Some were found, their heads in one place, & bodies in another, some with their eyes picked out, & noses cut off. One man's body was cut to pieces, and his entrails taken out and wound around his neck[;] one's heart was taken out & cut . . . to pieces." And then she wrote, "But our unworthy lives are still spared. Our heavenly Father has delivered us from danger, seen and unseen, whilst our neighbors (literally speaking) have fallen victims to the blood-thirsty savages." Many shared her views of Indians, trusting Providence for protection. Asher Edgerton, living in Quincy, wrote about the fighting on May 28, 1832, admonishing relatives in New York, "I wish some of your petty coat folks was here that are so troubled about the Indians being hurt. They would sing another song." Whites relatively close to fighting displayed scant sympathy for Indians.

The Chicago Massacre of 1812 and other previous Indian attacks seared perceptions. Responding to Black Hawk's incursion,
Hiram Beckwith's mounted volunteers hustled from Danville to
Chicago. At Chicago, he "saw the blackened stubs of the old fort
stockade just outside of the stockade, log pickets 15 ft. high paint-
ed white, and the graves of the massacred garrison." His next
observation implies much: "All the country between the Vermil-
ion and Chicago was Indian and hostile country." Of course, this
stretch was home to few settlers in 1832, but to call it Indian
country is revealing. Beckwith implied the region was beyond
Illinois' effective control and not merely middle ground; it was
Indian territory. Normally, settlers saw boundless opportunities
in vast spaces, but Beckwith saw dangers. Space belonged to Indians, and this frightened Beckwith and others.

Initial victories dispelled some of Black Hawk's pessimism.
Heartened, he coordinated attacks, dispatched scouts in several
directions, welcomed Winnebago and Potawatomi recruits, and
oversaw distribution of booty scavenged from Stillman's rout.
Nevertheless, while capitalizing on unexpected victories, he shunted the band's women and children to Wisconsin for protection.

He did so for good reason. By late May federal and state reinforcements positioned themselves to campaign against Black
Hawk. Commanded by General Atkinson, these forces included
a regiment of Regulars and 3,200 mounted volunteers. Settlers
erected blockhouses and other fortified structures from Lower
Yellow Banks on the Mississippi to Peoria on the Illinois. Supplies moved up these rivers to the massing troops. Upwards of
12,000 regulars and volunteers assembled in Illinois and neighboring states and territories to stop Black Hawk's band of several hundred.

Understanding the odds, Black Hawk and followers slipped
into Wisconsin to elude pursuit. Following vigorous rearguard
action at Wisconsin Heights, the dwindling band sought refuge
across the Mississippi, only to be intercepted just before crossing.
On August 2 the end came at Bad Axe on the Mississippi. His
followers hungry and exhausted, Black Hawk approached the
armed steamer *Warrior* to surrender, but he was denied permission to board. The *Warrior* then raked his followers with canis-

ter from a six-pounder and with musketry fire, while Regular Army units closed in. The end was swift.

Over 300 were killed or drowned in the Mississippi. Sioux Indians, ancient enemies of Sauk now employed by the Army, waited on the west bank, killing scores who swam the river. By day's end only about 150 of the band entering Illinois in April were alive, including Black Hawk and some 120 others who surrendered. General Atkinson lost eight killed and twelve wounded. Slain Americans since April totaled just seventy-two. The Sauk killed just thirty-three, less than half. Slain Indians numbered between 450 and 600.[14]

Defeated, forlorn Indians in September of 1833 conceded via treaty their last lands in Illinois and quit the state, superior numbers and power carrying the day. The middle ground's enfeebled mediating processes vanished, and with it the fur trade died. So thorough were Indian subjugation and removal that today's Illinois, unlike neighboring states, contains no Indian reservations.

Despite the war, the state census of 1835 revealed 269,974 Illinoisans. Dramatic growth is revealed by examining the increases at five-year intervals beginning in 1820. Between that year and 1825, the state gained 17,655, between 1825 and 1830 it gained 84,628, and between 1830 and 1835 it gained 112,529 people. Even allowing for high birthrates within Illinois, impressive waves of migration surged to frontier Illinois into 1835, and these waves accelerated very rapid change.

PART IV

THE FORMATIVE 1830s

IO.

EXCITEMENT IN THE LAND

Sweeping changes stripped many frontier traits from Illinois by the early 1840s. Horribly mauled in the Black Hawk War, Indians threatened no one, and soon soldiers escorted them across the Mississippi. Terror of Indians yielded to curiosity and even pity. Illinois lost its rooted Indian culture, and the middle ground vanished. Despite nature's buffeting and sharp economic distress, population in 1840 topped 476,000, ranking Illinois fourteenth among twenty-six states. Most Illinoisans in 1840 lived north of Vandalia, many north of the new state capital, Springfield, and by late 1839 the northern half of Illinois contained about half the state's 87 counties. Prairies became settled, steam-powered mills served many locales, education and reforms took big strides, denominations contended, and Chicago thrived. Rocketing land sales made the 1830s exhilarating. By 1840 steamboats serviced all navigable waters, the National Road finally reached Illinois, and railroads made an appearance. Illinois' ties to the East multiplied. All of this unfolded within the context of the emerging Second Party System, which consisted of Whigs and Democrats and lasted from about 1831 to 1855. Breathtaking, complex development marked the 1830s, enmeshing Illinois into ever-expanding regional and national economic and social arrangements.

Some changes were symbolic, some were substantive, and some were both. Some positive changes carried stiff prices, and some negative changes brought salutary chastening. Changes created their own momentum, sowing further transformations, which unfolded amid complex regional and national contexts, including continuing national expansion.

The Black Hawk War ended Indian resistance in Illinois. A treaty, signed at Chicago on September 26, 1833, ceded about 1,300,000 acres in northern Illinois, extinguishing the last Indian holdings in the state. Although individual Indians and households remained in Illinois, organized Indian presence faded.

The war produced other important consequences. For example, Stillman's rout sent hundreds of settlers scampering for safety. (Even Chicago's population dipped, from 428 in 1832 to 370 in 1833.) Many who never returned had southern roots, and Northerners quickly took their places.[1] Settlement surged. Southern flight and northern influx were significant events, cloaking northern Illinois with a decided Yankee hue, with profound social, economic, and political regional and national consequences. Southern culture in Illinois, once dominant, slipped in relative importance. The northern fourteen counties facilitated this transformation. Yankees, other Northeasterners, and foreigners—not Southerners—grabbed prime land in northern Illinois and sparked the region's boom.

Chicago grew rapidly. Patrick Shirreff, a Scot visiting Chicago in 1833, observed some 150 wooden houses lining the Chicago River, a bridge spanning the river, and brisk trade. He extolled Chicago's future, especially once a canal or railroad linked it to the Illinois River, adding, "Almost every person I met regarded Chicago as the germ of an immense city, and speculators have already bought up, at high prices, all the building-ground in the neighborhood."[2] In 1834 Chicago's population shot to at least 1,720, a 464-percent increase in one year!

Wars brim with contingencies and unintended consequences. As had happened during the Revolution and the War of 1812, soldiers traipsing across Illinois in pursuit of Black Hawk liked what they saw, and many returned to settle. One source, for example, stated, "The close of the Black Hawk war, and dispersion of the soldiers . . . called the attention of the country more generally to the natural advantages to be found in northern Illinois." These veterans, in fact, were among the very first who returned to claim land.[3] Rolling, well-drained hills and fertile and timbered valleys enticed veterans and their families.

In secure locales before the war, few pioneers worried about Indians, and this affected settlement patterns. For example, in Fountain Green Township in Hancock County in the 1820s, "The virtual absence of hostile Indians in the area did not demand a closely clustered population, and families [settled] . . . out of sight of their nearest neighbor."[4] In exposed regions, though, people settled in protective clusters. After Black Hawk's defeat, pioneers flooded across the landscape, oblivious to remaining Indians.

Conflict stretches technology's limits, as did this war. Federal authorities in 1832 chartered four steamships to shunt soldiers from Michigan to Chicago, with unforeseen consequences. Cholera forced two ships to turn back, but the *Sheldon Thompson*, carrying General Winfield Scott, and another ship steamed on, slipping thirty cholera victims into Lake Michigan. *Sheldon Thompson* reached Chicago on July 8, Chicago's first steam-powered visitor, the precursor to vast Great Lakes fleets. But it brought cholera, and nearly 100 soldiers died at Chicago, far more than Black Hawk's fighters slew. The disease then spread to civilians, including former Governor Ninian Edwards, stricken as he tended afflicted neighbors in Belleville. Cholera sliced through Illinois into 1834. Chicago's steam age had opened with death.

The war tested people who later shouldered heavy military responsibilities. Albert Sidney Johnston, Abraham Lincoln, Winfield Scott, and Zachary Taylor served. Governors of pioneer Illinois between 1834 and 1846, William L. D. Ewing, Joseph Duncan, Thomas Carlin, and Thomas Ford, also served in the war, as did John Wood, governor in 1860–1861.

Views of Indians changed. Before 1832 they were stereotyped as unpredictable, dangerous, indolent British lackeys. Because British agents advised and equipped Indians, few settlers regarded Indians as authentic players, capable of influencing their environments.[5] Immediately after the war, Black Hawk and other Indians were idealized and lionized. Black Hawk's autobiography, published in 1834, elicited much sympathy. Names of defeated chiefs and tribes adorned the era's most impressive symbol of power, the steamboat, and by 1832 *Black Hawk* plied waters with *Tecumseh*, *Tiskilwa*, *Choctaw*, and *Mohican.*[6] Indian place names also proliferated—the name "Illinois," the towns of Chicago, Kankakee, Pontiac, Ottawa, Peoria, the counties of Iroquois and Winnebago, and numerous river names are derived from Indian terms. Furthermore, some modern highways follow Indian trails, originally ancient buffalo trails. Long after Indians left Illinois, settlers continued to eat foods developed by Indian people and use Indian medicines and articles of dress. It was ironic that all of this occurred as Indians were vanishing. Of course, people of mixed ancestry continued to dwell in Illinois, as did some Indians who essentially gave up tribal ties and adopted white ways.

For observers like Eliza Farnham, writing a few years after the war, "the Indians were an embodiment of her belief that living in close, sensitive contact with unspoiled nature ennobled a man's spirit. Hence, she could only deplore what the white man had done to them."[7] She and others believed Indians lived in perfect harmony with nature. People both romanticized these wise, noble ecologists and called for their removal for their own protection. Neither this view, however, nor the savage-British-lackey view credited Indians with being independent agents. Neither view granted Indians full humanity, warts and all. In short, postwar Indians acquired distorted, non-human traits as they entered elevated mythical realms.

* * *

Peace spurred settlement. The federal census of 1830 listed 157,445 Illinoisans, an increase of 102,234 from 1820, for an average annual growth of just over 10,200. The state census of 1835 counted 272,427 Illinoisans, a whopping jump of 114,982 in just five years, for an average annual increase of almost 23,000, despite the Black Hawk scare. Then between 1835 and 1840 population sprang from 272,427 to 476,183, a gain of 203,756. Despite

TABLE 1: Sales of Public Domain Land at Illinois Federal Land Offices

Year	Acres sold	Number of Land Offices	Leading Land Office	Acres sold by Leading Office
1820	6,699	3	Edwardsville	2,649
1821	50,380	5	Edwardsville	35,243
1822	27,763	5	Palestine	16,474
1823	60,532	6	Springfield	38,720
1824	43,986	6	Springfield	22,339
1825	45,801	6	Springfield	26,767
1826	80,080	6	Springfield	56,122
1827	58,691	6	Springfield	33,398
1828	96,090	6	Springfield	45,206
1829	196,243	6	Springfield	86,492
1830	266,448	6	Springfield	101,933
1831	339,408	8	Edwardsville	100,350
1832	222,372	8	Edwardsville	80,713
1833	360,273	8	Springfield	109,642
1834	354,010	8	Edwardsville	124,302
1835	2,096,623	10	Springfield	478,976
1836	3,199,703	10	Quincy	569,376
1837	1,012,842	10	Vandalia	183,891
1838	778,556	10	Quincy	165,243
1839	1,132,872	10	Galena	229,471

economic depression beginning in 1837, the average annual gain topped 40,700, the vast majority of whom migrated to Illinois. (Even a stunning 4-percent birth rate in 1835 would have added fewer than 11,000 new residents, certainly offsetting that year's deaths, but accounting for only a fraction of the 40,700 increase.) Absolutely and relatively, the 1830s witnessed tremendous population growth.

Land sales reflected population growth. In 1820 Illinois' three federal land offices, located at Shawneetown, Kaskaskia, and Edwardsville, had sold just a few thousand acres of public domain land. In 1831 Illinois' eight federal land offices sold over

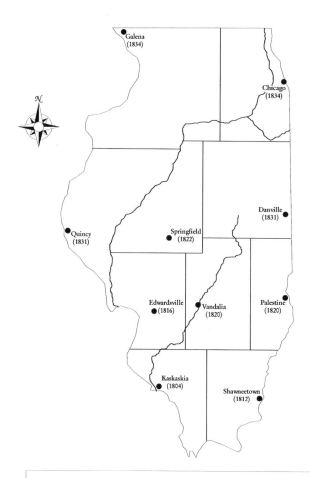

Land Districts and Land Offices--1834

0 10   25   50   100 MI.

- **Land District Offices** (Dates show when districts were legally established. Each district was named after the town in which the land office was located, except for the districts containing Galena and Chicago; Galena was in the Northwestern District and Chicago in the Northeastern District.)

one-third of a million acres. The Black Hawk War dented sales in 1832, but buying quickly rebounded, and in 1836 ten offices catapulted sales to well over three million acres. Though the following year's economic collapse slashed land sales, they began to rebound by 1840 (see table).[8]

Two locales illustrate war's impact. In 1832 in modern Joliet Township of Will County, migration totaled only 40 percent of the 1831 figure. Increasing slightly in 1833, migration in 1834 was seven times greater than in 1832. War also retarded settlement in modern Woodford County, migration in 1832 plummeting to less than half of what it had been in each of the three previous years. But it climbed in 1833 and jumped further in 1834 and 1835.

Significantly, war only slowed migration. For whites the war was hardly a prolonged slugfest triggering wholesale depopulation. Rather, slack land sales reflected reasonable precaution and good sense. Furthermore, even reduced sales signified willingness to invest in land—in the future—although war hovered. Buyers assumed conflict was transitory, a valid assumption. Above all, people contemplating settlement in Illinois were reassured. Illinois' attractions were persuasive. In New Haven, Connecticut, Levi Stillman, who had never visited Illinois, wrote about it on May 24, 1833. He could hardly contain his enthusiasm for the state, bursting out, *"I love Illinois* and want to be there very much. I have not given up the idea of going at some future period." He then mentioned friends who trekked to Illinois and liked it. His enthusiasm was far from unique.

The year 1835 ignited frenzied public domain land sales. From 354,010 acres in 1834, sales in 1835 shot to 2,096,623 acres—a nearly 600-percent increase in one year! This buying craze swept the country, one authority noting, "In the thirty months from the fall of 1834 to the spring of 1837, the American people generated the largest land office business in the history of the Republic."[9] Eager purchasers snapped up public domain lands from Maine to Michigan, down to Illinois, and in Mississippi, and elsewhere.

New land offices by 1835 in Galena and Chicago boosted sales. Brisk sales marked northwestern Illinois, the Military Tract (the land wedged between the Mississippi and Illinois rivers), and areas away from navigable rivers. Significantly, prairie lands sold well. Chicago's office in 1835 peddled 370,043 acres, topping combined sales in all offices the previous year, but Springfield led the pack, racking up 478,976 acres. Springfield's lead in 1835 among the ten offices, followed by Chicago and then Quincy, reflects quickening sales in northern and western Illinois, a fact borne out by

After suspicion of prairie faded, three or four yoke of oxen broke the tough prairie sod. From *A Guide to the Illinois Central Railroad Lands.* Chicago: Illinois Central Railroad Office, 1859. ILLINOIS STATE HISTORICAL LIBRARY, A DIVISION OF THE ILLINOIS HISTORIC PRESERVATION AGENCY.

increased land values and population. Reflecting massive Military Tract sales in 1835, Quincy's office dispensed 367,337 acres, exceeding by more than 1,000 percent the previous year's figure of 36,131 acres.

Several factors shaped settlement in the Military Tract: mounting steamboat traffic on the Mississippi, opening markets; the Erie Canal's continued success; Great Lakes steamboat activity by 1832; dumping by speculators onto market large blocs of Military Tract land; and guidebooks extolling the region. Pike County in the Military Tract attracted large-scale speculators, people who bought more than four quarter sections in one year. In 1821, forty-six large-scale speculators operated, thirty-six from the East, three Illinoisans, and only eight from southern states, including Kentucky and Missouri. In 1835 the tract's top sixteen speculators

included thirteen New Yorkers or New Englanders, two Illinoisans, one person of unknown origin, and no Southerners.[10]

Sprightly land sales continued through 1836. Land offices sold
3,199,703 acres, the most public land ever sold in Illinois, and an
increase of over 50 percent above the previous record year, 1835.
Sales in 1836, in fact, equaled nearly 31 percent of all acres sold
from 1820 through 1839, and combined sales for 1835 and 1836
topped 51 percent of the acreage sold during this time. In 1836 all
ten land offices, for the first and only time, had sales in six figures,
eight land offices basking in record sales. Quincy led, posting an
all-time record of 569,376 acres and reflecting settlement washing into the Military Tract.

Land values spurted dizzyingly, transforming ordinarily prudent people into expectant millionaires, who pumped successful
speculators for ways to achieve overnight success. On April 25,
1836, M. W. Ross wrote to his native Scotland from Rosscroft
in Kane County. After noting considerable success in farming,
he lamented, "Had I sufficient capital to go into the stock business I could make money very fast but I must get on by degrees."
Fortunes were to be made, Ross knew, and he chomped at the
bit to get his share. He reported that he had met in Chicago a
Charles Smith, from Britain, who had arrived in America about
two years previously with £1,000 and was now worth £40,000,
thanks to land speculation. Ross was impressed. Significantly, he
then noted, "I wished him to let me into his secret. He said he
should be most happy to point out a similar tract for me to follow." But caution prevailed; Ross added, "I have got a very good
subject in hand, however, and although it may be much slower
in its advance to fortune, it is still more sure, and I believe I shall
stick to it." Eager to prosper, Ross was nonetheless chary. Less
circumspect hopefuls rushed headlong, and some regretted it.

Speculation cut across class lines. The "poorest squatter and
the wealthiest nonresident found this activity attractive." Chicago frothed with speculation during the early and middle 1830s,
"speculators representing every classification . . . in the city, and
they competed actively with each other for both Chicago real
estate and choice farmland in close proximity to the city."[11] Speculative mania also ran amok in formerly calm rural areas. Specu-

lation in "every classification" of society is significant, suggesting widespread approval. Fast-paced sale and resale of lands helped buyers and sellers determine "true" value at any given moment. Federal legislation encouraged speculation. During plush times prior to 1837 sellers dumped much land onto the market. Large-scale nonresident landowners sold as land prices rose, realizing tidy profits and making lands available to other speculators.

William Cullen Bryant's investments in Princeton demonstrate the lure of town lot speculation. In 1837 this poetic Jacksonian Democrat bought two lots for five dollars each, and in 1865 he sold one for $1,600 and the other for $2,500. He made these killings while advocating inexpensive western land and protection for settlers from gyrating land prices.[12] On the other hand, he could have lost his investment, as many did.

In the financial bubble before 1837, "all who had any money could share in the sure rewards of enterprise by sending it along to be invested in the soil which soon would enrich them by its swiftly increasing values."[13] This process "brought capital to the West and enabled settlers and squatters, lacking sufficient funds to buy government land, an opportunity to make a home."[14] Borrowers confidently relied on expected farm profits, rising land values, and other gains to repay loans. Even absentee speculators who snapped up choice mill sites, town lots, and farm land elicited few complaints. Grim economic conditions by 1838 cooled such ardor.

The 1830s also witnessed wild speculation in towns. From 1835 to 1837 alone, over five hundred new town sites were laid out.[15] Towns were laid out in Jersey County in 1836 and 1837: Camden, Delaware, Grafton, Hartford, Jerseyville, Philadelphia, Pittsburgh, Randolph, Salisbury, Teneriffe, and Upper Grafton. All but Grafton and Jerseyville, though, became ghost towns; Jerseyville survived by becoming the county seat. A contemporary article recounted a Yankee who, visiting the West in 1836, saw rampant speculation amid natural beauty and richness. The speculation "infested all classes." If you greeted a farmer, this Yankee claimed, "before he returned your civilities, he draws from his breeches pocket a lithographic city, and asks you to

take a few building lots, at half their value, and earnestly presses you to buy as a personal favor conferred on you."[16] Many
speculative towns were still-born and others died in infancy. Pet
projects succumbed to harsh realities, and fragile towns met rack
and ruin. Investors accepted failure; they had seen opportunity,
seized it, failed, and then abided by results. Speculation, after
all, reflected both optimism and willingness to take risks.

The unwritten consensus governing reactions to failure was
both broad and binding. Instinctively, it seems, people knew it,
accepted it, and lived by it. The consensus even restrained losers
in contests in which skullduggery tipped the balance. Losers got
on with their lives, very few breaking the consensus.

Edward McConnell may have typified many settlers. He wrote
from Chicago on July 19, 1835, "I have been tolerable successful
in my speculations up here. I own about two sections of land in
different parts of the Canal route, some of which are said to be
very valuable. My selections here have all been good. I paid as
high as seven dollars per acre for some land near town which in
time I expect to realize something very handsome from. I have
invested all my means in land. I purchased a piece of floated
land (thirty acres on the south branch of the river within three
miles of town) which is very valuable. I gave 450 dollars for the
tract." McConnell added, "It is unknown the amount of money
that has been made at this sale. Such a field for speculation
never was known before in the western country. Nor probable
never will be again." McConnell had much company in 1835, for
Charles Joseph Latrobe in that year visited Chicago and wrote
of "land speculators as numerous as the sand."[17]

McConnell's letter also depicted improvements in Chicago. He
noted a new Episcopal church, a money-raising fair to finance
an organ for the church, a proposed theater, and construction of
an expensive tavern. He noted that Chicago attracted much investment: "There is a great deal of capital here. There are more
than a dozen who are worth upwards of a hundred thousand
dollars each. Chicago is entirely Eastern in manners and people.
Upwards of two hundred families landed last week from down
East." His reference to Chicago's being "entirely Eastern in manners and people" reveals growing northern influence.

Many settlers and others speculated in lots in real or imaginary towns. Public announcements heralded sales, but sometimes cabals schemed behind the scenes. Occasionally, nonresident speculators brandished detailed maps and other useful information about lands, to the chagrin of ordinary purchasers.[18] Finally, some speculation occurred in commodities.

One account indicates that the frenetic speculative mania that swept Illinois originated in Chicago. Speculation, it claimed, quickly transformed Chicago "from a mere trading-post to a struggling, bustling town of several thousand inhabitants—looking something like a flock of new barns had alighted among buggs [*sic*] and mud puddles and had most of them brought their stilts along to alight upon. . . . A spirit of gambling and adventurers and all were wild with a desire for sudden and splendid wealth. . . . The East caught the infection and every vessel coming West was loaded with people bound for these fairy cities of the West. . . . This rage for new towns was so general and the paper towns became so numerous that the wags began to say that the whole of the State would be just towns, with not enough room left for a single farm." The "rage for new towns" was so pervasive that prudent men became reckless, wise men foolish, and strong men weak. People surrendered their judgments to the dictates of the wildest imaginations. Wherever the craze started, it grabbed attention, focusing attention on frontier Illinois and luring streams of immigrants.

Another source described the speculative binge in succinct terms: "When money was abundant, credit had been extended to everybody. With the vast system of internal improvements, and the large circulation of the banks, this was the condition of our people. They were largely in debt on account of speculations, which proved to be delusions."

On February 20, 1837, Rufus Everett of Princeton, Illinois, wrote to his brother, Dr. Oliver Everett, of Dixon's Ferry: "Speculation runs high as ever in these parts. . . . Lots in town have risen greatly since I came down. Cyrus has sold twenty acres on the east end of his place for $25 per acre and ten acres from the other forty that he sold has since been sold for $30.00 per acre. A pretty high price for unimproved prairie."

Speculation in commodities apparently ruffled few settlers beyond generating some diffuse grousing about high prices. Writing to Levi Baker of Worchester County, Massachusetts, on December 26, 1838, Hannah Turner referred to speculators in Quincy: "There are 8 or 10 merchants in Q. They came to speculate, and sell their goods very high." Nevertheless, she did not condemn them.

Undoubtedly Hannah Turner and other pioneers understood the risks involved in bringing retail goods to such places as Quincy. The markup on goods arriving from such places as Pittsburgh or even St. Louis was high, but merchants incurred high transportation and storage costs and daunting fluctuating markets, causing many commercial ventures to sputter and then fold. Even so, speculators' organizing skills and capital put goods onto the shelves. Also, ordinary settlers themselves speculated, which probably tempered any impulse to criticize commodity speculation. Merchants cornering markets usually succeeded only temporarily, something people probably understood. Unbridled competition and numerous alternatives usually hobbled blatant monopolists. Thresholds for retailing were low, resulting in merchants darting in and out of various pursuits.[19] Essentially free markets provided competition and options, thwarting aspiring monopolists. Finally, exactly where handsome profits ended and speculative killings began was not always clear, and few condemned hefty retail profits.

Furthermore, seasonal market fluctuations, sporadic supplies, and uncertain lines of credit and value of money confused full understanding of economic conditions. Most people probably realized this. Apparently no settlers' associations arose to stifle speculation in commodities, and virtually no club law intimidated profiteers. Marketplace dynamics, most people believed, kept commodities on shelves.

But some speculation raised eyebrows and even fists. Settlers loathed professional, large-scale, nonresident insiders who connived and profited from privileged inside information, for example, ferreting out projected road routes and buying adjoining property or, worse yet, influencing routes of proposed roads and benefitting from them. Conniving through "connection" perverted republican principles. Many settlers detested these speculators as manipulative parasites, who operated cryptically through agents to ride roughshod over ordinary people, or at best regarded them as quick, alert entrepreneurs who capitalized on opportunity.[20]

On July 19, 1835, McConnell wrote from Chicago, possibly raising eyebrows: "I expect to leave here about the first week in August to attend the land sale at Green Bay, provided I effect a loan of money to speculate with. Several of the New York Capitalists have gone there already. It is said that upward of a million of money was taken back from here which could not find investment." Practically no one censured settlers speculating locally with their own money. On the other hand, nonresidents speculating with borrowed money were something else. The infusion of powerful New York speculators into the bidding process was another matter.

Resourceful settlers banded together to form voluntary associations to suppress blatant speculation by well-financed, nonresident bidders. Settlers knew their neighbors, scrutinized newcomers, and kept a sharp eye for troublemakers, so hired mercenaries, scofflaws, and misfits rarely found safe havens among them. Of course, specific locales in early stages of frontier life sometimes briefly harbored furtive lawbreakers and social misfits. Desperate people often lived undetected on society's fringes, mixing with local Indians and others. Almost always, though, advancing settlers and authorities relentlessly bore down on these transient societies, sending members packing or absorbing and subduing them. In any case, frontier Illinois did not sustain prolonged anonymity or fringe behavior.

Settlers neutralized troublesome non-settlers by forming various extralegal organizations to insure that their version of justice prevailed. These voluntary associations, generally loosely organized, sprang up like weeds to address local problems. In some locales, virtually all bona fide settlers either joined them or tacitly supported them. They went by various names: "Claim Clubs," "Claim Associations," "Settlers' Associations." They administered "club law," or "settler justice," or other forms of popular justice.

Some of these organizations operated at public domain auctions. Interlopers showing signs of bidding land prices up to unreasonable levels received popular justice. Delegates from a local association spotted such people, approached them, carefully informed them of the association's consensus concerning unrestrained bidding, and suggested bidding land prices above $1.25 per acre was *prima facie* evidence of anti-social behavior that would not go unpunished. Delegates brandishing clubs punctuated their points.

Individuals failing to heed this wisdom were sometimes initiated into the mysteries of club law. If they persisted, ostentatious displays of clubs and utterances of willingness to employ them usually convinced the benighted individuals to cease and desist. Rare, unswerving stubbornness elicited moderate beatings, non-lethal thrashings of sufficient intensity and duration to produce desired results.

Practitioners of club law believed their actions supported civil law. Regarding themselves as virtuous justice mongers, they never lost sleep over their actions. Instead, some proudly related their participation in memoirs and county histories, believing they operated in a legal vacuum, in the absence of effective law.

Northern Illinois saw scores of such associations sprout during the 1830s and 1840s. They enhanced settlement, secured land for yeomen, and induced feelings of justice and empowerment. A. D. Jones, referring to northern Illinois, wrote that when a half-dozen men settled in a given locale on public land and claimed rights of preemption, they then "formed themselves in an Association, each member signing a constitution by which they pledged themselves to abide. This constitution decides the manner in which claims shall be made in the territory—it embraces the quantity of land and the conditions on which it shall be held. They thus become necessary to each other, and stand by each other, while if any one of the Association fails to fulfil his part of the mutual contract, they permit and encourage any one to 'jump' or supersede him, and defend him therein." Jones added that members ploughed furrows completely around their claims, or staked them out in unambiguous ways. State government, he noted, knew of and approved associations' activities.

Jones made a telling point concerning unspoken consensus and law: "Every thing relating to the whole business is understood in the whole community, and the mutual laws which they have framed for their own management are sufficient, in the absence of all other law, as must necessarily be the case there, to restrain all violence and to protect each settler in his rights." In sum, broad consensus operated, commanding nearly everyone's allegiance. Furthermore, members drafted association laws "in the absence of all other law," not in violation of state or federal law. Claim associations created law where law flagged, established order amid incipient chaos, and founded grass-roots institutions to insure justice where few institutions existed. In short, members replicated the best of what they had enjoyed elsewhere— including order and justice—and they had no interest whatsoever in undermining the spirit of the law. These associations were essentially conservative, which probably accounts for government's tacit approval. Properly understood, they fostered stability and justice.

Jones observed the fruits of claim associations:, "Many have supposed that much difficulty exists in thus claiming lands. But I can assure my reader, there is not the least danger of losing title or life." This was hardly an exaggeration. Jones added that claim associations operated so smoothly that any observer would conclude that "every thing was ordered by a well regulated civil police—as indeed it is, only it is not supported and administered by government. I have seen no where more orderly, industrious, intelligent, peace-seeking inhabitants than I found among these same 'squatters.'" Significantly, Jones observed that most members were either Yankees or from Middle Atlantic states.[21]

In resisting nefarious speculation, squatters used Lockean arguments concocted decades earlier. Squatters on property owned by absentee large-scale investors claimed some rights through labor investments. Crafty squatters sometimes stalled court proceedings for years, meanwhile harvesting crops, timber, and wildlife. Absentee owners sometimes ran into roadblocks in ejecting squatters.[22]

Club law, however, sometimes failed to deter wealthy nonresident speculators, so settlers advocated improved preemption laws. Earlier federal preemption laws had helped, but settlers wanted additional protection. A. D. Jones, for example, in 1838 wrote in

Illinois and the West, "A pre-emption law framed alike favorable to government and the settler, would be a great and mutual bless- ing, and the time is not remote, I hope, when such an one shall be devised and successfully carried through both branches of the national legislature." He added, "The intention of a pre-emption bill is to protect the actual settler from the assaults of the mere speculator, so that he may have the right to enter and pay for his land before and in preference to any one else, at the government price of $1.25 per acre."[23] He and others wanted countless farm- ers—sturdy, independent Jeffersonian yeomen—to bring fertile lands into production.

In response to such desires a preemption law was passed in 1841. Although it elicited rejoicing, it was flawed. Speculators, for example, hired mercenaries to squat on prime farm lands, choice mill sites, town sites, and other prized property. The law lacked the means of thwarting such people, and even claim asso- ciations did not squelch this violation of the spirit of the law. Significantly, however, the first known professional writer to link speculation and dispossession wrote in 1847, late in Illinois' fron- tier experience.

Although settlers cooperated to insure that much land was sold at low prices, they competed in other ways, sometimes dishonor- ably. For example, on November 13, 1837, Andrew Fitz complained he could not find public land for sale around Schuyler and Ful- ton counties. Settlers there "will not inform you, wishing to enter themselves at sometime or other." Others searching for land were sometimes deliberately misled by local folk, who probably wanted the land for themselves. Still, these uncooperative acts did little to mar the record of significant and abiding cooperation and har- mony throughout frontier Illinois.

Not everyone, furthermore, valued claim associations, club law, and related activities. Referring to controversies in lands north- west of Chicago, William Waterman wrote from the Fox River on March 25, 1839, "For my part I should rather purchase deeded land, even if I had to pay pretty high for improvements. There is too much litigation, fighting and clubbing about claims here at present, to make society very agreeable. Indeed, there will be no end to contention, till the settlers obtain a deed from [the] Gov."

Of course, deeds were precisely what settlers wanted, but most also wanted land at the lowest possible price. While claim associations and occasional judicious application of club law ushered in order and forestalled destructive bidding and demoralizing speculation, other means were also employed to the same end. For example, after learning that moneyed eastern speculators had obtained huge tracts of land and were demanding exorbitant prices, settlers launched county-level initiatives. Voters assessed all land at 5 percent of value and required that property taxes be raised to build schools. Speculators holding unproductive land for years found such taxation onerous, so they unloaded their holdings at reasonable prices. In this way, voters pried idle lands from nonresident, large-scale speculators. Operating within the law, settlers discerned their interests and defended them by pushing buttons and pulling levers of county and state government.

Muscular accomplices occasionally accompanied claim jumpers to make fraudulent claims stick. Fist fights sometimes ensued, but settler-created ad hoc courts adjudicated most disputes peacefully. Varying in size, composition, and procedures, these courts listened to disputants, weighed conflicting testimony and other evidence, and then rendered decisions. These proceedings rarely included lawyers—some courts barred their participation altogether—and courts usually decided against transient claim jumpers and in favor of actual settlers, the people who clearly wanted to become permanent residents. Courts were especially unsympathetic to jumpers working for nonresident, moneyed speculators. Court decisions carried weight, a testimony to the respect people on the scene had for the courts and for the governing consensus. Court decrees, everyone understood, had the force of law. Rare individuals who bucked decisions incurred the community's swift wrath. Recalcitrant offenders were hustled to the boundary of the court's jurisdiction, warned never to return, and then expelled, sometimes with graphic descriptions of what continued defiance would elicit.

Informal, broad-based consensus channeled relationships between speculators and encroaching squatters. Wanting security and social mobility, people resolved to get land, brushing aside hesitant, spasmodic efforts to thwart squatting. By the early 1840s squatters in eastern Illinois risked eviction, but consensual and extra-legal measures shielded some: few land owners "will incur the odium attached to ousting a man from such a possession, without at least giving him the value of the improvements, i.e., houses, fences, and broken-up prairie, which he may have made upon it."[24] In short, people occupied public lands, appropriated soil and timber, and benefitted from improvements.

Customs often outweighed legal title and force of law. Knowing neighbors filched timber, nonresident speculators occasionally occupied their lands to protect their assets. More commonly, however, owners arranged with nearby squatters to prevent others from heisting timber, granting cooperating squatters a reasonable share. Local sentiment and custom restrained large-scale absentee owners, so they struck accommodations with local folk. Resident speculators, on the other hand, often protected vulnerable settlers, buying titles to tax-delinquent lands and selling them back to original owners, thereby keeping titles from grasping absentee speculators. As Siyoung Park observed, "In a sense, local tax buyers acted as mortgage loan officers, as no bank was yet in existence there," thereby encouraging settlement.[25] A central fact emerges from the evidence: large numbers of ordinary people obtained much land, and they got it with very little bloodshed.

II.

TRANSPORTATION, TOWNS, INSTITUTIONS

Improved transportation in northern Illinois during the 1830s spurred settlement. By 1833 Chicago enjoyed regular stagecoach service with Detroit, and in 1834 a state route connected Chicago to Galena. Older links improved with increased traffic, as did the Kellogg Trail, connecting Peoria and Galena in 1825. In the 1830s villages popped up where two or more trails met, or where a trail crossed navigable water.

The National Road ushered thousands westward from Wheeling, Virginia, through Columbus, Indianapolis, and beyond.[1] This broad, graded, well-engineered thoroughfare boasted dozens of fine bridges, many inns, and repair facilities. Although it had not yet reached Illinois, it funneled people, mail, and commerce in its direction. It belatedly reached Vandalia in 1836, an anticlimactic milestone conferring meager benefits on the community. Despite these improvements, however, most roads were still primitive. Furthermore, steamboats plying the Ohio's northern tributaries and canal boats siphoned freight and passengers from the National Road. Great Lakes steamers by 1832 coursed between New York and Chicago. Unlike the Ohio River, seasonal water levels in the Great Lakes barely fluctuated. William Oliver lauded the lake route as "the best route, not only for the north of St.

Louis, but for a large proportion of the state, in autumn, when the Ohio is apt to become too low for the passage of steamboats."[2] Clearly, evolving water competition buffeted the National Road before it reached Illinois, dissuading settlers and shippers from using it. Although faltering railroad competition in the late 1830s was premature, the handwriting for the National Road was on the wall. It faced tough competition before its tardy arrival in southern Illinois, just as migration flooded into northern Illinois. Had it arrived earlier—and in northern Illinois—its role would have been greater.

New bridges and ferries also enhanced travel. Steam-powered ferries replaced some horse-driven ferries during the 1820s.[3] In 1834 a rope ferry spanned the Chicago River. Individuals, businesses, towns, and counties operated bridges and ferries, under the state's regulatory eye. Regulations excluded competition and set toll rates and times of operation, making bridges and ferries quasi-public utilities. Usually ferries operated for a few years, traffic increased, bottlenecks occurred, and complaints mounted. These sometimes produced authorization for another ferry, but they also led to bridge building.

In 1818 *Walk-in-the-Water* introduced steam vessels to the Great Lakes, and packet service connected Buffalo and Detroit by 1833, giving Northeasterners new options in reaching Illinois. Some carried to Illinois New York residents who had farmed along the Erie Canal and whose land became so valuable they sold out and bought better, less expensive land in the West.[4] Passengers sailed to Detroit, from which they trekked on the Chicago Road to northern Indiana or along the Territorial Road to St. Joseph on Lake Michigan. They then settled in Illinois, mostly in northern counties. Others booked passage on steamboats from Detroit north through Lake Huron, past old Fort Mackinac, and across Lake Michigan to Chicago. Increasing numbers of steamers pulled into Chicago, disgorged settlers and cargoes, loaded produce and products of Illinois, and returned east.

Chicago basked in scheduled steamship stops by the mid-1830s. Only four Great Lakes steamers visited in 1834, but by 1836 some 450 steamers docked.[5] Steamboats chugged to Peoria in 1830, to Dixon in 1836, and to Rockford in 1838, and by 1839 packets linked the Rock River and St. Louis. By then, one source claimed, steamboats had largely killed off keelboats and flatboats, but the aura of rivermen lingered: "Flat and keel boats are now rarely seen on the western waters; but when they were the only means of transportation, they reared a hardy class, fit to fight with Indians, or to subdue the wilderness. This class, thanks to steam navigation, is now on the verge of extinction, and the valley of the Mississippi has seen 'the Last of the Boatmen.'"[6] This was true only in specific regions, however.

Public interest, political support, and converging technological breakthroughs hastened internal improvements. Improvements in steam power were paramount. After the War of 1812, high-pressure, deck-mounted engines and shallow drafts allowed western steamboats to navigate shallow waters, unlike their eastern cousins. Before 1820 the hoarse cough-chug of steamboats pierced streams barely four feet deep. Since western waterways generally became shallow just when autumn harvests needed shipment to market, these shallow-draft vessels served farmers well. High-pressure boilers sometimes exploded, with hideous results, but western steamboats continued to serve inhabitants. Coincidentally, steam power pumped water from the nation's mines, allowing miners to go deeper for metals used in steamboats, trains, canal gates, bridges, and other means of transportation. Improved shipping, packaging, storage, and scheduling after 1815 also enhanced transportation.

Interestingly, as late as 1835 boatyards in Ohio or Pennsylvania constructed over three-fourths of the 588 steamboats plying western rivers. Ohio supplied 226, Pennsylvania 216, and Kentucky and Indiana together provided 103. About fifty cities and towns constructed at least one steamboat prior to 1835, but only nine constructed more than ten. Pittsburgh led the pack, producing 173, and Cincinnati was second with 164 boats. Louisville and New Albany were next, with thirty-three and thirty-two, respectively.[7]

By about 1835, some 200 steamboats plied Illinois' rivers, the number topping 430 within a decade. Steamboats revolutionized life on western rivers far more than on the Great Lakes. Downstream traffic from Illinois had always functioned reasonably

Well into the age of steamboats, flatboats and other
vessels assisted westward expansion. From J. E.
Alexander, *Transatlantic Sketches.* 2 vols. London:
Richard Bentley, 1833. ILLINOIS STATE HISTORICAL LIBRARY,
A DIVISION OF THE ILLINOIS HISTORIC PRESERVATION AGENCY.

well, but steep costs inhibited upstream traffic. Keelboats and
other vessels moving upstream from New Orleans to Illinois took
six weeks or longer, soaking up labor and hoisting costs. Sails
were rarely used, narrow channels restricting tacking and reaching by commercially viable craft. Upstream costs for freight—
always the bottleneck in western commerce—plummeted to less
than 10 percent of pre-statehood costs, virtually extinguishing
upstream keelboat traffic. By the late 1830s, average speed down
the Ohio River was perhaps ten to twelve miles per hour; upriver,
perhaps six.

Wide expanses of the Great Lakes, on the other hand, allowed
the use of sails. Costs for westbound Great Lakes traffic, moreover, were not appreciably greater than for eastbound traffic. In
1835 some 225 schooners plied waters between Lake Erie and
Chicago. Both sail and steam helped Chicago boom, sail holding
its own for years.

Steamboats also affected settlement in unintended ways. By

the 1820s some western steamboats had been wrecked, and soon their salvaged engines powered mills.[8] Freed from dams, mill ponds, mill runs, water wheels, icing, floods, droughts, and other vagaries and expenses, steam mills became footloose and revolutionary, popping up all over and bringing milling anywhere fuel could be hauled. To be sure, steam mills sometimes depleted local wood supplies, but distant supplies arrived once local supplies became exhausted or prohibitively costly. Once pioneer aversion to settling away from timber subsided, steam engines heralded prairie settlement.

Other transportation developments spurred frontier Illinois. The Erie Canal, an impressive 363-mile feat of engineering and construction, opened in 1825. Cargo costs between Buffalo and New York City plummeted. For example, in 1817 a ton-mile on the Buffalo–New York City route cost over nineteen cents, but by the 1830s it cost less than two cents. In 1855 the value of canal freight exceeded $204 million, well above New Orleans' in 1860, which was $185 million. Fleets of sailing vessels and then steamships linked the canal to Lake Michigan.

Subsequent canal construction in Ohio and later in Indiana accelerated the transportation revolution by linking the Ohio and Wabash rivers to Lake Erie. Farm commodities from Illinois and elsewhere now flowed eastward. Western farmers buffeted eastern farmers with fierce competition, forcing some to abandon grain production and shift to dairy cattle, sheep, and orchards, or take up odd jobs, or sell out. Barges and steamers brought eastern manufactured goods to Illinois, supplementing goods from Pittsburgh and elsewhere and lowering costs. These increasingly lightened the burden of daily life. Marshall Jenkins ran a store in Jackson County into the 1840s. If his store was typical, consumers had a wide range of goods from which to choose. The store carried small luxuries and refinements: ribbons, patterns and edging for dressmaking, various buttons, mittens and blankets for winter, assorted dyes, materials ranging from fine silks to coarse linsey, ready-made shoes and slippers, such patent medicines as Godfrey's Cordial and World Salve and Sulphur, firearms and implements, kitchen tools and utensils, a wide assortment of books and pamphlets, nails and sails, lumber and paint.[9] Merchants in larger towns stocked even greater variety. Using canals and ships, New Englanders, Irish, Germans, and others glided westward with goods. Towns in Illinois like Barrington, Clinton, Barry, and Urbana attest to settlers' eastern origins. Northerners inundated the Military Tract; soon towns named Pittsfield, Quincy, Vermont, and Kinderhook and counties named Adams, Schuyler, Hancock, and Fulton dotted its landscape.[10] Clinton County honors Governor De Witt Clinton, the Erie Canal's foremost proponent. Conferring such place names, settlers honored eastern sites, figures, and memories, reflecting attachment to eastern culture and desire to spread it.

The Erie Canal forged growing commercial, migratory, and social ties between Illinois and the Northeast during the crucial 1830s and 1840s. Chicago prospered with the Erie Canal, hastening construction of the Illinois & Michigan Canal. Illinois' trade shifted from a north-south Mississippi River axis to an east-west Great Lakes–Erie Canal axis. Significantly, east-west commerce cemented social and political ties, a process abetted by settlers from New England and upstate New York. They stamped northern Illinois with Yankee values, institutions, and overall culture. Furthermore, the canal ushered Germans, Irish, and others to Illinois, strengthening ties eastward and giving vitality and power to northern Illinois. Slowly, eastern culture—especially from New England and New York—and foreign culture challenged southern influence in Illinois, with profound implications for the Civil War.

The Erie Canal, booming Chicago, the Illinois & Michigan Canal, and later massive railroad construction shaped northern Illinois. Without them, it might have developed like northern Indiana. Southern Illinoisans and Upland Southerners would have pushed up rivers, rolled onto prairies between Chicago and Iowa, and perhaps even flooded the northern fourteen counties. Had this happened Illinois' overall complexion would have approximated Indiana's; until quite late, Indiana received hefty settlement from slave states and relatively few Yankee or European settlers. Southern and northern Illinois would have been similar.

Handfuls of northern and European settlers would have been isolated, mere inconsequential drops in a southern sea. Illinois' ties with the South would have remained firm.

Transportation improvements created safer, faster travel, with inevitable major social consequences. Trips from New York requiring four weeks or more in 1825 took just ten or twelve days fifteen years later. Households journeyed west and settled intact in Illinois, often not needing chain migration or group migration. They communicated with friends back home, sometimes returning home to visit. And settlers disappointed in Illinois returned home relatively easily.

Visiting Chicago in 1839, Albert Parker wrote on October 25 to his mother that it took him eleven and a half days to travel from Groton, Connecticut. Near the end of the letter he wrote, "Tell Enos he must come out here and go into the staging business." This single sentence, while not promising assistance to Enos in getting settled in Chicago, was similar to countless comments in other letters; by referring to a specific person and suggesting success for that person in Illinois, he probably greatly encouraged Enos to at least consider migrating to Illinois. It is precisely these informal, offhand, and brief bits of encouragement that generated so much migration in general and chain migration in particular. Albert Parker himself came to Illinois via chain migration, after another brother, J. N., wrote their mother on December 3, 1838, from Chicago: "I think I shall want Albert to come on in the spring, if so I will write again to that effect." Similarly, after John Brees of Indian Creek wrote to his father on August 29, 1837, and urged him to come to Illinois, he added, "It will relieve your mind, and body, and be a source of much satisfaction." He then offered to make his father comfortable through the winter, noted enticing available foods, and indicated that the trip could be done via the lakes in under three weeks at low expense. These were elements of chain migration.

Quickened immigration drove internal improvements. Immigrants constructed canals and other arteries of transportation. The Illinois & Michigan Canal, twelve years abuilding, employed thousands of Irish and other immigrants. Canal promoters advertised in eastern and Canadian newspapers for laborers as late

as 1847, and canal agents scoured eastern cities for labor. Immigrant laborers and others built roads and bridges, or worked
on ships. They mined iron, copper, and coal, ingredients for internal improvements. In short, requisite labor sources coincided
with technological breakthroughs. Technological advances became intrinsically wrapped up in evolving social conditions and
politics.

* * *

From the time steamboats first visited Chicago in 1832 to the
surge of railroad construction by the mid-1850s, the two major
political parties of the Second Party System, the Whigs and the
Democrats, hammered at each other. Although they both practiced electioneering hype and deliberately raised bogus issues,
they also thrashed out important matters, including the proper
roles of government and public funds in sponsoring canals, roads,
railroads, and other internal improvements. Political assumptions, processes, and personalities defined and channeled sharp
conflicts. Specifically, as the Whig Party jelled in opposition to
Andrew Jackson and his followers, national and state Whigs, such
as Henry Clay and Abraham Lincoln, advocated internal improvements, protective tariffs, and a national bank. Borrowing
from Clay's American System, northeastern and Great Lakes
states financed, subsidized, guided, or regulated canal, turnpike,
railroad, riverine, and harbor projects, and banks. Clay, in turn,
had borrowed heavily from ideas and philosophy of the defunct
Federalist Party, the party of George Washington, John Adams,
and Alexander Hamilton. In general, in Illinois and nationally
the Whig Party was the minority party. Federalists and Whigs
usually favored a stable, structured, and literate society, one girded by plenty of institutions. Whigs generally favored a modern,
commercial, and urban society, and they welcomed government's
promotion of worthy social and economic projects, especially those
strengthening nationalism and modernity. Whigs differed from
Federalists, however, in fearing a strong presidency and in relying heavily on Congress.

The Whig Party's platform reflected Illinois' future. Within
twenty years railroads criss-crossed the state, telegraphs clicked

instantaneous news to remote villages, and other marvels dazzled residents. Henry Clay's Whig Party and then Abraham Lincoln's modern Republican Party used tariffs to protect American industry and American workers from foreign competition, garnering votes for decades from urban workers. President Abraham Lincoln, an ardent Whig-turned-Republican, created a new national banking system, which lasted until overhauled by the Federal Reserve System in 1913. The prairie lawyer lavished federal support on railroads and, borrowing from earlier Jeffersonian-Jacksonian ideas, he also backed the Homestead Act. Despite premature railroad activity in Illinois by 1838 and despite failures of the state's system of internal improvements and the state banks—all victims of the depression—these undertakings ultimately prevailed in Illinois and elsewhere, abetted by the Whig lawyer and state legislator from Springfield, who in 1861 became the country's first Republican president.

Andrew Jackson and Martin Van Buren led the national Democratic Party during the 1830s, and Stephen A. Douglas was becoming prominent in Illinois. Democrats borrowed heavily from their predecessor, the earlier Republican Party, the party of Thomas Jefferson, James Madison, and Aaron Burr. In general, Democrats followed Jefferson's ideas of society, especially valuing sturdy, independent yeomen farmers. Remote economic and political power, especially power associated with the federal government, worried them, as did national and even state projects, favoritism, insiders' schemes, and cities. Consequently, Democrats generally resisted federal activities, including internal improvements, a national bank, and protective tariffs. Fearful that connivers corrupted legislators, they sought fairness and protection via the People's Tribune, Andrew Jackson.

Jackson's ideas and actions concerning public lands, Indians, and the common man helped carry Illinois in the successful presidential campaigns of 1828 and 1832. Jacksonian Democrats, furthermore, filled Illinois' governor's office and elected most legislators, congressmen, and U.S. senators. Although dissension dogged Illinois' Democrats, they fared well.

Jackson did irritate Westerners by blocking such projects as federally sponsored roads. Nevertheless, in 1836 his protégé and

Vice President, Martin Van Buren, captured Illinois in his own presidential bid. Economic depression killed Van Buren's reelection bid in 1840, but he again carried Illinois. Whigs and Democrats jostled through the 1840s and beyond, until the Whig Party self-destructed in the mid-1850s over the Kansas-Nebraska Act and related issues. Nearly all Whigs then embraced today's Republican Party. This new, vigorous, northern-oriented party ousted Illinois Democrats, taking the governor's office, the legislature, and Congress. In 1858 and then in 1860, Stephen A. Douglas and Abraham Lincoln slugged it out in debates and elections. They addressed many issues, including the critical issue then shredding the country: racial slavery, its existence, and possible spread.

Inspired by the Erie Canal and federal improvements in lake and river transportation facilities at Chicago, state political figures erupted with enthusiasm. Even such Democrats as Governor John Reynolds and Democrat-turning-Whig Joseph Duncan pushed for internal improvements, Duncan favoring the Illinois & Michigan Canal. (Duncan believed private interests should construct railroads, so he vetoed legislation using state funds for internal improvements. His veto was overridden. He also opposed creating another State Bank of Illinois, favoring instead a national banking system.) Proponents of state support for internal improvements garnered ringing endorsements from pioneers in northern Illinois, most legislators, eastern lenders, and former Governor Edward Coles, who finagled financial arrangements from Philadelphia, the country's financial center.

By 1836 the state was sponsoring canal work, railroad schemes, and road improvements. On July 4, 1836, construction began on the Illinois & Michigan Canal, a grueling project delayed by depression, sickness, strife, and other problems. Canal laborers necessarily lived near disease-breeding water, and drinking water supplies brought death. Cholera sliced into the work force, displaying particular ferocity in 1845, whisking victims off in little more than a day. So many Irish immigrants died that one priest in La Salle observed, "The plague-stricken region was, with hardly an exception, Catholic."[11] Finally completed in 1848, the canal linked Chicago to the Illinois River, and with it the Mississippi River. Employing laborers, contractors, and hosts of allied people, it boosted towns like Ottawa and La Salle. It symbolized determination to join New York, Pennsylvania, Ohio, and Indiana in becoming enmeshed in developing regional and national economic systems. Transportation construction and breakthroughs helped settle northern Illinois, assisted by various levels of government which either funded them, or subsidized them, or even undertook them.[12]

Like the National Road in Illinois, the canal faced stiff competition upon completion, this time from railroads. As early as 1830, visionaries imagined trains whisking people and goods between the East Coast and Illinois. One bold prediction appeared on the front page of the *Hampshire Gazette* on December 22, 1830: "We shall breakfast at New-York, dine at Buffalo, sup at Detroit, and get to Green Bay early enough for parade the next morning." Railroads captivated public imagination. By 1839 twelve miles of track of the Northern Cross railroad linked Meredosia on the Illinois River to Morgan City, Illinois' first railroad and one of the first west of the Appalachians. Early western railroads usually connected rivers, lakes, and canals to each other or to towns. Even the ramshackle Northern Cross railroad, soon to be defunct, ignited alarm and jealousy. People worried about being left off its projected route.[13]

In 1839 a state legislative committee spelled out advantages of railroads, reporting that Illinoisans transacting business over 100 miles away normally consumed three days of travel each way, for a total of six days, and food for man and horse totaling $16.50. (These calculations omitted lodging costs and wear and tear on the horse.) Traveling the same distance via train would require less than one day each way, and cost just $13 for transportation and food.[14]

Private companies failed to raise sufficient capital to construct railroads, so lawmakers in early 1837 passed the Internal Improvements Act. It saddled Illinois with financial obligations for improvements worth $10 million, of which $3.5 million was dedicated to the Illinois Central Railroad.

This mammoth railroad was to run north from Cairo through Decatur and Bloomington, to the Illinois River and the western

end of the Illinois & Michigan Canal, and then stretch northwest to Galena. The legislature planned two east-west lines: the
Northern Cross Railroad, costing $1,850,000, linking Quincy,
Springfield, Danville, and Indiana; and the Southern Cross Railroad, costing $1,600,000, connecting Alton and Mt. Carmel, with
a branch forking southeast through Edwardsville to Shawneetown.

Planners also envisioned some shorter lines. One, projected to
cost $700,000, was to run from Warsaw on the Mississippi to
Peoria. At Peoria it would link with track stretching from
Bloomington to Mackinaw and Peoria, with a spur forking to
Pekin from Mackinaw and costing $350,000. Another line, to
cost $600,000, would run from lower Alton to Hillsboro and on
to the Illinois Central near Shelbyville. In the plan, it linked to
track running from the Illinois Central to Paris and then toward
Terre Haute, a line projected estimated to cost $650,000. A small
line was also slated to connect Belleville, Lebanon, and the Alton and Mt. Carmel line at a cost of $150,000.

Five facts about these plans deserve attention. First, it was a
true network, not just stray lines connecting unrelated places;
the design had system. Second, although proposed lines connected
river towns, the network would not merely supplement riverine
transportation, a role played by early railroads. Third, most track
would be in southern Illinois, where most people lived. This was
short-sighted, however, given northward waves of settlement.
Fourth, the railroads usually connected population clusters. Fifth,
no lines served Chicago or regions east and north of a line running from Danville to Decatur and north to Bloomington and
then Galena. Chicago was served by boats and roads and eagerly
awaited the canal. Poor drainage in eastern and northeastern Illinois inhibited developments there.

Lawmakers also addressed river transportation, appropriat-
ing hefty sums for river navigation improvements. The Rock,
Illinois, and Wabash rivers each received $100,000, the Kaskas-
kia and the Little Wabash $50,000 each.

The legislators had good intentions, charging the state with
creating and maintaining ambitious internal improvements. Prosperity and massive migration during the mid-1830s were heady,

encouraging speculation and risk-taking. Board members were dedicated, honest, and enthusiastic. Unforeseen defects, though, killed the railroad scheme and crippled other transportation projects.

The timing was terrible. The Internal Improvements Act of 1837 burdened Illinoisans with crushing debt and taxation in the very year in which economic depression engulfed the country. In 1838 the collapsing economy fell onto Governor Thomas Carlin, Joseph Duncan's successor. Commerce evaporated, demand for railroads plummeted, and Illinois' capacity to sustain construction flagged. Moreover, despite fine personnel, the project was highly ambitious, perhaps even for a robust economy. It outstripped existing engineering skills and technologies, materials and equipment, capital reserves, the labor pool, and managerial experience. Difficulties were insurmountable.

Only the track east from Meredosia, part of the Northern Cross, had traffic by late 1838, a frail train creaking along rickety track. By 1840 work virtually ceased, and lawmakers in 1840–1841 killed the scheme. Track finally reached Springfield in early 1842, far too late, and the line failed. Overall failure haunted Illinois for years.

* * *

A state bank was another unrealized dream, another victim of the depression. Ignoring the state's dismal record of a state bank in 1821, the Whig-dominated legislature conjured up another bank plan in 1834–1835, narrowly chartering the second State Bank of Illinois. Governor Joseph Duncan opposed it. Chartering such a bank in prosperous times was reasonable. Profits could be plowed into internal improvements. But times were anything but prosperous, and the bank soon exacerbated the state's economic woes.

Democrats and Whigs clashed over bank creation. Professing aversion to privilege, Democrats attacked the Second Bank of the United States in the election of 1832, later slaying it. Its demise spawned swarms of state and private banks, many undercapitalized, unregulated, and fragile, issuing worthless paper notes.

The State Bank of Illinois, headquartered in Springfield, had branches in Alton, Chicago, Galena, Jacksonville, and Vandalia, reflecting northward movements of population and commercial outlook of northern Illinois. In 1836 additional branches opened in Belleville, Danville, Mt. Carmel, and Quincy.

Capitalized at $1.5 million, with the state providing $100,000, the State Bank of Illinois appeared sound. But a cabal of self-serving insiders, including East Coast lenders, soon controlled the bank, and outside regulators had virtually no oversight. Speculation and cronyism dampened public confidence. Recognizing the institution's shaky condition, businesses in Cook County used private banks and private lines of credit, avoiding the Chicago branch.

Reeling from economic panic, the bank suspended specie payments by May. At the insistence of such Whigs as Abraham Lincoln and many Democrats, politicians refused to either scale back internal improvement projects or require the bank to surrender its charter, which it had violated by suspending specie payments.

Plans to secure eastern and European financial support failed, as did internal improvement projects. In mid-1841, the state defaulted on interest payments, killing confidence in bank notes. Many Illinoisans accepted only notes from Wisconsin and Indiana. Debt for stymied internal improvements and for collapsing state banks topped $15 million. Annual interest approached $800,000, crushing a state whose coffers took in less than $100,000 per year. Eventually, bank bonds were redeemed at forty-eight cents on the dollar.

Banks, state connections to banks, and paper notes so soured the public that for years demagogues frothed over state banks. Democrats leveled sustained fire against banks and bankers. National banking became feasible only when Republicans, the Whigs' successors, passed national banking acts in 1863 and 1864, providing order and stability for banks. Similarly, Republicans championed railroads and protective tariffs, old Whig planks.

The failure of the internal improvements schemes and the ongoing financial debt saddled the public, angering it. Despite the bipartisan birth of the schemes in the heady mid-1830s, people came to view the failed schemes as unwise, corrupt, and debilitating. Failed projects undermined public confidence in the legislature.[15]

* * *

Reflecting northward settlement during the 1830s, the state's center of population leaped from near Vandalia to a point directly east of Springfield. This was just southwest of the center point of Illinois' land mass, which lies on the boundary of Logan and Macon counties. Another ten years shifted the population center into Logan County, slightly east of Lincoln.

Macon and Macoupin counties were created in 1829, raising the total number to fifty-one, one-half today's total. A flurry of county-creation followed: Coles and McLean in 1830, and then Cook, Effingham, Jasper, La Salle, and Rock Island in 1831. Of thirty-six counties created during the 1830s, only eight were on or below the latitude of Springfield. The decade saw the creation of thirteen of the northern fourteen counties; the fourteenth, Jo Daviess County, had been formed in 1827 amid booming lead mining.

As population surged northward, Springfield became the state capital in 1839. It was a major economic and social plum. To win it, the town bested Alton, Jacksonville, Peoria, and Illiopolis. Springfield's location gave northern and central Illinois better access to government machinery, symbolized compromise between early southern inhabitants and influxes of Northerners, and reflected the northward-moving frontier. The capital's relocation testified that future settlement, prosperity, and power lay in northern Illinois. Fights over the capital's location were understandable, as were contests over county creation and county-seat location. Despite demagogic rhetoric and very high stakes for individuals and the disputing communities, the struggles were essentially peaceful. Quarreling partisans rarely administered or received whacks and bumps.

County seats and other towns often sparked controversies, but they also spawned schools, lyceums, and important meetings. Furthermore, river towns enjoyed unique functions until railroads appeared. River towns sported warehousing, brokerage,

forwarding, and insuring activities, and they repaired, outfitted,
and supplied steamboats. Steamboats consumed huge quantities of cordwood, which landings provided. River towns attracted
milling and manufacturing, powered by overshot waterwheels
and steam. Ferryboats and, later, bridges crossed the rivers at
some towns, funneling land transportation to them. Early railroads linked towns on navigable water with points inland. Only
railroads threatened river towns, and some languished or even
shriveled, then prospered wildly once tracks reached them and
crossed the river. The choices made by influential town leaders
shaped town growth.

Although towns played vital economic roles, they also exhibited social, cultural, and even ideological features. Many people
settled in towns to preserve cherished ways of life. For example,
New Englanders and then Germans settling in Quincy cultivated
transplanted values. Mormons chose Nauvoo, and then Icarians
planted their communal experiment there. New England's prairie colonies were far more than economic constructs. Towns reflected values, aspirations, decisions, and contingencies, not just
economic forces.[16]

* * *

A crucial fact affected the development of nineteenth-century
towns. During warm months, prevailing winds cross Illinois from
the west and southwest. In most cases, the finest residences and
stores, evidence suggests, expanded *westward* from the town's
center, *west* of business and industrial sections. Towns were
wooden, and fires could devastate them. Those living upwind—
to the west—from the central business district and manufacturing avoided wind-driven sparks. They also were spared, especially on sultry days after rain, odors emanating from the great
numbers of horses, mules, and other animals inhabiting towns,
and the stink of tanning, butchering, and other such operations.
Sharp westerly and southwesterly winds swept dried streets, blow-
ing dust and smells downwind into houses and buildings. These
often had long front lawns, giving some protection from airborne
nuisances, but houses upwind were spared entirely. Wood and
coal for heating, cooking, and manufacturing blanketed towns

in smoke. Even slight breezes prevented smoke from drifting upwind, sparing upwind residents from various ailments. Even with imperfect knowledge about disease, people wanted to live upwind from garbage, offal, smoke, and stagnant water. More-over, winds drove mosquitoes, flies, and similar pests downwind, to lee parts of town.[17] Similarly, for those living upwind, unpleas-ant noises were minimized. (Farmers understood prevailing wind principles, almost always building houses upwind from barn-yards, henhouses, and pigpens, and rarely putting barnyards to the north of barns.)

Fine residences not located upwind usually had other mitigat-ing factors, such as being built on hills. Regardless of their loca-tion in a town, higher elevations attracted wealthier people. Both floods and the stench of damp and unhealthy ground could be avoided there, and hill dwellers benefitted from breezes and lovely views. Further, living on "the hill" made a social statement. Poorer townsfolk generally lived in low-lying sections of towns.

The relative quantity of woodland and prairie influenced town site selection. In 1834 a region encompassing twenty-six counties ran roughly from Beardstown to Danville and from Decatur to Ottawa. Nearly all towns platted in this region were west of a line drawn from Decatur through Bloomington to Ottawa. (Dan-ville and Urbana were notable exceptions.) West of this line, wood-land was plentiful. Moreover, virtually all thirty-five towns plat-ted by 1834 west of the line were platted near the timber-prairie edge, the boundary separating woodlands from grasslands. Very few towns—or farms, for that matter—were founded far from tongues of woodland stretching into prairies. Between 1835 and 1837, 189 towns were platted in the twenty-six counties, the vast majority west of the line connecting Decatur, Bloomington, and Ottawa. Of the towns founded during the 1830s, 84 percent were near the prairie-timber margin. Few towns were platted in east-ern parts of the region, where Grand Prairie offered skimpy tim-ber supplies. Newspaper advertisements extolled prairie towns, depicting nearby prairies as rich, rolling, and beautiful—and well-drained. Even so, poor drainage afflicted the region's eastern parts, tagging them with a bad reputation. Some parts opened only with railroads in the 1850s, and railroads heavily influenced town

Smoke from a locomotive and a factory wafts above a
church steeple in a community fortunate enough to
secure rail service. *A Guide to the Illinois Central
Railroad Lands.* Chicago: Illinois Central Railroad
Office, 1859. ILLINOIS STATE HISTORICAL LIBRARY, A DIVISION OF
THE ILLINOIS HISTORIC PRESERVATION AGENCY.

location there. In short, several factors influenced town location,
the most important being proximity to the timber-prairie margin.[18]

These 189 towns illustrate much. Advertisements for the towns
emphasized fine soil, access to timber, good water, and similar
considerations. One study of advertisements associated with thirty
towns founded in western Illinois between 1835 and 1838 reveal
that four advantages appeared in over half of the advertisements:
rich land, distance from other towns, availability of timber, proximity to navigable water. Mentioned in from 40 to 50 percent of
the advertisements were roads, mill or water power, beauty of
site, and prairie.[19] Survival rates of the 189 towns, however, largely
hinged on one factor: proximity to competitors. Only 22 percent
of the towns platted within two miles of a competitor, 31 percent
of those platted five to six miles from competition, and 57 percent platted more than seven miles from competition survived.
In sum, increased distance meant increased chances of survival.
Clearly, survival required certain size hinterlands. Stiff, physi-

cally close competition compressed hinterlands, killing off poorly located towns. Probably over half the failures occurred by 1840, economic tribulation weeding out the unfit. Others expired by 1860, after failing to attract railroads. Towns surviving to 1870 tended to still exist in the 1970s.

With increased population density, though, only six or eight miles separated towns. By the early 1850s in sixteen central Illinois counties, the average distance between towns in nearly every county was between six and nine miles.

* * *

A few words on the development of several towns from the 1830s may shed some light on their success or failure. Alton, founded in 1814 by Rufus Eaton of Connecticut, had a promising start, thanks to Eaton's political connections and his eye for a good town site. Located about midway between St. Louis and the confluence of the Illinois and Mississippi rivers, just upstream from the Missouri's mouth, it boasted a good landing, limestone deposits, and nearby coal. Alton soon served surrounding communities as a wholesale and forwarding center, a place through which local businessmen sent goods to their ultimate destination. Eastern capital buoyed Alton's merchants, granting them sway over sizeable market areas. Its pork and beef packing industry flourished for decades. It was assumed that Alton would become the state's railroad hub. Eager to outstrip nearby St. Louis, Alton also vied to become the new state capital. But by 1837 its political aspirations had fizzled, and the death of the crusading Elijah P. Lovejoy (see chapter 12), accompanied by economic depression, scarred the town.

Jacksonville, founded as the county seat of Morgan County in 1825, hoped to become both state capital and Illinois' premier city. Although it failed in these two endeavors, it succeeded in others. Illinois' oldest continuously published newspaper began operations there in 1831. By 1833 Illinois College, the Ladies' Education Society, and the Jacksonville Female Academy (which merged with Illinois College in 1903) had been established. In late 1833 a Congregational Church, the fifth in Illinois, was organized. Governor Joseph Duncan, a Democrat from Kentucky who broke with Andrew Jackson, quietly became a Whig, and served from 1834 to 1838, and Stephen A. Douglas, a rising State's Attorney and prominent Democrat, both resided there. In 1839 Jacksonville obtained the Illinois School for the Deaf. Later it acquired the Illinois School for the Blind and the state insane asylum. All of these institutions provided a critical mass of educated people for other cultural activities, including music. Jacksonville's roles as county seat and regional forwarding point for a rich agricultural area enhanced growth and stability. By 1839 the Northern Cross Railroad, the state's first railroad, tenuously linked Jacksonville and the Illinois River, and the Jacksonville Woolen Mills took root in town. Population jumped from 446 inhabitants in 1830 to about 1,900 in 1840—not uncommon growth for a new town in the northern half of Illinois.

Capitalizing on a fine location, Quincy's population jumped from six hundred in 1834, its year of incorporation, to 1,500 by 1838, making it the largest settlement in the Military Tract. Kentuckians and New Englanders in about equal proportions made up the bulk of its population. Its surrounding rich agricultural land, trade along the Mississippi, early industries, and population mix served the city well. Quincy received fleeing Black Hawk War refugees, New Englanders in 1836, and Germans a year later. In 1837 some three hundred steamboats arrived or left. Quincy obtained a city charter in 1840, when milling, shipping, meatpacking, and retailing were important. Galena and Springfield also prospered during the 1830s.

Chicago contained just 150 residents and several rude huts in early 1832, the year the first steamboats docked there. In 1833, when it was founded as a town, it boasted some 350 residents and 150 houses. Reaching a population of 1,800 the next year, it had 4,170 residents in 1837, when it was incorporated.[20] Shrugging off economic turbulence, Chicago was poised in 1837 for its rise to prominence. On October 25, 1839, Albert Parker, a Bostonian, wrote that Chicago had no carriages or handcarts, only wagons; hogs, dogs, geese, and hens ran loose through the streets.

But during the 1830s fledgling Chicago lured energetic, visionary, and socially attuned settlers from New England and New York: men such as John Stephen Wright, "Long John" Wentworth, and Walter L. Newberry.[21] Wright dabbled in retailing, real estate, publishing, manufacturing, and myriad other activities. An unabashed booster, he lauded Chicago's virtues, attracting eastern investments and settlers. He founded the *Prairie Farmer*, which extolled the state's agriculture.[22] Wentworth joined him in entrepreneurial and booster quests. Six feet six inches tall and a recent graduate of Dartmouth College, he published the *Chicago Democrat*, agitated for a state charter for Chicago, and launched and boosted civic projects for over fifty years. Newberry speculated in urban lots, made a fortune, lavished money on his adopted town, and helped create the Chicago Public Library. He also left money to found the Newberry Library.

Others from the Northeast contributed in many ways to the growth of Chicago. For example, they promoted meat-packing, which helped define and channel Chicago's growth for generations. Large-scale slaughtering, salting, smoking, packing, and shipping of meat—especially pork—occurred as early as 1835. The indomitable Gurdon Saltonstall Hubbard, a Vermonter, spearheaded meat processing, and two other men with New England ties, Philip D. Armour and Gustavus Swift, augmented and extended Hubbard's efforts.

Born in New York in 1805, William Butler Ogden served in the New York legislature, advocating using state resources to construct the New York and Erie Railroad.[23] Persuaded by his capitalist brother-in-law, Charles Butler, he migrated to Chicago in 1835, immersed himself in real estate, made a fortune, and in 1837 became Chicago's first mayor. A city councilman for many years thereafter, he championed railroad construction, served as president of the Galena & Chicago Union Railroad, and backed educational, civic, and political projects. Russell Heacock of Connecticut became Chicago's first lawyer in 1827, and pushed temperance and abolition. In 1832 Elijah Dewey Harmon, a Vermonter, became the community's first physician.

In the 1830s, then, Chicago was not terribly impressive, but that decade paved the way for the village to become the Second City.

Numerous town foundings, mostly in northern regions, reflected settlement's hubbub in Illinois. Among them were Joliet (1831),

Aurora and Rockford settled (1834), Elgin, Waukegan, and Freeport (1835), Winnetka started (1836), Pottsville settled (1837), and Nauvoo founded (1839). Significantly, six of the state's seven most populous towns in 1840 incorporated after 1830. Only Alton, with 2,340 residents in 1840, incorporated before 1830.

Other older towns slumped, including Vandalia. An insignificant village, Vandalia failed to capitalize on being made the state capital in 1819, and stagnated. As settlement flooded northward and new counties were created, the capital relocated after twenty years. Springfield topped several rivals, partly because of its central location; Vandalia reverted to being county seat of Fayette County.

* * *

Meager financial resources and negative attitudes dogged education in early Illinois shortly after statehood. The state of formal education for years after statehood was deplorable; public education was virtually nonexistent. Southerners, moreover, expressed mixed views concerning the topic, and few favored taxation to support it. In 1825 state law provided for free common schools in each county, open to all white citizens to the age of twenty-one. In 1827, however, another law, declaring that no person could "be taxed without his consent," undermined tax-supported schools and resuscitated subscription schools—schools supported by parents' quarterly fees to itinerant teachers—which flourished into the 1850s, in the absence of state-supported education.

By the mid-1830s, prosperity, rocketing population, and influxes of Yankees and others augured favorably for education.[24] Although Woodford County was not created until 1841, school attendance there was impressive as early as 1836–1837: of 599 people between the ages of six and twenty-one years, a whopping 549 attended school, or about 91.5 percent. Almost 94 percent of the females in this group attended, as did just under 90 percent of the males. Woodford County was similar to other counties, being settled first by Hoosiers and upper southern folk, and then by many Northeasterners. Perhaps its attendance figures were typical. Another source notes that of 472,254 white persons in Illinois in 1840 only 27,502 over twenty-one years of age could neither

read nor write.²⁵ Almost certainly, among foreign-born Illinoisans the proportion of illiterate adults was relatively high. Interestingly, over decades school attendance may have declined.

The 1830s brought other transitions. A group of young men—
the Yale Band—from Yale College founded Illinois College in 1829
at Jacksonville, classes opening in January of 1830. In 1835 it
graduated Illinois' first college class, consisting of two young men.
One was Kentucky-born Richard Yates, who as governor of Illinois during the Civil War skillfully supported Abraham Lincoln
and the Union. Most residents around Jacksonville, though, had
southern roots, which embroiled some in controversy with Yankees over such matters as abolition.

Three institutions founded in 1833 enhanced education. The
Convent of the Ladies of Visitation was established at Kaskaskia by representatives from the mother house in Georgetown,
District of Columbia, and soon scores of students studied literature, math, and music. It opened in 1836, but the great Mississippi flood of 1844 forced its abandonment. The Illinois Institute of
Education, designed to bolster statewide education, met in Vandalia. To assist college students, the Ladies' Education Society
organized in October in Jacksonville. (It exists today, and is allegedly the country's oldest, continuously functioning women's
society.)

One member of the Yale Band, the Rev. Theron Baldwin,
stopped in 1834 at Captain Benjamin Godfrey's home, five miles
north of Alton. Both were New Englanders, religious, and promoters of education. After a career at sea, Captain Godfrey went
into business in Alton. Wishing to promote education for wom-
en, he, Baldwin, and others established Monticello Female Seminary, whose main building opened in early 1838. This seminary
in the town of Godfrey educated generations of women before
folding in 1971.

Asa Fitch of Greenville helped form the Greenville Polemical
Society. He wrote on December 6, 1830, that he had drafted a
constitution for the society patterned after debating societies he
had joined in the Northeast, but modified to fit the state of society in Greenville. A similar society appeared in New Salem. Although the village was predominately southern during its brief

existence, perhaps its northern residents spearheaded the New Salem Debating Club, to which Abraham Lincoln belonged.

Josiah Holbrook, a Yale College graduate, inaugurated the lyceum movement in 1826 in Millbury, Massachusetts. Various lyceum organizations in 1831 coalesced into the American Lyceum, and later that year the first branch was formed in central Illinois, at Illinois College. By 1834 over three thousand local branches peppered the country. The Sangamon County Lyceum was founded in 1833, and about two years later the Young Men's Lyceum was organized in Springfield. Lyceums provided forums for discussion and debate, accumulated libraries, and supported schools. Often meeting in schools and churches, they inculcated civic virtue and responsibility, qualities vital to the Republic's survival, and fostered young men's speaking skills and organizational talents. The Sangamon County Lyceum selected topics from five areas: history, health and medicine, culture, politics, and science. Specific topics included blood circulation, geological activity, phrenology, whether married people were happier than single people, and colonization efforts. Newspapers reprinted accounts of some meetings. Typically, lyceum leaders were Whigs, but local branches were nonpartisan. Lyceums supported civic events, including boisterous Fourth of July celebrations. In sum, these institutions nurtured keen and ambitious people, including Abraham Lincoln, who spoke at the Young Men's Lyceum in early 1838, shortly after arriving in Springfield.[26] As frontier Illinois faded, lyceums flickered out of existence, but colleges and Chautauqua events filled the vacuum.

Churches provided moral instruction. Roman Catholicism in Illinois, after years of neglect and decline, revived and grew. Other churches also harvested souls. The Episcopal Church founded its first parish in Illinois in 1832, in Jacksonville. The Congregational Association formed three years later, giving nascent Congregational congregations a statewide superstructure.

A massive construction at Alton instructed Illinoisans and signified both change and continuity; Illinois built its first penitentiary, a limestone, fortress-like structure, which welcomed its first guests in 1833. It made two important statements. First, dire labor shortages no longer afflicted frontier Illinois, so incarceration now awaited adult males convicted of non-capital offenses; convicts no longer received corporal punishment and then resumed work in society. Second, the penitentiary reaffirmed traditional values and assumptions. Scofflaws, people believed, voluntarily rejected wholesome lives and chose criminal careers. Accordingly, society incarcerated wrongdoers for three purposes: to protect law-abiding folk from predators, to punish, and to rehabilitate. The penitentiary impressed on criminals the wrongfulness of their crimes, the need for restitution, and society's rights. It isolated prisoners from each other and encouraged them to contemplate their transgressions. The penitentiary, people insisted, made convicts penitent. To produce penitents, the public brooked no schools for crime, no prisons producing hardened criminals. Rather, the penal system shielded new convicts from evil and demanded they toil fifteen hours per day, sufficiently fatiguing them so they had little energy for nefarious activities. Prisoners produced food, fiber, and other sustenance, more than paying for their upkeep and filling the state's coffers. The penal system helped convicts pay their debts to society.

* * *

By 1840 settlers largely overcame a natural barrier. Rational and irrational concerns about prairies had delayed settlement of the Military Tract.[27] Experience helped settlers lay aside irrational fears of prairies, and gradually, as early as the 1820s, Europeans, Northerners, and others strode directly onto prairies, hardly considering forests. Settlers thronged the Military Tract's prairies, and throughout northern Illinois pioneers snapped up prairie land. A new era in frontier Illinois dawned, especially after 1837 when John Deere, a Vermont native who settled in Grand Detour, manufactured smooth, self-scouring steel plowshares, which sliced open matted roots of prairie grass, turned rich soil, and enabled prairie farmers to plow and produce more.

Although improved transportation overcame distance and farms and towns helped tame the wilds, nature still packed a punch. The lethal, legendary Deep Snow punctuated 1830–31. Following downpours, deep, unrelenting snow blanketed Illinois, killing humans and animals and etching itself in personal and collective memories. Some persons simply vanished, while others' remains were found with spring's melt. Lingering cold hurt corn, game was scarce for years, and cotton fields in southern Illinois perished, never rebounding. Some Brown County residents gave up and fled. Stalwart residents of Pike County stuck it out, despite dangerously depleted liquor supplies. Indians slew immobilized animals, amassing extraordinary meat supplies. Spring melt water turned creeks into impassable torrents, restricting movement. From 1832 into 1834, cholera swept some survivors to their graves.

Nature struck again in late 1836. Snow melt covered Illinois with pools and slush. On balmy December 20 a fast-moving, icy front sliced eastward, freezing pools and slush solid in minutes. Persons caught in the open raced for shelter, many not making it. Cattle, hogs, birds, and other animals froze fast to the ground and died. One quick-thinking horseman sliced open his horse and crawled inside it to stay warm; there he was found, frozen to death.[28] Andrew Heredith, driving over 1,000 hogs toward St. Louis, reached a point eight miles south of Scottville when the cold front hit. He and his assistants fled by wagons to safety, barely making it, but anguished hogs piled upon each other for warmth. Those on the bottom suffocated, while those on the outside of the pile froze, creating a pyramid of 500 dead hogs. Surviving hogs suffered horribly.[29]

Nature's triple onslaught—the Deep Snow, cholera, and the Sudden Freeze—and the Black Hawk War were milestones. Of course, commonplace diseases brought grief, tree-tossing tornadoes rattled settlers, prairie fires blackened billowing grasses, floods swept victims to watery graves, and extreme heat killed people. But settlers never again underwent such ordeals by nature. They were defining moments, great divides. For decades, survivors reckoned dates of births, marriages, deaths, and other important events from the Deep Snow, or the Sudden Freeze. Survivors prided themselves on having borne nature's fury, considering themselves true settlers—the "Old Settlers"—and regarding later arrivals as untested upstarts.

12.

SOCIAL CLASHES AND ECONOMIC COLLAPSE

The 1830s saw individuals, households, and complete colonies arrive in Illinois. Colonial efforts were nothing new. New Design, for example, received groups of Virginians during the 1790s, English colonies alighted in Monroe County and Edwards County by 1819, the humane Ferdinand Ernst led German households to Vandalia in 1820 and 1821, and a cluster from Yorkshire, England, settled at Lynnville in 1829. Practicing chain migration, individuals and households migrated, got established, and helped relatives and friends migrate and settle. For example, in 1830 Jabez Beebe of New York wintered near Fort Edwards and then settled on a military bounty claim. In 1832 his sister, her husband, and their six children arrived from New York. Beebe housed them, sold them land, and helped them adjust.

Chain migration and group migration ushered many Yankees, other Northerners, and foreigners to Illinois, especially to the northern half—the booming half—stamping that region with unique imprints. Group migrations from the Northeast, England, Scotland, the German states, Belgium, Norway, Sweden, and even the Azores speckled the landscape with place names and other reminders of these undertakings.[1] Some colonies had religious impulses, some were social or economic experiments, and others were efforts of like-minded folk of similar backgrounds eager to settle in a strange land and form new lives together. Limited southern group migration continued, built largely around kinship networks and congregations and a few planters who rejected slavery and came north to free their slaves and start a new life.

Yankees cherished commerce, institutions, education, formal contracts, precision in speech, civic duty, work ethic, order, belief in progress, and involvement in larger society. They exuded a desire to pool resources and talents for common goals, enforce community norms, commit reforms, and form tightly knit societies. They shared many of these traits with Anglo-Dutch New Yorkers, members of a hybrid society that had its roots in the 1660s. Over decades, this hybrid Anglo-Dutch culture received infusions of westward-wending Yankees in upstate New York. Among most transplanted New Englanders, zealous Puritans had long since transformed themselves into questing, reforming, talented Yankees, people not unlike Anglo-Dutch New Yorkers. Perhaps settlers who came to Illinois from New York were more inclined to see the world in terms of win-win eyes than settlers who arrived straight from New England, who were more apt to bring ingrained assumptions, habits, and procedures, as well as focused, stern answers to life's questions and proper forms of worship and behavior. Even so, New Yorkers and Yankees shared many values as they settled in Illinois, often functioning in ways that were indistinguishable. Consequently, collective purpose, written constitutions, and other covenants often girded many northern colonies in Illinois. Even when a formal covenant was absent, many communities operated as though they had one.

Yankees reveled in a sense of mission, a fondness for community, and a passion to perfect themselves and (especially) their neighbors. Brimming with reformist impulses, they advocated many causes, including education, temperance, abolition, and humane care of impaired people. They comforted the afflicted, afflicted the comfortable, and throttled the degenerate. To advance, protect, and channel their undertakings, they spawned institutions, civic groups, and schools. They placed great stock in the printed word, order, moderation, thrift, and deferment of personal gratification. Living "under the full gaze of their ancestors," and devoted to both the past and posterity, they cheerfully endured today's hardships. Their powerful, indelible impact redirected regional and national history.

New Englanders pushed reform for several reasons. Chronic concern—even dread—about social havoc caused by ignorance, sloth, selfishness, alcohol, and slavery kept them agitated. Moreover, they sympathized with downtrodden and vulnerable people. Having divested themselves of grim Puritan views of humanity, many touted human potential for progress. They believed they could eradicate ills and attain lofty goals via education, reform, and personal regeneration. (Interestingly, Abraham Lincoln, a native of Kentucky, shared these concerns and hopes.) Having never felt the sting of Indian attacks, most showed little antipathy toward Indians, often idealizing them instead. They sometimes wore their ideas of social justice on their sleeves, thereby annoying others. Their sense of the commonweal—the overall good of the community—was highly developed, and they eagerly curbed individuals who threatened social harmony and well-being.

Many Yankees, moreover, felt beleaguered, giving urgency to the task of transplanting New England culture. Political decline, economic and social dislocations, and feelings of loss taxed them. The embarrassing Hartford Convention, the debacle of the Federalist Party, John Adams's death in 1826, President John Quincy Adams's defeat in 1828, and concern about national moral fiber weighed on them. In ousting Adams in 1828, Andrew Jackson, uncouth slaveowner upstart, swept the South and West, garnering Illinois' three electoral votes. Yearly, New England's population shriveled as a percentage of national population. Irish Roman Catholic immigrants in Massachusetts unleashed nativist fury. High taxes and increasing Great Lakes agricultural competition hammered Yankee farmers, some adjusting by turning to dairying, orchards, and sheep raising. Urbanization and industrialization beckoned Yankees' sons and daughters, disturbing many. *Nouveau riches* elbowed their way into power. Perceived western opportunities, moreover, beckoned New Englanders, dissolving increasingly lukewarm ties to their native states. In short, dislocations, relative decline, and anxiety motivated many Yankees to shore up Yankee ways and export them, with profound results in Illinois.

Various pressures in New England, combined with urgent social sentiments and lure of western attractions, convinced entire segments of communities, often groups of younger men and young households, to seek greener pastures in Illinois via organized colonies, often led by Congregational ministers, who imbued members with lofty understandings of mission. Although New England Puritanism transformed itself into Congregationalism and even Unitarianism by the early 1800s, thereby losing much of its stern religious stuff and dynamism, New England still spawned group undertakings of moral significance that imposed tight social and economic restraints on members and others. New England's towns, along with the region's colleges and seminaries, launched numerous group migrations, planting instant communities across northern Illinois. In addition, eastern speculators and other businessmen sponsored group migrations, seeking tidy profits.

* * *

Southern world views largely reflected Gallic-Celtic views, emphasizing certain traits: loyalty, family and clan, emotion and honor, standing against the world, and a desire to be left alone. Most Southerners had Scots-Irish, Scots, or Anglo-Celtic roots. Steeped in Calvinistic understandings of people and the world, tempered for some by pietism or Anglicanism, they also held many Jeffersonian notions of society, politics, and the crucial importance of yeomen farmers for the Republic's survival. Most ordinary southern settlers distrusted permanent institutions, other than local churches, and kept them at arms' length. Dreading arbitrary power and its abuses, they feared sustained collective uses of power, especially remote power over which they had little control. They relied on ad hoc, limited-purpose efforts to accomplish immediate goals. Indifferent to and even scornful of formal education, many southern settlers, even elites, had minimal schooling, harbored pessimistic and fatalistic thoughts, and suspected complex, interdependent society and modernity. Although southern elites often gravitated toward towns, most Southerners settled on the land and in tiny hamlets, preferring selective social involvement. Exhibiting little concern for the commonweal, they rarely joined voluntaristic organizations. Although southern settlers from all walks of life engaged in politics and church life, few had enough spare time, inclination, or wealth to form or join secular social organizations. Most were indifferent or hostile to reforms, but some touted temperance and personal regeneration, usually within a religious context. A few came north after either renouncing slavery and freeing their slaves or clashing with slavery and slaveowners, but far fewer became zealous cultural warriors, cloaked with righteousness and bolstered by ongoing support from native states. Appreciating and practicing oral traditions and artful stories, many disdained written contracts, relying instead on a handshake, good name, and honor. They generally kept to themselves, maintaining a few close friends, and defended family and personal reputation with zeal and even fury. Valuing being left alone, they left others alone. Many had little worldly success, often feeling buffeted by society, nature, or Providence. Many were traditionalists, people for whom ritual and stability were important. In short, they wanted to create few institutions—other than local churches—grind no ideological axes, and refrain from remaking their neighbors or the rest of society in their image. Success for some people, they lamented, meant failure for others; a win-lose worldview existed in their minds. They valued enduring—and often fierce—personal and kinship ties and feelings of independence. Frequently regarded by others as lethargic, they sometimes exploded impulsively. Many touted a high sense of personal honor and courtly behavior toward women. Finally, southern settlers had a keen sense of place, a strong affinity for the land, and a belief that association with specific locales provided people with identity and meaning.[2]

Most southern settlers were used to manual labor and outdoor life, eking out a fairly marginal existence. Men hunted, and many trapped and fished. Most farmed, some accompanying their produce to markets on flatboats and other river craft. Most women raised children, prepared meals, kept house, tended the infirm and dying, and served as mainstays for local congregations.

Into the 1820s and even beyond, southern settlers formed the cutting edge of frontier Illinois. Anecdotal evidence suggests that most footloose men living alone in the wilds or as members of small clusters of men on society's fringes hailed from the South. They had few traits Northerners valued. Although many southern settlers opposed slavery and fled to Illinois, Yankees resented efforts in 1823–1824 to graft the institution onto Illinois. Yankee-southern squabbles in Illinois involving slavery, culture, and other matters reached crescendo proportions between the mid-1830s and mid-1850s. Residual French and increasing numbers of foreigners compounded north-south spats.

Abhorring many southern traits, Yankees labored to either change Southerners or mitigate the effects of southern culture. At the same time they buttressed Yankee culture. Furthermore, New Englanders and others seized moral high ground, setting much of the national agenda from it. Yankees berated Southerners and others from pulpits, schools, public offices, and the press. For example, *The Liberator* began blaring abolitionism from Boston on January 1, 1831, the year Nat Turner's slave rebellion seared southern Virginia. But relatively few northern settlers in Illinois were outright abolitionists; for a variety of reasons, most just wanted to keep slavery from spreading.

After abolitionist forces shook the country in 1831, the South reacted by clamping down. Southern authorities squelched dissent, silenced or drove out dissenters, and fostered a garrison-state mentality. Reverberations of strife over slavery jarred frontier Illinois. Simmering tensions between early southern settlers and the increasing trickle of Northeasterners were brought to the boiling point during the 1830s, when abolitionist Elijah P. Lovejoy was killed by a mob. Although such violence was rare in Illinois, it sundered social fabric in countless ways, large and small, and brought intensity to the state's political and social life, the urgency mounting yearly.

Meanwhile, New Englanders wrote and rewrote history, extolling New England history, myths, and life. These writings combated a quartet of foes: slavery and its northern allies; pioneers who either gleefully abandoned social restraints and led dissolute lives or who tried and failed to replicate civilized society; Roman Catholicism, which had fretted New England's Puritans and which Yankees believed menaced the Mississippi Valley and America's future; residual French and Spanish residents of the Valley, Irish, and some Germans, whom Yankees sometimes regarded as ignorant, shiftless, often besotted, and potentially dangerous allies of Catholicism and agents of degeneracy.[3]

In concocting myth and rewriting history, Yankees highlighted three related New England images: village, village green, and sturdy yeomen. This trinity, Yankees asserted, planted civilization, assaulted nature, and furthered Puritan mission. They served up several social ideals: seamless social harmony, uplifting town meetings, tempered Whig resistance to tyranny, unbridled civic responsibility, burning thirst for learning, focused mission, and New England exceptionalism in American history. Timothy Dwight and other Yankees peddled such self-serving histories in the early republic. They consciously placed "the image of the New England village before the American public as the ideal model for domesticity and community."[4] Tidy village greens and sturdy yeomen had mastered wilderness inhabitants, and they could overcome spirited and spontaneous Southerners. This myth-making, this fabricated history, accompanied settlement in region after region.

Yankees and others assaulted traditional southern culture in various ways. After statehood they attacked near-monopolies which Southerners enjoyed in politics, society, and economics. These assaults did not swamp or submerge southern settlers the way waves of American settlers had submerged French society—Southerners were far too numerous, and their grip on political machinery was far too strong—but as the frontier faded during the 1850s southern influence was eclipsed.

Hard-driving Yankees and others feared nature's apparent chaos and accompanying sloth. In school texts, newspapers, sermons, and private admonitions, they warned themselves and others about indolence. Illinois was bountiful, but therein lay danger; abundance enabled shiftless folk to scrape by and degenerate.[5] As early as 1819, observers warned against the danger: "A living is so easily obtained in this rich country that the most industrious of the inhabitants soon grow indolent."[6] On July 7,

1834, Morris Slight expressed delight and concern over conditions along the River Du Page. Writing back to Dutchess County, New York, he enthused, "I never saw a place in the west I like better than this. Move my family and friends here I should never want to return. It is an easy country to live in." He then warned, "Tho the danger I see is that the people will grow indolent as the little labor it takes to provide abundance." Vienna Winslow wrote from Babcock's Grove (later Lombard) on November 25, 1852, to her sister, Statira, back in Maine. She described with disdain the ease of living and its impact: "People labour here about in the same way that I always supposed they did. They have time enough, no hurry. They lie in bed until 7, or half past in the morning & are sure to be found in bed by 9 in the evening."

Southerners in particular, Yankees carped, were susceptible to sloth and indolence, overlaid with decadence. For example, Ebenezer Welch wrote on September 19, 1841, from Monmouth to Monmouth, Maine. He described corn ten to twelve feet high, luscious melons, and other bounties of nature, adding, "Here in the west things grow almost spontaneously, at any rate they far exceed my expectations. I think a man can raise 10 bu. of corn with less labor than he can with one in Maine." He then pounced on southern settlers around Monmouth: "Their greatest desire seems to be to live easily. In their work they are slovenish, & care but little about improvements. . . . They think the Yankees are very extravagant in their living, building, dress, &c." Welch obviously believed Yankees could handle Illinois' abundance, but Southerners could not.

As was true of many Northerners, Ebenezer Welch and others jabbed at irritating southern cultural traits, not at southern stands on slavery or race. On July 25, 1838, the *New England Farmer and Gardener's Journal* discussed western drawbacks without mentioning slavery, race, or Elijah P. Lovejoy's recent death. Instead, it counseled against indolence. Some regarded Southerners as wastrels, likening southern culture to barbarism. Ardent Yankees saw "the Southerner as a lean, lank, lazy creature, burrowing in a hut, rioting in whisky, dirt, and ignorance."

Some Southerners did relax ostentatiously, even elevating relaxation to an art form. Ever-vigilant Yankees focused keen concern on them. One account extolled noble Yankee yeoman traits, by implication blasting southern ones:

> They were not broken down aristocrats; they were not dissolute members of powerful families; they belonged to the middle ranks of society; they were men of lofty virtue, iron wills; always consulting conscience, never policy; loving home and native land, they left both in search of freedom, and finding it, they cherished it with the zeal and devotion of martyrs. They hated civil and religious despotism. They sought a new home, not for plunder, not for conquest, but for liberty of conscience. The New Englander moved westward bearing with him his free-school system and printing press, and with these a Northern State is better than a Southern State, and the north end of a Northern State better than the South end of the same State, etc., etc.

This airy appraisal reflected views shared by many Northerners.

Southerners, they insisted, shuddered at the thought of education and its impact on clergy and others and measured the quality of preaching by decibel, ardor, and sincerity.[7] Many Southerners did fret about clergy who preached from notes, failed to get emotionally drained, and displayed telltale signs of book learning. Formal education, they feared, might lead the faithful astray.

* * *

Pilloried and scorned, southern settlers struck back. They disliked northern assertiveness in business transactions and zest in other activities. They believed Yankees and other Northerners were excessively sharp in dealings and unforgiving in their practices. To be "Yankeed" meant to be swindled by someone from the Northeast, or at least to have succumbed to the sales pitch of such a person. Stories of Yankee peddlers foisting off shoddy or misrepresented wares, such as wooden nutmegs, made the rounds, doing much to reinforce stereotypes. The occasional itinerant shyster from the Nutmeg State or elsewhere in New England lent credulity to anti-Yankee sentiment. Because so many Yankees preached reform and social concern, the sharp dealers and outright swindlers from the Northeast exposed all Yankees to charges of hypocrisy.

One source noted, "The Southerners regarded the Yankees as a skinning, tricky, penurious race of peddlers, filling the country with tin ware, brass clocks, and wooden nutmegs." Early southern settlers in Woodford County encountered Yankee peddlers who convinced them "the genuine Yankee was a close, miserly, dishonest, selfish getter of money, void of generosity, hospitality or any of the kinder feelings of human nature." They concluded that Yankees' "grand aim was to get money, and to cling to it with deathlike tenacity after they had got it." Southern settlers "would have welcomed as freely a colony of Hottentots or cannibals, and to have these 'Yankees' settle in their midst, they say, seemed at the time like a judgment sent against them for some mighty transgression." Yankees had elastic ideas of honesty, they opined, and palmed inferior merchandise off on gullible customers.[8] Not surprisingly, some southern settlers shied away from Yankee colonies.

People used the term "Yankee" to refer to anyone east of Ohio, but Southerners knew southern New England (especially Massachusetts and Connecticut) was the hearth of "Yankeedom." Yankees, they maintained, were grasping, scheming, smug, sanctimonious, and hypocritical, and whenever Yankees got together—which they did far too often—they compounded each other's vices. Displays of unified Yankee purpose, including settlements and reform movements, disconcerted southern neighbors in Illinois. Making matters worse, Yankees founded with abandon institutions that threatened to immortalize Yankee flaws.[9] They maintained a trail of connections back to eastern colleges, seminaries, churches, businesses, banks, and reformist groups. They often tapped outside credit and financial reserves, pooled their resources, and dabbled in agrarian and town speculation. The inns, mills, shipping operations, and other enterprises they ran in Illinois often had powerful, abiding eastern ties. Even in communities in which they were distinct minorities, they banded together and ran for office, enjoyed disproportionate influence, and became local elites. They advocated schools, churches, social organizations, and other common undertakings that pulled people together. These "Yankee" activities and mundane actions often irritated their southern neighbors.

In the 1820s Christiana Holmes Tillson married, left Massachusetts, and settled among Southerners in Illinois. One day she offered a neighbor woman a piece of Yankee pie. When Mrs. Tillson uttered the words "Yankee pie," the amazed neighbor sputtered, "I didn't think you would say the like of that; I allus knowed youens were all Yankees, but Billy said, 'don't let on that we know it, kase it'll jest make them mad.'" Her neighbor's concern amused the perceptive Tillson, but it illustrates social cleavage.[10]

Above all, perhaps, critics denounced Yankees as cultural imperialists, busybodies who delighted in remaking others, hypocritical prigs who rarely refrained from telling others how to live, cultural warriors whose mission in life involved imposing their norms and controls on others. Northern imperialism, Southerners insisted, often masked a grasping nature and base ulterior motives. As Yankees waged moral and social crusades, Southerners noted, many built up worldly treasure.

Wherever Yankees alighted, critics affirmed, they left indelible marks via reforms, institutions, and other cultural forces. New England settlers around Rockford, for example, "impressed their personality upon this community, and it has remained until this day [1877]."[11] Permanent imprints shaped innumerable communities and their hinterlands, particularly in northern Illinois. In Henry County in 1859, prospective settlers distrusted nearby Yankee colonies and "the feeling of exclusiveness [that] seemed to prevail among the colonists." In addition, travelers accused the "damned Yankees" of luring gullible Southerners into Henry County in order to fleece them.[12] These were strong words, but many settlers voiced similar criticism.

As vigorous as their defense was, the southern counterattack was disorganized, piecemeal, and unsustained. Splits among Southerners weakened southern defenses and efforts to strike back. Southerners shared many cultural traits—diet, reliance on

self and a few others, and desire to cling to timbered portions of
Illinois, for example—but they wrangled over important issues,
including slavery. Some believed slavery was immoral. Others
cared little for moral questions, but concluded that the slave system hurt them socially and economically. Many crossed the Ohio
to rid themselves of it. Relatively few stridently supported slavery and cultivated it in their adopted state. Although division
and even rancor sapped southern strength, southern leaders and
culture dominated most aspects of life in Illinois well into statehood.

Foreigners too sometimes found Yankees difficult neighbors.
In early 1851, for example, Carl Köhler visited near Belleville for
a few weeks. He wrote favorably of his neighbors, but warned,
"When doing business they have no conscience at all, and follow
implicitly the advice an Old Yankee once gave his son: 'Boy, make
money; if you can, make it honestly—but, make money!'" And
he added that local folk delighted in taking advantage of a good
"*Dutchman.*"[13]

William Oliver, a visiting Briton who witnessed rivalry between
Yankees and others, offered something of a balanced assessment.
Visiting Illinois in 1842, when depression lingered and relatively
more Northerners settled, Oliver encountered someone in Madison County who had just left Sangamon County. The man preferred Madison because "it was easier to fall in with a suitable
farm than in Sangamon, which was nearly bought up and most
peopled by Yankees, whom he did not like. This last objection I
had previously heard stated, and the western people generally
seem, I think unfairly, prejudiced against their eastern country-
men, who are decidedly the most enterprising farmers in the
West."[14] Visiting Britons often expressed affinity for enterprising
Yankees, so Oliver's view is hardly surprising.

Despite all the rhetoric, however, northern and southern settlers had much in common. Many migrated due to a economic
dislocation or the likelihood of future hardships. Most came to
Illinois via rivers or on foot. Sizeable numbers arrived by Great
Lakes shipping only in the mid-1830s. Yankees and Southerners
shared the uncertainties and opportunities of an evolving, fluid

society. Republicanism quickened and guided both views. Both feared corruption, arbitrary rule, and tyranny, and they believed in self-government, limited government. In a sense, though, northern republicanism harmonized with the future, the unfolding society and economy, while southern republicanism was more compatible with eighteenth and early nineteenth century America. Nevertheless, differences concerning republicanism were relatively slight.

Many prominent members of both groups, moreover, were strongly against the spread of slavery across Illinois, and most Southerners and Northerners believed blacks were inferior to whites in abilities and should not enjoy citizenship. Many diverse settlers favored colonization of blacks in Africa or the Caribbean. In fact, beginning in 1830 Vandalia's residents formed a society to facilitate black colonization, and colonization societies soon popped up in other towns. Motives ranged from wanting to help blacks obtain a better life to just wanting to rid the state of them. The whole idea, however, was scotched by blacks themselves, who examined possible colonization and largely rejected it. Moreover, although many runaways darted to Illinois to become free, Illinois authorities gave little encouragement to blacks: "Throughout the antebellum period the Illinois legislature went out of its way to prevent free blacks from settling in the state." In fact, "the legislature was far more concerned with helping masters recover fugitive slaves than with preventing the kidnaping of free blacks." By 1860 Illinois, Indiana, Oregon, and California were the only free states that prohibited blacks and mulattos from testifying in court against whites.[15] Shared ideas concerning race bridged gulfs between Yankee settlers and Southerners.

Furthermore, even as tensions between the two groups mounted during the 1830s, northern and southern children in Illinois drank from the same civic and moral fountain. The Rev. William Holmes McGuffey educated generations of youngsters, combining moral and secular instruction. This ardent Pennsylvanian graduated from Washington College, became a Presbyterian minister, and taught at Miami University from 1826 to 1836, where he crafted the First and Second McGuffey readers, both published in 1836.

Using these readers, students and others learned about the West through interesting, relevant, republican stories and lessons, and illustrations pitting right against wrong. Clarion examples of patriotism, civic virtue, and morality fortified generations of students.

A half a million copies sold per year by 1843, and eventually 128 million copies of McGuffey's *Eclectic Reader* sold in various languages around the world. In addition, settlers and teachers entering Illinois carried *Webster's Elementary Speller*. Far more than a speller, it moralized via fables, catechism, and vignettes.

Related works instructed children of all backgrounds. Children in early Montgomery County, for example, studied the New Testament, Kirkham's grammar, and Pike's arithmetic, as well as the *English Reader*, *Columbian Orator*, and *The Pleasant Companion*. Pike County pupils also used Pike's arithmetic and the New Testament, along with Webster's speller, Weems's *Life of Washington*, and Defoe's *Robinson Crusoe*. In Brown County, Webster's speller, the Bible, *Life of Washington*, *Introduction to the English Reader*, the *Life of Marion*, and *Robinson Crusoe* also instructed students. These and similar works inculcated in children of all of Illinois' residents honesty, steadfastness, hard work, thrift, restraint, patriotism, and overall civic virtue. Common foundations of vocabulary, stories and legends, and morality were laid for virtually everyone.

Mundane, petty differences fomented the most antagonism. Cultural warriors, for example, differed over speech patterns and accent, work ethic, diet—southern preference for white corn meal and Yankees' for yellow caused friction—dress, architectural styles, ways of working horses, methods of horse racing—"New Englanders in harness on an oval, Southerners astride on a quarter-mile straight track"—trifling differences in worship, and even modes of walking and standing.[16] Ebenezer Welsh, writing from Monmouth on September 19, 1841, criticized Southerners' food preferences: "Many of them live almost entirely on 'whole hog bacon,' cornmeal dogger, & much & milck." Even the ways Southerners buried their dead—in family plots and with little ceremony—offended some Yankees. But these points of contention

underscore a significant fact: generally, Northerners and Southerners (and others) bickered over commonplace cultural differences, not cosmic issues.

* * *

Covenanted Yankee communities often offended southern notions of individuality and fair play. Yankees labored to transplant their values in Illinois. Conceding New England's shrinking national roles, Yankees taught and preached, trying to save
Westerners from themselves. Pitying all those who lacked New
England ties, Yankees labored to convert them into right-thinking, proper citizens. Yankee colonies in Illinois, often sustained
by New England institutions, shone as cultural outposts, immu-
nizing pioneers against barbarism, southern culture, and Roman
Catholicism.[17]

Some Yankees blended reform and profit. The Rockwell Land
Company involved "that curious mixture of capitalist incentive
and reform zeal often found" in antebellum businessmen.[18] Yale
graduate and Connecticut entrepreneur John A. Rockwell studied western opportunities, dabbled in land dealings in Michigan,
and founded Rockwell in La Salle County with two goals: advance temperance, and make money. Claiming that alcohol bred
crime, poverty, and dysfunctional acts and that intemperance
was immoral and un-Christian, he banned the manufacture and
sale of alcohol in the town. He advertised for settlers who were
"pure supporters of good order and good morals." By early 1836
Rockwell bustled, people snapping up lots and erecting structures.

The problem was, by prohibiting alcohol and seeking to attract people of "good morals," John Rockwell constricted the pool
of potential settlers. In addition, he banned sales to outside speculators to protect actual settlers, and in so doing he restricted infusions of capital and stifled settlement. Worse, nearby La Salle,
a town platted in 1836, sapped Rockwell's economic base. Finally, two unforeseen events rocked the community. The depression of 1837 slammed Rockwell, leaving only 159 residents there.
Though aggressive recruiting among Northeasterners jacked the
number to 300 by mid-1838, in August of that year malaria and

possibly typhoid decimated Rockwell's residents, sending survivors scurrying to safer locales. By 1840 only twenty-six forlorn stalwarts clung to Rockwell, dashing John Rockwell's hopes of profit and moral uplift.

Reflecting community ties and a sense of commonwealth, Yankees often settled through organized groups, many of which espoused religious or social goals. Group migration furthered a mission, or some other cooperative venture, emphasizing economic, psychological, and spiritual security. At least thirty-six colonies planted themselves in Illinois, most during the 1830s, and New England or New York contributed twenty-five.[19] Such group migration usually involved planning, explicit purposes or missions, written covenants, committees, and clear lines of responsibility and authority. During the sluggish early 1840s, one planned colony from England arrived in Stephenson County, practiced communal ownership for a year, then divided their property and disbanded. Most colonists in this undertaking became successful. Many colonies begat additional institutions. Colonies, furthermore, often kept in touch with sponsoring organizations back East.

Efforts in Massachusetts to colonize Illinois are instructive, reflecting elements of society. On February 2, 1831, Northampton's *Hampshire Gazette* invited residents to a meeting of the Illinois Colonial Association on February 16 at Warner's Coffee House. On Wednesday, February 23, the newspaper printed the preamble to the association's constitution, enumerating principles, and reported that members had decided to "remove to some part of that State [Illinois]" the following spring. "Some part" implies members had picked no specific site, formed no trail-blazing vanguard, and did not practice chain migration, unusual conditions for migrating New Englanders. Nevertheless, that May the colony pushed west, settling in Putnam County and transplanting a Congregational church from New England.

Having covenanted for generations, New Englanders valued written constitutions and agreements for migratory groups. (Even groups migrating from Virginia, Maryland, and New Jersey crafted constitutions.) The preamble of the Illinois Colonial Association's constitution counseled "industrious and moral men" to populate the Mississippi Valley. Such men would uplift the continent's interior, thereby benefitting the entire nation, would prove impervious to sloth, indolence, and immorality, defects New Englanders believed abounded among western denizens. The preamble stressed that western settlement "is viewed to be of vast importance . . . by many of the sons of the Pilgrim Fathers of New England." This reference to Pilgrim Fathers is likely a coded plea: settle western lands before others—i.e., Roman Catholics, and perhaps Southerners—settle. The preamble expressed desire to replicate favorable conditions: "The privileges of a social, moral and religious character which they now enjoy, and which they highly value, can be made sure to them in their future residence." Taking its cue from the preamble's lofty sentiments, the newspaper admonished, "It will readily be inferred that the man whose sole object is to make money, and the man who wishes to emigrate in order to free himself from the salutary restraints of society, are not fit characters for this colony, and will not be received into it." Colonists screened out vulgar materialists, selfish misfits, and harmful individualists, stressing community norms, civic strictures, and self-restraint.

On March 23, the *Hampshire Gazette* announced a meeting in Northampton to organize a church, "to be hereafter located in Illinois, to which place the Colony are about to remove." A week later the newspaper reported results: a church organized, a sermon preached from Luke 7:32, church officers elected, and communion served. It printed extracts from the Constitution of the Hampshire Colony—as the organization was called—noting colonists aspired to take to Illinois "all the literary, social and religious privileges now enjoyed by them." To do this they subscribed to several articles. The first acknowledged "God as the Author and Source of all good," and promised, "we will support a faithful gospel Minister," orthodox Congregationalist stances. The second article observed that "knowledge is conducive to human happiness," and promised to support education. The third article underscored financial commitments for the gospel and related needs. Finally, members pledged "to abstain from using or dealing in any way, with Ardent Spirits excepting as medicine."

Religion, social uplift, and personal advancement happily conjoined in this grand colonial endeavor.

Many migrating groups attracted stray individuals and households. Some strays joined before groups started trekking, some joined en route, and others latched onto groups as they settled. Loosely structured groups without narrowly defined, exclusive goals took in strays, as did groups with diluted senses of mission. Groups warmly welcomed outsiders with such practical skills as building, healing, and milling.

But sometimes groups excluded outsiders. Perhaps Yankee groups were especially exclusive. Groups with finely defined, exclusive missions or elaborate rules viewed outsiders charily. Religious colonies, of course, often filtered out non-believers. Perhaps ironically, efforts to remain united and untainted sometimes irritated neighbors, as in the case of the English colonists who settled in Edwards County after the War of 1812, when memory of war was fresh, and perpetuated certain English traits—dubbing one village Albion and replicating the stratified English society. Northerners and foreigners undertaking collective projects and flocking to cities and towns alarmed Southerners, who harbored Jeffersonian misgivings concerning cities and sustained common projects. Similarly, Mormons in Hancock County distanced themselves selectively from neighbors, sparking resentment. After suffering twenty killed in Missouri in the Haun's Mill Massacre in late 1838, some 15,000 Mormons fled to Nauvoo, which quickly became Illinois' largest city. Non-Mormon neighbors and others soon bristled at Mormon exclusiveness, bloc-voting, military units (the "Mormon Legion"), intolerance of internal dissent, talk of polygamy, theocratic practices, and disputes over ownership of animals and land. In 1844 Joseph and Hyrum Smith were murdered, triggering in early 1846 the Mormon exodus to remote Utah. Exclusivity, self-righteousness, and displays of concentrated power had elicited deadly responses.

The 1830s birthed many colonies. In 1833, for example, Alvan and Ezra Lyman, brothers, led New Englanders and other colonists into Sangamon County. A New York colony settled in Henry County, and Connecticut colonists hatched Rockwell, La Salle

County. People from Weathersfield, Connecticut, established Henry County's Weathersfield community, the first colonist arriving in October 1836. By 1837 the settlement housed sixteen men, six with families, and by 1839 about one hundred settlers lived there. Each member received a quarter section of prairie, twenty acres of timber, and a village lot. Foreign groups arrived. Germans, fleeing turbulence in 1830, settled in St. Clair County. In 1834 the first Norwegian settlement in the United States planted itself in La Salle County.

Over decades New England generated colonies in a broad swath stretching from New York to Oregon and Hawaii. Colonial projects often succeeded, although not always in ways envisioned by their founders, backers, and members. Yankee colonization in Illinois during the 1830s coincided with southern colonization's virtual demise.

* * *

Foreign immigrants frightened Americans by the 1830s. Only 8,385 immigrants came to America in 1820, some 23,322 in 1830, and 84,066 in 1840, a ten-fold increase over 1820. Immigration averaged 60,000 per year during the 1830s and 171,000 during the 1840s. It reached 428,000 in 1854, the highest number before the Civil War. Rocketing immigration also became increasingly Irish and Roman Catholic. Having ingested anti-Catholic tales for generations, descendants of Puritans lashed at incoming Irish Catholics, and there was sometimes violence. Yankee reformers, regarding Catholicism as inimical to republican government and progress, believed Catholic-bashing was a salutary, progressive pastime.

They and others pummeled Catholicism in two arenas. One theater was northeastern port cities, where most Catholics landed, and where mobs sacked churches and beat priests, and public and private discrimination stung immigrants. Precursors of Know-Nothings sprang up, sworn to combat Catholicism. The other theater was the Mississippi Valley—the "Valley" or the West— where most people assumed America's future lay. Westward migration, new states, and efforts to relocate the national capital to the Valley underscored the region's importance. Battles shaping the nation's future erupted in the land of tomorrow, the West.

Roman Catholicism in Illinois withered between approximately the 1780s and the time of statehood. Americans engulfed demoralized French residents, who were served only sporadically by visiting priests. Conditions soon improved, however. In 1818 foundations were laid for St. Louis University, a Jesuit institution. The St. Louis diocese was established in 1826, and two years later the Sisters of Charity founded the first trans-Mississippi hospital. The next year, at Ruma, the first English-speaking Catholic congregation in Illinois was founded. In St. Louis the first Catholic newspaper west of the Mississippi began publication.

Rejuvenated Catholicism spread. One source noted, "Catholic activity, at first confined to a few French families and missions in the southern part of the state, was, in the late twenties and early thirties, beginning to follow the thickening population into central and northern Illinois."[20] In 1826 Catholics, mostly descended from French and French-Indians, clustered with other Illinoisans in southern Illinois. One devout contingent hailed from Kentucky, descendants of venerable Maryland Catholics.[21] Twenty missions operating from St. Louis served Catholics. During the 1830s, Irish and others settled in northern Illinois, augmenting thriving Catholic communities.

When Chicago incorporated in 1833, 90 percent of its residents were Catholic, mostly French or French-Indian in background. In early 1833, Chicago acquired its first resident Catholic priest, Irenaeus Mary St. Cyr, sent by the bishop of St. Louis. By autumn he said mass in Chicago's first Catholic church, St. Mary's, a plain chapel on the south side of Lake Street. By 1834 Catholic churches or missions served Galena, Joliet, and several other northern sites. In that year the new See of Vincennes obtained jurisdiction over eastern Illinois, western Illinois being attached to the See of St. Louis. In 1833 the Convent of the Ladies of Visitation was founded at Kaskaskia. In late 1843 Chicago became the See for the entire state, and months later the Right Reverend William Quarter arrived and assumed duties as Chicago's first bishop.

These events pleased Catholics, but alarmed Yankees and others, who sponsored colonization projects to combat Catholicism in the Valley and coincidentally make money. One dual-purpose project was Weathersfield, founded in 1836. Residents hoped the colony "would eventuate not only in a good crop of converted Catholics, the establishment of temperance, justice, charity, and other moral characteristics; but that a fair return in the shape of dividends in kind, upon the money invested, would also accrue."[22] They sought God, reform, and gold . . . not necessarily in that order. West of Weathersfield, residents of Andover, founded in 1836, had similar goals, but their efforts yielded unintended consequences. Prospective settlers looked askance at Andover and went elsewhere. Clearly, "the concentration of Yankee colonies in Henry County was the primary reason for delayed settlement of the county and persistence of frontier conditions" as late as 1850. Few people wanted close-knit, intrusive colonists as neighbors.[23] Prominent leaders, including Abraham Lincoln, tiptoed gingerly around religious and nativist issues.

Catholicism fretted Yankees, but so did barbarism. Raw frontier beauty was striking, but harshness, sickness, and anxiety belied romantic vistas. The frontier was temptress, luring even virtuous citizens to degradation. Open space, embryonic social restraints and ennobling institutions, loneliness, and drudgery, warnings intoned, seduced even New Englanders and other upright pioneers. Writing to relatives in Pennsylvania on April 23, 1836, Mary Boone Perry complained about how people around Peoria observed the Sabbath: "They go fishing, sail on the lake, and guns are heard in every direction, almost, all the day"— telltale signs of incipient barbarism. Offspring born in Illinois, moreover, often degenerated even further, having known little civilization amid the wilderness.

Ever vigilant, Yankees saw barbarism everywhere. Some attributed barbarism to Southerners, depicting them as ignorant, militant, louts. Southerners, Yankees charged, shirked education, social ties, steady habits, or concern for the commonwealth. Southerners, valuing honor and family name, concluded deals with manly handshakes, eschewing legal contracts. They mixed anti-intellectualism with inordinate fear of power and suspicion

of non-religious institutions. Holding kin in esteem, they maintained few loyalties, except for kinship and church. Often unkempt and occasionally violent, especially after downing adult
beverages, they displayed considerable fatalism and even superstition.

* * *

Some crusaders regarded their jihad in stark, uncompromising terms. Their cause was holy, they believed, and opponents
and even equivocators were perverse and sinful. Armed with a
divinity degree from Princeton Theological Seminary, the Rev.
Elijah P. Lovejoy, a crusading Puritan from Maine, sallied forth.
His newspaper, the *St. Louis Observer*, savaged Catholicism while
it decried mistreatment of blacks. Enraging a wide spectrum of
folk, he scooted to Alton.

Unswervingly devoted, Lovejoy also flailed against dancing,
Sabbath breaking, licentiousness, and other choice targets. His
newest target, though, was slavery. Exasperated, Altonians and
possibly others destroyed his printing presses twice in late summer of 1837. Lovejoy remained steadfast, egged on and encouraged by friends. Late on November 7 a menacing crowd milled
near a stone warehouse containing another press, Lovejoy, and
armed followers. A shot pierced the night, mortally wounding
someone in the crowd and sending others scurrying for firearms.
Armed with courage, conviction, and perhaps a rifle, Lovejoy
eventually darted from cover, possibly to pick off another ruffian.
Suddenly, five shots hit Lovejoy, creating a martyr to abolitionism and the First Amendment and horrifying moderate people.
Irate students at Illinois College protested his death.[24] Clearly,
highly contentious national struggles were enlisting Illinoisans,
ultimately drawing them toward the maelstrom.

Of great significance, Yankee onslaughts against Catholics and
others in Illinois killed practically no one. State and federal constitutions, economic arenas, and boundaries of decorum shaped
and channeled struggles. Disputants employed economic boycotts, stinging sermons, cutting speeches and editorials, name
callings, and snubs and slights. Occasional shoving matches rarely
detonated violence. No mobs torched Catholic churches, ran-

sacked convents, or beat priests, unlike ugly violence jolting eastern states in the 1830s and later. Similarly, earnest Yankees thundered at low-life behavior, trying to tame or shame barbarians
and proslavery elements, but this rarely generated violence. The
Lovejoy incident shocked people precisely because the shootout
was so exceptional, so untypically violent. Although zealous
preachers, utopian dreamers, and ardent cultural reformers occasionally provoked wrath, most Illinoisans generally humored,
ignored, or shunned extremists. Courtrooms, lawsuits, debates,
pamphlets and newspapers, economic coercion, occasional mild
intimidation, and much unspoken consensus shaped, channeled,
and mitigated controversies, keeping most disputes amazingly
tranquil.

Slavery's last gasp for long-term survival had been the failed
referendum of 1824. It fatally wounded de facto slavery mas-
querading as indentured servitude, which largely disappeared
by 1840, hostile laws speeding its demise. Still, struggles over
race and slavery continued to distress Illinoisans. Sternly worded
laws, sometimes circumvented, curbed movements of blacks into
the state. Struggles over runaways and race frayed social fabric,
but rarely sparked lethal violence. Continuing prosperity probably allayed tensions and fueled hope. (Perhaps the fact that
Lovejoy's murder occurred during a sharp economic downturn
was no mere coincidence.)

* * *

Although land sales remained brisk into 1837, severe economic
malaise settled on the East and spread westward, largely a product of President Andrew Jackson's triumph over the Second National Bank and resulting speculative mania. Sales at federal land
offices in Illinois plunged from nearly 3,200,000 acres in 1836
to just over 1 million acres in 1837. Sales in 1837 plummeted at
all offices but one (for some reason, Vandalia's sales actually
climbed). For the first and only time, Vandalia led all ten offices
in sales. Offices with incredible sales spikes during 1835 and 1836
languished in 1837. Chicago, for example, sold 436,992 acres in
1836, but only a paltry 15,618 acres in 1837. Galena sold 280,979

acres in 1835 and 202,365 acres in 1836, but only 35,764 acres in
1837.

The plunge continued through 1838, only 778,556 acres of public land selling in Illinois, a decline of 234,286 acres from 1837. Quincy led sales, with 165,243 acres, a far cry from its sale of 569,376 acres in 1836. Dismal sales at Chicago persisted, where a minuscule 17,640 acres sold in 1838, a shadow of the 436,992 acres sold in 1836. Galena was the one bright spot in bleakness, spurting from 35,764 in 1837 to 87,891 in 1838 and reflecting revived growth in northwestern Illinois.

With economic downturn in 1837, wealthy nonresident speculators withheld properties from market, believing prevailing low prices did not reflect true land values and hoping for higher prices.[25] This tactic did not work, however. Times were tough, debts were onerous, buyers were few, prices were stagnant, and ordinary people with spare money found bargains. For example, John C. Newton taught school in Versailles. On December 12, 1838, he wrote about his inability to collect his fees: "I have been very unsuccessful in collecting and I don't know when I shall get it. The people cannot get market for their pork and there is no money in the Country." He had plenty of company.

Land sales started to bounce back in 1839, some 1,132,872 acres selling, but this recovery was uneven, Chicago and Galena being the biggest gainers. Chicago sprang from 17,640 acres to 160,154 acres, and Galena jumped from 97,891 acres to 229,471, making it the top office in 1839.

Property values in Chicago, which had rocketed to unrealistic levels through speculation, collapsed. Chicago's population slipped from 4,349 in 1837 to 4,220 the following year.[26] Work on the Illinois & Michigan Canal, started with high expectations on July 4, 1836, sputtered and then ceased altogether in 1842. The canal, scaled down, finally opened in 1848, the year a train first carried prairie grain into Chicago. Ambitious railroad plans faltered. The Galena and Chicago Union Railroad, chartered in 1836 to link Galena to Chicago, stalled. The Northern Cross Railroad folded, its sale bringing only $21,000, not a tenth of its original cost of $250,000. Railroads, enthusiasts hoped, would dissolve ties between northern Illinois and St. Louis and replace them with ties to Chicago. This eventually occurred, but depressed conditions postponed the day.[27] Land values tumbled, money became scarce, bartering and private credit flourished, and employment slumped, all aggravating sluggish times. Economic woes persisted, not really ending until perhaps 1846.

Adam Davis wrote on September 5, 1839, from New Boston, Mercer County, to Dan Weed of Marblehead, Massachusetts, "Pattented Land is in poor demand here these times on the acount of hard times and plenty of gov't land to be had at Congress price here and the many difficulties in the titles also the tax tithe on this will be a considerable incumbrance." Neighbors helping themselves to his timber bothered him, he added.

On May 1, 1840, John Dickson, writing from Knoxville, provided context for local depressed conditions: "I was not a little rejoiced to hear of your design to come here. I believe it would be fully as pleasant for you and much more to your advantage than to stay where you are." He then noted, "Although this country feels the effects of the times, it is only in a slight degree compared to yours. Money is scarce but is chiefly owing to the land being in market and money being principally invested in property, and there is not much prospect of a decline in the price of property when it is but $1.25 per acre." Necessities in Illinois, he found, were costlier than comparable necessities in Pennsylvania. Common laborers in Illinois, he reported, received seventy-five cents per day "and board, &c." John Dickson's letter suggests two valuable views: Illinois was better off than the East; both scarce money and high prices accompanied economic slowdown. Illinoisans still commanded respectable wages, which was amazing, given destitution in eastern cities.

Lucy Maynard penned views of depressed times from La Harpe on July 15, 1840. Admitting rust damage to wheat, she noted the "corn and hay look beautiful." Referring to slowed construction of a nearby house, she mused the builder "may be disappointed about that as well as many other things. [In] these hard times, every body, almost, owes money and there is nothing that we raise on the farm [that] will command money, and it has brought the people into a bad fix." She then inquired about money owed

to her, asking how much was due her and when it would arrive,
common questions in these depression years. James Brown, writing from Quincy on February 24, 1841, reported economic malaise: farmers, in debt, only had "wheat, corn, oats, pork, beans . . . which they have to barter."

Responses to hardship varied, some finding opportunity, others dwelling on pain. Economic misery sent some people packing. Still, evidence suggests no wholesale flight from Illinois. Desire to own land remained strong. Farmers and others reverted to subsistence agriculture, bartering, and local credit arrangements, and made do. Economic stagnation was national, so few alternatives existed elsewhere. Cities suffered greatly, dampening urban growth and propelling some townsfolk to seek relief in Illinois. In short, economic sluggishness stymied population growth here and there, but the state's population still grew.

Residents of nine northernmost counties, chafing under the state's heavy debt and feeling powerless and forlorn, flirted with secession. They sought congressional permission to join Wisconsin, maintaining that Nathaniel Pope's obtaining for Illinois the northern 8,000 square miles violated the Northwest Ordinance. Although Wisconsin encouraged these would-be secessionists— it needed more people in order to apply for statehood—Congress scotched the idea. The northern border stayed where it was, and Wisconsin had to wait until 1848 for statehood.[28]

Perhaps people's outlook on life, self-identity, and overall resources shaped their responses. Even as woes accelerated, some persons anticipated selling lots in paper towns, riding property values to dizzying heights, and making quick fortunes. As fledgling villages withered and paper towns were stillborn, Henry Warren cranked out advice on founding a village. Writing amid bleakness on August 14, 1838, he revealed understanding of central place theory, settlement diffusion, social psychology, and other aspects of human activity: "The way to make a village is to select a good plot of prairie in a rich area some 10 miles or so from any considerable village. As the farmers all want to get some woods on their farms they settle all round the borders of the prairie & leave the center, which may be taken at government prices & answers well for a village. They buy its outskirts lots. But you must have two or three or a dozen who will agree to put up houses. You must have a tavern & a store & if possible a post office."

Warren's advice to locate a village ten miles or so from a "considerable village" demonstrated intuitive understanding of central place theory as later propounded by Walter Christaller; each village required a hinterland for its activities to service. Warren understood settlement occurred on the fringes of prairie, near timber, which gave settlers two resource bases, and the prairie's center would contain the village. The need for tavern, store, and post office was obvious to observant settlers.[29]

J. H. Smith joined Henry Warren in dreaming of town growth during stormy times for most towns. Writing on May 27, 1838, from Jo Daviess County, Smith noted that the town of Savanna savored very rapid growth and a flurry of construction. Town lots, he added, "are selling from $50 to 600 and I think its haserding but little to sa that lots that could be bought for $150 now will bee worth $1000 in five years." Such dogged determination—such optimism—was not all that uncommon. Many peered beyond current troubles to better times, and this optimism paid off. Memory is short, and hope springs eternal.[30]

Despite misery stalking the land, ordinary settlers accepted responsibility, stayed tenaciously optimistic, and looked to the future. Traces of optimism surfaced in Hannah Turner's letter, written from Quincy on December 10, 1838: "if any of you can come, we shall be glad to see you. We live in a slab house yet. Mr. T. thinks of building this year if he can, but it is a very hard time for money." She added that several months of drought compounded the difficulties. Thoughts of building reflected optimism. Abraham Lincoln's views were that, "possessed of a fertile soil and a salubrious climate, surrounded by navigable rivers and lakes, we look forward to the brilliant destiny that awaits her, with a confidence undisturbed by the present disastrous condition of our beloved country."[31] Spectacular population growth from 1835 to 1840 indicates that others shared Lincoln's confidence.

On March 1, 1841, John Dickson of Knoxville ably depicted regional problems and opportunities: "Every thing is now favorable for the emigrant. Materials necessary for improvement are all low." He added, "The price of farm labour has come down

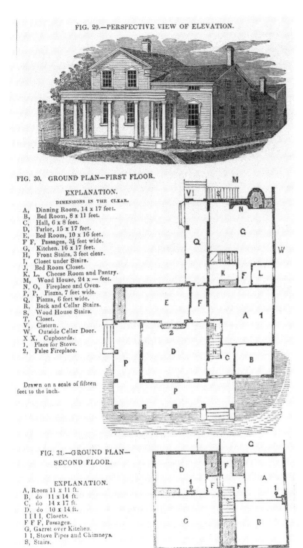

FIG. 29.—PERSPECTIVE VIEW OF ELEVATION.

FIG. 30. GROUND PLAN—FIRST FLOOR.

EXPLANATION.
DIMENSIONS IN THE CLEAR.
A, Dinning Room, 14 x 17 feet.
B, Bed Room, 8 x 11 feet.
C, Hall, 6 x 8 feet.
D, Parlor, 15 x 17 feet.
E, Bed Room, 10 x 16 feet.
F F, Passages, 3½ feet wide.
G, Kitchen, 16 x 17 feet.
H, Front Stairs, 3 feet clear.
I, Closet under Stairs.
J, Bed Room Closet.
K, L, Cheese Room and Pantry.
M, Wood House, 24 x — feet.
N, O, Fireplace and Oven.
P, P, Piazza, 7 feet wide.
Q, Piazza, 6 feet wide.
R, Back and Cellar Stairs.
S, Wood House Stairs.
T, Closet.
V, Cistern.
W, Outside Cellar Door.
X X, Cupboards.
1, Place for Stove.
2, False Fireplace.

Drawn on a scale of fifteen
feet to the inch.

FIG. 31.—GROUND PLAN—
SECOND FLOOR.

EXPLANATION.
A, Room 11 x 11 ft.
B, do 11 x 14 ft.
C, do 14 x 17 ft.
D, do 10 x 14 ft.
1 1 1 1, Closets.
F F F, Passages.
G, Garret over Kitchen.
1 1, Stove Pipes and Chimneys.
S, Stairs.

House plans in the September 1841 issue of the *Prairie Farmer* reflect a taste for touches of classical architecture and a desire for order, stability, and permanence.

from $20.00 to $12.00 per month. Mechanical labour is also much lower than formerly. Dry goods and groceries are also reduced. This is all owing to the scarcity of money. In fact, I think the emigrant could not have a better time. Land also can be had very low." Dickson added, "People are learning to live without money. They are thankful for the necessaries of life without the luxuries. They can raise their own tobacco, make their own sugar or do without, drink corn coffee, and many of them can let their children run without shoes and stockings through the winter." Wonderful opportunities, he insisted, awaited settlers: "If I wanted to make the western country my place of residence, and owned property in the east, I would rather suffer a reasonable sacrifice than miss the present opportunity of investing funds in the west." Finally, he touted Illinois' strengths, adding, "Don't be frightened. You can have any thing you want if you have the cash. Money, I presume, can be loaned at 25 percent [per year] readily, yet with good security. This is better than 4 or 6 percent. I believe this country has many advantages with but few disadvantages. Sickness is the only objection I can have to it. Many, however, come here for health and obtain it." On March 25, 1841, Samuel Knox wrote from Green Plains to Dan Weed, observing, "Money here is very scarce, and in consequence of that land is becoming low in value. Some are offering their land at government prices such as has been held up at 3 or 4 dollars per acre." Clearly, amid distress, people with spare cash enjoyed economic opportunities.

Early stages of the economic slump jolted John Bailhache. He bought half interest in the *Alton Telegraph*, and took charge in early 1837. The newspaper, he lamented, had been represented to him "as being in a most prosperous state." But Bailhache admitted he had "bought and paid for one half of the establishment before I examined it, or knew anything whatever about its condition or prospects except from report." Perhaps euphoria of the exhilarating 1830s had swept him along. He added, "I took charge of the paper early in May 1837, just before the general suspension of specie payments, and the almost universal ruin which followed. It soon became apparent that I had taken a very injudicious, if not a fatal step." Bailhache reorganized the newspaper, hired new personnel, and stayed afloat.[32] Others who had invested paid more dearly for their rashness.

The *New England Farmer and Gardener's Journal* in July 1838 depicted speculative mania and ensuing collapse. Surveying nature's bounty and deleterious effects of prosperity, it sermonized: "The Great Danger in the West is, that the soil is so fertile, and so remote from the ultimate market for its produce,

that there will not be sufficient inducements to industry, to insure moral and physical health to its population. Where men can
earn enough in two days to support them seven, they are too
much inclined to spend the five in indolence. . . . And when a
people are idle, from whatever cause, they readily, though often
imperceptibly, slide into indulgences and habits which are the
base of individual and public virtue." The newspaper then mused,
"It requires far more philosophy and fortitude to resist the smiles
of prosperity, than it does to bear the frowns of adversity."

Some settlers discovered salutary chastisement in hardship.
The newspaper's editors, the article reported, had received a letter "from an esteemed friend in West Wisconsin (Ioway), an ex-
tract of which we subjoin." The letter opined, "Until the recent
healthful check of the 'times,' the West was intoxicated with the
full spirit of speculation. Labor and industry were looked upon
as too slow and tame a way of making money. The 'royal way' of
making a fortune by speculation infested all classes; and, as a
consequence, the main pillar and ornament of a state was almost
entirely neglected." The letter hoped that suffering "may correct
the delusions of the day, and impress upon the minds of the community this fact, that *there is no accretion to individual or national wealth, without the exchange of labor and skill.*"[33] Concern about alleged unproductive speculation undermining steady
habits recurs in frontier history.

Beginning in 1837, harsh economic reversals shocked speculators. Land value plummeted, fortunes evaporated, towns vanished, and uncollected debts mounted. To some, however, the
depression was salutary, chastening people with unbridled passion for quick gain. Some speculators repented, and some would-
be speculators witnessed the fate of high-rollers and resolved to
walk the straight and narrow. The deep, prolonged economic
downturn kept before the public's mind the lessons taught by
hardship.

Distress made preemption urgent and important. Lines of credit
withered and confidence waned, keeping many from getting established in farming. Sluggish economics restricted urban opportunities, highlighting the need to make land available to ordinary people. In 1838 and 1840, new federal laws gave preemption

rights to squatters on public lands. Even so, this fell short of guaranteeing squatters the right to purchase land at minimum price, $1.25 per acre. In other words, they could lose lands they had improved to moneyed speculators.

Building on log-cabin imagery from William Henry Harrison's 1840 presidential campaign and swapping votes on tariffs, advocates of improved preemption laws finally succeeded in late 1841. Now, settlers could take up public domain land, gloss it with visible improvements, scratch a living from it, and then purchase it for minimum price.[34]

The era's speculation binge brought mixed results. Speculation highlighted perceived opportunities and attracted capital and emigrants. It quickened initiative, enterprise, and boosterism, rewarding flexibility, agility, and risk taking. "Getting there first" and "try anyway" were valued. These activities, traits, and attitudes sired useful investment, much construction, and general productivity.

On the other hand, speculation carried costs. Railroads and other socially worthwhile projects that ultimately benefitted society often faltered in infancy. Skittish investors withdrew capital after realizing no immediate profit. In addition, individual gain often did not generate social gain. Scrambling for wealth sometimes weakened the invisible glue so necessary for community well-being.

* * *

Nineteenth-century Illinois contained two major frontiers, with the 1830s forming the watershed. The first frontier consisting largely of Upland Southerners, held sway through the 1830s. It featured settlement of southern Illinois via rivers, strong ties with New Orleans, and revolutionary steamboats. The second consisted largely of Northerners and foreigners, and flourished between the Black Hawk War and the Civil War. It rolled across prairies of northern Illinois, created dozens of counties, moved the capital to Springfield, and became increasingly enmeshed with the East Coast through Chicago, Great Lakes steamers, and railroads. Observers saw dynamics of the two frontiers. In 1842 John Regan visited Ellisville, on the Spoon River, in northwestern Ful-

CHURCHILL & DANFORD'S
HARVESTING MACHINE.

Churchill and Danford's Harvesting Machine. Some
early farm machinery pushed the limits of technology,
often proving impracticable and unreliable. The
Prairie Farmer, August 1841. ILLINOIS STATE HISTORICAL
LIBRARY, A DIVISION OF THE ILLINOIS HISTORIC PRESERVATION
AGENCY.

ton County. He noticed the village's economy was oriented toward two places, New York and New Orleans. He wrote, "Ellisville is a bustling little place. Although there were not more than
a hundred and fifty houses in it, and none of them very large,
there was yet a respectable amount of business going on. In one
workshop five or six coopers were rattling away with might and
main, making up barrels for transporting the wheat of the approaching harvest to Chicago, New York, and New Orleans."
Significantly, Regan witnessed production for distant New York
in 1842, six years before the Illinois & Michigan Canal was completed. Clearly, the 1830s brought fundamental changes to frontier Illinois.

A central fact springs from frontier Illinois during the 1830s:

innumerable settler households obtained land and succeeded. This dominant fact distinguishes Illinois from Kentucky and other frontier states. In frontier Kentucky, "the distribution of land betrayed the expectations of most Kentucky settlers. It reflected the stranglehold of landlords, primarily absentee, over Kentucky." Many settlers in Kentucky lived on the margins, as squatters or tenants, and railed against speculators and land jobbers, seeing them as oppressors. They felt a sense of victimization that was hardly known in Illinois. Over time preemption rights softened anger, and "liberalization of land laws reduced the insurrectionary fury of trans-Appalachian pioneers."[35] Public land was readily available in Illinois, a stark fact luring Kentuckians and others. Illinois speculators hardly dented settlement, unlike in central and northern Indiana, where major speculators demanded an exorbitant $5 per acre, throttling settlement to a trickle. In Illinois efforts to corner the market or substantially inflate land prices foundered; too many alternatives existed. Illinoisans bought millions of acres of public land, and development proceeded apace. Steel plows sliced prairies, towns dotted prairies far from rivers and even far from timber, and ingenuity addressed vexing fencing problems. Of course, settlers in Illinois vied for farmland and town lots, but the playing field was comparatively level. Marketplace forces, claim clubs, and preemption laws either obviated obstacles or swept them away. Moreover, people clung to land, riding out tough times. In short, tested Illinoisans gained much.

Frontier Illinois was spectacular in another way during the 1830s. Farms, hamlets, and villages covered nearly all the state. In 1830 nearly half the state had fewer than two people per square mile. The entire region above an east-west line drawn across Illinois through Peoria was practically unsettled, the Galena area and a few isolated hamlets being exceptions. Moreover, a broad tongue of land from McLean and Ford counties all the way down through Richland County had fewer than two people per square mile. Only about one-fifth of Illinois contained more than six people per square mile, virtually all confined to two areas. One area was a ribbon stretching along the Wabash and the Ohio, from Edgar County to eastern Massac County. The other area ran from southern Pike County along the Mississippi River through Union County, with a bulge running into northwestern Clinton County and Bond County and another bulge stretching through Green County northward through Cass County and then eastward into portions of Logan and Christian counties.

By 1840 only one patch of Illinois had fewer than two people per square mile, a region consisting of Livingston, Ford, Iroquois, and Champaign counties. This area was generally poorly drained, permitting little settlement or even movement through the area. About 60 percent of the state contained over six people per square mile.

Simply put, Illinois was quite thoroughly settled by 1840, exceptions being a patch of water-logged land in the east and stretches in the far north. Farms, hamlets, towns, and churches, schools, mills, bridges, and other tangible evidence of settlement speckled almost every corner of Illinois. Settlement in Illinois never stalled.

Illinois in 1840 was truly decades removed from Illinois of 1830. Whirlwind activities during the 1830s terminated or at least tempered frontier characteristics. Perhaps the most important, permanent change was the maturing of the state. Its surging population was increasingly urban, commercial, diverse, sophisticated, and agile. Responding to market demands, for example, farmers steadily replaced stolid, durable corn with riskier, fickle wheat. Wheat involved greater risks and more labor, but it commanded top dollar in distant markets. Diverse people generated friction and sparked open conflict—and, occasionally, violence—but underlying consensus about basic matters greatly strengthened the fabric of society.[36] Snarling, shifting factions had swirled over contentious issues in the capitol in Vandalia and then Springfield, and now they received the Second Party System's discipline. Depression was painful and sobering, but it injected into economic and political proceedings healthy doses of realism, and continued growth buoyed observers. Illinoisans entered the next decade wiser. For Chicago's founders, "the belief in indefinite perfectibility took the form of developing a city set in a garden, of effecting an ideal reconciliation between the first generation of modern technology and a previously unexploited nature."[37] This was true everywhere, as steam power and other technologies spread across Illinois.

It was not true of Indiana, Michigan, Wisconsin, Iowa, or Missouri. These states had stalled frontiers. In 1840 only a tier of three or four southernmost counties in both Michigan and Wisconsin were truly settled. Above these tiers isolated communities and marginal farms dotted rivers and lakes, not real belts of settlement. Perhaps only one-fifth of Michigan was settled and possibly just one-sixth of Wisconsin. In Iowa settlement huddled in counties touching the Mississippi.

With better times by the mid-1840s visions of sparkling new towns flickered in hopeful imaginations. Writing on June 6 of either 1844 or 1845, G. R. Clark of Jerseyville, for example, advised Samuel Clark of Dover, New Hampshire, about speculative towns: "I want to get hold of a section (640 acres) near Burlington or Bloomington near which places real estate is destined to become valuable and that in a short time. Come out here if you want to make a fortune. I will learn you what I can." His specific advice paralleled Henry Warren's advice: "Go to Iowa, enter a section about 30 miles from any town, lay out a town on your land. Get a lithographed map of the place, give away a few lots on condition of their improving them, sell at a moderate rate at first & gradually add to the price. Then crack it up in the newspapers, sell lots in the East, petition the legislation for a county seat. Gain it & your fortune is made. Lose it & the next chance try again." This string of advice contains remarkable insights.

Like Henry Warren, Clark understood central place theory, including the need for towns to have adequate sized hinterlands, in order to prosper. As early as August 7, 1821, Horatio Newhall predicted that Greenville would flourish and triple or quadruple its population in a few years. After noting that Greenville had recently been chosen county seat of Bond County, he added that Vandalia was eighteen miles to the east and Edwardsville was thirty-two miles to the west, distance enough to ensure Greenville's future. Towns, moreover, increased the value of nearby land.

The last half of Clark's letter reveals much. Following economic revival in the 1840s, Illinois witnessed frantic crescendos of frontier activity, confined largely to northern counties and some eastern locales. But during this finale, frontier processes flourished in Iowa, Wisconsin, Minnesota, and elsewhere. Significantly, G. R. Clark urged Samuel Clark to go to Iowa, not Illinois. He knew frontier opportunities were drifting westward, leaving Illinois and crossing the Mississippi. In short, following revival from depressed conditions, frontier Illinois burned brightly before dying out. Coincidentally, railroads haltingly appeared from the late 1830s into the 1840s. But frenetic railroad construction from 1849 through the 1850s both caused and symbolized frontier Illinois' demise.

Moreover, Clark was willing to push buttons and pull levers to promote towns, a willingness shared by others. He understood the need to "crack it up in the newspapers," prime the pump by giving away a few lots, and lobby legislators to garner the county seat. His recommended media blitz and public relations campaign had roots in French and early American activities, but his promotional efforts display elements of modernity, whiffs of Madison Avenue.

Finally, his last two sentences are significant. Opportunity, he understood, implied possible failure. Even so, he opined, failure need not be permanent, and he urged the reader to "try again." This "go ahead" spirit animated settlers and sustained them in defeat, contributing mightily to the frontier's overall success. Hope, vital for success, always lay over the horizon. From the late 1840s until political crises of 1860, the frontier matured with the rest of Illinois, but as it did so it faded and largely disappeared.

PART V

COOPERATION AND CONFLICT

13.

Race, Ethnicity, and Class

As members of an antislavery group operating in Jersey County in the twilight of the frontier, Thomas Ford and Harley Hayes wanted to help a runaway slave hiding along the Illinois River in neighboring Calhoun County. But they suspected local proslavery men, including one named Bentley, who tracked and captured escaped slaves, were lurking nearby.

Ford and Hayes went to Mason's landing, skiffed across the river, found the runaway, and recrossed the river around dusk. When they landed, Bentley confronted them, seized the black man, hustled him into his wagon, and sped toward home, about seven miles away. Only after Bentley reached home was the truth revealed: his "captured runaway" was none other than Harley Hayes, who had blackened his face and hands. Meanwhile, Thomas Ford escorted the real runaway to Jerseyville, from which he was spirited to Canada.

What happened next is highly significant: essentially, nothing. No evidence whatsoever suggests Bentley vented his frustrations on Hayes. A minor incident involving resistance to slavery had been played out, Bentley had lost, and the matter was closed.[1] This incident illustrates something profoundly true about frontier conflict: the framework—the consensus—in which struggles occurred permitted subterfuge and moderate intimidation, but ordinarily not physical violence. Unspoken, understood rules governed disputes, and most violence was beyond the rules, beyond consensus. Bentley as well as Ford and Hayes knew the rules and abided by them. He played the game, lost, and accepted the outcome. Such peaceful acquiescence in defeat molded frontier society.

This incident also highlights cooperation bred by conflict. Among groups struggling to either weaken or sustain slavery, cooperation abounded. Freedom for the runaway who avoided Bentley's grasp did not just happen; numerous people cooperated to spirit him to Canada. Similarly, men like Bentley joined with others to snare and return runaways. Amid crises and conflict, it is clear, basic consensus and cooperation flourished.

Residents near early Danville managed, channeled, and practically choreographed violence, dedicating a special field and certain days for fighting. On these festive days, people wishing to fight showed up and had their fights, some fighters not knowing their opponents or even why they were fighting. Unspoken consensus precluded using knives, pistols, or other weapons. Sometimes a dozen brawls raged simultaneously, and local residents strolled from one contest to the next, giving pugilists advice and encouragement. After the fights finished, bruised participants cleaned up, shook hands, quaffed whiskey, and then sometimes watched horse races. A good time was had by all, and no hard feelings festered.

Wrathful individuals in Christian County headed to Taylorville, the county seat, where someone "harboring ill-feeling or any grievance against a neighbor would, on meeting him, throw out a challenge to meet on 'muster day' or some other public occasion and settle the matter. Time did not seem to abate their hostility . . . and public opinion deferred to this mode of settling old grudges." At the agreed-upon times, pugilists appeared, crowds formed, and fighting commenced. Some days were graced by a half a dozen fights, and "some of the most prominent men in the county would be engaged in these melees." Consensus proscribed the use of weapons, and the ban held.² Not one scintilla of evidence suggests that a combatant ever limped away, returned with a gun, and fired at an opponent.

In fact, roughhouse behavior probably vented steam by directing frustration, aggression and anger into socially acceptable outlets, much as mass sports did decades later. Moderate, contrived hell-raising probably squelched tendencies for real hell to well up. This was largely ritualized violence, violence circumscribed by consensus, which harmed neither fighters nor society. This unspoken understanding channeled fights, curbed unsportsmanlike behavior, restricted use of weapons, defined victory, and often prescribed postbellum handshakes and other rituals. Jersey County's runaway slave incident and Danville's and Taylorville's ritualized violence reflect three realities about frontier conflict: most was highly visible; most occurred within broad, tacit consensus; and people accepted the results.³

* * *

One central fact marked conflict since at least the 1760s: few Illinoisans died violent deaths. The largest single documented loss was the Fort Dearborn Massacre in 1812, where several dozen soldiers and settlers and perhaps a dozen Indians died. Even fewer died in Illinois in 1832 during Black Hawk's incursion. Perhaps only thirty died in scattered Regulator-bandit clashes during the half century from 1816 to 1866.⁴ Over the years cutthroats murdered an unknown number at Cave-in-Rock on the Ohio River. But these tolls are trifling compared to perhaps 1,000 or more soldiers who died in just two battles in Ohio in 1790 and 1791. Fighting in Michigan and Kentucky also produced truly grim death tolls.

Murder rates underscore frontier Illinois' tranquility. The federal census of 1850 contained statistics on social conditions among the country's 23 million inhabitants. *Mortality Statistics of the Seventh Census of the United States, 1850*, classified deaths occurring from June 1, 1849, to June 1, 1850. The census revealed 227 murders during these twelve months. Illinois' population was 851,470, about 3.66 percent of the national total. Census figures revealed seven murders in Illinois between June 1, 1849 and June 1, 1850, or about 3.08 percent of the nation's murders.

It must be remembered that parts of Illinois still had frontier conditions; settlers tended to be relatively young and male, a group relatively prone to violence; newcomers from practically everywhere, with diverse languages, religions, ideas about justice, and overall backgrounds, flooded into these counties; fluidity, some chaos, and extralegal activity marked some frontier regions.

The federal census of 1850 divided Illinois into three sections. The northern section consisted of thirty-two counties with 317,710 people, the middle section thirty-three counties with 298,236 people, and the southern section thirty-four counties with 235,524 people. The northern section contained frontier regions and Chicago's 30,000 residents. The middle section was post-frontier or in very late stages of frontier development. The southern section was definitely post-frontier. Significantly, between June 1, 1849, and June 1, 1850, the northern section—containing 317,710 people, crescendos of frontier activity, and Chicago—experienced *one* murder. Just one murder—in twelve months! (The victim was a young boy.) The middle section also had just one murder. The southern-oriented, post-frontier southern section, now relatively sparsely populated, experienced five murders.[5] Frontier Illinois suffered remarkably little mayhem.

Other frontier regions at this time were also highly peaceful. The state of Iowa suffered no murders during the twelve months, while the state of Wisconsin suffered just one. Murders in the territories of Minnesota and Oregon totaled, respectively, zero and one. No one in Utah was murdered during the twelve months. New Mexico and Texas, on the other hand, lost via murder seven and nineteen people, respectively.

Of course, as is true today, not all violence was reported. Even so, huge amounts of anecdotal evidence support the federal census reports concerning violence. Settlers, simply put, operated within constraints that produced frontier tranquility.

Foremost among constraints, it appears, was powerful consensus. It included basic understandings on important matters: humankind's fallen nature; fear of God; the absolute necessity of virtuous citizenry in republican society and institutions; restraint as the core of republican virtue; reluctance to push matters too far; the value of self-government and limited government; widespread ownership of land; factors legitimizing government; belief in a nonpoliticized society, one with much civil space; presumption of innocence, and faith in judicial processes and guarantees; need for broad tolerance, if not acceptance; subordinate positions for blacks; and belief that Indians, whatever their virtues, would make way for advancing American civilization. Even among Indians, blacks, and whites, however, some basic consensus facilitated commercial, social, and legal interaction.

* * *

Slavery and race spawned much tension and some violence. The Northwest Ordinance, the state constitution, and proslavery failure in 1824 hammered slavery. In addition, southern settlers joined vociferous Easterners and Europeans in flailing the foundering institution. Illinois' Underground Railroad shunted runaways northward. Conductors, stations, and lines concentrated in corridors running northward from Alton through Jacksonville, Pittsfield, and Quincy, on to Knoxville and Bloomington, and then to Joliet and Chicago. Unlike other northern states, Illinois never resisted the Fugitive Slave Law of 1850 by passing personal liberty laws, but Illinois State Supreme Court decisions from 1825 to 1852 killed slavery and indentured servitude, a quasi-slavery. The state supreme court eliminated remnants of slavery in Illinois in 1845 via its decision in *Jarrot v. Jarrot*. Many slaves entering Illinois attained freedom, and few Illinoisans mourned slavery's demise.

Consensus in Illinois blocked slavery's expansion, and by the 1840s outright slavery in Illinois vanished and de facto slavery via indentured servitude tottered. Of course, consensus consigned most blacks to limited social roles, but it also restrained most who fought over slavery, abolition, and roles of blacks. Sharp fights tested consensus, but only occasionally broke it. Slave trackers, though, sometimes shattered consensus and politicized previously uninvolved bystanders. They burst into homes and dragged away suspected runaways. Far worse, trackers sometimes shanghaied almost any black, including some who had never been slaves. This violated common decency, stirring up a hornets' nest, even justifying violence to free kidnaped blacks.

A poignant kidnaping incident in Bond County illustrated consensus' complexities. A Kentuckian master arrived with slaves, including a woman named Fanny and her son and daughter, but not Fanny's husband. The owner returned to Kentucky, but Fanny was sick, so she and her children stayed behind for months while she recuperated. In a county brimming with southern settlers, she found work and acceptance. Neighbors, in fact, informed her she was now free, since she had resided in Illinois for sixty days without her master.

A Kentuckian named Magoon, however, soon announced he had purchased Fanny and her offspring, and prepared to return them to Kentucky. Local people cautioned Magoon that they were free and hustling them from Illinois would violate law. But Magoon was adamant, and he conspired with two local fellows to kidnap the trio. Magoon and his accomplices spirited Fanny and her offspring away. But authorities caught them in Madison County, released Fanny and the children, and charged the kidnapers, who posted bond.

But, evidently, the kidnapers never faced trial. Perhaps public sentiment in Madison County would not countenance such a trial. People sympathized with Fanny, but probably frowned on prosecuting the two local fellows. Magoon left, continued plotting, returned, and arranged the kidnaping of Fanny's son. Inflamed, a pack of howling locals set off in hot pursuit, but after several days the trail grew cold.

This ugly incident both reinforced and severely tested consensus concerning blacks, slavery, runaways, kidnaping, slave trackers, law, and common decency. Residents certainly expressed divided opinions. Few were abolitionists, but people liked Fanny and probably felt sorry for her, making this slavery incident personal and immediate. In addition, Magoon clearly overstepped himself, and he was probably not likeable. People saw firsthand slavery's basic unfairness, its callous inhumanity. For some, this justified radical measures to uproot it. Other folk disliked slavery, but were squeamish about inflaming passions, breaking laws, or using violence.

The Fugitive Slave Law of 1850, and "black laws" passed by Illinois in 1853, which reinforced similar laws of 1819 and 1829 in restricting blacks and discouraging settlement, were patently unjust and had the effect of angering heretofore uninvolved people. While most probably implicitly assented to these laws, some Illinoisans detested them, and their enforcement was sporadic, despite some severe penalties. In Bureau County, these laws repelled nearly everyone and they were treated with contempt. Some Will County residents believed laws enforcing slavery were "against the law of God . . . however they might be enforced by human courts. It was an easy corollary to this belief that to help a man who was fleeing was a duty—that to aid in his capture was a crime against God and man."[6] Responses to free blacks and runaways hinged greatly upon sentiment in specific locales.

An incident involving a fugitive slave in Jacksonville illustrates much about threats, fear, violence, consensus, and law. In late 1842 Sarah Lisle traveled from Kentucky with her slave maid, Judy Green, for a lengthy visit in Jacksonville. Judy slipped away in February 1843, and Samuel Willard, a student at Illinois College, and his father helped Judy flee town, aided by the Wolcott and Carter families. Soon Samuel Willard and his father were charged with harboring slaves, and proslavery elements and others in the largely southern town pursued Judy.[7] Samuel Willard noted "hostility" to abolitionists, and W. Chauncey Carter later commented on "hatred" directed against abolitionists. During the episode, anti-abolitionists kicked and hit one of Samuel's helpful friends, whacked another with a stout stick, employed known ruffians, and brandished a pistol. One Sunday evening members of the Old School Presbyterian Church muttered about tarring and feathering the Willards. Peer pressure dissuaded David B. Ayers and Murray McConnel from helping Willard.

But no terrible physical violence occurred. Samuel Willard observed that throughout "all this affair the officers of the law treated me courteously, even kindly." He was housed not in jail, but in the Mansion House, a leading hotel. Although a ruffian forced his father and Judy to return to Jacksonville at gunpoint, no shots were fired. One of the constables in Jacksonville, Archibald Dixon, told Willard that he would have let him go were it not for public opinion. Willard enjoyed cool, low-key discussions about slavery with both Dixon and the county jailer, normally a volatile fellow. When proslavery folk formed an "Anti–Negro Stealing Society" to thwart abolitionists and noted that Willard and two other Illinois College students had tried to free Judy, the treasurer of the college defended Willard, and the faculty supported Willard unanimously, even if one of the college's trustees did not. When Presbyterians discussed tar and feathers, one spoke against it, "and the matter was dropped at once." When a young man from Boston who was "a Garrisonian abolitionist" stepped forward to offer Willard his small savings, Willard deemed him to be "of that pestilent breed" and sent him away; Willard and others shunned radical troublemakers. A state supreme court judge, Samuel Drake Lockwood, quashed five of the six counts of the indictment against Samuel Willard's father, found him guilty on the remaining count, and fined him lightly. Samuel Willard pled guilty and was fined one dollar. Although the unsuccessful fight to keep Judy from being sent back to slavery generated strong feelings, public sentiment and reason tempered actions and restraint and law prevailed. Judy's dashed hopes and reenslavement constituted the episode's major violence.

Sometimes things turned out more satisfactorily for the enslaved. On May 6, 1827, William Drury made his mark on a document that read, "I William Drury of Prairie du Rocher . . . have covenanted and agreed and by these presents do covenant and agree with my mulatto woman, Mary, who now lives with Mr. James L. Lamb in Kaskaskia, that whenever she shall pay to me the sum of seventy-eight dollars she shall from that day be free and at liberty to control and be controlled with the same manner that any free person may do." On the back of the document is a witnessed statement with William Drury's mark on it indicating that on June 2, 1828, the amount was paid in full. Evidently, this manumission was satisfactory to all parties.

Unspoken understandings shaped much conflict and cooperation concerning slavery and race. Richard, for example, was a

Kentucky-born slave, brought to Oquawka by his third owner, Captain William Phelps, where he aided Phelps in trading with Iowa Indians. He once saved Phelps's brother and family from fire, himself suffering injuries, which made him forever welcome in the Phelpses' households. He became a trusted aide in the Phelps brothers' trading businesses. Richard never became free—apparently no manumission occurred—but he enjoyed great latitude. He traveled widely, traded, carried a gun, interacted with Indians, and became de facto junior partner in the Phelpses' businesses, all without explicit agreement or contract. When he grew old, the Phelps brothers put him "on the retired list, with pay and rations." He gained much freedom because the Phelps brothers allowed it, others tacitly consented, and he exerted himself.

If Richard's latitude was remarkable, William Cooper's in Cass County was astounding. When Cooper, a black man, settled around 1821, virtually all his neighbors were Southerners. In 1826 he claimed and purchased land. Local people accepted him, as well as his white wife. Evidently, he and his family attended local Methodist services. Perhaps his personality traits deflected or even obviated outrage. Maybe he had some prized skill or knack that helped neighbors overlook skin color and intermarriage. In any case, they were Cass County residents for years, which suggests that they fit in quite well.

Born a slave in 1777, in 1795 Frank "Free Frank" McWhorter was brought to Kentucky, where he married Lucy, also a slave, in 1799. Intelligent and ambitious, he managed his master's farm and became an entrepreneur. He purchased his wife's freedom in 1817, his own two years later, and that of many family members over years. In 1830 he and his family moved to Pike County, Illinois. During the 1830s he and his two sons bought 800 acres for over $2,000. In 1836 he platted New Philadelphia, a biracial community and one of twenty-three towns founded in Pike County between 1834 and 1837. Outside of Chicago, only four towns in 1840 had black populations approaching 100: Alton, Jacksonville, Quincy, and Springfield. New Philadelphia became a nodal point for regional black activities. In 1850 it contained only fifty-eight of Hadley Township's 1,170 residents, but it was the township's only town. It sported typical frontier town functions: blacksmith, general store, post office, stage stop, wheelwright, cabinet maker, and two shoemakers, all serving New Philadelphia's hinterland and transient traffic. Its remoteness helped it, minimizing competition. The community reflected the creative energies of determined, talented people, who overcame tremendous odds.[8]

Free Frank functioned amid racism and kidnaping threats, surmounting illiteracy to raise stock and speculate. Displaying skill, determination, and integrity, he impressed white neighbors, who were too busy obtaining land and making a living to pick on him and his kin, had they been so inclined. Finally, some neighbors, such as Abraham Scholl, were antislavery Southerners who openly encouraged him.

Richard, William Cooper, and Free Frank obviously possessed skills and traits necessary to succeed. Another Pike County black man, however, evidently lacked them. In 1832 or 1833 he cast eyes on a white woman, hinting at marriage. Local folk literally ushered him from the region. Maybe he was socially maladroit, or possibly Pike Countians were less tolerant than Cass Countians about intermarriage. Also, Cooper had arrived in Cass County already married, unlike this hapless suitor, who misread powerful consensus and suffered the consequences.

Emancipated slaves in Illinois had some latitude. In Warren County in 1834 Joseph Murphy appeared in court to manumit a slave who desired to leave for Liberia. Murphy put up bonds of $1,000 to insure the freedman's not becoming a public charge, and then freed the slave, who assumed the name of Richard Murphy. Then something significant happened: Richard Murphy not only did not head to Liberia, but he stayed put in Warren County, becoming "one of the best citizens therein" and fairly wealthy.

As frontier Illinois faded, a Wabash County abolitionist resisted assault in Mt. Carmel, killing one assailant and wounding another. This incident reflects decades of unexpected twists and turns. In 1818 the area that became Wabash County in 1824 contained at least twenty-five indentured servants, quasi-slaves brought from the South just before statehood. Local sentiment, it appears, helped emancipate most servants, one freed as early as 1822. About the same time, a black man named Bunting ran a tanyard near Mt. Carmel. The census of 1850, remarkably, showed two Mt. Carmel black students in public school, an anomaly in America. Although Wabash County hardly seethed with abolitionists, it contained freed slaves, Bunting, and black students, products of unspoken and powerful sentiment. Moreover, the abolitionist's lethal self-defense *was* deemed justified.

Threats and occasional violence marred racial issues. Hiram Beckwith recalled courageous people bucking prevailing sentiments in Danville. Noting unpopular abolitionist views of a local minister, the Reverend Kingsbury, he remembered "when both Whig and Democratic parties, and all other shades of political opinion, held that slavery was right, and that any person who held the contrary opinion was regarded as a disturber of the peace, and liable to be pelted with rotten eggs, if not subjected to severe bodily harm." People blamed abolitionists for fomenting trouble in frontier Bloomington, Albert Dodd depicting the tension on November 30, 1843: "There is nothing very new going on here. Abolitionism is making some fuss. There is to be a convention of them here next Wednesday & the people of the county are resolved they shall not get a foothold in it. As the majority of the people are Kentuckians they will be apt to do all that is necessary to stop their meeting, & I anticipate a considerable row if they cannot be prevented peaceably." The year, 1843, is significant, for slavery in Illinois was moribund. Nevertheless, national struggles found their way into Illinois.

Although Kentuckians around Bloomington in 1843 opposed abolitionists, probably none aspired to own slaves. Very likely they quit Kentucky to escape slavery and everything associated with it. Perhaps Bloomington's tensions cloaked the real conflict, a cultural conflict. Even Southerners who opposed slavery wearied of hearing abolitionists carp about it. The struggle, moreover, involved two visions of America: on the one hand, Jeffersonian assumptions, values, outlook; and, on the other, a modernizing America, a Hamiltonian America embracing commerce, transportation, urbanization, and interdependency.

Even after the Compromise of 1850 crumbled, consensus still channeled struggles. In Jacksonville, for example, merchants sympathetic to abolitionism were boycotted, pressured socially, and ostracized. Timothy Chamberlain, who sympathized with runaway slaves, realized that whenever he left his wagon unattended it moved, which did not amuse him. A Yankee physician in Jacksonville, allegedly combating slavery, took to walking down the centers of streets when he ventured forth at night, worried that darkened recesses harbored enemies. Heightening his fear of darkness was his conviction that arsonists had tried to torch his house one night.[9]

Boycotts, social pressures, and wandering wagons lay within consensus. Arson did not. Neither did kidnapings of suspected runaways, especially popular runaways. Since ardent partisans saw slavery in moral terms, some pushed matters to extremes. Knowing exactly what they were doing, they hoped to provoke crisis, confident that the ends justified the means. Still, even in emotional fights involving moral issues, nearly everyone fought within consensus, not using arson, for example. Spates of violence occasionally tore social fabric, horrifying settlers, but massive strife never convulsed Illinois.

Such spates were typically brief, isolated, and shocking, usually eliciting harsh condemnation and often backfiring. In 1824 the proslavery drive stalled in the state legislature. A contested election in Pike County heartened proslavery folk, whose candidate, John Shaw, sought to oust Nicholas Hansen, the incumbent representative. In Vandalia, the state capital, fiery speeches and riotous mobs intimidated lawmakers, producing Hansen's ouster. Jubilant mobs stormed through town, berating Governor Coles, who backed Hansen, and hurling invective outside Coles's house and lodgings of pro-Hansen legislators. But these tactics backfired. Finding backbone, legislators condemned Hansen's removal. Even proslavery people denounced mob action as illegitimate pressure. Sharp fighting within political arenas was one thing, but intimidation of legislators was another. Reaction set in, proslavery support evaporated, and in 1824 a solid majority of voters unexpectedly buried proslavery hopes.

Straining consensus mightily, unexpected allies helped abolitionists. For example, some authorities dragged their feet, obstructing the capture of runaways. Some foot-dragging was blatant and public, and some was covert and implicit, accomplished with a wink and a nod. Authorities indicted Joseph Morse, a renowned Woodford County abolitionist, for guiding runaways northward. Morse rejected bail and help from solicitous friends, seeking jail instead. But Woodford County had no jail, so authorities transported him to neighboring Tazewell County, where the jailer rejected him, claiming that he lacked the requisite forms.

Sometimes profit motives clouded abolitionism. James Brown wrote from Quincy on February 24, 1841, to Dan Weed in Marblehead, Massachusetts. After investing considerable capital, he and Weed marketed sugar beet machines to process beets from western Illinois. Brown also dabbled in abolition. He wrote, "As we have a number of Abolitionists hear [*sic*], we would like to have the sugar of our own manufacture so as not to need the products of slave labour in that respect." By providing a substitute for slave-produced Louisiana sugar, Brown's machines would please conscience, palate, and wallet. Similarly, David Robson measured slavery's pulse as he sought opportunity. On July 25, 1823, he predicted the impact on land values in Edwards County of efforts to amend the state constitution to allow outright slavery: "About this time twelve months it will be known whether this will be a Slave State or not, but the most knowing people think there is no doubt but it will." Slavery, he added, would boost land sales. Maybe he opposed slavery, but prospects of brisk land sales enticed him.

Controversies surrounding slavery, abolitionism, and race flickered for decades. Although they sparked occasional violence, they also fostered voluntary associations and keen cooperation. A few voluntary networks, for example, either shored up slavery or promoted overall southern interests. Similarly, patchworks of organizations, ad hoc activities, and individual efforts, operating under umbrellas of consensus, eradicated slavery and indentured servitude. Formal constitutions guided some voluntary associations combating slavery. In any case, caution and muted activities marked many antislavery associations, commonly transcending individual interests and strengthening social fabric.

Some antislavery organizations popping up were affiliated with national organizations. Varying greatly, they hid and shunted runaways northward, lobbied politicians, educated the public, and ameliorated lives of free blacks, almost always functioning within broad consensus so as to not antagonize people. The St. Clair Society for the Prevention of Slavery in Illinois was formed early, on March 22, 1823, spearheaded by the Rev. John Mason Peck, a Baptist from Connecticut. Although he abhorred slavery, he also condemned militant abolitionists. At the same time, though, he favored expanded freedom for free blacks.[10]

Another early antislavery alliance, the Morganian Society, organized in Morgan County by 1824 to stifle that year's crucial proslavery drive. Its constitution was remarkable, given the county's overwhelming southern mien. The preamble illuminates political philosophy, social views, and concerns about slavery: "Under a free government public opinion gives energy to the laws; happiness and security of the community being the legitimate end, every good citizen thereof has an interest in its support; under its fostering wing, his moral, his religious, and his political rights are maintained; virtue and inteligence [*sic*] should be its bond of union." These republican sentiments energized frontier laws.

The document continued its truths: "But as man is naturally prone to abuse power, it is rendered necessary for the security of the whole, that this dangerous propensity should be well guarded against." Virtually all Americans feared unchecked, abusive power. So great was this fear, in fact, that even those ardently favoring reform, including abolition, usually opposed governmental involvement, preferring the Morganian Society and other private undertakings.

The document paraded its specific purpose: "Therefore, we, citizens of Morgan County, have thought it advisable to form a society for the purpose of concentrating public opinion; and by a frequent interchange thereof to enlighten and direct each other. When entering into association it becomes an indispensable duty to adopt a regular system of establishing order. It is the declared design and intention of this society, to promote the public good, by using all honorable means to prevent the introduction of slavery into this state; by maintaining the purity of elections, by cherishing political harmony, and by restraining vice and immorality." The phrases "regular system of establishing order" and "honorable means," "maintaining . . . purity," "political harmony," and "restraining vice" are instructive. The document displayed 131 men's signatures. (Women sometimes affixed signatures to documents chartering local congregations and certain social organizations, but constitutions of political movements—especially those of contentious causes—rarely had women's signatures.)

The constitution contained fourteen articles. The first stated that the Society existed "for the dissemination of political knowledge, and the maintenance of the inalienable rights of man." The second restricted membership to any man who had "attained the age of eighteen years, is averse to slavery, and is a citizen of this country." Stipulations of citizenship and age are noteworthy. (The state constitution conferred suffrage on all *adult* white *male* residents of Illinois.) Perhaps Society members worried that non-citizen membership would ignite corrosive controversy. Article eight tasked a standing committee to block slavery's introduction "by using all lawful means." Antislavery partisans would fight within law. Clearly, members were not willing to destroy society to save it from slavery. Finally, articles eleven, twelve, and fourteen arranged for elections, removals from office, and amending the constitution. Implicitly, these articles addressed potential conflict, facilitating smooth operations, consensus, and order.

Through the organization, 131 cooperating men resisted an advancing threat. The state constitution hobbled slavery, so continuation of the status quo promised slavery's extinction. Recognizing this, the voluntaristic, cooperative Morganian Society was an instrument—a weapon—for controlled conflict in *defense* of the status quo, which countenanced lingering vestigial slavery for a finite time. In resisting full-scale, robust slavery in an orderly fashion, it sought slavery's quiet demise. The Society's constitution, procedures, and desire for status quo stressed consensus.

By the late 1830s, though, consensus crumbled. The Illinois State Anti-Slavery Convention met in Alton October 26–28, 1837, amid escalating tension. Mobs had destroyed printing presses operated by the Rev. Elijah P. Lovejoy, who would soon die defending a new press. Stridently, the Convention demanded immediate national abolition. But the Convention's minutes, reflecting internal dissension, recorded a delay the first day, "the intrusion of a number of disorderly persons," and a contested presidential election, won by the Rev. Gideon Blackburn, a Carlinville resident from Virginia. The Convention differed markedly from the Morganian Society.

President Blackburn read a communication from a local church:

> Sir,
>
> When application was made to us as trustees of the Presbyterian Church for permission to hold the Convention in their house, our understanding was that the deliberations of that body, as well as the discussions of the same were to be free to all *orderly well disposed persons* who were *opposed* to slavery, and were willing to be governed by proper rules and regulations in debate. If therefore the discussions of your body should be otherwise we protest against the house being used for a one-sided discussion.[11]

Three trustees signed it. Its call for orderly, free discussion implies that such discussion was jeopardized. A revealing item was penned beneath the minutes: "Note: This communication brought forth the loud shouting and stamping of the mob, who then professed great zeal for *free* discussion. But who that very day foreclosed all discussion so as they had it in their power, by adjourning the convention *sine die.*" The stamping and shouting, concern over property use, and dilemmas of allowing dissenting voices indicate tensions and turbulence. Consensus concerning the first amendment, common courtesy, and related matters decayed, soon snatching Lovejoy's life.

His death further split abolitionists. Some abolitionists rattled other opponents of slavery. For example, on February 16, 1838, J. Buchanan, a prominent Macoupin County abolitionist, noted that David A. Smith, another abolitionist, denounced abolitionist newspaper attacks. Writing in the *Alton Observer* shortly before Lovejoy's death, Smith claimed that these attacks forced slaveowners to clamp down on slaves. Buchanan, writing about Smith on February 16, 1838, noted,

he had hitherto manifested, not only no desire, but a positive aversion,
to read Anti-Slavery publications. I have once or twice offered him
the *Philanthropist*, but so afraid, it seems, was he of contracting
some smell of "Incendiarism," that he never as much as looked over
a single no. In addition to these things, he has professedly given his
support to the *Observer* only through a desire to sustain the freedom
of the press. Last summer he was of the opinion that the paper
contained too much Anti-slavery matter, thought that the paper did
not partake sufficiently of the character of a Religious newspaper. In
fine, he was decidedly of the opinion that Mr. Lovejoy had violated
his pledge originally given to the citizens of Alton.

And then Buchanan quoted Dr. Blackburn, noting that he would
rather contribute funds to prosecute those who had destroyed
Lovejoy's presses than donate piddling sums to continue the newspaper. Clearly, Blackburn favored prosecuting vandals, but he
believed abolitionist newspapers had limited value, possibly negative value. Personality clashes and differences over tactics rent
many organizations. Hyperbole and demonization of opponents
during the waning of frontier Illinois detonated sporadic violence,
helping destroy the Whig Party.[12]

* * *

Yankees and others expressed anti-Catholic and anti-immigrant feelings by the 1830s, years before torrents of Irish and
Germans arrived. In 1846 one publication urged Protestants to
found colleges in the West, forecasting, "The North American
continent is now to be populated with swarming millions. Forest
and prairie are to be converted into cornfields, and cities are to
rise amid the solitudes of six thousand years." It warned, "Rome
pursues with sleepless vigilance the German or Irish emigrant
. . . wherever she finds him employed, in constructing our railroads, digging our canals, or becoming the hewer of wood and
the drawer of water to the more opulent inhabitants of our populous cities," and then admonished, "The mingling of these foreign elements with our population is almost the whole secret of
her power: and well has she shown that she understands its value.
She is expending her treasures in strengthening, encouraging,
and extending it, free as the waters of our great river."[13] This

alarmist evaluation contains two points: America's future lay in the Mississippi Valley; there progressive, enlightened forces contended with dark, reactionary forces. Some believed battles in the Valley would determine America's soul. But although the Valley was home to serious struggles, practically no one died in the fighting. The stakes were enormous, but the violence was minimal.

Probably the worst single conflict not involving Indians erupted along the Illinois & Michigan Canal route in 1838, a depression year. Canal laborers endured economic decline, wretched working conditions, scruffy shanty towns, and fatal diseases. Violence flared between two factions of Irish immigrant laborers, Catholic Corkonians and Protestant Fardowners, or "Leinster men." Believing Protestants received favoritism in hiring, some two hundred seething Corkonians rampaged through La Salle, guzzling liquor and beating people. After three days of disruptions, a sheriff's posse confronted Corkonians near Buffalo Rock, tried to subdue them, and fired. Between ten and fifteen died, some shot while fleeing.[14] Depression and prejudices prompted the shootings, but ancient hatreds imported from Ireland set the stage for the bloodbath, a significant fact. Although Yankee Illinoisans strode zestfully into cultural conflict, they and their foes committed little mayhem.

Yankees viewed immigrants with misgivings. For one thing, some of them, especially the Irish Catholics laboring on the Illinois & Michigan Canal, were scrappy imbibers. (During the 1830s and later, the Whig Party harped on recent immigrants, campaigning against allowing them to vote in general elections. Such actions wedded many Irish to the Democratic Party.) For another, immigrant women did more field work than Yankee women. Although Yankee women toiled ceaselessly, they neither cherished nor performed much stoop-work.[15] Furthermore, Yankee women were relatively well-schooled, at least compared to immigrant women and southern women. The prospect of swarms of illiterate immigrant women laboring in western fields alarmed New Englanders and others; they raced to plant correct values and institutions in the Mississippi Valley. They envisioned the Valley containing a huge population, maybe even as the national capital. They knew Valley society was still embryonic, still malleable, with competing ideas scrambling for dominance—in short, up for grabs. Newcomers, moreover, heavily influenced evolving society, heady stuff to two categories of people: those with strong, defined missions, and those with little prior social influence.

Morris Birkbeck, a prime backer of the English Settlement in Edwards County, wrote from Illinois on November 29, 1817: "Society is made up of new comers chiefly, and of course must partake of the leading characters of these." He added, "Where we are sitting, society is yet unborn as it were. It will, as in other places, be made up of such as come, among whom English farmers, I presume will form a large proportion." Birkbeck wished English settlers success in Illinois, but he also believed they would benefit the state. Even relatively few English farmers, he realized, could greatly alter the state's future. Frances Landon Willard championed certain values and institutions. In 1846 this toiling Christian from Vermont opened in Chicago a "female seminary" to uplift Illinois by properly influencing "the heterogeneous mass of populations from whence our pupils are collected."[16] She stressed Christian morality, self-control, and responsibility. A primary goal was "the amalgamation of classes," by which "the *poor* girl takes a high rank" and the affluent girl learns "to understand and be humble." Willard claimed class amalgamation undergirded American society and republican government. Correct education, she believed, strengthened social harmony, thereby obviating class conflict. This Yankee admonished right-thinking people to join the fray to shape the West, knowing a few strong individuals could make a big difference.

Some believe frontier America throbbed with oppression, violence, and exploitation, with predators stalking the landscape, committing mayhem and murder. Some maintain conflict—even germ warfare—spewed corpses across the landscape. Although the issues and the conflicting foes changed over time, this argument runs, violence was the defining element of frontier life. Decades of movies, television, and pulp novels reinforce these claims. Still, these apocalyptic versions generally pertain to trans-

Mississippi frontiers, not to frontier Illinois, and most allegedly occurred after 1860, after frontier Illinois faded.[17] Mounting evidence points to frontier tranquility.[18]

* * *

Visitors marveled at Illinois' diverse immigrants. In 1842, for example, William Oliver visited Randolph County, observing people from many quarters of the world, including "Dutch, Germans, Swiss, Yankees, Irish, Scotch, a few English, and a number from the more southern states."[19] Very likely, during the 1830s more Yankees and Southerners mixed in Illinois than elsewhere. Simeon Francis wrote from central Illinois on July 6, 1831: "Our population is of every color that you can imagine and almost of every nation." People of French, French-Indian, Indian, German, southern, Yankee, English, black, mulatto, and other extractions interacted there. On December 3, 1834, unsettled social conditions near Canton impressed Lucy Maynard. In frontier Illinois, she lamented, "everything is so different—the people, their manners, their mode of living." Maynard initially regarded her unusual neighbors negatively, but she adjusted. Social diversity was impressive, even if it troubled some. An anonymous letter written on January 19, 1836 to the Rev. William Irving, of England, indicates abiding dissatisfaction with frontier diversity. The writer, almost certainly a fellow Briton, cautioned Irving, "From the mingled multitudes who come from all quarters and from all denominations you must gather together the few (from their knowledge of the scriptures and of our worship learned in the counties whence they emigrated) who will hear your first call." Diversity, the letter lamented, daunted those who sought to establish right worship. The letter added, "As to the peculiarities of the people to whom you will thus minister in holy things, I leave you to judge yourself after repeating to you that they come from the Atlantic states of America, from Canada, from Ireland, from England & in vast numbers from the first settled of the Western States. On the whole they are a people of all characters and classes, & speaking the English language." The letter admitted that many settlers were able "to appreciate whatever is excellent in gospel truth or in eloquence of diction or soundness

of reasoning." Settlement in Illinois and surrounding frontiers
was "one of the most interesting spectacles, in point of future destiny, in the scale of civilized beings perhaps to be found on earth." Because the socially diverse Mississippi Valley could sustain one hundred million people, correct religion was supremely important. Finally, the lead mines of Galena attracted people literally from all over the world, "the most wonderful mixture of humanity that I ever beheld."[20]

Others noted the influx of various peoples. On September 5, 1836, Griswold C. Morgan wrote from Chicago, singing the praises of Rock River Valley and adding, "it is now fast filling up with people from the states of Ohio, Indiana, Kentucky, Tennessee, and Illinois." Charles Joseph Latrobe, visiting Chicago in the early 1830s, saw people who were "white, black, brown, and red—half-breeds, quarter-breeds, and men of no breed at all."[21] Roland Tinkham penned a letter from Chicago on August 23, 1831, telling of pirogue operators who transported him from Michigan to Chicago: "We employed a mongrel Frenchman and his Lady to paddle us and our baggage round the south end of the lake to Chicago. By the way, the people there are more than half French, and they are as much as half-Indians." People of mixed French-Indian ancestry intrigued travelers.

Settled counties sported diverse populations. For example, Indians, settlers from the Carolinas and Georgia, and Kentuckians and Tennesseans inhabited Washington County, formed in 1818. They were of Irish, Scottish, Welsh, English, German, and African extraction. Later, organized groups arrived from Germany, Poland, and New England.

Guidebooks touted the West's diversity. In 1832 one observed, "The population of the Valley of the Mississippi is exceedingly heterogeneous, if we regard the very great variety of nations of which it is composed. There is not a country in Europe which has not furnished some portion of its population." It then noted the variety of states supplying population to the West. Finally, it observed that some population streams entering Illinois from such places as Pennsylvania brought Germans, Scots, and others.[22]

Demographic changes increased heterogeneity by 1850. In 1818 some 38 percent of Illinois' 35,000 to 40,000 inhabitants hailed from southern states. About 37 percent were natives of western states, Kentucky contributing over half and Tennessee a hefty portion. A paltry 3 percent were born in New England.[23] Thirty-two years later, in 1850, census figures revealed 851,470 Illinoisans. Of that total 331,089, or 39.18 percent, were born in Illinois. Those born in other states numbered 399,733, or 47.25 percent. New York, the largest donor state, contributed 67,180 to Illinois' population. Ohio was a close second, with 64,219. Kentucky, the largest donor state in 1818, now occupied third place, contributing 49,588. Of the top ten donor states, six were north of the Mason-Dixon Line and the Ohio River, and four were south. Still, these figures are somewhat misleading, for many arriving from Indiana and Ohio had southern roots, as did most native Illinoisans. Nevertheless, a massive demographic shift had occurred. Reflecting this change, power either slipped from southern hands or became modified in the hands of Abraham Lincoln, Richard Yates, and similar Southerners. Foreign born in 1850 totaled 111,860, or 13.22 percent. The birthplaces of 3,352, or .40 percent, were unknown. Of the foreign born, only 51,647 hailed from the British Isles, including 27,786 Irish. Germans totaled 38,160, Canadians 10,699. Of the state's 851,470 residents in 1850, perhaps just 144,809 were born south of the Mason-Dixon Line and the Ohio River, or approximately 17 percent, a plunge from about 71 percent just thirty-two years previously.

* * *

Ethnic differences sometimes exacerbated other troubles. For example, in 1821 Edwards County, organized in 1814, consisted of modern Edwards and Wabash counties. Stagnant water made Palmyra, the first county seat, a hellhole by 1821. Everyone was clamoring for a new location. Albion was chosen over Mt. Carmel, unleashing "the first serious county seat controversy in Illinois and one of the earliest anywhere."[24] When searing memories of Anglo-Indian attacks were still fresh in American minds, George Flower and fellow British had founded Albion in 1818. Albion lacked timber, good water, and was only about four miles from the county's western border. Moreover, its very name miffed neighbors. Besides, people living east of Bonpas Creek realized that Albion's victory benefitted Albion's English immigrants and hurt Mt. Carmel's American settlers, some sixteen miles away. Finally, in September of 1821 Albion's partisans had the county sheriff arrested for not returning some public records to Albion.

Aggrieved Americans saw a solution: muster the militia, march on Albion, pry remaining county records from the cheeky Brits, and return them to their rightful place, Mt. Carmel. Americans drilled four militia companies near Mt. Carmel, marched toward Albion, monarchy's subversive bastion, and camped for the night. Next morning the march resumed, but the militia quickly ran headlong into a pack of peacemongers from Albion, a delegation authorized to negotiate. Good sense prevailed, tensions subsided, and people went away. Albion retained the county seat, a significant achievement.

Foreigners understood the importance of county government's functions. William Newham Blane, a visiting Briton, observed Albion was "considerably benefitted by having been lately elevated to the rank of a county seat; and it will, no doubt, some day or other, become a place of importance." In 1824 Wabash County was cleaved from Edwards County, Mt. Carmel obtaining the county seat. Peace brought desired results not possible from marching militia companies.

Unlike most county-seat tiffs, this one involved potentially explosive ethnic animosity. Efforts at Albion to replicate English deference and class arrangements affronted republican Americans. The militia's march toward Albion highlights another ingredient for disaster on the frontier: many ordinary men went about armed. William Blane saw much and liked a great deal, but he noted, "A custom much to be blamed among the better class in the Western States, is that of wearing concealed weapons."[25] Blane and others deplored concealed weapons, but it is possible that an armed society is a polite society, even if some tiffs quickly escalate into tragedies.

Often spats among immigrants erupted. In the 1830s and 1840s the zealous Daniel Scherer, a Lutheran missionary, labored in Illinois. His parishioners cut contributions, balked at repairing his well, and generally grumped. What really riled Scherer, though, was poor attendance at his Saturday confirmation classes and preparatory classes for Communion; many parishioners attended horse races, instead. He waded into other controversies as well. Referring to Lutheran clergy, Scherer wrote, "They ought either to be native Germans or able to speak the language with perfect correctness, free from all American admixture." The Lutheran church in Illinois and elsewhere "became deeply ensnared in a web of language and ethnicity that severely hampered denominational growth." Lutherans decided to minister only to Germans and their descendants, and only in the German language. Deleterious effects of these self-imposed restrictions were "compounded by synodical alliances and by personal, state, and nationalistic rivalries—to say nothing of the theological and liturgical disputes that divided German Protestants into conservative and moderate camps." Such discord sometimes spilled into larger society.

Internecine conflict rent the English community in Edwards County, superseding bickering between George Flower and Morris Birkbeck. The rift involved two towns: Albion, Flower's stronghold, and Wanborough, two miles away and Birkbeck's bailiwick. In addition, conflict involved laborers, contractors, merchants, and others. Allegations of sexual misconduct flew, and slander and gossip foamed. Accusations of trespass, assault, and battery brought costly litigation and hastened ruin. Albion's economy faltered, and Birkbeck's accidental drowning impaired the entire colonization undertaking. Even so, in another sense the colony succeeded, for Edwards County attracted English immigrants for decades.[26]

One grim, prolonged conflict pitted determined Indians against inexorably advancing settlers. Given existing realities, perhaps this cultural collision was irreconcilable. Further, it is probable that American views, superior numbers, and technology virtually precluded true consensus. The amalgam middle ground, however transitory, mediated and tempered some conflict, Indians and Americans mingling on rough equality. Cultural chasms still separated the two societies, but vigorous contact and cooperation did occur in the middle ground. Even before Americans settled Illinois, a middle ground functioned in the East, and "within that zone, the contact of peoples was a protracted process of cultural exchange."[27] Intercultural, or transcultural, features of Illinois' middle ground operated over years, fostering cooperation and mitigating troubles, even as foundations for middle ground life crumbled by 1815 and disappeared by 1832.

But troubles brewed over differing ideas concerning land ownership. Indians believed they had *use* of land and land's products, and did not *own* the land itself. Sale of land, they assumed, conveyed *use* of land and land's products, not sole and exclusive ownership of land. This assumption clashed with American ideas, which maintained land purchases conveyed outright ownership of land. Consequently, misunderstandings and cries of injustice surfaced. Indians sometimes compounded difficulties by selling a parcel of land two or three times.[28] Furthermore, uncertainty about *which* Indians truly had authority to sell land clouded sales.

The two cultures also differed over judicial assumptions and processes. Indians practiced a kinship-centered system, in which a murderer either paid the victim's relatives to "cover the dead," or the relatives extracted frightful retribution. Such justice differed sharply from American justice, in which the state dispensed justice. Still, when Americans accused three Winnebago of killing two Americans near Fort Armstrong, chiefs delivered up the trio to authorities at Prairie du Chien, and witnessed justices of the peace interrogate them. Although misunderstandings produced some tense moments, the trial began on May 12, 1821, over a year after the killings. Before the trial started, however, authorities released the youngest defendant, convinced he had tried to prevent the killings. A jury found the other two defendants guilty, and the next day they were sentenced to hang. Eventually, both President James Monroe and Secretary of Defense John C. Calhoun intervened, delaying the executions, weighing pardons, and trying to insure justice. One Indian died in prison, and the other was hanged at Kaskaskia. To forestall possible revenge, the War Department paid the families of the two dead Indians. Indians adhered to tribal ideas of justice, causing Naw Kaw Carimani, the last Winnebago to claim tribal-wide chieftainship, to view the hanging as unjust. Perhaps the two views of justice were simply irreconcilable, but in this trial authorities tried to insure justice, demonstrating concern for basic fairness.[29]

Sometimes reflective minds and common sense staved off potentially lethal conflict. For example, in 1824 Keokuk led a large force through Pike County to fight other Indians in Missouri. Realizing the presence of such a force might distress local residents, he sent word ahead to allay concern. This understanding worked, the force passed through, and trouble was averted.

Growing frontier diversity, perhaps ironically, helped strengthen consensus. By the 1830s or so, no single social or political segment could dominate all others. Like it or not, people were stuck with each other. Of course, southern influences continued, but they were far from complete, given southern fissures on many issues. By the late 1830s Illinois—especially the northern two thirds—was an admixture of French, French-Indian, southern, Yankee, English, Irish, German, and other folk, as well as offspring of countless mixed marriages. This mixed population resembled that of the Middle Atlantic region during colonial times and later. Like that region, Illinois experienced social and political strife, which led to fluid coalitions, fragile compromises, and cautious restraint, but not horrendous conflict. Consensus often emerged because factions realized that pushing things to extremes was neither possible nor desirable. Furthermore, a toleration, however grudging, of strange neighbors became the norm, not the exception. Toleration did not imply acceptance, but it did mean that pragmatic live-and-let-live sentiments pervaded society.

Marriage fostered cooperation and consensus, creating new ties and social and economic arrangements. Business arrangements, private agreements, and other cooperative acts sprang from marriages and friendships. Marriages and friendships produced, for example, lines of credit, partnerships, and managerial skills. In other ways, as well, households and intermarriage between households strengthened frontier society. As one source put it, "Intermarriage between the children of settlers naturally cemented the pioneers into a more compact body, and greater unity and contentment prevailed in their home relations, social enjoyments and religious observances."[30] Cooperative acts originated among relatives and friends curbed or channeled discord.

Settlers' offspring tended to intermarry, smoothing differences and bridging cultural gulfs. Indian-French marriages were common, so were Anglo-French marriages by the early 1800s, and on

December 13, 1820, N. Burton wrote that men from Kentucky
actually preferred Yankee wives. David Carpenter noticed intermarriage among diverse people, indirectly approving such unions.
On June 20, 1834, he wrote to Josiah Scofield of Saratoga County,
New York, urging him to come to Pekatonika, adding, "Should
you wish to avoid the expense of moving a help mate, I think
you may find a better half among us; as our place is settled almost exclusively by eastern people, besides you would have your
choice of selecting one among the Buckeyes & Hoosiers." Carpenter's reference to Buckeyes and Hoosiers reveals the era's strong
attachment to one's original state. New Yorkers marrying Hoosiers hurdled great barriers, but their offspring married almost
anyone within their race, religion and class being only moderate
deterrents. Intermarriage defused many ancient animosities between English and Irish, British and French, Catholic and Protestant, Scot and English, and others, helping to create a hybrid
culture and prevent balkanization of Illinois and the Valley.

In general, formation of new culture in Hancock County mirrored similar developments throughout Illinois: diverse farm traditions took root, and "we can see how these regional cultures
interacted to form a hybrid farm culture distinctive to the immediate region."[31] This culture was not merely a mixture of various
elements in Illinois. Rather, migration, settlement, adaptation,
fluid frontier conditions, and blending of various cultures bred
new culture, Illinoisan hybrid culture. Nowhere did this culture
flourish more than in towns, where transportation arteries crossed
and various people mingled, rubbed elbows, learned new ways,
and adapted. Certain towns acquired reputations for having expertise in specific occupations. The "knowers" in various walks
of life clustered to draw upon each other's expertise, tapping existing structures, inputs, and markets. In this exchange, ethnic
and other distinctions faded somewhat.

Intermarriage, blurring ethnic distinctions, helped diverse
people learn and live. Most settlers learned eagerly. Ideas concerning farming, for example, flowed freely, much adopting and
adapting occurring. In 1828 James Ross left Pennsylvania and
came to Pike County. Pennsylvanians cut wheat with cradles, so
Ross used one, which intrigued his neighbors, who had never

seen one. In Woodford County the Betteyune and Snyder households were "Pennsylvania Dutch," people of German ancestry. They introduced solid, practical barns, which enhanced farming success. The Pennsylvanians noted, "Barns will soon pay for dwelling houses, but dwelling houses never pay for barns." Germanic work ethic, sense of order, and attention to detail impressed Illinoisans, many emulating Pennsylvania Dutch traits and techniques.

Diversity probably mitigated white-Indian conflict. Perhaps German immigrants got along better with Indians than did Americans, and by the time sizeable numbers of Germans had arrived in Illinois, most Indians had left. German Romanticism valued nature and natural men, including Indians. In any case, "Germans lacked any consistent fear of Indians," and maybe this fact facilitated peaceful relations.[32] Unlike Germans, Americans grew up on stories of massacre, which set them against Indians. German proclivity to settle in colonies probably heightened their security, making them less itchy about nearby Indians. Finally, perhaps experimental features of many German settlements—whether religious or secular—facilitated peace with nearby Indians. In fact, romanticism, progressivism, and other German values probably helped Germans avoid trouble with Indians.

In part, Germans and other foreign-born settlers got along in the fluid, emerging society because they *tried* to get along. They had chosen to come to America, not to another country, and it was generally good to them. Unlike Europe, America had few artificial restraints. Unlike most Europeans, foreign-born Americans voted, ran for office, worshiped freely (or not at all), traveled anyplace, entered no army, paid virtually no taxes, and owned property. Most importantly, these heady, liberating experiences struck off mental shackles, liberating European settlers, expanding horizons, and enhancing awareness of one's innate worth.

Some leaders of foreign colonies were oblivious to liberating forces, which often generated both friction and healthy change. Ferdinand Ernst wanted the best for his colony of nearly 100 Germans near Vandalia in 1820, but he failed to understand the frontier's liberating potential. The basic social cohesion holding the colony together was financial obligation owed to Ernst, not ideological unity or mission. Consequently, as soon as debts were paid, things unraveled. Some indentured servants quickly paid off their indenture, others married neighboring Americans, and many prospered. Others cheerfully reneged on their obligations and moved into American society. Ernst Ludwig Brauns, analyzing Ernst's failed colony, displayed keen insight: "In America, the emancipated dayworkers and farmers . . . after drinking from the fountain of freedom, did not want to tolerate any longer the absolute peremptory commands of a German magistrate, which Ernst should have thought about beforehand."[33] Many colonies, especially foreign-spawned, foundered when members embraced Americans conditions and values, jettisoning oppressive practices and rigid leaders. Folding colonies and successful individuals were often linked causally. Failed colonies yielded success by bringing thousands to the frontier, exposing them to abundant land and other liberating forces, narrowing gaps between them and American neighbors, and oftentimes freeing them from outdated, stifling, or impractical group practices or bumbling, tyrannical colonial leaders.

Within a decade of statehood, Timothy Flint recorded frontier society's pacifying features. This intrepid observer of western society focused on a region running roughly from Cincinnati to St. Louis. He wrote, "The people of this valley are as thorough a combination and mixture of peoples of all nations, characters, languages, conditions, and opinions, as can be imagined. Scarcely a state in the Union, or a nation in Europe, but what has furnished us immigrants." Each ethnic group and class brought its own views, prejudices, and local attachments. Even so, migrating, settling, and adjusting in fluid society worked a wondrous effect: "Pride and jealousy give way to the natural yearnings of the human heart for society. They begin to run off mutual prejudices. One takes a step, and then the other. They meet half way, and embrace; and the society thus newly organized and constituted, is more liberal, enlarged, unprejudiced, and of course more affectionate and pleasant, than a society of people of *unique* birth and character, who bring all their early prejudices, as a common stock, to be transmitted as an inheritance in perpetuity."[34] In 1835 the Page family came from New Hampshire to Woodford County, where they encountered Hoosiers. One day the Pages or other New Englanders were trying unsuccessfully to wash clothes in hard water. Eventually they asked for help from the Hoosiers, who replied, "I seed yer didn't know nothing. Ef yer'd axed me, I'd telled yer all about it." Basic human decency overcame language and other cultural barriers, and "from little scenes like these, friendship soon sprang up between the two elements." As a native of Portage County, Ohio, Eleanor Robbins was prejudiced against Southerners. But even as she wrote from Rushville on May 26, 1836, to assail their ignorance, she admitted they had redeeming qualities: "The people hear are prinsaply from the South they are a verry ignorant peopple thare is many among tham that cannot read nor write but they are verry kind and friendly." Mingling, intermarriage, and other links soon overcame barriers and even created bonds among diverse settlers.

Once language obstacles faded or became unimportant, other differences were generally ignored. Furthermore, virtually all immigrant groups assimilated to a large degree. The least assimilable feature was religion, but the First Amendment and public sentiment made religion a fairly innocuous issue, a few glaring exceptions notwithstanding.

Clustering, settlers learned one thing well: other people, however strange, were not so bad. Kentuckian men married Yankee wives, and dissimilar people struck business deals, cooperated in innumerable ways, and formed the glue of community. People saw a new society, a new beginning, and a chance to bury the past. Illinois was not a new arena in which old grievances were nursed, inflamed, and used as pretexts for fighting. Quite the opposite. It was for many a slate from which the worst from the past was erased and onto which the best from the past was rewritten. Perhaps frontier Illinois' greatest product was regeneration, eternal renewal, and endless tomorrow. For people of goodwill, countless frontier laboratories yielded understanding, tolerance, and even acceptance. Arriving from New York, Sarah Aiken sniffed at neighbors near Peoria, but she came to appreciate prairie society. Similarly, Eliza Farnham was initially snobbish toward rustic Illinoisans, but she mellowed and became less judgmental. This softening process, occurring countless times,

facilitated frontier tolerance and reduced the likelihood of violence.

Timothy Flint, knowing the frontier intimately and understanding its impact, asked, "What mind ever contemplated the project
of moving from the old settlements over the Allegheny Mountains . . . without forming pictures of new woods and streams,
new animals and vegetables, new configurations of scenery, new
aspects of men and new forms of society?"[35] In contemplating
new aspects of humanity and new forms of society, individuals
undertook self-liberation. People envisioned themselves in new
lands, tapping new possibilities, free from stultifying social burdens. Thinking about frontier life, trekking westward, and settling among others caused them to cast off old habits and adopt
and adapt from materials at hand in new lands. People put much
of their pasts behind them, including failures and old animosities, and brought forth new lives. For decades of settlers, possibilities became realities.

This happened among the wide assortment of overlanders who
trekked to California in 1849 and later. Something similar occurred in the crucible of the Civil War, America's Iliad, when
men from dissimilar states and different countries fought side by
side. Old Settler Societies, Overland Societies, and the Grand
Army of the Republic and other veteran groups testified for decades to lasting camaraderie produced by hardships.

* * *

Illinois' landscape is gentle. It lacks craggy mountains, bold
coasts, and plunging rivers. Little suggests awesome forces or
cataclysmic struggle. Even the ponderous Mississippi River and
broad Lake Michigan usually lie dormant. But these appearances
are deceptive. Portentous New Madrid earthquakes heralded the
War of 1812, heaving and jolting the gentle landscape and its few
inhabitants. Rare in most of North America and Europe, tornadoes spewed death and devastation across miles. Summer's
heat and humidity enervated, and winter's blasts paralyzed. Massive floods on the Mississippi, Illinois, and Wabash rivers dwarfed
floods settlers had known elsewhere. Orange flames shimmering
against inky nights blackened miles of prairies overnight. Will-

iam Oliver noted that thunderstorms were "much more frequent, and more severe, than in Britain."[36] When he strolled at night, his way was lit by unremitting flashes of lightning. Most dead trees he saw, he maintained, had been slain by lightning. And during his visit to one locale, lightning bolts dispatched a young man, some houses, and a barn.

Some natural forces provided quiet, dramatic conflict. Glaciers scoured southward across nearly all Illinois at one time or another. Halting, they formed terminal moraines. Retreating, they contrived to lay down rock, sand, and glacial powder in thick deposits over scoured bedrock. These deposits formed outwash plains, till plains, recessional moraines, eskers, drumlins, kettles and kames, and other landforms that cover nearly the entire state. Glacial meltwater influenced the locations and features of the state's drainage systems, nearly all of which feed into the Mississippi and Ohio rivers. Forming the Great Lakes, glaciers provided a water route to the Atlantic Coast.

Other conflicts occurred in nature. Long before settlement, annual late-summer and autumnal prairie fires swept undulating landscape, ignited by lightning or by Indians driving game. These fires retarded the spread of trees and bushes into prairies, keeping northern Illinois in billowy seas of grass. Local environments tested plant life brought by settlers. Animals contended for domain in forests and prairies.

Humans and nature clashed. Around 1800, when American settlers numbered a few hundred, the last buffalo died out or left. Generations of hooves etched trails, pathways later used by Indians, then by pioneers, and finally by road builders. Few settlers ever saw buffalo, but many saw or heard wildcats. Called panthers, or "painters" in local parlance, they were the stuff of legends. County histories and memoirs mention them, marking the frontier's demise with the passing of the last wildcat. They threatened livestock more than settlers, stalling settlement in many regions. So long as they and wolves lurked about, sheep raising was chancy and wool production languished. Alfred Chadwick, living in Morgan County, wrote on September 3, 1830, "Wool also will engage the attention of our agriculturalists as soon as the country becomes more cleared of wild animals which destroy our sheep." Settlers contended with rattlesnakes and other snakes, especially when plowing virgin prairie grass and clearing forests. Prairie fires devoured crops, fences, stock, farmsteads, hamlets, and occasionally humans until plowing created "fire lanes" and sharply reduced supplies of prairie grass. Conflicts between people and nature took many other forms—swollen streams, heat stroke, deadly ice storms, flies and other bothersome insects—and they continue.

Nature was present in frontier Illinois as both earthly Garden and cultural Desert, as sustainer and destroyer, as comforter and tormentor, as familiar and exotic, and as hope and despair. In 1843 Margaret Fuller found harmonious, contented communities in northern Illinois. But she echoed Sarah Aiken in looking beyond the benefits of bounteous, beautiful nature to glimpse a cultural desert, one all too frequently inhabited by "swarms of settlers whose aims are sordid, whose habits thoughtless and slovenly." In the battle between savagery and civilization, Fuller opined, the burden fell heaviest on women, who enjoyed little dependable domestic help and whose backgrounds sometimes ill-fitted them to combat nature's denizens. Daily, commonplace chores placed lengthy workdays on women, year in and year out. For many women, toil at the washtub precluded leisurely time with books, writing, and music. At the same time, however, settlers strove to establish culture in the wilderness. A literature, Fuller hoped, would spring from western soil to reflect the "new frontier society, free, open and democratic."[37]

Nature may destroy or inspire today, but settlers looking at nature saw the future, a bright future. Early generations gazed upon lands between Lake Michigan and the Illinois River's headwaters and saw a connecting canal. Settlers felt sharp westerly winds and dreamed of harnessing their power. Some looked beneath tough matted roots of tall prairie grass and saw rich soil yield bountiful harvests. Others saw vessels coursing the Great Lakes. Settlers envisioned farms, roads, settlements, and other signs of progress dotting the landscape. For example, Ferdinand Ernst studied dense, foreboding wilderness around Vandalia and exclaimed, "But how it will have changed in 10 or 20 years! All these huge forests will have then disappeared, and a flourishing city with fine buildings will stand in their place. A free people will then from this place [the future state capital] rule itself through their representatives and watch over their freedom and well-being."[38] Nature enticed settlers to see in Illinois endless tomorrow, progress, and unfolding bright futures.

From the start, Illinois abounded with ingredients for outright disaster. Indians pummeled Indians, French and Indian contested British, Americans ousted British, and various American interests vied for dominance. Contending players and issues changed over time, adding to the frontier's dynamism. Some struggles and conflicts originated wholly within Illinois, some originated outside, and some originated both within and without. Wherever conflicts originated and however they were resolved, few ended in total disaster, extermination, or obliteration; too many alternatives existed for these to occur. Even warring parties rarely took matters to extremes. For example, Britain deliberately chose not to wage cultural warfare against their longtime and lethal enemies, the French. Only the Indians had to yield control of land, give up basic culture, or march from the state, and even then Indian place names cover the state. Usually, mitigated conflict, compromise, and consensus prevailed.[39]

Frontier conflict and cooperation need more study. Frontier Illinois needs to be compared to other North American frontiers, Atlantic Coastal regions, and frontiers in such places as Australia, Russia, and Brazil. Such systematic comparisons would give comparative perspective and context to understandings of cooperation and conflict in emerging Illinois. Canadian settlers probably faced less conflict than contemporary settlers in Illinois, but Illinoisian settlers probably faced much less violence than pioneers in Australia, Russia, or Brazil. Perhaps, in fact, cooperation and conflict in frontier Illinois made society there similar to today's Swiss society. Like today's Swiss, pioneers were sharply divided by religion, language, customs, and ethnic origins—and like today's Swiss, they were armed—and yet they elected to live, conflict, and cooperate within powerful consensus. Like today's Swiss, they were horrified by murders and other acts of violence, which indicates that these were not commonplace events. They chose to abide by the outcomes of contests, even when ruin resulted, and show much restraint in their lives. They longed for security, predictability, and peace, knowing these ingredients generated prosperity and overall success. In conflicting and co-operating, they minimized destructive conflict and enhanced dynamic tranquility. These choices helped produce a prosper-ous, dynamic society, one that was generally inclusive, just, and highly attractive to hundreds of thousands who made choices to settle in Illinois.

14.

CONFLICTS AND COMMUNITY

Intense, high-stakes fights involving growing counties erupted chronically. Even in moderately sized counties, some people required two days to reach their county seat to transact business, given miserable roads and inclement weather. This increased costs and flattened their property values. Moreover, population spurts far from county seats prompted efforts to either create new counties or move existing county seats. Creation of new counties and relocation of seats radically affected donor counties, the newly formed counties, and neighboring counties. Consequently, these high-stakes activities caused great agitation.

Land for new counties came from five sources.[1] Unorganized territory provided land for relatively few counties, all but three of which were created before 1832. Land from unorganized counties and land from existing counties were combined to create other counties. Half of these counties were created before 1832, and half afterwards. Land lopped off an existing county formed a new one in many instances. The majority of these were formed after 1832. Parts from two or more existing counties created almost as many, most of them formed after 1832. Finally, only one county (Gallatin) was formed by combining two complete counties (Saline and Gallatin), resulting in an enlarged Gallatin County.

Beginning in 1790, proclamations by territorial governors created five counties, the last three in 1812. Enabling acts by territorial legislatures created ten, only two before 1816. After statehood in 1818, General Assemblies created the rest.

The processes by which ordinary citizens advocated new county formation varied. Essentially, after statehood, individuals wanting to form a new county—or block the creation of a county—wrote petitions, gathered signatures, and got the signed petitions to state legislators, who sent them to the appropriate committee. Until the late 1830s, the appropriate committee was ad hoc and usually consisted of appointed legislators from the affected regions, often appointed by legislative leaders. By 1838 standing committees in both houses handled petitions. These committees drafted enabling bills and sent them to the floor with recommendations. Floor debate sometimes changed boundaries, names, and other features of proposed counties. Gaining floor approval in both houses, enabling acts then went for approval to a council of revision prior to 1848 or to the governor after 1851. After receiving approval, counties were authorized to organize, requirements for organization sometimes appearing in enabling acts and sometimes in separate legislation.

More than half of Illinois' counties were formed before local residents received the right to vote on county creation. Bureau County, formed in early 1837, was the first county on which residents agreed via a "yes-no" referendum. Before such popular voting became mandatory in 1848, however, of thirty-five counties created between 1838 and 1848 only eleven had yes-no votes. In three cases, moreover, the legislature allowed only some residents in the affected region to vote, not all.[2]

Similar developments occurred in selecting sites for county seats. The General Assembly designated fourteen sites, ten before 1840. However, commissions consisting of three to five men selected most sites. The referendum method of selecting sites, first used in 1837 to select Cass County's seat, largely replaced commissions, which were not used after 1843. Winning towns had to have either a majority of votes or a plurality. Replacement of commissions by popular vote probably reflected widespread suffrage and participation in the Jacksonian era.

Sometimes, new-county creation met little resistance. Residents wishing to form a new county met, petitioned, possibly voted on the matter, and sent the results to the state capital. Although only state action could create new counties, legislators usually deferred to demands for them. Even those standing to gain nothing by new counties usually offered just token resistance. One reason for approving is clear: by the time remote areas of a county became populated enough to generate new-county movements, the rest of the county was also growing and prospering. In short, both the new county and the truncated donor county prospered; it was win-win for both. Usually only counties with small areas stood to lose by giving up some land.

Sometimes, however, new-county drives provoked fierce opposition, especially if existing seats were threatened. Often, for example, calving counties changed the relative location of the donor county seat, shifting seats from central positions to peripheral locations, which tempted rivals to vie for the seat. Understandably, partisans of existing seats sometimes aborted new county formation. Sometimes, contests exhibited Byzantine qualities, residents in one village, for example, acquiescing in secession by part of the county to weaken a rival village's claim to the seat. Often four or five towns over decades vied for county seat. State lawmakers authorized new-county and county-seat elections, but lobbyists, county commissioners, and other politicians shaped decisions. On January 23, 1837, for example, Rufus Everett wrote from Princeton about the possible division of Putnam County: "There is a good deal of excitement in this section about the division of this county. Princeton has three members in the lobby at Vandalia [the state capital]." He added, "There is strong opposition at Henipen [the county seat of Putnam County]. They leave nothing undone to defeat the objects and wishes of the Princeton people." Princeton's lobbyists succeeded, however, and on February 28, 1837, Bureau County was created from Putnam County, and Princeton became the county seat. Sometimes a new county carved land from two or more counties, complicating matters. Bizarre twists marked struggles, producing delightfully weird results and bemusing contestants and historians.

Victors in county-seat fights anticipated growth, prosperity, and prized stability. Winners garnered the official records and lucrative and influential county positions, including county clerk, sheriff, judge, assessor, jailor, bailiff, and county treasurer. Winning towns attracted swarms of lawyers, realtors, surveyors, office-seekers, merchants, contractors, laborers, and those coveting amenities normally accruing to county seats. Builders and others got contracts for constructing and operating courthouses, county jails, and other structures and services. County residents frequented county seats to conduct business involving land, taxes, justice, and related matters. They also bought goods, milled, bartered, and just visited. These activities enriched inns, taverns, restaurants, liveries, and hotels, the finest of each usually clustering near the courthouse. Invariably, county seats boasted the county's finest restaurant, poshest hotel, best-stocked retail stores, and best fairs and other exhibitions. Seat newspapers became organs of record, publishing government notices, records of meetings, announcements, and other official information. The county's best roads, sturdiest bridges, and similar amenities graced regions immediately around seats. On the other hand, towns losing county-seat fights were usually consigned to relative isolation, stagnation, or decline, some losers disappearing completely. Finally, these fights interested residents of neighboring counties, the outcomes often affecting their economic and social conditions and generating annexation movements.

Knowing the stakes, wrangling competitors employed subterfuge, chicanery, and bribery, bent or circumvented laws, occasionally intimidated, brandished weapons, and even resorted to scrupulously fair elections. Realizing that physical possession of court records was crucial, partisans spirited them away in the dead of night. Some county seats lodged in four or five communities before finding a permanent home.

County histories bulge with accounts of county formation and county-seat contests. Aging settlers had vivid, if flawed, memories of contests, and authors of county histories delighted in recounting these struggles. Winners basked in victories, while losers nursed wounds, some tussles remaining contentious decades later.

These high-stakes, emotionally charged fights, often bringing personal and community ruin, had one thing in common: they were peaceful. Consensus demarcated the parameters of struggle, guided tactics, and channeled combat. Contestants sometimes labored for months and even years, tried everything to snag the county seat, worked up emotional and political lather, and then lost everything and quietly left the arena, accepting defeat and even ruin. Losers labored within political structures, including new elections, to undo defeat. Even those who teetered on the precipice of ruin said to themselves, "This far and no farther." Society's invisible glue—the broad, unspoken consensus and ingrained republican restraint—held, throttling visceral reactions and enjoining everyone to accept results. Several county contests illustrate much.

In 1821 state legislators combined parts of Bond, Clark, and Madison counties to form Pike County, making Coles Grove temporary county seat. The enabling act creating Pike County appointed five commissioners to select a permanent seat, "taking into consideration the condition and convenience of the people, the future population of the county, and the health and eligibility of the place." The act authorized them to receive donations of land for county use. Two men donated land, attracting the county seat to Atlas in 1823.

But this caused trouble. Only three commissioners signed the report naming Atlas the seat, and law made no provision for majority decisions in these matters. Furthermore, because the commissioners filed their report late, a court ruled to void their choice, ordering Coles Grove to remain county seat. Another court reversed this decision in 1824, making Atlas the seat. Atlas built a rickety log courthouse, followed by a much better structure, and basked in a sparkling future.

Central and eastern regions of Pike County, however, disliked Atlas's western location. Commissioners elected in 1827 to relocate the county seat dragged their feet, but sentiment for relocation stayed warm. It ignited during the winter of 1830–1831, when fire of uncertain origin destroyed Atlas's courthouse.

The state legislature in its 1832–1833 session selected a commission to relocate the county seat. The commissioners reported
in early 1833 that they had examined "said county of Pike, having a due regard to the present as well as the future settlement
and prospective growth of said county," and had chosen a site
"to be known and designated by the name of Pittsfield," which
was centrally located.

No popular vote influenced relocation decisions, but the choice
made sense. Meager population growth in western Pike County
undercut Atlas's grip on the seat. No public outcry greeted Pittsfield's selection, not even from Atlas's residents, it appears. In
short, the choice occurred within prevailing consensus and probably reflected popular sentiment, even if a few corners were cut.[3]

Warren County was created in 1825, with Oquawka its temporary seat. The state legislature in January of 1831 picked three
men to locate the permanent seat. On April 7, 1831, they reported
they had selected a site they named Monmouth. People in western Warren County groused about the distance to Monmouth.
Failing to transfer the seat back to Oquawka, they agitated to
create a new county, and Henderson County was sliced from
Warren County in early 1841, Oquawka the county seat. Now virtually everyone was near a county seat, and budding politicians
in both counties salivated over numerous county offices.

Complexity and tranquility marked the selection of Carroll
County's seat. According to enabling legislation creating the
county in 1839, Savanna became temporary county seat, pend-
ing selection of a permanent one. The legislation mandated a
vote in April on the seat's location, which Savanna won with 126
votes to Elkhorn Grove's 86. But the legislation required the permanent site's residents to donate town lots for the courthouse
and other public functions.

Savanna failed to donate the town lots, so victory was fleeting.
Worse, Savanna sat at the county's western edge, on the Mississippi, while Mount Carroll was centrally located. By 1842 Mount
Carroll's prosperity motivated its financial leaders to try to garner the county seat, businessmen enticing county officials with
pledges of town lots.

Mount Carroll's boosters entreated state legislators, who during the 1842–1843 legislative session passed "An act to re-locate the county seat of Carroll County." To find a site that "shall give the greatest amount of good to the greatest number of inhabitants of said county," the act appointed three commissioners, one each coming from Lee County, Jo Daviess County, and Rock Island County. Presumably, this trio was close enough to Carroll County to select wisely, but far enough away to be free of unseemly influences. The act stipulated a county election in August 1843, between the existing county seat, Savanna, and the commissioners' nomination, Mount Carroll.

Mount Carroll received 231 votes, Savanna 190. (Inexplicably, six people in Savanna precinct voted for Mount Carroll; perhaps they had financial interests there, or perhaps they wanted Savanna to remain free of lawyers, defendants, and others who frequent courthouses.) Savanna accepted the outcome, and government transferred smoothly from Savanna to Mount Carroll.

Twists and turns marked Woodford County's birth and Hanover's county-seat victory. Woodford County's proponents got the legislature to abort a fetal competitor conceived at Washington. Possible trickery may have backfired by violating basic fairness, leading commissioners to bestow the seat on Hanover, where it stayed before moving to Eureka in 1894. At no time in the convoluted process, though, were threats uttered or weapons drawn.

After Rockford partisans grabbed the county seat of Winnebago County from Winnebago in an honest, lopsided election in 1839, they tried to reconcile the vanquished, throwing a lavish party at the Rockford House, where former adversaries pledged goodwill. Good intentions, however, failed to make amends, and ill-will worsened when Winnebago declined and flickered out of existence. Even so, Winnebago's crushed investors accepted loss, many just going away and none taking dire action.

Tazewell County was organized in 1827. Mackinaw became county seat, its central location commending it. Town lots commanded top dollar in brisk sales in June of 1837, and residents "looked forward with fond expectation for a bright and prosperous future for their capital." Soon an imposing log courthouse graced Mackinaw, costing $125 and sporting glass windows. Unfortunately, hogs wallowed under it; porcine fragrance wafted upward and grunts and squeals pierced carefully crafted arguments of courtroom lawyers, so the courthouse endeared itself to few, weakening Mackinaw's grip on the county seat.

In 1830 McLean County to the east was calved from Tazewell County. Mackinaw was now near the eastern extremity of truncated Tazewell County, a distinct liability. In 1830 neonate Pekin tried to wrest the county seat from Mackinaw. A chief architect of the law creating McLean County was William Brown, a state representative from Pekin. In early 1831 state lawmakers picked a three-man commission to locate the permanent seat, decreeing Pekin as temporary seat. This miffed Mackinaw's residents, who saw personal and civic aspirations being dashed.

Commissioners engaged in masterful delay for years, keeping the county seat in Pekin. Fed up, the legislature in 1835 appointed another three-man commission. At this point, Tremont entered the contest, impressing the trio by offering Tazewell County land and cash subsidy in return for the county seat. In 1836 the commissioners selected Tremont, noting its central location with respect to current and probable population patterns. Pekin nevertheless continued to do well.

By 1839 Tremont and Pekin exchanged snarls. Tremont initiated defensive measures to retain the seat. Perhaps it collaborated with factions wanting to weaken Tazewell County. In 1841, in any case, portions of southwestern Tazewell became Mason County, and parts of Tazewell County were added to McLean County. In 1843 voters thwarted an effort to slice more of Tazewell County and give it to Woodford County. And the same year the legislature authorized a vote on Pekin's drive to pry the seat from Tremont. Voters disappointed Pekinese. Undaunted, Pekin kept plugging away, and the town kept growing. In early 1849 another vote gave Pekin the prize.

Pekin beamed and conjured up a splendid new courthouse, but its victory was pyrrhic. Growth slackened and a rival, Peoria, outstripped it. Years of corrosive feuding left Tremont and Pekin enervated, squandering frontier ebullience and sowing uncertainty and negativity. Civic leaders, engrossed by endless spatting, ignored true community well-being and rising Peoria. In any event, internecine struggles crippling the once-promising towns never degenerated into violence.

Logan County's story is complex, replete with technology's impact. A site enchanted Russel Post, a speculator, who founded Postville in 1835, soon an overnight stage stop on the Chicago–St. Louis route. With Logan County's establishment in 1839, commissioners named Postville the county seat. Centrally located, it thrived, its future apparently bright.

Still, residents in Logan County and neighboring DeWitt and McLean counties tried to carve a new county from all three counties, with Waynesville, in western DeWitt County, as county seat. But nearby Mt. Pulaski balked at this, and in 1847 voters switched the seat to Mt. Pulaski. Postville languished. But folk in northern and western Logan County disliked Mt. Pulaski's inconvenient location. They touted Postville, whose central location commended it. At this point, though, technology intervened: the Chicago & Alton Railroad, which was scheduled to link Alton and Bloomington in 1853. Residents of Lincoln, founded in 1853, and others advocated locating the county seat on the railroad. (The railroad was slated to run through Lincoln.) Lincoln's boosters hurriedly donated four prime town lots to the county, designating one for a courthouse. Thus enticed, voters in late 1853 bestowed the county seat on Lincoln.[4]

As different as these stories are, they have a common thread: contestants played by the rules, more or less, and abided by the outcome, however produced and however painful.

* * *

Napoleon Murat, visiting the West in 1826, saw squatters and others dispute. Settlement, he noted, outpaced law's reach, throwing people back on themselves to choose solutions to problems. They chose fighting, and "every dispute is amicably terminated by the fist." (Almost certainly, Murat exaggerated. Not "every dispute" was, in fact, settled by fists; on one occasion, two adversaries settled *their* dispute by standing ten paces apart and hurling rocks at each other.)[5] Murat's terms "amicably" and "terminated" reflect keen awareness that fights truly ended quarrels.

Some facets of frontier society appalled Murat, but disputes "amicably terminated by the fist" pleased him.

Frequent fist fights suggest a violent society, but perhaps the opposite is true. Only fists were used, consensus channeled most fights, and the end of the fight generally terminated the dispute. Republican restraint, self-governance, and deference to community norms minimized truly lethal fighting. These traits mark a self-governing society, not a horribly divided, violent one. Binding consensus, the glue of society, was robust, making ghastly violence both unacceptable and rare.

J. H. Oakwood remembered that on occasion near Danville sometimes a dozen fights raged simultaneously. Impugned honor, unpaid bets, slights, besmirched family, sullied women's reputations, or questioned masculinity may have ignited them. Religious beliefs, political theory, or other ideological issues or abstractions rarely caused strife; most conflict had low ideological content. This helped people accept the results of fist fights, court decisions, and other outcomes. A handshake usually ended feuds for good.

Excessive imbibing often led to problems on the frontier. Whiskey fueled spirited behavior at political campaigns, election days, militia musters, Fourth of July and other celebrations, barn and house raisings, huskings, races, parties, and trials in "court week." From the 1790s until about 1830, per capita alcohol consumption in America peaked. In Bond County at public events "drunken men were so common, that sober men seemed to be the exception." Election days were splendid opportunities for fights. As county residents congregated to vote in Greenville, they spotted acquaintances, renewed ancient grudges, bickered, and then fought. Sometimes three fights simultaneously graced elections. One source noted, "At any time between the years of 1830 and 1845, it was nothing unusual to see twenty or thirty men at one time, on election day or muster day, in Greenville drunk . . . the majority of them with coats off and sleeves rolled up, wanting to resent an insult which they fancied they had received from some one whom they were trying to find." Such behavior occasionally threatened or injured innocent people: "And woe be unto the luckless individual who was mistaken for the aggressor. Many an inoffensive, respectable citizen received rough treatment under such circumstances, and astonished his better-half by returning home from an election, or muster, with a smashed hat, black eye, or bloody nose, to satisfactorily account for which, required, in some instances, no ordinary amount of explanation." Alcohol lubricated much spontaneous fighting.[6] On muster days militia companies drank and goaded their finest fighters to fight other companies' finest. Consequently, in a typical year Illinois militiamen inflicted far more bruises on each other than on Illinois' enemies. Arguments in courts and decisions rendered sometimes sent tipsy bystanders flying against each other.

Residents of Jasper County drank and fought at horse races. Bets of whiskey facilitated fighting in which "a great many peeled heads, bloody noses, black eyes" and more serious injuries abounded. Alcohol-induced troubles stigmatized Newton, in Jasper County: "The village was in moral quarantine. Its reputation was known far and near. Settlers avoided it, and even travelers avoided it on their journeys so far as possible." Degenerate, emboldened toughs, led by Lewis Jordan, the county sheriff, accosted unwary travelers, demanded they treat in saloons, and threatened those who refused. This behavior ended when a traveler, not amused by this custom, nearly killed the sheriff, who finally slithered away, along with some of his confederate toughs. Civilized townsfolk surfaced, and the villains quieted down.

Extorting drinks was one thing; extorting land was another matter. In Winnebago County, for example, some settlers spotted attractive land, decided to claim it, and slept there to keep others from claiming it, only to awake and discover that during the night intrepid claim jumpers had hauled by wagon a ten-by-twelve-foot shanty to the site and quietly offloaded it. The previous claimants were confronted with a *fait accompli* "cabin," evidence of a superior claim to the land. Such daring acts, intimidation, and even physical force occasionally brushed aside legitimate claimants, but they typically banded together and either expelled the interlopers or took them to court, where such brazen shenanigans seldom fared well. These courts and actual settlers were further galled whenever they learned that powerful eastern speculators had engineered these nefarious acts.

Consensus shaped and mitigated conflict. For years after Tazewell County was formed in 1827, its residents enjoyed fist fights.
One source noted, "The pioneers enjoyed a 'free fight' and entered into sport of a pugilistic nature with great interest, seldom
resorting to knives or pistols." A good time was had by all. Consensus proscribed knives or pistols, disallowed certain punches
and kicking and biting, determined what fighters could do to
downed opponents, and devised protocols to end fights, to confer
finality on "fair fights."

* * *

Settlers' faith in frontier justice, in its legitimacy and equity,
minimized violence. In 1826 Napoleon Murat reported on courtroom activities:

> No court-house is yet in existence; the judge therefore selects the
> largest room of a tavern or a spacious loft. . . . The sheriff opens the
> court and calls the cases, the noise ceases. Upon a couple of planks
> are ranged twenty-four freemen, heads of families, housekeepers,
> forming the grand jury. What an assemblage! From the hunter in
> breeches and skin shirt, whose beard and razor have not met for a
> month—the squatter in hat, and dressed in stuffs manufactured at
> home by his wife—the small dealer . . . sitting beside the blacksmith.
> . . . The judge makes his charge with as much dignity as if he sat in
> Westminster, and the verdicts savour nothing of the whimsical
> appearance of the court and jury.[7]

Despite informalities and rough appearances—or perhaps *because* of them—court proceedings commanded great respect. In
any case, frontier courts provided equity, order, and structure for
fluid, transient society, serving as a social safety valve and sustaining hope.

The nature and resolution of court cases during the 1840s illustrate much. In Knox County 80 percent involved civil actions,
and only 20 percent involved criminal prosecution. Given the
sluggish early 1840s, civil cases often involved debts and related
matters. Murder generated three cases, but none came to trial.
(A defendant's escape from jail terminated one murder case.) Of
eighteen assault cases during the decade, six came to trial. Juries

acquitted all six. In thirty-four burglary cases, three defendants pled guilty at arraignment. One got two years, one got three and a half years, and one received just six days in the county jail, a youth of eighteen years, whose sentence included restitution. Eight burglary cases came to trial, producing three convictions. Two received one-year sentences, and the third got thirteen months. (State law mandated burglars serve between one and ten years in the state penitentiary.) Liquor violations and morals charges were rare, and convictions rarer. Insufficient evidence produced some acquittals.

Clearly, jurors took their responsibilities seriously and were not rubber stamps for prosecutors. Cases producing 100-percent conviction rates included wantonly burning prairies and obstructing transportation. Perhaps these cases involved blatant guilt, but disparities in conviction rates likely reflect laudable reluctance to wrongfully convict for serious wrongdoing. Furthermore, no evidence suggests that intimidation of witnesses, suborning of jurors, bribery, or other corruption sapped justice in Knox County. The circuit court performed "its duties competently and professionally."[8]

Close ties between citizens and authorities and respect accorded judicial proceedings impressed Elias Pym Fordham, an insightful Englishman, who wrote from Shawneetown on November 15, 1817: "I wish I could give you a correct idea of the perfect equality that exists among these republicans. A Judge leaves the Court House, shakes hands with his fellow citizens and retires to his log house. The next day you will find him holding his own plough. The Lawyer has the title of Captain, and serves in his Military capacity under his neighbour, who is a farmer and a Colonel."[9]

Many settlers eagerly attended "court days" for entertainment, but they gained renewed respect for frontier justice, respect tinged with genuine awe. This reassured settlers, encouraging them to stay on the frontier and settle differences via legal channels. Close ties between citizens and authorities amazed Richard Flower, who spearheaded English settlement in Edwards County. After hiring a man to plow for him, Flower wrote, "I went into my field the other day, and began a conversation with my ploughman: his manner of speech as well as his conversation surprised me. I found he was a colonel of militia and a member of the legislature." John Palmer echoed these sentiments in 1817 in Ohio, but they also rang true for frontier Illinois. He met a Judge Lowe, who also kept a tavern: "It no doubt seems singular to the English reader, to hear of judges and captains keeping taverns . . . but it is very common in this republican country."[10] Frequent contact with authorities and confidence in republican institutions reinforced each other. Settlers plunged headlong into politics, often for the first time. Closeness to governance made palatable defeat in courts, elections, land squabbles, and even fist fights.

* * *

Admittedly impressionistic evidence suggests crime peaked during two stages of frontier development. In the beginning, amid sparse population in isolated locales, social flotsam and jetsam, often on the lam, clustered and eluded social restraints and the force of law. Although they robbed, counterfeited, even murdered, over decades some acquired mythical status among Old Pioneers musing on bygone years. Crime peaked again during the twilight of the frontier, when numerous strangers crowded in from various far-flung lands, straining consensus. Growing numbers of tenants, rural laborers, and single males also frayed yeoman social fabric. Sectional strain heightened social tensions. Growing anonymity of diverse populations in fully settled counties, swift links to the outside via railroads, and weakening social bonding and self-restraint abetted criminal tendencies.

Court activities in Knox County, established in 1825, illuminate peaks and valleys in crime and justice. The Fifth Circuit Court began functioning on October 1, 1830, handling administrative details and hearing a grand jury report concerning the county's log jail. Lacking other business, the court adjourned the next day. One case was heard during 1832. Other years had similarly light dockets, reflecting scarcity of serious crime. The 1840s brought change, however, as Knox County's population nearly doubled. On average, judges in Knox County Circuit Court now heard 108 cases per term. Perhaps this spurt reflected increased population, but more likely it reflected population composition. Many people hailed from border states and Indiana, while others were Yankees. These people "differed as widely in essentials, in all that constitutes philosophy of life, as though they belonged to different races, which they did not." Checkered economic times, marked by bankruptcies, also produced court cases.[11]

Nettlesome counterfeiters, whose sideline was horse-thievery, infested Jasper County (est. 1831). Victims followed the trail of Cornelius Taylor, a ferry operator in Lawrence County, who made wagon trips to St. Louis, after which bogus coins and paper money circulated locally. They followed Taylor to Acre Williams, whom they hung by the neck a couple of times and questioned ardently, until he revealed names of associates and locations of molds and dies. The principal associates scattered, but the seizure of the materials terminated counterfeiting activities. This incident illustrates angry, rough, effective response to crime.

Swindling blemished the frontier. Near Indian Creek in Bond County a stranger named Gaylor convinced others he had discovered a lode of silver, and he conned Samuel Hunter into constructing a furnace. Soon, however, neighbors realized Gaylor was refining little or no silver, so they confronted him. They uncovered the scam and lodged Gaylor in the local jail. Interestingly, he quickly secured his release. Perhaps victims were too embarrassed to press the matter.

Unlike swindling, much serious crime during the frontier's heyday was unplanned. Human nature, opportunity, and desperation misled people. For example, in 1835 Elias McFadden and his son David farmed in McDonough County, created in 1826. One day the sheriff and John Wilson, a farmer, appeared with an execution to levy on a crib of corn and a wagon to haul the corn away. Elias McFadden physically resisted, and then David McFadden shot from the McFaddens' cabin, killing Wilson. The McFaddens were arrested, tried, found guilty, and hanged in June. David McFadden's impulsiveness unleashed severe retribution, in keeping with public thinking concerning crime. Self-governing republican citizens, citizens knew, were expected to govern themselves, to restrain rash impulses.

Some violent crime was planned. Some thugs, thieves, counterfeiters, and murderers were cold-blooded. And some were accomplished in violence, innocent of moral instruction, and ever eager to explore new depths of debauchery.[12] George Ray of Woodford County drove cattle to Wisconsin, often traveling alone. One evening he took lodging in the loft of an isolated cabin along the Kishwaukee River, fifty miles north of Ottawa. The cabin reputedly housed a family of cut-throats, grown sons helping the family patriarch commit despicable deeds. During the night they repeatedly started up the ladder to Ray's loft, but each time he stirred to let them know he was awake. They backed down, and he survived. Months later local folk raided the place, killing the patriarch, chasing the sons away, and breaking up the homicidal household.[13] This den of mayhem and others like it at Cave-in-Rock and elsewhere, while rare, did take lives.

Reuben Fenner settled in Fulton County, married a neighbor, and soon indicated willingness to share his wife's affections with his brother. Horrified, his wife objected, so the brothers whipped her and mistreated her horribly, and she died. Suspicious authorities opened the coffin, discovered ghastly wounds, and locked the brothers in Lewistown's jail for trial. They escaped with help from friends. Flimsy jails saved comparatively many loathsome people from the hangman's noose, secure lockups remedying this only as the frontier waned.

Horse thievery, often organized, thrived during the frontier's twilight, anti–horse thief societies popping up even in otherwise tranquil counties. Cass County, formed in 1837, suffered organized horse thefts in 1852. Worse, gang members murdered one member who turned state's evidence. Although murders were few, comparatively many occurred among acquaintances. On August 14, 1838, about thirteen years after Schuyler County's creation, H. Warren of Rushville wrote about a laborer who saved hundreds of dollars in gold and was murdered after being seen with a co-worker, who then vanished.

* * *

At times, settlers took to carrying weapons for personal protection. Edwin G. Barker wrote from Hennepin on July 25, 1837, "I always take my pistols. A man was murdered a few days since on a road I have traveled a doz times & robbed of better than $10.00 which has rather scared me." Even so, very few settlers ordinarily carried weapons in conducting daily business.

A string of nasty—even gruesome—conflicts pitted predatory gangs against outraged citizen coalitions, the Regulators. Dispensing popular justice, Regulators flourished from the late 1830s into the 1850s. Previously, applications of popular justice had been brief and limited, and distinctions between dispensers of popular justice and law-breakers were crystal clear.[14] Regulators, however, blurred distinctions. Lawless elements embedded themselves in Massac, Pope, Ogle, DeKalb, and other counties, where they preyed on passersby, suborned or cowed officials, eliminated some, counterfeited, stole horses, and murdered. Regulators who rashly tried and executed bandits clouded the picture, but indicting Regulators for dispensing rough justice sometimes inflamed public sentiment.

Conflicts varied, many being quarrels over tactical matters, not fights over fundamental differences. Many were sporadic, limited in scope and scale, and often avoidable. Some were essentially personality clashes. A few conflicts, though, sprang from fundamental, long-standing, and essentially irreconcilable differences. They involved *basic* assumptions and values, and reflected vast gulfs between contending cultures. They had systemic features, usually involved institutions, and sometimes involved several players and complex issues. These contests involved questions of *whether* certain things should be done, not merely *who* should do them or *how* they should be done.

Potential for catastrophe was enormous, but various factors largely negated it. Broad, powerful, unspoken consensus on vital matters was extremely important in averting disaster. Consensus shaped and defined conflict and even violence, usually allowing them to unfold within understood parameters. Even desperate, emotionally charged battles involving slavery almost always occurred within unwritten rules and understandings, throttling passions and enabling Illinois to escape the bloodshed that rocked Kansas in the 1850s. Simply put, most conflict among pioneers occurred within broad, sustaining consensus, toning down violence's ferocity and scope.

Consensus predated statehood. Although bickering and rancor marred territorial politics, peace predominated. One source notes, "In other territories politics were punctuated by dueling, malicious newspaper charges, and calls for congressional investigations of territorial officials. However, in Illinois the governor and delegates were allied through kinship and political history, thus defusing a possible area of conflict." Furthermore, important issues bonded people: "The major issues of land acquisition and frontier defense united rather than divided most territorial citizens. Only political patronage and the legalization of slavery divided citizens and politicians. Neither generated much heat prior to 1818." Of great importance, "Peaceful politics distinguished Illinois from its contemporary territories."[15] Consensus-guided politics augured well for frontier life after statehood.

Other devices curbed licentiousness. Federalist founding fathers, including George Washington and Alexander Hamilton, wanted an orderly West integrated into larger society. They hoped transplanted, rational systems of power and order, based on law, would enhance order, protecting private property and encouraging genteel society. Trans-Atlantic economic structures, they further hoped, would guide the region's economy. The ordinances of 1785 and 1787 facilitated orderly settlement, inducing responsible and industrious New Englanders to settle.[16] Spurred by secular and religious missions, these stalwart folk transformed the region.

Some actions strained consensus. For example, consensus disallowed premeditated theft. And yet, occasionally consensus stretched to enable thief and victim to look the other way, both becoming better people. In early Sangamon County stealing was rare, local folk usually assisting needy newcomers until they got established. Therefore, meal and flour disappearing from a mill perplexed the miller, who resolved to catch the culprit by hiding in the mill. A man with an empty sack entered the mill, and then did something highly unusual: he knelt and prayed ardently for forgiveness for the theft he was about to commit. His prayer spilled out problems he had in earning a living, asking for a way out of his predicament. He then put into the sack just enough flour for immediate needs and started to leave. The miller recognized him as a respected resident and called for him to stop, which he did. The miller then told him to fill his sack. The two men had been friends before, and after this incident they became even better friends, remaining so for the rest of their lives.[17]

In the miller's mind, the era's consensus accommodated the thief's actions via the concept of the deserving poor. The miller judged the thief to be a deserving poor person, someone who tried to play by the rules but who was overwhelmed despite his best efforts. His good traits and potential, the miller believed, outweighed the transgression. This belief required forgiveness, understanding, and even assistance.

Some acts broke consensus, triggering very different responses. Visiting Kentuckian pugilists who gouged eyes brought opprobrium on themselves. By perhaps 1830 gouging faded, as did whipping. In some fights weapons were permitted, and some duels occurred. Illinoisans, however, banned duels, few occurring after about 1821. Scattered gunfights continued.

Other pressures damaged consensus. For example, federal land offices dispensed property, but sometimes offices reeked of favoritism, deceit, and blatant corruption. Wealthy and well-connected people literally came through the back door and got choice parcels of land. Local officials twisted laws to benefit specific people, including Congressmen. Gross inefficiencies, lost records, delays, and other frustrations worsened conditions.[18]

Other irregularities cheated people. Still, consensus governed victims' responses to unfairness. Avidly, they lobbied Congressmen, petitioned, and complained within established structures. Aggrieved land seekers almost never inflicted injury on crooked insiders and blundering bureaucrats.

Perhaps some were "silent sufferers," people seething with rage. If so, they joined innumerable "silent sufferers" throughout the world, some of whom sought redress in frontier Illinois. Edward Burlend, for example, had suffered silently in Yorkshire, England. After settling in Pike County, he spotted horses feeding for the third time in his fenced corn field. When he went to expel them, a local tough objected and whacked him across the forehead. Burlend might have retaliated in kind, but he had a household. (His self-restraint was fortunate, for the bully was a dirk-toting thug.) The Burlend household suffered injustice silently, not even resorting to courts. Things soon brightened, however, when the bully left the area. Silent suffering allowed some to remain on the frontier.[19]

Sometimes settlers' acquiescence in adverse decisions was selfless, even heroic. For example, Samuel Turner arrived in Schuyler County in 1823, and after buying and selling land he built a cabin in 1825 on land in Buena Vista township, into which he poured labor and prospered. He married, but in 1834 he lost the property and improvements to someone presenting superior title. No evidence whatsoever suggests Turner threatened the person holding superior title, or resorted to violence. Losing the land, he moved to a nearby farm, where new problems hounded him; in fact, before obtaining uncontested title to the new farm, he paid for it three times. Again, no evidence indicates he railed against injustice or fondled his rifle for redress. Instead, he toiled diligently, raised children, and died peacefully in 1855.

Samuel Turner's responses to disappointing justice were moving, but not untypical. Everywhere, defeated individuals abided by terms of defeat, either trying to recoup losses or going elsewhere. They accepted their lot in life, at least temporarily, sustained by several beliefs: society was basically just; legal and extra-legal proceedings functioned well; defeat was reversible; starting over was possible, thresholds of skill and capital needed for most undertakings being low; fellow citizens treasured justice and order, even those trying to begin anew. Finally, settlers accepted responsibility, believing they had free will.[20] Migration, settlement activities, and participation in unfolding society usually kindled or reinforced these beliefs. The frontier probably attracted people with these traits, and it probably instilled them. They helped people withstand buffeting forces.

Pioneers craved orderly, predictable, and dynamically tranquil society. Samuel Turner and others who lost heavily and repeatedly responded calmly. Believing the moral universe was just, they stayed within consensus, getting on with their lives. Their cravings and measured responses to defeat enhanced settlement and prosperity, whether people wanted to replicate previous conditions or to begin anew. Moreover, when criminal activities surged, settlers moved swiftly to crush the offenders. Given these factors, the profound tranquility and justice of frontier Illinois surprise no one.

Illinois' silent sufferers often had recourse. For its day, frontier Illinois was highly democratic; virtually all white males had suffrage. Society was comparatively open, fluid, and fair. Sufferers like Burlend obtained land, started businesses, occupied political office, experienced physical and social mobility, and waited. Others left. As was true for Abraham Lincoln and Mary Todd, frontier marriage often bridged social chasms and fostered mobility to degrees rare in the East and virtually unknown in England. Evolving and fluid society allowed settlers arriving with virtually nothing to rise. Perhaps sufferers' greatest recourse was abundant hope, confidence that things would work out. Even those who failed to rise far, nourished the hope and expectation that their lot would improve eventually. Such crucial intangibles undergirded consensus.

Consensus and common sense guided judicial proceedings and extra-legal activities. Settlers cut corners and technically broke laws, but they rarely violated the spirit of law. Pioneers, in fact, regarded willful lawbreaking as assaults on society, and most favored crushing outlaws swiftly and thoroughly. Even so, settlers distinguished between reasonable, legitimate, and beneficial laws and irrational, illegitimate, and deleterious laws, gleefully circumventing the latter. For example, after joy-leeching legislators outlawed playing ninepins, settlers complied. But they deemed the law goofy, so they added a pin, and everyone played tenpins.[21] Winking consensually at violations of inane law, pioneer society sparkled.

Sometimes common sense allowed killers to escape prosecution. This happened twice in Bond County in the late 1830s. In 1838 Jack Wood and a man named Rutter bickered. Wood said he wanted no trouble and walked away, but Rutter became vitriolic, followed Wood, and attacked him. In fending Rutter off, Wood swung once, hitting and killing him. Around 1838 Nathan Harmon, a troublesome sot, insulted a stranger. Wisely, the stranger chose not to take umbrage, but Harmon pursued him and pounced at him, only to receive a flurry of punches, which killed him. Neither Wood nor the stranger was charged. Reasoned allowance was made for those unintentionally killing tormentors in self-defense. Such conflict resolution, harsh as it was, likely reduced violence by deterring bullies. Applications of common sense helped settlers truly esteem law.

Even informal, ad hoc justice rested on good sense. One day, for example, a German settler saw people chase his dog, shoot at it, and kill it. Having killed seven neighboring sheep, the criminal dog had reaped swift, terrible retribution, but "by mutual agreement among local farmers" no morose sheep owners received compensation. Moreover, via this "mutual agreement" the same punishment quickly dispatched a canine accomplice "to prevent future calamity."22

Authorities generated confidence by suppressing true lawbreakers, even during peak frontier years. For example, although settlers surged into Stephenson County into the 1840s, it "was scarcely a comfortable locality for the outlaw or one of felonious propensities." Nevertheless, if scofflaws arrived in a "born again" condition, they were welcomed. Schuyler County, founded in 1825, suffered its first murder in 1831, when David Morgan shot George Everett. After elaborate and lengthy courtroom proceedings, Morgan was hanged in January 1832. In Logan County taking pot shots at the driver of a passing stage landed a fellow in jail, who "was an exceptional villain, shrewd, cunning and brave, and noted for his adroitness in escaping." He did escape, but was soon recaptured and died in the penitentiary. In Bond County, organized in 1817, some toughs operated, but "the laws were, with few exceptions, strictly and promptly executed, without any serious resistance or attempts at lynching." A few years later, a man named Baker stole a horse, was caught, whipped, and expelled from the county. Stealing another horse near Vandalia, the inveterate criminal was pursued, overtaken, and shot.

In part, crime was low because "neighbors knew everything about each other," which deterred aspirant criminals and helped catch wrongdoers. Social anonymity—social space—for wrongdoing was lacking, making malefactors stand out. Neighbors spotted suspicious newcomers. They often knew when others lied, and did not take kindly to it. Criminals on the lam simply found few good hiding places in frontier society. When the countryside reached a certain population density, culprits found the going rough. Some fled to the middle ground, the Indian-white hybrid society, but even there social controls restrained them. Some law-breakers flitted to cities, where anonymity cloaked numerous scofflaws.

Sometimes governmental machinery either creaked inefficiently, failing to keep pace with settlement, or did not act promptly where newcomers scrambled after prized land. In those instances, settlers instantly created quasi-legal institutions. Settlers coalesced, created popular ad hoc institutions, imbued them with the force of law, and acted decisively. Resting on broad consensus, these institutions almost invariably either prevented conflict or mitigated it. Prime examples of such institutions abound, perhaps especially in northern Illinois after approximately 1832. They included wolf drives, sweeps against outlaws and other miscreants, and campaigns to lure railroads. Some organizations functioned closely with existing governmental structures, but often they functioned autonomously, in the *absence* of effective government.

Popular institutions adjudicated conflicting land claims during the 1830s. In Winnebago County, for example, some newcomers selected land, went back to get their families, returned to the claim, and then learned that others had just claimed the land, something quite common. These interlopers, "claim jumpers," annoyed and angered original claimants, sometimes prompting petty violence, but seldom becoming lethal. Accordingly, settlers created "settlers' courts" to insure justice, some of which barred lawyers from participating. Court size, methods of formation, and procedures varied somewhat. Disputants appeared before the courts, made their cases, produced witnesses, grilled each other and opposing witnesses, and awaited decisions.

Most courts unabashedly decided in favor of those intending to actually settle the land. These courts were not absolutely fair, but decisions came quickly—the jurors and court officials having pressing work to do on their own claims—and few actual settlers complained. Instead, contemporary manuscripts, recollections, and country histories heap praise on them, regarding them as both legitimate and eminently fair. In short, they were quasi-legal and possessed the moral force of law.

They also had the physical force of law. Individuals bucking court decisions quickly jeopardized themselves. Stubbornness would be futile and costly, courts warned, and those persisting in frustrating court decisions sometimes found themselves and their possessions hauled away and dumped at some spot remote from the contested land. Stern warnings not to persist in defying the court punctuated this act. This usually sufficed; even dullards got the message. Clearly, those who bucked court decisions found solid, determined consensus backed the courts.

Sometimes courts were proactive. When Galena's land office began selling land in 1839, for example, settlers gathered in Rockford, almost seventy-five miles eastward. They selected a three-man committee to visit Galena "and adjust and settle any dispute or controversy that might arise in regard to claims, etc.," swore the three, and sent them. They held court in Galena during land sales, settling disputes. One settler witnessing the entire procedure credited the court with preventing trouble and subsequent litigation.[23] Underlying consensus and precise cooperation in Rockford and Galena crowned this proactive measure with success.

Other proactive measures also obviated problems. For example, in Lake County settlers signed agreements pledging that when land was surveyed and sold the signers would deed to each other any parcels that might be within the lines of staked claims. These agreements usually held. Similarly, in Libertyville in late 1836 settlers drafted a compact to unite settlers against potential trouble from late arrivals, people who might jump claims. The agreement divided the county into three districts, a board of three commissioners holding sway in each district. Differences of opinion concerning claims went before these boards. Some trouble arose, however, but mostly from non-signers who questioned the compact's authority.[24] Most proactive systems worked fairly well.

Monied nonresident speculators distorted settlement in Kentucky, driving small-scale farmers across the Ohio, and provoking furious populist reactions. Although Indiana suffered similarly, Illinois avoided this fate. Some partially successful large-scale speculation afflicted central Illinois as the frontier waned, but little damage was done. Generally, Illinois resembled Iowa, where speculators did not withhold land from market, restrict settlement, or foreclose delinquent farmers. Consequently, in Illinois little violence occurred between settlers and speculators.[25]

* * *

To some degree, abundance and ease laid foundations for co-operation and consensus. Incredible soils, lengthy growing seasons, and adequate rainfall at critical times made Illinois a garden, sustaining settlers. Settlers brought flora alien to Illinois, even as they destroyed forests. Similarly, Illinoisans helped drive buffalo away by 1800, suppressed wolves, and hunted other animals to near extinction, but they also imported sheep, oxen, hogs, honey bees, and innumerable other animals. Abundance, mobility, and resulting hope softened class distinctions, settlers rarely fracturing along class lines. No social segment became so utterly destitute that it grossly shattered consensus.

Some frontiersfolk, of course, knew poverty, but relatives, neighbors, and churches ameliorated their lives, keeping them from desperation and helping them stay put. So did local government. For example, in 1830 Tazewell County court officials placed Sarah Stout, the county's first pauper, in Nathan Dillon's custody, who agreed to care for her, a common practice. Once this arrangement expired, the court let her out to the lowest bidder for her care. Of course, she was expected to work while living with others. Two years later Nicholas Miller—"Old Man" Miller—became the ward of John Summers, who received $78 for keeping him. Within three years, however, this veteran pauper's value tumbled, and no one bid on him, so he lived entirely at county expense. In any case, Sarah Stout and Nicholas Miller, two largely dependent people, remained in frontier society with public assistance.

Nevertheless, some left, and their leaving constituted a safety valve, diminishing the frontier's social stress. Some returned East, a few returning to Europe. Some discouraged elderly folk in Winnebago County returned "to their homes in the east to die." Into the 1830s, return trips often consumed several dangerous,

costly, and uncertain weeks. Soon, however, Great Lakes packets reduced costs, improved safety, and sped travelers eastward
in ten days or less. And by the frontier's twilight in 1860, settlers
zipping to Pennsylvania required hardly more than a day.

Other options unfolded for discouraged settlers. By the 1830s
and 1840s, for example, they could head to new frontiers in Iowa,
Minnesota, and even Oregon and California. If they had had their
fill of agrarian frontiers, they could flock to Chicago, St. Louis,
and other beckoning towns. Their departures removed potentially combustible social discontent.

A note of caution, however. Many who left were not dissatisfied.
Some, for example, returned to childhood surroundings as victors to retire among old acquaintances. George Smith, born in
Scotland in 1810, prospered in Chicago, and in 1857 returned to
Scotland, demonstrating that "Chicago's environment did not alter everyone's values."[26] Similarly, those going to towns or to frontiers farther west often did so after acquiring valuable skills and
experience as Illinois pioneers. They now sought new challenges.

In addition, some dejected settlers retreating eastward returned, after difficulties passed. For example, vexing Indians rattled Isaac Greathouse and family in Edwards County, so they
prudently scooted to a nearby fort, and then to Kentucky. They
returned to Illinois in 1821, staying. Poor drainage in Cumberland
County discouraged Daniel Kingery, so he returned east, but he
returned for good in a year or two. Since youngsters had little
say in migration, some seized the first opportunity to return east.
Some who did so, however, later returned to Illinois. Young Adino
Page returned to Massachusetts upon turning twenty-one, worked,
married, and in 1859 settled in Woodford County. By the 1850s,
improved transportation whisked returnees back to fresh lands
for another try.

Everyday, freely given courtesies lubricated social interaction.
William Oliver, a visitor from Britain, claimed "the inhabitants
are much more courteous than the peasantry of Scotland or England, and maintain an ease and self-possession which is seldom seen, amongst what may be reckoned their equals." Oliver
added, "In the West, distinction of classes is little known and
seldom recognized. I have seen a veritable major invited to a

corn-shocking; and the major went."[27] Majors went, especially if they were candidates. Candidates flattered, conferred favors, and soothed disappointments, something notably lacking in Europe, where practically no one voted. Blurred class distinctions, much vertical and lateral mobility, and common courtesies minimized class friction.

As the frontier faded, even nature contributed to potentially explosive situations. Settlement south of Otter Creek began in 1830, nine years before Jersey County calved off of Green County. In 1853 bad corn harvests and meager hog feed supplies led farmers to drive their swine into woods south of Otter Creek to dine on mast. This region was still public domain land, called "Congressional" land. Nearby hog owners claimed the mast properly belonged to their swine, not to interloper hogs. The disputing owners literally armed themselves for a showdown. But a trespass lawsuit and a change of venue provided time and perspective for reflection. Owners of outlander hogs drove them home, defusing the situation.

Most quarrels ended this way, despite blustery shows of weapons. The incident illustrates attitudes toward public domain lands and law. The mast forests were Congressional lands, but neighboring folk assumed "ownership"—proprietorship—of the mast, treating it as their cache. They claimed access to public domain resources, perhaps especially wood, mast, and other perishable, renewable resources. They believed local folk deserved first use, a belief punctuated by threats. Nevertheless, cooler heads prevailed, judicial procedures functioned, and no hog war erupted.

Frontier conditions generated powerful social cohesion from immense diversity. Disparate migrants forged durable ties before they headed west. Intense interaction preceded most treks, prospective settlers meeting to form organizations, draft rules, determine destinations, means of conveyance, routes, possessions to take and things to leave behind, and innumerable other facets of migration and settlement. They shared booklets and settlers' letters, pooled resources, and in myriad other ways cooperated. Very few trekked and settled entirely alone. Even rugged individuals interacted with others constantly, giving and receiving help and establishing webs of mutual obligations. Planning, migrating, and settlement for many were heady, life-changing processes, brimming with novelties and problems.

Migration's challenges cemented ties. Settlers saw westward treks as noble and heroic odysseys, part of a national cavalcade. Stray households and individuals achieved instant community by adhering to groups, usually guided by informal ground rules of behavior. Trekkers shared each other's burdens and resources. Close ties impressed participants, who nevertheless knew most successful traveling communities quickly disintegrated. Most were merely functional ad hoc mobile communities, ushering volunteers westward and dissolving upon arrival. Even tight communities vowing to travel, settle, and live together disintegrated. Despite the ephemeral nature of migratory groups, common experiences produced strong ties, friends basking for decades in shared memory. Significantly, bonding was highly portable, loyalties transferring readily to nascent frontier towns. Moreover, as settlers moved from town to town so did loyalties.

Perhaps organized homogenous groups with clear missions and detailed rules experienced the tightest bonding, at least initially. Extremely tight structures and strictures, however, made groups brittle, colonies fracturing and members defecting. Their contributions to frontier society were often either ephemeral or minimal, or worse, lasting and grotesque. Moreover, they often stupidly quarreled with neighbors.

Traveling with strangers by ship and train from New York to Chicago, Vienna Winslow experienced camaraderie, which seemed to surprise her. On November 25, 1852, she wrote to her sister, commenting on "being together so long we felt quite attached to each other, & although we were meeting with strange faces in a strange land, yet I found many kind and interesting friends, willing to lend their assistance when needed."[28]

Trekking westward on roads produced analogous stories. Perfect strangers voluntarily lent assistance. Travel and camping for the night strengthened social fabric among fellow travelers. Although women, children, and the sick sometimes slept in inns or nearby farm houses, men dozed in wagons, guarding possessions and tending stock. Children, the elderly, and others gathered grass, water, firewood, wild fruit, nuts, and other necessities.

River travel established similar ties. Individual households headed to Pittsburgh or Wheeling, where they coalesced into groups and then either purchased or built river craft. Sometimes for mutual assistance a dozen households lashed several flatboats together, livestock, wagons, supplies, and equipment cluttering decks. Travelers kept sharp watch for steamboats, as well as for sawyers and planters. Lashed vessels provided security, division of labor, and overall satisfaction. Constitutions or written rules guided few riverine groups, and social arrangements were informal. Although these journeys often lasted just ten days, close ties formed. Some groups remained intact after landing, pushing inland to settle.

Travel via western steamboats, commercial flatboats, and canals built consensus. Timothy Flint reported travel's impact on immigrants and visitors: "They have passed through different states and regions, have been more or less conversant with men of different nations, languages and manners. They have experienced that expansion of mind, which cannot fail to be produced by traversing long distances of country and viewing different forms of nature and society." Although temptations beckoned and state and religious power en route to Illinois was weak, Flint observed, "it is honorable to the character of the West, that these voyages are generally terminated in so much quietness, morality and friendship."

Downstream passage had additional significance. Innumerable young men manned flatboats from Pittsburgh and Wheeling to Illinois, or from Illinois' waterways down the Mississippi to New Orleans. These journeys were rites of passage, in which young men such as Abraham Lincoln left home, fended for themselves, saw the world, became part of something larger than their locale, and grew up. Timothy Flint claimed these trips gave "to the young people, and those who impart authority, impulse and tone to fashion and opinion [and] an air of society, ease and confidence."[29] Western waters moved cargo, but they also guided boys into manhood, strangers into friendship, rural folk into towns, locales into the nation, and the nation into the West. Rivers blended people and encouraged cooperation, cohesion, and friendship.

Mundane assistance among perfect strangers in frontier Illinois cemented ties. William Oliver observed, "Travellers, when
they meet in the wilder districts, mostly stop and chat for a time,
as each can give to the other some information about the route
he has come. . . . People in the backwoods are capital in giving
directions to a traveller for the route he is to follow." On the
frontier Oliver was misled only once, when a German sent him
straight into a marsh, from which he had trouble extricating himself.[30]

These cooperative acts generated such social cohesion that
community commonly preceded effective government. Without
fanfare, neighbors greeted newcomers, offered assistance, and
raised houses for them. Together, they girdled trees, built fences,
and plowed. Bees, frolics, barn raisings, harvests, and butchering cemented settlers, as did harvesting for the infirm. They
butchered hogs, hunted, tracked predators, and erected community defenses. Dancing, story-telling, drinking, and much merri-
ment punctuated this community labor. Pioneers borrowed and
swapped tools, teams, and other necessities. After autumnal fires
cleared substantial regions of vegetation, neighbors conducted
wolf drives. When fires threatened, whole neighborhoods mus-
tered to fight them, the exhausting battle often raging all night.
No one coerced settlers into such efforts, and some absented themselves, but social cohesion stiffened by enlightened self-interest
roused volunteerism. Life-long friendships sometimes sprang from
a few days' common effort.

Cooperation, though, produced far more than buildings, friendships, and rollicking times. Botscharow-Kamau's superb study
of conflict and cooperation of frontier society in Indiana noted,
"Most importantly, by participating in these events, neighbors
demonstrated their good will to each other, and they also expressed and helped create the social solidarity of the neighborhood. Through the exchange of labor and food, the participants
not only did something important, they also said something important." Assistance, obligations, and discharging social debts
created and strengthened social fabric, producing harmony,
smooth relations, and continued cooperation. Botscharow-Kamau displayed insight of frontier society: "Harmony and bond-

ing were fundamental to frontier society, and acts defined as neighborly meant much more than simple friendliness or helpfulness. In part, this was dictated by necessity; but settlers also valued neighborliness in itself." The study added, "Good neighbors engaged in a good deal of social interaction, gift-giving, and mutual aid." These ties, moreover, operated across distinctions of class and wealth, and "families for miles around were linked together as one neighborhood by the social customs of the times, which, in the spirit of democracy, drew the line at moral worth alone."[31]

Informally and indelibly, people kept unwritten ledgers of assistance, swapping, loaning, and other communal transactions. Debtors not repaying in timely fashion suffered retribution.[32] Cooperation was voluntary, but refusal to reciprocate produced friction, even ostracism.

German millenarians who founded the Harmony Society in 1814 on the Wabash learned this harsh truth. Ironically, Harmonist codes stressed mutual assistance and harmony, something they failed to extend to non-members. Collectively aloof and refusing to exchange mutual assistance with non-Harmonist neighbors, they authored antagonism, helping doom their utopian experiment. Needlessly bucking powerful unwritten frontier social codes, they lost and suffered.

Shared suffering, privation, and crisis brought out people's better angels, fostering consensus and community. Settlers huddled in strongpoints during Indian scares. Indian threats plummeted after 1814 and vanished in 1832, but memories of threats nourished cohesion for decades. Moreover, nature's threats triggered instant cooperation. During the Deep Snow winter and the Sudden Freeze, neighbors opened doors and saved lives, fashioning ties of obligation and experience, creating lasting community.

Most problems facing pioneers engendered cooperation. Most were tangible, clear-cut, and apparently manageable, not abstract, nebulous, or unmanageable. People from all quarters of the world understood the need to overcome predators, fires, poor transportation, and similar obstacles. Believing that redress existed, perfect strangers banded together. Jointly solving problems bound wildly disparate elements of society with invisible glue.

In Brown County the Deep Snow produced indelible memories and life-long ties. In late 1830 few settlers inhabited western Illinois. When marooning snows hit, Benjamin Gristy's family, safely ensconced in their snug cabin, saw two people struggling through drifts. The Gristys took them in, saving them, and "The friendship here formed lasted for a life-time . . . these neighbors had the pleasure of enjoying each other's confidence while they sojourned together down the lapses of time."[33] That winter similar acts and shared challenges bonded innumerable pioneers. As one source put it, "The first settlers hung together. They had passed through too many trials and hardships to desert each other."[34] For virtually everyone, commonplace and spectacular hardships and freely rendered assistance forged durable ties.

In fact, early communities often thrived on threats, difficulties, and "times of troubles." Cooperation and eagerness to participate bubbled among strapped settlers, where "the basic problems of organization were intimately connected with matters of life and death."[35] Serious natural and human threats repeatedly threw settlers back on themselves, as did commonplace activities like harvesting, raising buildings, and providing for schools and churches, which helped them become informed, vital, democratic frontier residents and republican citizens.

Hardships did not cause diversity to degenerate into fragmentation. Common privations helped people—even antagonists—conclude that others were not so bad. When southern settlers in Woodford County, for example, through "that sympathetic feeling born of the privations endured in a wilderness home" got to know dreaded Yankees, "they buried their former prejudices, and cultivated a friendship with this hitherto detested race." One observer noted that the "wilderness is not the place to indulge in hostile feelings and prejudices, and upon acquaintance being thoroughly established between them, the Southern people, finding New Englanders to be men like themselves . . . gave them the right hand of fellowship, and a bond of reciprocal affection was formed." Major crises and petty problems shoved pioneers together, forcing dissimilar people to shed lingering animosities and pull together. Carl Köhler, a German visitor in Belleville, wrote that residents had a choice: either pay light taxes, or work on local roads. He joined forty others in road work, building a solid bridge across a creek in an hour.[36] Such everyday occurrences smoothed cultural differences and further fostered broad toleration, even acceptance.

Having himself experienced the frontier's privations and the horrors of Civil War combat, Professor B. J. Radford of Eureka understood that hardships and mutual assistance created community. Stressing that pioneers fell back on themselves to meet challenges, he asked, "What is it that binds the bonds of household together? What is it that binds neighbor to neighbor?" He answered by noting his lengthy Civil War service. Unit reunions, he reported, produced much discussion on "the hardships, the long marches, the tough battles they had." He added, "These are the things that make men comrades, working together, unselfishness and helpfulness where help is needed." And then he applied these principles to more universal settings: "These are the things that make neighborhoods." Concluding, he maintained neighborly ties require "mutual helpfulness that brings them together in unselfishness and mutual self-denial." Radford's astute observations underscore stark relationships between common hardships, mutual assistance, and social cohesion in frontier Illinois.

PART VI

FRONTIER ILLINOIS FADES

15.

TIES THAT BIND

Between the Mexican War in 1846 and the Civil War in 1861, frontier Illinois changed, faded, and largely disappeared, leaving memory and myth. Telltale signs, events, and developments pointed to the frontier's disappearance, some of them symbolic, some substantive, and some both.

Specific memorable occurrences, often traumatic events, signified its passing. For example, Old Settler societies designated people who settled before the Deep Snow of 1830–1831 as Old Settlers, implicitly regarding later arrivals as less than fully authentic pioneers. An Old Settlers' meeting in Logan County made finer distinctions, labeling those who had arrived before 1840 Old Settlers, but conferring special honor on those who had endured the Deep Snow. Each Deep Snow man and woman in attendance received a handsome cane and the title of "pioneer." Elsewhere, the signal event separating true, authentic pioneers from later arrivals was a railroad's appearance, violent incident, fire, struggle, or similar event. Many such events marked the passing of defining features of frontier life.

In addition, pioneers associated salient events with overcoming hardships and with progress and overall growth. Population figures reflected such change. Illinois climbed from twentieth

During the 1850s, steam-powered threshing machines displaced animal-powered machines. Transportation improvements sped machinery to farmers from distant manufacturers. Advertising whetted farmers' interest. The *Prairie Farmer*, March 3, 1859. ILLINOIS STATE HISTORICAL LIBRARY, A DIVISION OF THE ILLINOIS HISTORIC PRESERVATION AGENCY.

most populous state in the Union in 1830 to fourteenth in 1840, eleventh in 1850, and finally fourth in 1860. The state's population during the 1850s spurted from 851,470 to 1,711,951, sweeping away the last major vestiges of frontier life. The total increase in Illinois of 860,481 was larger than the increase of any two other states of the Old Northwest. Live births in Illinois accounted for 306,950 of the increase. Migration accounted for 553,531. Of those migrating into Illinois, some 318,402 were natives of the United States, and 235,129 were foreign-born.[1] Rapid growth, however, spawned disruption.

As frontier Illinois moved from south to north, southern counties passed through frontier stages before northern counties. With statehood in 1818, in fact, portions of southern Illinois were already post-frontier, but northern Illinois contained very few settlers. Pioneers in southern regions endured slow, costly, and uncertain transportation, often taking days to reach their county seat and investing eight laborious weeks and a tidy fortune traveling to the East Coast. In the 1850s, by contrast, trains safely

and inexpensively sped settlers and their produce in just two
days from northern Illinois to the coast and returned with people
and goods from the East. Indians generally confronted pioneers
in southern forests, not in northern prairies. Few pioneers in southern counties knew steel plows or mechanical reapers, but later
settlers farther north used them. No telegraphs or railroads crossed
frontier southern Illinois, but they later sliced through sparsely
settled northern counties. Settlers from slave states and some
blacks filtered into southern regions, while Northerners and Europeans flocked across northern prairies. Few settlers in southern Illinois embraced national reform movements, but residents
farther north did so. Most southern counties shed frontier characteristics only slowly, but northern counties often lost them in
just a decade or two. Clearly, southern regions had significantly
different frontier experiences from northern regions.

Crescendos of transportation and communication developments helped kill frontier Illinois. Steamboat traffic steadily increased through the 1850s. In 1834 some 230 steamboats coursed
the Mississippi and its tributaries, in 1840 some 286, and by 1848
about 1,300. Private, state, and federal projects lessened some
hazards. More and bigger vessels slashed transportation costs and
time for goods and passengers upstream. One observer at mid-
century noted that in 1817 passenger fare for a trip between Louisville and New Orleans was between $125 and $150. Despite
inflation during ensuing decades, the fare for that journey by
mid-century was "not more than $25."[2] Travel from New Or-
leans to Pittsburgh, once a three-month ordeal, now took two
weeks. Finally, by about 1840 authorities had cleansed waterways of most pirates and other cutthroats.[3]

Soon after Chicago first heard the chugging of steamboats in
1832, Great Lakes shipping linked the town to eastern points via
the Erie Canal. Buffalo became the break-in-bulk point for goods
that arrived by ship and then were offloaded to canal barges for
shipment to New York City and elsewhere. Illinois products constituted a large portion of goods streaming eastward along this
booming lake-canal system. In 1851, for example, Chicago shipped
nearly 40 percent of the corn entering Buffalo, over 42 percent
of the oats, over half the wheat, nearly 54 percent of the bacon

and hams, nearly 57 percent of the beef, and nearly two-thirds of the corn. Chicago, moreover, shipped over 22 percent of the furs, nearly half the hides, and over 99 percent of the buffalo robes, reflecting Chicago's initial advantage, continuance of early frontier activities, and increasing ties with western plains and forests. In 1837 Chicago shipped about 100 bushels of grain, in 1847 some 2,243,000 bushels, and in 1857 upwards of 18 million. Clearly, canals and interlake vessels transformed Chicago into a very major shipper. By 1845 Buffalo's brisk trade in livestock, grain, and flour was greater in volume than that of any other American city, primarily due to Chicago.[4]

One author notes that "modern Chicago was born in 1848."[5] In that year telegraph lines reached the town, the Illinois & Michigan Canal opened, construction started on Chicago's first railroad, the first oceangoing ship docked, wooden turnpikes reached into the nearby countryside to tap foodstuffs, the city's first stockyard began operating, and Cyrus McCormick arrived from Virginia. But the city's greatest asset was its assertive, inventive, visionary, and youthful residents. They zestfully exhibited the greatest resource people can have: hope.

Steamboats, then canals, and finally trains whisked migrants to Illinois in relative comfort and security. This lessened the need to travel in groups, even though group migrations continued for ideological reasons. Vienna Winslow wrote on November 25, 1852, about a voyage across the Great Lakes to Chicago. Although the lakes were choppy and passengers were seasick, she wrote with satisfaction, "There was a table of books, & every luxury you could wish for at the table to eat; then the tables were cleared and a dessert of ice cream & jelly, nice apples & nuts, & raisins." Such fare would have been unthought of just twenty years earlier, and overall conditions were markedly better. By the 1840s, in fact, women traveled either alone or with small children, something practically unknown just twenty years earlier. Moreover, passenger fares on Great Lake steamers were lower: for instance, fares between Buffalo and Chicago were $20 in 1840 but only $10 a decade later, with steerage at half price.[6] Being of an anticipatory nature, Vienna Winslow predicted, "But we shall not be

obliged to cross the lakes for the future. They have got the railroad completed around the lake."

In April of 1848 the Illinois & Michigan Canal finally opened,
a monumental accomplishment nearly twelve anguished years in
the making. Although lack of state funding stalled the project in
1841, Governor Thomas Ford badgered legislators to restructure
its debt, British and eastern financial interests breathed new life
into the project, and Governor Augustus French taxed to sustain
the project. Investments nearing $6,500,000 finally produced an
engineering marvel, which included twenty-five bridges spanning the canal, fifteen locks, dams, aqueducts, towpaths, and
locktenders' houses. The canal was sixty feet wide at water level,
thirty-six at the bottom, and six feet deep. Each lock was 110 feet
long and eighteen feet wide. Stretching from Chicago to La Salle,
its total length topped 101 miles, and its sixty-foot width allowed
barges easy passage. Soon cargo and passengers glided in both
directions. Very substantial traffic graced the first year's 180 days
of operating season, 162 licensed boats garnering $88,000 in
tolls. Moving goods and people when nearby trails were impassable strips of mud, the canal presaged impending railroads. Linking the Great Lakes and the Mississippi River Valley, for decades
the canal moved grain, lumber, sugar from the South, metals,
fuel, and other bulk commodities. Chicago benefitted immensely
from it.

Vessels plied its placid waters, tolls washed into the state's
treasury, and prosperity buoyed towns along its path. Lockport,
Joliet, Ottawa, La Salle, Peru, and cities as far south as Beardstown thrived. This string of towns transformed their hinterlands,
uplifting them and further drawing them into burgeoning regional and national economies, eroding frontier conditions and
frontier mentality. McCormick's reapers, produced in Chicago,
floated on barges to customers.[7] Farms along the Illinois and
Mississippi rivers and their tributaries spewed food and fiber to
eastern consumers. Eastern goods returned via the canal to western customers. The canal helped Chicago draw from the upper
Mississippi Valley, siphoning grain traffic away from St. Louis.

The canal brought additional changes. Thousands of Irish and other laborers toiled on it. When canal work slackened, many laborers took up farms along the canal and the Illinois River clear to Peoria. Lacking money, canal directors had issued workers canal scrip, which was accepted only at a discount. The state of Illinois accepted scrip in payment for state lands, which resulted in many Irish laborers settling along the waterway. In Will County Irish canal laborers dominated the new town of Troy. Chicago attracted many Irish and other immigrants, as well as New Englanders and New Yorkers. Its spectacular growth well into the 1850s, sustained in part by the canal and labor pools, hurried the frontier's demise.

Soon a burgeoning transshipment point, Chicago boomed as a break-in-bulk center, with cargo moving from one kind of vessel to another. Products of farms and forests entering Chicago encountered three alternatives: they were offloaded and then transferred to waiting Great Lakes vessels; offloaded and processed; offloaded and then stored. Similarly, northern lumber flowed to Chicago, there to be processed, stored, or transshipped on the canal.[8] Replacing log structures and symbolizing the frontier's demise, sturdy balloon-frame buildings across northern Illinois testify to huge shipments of northern lumber, creativity, and desire to save lumber costs. Tanneries, natural byproducts of meat-packing operations, sprouted along the Chicago River. Break-in-bulk activities saw products warehoused, transported across town, sometimes processed, insured, protected, bid on, and usually shipped out. Chicago's residents consumed only a fraction of the grain, meat, leather, timber, and other products entering the city and processed in it, most products being sent to customers elsewhere. Processing, storing, and selling were essentially city-building activities, not city-serving activities. City-building activities created an ever-increasing hinterland, providing employment and wealth for Chicago. Soon railroads vastly extended Chicago's hinterland.

Nevertheless, farmers around Chicago groaned under high costs and delays in getting their produce to Chicago and hauling manufactured goods to their farms. Wagon travel was slow, expensive, and subject to capricious weather. Meltwater in spring and storms in summer and late autumn made roads impassable for weeks.

DANFORD'S IMPROVED IRON REAPER AND MOWER.

In the waning years of frontier Illinois, a mechanical
reaper and mower complements a prosperous, neat
farm. Note the ornamental shrubs and post-and-board
fences. The *Prairie Farmer*, June 30, 1859. ILLINOIS STATE
HISTORICAL LIBRARY, A DIVISION OF THE ILLINOIS HISTORIC
PRESERVATION AGENCY.

Moreover, gaping holes in roads snapped axles and shattered
wheels.

Creative minds boldly addressed these problems. In the late
1840s near Springfield, for example, one enterprising fellow built
a steam-powered prairie car. Twenty-six feet long and nineteen
feet wide, James Semple's contraption actually chugged from
Alton to Springfield, thrilling Semple and helping him envision
steam-powered vehicles towing strings of cars across prairies.
Despite its basic merits, though, it was underfinanced and failed.

As counties filled up with settlers, innumerable ordinary local improvements significantly enhanced transportation. Everywhere, countless paths connecting farms to each other and to
roads were upgraded by neighbors and townships, becoming small
roads. Over time, trails became serviceable roads. Makeshift
bridges spanned creeks, enabling farmers to visit each other without wading. Wagons and carriages now linked farmsteads, im-

proving bartering, local commerce, and social intercourse. Journeys to town, church, and school became easier and safer. Local vagaries hampered some improvements. William Oliver, a Briton visiting eastern Illinois in 1842, praised bridge construction, but then sniffed at local roads. He saw a state-maintained road marred by a huge hole, excavated by local people seeking clay with which to daub chimneys. He also encountered roads blocked by recently built fences. He noted rural areas, "where the country is getting peopled up," had satisfactory roads. But he criticized patchwork road building, claiming roads "are flung about from one farm to another, in a manner perfectly vexatious and perplexing." He predicted people would not put up with such bewildering confusion for long.[9] In reality, however, local folk generally understood local conditions and topography well and laid out roads rationally.

Visiting St. Clair County from Germany in 1851, Carl Köhler echoed Oliver's sentiments. He found American roads were inferior to German roads, noting difficulties farmers had in reaching nearby markets and claiming roads "in winter are not at all passable." Consequently, he noted, farm location was extremely important. Farmers far from town raised only livestock, which walked themselves to market.[10] Clearly, road quality varied from place to place, but in many locales it improved markedly by the 1840s. Even assuming Oliver and Köhler's observations were accurate, roads became better over time.

Bridges further banished frontier isolation, saving lives, speeding travel, and replacing ferries. Carroll County in 1853 appropriated $2,000 to bridge Plum River near Savanna, constructing it the next year. Elsewhere, improved bridges replaced rickety structures. Bridging streams was challenging; a trestle bridge thrown over the Kaskaskia in 1824 in Randolph County collapsed after about a year. Undaunted, the Kaskaskia Bridge Company built a three-span bridge, which collapsed in May 1843, before it opened. These and other setbacks aside, solid bridges spanned streams, especially near county seats and other important towns.

Getting grain to functioning mills challenged settlers. Poor roads and cumbersome ferries delayed grain-bearing ox carts and horses. Low water, mechanical breakdowns, and sickness among oxen and horses treading inclined-plain mills often stymied milling and delayed patrons, sometimes for days on end. Steam mills, operating by the 1820s, alleviated some bottlenecks. With better roads, ferries, bridges, and other improvements by the 1840s, and railroads soon after, grain reached mills faster, cheaper, and more regularly.

Reliance on horses, carts, and wagons diminished. Fewer rural folk walked to town, rode oxen, or rode three or four on one horse. Of course, farmers and others still moved cargo by wagon, and on Saturday evenings they and their families came to towns in wagons to trade and visit. But carriages, buggies, and other spring-equipped vehicles appeared, further signaling the frontier's passing.[11]

Farmers and others agitated for plank roads. Introduced from Russia to Upper Canada in 1833, plank roads appeared in New York in 1844, spread quickly, and by 1857 some seven thousand miles of plank roads linked hinterlands and towns, mostly in Middle Atlantic and adjacent states.[12] In 1847, however, Illinois became the first state to approve incorporating plank-road companies, dozens quickly spawning across northern Illinois, many serving Chicago. In late 1848 wagons clanked along the eight-foot wide road stretching ten miles between Riverside and Chicago, generating hefty profits and a spate of road construction. Shortly, plank roads joined Chicago to Genoa, Elgin, Sycamore, Oswego, and Naperville. Others linked steamboat landings all along the Illinois to nearby hinterlands. As late as mid-1855 the Lockport, Plainfield & Yorkville Plankroad Company formed in Will County. At their peak, in the early 1850s, plank roads totaled a few hundred miles, but they served primarily local needs.

Problems soon bedeviled them. Stringers set into the ground supported three-inch planks, but freezing-thawing dynamics played havoc with them, and blistering sun dried and warped planks. Maintenance costs devoured profits and drained scant reserves. Moreover, mere planning for railroads stifled road construction. For example, plank road projects south of Chicago fizzled after the Illinois Central Railroad announced plans to lay track there. Although brutal railroad competition overwhelmed them, plank roads served the public by raising expectations for better transportation and forming labor pools, men who soon worked on the railroads.

As early as the 1830s, visionaries foresaw a thriving metropolis on Lake Michigan tied by iron rails to Lake Erie and points eastward. William B. Ogden, formerly enamored of steamboats, was smitten by railroads. He announced his vision: "Continuous railways from New York to Lake Erie, and south of Lake Erie, through Ohio, Indiana, and Illinois, to the waters of the Mississippi, and connecting with railroads running to Cincinnati, and Louisville in Kentucky, and Nashville in Tennessee, and to New Orleans, will present the most splendid system of internal communication ever yet devised by man."[13] Ogden's prescient view was stated in 1835, while he was a New York State legislator, before settling in Chicago. Two years later, economic depression foiled Ogden's dream for about twenty years. Others, however, eagerly awaited railroad track. On July 16, 1848, years before Rockford saw a train, Oren W. Fisk wrote about lands being sold to generate capital "to make a rail road to Chicago and a telegraph, which is nearly done." Such anticipatory comments were common.

Around ten years after the Northern Cross Railroad prematurely linked Springfield and the Illinois River, railroads again captured public imagination. Work on the Galena and Chicago Union Railroad began in the summer of 1848, and by November 21, passengers and freight moved along eight miles of track. One passenger, Jerome Beecher, a shoemaker, rode and met a farmer carrying hides to Chicago in an ox-drawn wagon. When Beecher purchased the hides, a new age for Chicago dawned. Two additional miles were added to the line by year's end.[14] Although by early 1849 Illinois had fewer than eighty miles of track, the Galena and Chicago Union line soon operated fourteen miles of track from Chicago toward Elgin, while the Sangamon and Morgan Railroad (successor of the defunct Northern Cross) linked Springfield to the Illinois River. In 1850 tracks reached Elgin, and the Chicago and Aurora line forked off the Galena and Chicago Union line and covered the ten miles to Aurora. Slightly over one hundred miles of track served Illinoisans. Railroads assaulted distance and other natural barriers, giving people options concerning resources and markets. Furthermore, railroads mediated between humankind and nature, bringing them together. In sum, railroads cut transportation costs and time and made travel relatively certain, predictable, year-around, and safe. By 1853 they tied Illinoisans to contiguous states, the Gulf of Mexico, and to the East Coast. Furthermore, by the early 1850s postal rates for letters plummeted to three cents thanks to railroads, promoting writing and other communication.

Before most people heard locomotives roar by, however, they heard telegraph transmitters clack. Telegraphs reached St. Louis by December of 1847, and by early 1848 telegraph lines linked Chicago, Springfield, and St. Louis. Railroad construction soared in 1852, tapping telegraphers heralding their arrival. They helped avoid collisions and disasters at weakened bridges, and fostered railroad efficiency, manufacturing specialization, and economic integration and coordination. They flashed stories to newspapers and sped investment orders. They drew people together economically and socially. Before the arrival of telegraphs, newspapers usually printed legal notices, local items, and articles that were "exchanged" among newspapers. Obviously, no up-to-date national news could be printed. After telegraphs arrived, newspapers rushed current news into print from distant sources.[15] Overnight, telegraph offices became community hubs, nerve centers rivaling post offices. Clearly, these revolutions assaulted isolation, helping end frontier life.

Visionaries saw a bright future for railroads. Technological breakthroughs, amassed capital, managerial skill, and expanding markets spearheaded Illinois' railroad surge by 1855. Waterways continued to carry nonperishables and bulky goods, but railroads had several advantages: speed; ability to slice through regions not served by waterways; and increased ability to operate in all weather and seasons.[16] Railroads provided inexpensive, comfortable, fast, safe, and dependable transportation. They allowed massive, rapid settlement of remaining uninhabited regions, regions either too far from navigable water or too waterlogged. Railroads, furthermore, sharply curtailed long-distance stage and wagon traffic, lingering and costly frontier vestiges.

Railroads affected roads. Carrying most of the nation's mail to local post offices, fast-moving stagecoaches required sweeping curves in roads; slowing for right-angle curves stole precious time. Sweeping curves, however, trimmed corners and confused property lines, annoying farmers. But after railroads put most stages out of business, farmers petitioned to realign the roads. Sluggish wagons and even buggies needed no sweeping curves. Soon roads hugged section lines and made right-angle turns, pleasing farmers and accentuating the checker-board pattern inherent in the Ordinance of 1785.[17]

The disappearance of public land was perhaps the most significant indication of the frontier's passing. In 1849 about 40 percent of Illinois' area consisted of U.S. public domain lands, mostly in isolated prairies far from navigable streams in central and east-central Illinois, some in the far north. Railroads laced Illinois by late 1855 and more were under construction. They helped settlers gobble up remaining chunks of government lands, a significant nail in the frontier's coffin.[18] Brisk sales of government land almost always preceded the arrival of railroads, purchasers anticipating rising land values. For example, in 1851 as tracks approached Sugar Creek, buyers avidly snapped up nearly every acre of unsold land within ten miles of the route. Within a year after track was laid, nearby properties doubled in value, and by 1856 prices ballooned nine-fold over pre-railroad prices. In McLean County, as late as 1849 settlers still clung to groves. But in 1850 the Illinois Central Railroad received a charter to select government land on which to lay track. Over night, land values rocketed, "all the prairie within many miles of the railroad was entered immediately," prairies were settled, and a necklace of small towns graced the rail line. Although professional speculators bought lands, holding some until the late 1860s, many ordinary people also bought and speculated. Buyers snapping up land in anticipation of railroads sounded the frontier's death knell.

An advertisement printed in 1855 by the Illinois Land Company predicted rising land values. It offered 30,000 acres in central Illinois, served by four railroads, and quoted from a letter written from Vandalia on June 13, 1853, by James M. Davis, the Land Register for the Vandalia District. After noting his lengthy service as register of lands, he touted the offerings' rich soil and

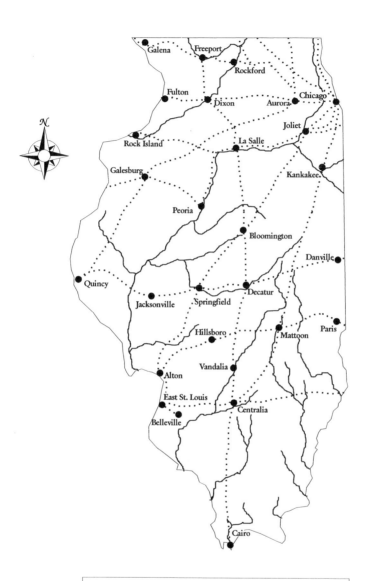

Illinois Railways c. 1855

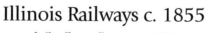

ready markets via railroads: "I feel sure that these and all other lands situated near these great lines of Rail Road communication, must, within a very few years, become very valuable." He then added, "The day is not far distant when . . . in Illinois Government land is all taken up; and in the hands of individuals, and the increase of immigration and Rail Roads, cannot fail ultimately to make land in Illinois immensely valuable." The publishers appended a note, observing, "It must be borne in mind that the above letter was written more than two years ago, and before any of the Rail Roads mentioned were completed. Since which time lands have advanced more than four hundred per cent."[19]

Railroad companies copied the Illinois & Michigan Canal in scouring eastern cities for laborers, many of them immigrants. Advertisements and agents in the East attracted labor for work on railroads, and railroad promoters hired firms in New York and elsewhere to recruit workers. In addition, recruiting occurred in Europe. Perhaps some 100,000 men worked at one time or another for the Illinois Central. And as was true of canal workers, cholera cut down thousands of railroad workers, one crew at Peru losing 130 in two days. Fifty-two laborers who died in 1853 while constructing the Mississippi and Chicago line near Funk's Grove are said to be buried in a mass grave nearby.[20]

Illinois' speculative rail construction during the 1850s contrasted sharply with deliberative railroad construction around Toronto, Canada, which promoted traditional values and bucolic landscape. As tracks radiated from Toronto during the 1850s, Torontonians agonized over railroads marring pastoral scenes, horrid accidents, and disruptions of decorum. They dismissed ideas Chicagoans took for granted, including laying track through uninhabited regions. In short, stodgy conservatism guided Torontonians in railroad matters. Toronto's existing character and structures heavily influenced railroads. Railroads, on the other hand, body-sculpted adolescent Chicago, defining and directing its growth.[21]

Railroads radically reordered townsite advantages. Previously, town founders sought sites on navigable water, preferably near forests or groves. Illinois' earliest railroads connected existing communities to nearby landings and ports, improving water-borne traffic. By 1852, however, track shot across bleak prairies far from rivers, immediately spawning villages and hamlets at intervals, which provided water, fuel, support facilities, and storage areas. And each station or loading platform serviced rural people in its hinterland. James Caird, a visiting Briton, observed in 1858, "In England we make railways to facilitate an existing traffic." This was true of practically all railways in Europe. Caird then added an insightful comment, "But in the Western States of America railways are made for hundreds of miles through the wilderness, not to accommodate but to create traffic."[22] Even more impressive, during the 1850s rails traversed previously inaccessible wetlands in eastern Illinois, permitting settlement, especially near stations. Drainage of wetlands in Iroquois County and elsewhere followed, and soon farms and towns dotted eastern flatlands.

Many townsites enjoyed no economic advantage before track arrived. With track, though, advantages sprang up. Kankakee did not exist in 1850. Railroads arrived and a town appeared, containing 3,640 inhabitants in 1856 and 4,900 by 1859. No one lived at Centralia in 1850. After track arrived, some 1,900 people lived there in 1856 and 2,500 by 1859. Mattoon did not exist in 1850. The site attracted tracks and 472 people by 1856, swelling to 1,400 by 1859. Du Quoin was nonexistent in 1850. The railroad and some 300 people arrived by 1856, the population quadrupling to 1,200 by 1859.

Railroads generated business for themselves, seemingly out of thin air. Warren County debated donating $50,000 toward building the Chicago & Burlington line, igniting strenuous assertions that Warren County's entire annual agricultural production would not fill one train. Opponents claimed not enough county residents would ride the train to justify the $50,000 subsidy, arguing that stages passing through the county seat were only half full. After track was laid in 1854, however, "there was more freight at Monmouth waiting shipment than the most sanguine had dreamed," and the county's population surged. Railroads swept aside pessimistic concerns, ushering in prosperity and justifying bestowed subsidies.

Existing communities spurted when railroads arrived. Drowsy
Urbana, for example, contained in 1850 about 500 souls, obtained
tracks, and by 1856 had 3,285 people. Cairo, home to 300 residents in 1850, got track and contained some 3,000 residents by
1856; about 5,200 lived there in 1859.²³ Supine until 1854, Monmouth in Warren County obtained the Chicago, Burlington &
Quincy railroad. With that, "the town sprang into active life, and
improvements of every kind began to be made. The next year the
college . . . was located, and gave an additional impetus to persons looking for an intellectual home. A few years after, the library was founded, and made another prominent attraction. Good
hotels were built, fine stores appeared, and the Union Hall, one
of the largest in this part of the State, was erected." Trains brought
northern lumber to Monmouth, and hauled away the region's
grain and meat, a common story during the 1850s.

Improved harbor and dock facilities and external transportation links boosted Chicago. By 1861 eleven railroad lines rushed
nature's treasures across great distances to Chicago and dispatched
the city's goods and services to distant consumers. Chicago tapped
and served various hinterlands, which was nothing new. In the
1840s, for example, coopers in Virgil in Knox County had prospered making barrels to transport local wheat to Chicago, New
York, and New Orleans.²⁴ The advent of railroads, however, wedded remote farms and villages to Chicago. Economic functions
became complexly interconnected. Illinoisans and others fed goods
into Chicago, handled products from Chicago, or serviced the
railroads and telegraphs connecting local centers to the thriving
lake city, and the city flourished. Home to nearly 30,000 people
in 1850, it was Illinois' largest city. It contained 80,000 by 1855,
nearly 110,000 in 1860, about half foreign born. Its growth was
fearsome: "During the nineteenth century, when Chicago was at
the height of its gargantuan growth, its citizens rather prided
themselves on the wonder and horror their hometown evoked in
visitors. No other city in America had ever grown so large so
quickly; none had so rapidly overwhelmed the countryside around
it to create so urban a world."²⁵ Matching Chicago's rise, the
city's collar communities grew, nourished by railroads. For example, in 1854 the Chicago and Milwaukee Railroad created

Evanston, and in 1856 the Illinois Central spawned Hyde Park. Soon, strung parallel to railroad tracks, there were summer homes and villas.

The 1850s cemented strong ties between Chicago and the East. When the Michigan Central Railroad reached Chicago in 1852, two daily trains clanked in each direction between Chicago and Detroit. Travel time between New York and Illinois plummeted from three weeks, under favorable conditions in the early 1830s, to just two predictable days, and costs similarly declined. By 1856 Chicago had access to thirteen railroads and the services of 104 trains daily. The next year saw some 120 passenger trains daily enter and leave Chicago.[26] Although the Illinois Central line reinforced connections between Illinois and the South, most new track reinforced Illinois' east-west links.

Backed by eastern capitalists eager for Chicago to surpass St. Louis, the Hannibal and St. Joseph Railroad in northern Missouri was oriented to transfer northern Missouri from St. Louis' hinterland to Chicago's. The Chicago, Alton & St. Louis Railroad was the first line from Chicago to reach the Mississippi, arriving by 1853 at Alton, some twenty miles upriver from St. Louis. Relying on predictable rails instead of fickle river conditions, many shippers left St. Louis' market and entered Chicago's. St. Louis' northern hinterland shrank under pressure from dynamic, expanding Chicago. On April 21, 1856, a locomotive of the Chicago and Rock Island line bridged the Mississippi, a great milestone, one symbolizing Chicago's lengthening economic reach. Simply put, Chicago tapped ever-increasing hinterlands, drawing grain, lumber, and other sustenance. Reapers, processed meats, prefabricated homes, and myriad other products from Chicago's factories and shops raced via rail into ever-expanding markets. When aging settlers reminiscenced decades later, not unexpectedly they touted roles played by early railroads, telegraphs, schools, and churches in overcoming rough conditions.

Illinois foodstuffs reached eastern consumers in ever-increasing quantities, also reflecting technological and economic maturation. One British visitor in late 1858 witnessed efforts to apply steam power to prairie farming: "We passed a steam plough which was moving itself along a prairie road to a farm where it was about to be tried." The visitor speculated that low costs of feed for draft animals would inhibit the application of such machinery to farming.[27]

Improved *quality* of foodstuffs reflects additional maturation. Hurrying to establish grain standards before city officials imposed their own standards, wheat dealers in 1846 organized the Board of Trade. This board was soon hotly criticized for driving down prices paid to wheat farmers. By the 1850s, a reformed Board of Trade tried to insure standards, grading moisture, weight, and color, thereby allaying eastern concerns about mixed lot shipments. By 1860 it appointed a chief inspector, examined grain entering Chicago, examined departing grain, and held warehouses liable for defects of grain shipped. Chicago's reputation for quality grain rocketed, garnering top dollar for shippers and forging new Illinois-eastern ties. The 1850s also witnessed the birth of a "futures" market.

Businessmen traded between Boston and Chicago via railroad and telegraph. For example, in Chicago footwear retailers from Massachusetts depended upon Bostonian suppliers, and this connection facilitated Chicago's regional footwear dominance. Illinoisans eagerly anticipated eastern markets and eastern goods and services. John Barker wrote on March 21, 1857, from Carroll County to David Ports of Maryland, predicting, "The railroad will be completed this fall; then we shall have a road to the eastern market." Four years later, such ties reinforced Illinois' adherence to the Union cause.

Railroads altered trade patterns with New Orleans and the East Coast. In the early 1850s, Cincinnati shipped over 30 percent of the flour reaching New Orleans. Between 1855 and 1861, though, after rails crossed the Appalachians, Cincinnati supplied only 4 percent, on average, of the flour. Perhaps distance kept Illinois' trade pattern from being as severely affected by trans-Appalachian railroads, but the pattern did change.[28] In fact, with crop failures and repeal of Britain's Corn Laws, Illinois' foodstuffs found European markets. By the 1850s trains hustled Illinois' grain, meat, and other products toward Europe, alleviating food shortages caused by the Crimean War.

Freight and passenger rates fell dramatically. Generally, passenger rates were under three cents a mile. Competition reduced rates by the late 1850s, travel between Rockford and Chicago costing just a dollar. Trains clicked along at sustained speeds of thirty or forty miles per hour, increasing during the decade. Stagecoach speeds just topped six miles per hour for long trips, and wagons lumbered at two or three miles per hour. Trains operated in all but the foulest conditions, unlike coaches, wagons, ships, and canals, and were stopped only occasionally by drifting snow or massive flooding.[29] Trains plugging through inclement weather greatly enhanced commerce, large lanterns making night travel safer by the mid-1850s. Despite some ghastly railroad accidents, trains on the whole saved lives.

Sharp reductions in high, distance-graduated postal rates by the early 1850s curbed frontier isolation. For example, mailing a one-sheet letter beyond 400 miles cost twenty-five cents in 1815, when laborers earned just sixty or seventy-five cents per day. Such a letter still cost twenty-five cents by 1845, when laborers often earned a dollar or so per day. Postal rates dropped beginning in 1845, and mailing a letter not weighing over half an ounce now cost just ten cents beyond 300 miles.[30] And by 1851 the cost collapsed to just three cents up to 3,000 miles. Perhaps these sharp reductions reflect two developments: economies realized by the spread of railroads across the county, and keen competition from nascent telegraphs. Now, even frontier laborers, many earning over a dollar per day, sent letters back and forth, dissolving loneliness and informing others about frontier Illinois. A similar reduction in postal rates for printed materials, including newspapers, further reduced frontier isolation. Even tiny post offices tucked away in stores attracted patrons from outlying regions.

A letter written on October 16, 1857, from Spring Garden by Samary S. Sherman to her cousin, Lucretia C. Sibley of Massachusetts, illustrates the change. She wrote, "I will again resume my pen to write a few lines to you, to present our united and sincere thanks to you for the bundle of papers that you were so very kind as to send to us." She added, "They have afforded us a great many feasts on perusing them, and a great many tears have been shed over them on reading and sympathizing with the misfortunes of others." The "bundle of papers" reflects technological breakthroughs in newspaper production, along with reduced costs, but it also suggests lowered postal rates, as does Samary Sherman's "again" resuming her pen. She mused about possibly subscribing to the newspaper, an indication of acceptable postal costs and predictable, speedy delivery, services only recently available to Illinoisans. Trains, lowered postal rates, and federal subsidies produced results.

Low postal rates killed three practices. Into the 1840s individuals could mail letters postage due. Typically, postmasters held such letters until addressees paid the steep postage, many letters languishing for months until addressees scraped up enough cash to redeem them. Another practice was a conspiracy between letter writers and recipients, who devised codes consisting of dots, dashes, and other symbols. Writers penned letters, folded them, and then on the outside wrote the real message in code. Recipients learned these letters awaited them in local post offices, asked to see them, read the coded messages, and then rejected the letters. The third practice was implemented to save paper (mailing extra sheets cost more). Writers finished a page, turned it at a right angle, and then wrote new lines at a ninety degree angle over the original lines, sometimes in different colored inks. Such crosshatched letters were nearly indecipherable. Postal rate reductions by 1851 virtually ended these practices.

Widespread commercial use of telegraphs to send important, up-to-date information indicates time was money. Three more decades passed before telegraphs and railroads produced standard time zones, but such needs became apparent during the 1850s. This was also true in mail. By the 1840s private express mail service cropped up. By the early 1850s express firms in Illinois sped letters, contracts, bank notes, bills, newspapers, and relatively small packages to recipients. (The U.S. Post Office began parcel post service only in 1912.) Speedy delivery coincided with a flickering frontier and a maturing state.

Transportation breakthroughs radically changed Quincy, a town on the Mississippi. Settled in 1822, seat of Adams County in 1825, Quincy obtained a federal land office in 1831, during massive land sales in the Military Tract. Quincy's salient advantage: it was the only point on the Mississippi's left bank for 150 miles at which the bluffs reached the river and low-water was still deep enough for steamboats. About 1,000 steamboats docked there by 1841, over 2,900 by 1856.[31] Between 1841 and 1849 its shipments of wheat, corn, and oats basically doubled. Busy mills produced 55,160 barrels of flour in 1847, some 132,000 in 1857. Pork packing thrived in Quincy as a cold-weather industry, most hogs butchered between the first frost and sometime in January. Cooperages, distilleries, soap-making firms, brickworks, machine shops, and allied industries either provided services and products for grain and meat industries, or they used grain or meat products. These forward and backward linkages for agrarian production helped Quincy prosper. Packet lines connected the city to St. Louis and Keokuk, and in 1852 Quincy obtained daily mail. The next year Quincy became a port of entry, foreign ships soon docking there, and its far-flung waterborne connections were vibrant. Most shipping occurred between late summer and late autumn, before ice choked the Mississippi.

Railroads, however, brought a sweeping revolution, linking Quincy by early 1857 to the Illinois River, Chicago, and eastern North America. It became just one of many towns north of the Ohio railroads oriented eastward. Despite difficulties with differences in track gauges and with poor bridges, "the integration of the regional railroads with the eastern trunk systems increasingly attracted trade that had formerly moved to eastern markets by way of New Orleans."[32] Symbolizing this growing commercial unity, Massachusetts shipped a codfish directly to Quincy. Enhanced connectivity, prosperity, and Civil War business made this rail hub in 1870 the state's second city.

By the late 1850s the Illinois Central Railroad substituted abundant coal for vanishing wood: "This important combustible will be found so widely distributed throughout the prairie region of Illinois, that the absence of densely wooded tracts will subject the settler to no serious inconvenience." The attempt to entice settlers into treeless regions continued: "The Illinois Central Railroad Company, with an ample supply of wood at their command, at a cost not exceeding $2.50 per cord, are substituting, as a matter of economy, and convenience, coal burning, in place of wood-burning, locomotives on their road, and other railroads are following their example."[33] Clearly, coal altered settlement dynamics in the 1850s.

Railroads starkly affected Montgomery County in 1852. The Terre Haute & Alton railroad was constructed along the south line of North Litchfield Township, which inspired the founding of Litchfield and other important changes. As one sources notes, "with the laying out of Litchfield and the opening of a market for grain, and the consequent appreciation of land, a new era dawned. The vacant prairie began to be fenced and brought into tillage. A salient feature of this decade was the creation of the village of Litchfield, with a population of 1,500, many of them of different nationality, and widely differing in manners and customs." Again and again, railroads secured markets, hoisted land values, brought new land under cultivation, birthed towns, and jumbled together diverse people.

Sometimes infusions of outsiders brought mixed results. Railroad laborers, including many Irish, settled along the lines, often crowded into makeshift quarters near tracks. Their ethnicity, religion, and modes of living sometimes distressed local people. Even so, some settled, married, and adjusted well. For example, in 1851 Irish laid track through Sugar Creek, south of Springfield. Nine years later Irish-born young men comprised almost a quarter of the population of Sugar Creek's two villages, Chatham and Auburn. Other outsiders were far less welcome. Con artists and rings of thieves, often from larger cities, used trains to descend on a town and make their getaway. On the other hand, Jasper County did not "lose its early reputation of lawlessness and low standards in morals" until after railroads arrived. According to some, infusions of outside influences brought mixed results.

Fearing railroads would be inherently undemocratic, residents near Chicago awaited tracks with trepidation. Only the wealthy, they argued, could use them and benefit from them. Moreover, people near tracks would gain unfair advantage over those farther away. Some nervous businessmen quaked about railroads' net impact, some in outlying towns expressing misgivings about close ties to Chicago. Most people, nevertheless, fervently supported the era's high-technological wonder.[34]

Horrific railroad accidents marred the frontier's twilight. Trains inflicted grisly deaths on wandering livestock. Worse, people fell victim, including a five-year-old farm girl killed in 1855 south of Chatham. One ghastly accident occurred in Will County, near Rock Run, on November 1, 1854. A Chicago and Rock Island Railroad train ran off the track, the first two cars landing on the derailed locomotive. Steam burst from the locomotive, "terribly scalding sixty-two of the passengers, literally cooking some of them alive. Twelve of this number died within a few minutes." Hours passed before scalded survivors could be brought back to Joliet, "and the scenes of suffering presented at the depot were indescribable and sickened the heart of every beholder." Joliet's residents, especially women, alleviated pain, but four more people died.[35]

Railroads hurt more than people. They retarded the Illinois & Michigan Canal, killed plank roads, and undermined Wabash steamboat traffic, which flourished between 1832 and 1856. Unlike plank roads, however, the canal hauled bulk cargo efficiently and survived, even if stunted.

In addition, railroads crippled towns they bypassed. A Chicago & Alton train vitiated Auburn in 1852 when it pulled into nearby Wineman, which also had a telegraph. Auburn's robust stage service vanished by 1853. Bypassed Auburnites responded by lifting their homes onto ox-drawn sledges and dragging them to Wineman. With Wineman's incorporation in 1865, it changed its name to Auburn, probably to console former Auburnites. To avoid high costs of construction and to reward investors in land, some railroads avoided established towns. For example, a branch line of the Illinois Central bypassed the French town of Bourbonnais and other nearby French settlements and overnight created Manteno, Chebanse, and Kankakee. This benefitted the Associates Land Company, an organization of railroad directors who speculated in town sites. In 1853 Kankakee bested Bourbonnais as country seat of newly created Kankakee County,

Bourbonnais shriveling over time into a sleepy village. Ushering in additional change, the new railroad enticed Yankee farmers to the region.[36]

Tapping Mississippi River commerce, Oquawka bustled. By 1856 it sported a fine distillery, first-class hotels, secure warehouses, saw and grist mills, streets clogged with grain-laden wagons, and a plank road and ferry boat for trade in Iowa. By 1857, though, its poor decisions persuaded the Chicago, Burlington & Quincy railroad to bypass the town. Burlington, Monmouth, and Galesburg prospered, but Oquawka withered and languished, its plank road and ferry service folding.

Knowing their advantages, towns vied for railroads and other internal improvements. Even tiny towns sent "swarms of delegates" to sway railroad officials and "legislative sessions were inundated with hopeful agents" from innumerable communities.[37] These competitions "revealed the life and death perception of the need to acquire the latest transportation facilities." They were analogous to county-seat battles. To entice railroads, towns offered free rights of way, near guarantees of profits, and other enticements.

Even victorious towns, however, sometimes paid a price from laws of unintended consequences. By the early 1850s, for example, before railroads boomed, the river towns of Peoria, Pekin, Beardstown, Meredosia, Oquawka, De Soto, Alton, and Quincy were Illinois' major pork packing centers. Illinoisans also used packing facilities in Hannibal and St. Louis in Missouri, Keokuk and Burlington in Iowa, and Terre Haute in Indiana. Each of the thirteen facilities dwarfed Chicago's. Railroads, though, quickly extended markets for dressed hogs and then live hogs, and hogs arrived from ever greater distances. Chicago's pork hinterland expanded, crippling packing operations in other towns. Chicago's economies of scale and other advantages allowed packers to pay hog producers top dollar. The mid-1850s saw railroads speed twice as many hogs to Chicago as to Peoria, Chicago becoming the state's leading packing center and then the greatest in the Old Northwest. Most centers annually processed fewer than 50,000 hogs—even St. Louis handled fewer than 100,000—but Chicago in the late 1850s annually packed over 200,000, and by

1859–60 some 350,000 hogs arrived annually by rail, of which Chicago packed 66 percent, shunting the rest elsewhere for processing. Railroads, in short, centralized hog packing, which elevated Chicago and garroted smaller packers.[38]

Railroads undermined or skewed other economic activities, as well. For example, in pre-railroad years, drovers often spent several weeks coaxing livestock to market and returning home. (Waterways transported some herds part of the way.) Now trains sped livestock to market. Coaches and inns still serviced passengers, but largely on roads remote from tracks. Since before statehood itinerant pack peddlers on horseback and on foot had plied farmsteads and hamlets with cutlery, pots and pans, pins and needles, and other supplies. As paths turned into real roads, railroads supplied huckster wagons, which bounced along increasingly regular circuits, providing bolts of denim and cotton goods, seasonings and candies, medicines, kerosene, and ammunition— items routinely offered by pack peddlers. Nevertheless, some households purchased very few items from huckster wagons, electing instead to remain largely outside the commercial economy by producing in the home most of life's necessities and many luxuries.

By the 1850s rural folk hopped trains to nearby communities to get tools and knives sharpened, buy household goods formerly distributed by peddlers and hucksters, and sell produce. No longer did Isaac Funk and Robert Stubblefield of McLean County carry plow irons sixty miles on horseback to get them sharpened. Trains, moreover, brought sustained supplies of patent medicine, and home-brewed folk medicines waned. Peddlers, hucksters, long-haul teamsters, and long-distance drovers disappeared in many places. In sum, railroads eradicated specific occupations, but expanding economic opportunities buoyed those dislocated by railroads.

In addition, families used railroads for recreation, riding for enjoyment, for family outings. Recreational use had counterparts in uses of omnibuses and streetcars in cities, families riding Sunday afternoons decked out in their finest. Rail proliferation strengthened ties between rural areas and myriad towns and cities, drawing farm and hamlet into regional and national networks. By the early 1870s, for example, residents of Sugar Creek, south of Springfield, were within five miles of a freight depot, something true through much of the state. By 1860 Illinoisans, for good or for bad—and often for both—became increasingly enmeshed in far-flung railroad connections, with profound and permanent results.

In addition, railroads had great intangible and symbolic significance. Railroad images and nomenclature captivated public imagination, as high technology often does. People employed metaphors of locomotives, rushing trains, and endless track. Arch-Democrat Stephen A. Douglas, senator from Illinois, joined Republicans in advocating railroads. Ironically, therefore, during his reelection bid in 1858 a Republican banner depicted a train hurtling toward him, suggesting he was a figure of the past powerless to influence the future. Railroads captured imagination in ways that even steamboats had not. Steamboats went only where nature's rivers flowed, where they encountered shabby flatboats and even lowly canoes, reminders of yesterday's technology. Worse, sandbars, ice jams, floods, and sawyers and planters endangered them. Trains, on the other hand, hurtled through time and space, prairie and forest, largely oblivious to nature's whims. Joining telegraphs in annihilating distance, they symbolized boundless progress blessed by science, the inexorable wave of the future.[39] By 1860 Illinois ranked second among the states in track mileage, boasting 2,799 miles. Clearly, Illinois subscribed to the future.

Business advertisements reflected rising expectations for railroads. Anticipating railroads, merchants regaled potential customers with railroad imagery. For example, in Freeport on November 17, 1847, D. A. Knowlton informed readers of the *Prairie-Democrat* they should "Clear the Track!" for the Galena & Chicago Railroad, then barely in planning stages. Freeport, Knowlton intoned, "is destined to be one of the most important depots on the great G.&C.R.R." Readers learned his store in Freeport, which he termed "a perfect Depot," brimmed with "New Goods! Of all kinds and styles," and could replenish stocks of merchants and peddlers. Railroads undermined peddlers, so the use of railroad imagery in appealing to peddlers is ironic.

But linking business to railroad terminology made sense, given railroads' grip on public imagination.

Communities obtaining railroads celebrated their good fortune. For example, when on January 11, 1855, the first train pulled into Waukegan from Chicago the good townsfolk knew how to welcome it. As the train arrived at 12:30 p.m., cannon roared a salute, church bells pealed, a band from Milwaukee cut loose, and speeches began. A dinner was then served for 300 guests, replete with more speeches. And for those guests not returning to Chicago that day, a grand ball awaited them that evening.

* * *

Towns by the 1850s revealed various maturing forces and conditions. Some towns had their first boardwalks by the 1840s, and by the mid-1850s some lit streets by gas. Many replaced decaying wooden or log courthouses with brick or stone structures. Secure lockups replaced early jails, flimsy structures that invited escapes; it would not do for respectable towns to have rickety jails. Town ordinances expressly forbade hogs, cows, sheep and other domestic animals to wander and loiter. (Effective enforcement, however, sometimes lagged.) As early as 1839 Mount Carmel in Wabash County passed ordinances curtailing perambulating hogs, similarly addressing dogs in 1841. Later, laws restricted strolling horses and sheep. In 1851 Mount Carmel passed a tougher anti-dog ordinance. Sometimes town ordinances failed in improving towns, so private safeguards were employed, often with success.

For example, Pana sprang into existence at the juncture of the Terre Haute and Alton Railroad and the Illinois Central Railroad. On May 2, 1855, Milan S. Beckwith wrote that town lots were selling briskly, adding, "In the certificate of sale is a provision that the purchaser shall in one year from the time of purchase erect buildings worth not less than three hundred dollars." Clearly, those who laid out Pana wanted order, attainable standards, and safeguards for their efforts, hopes shared by town lot purchasers. Such private covenants were designed to guarantee the quality of new buildings, stimulate the purchase of building materials, and possibly screen out undesirable individuals.

The *Prairie Farmer* of June 30, 1859, depicted efforts to harness prairie winds. ILLINOIS STATE HISTORICAL LIBRARY, A DIVISION OF THE ILLINOIS HISTORIC PRESERVATION AGENCY.

In 1840 Mount Carmel's Main Street sported boardwalks, and three years later a bridge costing $11.70 graced the intersection at Market and Seventh Street. A hook and ladder company safeguarded the community by 1848. In 1857 the town graveled one block of Main Street, covering up telltale evidence of raw frontier life. The same year in Wabash County three additional signs of maturation appeared: dire need for a new courthouse, since the old one burned that year; a county subsidy to the Ohio and Wabash Railroad; a county-created Vigilance Association to thwart horse thieves. Finally, in 1860 Mount Carmel obtained Illinois' first cannery, reflecting regular bumper harvests and dependable transportation. Within thirty-five years the town had shucked off many frontier traits, achieving post-frontier status.

Urban changes were stark and dramatic. New retail stores and new homes, often built of brick or stone, added luster to towns, corner stores usually being the biggest and most imposing. Brickyards, quarries, and marble works cropped up, attesting to perceived need for stone or brick public buildings, new banks, monuments, and fashionable homes. Stone and marble buildings indicated the ability to transport raw stone to distant work places and then to consumers. Some builders dubbed stone or brick buildings "fireproof," a claim that frequently went up in smoke as buildings burned. Pekin got its first "fireproof" building in 1859. Still, towns remained largely constructed of wood, producing spectacular fires. Worse, as frontier towns matured, their buildings had less space between them, enabling wind-driven fires to consume whole sections of town, some towns' worst fires occurring late in the frontier era. Libraries sprouted as the frontier died, Metamora founding one in 1857, for example. By the late 1840s towns boasted daguerreotype shops. Asa Smith opened one in Oquawka in 1846, while also running a bookstore. Towns built waterworks, water pipes, and other facilities to improve water quality. By the 1850s creative minds in towns and on farms concocted devices to tap wind power.

A thousand small improvements made life in towns more comfortable. Carl Köhler noted that in the town of Lebanon people could purchase white oil paint, precut windows, glass, putty, and other necessities. At the same time, however, he stressed the volume of bartering, homemade clothes and food, and the tendency for farmers to build their own homes.[40]

Throughout most of the frontier era pioneers lit their cabins with grease in a saucer with a floating wick, greased paper over window openings, fireplaces, butterwood balls soaked in fat, and other primitive means. Candles were expensive to buy or make and were used only by fairly wealthy people. In any case, poor lighting ended the work day and sent people to bed. Around 1830 the oil lamp, burning whale oil, appeared. In cities by the 1850s gas provided vastly improved lighting, at least for people of means and for some streets. Gas illuminated Quincy's streets by Christmas, 1854. During the frontier's gloaming, kerosene was replacing whale oil. For the first time ever, ordinary Illinoisans enjoyed decent interior lighting. Pioneers read and worked after sunset, breaking nature's ancient rhythms and dictates.

Early settlers ate meals on stools or puncheon benches, often sharing a common knife. Pioneers' shoes were often made from leather of their own tanning. They donned home-made linsey and flannel and other homespun items. Sunbonnets were common, and some women sported calico dresses. Few wore boots, some wore shoes, and many went barefoot much of the time in moderate weather. Toward the close of the frontier, chairs replaced stools and benches. Furniture shops in numerous towns reflected improved transportation, reviving conditions, and people's desires. Townsfolk and even farmers in northern counties, especially, bypassed local craftsmen and bought manufactured furniture. Pianos, organs, and even sewing machines replaced looms and spinning wheels. Of course, some women continued making clothes and men still worked on leather goods in winter's relatively idle months. Raising sheep became feasible once wolves and other sizeable predators were suppressed. One biased contemporary source, prematurely optimistic, claimed in 1859 that predatory wolves were extinct.[41] Reflecting the belief that wolves no longer menaced sheep, innumerable woolen mills, including converted grist mills, appeared throughout Illinois by 1850, mostly steam-powered. Wool prices tumbled, more woolen clothes appeared, buckskin vanished by the 1840s, and settlers put aside homespun and adopted store-bought clothes, improved transportation making this possible. In general, by perhaps 1850 household labor and time were too valuable to squander much time making homemade items. In addition, maturing society produced increasingly fine divisions of labor, leading to more tailors. On December 24, 1839, James H. Smith advised David Ports, a Marylander thinking of settling in Illinois: "If you are in need of clothes get the stuff [fabric] and get them made after you get here." By the 1840s clothing was increasingly varied, store-bought, and inexpensive. By the 1850s, barefooted adult pedestrians were a rarity; boots and shoes were common, for even the poorest, although barefoot youngsters still scampered about.

The railroad revolution, improvements in other modes of transportation and communication, and increased urbanization transformed Illinois. In doing so, they eroded frontier Illinois and banished many frontier traits.

16.

CHANGING ECOLOGY, EVOLVING SOCIETY

With Indian removal by the late 1830s, most Indian-white middle ground culture vanished. New middle ground culture developed, however, in which agrarian values melded with onrushing modernization. Commercial agrarian society and supporting farm towns formed this new middle ground, a place of mediation and commingling of nature and advancing American culture. Railroads, other technologies, and institutions largely defined and shaped this middle ground, where farmers who valued rural life harmonized with latest technologies and town life. Technology and science augmented nature's bounty, and railroads and vessels sped foodstuffs and other commodities to consumers. Rural dwellers enmeshed themselves in evolving national economic and cultural systems, a process most welcomed. Tensions between nature's environment and human achievements changed, sometimes abating, and signs of harmony and reconciliation appeared.[1]

Ecological changes by the 1850s signified eroding frontier conditions. Newcomers, checking prairie fires, planted fruit trees, bushes, flowers, and other plants they brought from distant places to grace farms and villages, softening life, providing variety, and giving pleasure. Songbirds flourished amid the new vegetation. Honey bees, dubbed "the white man's fly" by Indians, having preceded advancing settlers by a few score miles, now buzzed throughout Illinois. Oxen, cattle, horses, swine, sheep, poultry, and other non-indigenous animals inhabited every region.

By the 1850s settlers used saplings from New England and elsewhere to establish sizeable professional orchards, especially in northern counties. Trains rushed fresh fruit to Chicago and other markets. Professional nurseries also arose during the decade, reflecting rising discretionary income and desire to spruce up property. Bureau County's nurseries were established in the 1840s. Commercial ornamental shrubs, flowering trees, ivy, fruit trees, and flowers marked passing frontier conditions. In York Township in Carroll County, for example, N. D. French set out a nursery in 1851. Construction and steam engine requirements denuded Illinois timber, but new and diverse fruit and decorative trees and bushes enhanced life.[2]

In 1840, Illinois' orchard production was worth just under $150,000. By 1850 it climbed to $446,000, and by 1860 it topped $1,126,000. Even accounting for moderate inflation, the increase of 750 percent between 1840 and 1860 far outstripped population growth. Indiana and Michigan also registered impressive gains, Indiana's value increasing over nine-fold. For the most part, the greatest increases in absolute and relative terms throughout the Old Northwest occurred during the 1850s, when the Illinois frontier faded, transforming itself via increased acreage in cultivation and via transportation and mechanization revolutions.[3]

Much in Illinoisans' diets remained, however: wild game, fish, wild lettuce, poke, narrow dock, watercress, black mustard, dandelion wine, mushrooms, grapes, berries, plums, and other wild fruit and vegetables, and milk, often a source of sickness. But maturing Illinois consumed a broadening selection of foods and even delicacies. Varied, refined, and balanced diets heavily supplemented or largely replaced limited, rough "natural" diets, even in late winter. People now consumed finely milled flour and purchased meats, and apples and other fruit from commercial orchards. Fruit, recently introduced animals, and grains became dietary mainstays. Around the year 1800 potatoes were virtually unknown, but after 1850 they were common. After the suppression of predators, enough chickens survived from year to year to

insure growing supplies of eggs. Improved processing and storage methods removed many seasonal limitations. Through can-
ning, salting, and smoking, Illinoisans enjoyed vegetables, grapes
and other fruit, and prepared meats year-round. Supplies of salted meats, cider, and grains laid in at harvest time lasted into late
summer, as did carrots, potatoes, and onions, when stored properly. Traditional seasons of feast and scarcity abated, diets becoming more uniform year-round. Even people of moderate means
enjoyed more spices, tea, mustard, coffee, rice, and sugar—foods
brought by train and ship.

For decades both sexes and all age groups had quaffed copious quantities of whiskey, youngsters often sipping some before
trundling off to school. Often costing around thirty cents per gal-
lon, whiskey graced even religious households and flowed freely
at house raisings, hog slaughters, dances, and on innumerable
other occasions. Its widespread use reflected early southern culture and poor, expensive transportation, which necessitated turning surplus grain into a commodity capable of withstanding transportation costs. It also testified to grim facts of painful teeth, sore
gums, arthritic joints, aches and pains from malaria and accidents, and overall discomfort, which tempted people to take frequent nips. In Logan County, for example, people thought liquor
mitigated malarial aches, known as ague, "so every one attended
to that." In 1851 lawmakers clamped down on casual drinking by
setting a minimum sale of hard liquor at a quart and forbidding
sales to youngsters under eighteen years of age. Much of the furor over drinking involved immigrants, nativism, and religion,
which were often the thinly veiled targets of temperance advocates and other reformers. During the 1850s, nevertheless, cider
and other beverages partially displaced whiskey as a common
drink, a sharp change from frontier days.

Thorough settlement decimated certain species. Early settlers,
for example, howled about ferocious insects. In early Logan
County farmers hauling corn to distant Edwardsville for milling, traveled at night "on account of the flies being so bad, for
at daylight they had to build a fire near the horses and keep the
flies off until night." Greenhead flies, dubbed prairie flies, infested marshy places and were particularly tormenting in late

summer, attacking in swarms, drawing blood from horses and other animals, and stampeding frantic victims. Bites actually killed horses, and wary travelers avoided these hellish creatures by traveling at night. Malaria-carrying mosquitoes afflicted soggy lands in eastern counties. Malaria was Illinois' most prevalent disease between 1780 and the 1850s. As late as the 1840s, a visiting physician noted, "the whole prairie was saturated with malaria. In fact, the entire area of central Illinois was a gigantic emporium of malaria."[4] However, during the 1850s drainage and cultivation markedly reduced numbers of mosquitoes, sickness abating. Similarly, rattlesnakes for untold centuries thrived on prairies, but by 1850 innumerable fatal encounters with sod-busting settlers and thick-skinned hogs, impervious to snake bites, thinned their ranks. Plowmen dispatched scores daily with long whips. In short, settlers altered and sometimes enhanced frontier life by draining, farming, introducing some new species, and decimating others. One memoir claimed that deer were plentiful in McDonough County in 1850, but rare in 1860.[5]

Other events heralded the frontier's passing. For ages, annual prairie fires killed saplings, bushes, and other vegetation that spread onto prairies from woods; generally, only water courses sustained such vegetation in prairies. Settlement and resulting widespread plowing checked raging prairie infernos. Deliberate plowing in strategic places, backfires, and creative fire-fighting further checked fires. Early settlers saw blackened prairies, but later arrivals rarely did. The last major autumnal fire was a milestone, the harbinger of additional swift changes. In McLean County, "sometimes the settlers protected not only their farms from fire but a considerable prairie. The prairie so protected soon became covered with a growth of timber." One British visitor in the 1840s discovered fire-damaged trees: the fire "materially injures them, and on the ridges and in the groves, which from their situation, must have been frequently exposed to fire, the old timber is invariably unsound, and much of it is hollow." He noted, however, "wherever the fire has been kept out for a few years, and in this country, where vegetation proceeds with a rapidity quite astonishing to the native of Britain, many kinds of trees, at the age of three or four years, have attained a height of from eight to twelve feet."[6] Even before fires abated, settlers planted small orchards and various trees and bushes around houses and between fields, providing cover and sustenance for animals. Alien trees, bushes, flowers, and other imported vegetation meant new habitats for animals, new ingredients in the ecological equation. Imported flora and fauna and altered native flora and fauna created new environments, new opportunities.

Settlers planted "artificial" groves. These provided the owners with steady supplies of wood products, and they also provided settlers and visitors with beauty. At least a few planters and others believed such groves ameliorated climate, making winters milder and summers less oppressive.[7]

Some unwelcome species arrived as the frontier matured. Tazewell County, for example, was for years the nation's garden spot, free from parasites that afflicted crops. But over the years smut, rust, chinch bugs, and other parasites from various places entered the garden. The need to battle pests unknown to early pioneers marked the frontier's passing. Burgeoning towns brought unhealthy nuisances: "Rats have recently made their appearance in the cities, and may hereafter be regarded as permanent residents."[8]

Settlers' concerns about prairie settlement slackened by the late 1830s and disappeared entirely before frontier Illinois vanished. Steel plows sliced tangled prairie grass roots. Members of Bishop Hill colony, the Janssonists, broke prairie sod by "assembling a large herd of oxen to pull sod-breaking plows," and they overcame wood shortages by making brick for buildings and experimenting with sod fences. Then they adopted broom corn as a profitable commercial crop and operated mills, workshops, a hotel, and a store to provide goods and services for area customers.[9] Poor drainage afflicted Henry County, as well as the east-central counties. Pioneers from Holland, the Frisian Islands, wetlands ringing the Baltic Sea, and the English fens performed wonders in reclaiming land and making it productive. Sweet water filling prairie wells dispelled concerns about the quality of prairie water, but not without difficulty.[10] Ships and then trains by the 1850s brought pine from Michigan, Wisconsin, and Minnesota for fencing, housing, and other needs. Hungry settlers gobbled up the last major prairie lands by 1860.

The 1850s saw Illinoisans push to new frontiers farther west. Perhaps awareness of good lands farther west led Illinoisans to disregard soil conservation. Germans and others, though, had histories of soil conservation, and they marveled at settlers' callous misuse of the soil. Carl Köhler, for example, saw a farm near Belleville that had been farmed for twenty-five years without fertilizer. Manure pits, common in his native Germany, were absent in Illinois. He noted, "The American farmer does not think of leaving productive land to his children. They can find land elsewhere. Indeed, there are still billions of acres in the West, awaiting only plow and seed to make them bloom. He tries rather to get as much profit as possible in his lifetime."[11] Pioneers, of course, knew Illinois' soil was incredibly fertile, which led some to abuse it.

Settlers occupying the last major chunks of land meant extinction for certain animals. Deer, wolves, wildcats, and other animals retreated to thickets and overgrown river bottoms. From these hideouts, predators pounced on sheep, hogs, and other livestock, and occasionally attacked or frightened people, which triggered massive, day-long drives to track them down and kill them. In 1851 Henderson County's residents organized a huge wolf-hunt, but in 1857 a large wolf turned up and made off with a hapless porker. Wolves were hunted, poisoned, ensnared in traps and pens, chased down by mounted men carrying clubs, and pursued by bounty hunters. By the middle 1840s, one publication observed, "The buffalo and elk have left the State for the boundless prairies west of the Mississippi. The bear is seldom met with. The panther and wild-cat have mostly disappeared, as have the beaver and otter."[12] A visitor to Illinois in 1842 noted that buffalo, elk, and beaver were virtually extinct, bear and wildcat had retreated to dense forests, and relentless struggles continued against such predators as wolves and raccoons, the latter devouring huge quantities of corn. On the other hand, quail increased in numbers as settlement occurred, perhaps sustained

by insects, worms, and bugs in newly created treelines.[13] Wabash
County residents killed their last wildcat in 1838, their last bear
in 1850. Killing or expelling the last wolf marked a milestone in
frontier maturation. Although certain animals became rare, especially large predators, game remained plentiful before the Civil
War. Visitors found turkeys, partridges, prairie chickens, and
rabbits in "superabundant" quantities.

Predators reeled from human pressures, but benign animals
also suffered from relentless settlement and wanton practices.
Eliza Farnham, a sensitive and intelligent observer of Illinois'
frontier, lamented mindless destruction of wildlife. Although she
visited during the late 1830s and early 1840s, even then she witnessed destruction. She noted deer trapped in snow: "In this
dreadful condition, the terrified creatures are overtaken, and often cruelly beaten to death, by barbarians whose only object is to
destroy them." Of course, she did not suffer losses from crop-
devouring deer, but her basic point had merit. She recoiled in
horror from indiscriminate slaughter of waterfowl and other creatures.[14]

Perhaps her pleas and others' took effect, for in 1855 legislators passed the state's first game law, however feeble and quirky.
It read, "It shall be unlawful for any person to kill, ensnare or
trap any deer, fawn, wild turkey, grouse, prairie hen or chicken,
or quail, between the fifteenth day of January and the first day
of August of each and every year." Fines were to be divided between the complainant and school trustees in the township in
which the offense occurred. Although the law exempted fifty-
eight counties, these first game laws anticipated a time when
various animals faced extinction. The law sought to conserve some
of the frontier's wilder, natural features, a desire mounting with
the frontier's passing.

As late as the 1840s, some defended profligate use of resources,
including the soil. One British traveler, for example, noted, "It
ought always to be kept in mind, that in a country where labour
is so dear, land so cheap, and nature so liberal, it is better to do a
great deal in a middling way than to do a little well. The outlay
consequent on tilling land with care is not met by a correspond-

ing return."[15] So long as good land seemed to exist in inexhaustible quantities, concern about scarce human labor trumped concern about land.

* * *

Many wanted to eradicate or at least downplay Illinois' frontier features. Speculators and other landowners knew that increased population boosted land values and productivity. Raw conditions, they feared, would deter prospective settlers, so they proclaimed the frontier's demise: progress and civilization were banishing lingering traces of crude, dangerous wilderness.[16] Railroad construction, especially, was touted: it ended debilitating isolation for those living away from navigable rivers and created vast markets. By the 1850s, in fact, boosters lauded Illinois as a post-frontier society, one just slightly less developed and refined than the East.

In 1855 the Illinois Land Company advertised 30,000 acres for sale. The advertisement included selections from a letter the Rev. John S. Barger of Clinton wrote on January 22, 1855. After claiming eastern farmers and their sons would fare better in Illinois than in the East, Barger opined, "This is not a wilderness. They will find schools and churches springing up in almost every settlement made, and now being made, throughout the State. Illinois is not a moral desolation. It literally and spiritually 'blossoms as the rose.'" After advising readers to visit Chicago, Galena, and Cairo, he encouraged them to take in rural regions: "The Illinois Central Rail Road and its branches traverse the finest portions of the globe. Let them glide through our State on these and other roads, now chequering almost the entire of this 'garden of the Lord,' and stop where they will" to examine land. Then followed a letter by B. G. Root, noting strong connections between farmers and outside markets and supplies: "We receive, in excellent condition, fresh fish from the lake via Chicago, and tropical fruits via New Orleans and Cairo. The facility with which we dispose of whatever we have to sell, and procure whatever we wish to purchase, the mildness of the climate and the fertility of the soil, render this a most desirable residence." And then Root alluded to competition from more recent frontiers: "If you will once visit us, you will abandon all idea of settling in Iowa." Clearly, boosters suggested the frontier's favorable features, including good land at reasonable prices, still existed, but they insisted the worst features, including isolation and "moral desolation," had faded.

Perhaps events around the river town of Warsaw convinced people that frontier conditions had ended. Beginning in 1858 boating regattas were held on the Mississippi River, "a silver goblet lined with gold" being the prize that year. Thousands lined the banks to watch the races. Boats built by Andrew Wiard's boatyard in Warsaw competed.[17] Veteran river crews probably reflected on the regattas, sensing the passing of frontier conditions. Entertainment and enlightenment from the outside helped banish frontier isolation. For example, as early as September 4, 1841, the *Illinoian* announced that between September 8 and September 13 a "Circus and Caravan" of a "moral character" involving wild animals, a giraffe, an elephant, a gymnastic performance, and equestrians would present shows in Berlin, Jacksonville, Winchester, Whitehall, and Carrollton, a schedule that reflected improving transportation.

Applying science and technology to agriculture, agricultural societies and fairs further banished the frontier. Of the 114 societies known to have functioned about 1820, all but sixteen were in New England, clustering around Pittsfield, Massachusetts. Nevertheless, the idea of agricultural societies spread from its Massachusetts hearth to Illinois and elsewhere, and by 1860 the Old Northwest states, with only 22 percent of the nation's population, had nearly 34 percent of its agricultural societies. These states promoted many societies because of their New England ties, numerous proprietor farmers, and high agrarian production.

As early as October 24, 1836, the *Illinois State Gazette and Jacksonville News* featured the "Illinois Agricultural Society" in a lengthy article and devoted one and one-half columns to printing the names of the winners of that year's competitions. (The April 13, 1836, issue announced the formation in Jacksonville of the Diamond Grove Jockey Club, dedicated to improving the stock of horses.)

Improving economic conditions during the early 1840s launched a wave of midwestern societies. (Nationally, societies probably peaked in 1858, when 1,367 functioned.) Even before depression dissipated, Illinoisans founded societies. The Union Agricultural Society, founded in Chicago by 1840, assisted "instruction and science, and improvements in scientific and practical agriculture and the mechanical arts" around Chicago.[18] In Winnebago County, the Agricultural Society functioned in April of 1841, and that October its exhibition bestowed awards for outstanding livestock, cultivated land, butter, cheese, flannel, sewing silk, and sugar. Fair prizes also rewarded music, art, and other endeavors. John Regan, a Scot, won first prize for oil painting in October 1854 at the Knox County Agricultural Fair.[19]

Some counties organized agricultural societies prematurely. For example, Winnebago County, organized in 1836, witnessed in early 1841 the formation of a society, which chose officers, gathered funds, and in October held an exhibition. Displays of garden produce, grain, livestock, domestic articles, manufactured items, and other products delighted visitors. Contestants won awards for superior livestock, cultivated land, butter, cheese, flannel, silk, sugar, and other accomplishments. This exhibition featured the first cattle show in northern Illinois. After functioning for several years, however, this society flickered out of existence. Nevertheless, the germ was planted, and perhaps efforts in nearby counties goaded residents of Winnebago County to try again, for in 1852 a new society took shape. It thrived and conducted many exhibitions over decades.

Even in their infancy, fairs fostered learning and progressive practices. They helped overcome isolation and backwardness, helping vanquish frontier conditions. Typically, early county agricultural societies did several things: organized, held exhibitions, made awards, bought and laid out land, erected buildings, and tried to survive. Significantly, they explicitly reminded agriculturalists and others that excellence was valued and might be rewarded.

Several examples illustrate the wave of county fair foundings. The Warren County Agricultural Society, organized in August of 1852, attracted a thousand visitors at its first fair, held in the courthouse. Eventually, the society bought spacious grounds and built impressive buildings. The Ogle County Fair began in 1853, and the Fair Association purchased forty acres adjacent to Oregon, where the fair was held for many years. The Carroll County Agricultural Society organized in 1853 "to represent the interests of Agriculture, Horticulture and Mechanics." Its first fair was held south of Mount Carroll in late 1854. In Montgomery County an agricultural association formed about the year 1850, had a checkered career, and on July 3, 1857, the Montgomery County Agricultural Society superseded it. In June 1856 the Richland County Agricultural Society was formed. It held fairs near Olney's depot, in 1858 it rented ten acres east of Olney, and in 1860 it bought this land and held fairs there.

As fights over county formation and county seats tapered off, squabbles over locations of county fairs erupted. Hillsboro and Litchfield, for example, vied for the Montgomery County Agricultural Society, Hillsboro winning. The way Hillsboro won miffed the people of Litchfield, who organized the Litchfield Agricultural and Mechanical Association. This organization sputtered for several years, ran into difficulties, and folded.

Fervid, focused men organized the Logan County agricultural society and fair in 1856. They met in late June, adopted a constitution, appointed officers, planned a fair in October, and organized a drive for funds. The drive fizzled and time ran short, so some officers and members formed an association, a joint-stock company of sorts. Each member chipped in $100, receiving stock certificates. The association purchased land, fenced it and threw up stalls, and in October held its first annual fair, a stunning success. Only five months later, in March of 1857, it held its second annual fair, an even bigger success, as measured by exhibits, attendance, receipts, and other indicators.

In 1851 farmers met to form the Randolph County Agricultural Society, which they organized on January 9, 1852. They elected officers, and held the first Annual Fair, or Exhibition, in October on James Craig's farm, which also hosted the second Annual Fair the following October. The third fair, October of 1854, moved to William Robertson's farm, but residents around Sparta wanted a better site, so they banded together, pooled money, bought boards, and fenced a lot in Sparta, which Matthew McClurkin donated for five years. This fenced lot hosted three increasingly successful fairs from 1855 through 1857, after which growing attendance again necessitated a larger site. The society's Executive Board purchased ten acres of land at Sparta for $2,000, fenced it, and built stables and exhibition buildings. The fair moved there in October 1858, and featured mechanical gadgets, livestock, produce, and ladies' crafts. Succeeding years brought improvements. Permanent, constantly improving sites, complete with impressive buildings, contrasted sharply with earlier ad hoc efforts. By 1860 fairs and sponsoring societies were influential.

County agricultural societies and fairs preceded state-sponsored fairs. The Illinois State Agricultural Society, a private organization, functioned before 1853. A bill incorporating the organization passed in February 1853, and the first state fair graced Springfield for four days in early October, supported by a state subsidy. For decades the state fair rotated among a dozen cities. Held in Centralia in September 1858, the fair featured a novel event: each evening a Professor Wilson ascended in a hot-air balloon "for the edification" of fair goers. The fair found its permanent home in Springfield in 1894.

Ideas from state and county fairs improved agriculture and rural life. Although some settlers had some full-blooded stock as early as the 1830s, county and state societies and fairs stressed the importance of blooded stock. Stray livestock, however, frolicked around, degrading the bloodline. Fencing from Great Lakes lumber and more stringent enforcement of evolving laws requiring livestock to be fenced eventually curbed this.

Undergirding impressive progress in agriculture, science, and the arts was the *Prairie Farmer*, founded as the *Union Agriculturalist and Western Prairie Farmer* in 1841 by John S. Wright, a Chicago sparkplug. This newspaper advocated and disseminated improvements in agriculture and rural society, teaching rural folk about mechanization and scientific farming. Because farmers wrote most articles, the organ earned widespread credence.

Frontier Illinois promoted invention and innovation, especially as diverse people mingled, exchanged ideas, and learned from each other.[20] As one observer noted, labor shortages and high wages spurred labor-saving inventions and innovation: "Where labour is so valuable, people naturally attach much importance to despatch, and any method which serves to abridge labour, is seized upon with avidity."[21] For example, in 1839 Hiram Waddams of Stephenson County thrashed wheat with a mobile wheeled thrasher, fascinating his neighbors. Perhaps the late 1840s witnessed a critical mass of inventors, capital, technological breakthroughs, and demand, gadget following gadget, many fathering additional offspring. In 1848 Pells Manny, also of Stephenson County, constructed a harvester that cut the heads off grain eight inches below the hulls. This harvester became popular, and by 1854 Manny's sons operated a successful company at Rockford.[22] Others tinkered with gadgets and implements, and their efforts paid off. The first thresher and cleaner machine operated by late 1847 in Carroll County. That year Cyrus McCormick built his steam-powered factory in Chicago, heavily financed by John S. Wright, and labor-saving reapers soon sold briskly in northern Illinois. Wright also sponsored the Atkins Automation, a reaper uniquely able to rake, and by 1854 reapers sped to farmers from Chicago on six railroads, which rushed grain back to the city. In addition, mechanical corn planters and mowers appeared on prairies. During the 1850s, trains raced from Chicago, laden with factory-produced implements destined for farmers in several states. By 1860, in fact, Illinois produced more agricultural machinery than any other state, McCormick producing over 4,000 reapers in that year.

Many businessmen were owner-inventors, small-scale entrepreneurs who dabbled in invention as they adapted technology to frontier realities. Some independent inventors, though, fed ideas to companies. During the 1850s, inventing increasingly became a full-time activity, many inventors working directly for corporations.

Personal observation, word-of-mouth testimony, articles, and advertising convinced farmers to try evolving improvements. Agricultural machines and techniques displayed at county and state fairs dazzled and enticed farmers. The trusty *Prairie Farmer* informed thousands and overcame innate rural conservatism. McCormick and other manufacturers created systems of knowledgeable dealers, advertised, offered credit to purchasers, and during the late 1850s annually sped via trains thousands of reapers and other implements to distant consumers. Each year the market region expanded, forging new links between Chicago and farmers and further overcoming the frontier's isolation and other characteristics.

Symptomatic of the frontier's passing, supplies of timber along rivers and in groves dwindled, depleted by construction of homes, outbuildings, fences, furniture, and implements, and by use for cooking and heating. Steamboats, steam mills, and then trains consumed immense quantities. Railroads needed wood for fuel, ties for tracks, bridges, and buildings. Tanners barked trees to secure needed chemicals. Some people in southern Illinois, still viewing woods as obstacles, girdled, chopped, and burned offending trees to make way for crops. Attitudes in early Jefferson County probably reflected most thinking: "It seemed that the timber never would be cleared away, notwithstanding everybody in those days used only wood for fuel, building, fencing and nearly everything else." People voraciously devoured public domain timber, annihilating entire groves, these assaults accelerating during the 1850s.

On the other hand, many settlers on prairies appreciated remaining timber supplies. P. R. Bryant wrote from Jacksonville on December 30, 1830, that farmers within three or four miles asked ten dollars per acre of farm land, about eight times the price of nearby public domain land. He added, "There is excellent prairie land within that distance belonging to the Government; but good timber land cannot be had." And then he made an observation shared by others over decades: "Every one has made free with the timber on Congress lands instead of cutting his own. Enough for fuel and other common purposes can however still be obtained."[23] Filching public timber shows settlers understood timber's value and wanted to conserve their own. Still, axes continued felling trees on both private and public land.

Others expressed concern about shrinking timber supplies. Writing from Spring Garden, Illinois, on January 17, 1860, Samary S. Sherman assessed timber reserves: "although there has been a great deal of timber taken off of this place . . . still there is a great abundance left, enough to keep a mill going for several years. People say that the whole town of Spring Garden and other houses have been built off this place." She understood mills' voracious appetites for wood. She and others kept an eye on vanishing timber, some lamenting its profligate use. In Jefferson County, for example, "Ash, white and black oak, post oak, black walnut, hickory and cherry" abounded, and the basic problem was how to clear it for farming: "The woods and fields used to be illuminated by the burning of logs, simply to get rid of them." Railroads worsened the problem: "After the coming of the railroads, this vicious timber slaughter became more contagious and the whole population felt at liberty to chop down any and everything that would make a railroad tie or a mine prop."

Vanishing timber worsened fencing problems.[24] Farmers and others placed great emphasis on the quality of fencing, arguing that good fencing made good farms. Traditional fencing in the early nineteenth century, the Virginia rail fence—also called the worm fence and the snake fence—consisted of split rails and was comparatively easy to erect. After splitting rails, farmers laid them in a zig-zag manner, making frequent minor repairs. These rail fences, when well maintained, generally kept livestock out of crops and away from each other. By the 1830s and the 1840s, they zig-zagged their way across the southern two-thirds of the state. But these fences consumed much wood, were labor-intensive, took up too much land, were not fully animal-proof, and required constant maintenance. Some settlers built post and rail fences (or straight-line rail fences, as they were known), saving wood and land, but these took even more labor. People experimented with wild apple, plum, locust, grapevines, and Osage orange, fashioning them into hedge fencing. As early as the early 1830s, Jonathan Baldwin Turner labored in central Illinois to perfect Osage orange hedge fencing. These fences, though, consumed even more land than worm fences, soaked up much labor for trimming, and were not animal-proof. The severe winter kill in 1855, furthermore, discouraged experiments in hedge fencing. Temperature extremes also snapped thin wires some used for fencing. Some farmers constructed turf (or sod) walls and ditches. On July 13, 1844, J. M. and Sarah Smith of Cherry Grove wrote to David Ports of Washington County, Maryland, about his fence: "You may perhaps wish to know how you can fence a farm without timber. I am fencing mine with sod 2½ rods of which I can make per day[.] this is faster than I could make a rale [*sic*] fence at the distance I am from timber." Like hedge fences, sod fences were labor intensive and ultimately unsatisfactory. Also, they placed adjacent land in shade, reducing yields. The need for inexpensive, practicable fencing was pressing.[25]

Construction methods also had to adjust to lumber shortages. Lightweight, tree-saving, balloon-frame houses, mass produced in Chicago by the 1850s, arrived via railroads at ready markets on prairies. These used studs, joists, and rafters, held together by nails. In fact, when the Illinois Land Company advertised 30,000 acres in 1855, it advised potential buyers, "Houses can be bought ready for fitting together (at Chicago) at from $150 to $200 each, containing five rooms and a kitchen, neat and substantially built."[26] Metal, furthermore, increasingly replaced wood in implements, buildings, boats and other means of transportation, furniture, and myriad other household and commercial items. And by the 1840s coal began replacing wood for heating, cooking, and then in locomotives, steamboats, and factory boilers.

Radically improved transportation alleviated timber shortages. In 1841 J. R. Lockwood floated the first raft of pine lumber from Wisconsin to Henderson County, and other men guided rafts to other counties. With this success, word spread and demand quickly soared, high prices notwithstanding. Chicago began receiving pine shipments, and throughout northern Illinois balloon-frame houses replaced crude log cabins. High costs and risks plummeted during the 1850s as railroads and improved shipping sent vast quantities of lumber into the maw of Chicago and other places, including landlocked towns. Pine lumber found its way into countless homes, buildings, and fences, board-and-post fences replacing older worm fences.

One visiting Briton observed in 1858 that posts were made of cedar, seven feet long, and the boards were pine, adding that both "are prepared in the forest, so that the settler buys them ready for his purpose," often at the nearest railway station. "The

A bucolic scene of cows, poultry, and a sleek horse, post-and-board fences, a tidy farm, and decorative shrubs, and an unobtrusive train in the distance reflect prosperity, progress, and order. *A Guide to the Illinois Central Railroad Lands.* Chicago: Illinois Central Railroad Office, 1859. ILLINOIS STATE HISTORICAL LIBRARY, A DIVISION OF THE ILLINOIS HISTORIC PRESERVATION AGENCY.

holes for the posts are not dug out as with us, but are bored with an auger made for the purpose, and the work of fencing thus goes on with much neatness and regularity, and the fences, being all made in the same manner and with timber of the same dimensions, are very uniform and substantial." He added that neighbors cooperated greatly in this project, dividing up the tasks and working smoothly.[27]

Assisted by improved fences, evolving laws clamped down on owners of stray livestock, shifting responsibilities for keeping these animals out of fields and gardens from land owners to livestock owners, with some success, spurring livestock breeders to invest in pure breeds—another mark of the transition to a post-frontier era.[28]

Accompanying all of these changes, migration into many frontier locales slackened, population growth rates stalled, and some counties leveled off. This signified that the locale's carrying capacities were being reached, given existing technologies and social and economic realities. Rising land values, vanishing public lands, consolidation of land holdings, increased efficiencies, and alternative opportunities persuaded some prospective settlers to bypass frontier Illinois and some Illinoisans to leave it. Displaced Illinoisans responded in several ways: many despaired of ever owning land and trooped to towns; some became farm laborers or tenant farmers, hoping to buy land someday; others pushed farther westward, seeking opportunities in emerging frontiers; others just sank, becoming burdens to others.

Ordinarily, as agricultural output climbed and land was farmed more intensively, the demand for farm laborers held steady. Agrarian families maintained high birth rates, bucking the nineteenth-century national trend. But with mechanization, increased production, sagging birth rates in towns, and departure, county populations tapered off and then declined. In fact, nine counties peaked in population by 1870, after the frontier ended: Boone, Hancock, Henderson, Jo Daviess, Knox, Marshall, Putnam, Schuyler, and Warren, all either lying west of the Illinois River or traversed by it. By 1880 populations peaked in another twenty-five counties, two-thirds of which lay east of the Illinois. In short, processes unfolding during the 1850s caused thirty-four—one third—of Illinois' counties to peak by 1880.

Migration from Illinois, or within Illinois, was nothing new. Indians, French, and American settlers had fled crises. Even in tranquil times, heavy out-migration from some counties began just a decade or two after initial settlement. For example, Edwin G. Barker wrote from Hennepin on March 10, 1838, commenting on a party "of about 40 or 50 organizing for the Rocky Mountains." In Morgan County, Joseph King, a native of England, wrote on October 8, 1839, about selling some land, adding, "We are not certain what we shall do with the money. Probably we may loan it out in other lands. I intend going into the Countries west of the Mississpy as soon as I can . . . to see what are the prospects." In 1819 Josiah Fulton became the first permanent white settler in Peoria, and in 1839 a party of at least a dozen men from Peoria trekked to the Oregon Country, motivated by patriotism, religion, and hopes of personal advancement.[29] The departure of these energetic men jolted the young settlement, but into the

1840s the drain across the Mississippi was still comparatively light. Mormons, facing lethal hostility, abruptly departed for Utah beginning in 1846. Overcrowding and perhaps wanderlust caused some flight. For example, in 1847 Joel Tullis of Schuyler County, "becoming restless from the encroachments of the rapidly increasing population," sold his home, loaded his family and possessions into an ox-wagon, and headed to Oregon. With the Mexican War in 1846 and the Gold Rush in 1849 and later, many forsook Illinois for lands farther west, both a sign frontier Illinois was passing and a cause of its demise. In 1849, for example, perhaps 15,000 men left Illinois for California, helping make California's population 92 percent male in 1850.[30] Hundreds of overland companies formed throughout the state, perhaps especially north of Vandalia, and went west. In early 1850, nearly four hundred people left Will County for California's goldfields, prompting the worried editor of the Lockport *Telegraph* to belittle the exodus and advise residents of Will County to stay put and be content.[31] Other counties experienced similar losses. Pike County thought of itself as "the mother of states to the west of Illinois," because it exported so many people. Many eventually returned, but strong streams flowing westward produced both positive and negative economic dislocations. Other settlers did not forsake Illinois for other places; they never came to Illinois in the first place.

By the 1850s, settlers contemplated bypassing Illinois for Iowa, Minnesota, and places further west. Samary S. Sherman, for example, wrote from Jefferson County on August 4, 1854, to Lucretia C. Sibley, her cousin. She referred to the Wallace family of Steubenville, Ohio, and their possibly moving to Chandlersville in Cass County, Illinois. She wrote, "Mr. Wallace owned a woolen factory there, but has now sold out for about 40 thousand dollars and intends to remove to this State or Minnesota. He wishes to purchase a Sheep farm. I should like to know what kind of a country it is about Chandlersville. Perhaps the country and soil would suit him there." On July 27, 1855, Edward Eno wrote to his brother, a resident of New York, about his wanting to speculate in Minnesota: "The southern part of Minnesota comes into market this fall. It is a splendid country & filling up rapidly." People from Ohio and other easterly places continued to settle in Illinois, but Minnesota and other new frontiers also attracted settlers, including Illinoisans. Many departing Illinoisans were not under duress. They were doing well enough, but they longed to see new places and undertake new challenges. Clearly, maturing Illinois exported many people, especially those between fifteen and twenty-four years of age, which reflected fading frontier conditions.

Though some poor folk, after tasting defeat, pulled up stakes and left, many others, nevertheless, stayed put. From the beginning, Illinois contained defeated settlers. Many unable to care for themselves were unable or unwilling to leave Illinois. They stayed, often receiving assistance in staying.

Shortly after statehood, when labor was scarce, counties "bid out" paupers. Farmers wanting the labor of a healthy county pauper "bid" low on the person. Winning low bidders received county stipends to care for the paupers, hoping in return to obtain valuable labor from them. Winning bidders also often promised to teach paupers skills, clothe and feed them, and help them in other ways. Some healthy paupers cost early Wabash County only 37 ½ cents per week, but invalid paupers with little work potential cost $2 per week. Officials in Warren County paid relatives of paupers to look after them. Usually these arrangements worked out satisfactorily for all parties, but sometimes they permitted abuse. If Tazewell County is any indication, expenditures for paupers constituted over 23 percent of the county's total annual budget in 1832.

This system, though, died out as the frontier vanished. In Warren County, the "bidding out" system ended in 1857. County poor houses and poor farms replaced it. They were communities consisting of a dozen or several dozen paupers living dormitory style in specially constructed buildings, often a short distance from a town. Some poor farms appeared before 1850, Tazewell County's forming in 1847, but poor farms multiplied during the 1850s. Henderson County's was founded in 1855 and Warren County's in 1859, for example. Infirmity, age-related problems, general poverty, and the absence of supporting family filled poor houses and farms. Overseers superintended care of the inmates, resident supervisors living at the sites. Poor farm inmates raised

their own vegetables, livestock, poultry, dairy products, and fruit.
When inmates died, counties spent around $3 for the coffin and
possibly $10 for the complete burial, not inconsiderable sums.
Often self-contained communities, successful poor farms provided
security and personal support for inmates. They also removed
the poor from daily view of local residents.

The state also supported some indigent folk. During the year
between June 1, 1849, and June 1, 1850, some 797 people in Illinois received support as paupers, 376 of whom were native and
421 of foreign birth. On June 1, 1850, some 434 paupers received
state support, of whom 279 were native and 155 were foreign
born. State-supported paupers during the year received $45, 213
in assistance.[32]

By the 1840s the state assumed responsibility for caring for
people with conspicuous special needs. It established the Illinois
Institution for the Education of the Deaf and Dumb in 1839, the
State Hospital for the Insane in 1847, and the Illinois Institution
for Education of the Blind in 1849—all in Jacksonville. Strong
political connections and vibrant booster energy helped Jacksonville snare these coveted institutions. The Illinois Institution
for the Education of the Deaf and Dumb was the second state-
founded and state-operated institution, the Alton Prison being
the first, founded in 1827. From 1843 to 1848 the state's first medical
school operated at Illinois College in Jacksonville. All of these
institutions helped usher Illinois into its post-frontier era.

Poor farms and houses and state institutions were milestones
in the frontier's demise. Not everyone, however, who manifested
problems ended up in these institutions. Instead, some became
farm laborers or tenants, who were farmers without farms. Nationally, in 1860 for the first time wage earners outnumbered independent proprietors, and many laborers were farm laborers.

Laborers were generally associated with frontier conditions.
In 1860 Illinois contained 143,310 farms, 153,646 farmers, and
47,216 laborers. (Probably some listed as farmers were, in reality,
glorified farm laborers.) Numerically, farm laborers in Illinois
exceeded 30 percent of the farmers. Generally, among Old Northwest states, the more recent the frontier experience, the greater
the relative number of laborers. In Wisconsin and Michigan, still

frontier states in 1860, farm laborers topped 33 percent and 40 percent of the farmers, respectively. In 1860 in Indiana, which entered the Union before Illinois, laborers were under 22 percent. Clearly, states with persisting frontier conditions needed farm laborers to bring land into cultivation, dig wells, drain lands, remove stumps and other obstacles, erect buildings, fences, and other structures, and do other necessary rough work. Ohio, though, was an apparent anomaly in 1860; there, farm laborers exceeded 34 percent.

Two factors may explain this. From 1840 through 1860 Ohio led the Old Northwest states in the value of orchard and market garden produce and wine production, all of which are labor-intensive but which require little machinery. Also, during the great economic slump beginning in 1857, desperate urban unemployed worked as farm laborers, and more major cities were closer to Ohio than to Illinois.[33]

Tenancy flourished in the late stages of frontier Illinois. Around Sugar Creek, for example, between 1850 and 1860 the number of tenants quadrupled. Many young single men and recently married men became tenant farmers. Some remained tenants, but for others tenancy was only a temporary stint, a stepping stone to something better, including owning land. Even so, spurts in tenancy indicated a flickering frontier; inexpensive public land became scarce during the early 1850s.

Contractual terms of tenancy varied, but they usually approximated the following. A tenant providing his own housing, tools, seed, and draft animals kept two-thirds of the harvest, the landlord getting one-third. A tenant providing just his own housing kept only one-half the harvest. A tenant providing only his labor kept just one-third. Terms of tenancy sometimes also spelled out grazing, hunting, and gathering rights.

William Scully came to America in 1850 and acquired a tenant-based agrarian empire in Logan County. He had little difficulty hiring tenants and laborers, a new reality that clearly demarcated the frontier era from the post-frontier era. But unfavorable restrictions on tenants sapped their motivation, which degraded Scully's vast holdings. Scully paid tenants nothing for permanent improvements they made; consequently, they planted few trees and did little hedging. They constructed few good houses or fences, built practically no churches or schools, and created few institutions. Because they were disinterested and of- ten transients, they raised corn year after year, damaging the soil. Since it was they, not Scully, who paid the taxes on the land, it was not in their interests to improve it. Widespread, unrewarded tenancy depressed natural and social environments. In sharp contrast, adjoining townships in Logan County, where there were numerous resident land owners, sparkled with "neat and sub-stantial dwellings, many of them brick, usually two stories high; large, roomy barns, cattle-sheds, orchards, neat lawns with ever-greens and all the other appurtenances and aspects of an ideal Illinois farm."

The fact that tenants founded relatively few schools probably contributed to declining school attendance in post-frontier re-gions. For example, in Schuyler County in 1861 about 63 percent of all youngsters under twenty-one years of age attended school. This figure tumbled to just 56 percent by 1871, and slipped to under 55 percent by 1881. This decline occurred despite state laws designed to encourage education. Whatever the precise causes of the decline in Schuyler County, tenancy wherever it took root discouraged education.

Nevertheless, tenancy did confer benefits. It gave poor people a chance to break into farming. "Tenancy granted them time to investigate a region, break land of their own, and accumulate capital." It was somewhat analogous to squatting. Furthermore, "on the Midwestern farm frontier, tenancy reflected rational re-sponses to economic conditions more than individual failure." In addition, tenants leaving farming for other pursuits were not necessarily failures. Although they and other laborers were often socially marginal, seldom leaving family-name impressions on the landscape and rarely appearing in local and county histories, they toiled and kept their eyes open, learned of opportunities elsewhere, and made rational choices concerning them. Perhaps of greater importance, however, others did not perceive them as failures.

Innumerable landless people avoided entering poor houses or becoming tenants or agrarian laborers. During the economic upturn of the late 1840s and 1850s, they and others thronged to thriving towns, often in northern Illinois. Moreover, these towns beckoned swarms of Easterners, Europeans, and others. They were part of vast streams of people seeking opportunities in the country's urban places. As urbanization proceeded, many people ignored rural attractions and headed straight for Chicago or other urban centers, a sure sign frontier Illinois was closing.

During the depression of the late 1850s, rural residents also headed to towns. Frontier expansion waned during economic slowdowns. If the history of neighboring Iowa from 1840 to 1895 is any indication, "strong grounds exist for suggesting that western rural-to-urban migration was an early and significant force in the growth of frontier areas." Rapidly growing towns, moreover, lured new and recent settlers from rural areas, even when land was readily available.[34] In short, some settlers in prosperous times obtained land, encountered economic troubles by 1857, considered alternatives, and moved to towns.

Ironically, by the 1850s economic inequality in Chicago was growing and becoming entrenched. Urban propertylessness was widespread. Chicago's distribution of wealth was skewed, even when compared to eastern cities. For example, in Chicago in 1850 the wealthiest one percent of the population owned 52 percent of the wealth. In New York City, Boston, and Brooklyn, the wealthiest one percent in each city owned 40, 37, and 42 percent, respectively.[35] Furthermore, at mid-century over 80 percent of Chicagoans worth over $25,000 had arrived in Chicago before 1839. Most of these arrived either with considerable wealth or with access to others' wealth. Clearly, many wealthy people who were at the top in 1850 either started near the top or arrived during Chicago's effervescent early years, or both.

Laws passed during the 1850s reflected growing class cleavages, another mark of the frontier's passing. For decades settlers tapped timber, game, and even soil on public lands and the lands of nonresident owners. Moderate pilfering of these resources was overlooked, or at least tolerated. Settlers regarded such idle lands and resources as commons, to be used to benefit actual residents, especially if the owner resided far away or was Uncle Sam. These practices, though, faced stiff legal challenges during the 1850s and generally vanished by the Civil War. One source notes, "Stock, timber, and hunting laws, passed in the late 1850s, restricted tenants, laborers, and poor farmers from grazing their herds on prairie meadows or helping themselves to the fruits of the countryside."[36]

Economic depression, economic disparity, and class strains generated experiments in maturing Illinois. Beginning in 1843, colonies based on the ideas of the French utopian theorist Charles Fourier sprouted in Illinois and across the Upper Mississippi Valley. Fourier and his leading American disciple, Albert Brisbane, believed each colony or "phalanx" should blend capitalism and socialism, promote social harmony, and contain between 1,500 and 3,000 people. Illinois' first phalanx, the Bureau County Phalanx, appeared furtively in 1843 and then folded. Fulton County spawned a phalanx, and Sangamon County three. Despite dedication and hard work, all Illinois' phalanxes failed within months.[37]

Squatting, a common frontier practice, declined for several reasons. The last public lands were taken in the 1850s, restricting available land. New laws, furthermore, protected unused property. Worse, squatters received private warnings from powerful interests, warnings not to purloin unused resources. This undercut the basis of squatting, which had been relatively painless for most people. In Sugar Creek into the 1840s, for example, squatters farmed idle land and grazed livestock on others' grasslands. New laws, moderate speculation, increased land prices, and warnings dissuaded them, and from 1840 to 1850 only one in four squatters around Sugar Creek bought land and persisted to 1850. Furthermore, nearby kin and friends assisted most purchasers. From 1850 to 1860 only 20 percent of the purchasers present in 1850 persisted to 1860. Perhaps squatting was more difficult on prairies than in woods. In prairie regions, game, wood, fuel, and other means of scratching out a living were either scarce or uncertain. Finally, many early squatters were Southerners, people generally seeking admission to Jefferson's yeoman society. But as more New Englanders and other non-Southerners arrived, their propensities for order and procedure probably inhibited them from squatting and caused them to oppose those who did. For various reasons, squatting faded with the dying frontier.

As the frontier faded, especially as available land in Illinois dwindled, absentee owners became increasingly resentful of the way they were treated. Even as early as 1846, however, Britons grumbled about onerous burdens placed on lands they owned in Illinois. To be sure, neighbors often gleefully pilfered timber and other resources both from public land and from lands held by absentee owners, perhaps especially foreign absentee owners. But these were petty annoyances compared to heavy taxation. Robert Leslie of London, England, wrote on September 28, 1846, complaining about "policies" of Illinois that "harass & throw every obstacle their imagination can devise in the way of nonresident holders of land." He maintained that the slightest error, by anyone, in a foreigner's purchase of land caused the land to be forfeited. Nonresident land owners, Leslie insisted, were subject to heavy state taxes. Adding to this burden, he claimed, were the rates levied against the land at the county level by envious "neighbors who are much prejudiced against foreign holders of land." Perhaps Leslie's points were true. Even so, foreigners who came to settle on the land faced few such problems; only nonresident, and perhaps wealthy, land owners riled settlers, and had to suffer their retaliation.

By the middle 1840s, depressed economic conditions lifted. Hope was in the air—and with it, speculation. Diminishing wood supplies in Illinois and insatiable growing appetites in prairie regions for lumber caused people to cast speculative glances toward Wisconsin's pine forests. On November 1, 1845, for example, George E. More wrote from St. Charles, on the Fox River, to Francis Craig of Ticonderoga, New York, "I calculate on saving again this winter a little and speculating, etc., etc., and making sure to leave in the spring. My trade shall be all lumber, cash up on the nail. I shall wish Fox [River] more water and a quicker trip next spring." The previous spring, he noted, travel on the Fox had been slow. He added, "I am in for the lumber speculation this winter. I wish to go in as steep as possible." He then asked Craig to try to raise some capital for him in the East, adding, "Lose no time in attending to this." Clearly, imaginations quickened with returning prosperity, and strengthening commercial and personal ties with East Coast interests fostered speculative undertakings.

During the exuberant 1850s, speculation became increasingly
sophisticated. Edward Eno wrote from Jacksonville on January
5, 1855, to his brother in New York: "If you were here now I
would try to get you into a corn speculation in which I know we
could make a pile." Then he suggested a different form of speculation, one dealing in futures: "25 per cent advanced would buy
corn to be delivered in June & July that would be sure to advance
20 to 30 cents a bushel." Eno's correspondence brims with the
era's speculative ideas, which were often facilitated by railroads
and telegraphs.

Telltale political signs also marked the frontier's passing, indicating social and political maturity. The last four counties—Saline, Kankakee, Douglas, and Ford—formed in 1847, 1851, 1857,
and 1859, respectively. Three events encouraged new courthouse
construction: recent relocations of county seats; obsolete or dilapidated existing structures; destruction of existing structures,
fire destroying Wabash County's in 1857, for example. Statewide,
the finishing touches in 1853 on the new State Capitol Building in
Springfield formally and symbolically anchored the capital there,
terminating its northward ambles.

The adoption in 1848 of a new state constitution, the second
since statehood, hinted at a fading frontier, warranting new political arrangements.[38] The Constitution of 1818 granted suffrage
to "all white male inhabitants above the age of twenty-one years"
who resided in Illinois for six months before elections. In 1848,
however, Whigs and conservative Democrats pushed through a
constitutional provision restricting suffrage to citizens, not just
inhabitants. In the Constitution of 1848, Article VI, Section 1,
stated that every "white male citizen above the age of twenty-
one years, having resided in the State one year next preceding
any election, shall be entitled to vote at such election." American
settlers gained suffrage after a year's wait, not six months, and
aliens no longer voted. This suggested that acute labor shortages
had ended, sharply diminishing the need to attract newcomers.
Furthermore, by 1848 concern over immigrants was rising.[39] Less
democratic in provisions and tone than its predecessor, the new
constitution nevertheless realistically reflected ongoing social and
economic changes, including declining need for unskilled labor.

Significantly, anger and financial burdens created by the state bank and, especially, internal improvements fiascoes during the 1830s produced stringent prohibitions against lawmakers plunging Illinois into debt to finance banks and internal improvements. The new constitution, though, did allow state-chartered private banks.

Reflecting disgust with career politicians and visceral distrust of government—especially the legislature—provisions severely limited officials' salaries and sliced in half lawmakers' daily reimbursement when legislative sessions ran forty-two days. Half pay after forty-two days spurred legislators to finish necessary tasks and then go away. Citizens feared that loitering politicians generated much mischief.

All seven sections of Article VII addressed counties, their formation and size, possible county divisions, and methods to fix county seat location. Section 6 allowed voters to adopt or reject township government. The constitution required elections for all county and state offices. It abolished the County Commissioners' courts, replacing them with courts consisting of three county judges elected to four-year terms.

The Constitution of 1848 required secret ballots in elections, an apparent improvement. Although Illinoisans had used secret ballots from statehood through 1830, during the heyday of frontier Illinois and during the great surge of Jacksonian Democracy Illinoisans cast their votes *viva voce*, that is, with a "live voice." Voters literally stood near election officials and called out the names of candidates they wanted, and each voter's name and his choices were duly recorded in a poll book. People within earshot heard the names called out, and poll books were open to public inspection. Without doubt, people knew how others voted.

On the one hand, secret balloting was a reform, which shielded voters from pressure. On the other hand, it tacitly admitted defeat. It departed sharply from the early Republic's assumptions, shared by settlers, that citizens voting *viva voce* did not buckle under pressure. Voters were deemed to be stalwart, *independent* individuals, republicans who fearlessly expressed political sentiments. Secret balloting indicated that the belief in self-sufficient and *independent* farmers was fading, along with the frontier.[40] Hired hands, tenants, and other employees lacked the economic independence of Jeffersonian yeomen; employees voting *viva voce* could be pressured. Reflecting this reality, secret balloting provided protection.

For decades southern-born leaders dominated politics. Over time, however, increasing numbers hailed from New England, New York, and other northern places. Having experienced township forms of government, Yankees advocated it in Illinois. Constitutional convention delegates from the northern third of Illinois supported township government nearly unanimously. Beginning in 1849, dozens of counties held elections, and counties opting for township government reflected growing Yankee strength.[41]

Northeastern counties adopted township government, as did a few counties along the Illinois and three western counties. Throughout the 1850s additional northeastern and east-central counties adopted it, but relatively few counties in the southern third of the state did. The adoption pattern is significant. Before the new constitution, all counties had county commission government, a southern import with origins in Virginia. Eventually, only fifteen counties did not adopt township government, nearly all in southern Illinois, reflecting ascending northern influence, a crucial fact in turbulent years before the Civil War.

The constitutional convention split along sectional lines on racial matters. Although slavery for all intents and purposes died by the middle 1840s, delegates crushed efforts to confer suffrage on blacks by 137 to 7, probably reflecting public sentiment. In addition, Article XIV directed the General Assembly in its first session to pass laws prohibiting black migration to Illinois and manumission.[42] Illinoisans opposed both slavery and political equality for blacks.

Growing Yankee strength was evident in Illinois' politics. From 1840 to 1862, forty-six different men were elected governor, U.S. senator, and congressman. The origin of ten of these men is uncertain. Of the remaining thirty-six, only one-fourth hailed from slaveholding states, Kentucky providing seven of the nine. Significantly, New England provided nine. Political tides had shifted. Although this shift was not reflected in political acts favorable to blacks, slavery was killed off in Illinois during these years.

The seven debates between Abraham Lincoln and Senator Stephen A. Douglas in the summer and fall of 1858 reflected these political shifts and political maturity. Though narrowly winning reelection to the Senate, Douglas damaged his presidential chances in the debates, while Lincoln gained national exposure. The debates did not always inspire, but the two Illinoisans occupied the political limelight and shaped national discourse on slavery, race, and territories, helping Illinois shed its frontier image and presaging Illinois' role in the upcoming Civil War.

In 1851 the West Jacksonville school district became the first in Illinois to offer free, public high school education. Five years later, William H. Wells came to Chicago from Massachusetts and organized that city's first high school, which admitted both sexes. Meanwhile, vigorous lobbying of lawmakers and repeated efforts in the legislature to create a statewide system of education bore fruit.

State lawmakers in 1855 assumed overall responsibility for education by levying a tax of two mills per dollar annually on all taxable property. This foundation for financing public schools and ensuring quality education was buttressed by sales of the sixteenth section of each township, the "school section." Although many sections had been sold previously, some townships refrained from selling their sections until years later, after land values increased. The legislation of 1855 required townships to operate schools for a specific number of months per year, penalizing recalcitrant townships by withholding funds from the "school section" and the two-mill annual tax. Each county's school commissioner, soon renamed school superintendent, was tasked with visiting every school at least once a year. A state superintendent oversaw the system's operation. Sadly, Illinois failed to fund the basic plan, and it did not require school districts to adequately fund schools.

Still, the 1855 legislation placed every school-age youngster in a school district, with a right to publicly financed education. Prior to 1855 most schools were subscription schools, formed by parents banding together and hiring teachers, who commonly roomed and boarded around with students' parents. Many schools operated only a few months per year, no uniform standards existed, and results were checkered. Broken contracts and firings snapped continuity. Some teachers were itinerant workers, moving from job to job, never establishing strong ties with local communities. The legislation of 1855 extinguished most subscription schools, made education less capricious, and improved quality. In so doing, it heralded the frontier's passing.

Meanwhile, institutions of higher learning burgeoned. Nearly all were private, church-affiliated institutions, having unabashed religious missions. County seats, with inns and relatively good transportation, generally competed successfully in attracting colleges. By 1848 several colleges existed: Illinois College, in 1829; Knox College, 1837; McKendree College, 1837; Illinois Conference Female Academy (later MacMurray College) 1846; St. Xavier College, 1846; Rockford College, 1847; and Rosary College, 1848. Several institutions founded before 1850 have since closed their doors: Shurtleff, 1832; Monticello Seminary for Young Ladies, 1835; Canton College, 1836; McDonough College, 1836; Jubilee College, 1841; and several others. All colleges operating by 1850 were in the western half of Illinois.

A flurry of foundings followed in the 1850s: Illinois Wesleyan University, 1850; Northwestern University, 1851; Monmouth, 1853; Shimer College, 1853; Eureka, 1855; Blackburn, 1857; Illinois State Normal School (later Illinois State University), the state's first "Normal" college, 1857; Almira College (later Greenville College), 1857; Lake Forest College, 1857; Quincy College, 1860; and Wheaton College, 1860. Perhaps twenty-five institutions making claim to collegiate status popped up during the 1850s, but most failed within a few years.

In their early years, some colleges had few students who were true college students; some operated as preparatory schools for a few years. Although these schools varied in quality and many struggled to stay afloat, some did attract East Coast and other out-of-state students.

In approving the Illinois State Normal School, the General Assembly created Illinois' first tax-supported college and the first teachers' college in the Mississippi Valley. This reflected state government's growing commitment to promote solid teaching throughout the state.[43]

In addition, schools offering highly practical business courses appeared. In Rockford, for example, on February 5, 1856, William S. Brown wrote to a friend that he "commenced a course in Book-keeping last week. Have run through single entry, of which I had already a better knowledge than I supposed, and am now peering into the mysteries of double entry." Brown was a printer-entrepreneur who sought to improve his professional skills.

Other institutions shoved aside remnants of the frontier. In Oquawka in early January 1860, a group met to form the Oquawka Historical and Geological Society. They intended to display a collection of geological specimens and oddities, purchase a library of literature, and secure talented lecturers. Similar undertakings occurred throughout much of Illinois.

The founding of myriad social institutions was supremely important. Perhaps no other single factor did as much to obliterate frontier traits. Most institutions were local and voluntaristic, attracting like-minded people united for common purpose. Some were largely utilitarian in purpose, founded to achieve practical goals. Others were formed for cultural and moral reasons. Many reflected needs for music, reading materials, lectures, fellowship, and moral foundations, sweeping aside much frontier isolation.

Towns and villages sported chapters of Masons and Independent Order of Odd Fellows. In Hillsboro the first Freemasonry lodge was organized in 1840, the first I.O.O.F. in 1848. In Rushville, the Masonic lodge was chartered in October of 1842, and the I.O.O.F. in early 1847. In Mount Vernon the Masons and the I.O.O.F. organized the same year, 1845. During the 1850s Germans organized *Turnvereine* (called "Turners" popularly) in towns, which fostered bands, choirs, debates, lectures, and other activities. The first two Turnvereine in Illinois were at Peoria and Chicago in 1851, and others were soon formed at Belleville and Springfield. Issues affecting America and Americans, not Germans, were discussed at meetings, helping German newcomers to focus on their new homes. In Chicago the *Illinois Staats-Zeitung* began publication in 1848, reflecting German quest for identity

and culture.[44] Helping Irish immigrants in Illinois, the Chicago
Hibernian Benevolent Emigrant Society began operations in early
1848. Private associations and clubs popped up all over, further
vanquishing underdeveloped frontier conditions.

Women organized associations, extending their social roles and
further banishing frontier conditions. In early 1856 in Greenville,
for example, women wanted to improve themselves and their
town's intellectual and moral conditions, so they organized the
Social Circle, drafted a constitution and by-laws, met afternoons
weekly to sew and knit, and gathered the same evening to dis-
cuss members' essays. They sponsored dinners and concerts. Using
profits by August to outfit a library, they changed their name to
the Ladies' Library Association and continued over decades to
promote the town's library. Such non-church organizations founded by women are significant. Since Puritan days, when the church
was insecure and threatened, it "valued women as allies. When it
became more secure politically, it left women to their husbands
and fathers." Women enjoyed fewer significant roles in secure
churches.[45] In early frontier Illinois, struggles against darkness
were uncertain, and women's contributions were valued. By the
late 1830s and even more manifest by the 1850s, fading frontier
conditions curtailed some women's roles. But as the frontier
slipped away women founded many non-religious social organizations.

In 1849 Miss Virginia Corbett organized the Jerseyville Young
Ladies Seminary with sixteen young women from the region,
enrollment reaching seventy in 1856. Five unmarried women assisted her. Perhaps the state school act of 1855 undermined this
seminary, for Miss Corbett closed it in early 1856. But during the
frontier's waning years, it typified similar activities around Illinois.

Newly founded organizations suggest several things. The raw
days were past. Growing physical comforts and security provided
resources and time. Unlike churches, founded in early years, the
numerous social institutions founded largely in later years met
special needs. Class consciousness—or cultural consciousness—
accompanied societies' formation. Discussion groups, for example,
usually consisted of the "better" elements of society. Moreover,

some institutions—temperance groups, for example—often targeted specific social groups for moral reformation, often immigrant or ethnic minorities. Some founded societies to replicate social conditions they had known elsewhere, to transplant culture to Illinois. Finally, some local organizations were chapters of national organizations, which spoke of vastly improved communications and increased national outlook.

The founding of institutions probably reflected another need. With Chicago spearheading the headlong rush to embrace technology and modernity, Illinois enmeshed itself in the national economy. Prosperity and growth brought increased complexity, ever-larger scales of production, and powerful remote forces. An example of this, one involving women, occurred in the 1850s, when sewing machines appeared in homes, costing about $50 each, payable in installments. For centuries hands had stitched shirts in homes, one shirt taking up to fourteen hours. Machines slashed that time by 90 percent or more. And sewing machine companies needed agents, just like companies which produced reapers and planters. Soon networks of women appeared, most full-time agents living in larger cities.[46] Sewing machines were local links in ever-larger systems of production and distribution.

Modern efficiency, however, generated anxiety among people who had traditionally reveled in a sense of control. People literally cheered railroads, telegraphs, and distant financial institutions, but these radically changed daily life. Although forces of modernity brought prosperity, they also jarred, disrupted, and shredded social fabric.

Consequently, founders of local organizations sought to regain control, to stake out space in daily life free from the grip of remote forces. As one source noted, "As a corollary of their scramble for wealth, Chicagoans like [William] Ogden continually attempted to fashion a more cohesive world, to ameliorate the scramble for wealth with the balm of tradition. Cohesion, they hoped, would come from such practical organizations as the Young Men's Association (YMA) and its successor, the YMCA." One founder of the YMA was Seth Otis, who had enjoyed a reading club in Albion, New York, and wanted to recreate one in Chicago.[47] Associations for reading, discussing, and other activities indicate longing for a cohesive, known, and controllable world. This was crucial for Chicago, which did not blend continuity and success the way Toronto did. Chicagoans knew how to make a living, Torontonians knew how to live, and perceptive people in both cities understood the difference. Powerful Chicagoans wanted to blend the two worlds, which would erase remaining frontier traits and provide some control.

If the fading frontier in Kane County is any indication, women tried to control their lives in other ways. Organized in 1836, Kane County displayed frontier characteristics well beyond 1840. During the 1830s and through 1842, the divorce rate was under three per thousand per year. Twice during the 1840s the rate spiked to over four per thousand, but the great surge came during the 1850s, when the rate topped eight per thousand and when the frontier faded abruptly. Interestingly, between 1837 and 1869, women were plaintiffs 61 percent of the time, and for both men and women desertion was by far the leading cause of divorce, with men and women deserting at about an equal rate. (Women stood a better chance of being granted a divorce for desertion than men.) Desertions occurred when some women balked at migrating to Illinois or returned home shortly after settling in Illinois. Some men who rushed to California's goldfields just never bothered to return, and a few women deserted their husbands and took off for California. Adam Copelman took his wife, Betsey, to Chicago so she could then travel to New York to visit relatives. Betsey simply stayed in New York, never returning to Illinois. In any case, divorces were rare during the strenuous frontier years, but in the frontier's twilight divorce became more common.[48]

Grounds for divorce increased in number after statehood. In 1818 the only grounds were adultery, bigamy, and impotence, but by 1845 the General Assembly had added willful desertion, extreme and habitual cruelty, habitual drunkenness, and conviction on a felony. In Sangamon County from 1837 to 1860, women filed for divorce in 63 percent of the cases. They were successful 79 percent of the time, while men were less successful, obtaining divorces in 72 percent of the cases in which they filed. Moreover, women from all economic backgrounds successfully filed for divorce. Meanwhile, society's valuation of children underwent a change before 1860. Instead of occupying an economically subordinate position within a patriarchal family, they were now perceived as distinct members of that family, with rights of education and protection via state statutes. The family and the state came to hold children in trust for the republic and for the republic's future.[49]

Some county medical societies trace their origins back to the 1850s. In various counties physicians associated to insure regular professional contact, improve medicine, and eliminate competition by raising professional thresholds. Medical schools backed these efforts. Some physicians tried to organize a statewide organization.

Some reform was designed to control urban life. Surging immigration, trade unions, urban disturbances, and other signs of social disharmony scared Illinoisans, heightening fear of cities, and the arrival of rural folk added to the strain. Attempts to shape and improve urban life in the 1850s were proto-Progressive activities, efforts by educated, white-collar, old-line elites to forestall urban troubles.

The sex ratio changed during the frontier's twilight. In very early frontier years, men temporarily outnumbered women. This yielded unusual social activity. In Carroll County, for example, at a place later known as Stag's Point, men constructing a mill wanted to dance. But no women were nearby, so the "male dancers had males for partners," with no ensuing stigma. As women settled and the sex ratio became more balanced, these fellows forsook their male dancing partners and danced with women. In the frontier's last stages, though, males again outnumbered females. Rising land prices in Illinois shunted some ordinary households to lands farther west. Furthermore, as inexpensive land disappeared, many single men postponed marriage and became laborers or tenants, hoping to get land. Another factor helped tip the scales. Orchard and market crop production rocketed, as did wheat production and sheep raising, activities requiring intensive labor. Young men, often unmarried, met the demand.

Social diversity and complexity marked the passing frontier. The 1850s saw new ingredients added to the older mix of Southerners, Northerners, French, and blacks. During the late 1840s waves of Irish and Germans entered the state, joined by contingents of Portuguese, French Canadians, Norwegians, and others. The Portuguese were Protestant convert exiles from the island of Madeira. They arrived in late 1848 in Jacksonville and Springfield, were industrious and thrifty, prospered, and preserved much of their culture.

Spurred by alleged excessive drinking among immigrants, temperance societies mobilized and veered toward prohibition. Women and churches often spearheaded these societies. Campaigns against alcohol spilled into larger cultural battles. For example, many folk favoring temperance also favored regulating immigrants, especially Irish and German immigrants. The Know-Nothings were adamantly anti-immigrant and anti-Catholic, but they also attracted people concerned about society's overall health.

Religious and related ethnic battles continued to flare in Illinois into the 1850s, some of them instigated and fueled from the East. As the Valley was populated, urgent cries from cultural warriors in the East continued to be heard. For example, one publication in 1849 noted that piety and self-denying devotion among Protestant women were "without fitting and worthy spheres of action. The policy of the Roman Catholics in this respect has been wiser than ours; though some of their methods are objectionable. We should open wide to these devoted female spirits the honorable sphere of instruction, for which nature and grace have specially fitted them." The publication continued, "We should organize and encourage orders of sisters of Education—the noblest charity—to go forth and labor under the bonds, not of an awful and irrevocable vow, but of their own free love and voluntary devotion."[50] Spats between Protestants and Catholics included differences over drinking, activities deemed permissible on the Sabbath, and other social issues.

William S. Brown, writing in Rockford on February 5, 1856, captured the tone of Yankee society there. He claimed the town's population was about 7,000, and with approval he noted, "a large portion of which is composed of *young men*, from 18 to 35 years of age, most of them keen, *trading* Yankees, full of great *projects* and *hopes*, and working faithfully to accomplish them." Youthful, focused, diligent Yankees working with hope on projects earned respect and admiration from many, and by the 1850s they helped northern culture to largely displace and subordinate southern culture in Illinois.

Abolitionists and many others fumed after Congress enacted the odious fugitive slave law as part of the Compromise of 1850. Although numerous reform movements continued into the 1850s, including education and other uplifting drives, most were eventually subsumed under the all-absorbing fight over slavery.

Jarring trends accompanied the frontier's closing. Although the very early stage of frontier life attracted some questionable folk who transgressed against customs and laws, this stage passed quickly and social control became highly effective. Persistent turbulence was rare. Settlers craved order as a necessary ingredient for prosperity and progress. These yearnings were so strong that some counties experienced their first murders only many years after county formation. Tazewell County, organized in 1827, suffered its first murder in 1844. Henderson County, organized in 1841, witnessed its first murder indictment in 1859. Macon County's first murder was seventeen years after the county was formed. Sugar Creek's first "road crime" occurred in 1842, about twenty-five years after settlement began. In other places, as well, no serious crime occurred until well after counties were organized, after population densities reached comparatively high levels.

Early Stephenson County may have avoided serious crime because of "the sturdy character and unflinching integrity of the early settlers." Pioneers' moral fiber did inhibit crime and crush it when it surfaced, but another factor maintained order. Most settlers had a stake in society, something to lose. Even those currently without property had a stake in the future; they had hope. Consequently, residents guarded against suspicious characters, and justice for scofflaws was usually swift and condign.

Occasionally, severe and brutal fights involved gangs who terrorized the countryside and subverted or awed authorities. Organized bands of citizens, known as Regulators, opposed them. For example, from 1837 into late 1845 Regulators in Winnebago County waged protracted campaigns against robbers, counterfeiters, horse thieves, murderers, and other miscreants. Vicious civil strife rocked Massac County in 1849. Related conflicts sputtered intermittently here and there during the 1840s and even into the 1850s. Although all of these outbreaks claimed only a few lives, they followed frontier tranquility, shocking people. Equally shocking, moreover, these struggles blurred clear-cut distinctions between willful miscreants and solid citizens, many of the latter committing dastardly deeds. As was true with earlier Regulator activities, causes of such popular outbursts varied. Regulators had various motives, self-perceptions, and goals, but undergirding everything was an ardent desire for order and justice. Perhaps they were traditional conservators, who wanted to keep local, familiar, and static social and economic ways and systems and who felt both frustrated and threatened by dynamic elites and other forces beyond their control.[51] In any case, these corrosive movements indicated that the frontier was waning, and along with it frontier tranquility.

As the countryside became more thickly populated and social cohesion loosened, horse theft increased, arousing burning anger and concern.[52] Montgomery County suffered from horse thieves from 1867 to 1875, the thefts being the work of gangs based in cities. Many other counties had little horse stealing before the Civil War, but suffered from a flurry of thefts for years afterwards. Anti–horse theft societies sprang up to combat both organized and spontaneous theft. In southeastern Warren County, the Greenbush Mutual Protecting Company formed in 1850 to protect members from horse thieves and counterfeiters. Unlike some Regulator societies, it consisted of prosperous citizens and it had a printed constitution. Members evidently believed their actions were legal and strengthened the law. To pursue, arrest, and punish horse thieves, residents of Wabash County in 1857 also organized a Vigilance Association.[53]

Rising crime and suppressive measures signaled the frontier's passing. Some harried Chicagoans and others hungered for quieter, less hectic times. On May 21, 1853, the *Chicago Tribune* noted a lust for gain, observing, "Mammon sits at the helm and drives us on. We hasten from our coffee to plunge into the strife of business. Is this *life?* It is breathing and working, but is it *living?* Of the sacredness and divine influence of the home we know but little." Furthermore, Chicagoans visiting Toronto were struck by its less frenetic, more orderly, and higher quality of life.[54]

Longing for bygone treasured frontier traits and hungry for manifestations of tradition, aging men and women formed Old Settler societies, with membership typically restricted to settlers who had arrived before some salient event or date in regional history. A very early Old Settlers' Society formed in Sangamon County in September 1859, in the frontier's final months. The next month elderly Chicagoans founded an organization open to those residing there since 1834. Perhaps this requirement was too stringent, for the organization later bumped up the cut-off date to January 1, 1837.[55] Bureau County had Old Settlers' meetings by 1861. Dates and terms for membership varied, but by the late 1870s Old Settler societies graced most counties. Telling and re-telling stories from early years helped to reconnect to a simpler, purer past. Old Settler societies recreated a frontier past as members remembered it, or wanted to remember it.

These societies sprang up shortly before the Civil War, when the depression of 1857 still saddled the country, John Brown's Raid rocked the country, the Democratic Party dissolved, and similar events jolted confidence. Not unexpectedly, aging pioneers yearned for a golden age, a time when life seemed safer, simpler, and more predictable, and when the image of the romantic Garden glistened.[56] Perhaps ironically, therefore, others later remembered this very era—the frontier's twilight, the years of national economic and political crisis—as the golden age. Francis Grierson, for example, by 1909 wrote about an idealized world, the world of Springfield of 1858. Probably laboring under an emotional debt to rural Illinois, Grierson believed he had dwelled in the Garden in 1858, a pre-modern Garden swept aside by modernity's powers, a Garden offering renewal. This vision of the golden age and renewal combated encroaching modernity. But those waxing nostalgic just before 1860 over the vanishing frontier experienced far more frontier conditions than those who looked back to 1858 from 1909.

Nevertheless, conjuring up in 1909 a mythic antebellum frontier is significant. Clearly, the frontier, the constantly reworked memory of it, and its presence in twentieth-century minds helped shape modern America. They helped Americans cope with ongo- ing self-definition, withstand bewildering economic and social changes, and understand their past. In 1893 Frederick Jackson Turner redirected national thinking about American history, focusing attention on roles played by the American frontier. He and others who experienced fading frontier traits reflected on American life, and frontier experiences shaped their thinking.

One source noted of Carroll County, "As the years increased, the productions of their farm and stock increased, and the memories of the scanty meals and scanty wardrobes, physical hardships, etc., of their pioneer days were sweetened in the contemplation of farms and houses and barns and other surroundings of comfort their industry and perseverance had brought forth from the prairies and forests, that but a few years ago had been the grazing places of the buffalo, the elk and other animals natural to the wilds of the northwest, and the undisturbed hunting grounds of the red men." Settlers regarded the early years as a golden era, yet they delighted in sweeping changes, doing their utmost to bring them about.

* * *

Although frontier Illinois faded, much remained the same.[57] Households remained the basic social and economic block. Interdependency and diversity loomed larger every year, but residents tended gardens, raised poultry, and supplemented diets with wild game, fish, and wild berries and nuts. Some southern settlers did not retain traditional southern political and economic positions, but many clung to southern culinary habits, speech patterns, and forms of worship and entertainment. Moreover, settlers from everywhere continued to use spinning wheels, hand looms, and other traditional tools long after cheaper, mass-produced products rendered these tools unnecessary for all but the poorest folk. Similarly, fireplaces in the older parts of rambling homes constructed over time sometimes supplemented new cast-iron stoves in heating and cooking. People concerned themselves about friends, household members, church, school, work, and other personal facets of life. There were marriages, births, sickness, death, church, employment, ice cream socials, school plays, and Fourth of July celebrations. People were still born at home, received much education around home, got medication from home, married at home, and were buried from home. Many still worked in or around the home. Traditionally, women tended the ill, the dying, and the dead. One observer noted in the early 1840s, "Unless the death is very sudden, the news of it are speedily conveyed through the neighborhood by the women, who evince great alacrity in attending and sympathizing with the sick, it matters not whether strangers or friends."[58] Neighbors assisted survivors in traditional ways: providing food, attending the funeral, offering to take in children, planting or harvesting crops, tending to livestock, and buying land from the bereaved family. Most people died at home, and when death occurred neighbors "sat up" with the body all night every night before burial. In the frontier's final years, relatives buried dead in fine clothes, not in burial shrouds, a change barely noticed.

Although plows increasingly cut into remaining prairie lands, as late as the spring of 1855 a perceptive soul echoed Sarah Aiken in responding to prairie grandeur. Spring, he wrote to his lady friend, was "the most lovely part of the year. Reanimated nature is beautiful to behold. The broad expansive prairie, as far as the eye can reach, presents one unbroken surface of verdure, save here and there a grove which dots the landscape, like islands in the sea." He then predicted, "Two weeks hence it will bloom like a rose. Even now the violet Sweet William, Indian Paint and other wild flowers are beginning to blossom. But when the thousands of wild flowers are in full bloom, the undulating surface of the prairie looks like one vast garden and cannot fail to impress upon one's mind the sublime idea that these are the beautiful works of the great Architect who so wisely planned all things."[59] Even during the waning years of the frontier, as the prairie yielded to the plow, others sensed their grandeur.

Even the Ohio River, as it brushed southern Illinois, retained features known to early Indians, *voyagers*, and flatboat crews. In 1852, for example, Henry Arthur Bright cruised toward Cairo, penning his impressions as he slid through the night on the broadening stream: "There were no houses on the bank, no boats upon the water, and were it not that the heavy pulsing of our

Despite innumerable technological advances during
the 1850s, harvests still required much human labor. *A
Guide to the Illinois Central Railroad Lands.* Chicago:
Illinois Central Railroad Office, 1859. ILLINOIS STATE
HISTORICAL LIBRARY, A DIVISION OF THE ILLINOIS HISTORIC
PRESERVATION AGENCY.

engine reminded us that we were, after all, in a civilized land,
and on a much frequented track, we should have half expected
to see some Indian canoe shoot along from under the bushes that
fringed the river."[60] Despite impressive human achievements in
altering the landscape, a great deal remained unchanged.

Though much had changed since Sarah Aiken entered Illinois'
frontier in 1832, she would have felt comfortable there in 1860,
when differences between rural Illinois and her native rural New
York were far smaller than they had been in the early 1830s. Almost certainly, she would have embraced labor-saving devices,
railroads, institutions, reforms, education, and other signs of
material and social progress. Railroads by 1860 offered two-day
travel to Julia Keese, her childhood friend back in New York,
and knowledge of this might have alleviated her loneliness. Life
evolved within acceptable parameters.

But changes sweeping Illinois and the nation were important

and indelible. They were modernity's cutting edge, propelling Illinoisans and the nation headlong into lives undreamed of by early settlers. The frontier itself changed radically as it churned across the arid, railroad-dominated Far West. And as the frontier left Illinois and became the trans-Mississippi Great West with new states—Minnesota in 1858 and Oregon in 1859—the nation convulsed with wrenching, insoluble problems. As frontier Illinois faded, memorialized by Old Settler societies, aging settlers and the nation focused on ominous sectional rumblings. The ensuing Civil War brought far-reaching, unintended, and unforeseen changes. The America emerging from war's caldron in 1865 was decades removed in crucial ways from the America that stumbled and lurched into war in 1861. Veterans entering the Far West found a frontier far different from the one that had graced Illinois for decades. Many features of the trans-Mississippi frontier America world would have mystified and shocked Sarah Aiken.

The demise of frontier Illinois ended a highly important era, one in which Illinoisans laid enduring foundations. No longer in its infancy by 1860, Illinois had 1,711,951 residents, ranking it fourth in the nation. Its nearly 2,800 miles of railroad track ranked it second among states. Abraham Lincoln, Stephen A. Douglas, and indeed all Illinoisans stood on the cusp of another highly significant era, the cataclysmic Civil War era. Acerbic and heated rhetoric over important issues during the 1850s politicized society, generating high voter turnout and dissolving consensus and willingness to compromise. Still, qualities that shaped frontier Illinois—willingness to venture into the unknown, inventiveness, flexibility, optimism, voluntarism, broad tolerance, ideas about race, cooperation, desire to replicate, limited and channeled conflict, determination, and risk-taking—influenced Civil War leadership, the nature of combat, and the war's resolution and Reconstruction. Although Illinois by 1860 had outgrown and shed salient frontier traits, its frontier experience influenced how its citizens would address crises, war, and the general future. Reversing chronological order, the lengthy and varied frontier experience for Illinoisans and others was an Odyssey, one which heavily influenced the Civil War, the national Iliad, and much of American life.

Notes

Journal Abbreviations

AAAG: Annals of the Association of American Geographers
IHJ: Illinois Historical Journal (formerly the *JISHS*)
JAH: Journal of American History
JER: Journal of the Early Republic
JHG: Journal of Historical Geography
JISHS: Journal of the Illinois State Historical Society (now the *IHJ*)
JSH: Journal of Social History
TON: The Old Northwest: A Journal of Regional Life and Letters
W&MQ: The William & Mary Quarterly
WHQ: Western Historical Quarterly
WIRS: Western Illinois Regional Studies

Prologue: Three Observers

1. J. D. B. De Bow, *Mortality Statistics of the Seventh Census of the United States, 1850,* 81. This significant fact is discussed at length in chapter 13.

1. The Shaping of Settlement

1. The American Bottom is a stretch of rich floodplain running about 100 miles from above Cahokia to the mouth of the Kaskaskia River. The term was coined by the late 1770s to distinguish this stretch from Spanish-held bottomland directly across the Mississippi.

2. For global views of frontier-building activity and imperialism and resistance to these activities, see Walter Nugent, "Frontiers and Empires in the Late Nineteenth Century," in Patricia Nelson Limerick, Clyde A. Milner II, and Charles E. Rankin, eds., *Trails: Toward a New Western History.* Stressing developments from 1870 to 1914, Nugent

places the American frontier in contexts of global frontier activities, focusing on roles played by demography, disease, motivation, timing of frontier or imperial surge, and type of frontier in influencing settlement undertakings.

3. For example, in late October 1818, Elias Pym Fordham described a prairie fire in southeastern Illinois, "It was the most glorious and most awful sight I ever beheld. A thousand acres of Prairie were in flames at once;—the sun was obscured, and the day was dark before the night came." And then he added, "There are five large fires visible tonight, some many miles off." Fordham, in Frederic Austin Ogg, ed., *Personal Narrative of Travels in Virginia, Maryland, Pennsylvania, Ohio, Indiana, Kentucky; and of a Residence in the Illinois Territory, 1817–1818*, 235. Visiting Illinois in 1821 from Massachusetts, George W. Ogden stressed wanton roles hunters played in starting fires to drive game, claiming farmers often suffered "from the all-devouring flame." Ogden, in Reuben Gold Thwaites, ed., *Early Western Travels, 1748–1846*, vol. 19, 56–57.

4. John Mack Faragher, *Daniel Boone: The Life and Legend of an American Pioneer*, illustrates conflict in Kentucky and then Missouri. Faragher's narrative is not simply an account of violence between Indians and Indian-haters. Rather, it uncovers layers of conflict, intricate personal relationships, and the struggle's complexities. Virtues and flaws abound on all sides in Faragher's account, with leading players displaying human traits throughout. Boone, moreover, held Indian foes in higher regard than he did elements of white society. A legislator, judge, and speculator, he spewed vitriolic comments at lawyers, politicians, legalities, and speculators. Overall, Boone occupied various positions somewhere between Indian society and white society, somewhere in a middle ground, and he regretted killing three Indians during his long life. Nevertheless, he and his companions fought severe and brutal battles. Mutual savagery, hatred, and rage intensified prolonged combat in Kentucky and regions north of the Ohio, sentiments generally absent from Illinois. The absence of large-scale, set battles in Illinois may help account for the difference.

2. Commingling Cultures

1. Reuben Gold Thwaites, ed., *The Jesuit Relations*, vol. 59, 127, 129. Father Gabriel Marest, living at Kaskaskia in 1712, wrote that Indians usually conducted two annual hunts. Heat and debilitating fatigue limited the summer hunt to just three weeks. The winter hunt, often lasting four months, saw Indians form into bands and scatter to hunting camps and villages from which they tracked Buffalo and other game. Thwaites, ed., *The Jesuit Relations*, vol. 66, 231 and 253.

2. Raymond E. Hauser, "Warfare and the Illinois Indian Tribe during the Seventeenth Century: An Exercise in Ethnohistory," *TON*, Winter 1984–85, 368. Indians acquitting themselves poorly in warfare were disgraced. Jean-Bernard Bossu visited Fort de Chartres in 1752 and observed, "Those who run away or desert in an action concerning honor or the defense of the tribe receive no physical punishment, but they are considered a disgrace to the human race." They could only regain status by performing some very heroic deed. Seymour Feiler, ed., *Jean-Bernard Bossu's Travels in the Interior of North America, 1751–1762*, 82. Indian licentiousness sometimes shocked French priests and others, Father Gabriel Marest lamenting, "Gluttony and the love of pleasure are, above all, the vices most dominant among the Savages; they are habituated to the most indecent acts before they are even old enough to know all the shame that is connected with them." He added that, for that reason, they were "very little inclined to submit [themselves] to the yoke of the Gospel. But the more averse they are to the Kingdom of God, the more ought our zeal be quickened to draw them near, and cause them to enter it." Nevertheless, he saw value in this independence, observing, "It is true, there are Chiefs among them, but the Chiefs have no authority; if they should use threats, far from making themselves feared, they would see themselves abandoned by the very men who had chose them for Chiefs." Thwaites, ed., *The Jesuit Relations*, vol. 46, 221–222.

3. Thwaites, ed., *The Jesuit Relations*, vol. 59, 129, 131. When some Tamaroas in 1682 mistook Henri de Tonti's party for dreaded Iroquois and attacked, Tonti stymied the assault by displaying the calumet, the Tamaroas not "doing us any harm." Henri de Tonti, "Memoir on La Salle's Discoveries, By Tonty, 1678–1690," in Louise Phelps Kellogg, ed., *Early Narratives of the Northwest, 1634–1699*, 304.

4. Thwaites, ed., *The Jesuit Relations*, vol. 59, 127. The Illinois Indians acquired brass kettles from French traders at Green Bay as early as 1669. Between 1680 and 1719 the Illinois ceased to produce their own pottery, turning instead to metal and ceramic vessels of French manufacture. After French arrived in Illinois, Indians adopted French-made goods, often adapting them for special use. John A. Walthall, "Aboriginal Pottery and the Eighteenth-Century Illini," in John A. Walthall and Thomas E. Emerson, eds., *Calumet Fleur-de-Lys: Archaeology of Indian and French Contact in the Midcontinent*, 168–170. In 1682 Henri de Tonti described Indians along the Illinois: "The savages there are quick, agile, and brave, but extremely lazy, except in war, when they think nothing of seeking their enemies at a distance of 500 or 600 leagues from their own country." He claimed they harassed Iroquois at his instigation, but they probably needed little encouragement to seek revenge. Tonti, in Kellogg, ed., *Early Narratives*, 303.

5. Hauser, "Warfare and the Illinois Indian Tribe during the Seventeen Century," 368.

6. Judith A. Franke, *French Peoria and the Illinois Country, 1673–1846*, 22–27, and Carl J. Ekberg, "Marie Rouensa–8cate8a and the Foundations of French Illinois," *IHJ*, Autumn 1991, 146–160. Writing in Kaskaskia in 1712, Father Gabriel Marest reported marriages between three French men and Illinois women. He also observed many Illinois Indians raising chickens and pigs, "in imitation of the Frenchmen who have settled here." Thwaites, ed., *The Jesuit Relations*, vol. 66, 231, 255. Father Jean Francois Buisson de St. Cosme visited the Lake Peoria area in late 1698 and found marriages between French men and Indian women: "We saw . . . women savages married to Frenchmen, who edified us by their modesty and their assiduity in going to prayer several times a day in the chapel." St. Cosme, "The Voyage of St. Cosme, 1698–1699," in Kellogg, ed., *Early Narratives*, 351. Sometimes Indians' mimicking of French ways was amusing. For example, Indians honored French visitors by solemnly pacing back and forth with muskets shouldered in European style. Such pacing was so uncharacteristic of Indians that one French priest referred to the honor guards as "Frenchified." Thwaites, ed., *The Jesuit Relations*, vol. 55, 189.

7. Natalia Maree Belting noted that French got along with Indians, far better than the English did. Nevertheless, she observed, even French harbored negative attitudes toward Indians and a chasm separated the two cultures, and she noted that French culture destroyed much Indian culture, however inadvertently. Belting, "The Native American as Myth and Fact," *JISHS*, May 1976, 121–122. Moreover, the French had terrible problems with Iroquois and then Fox, hobbling settlement efforts in Illinois. Despite French alacrity in adapting to life on rivers and in forests, not all became smitten by the outdoors. For example, Father Marest wrote that "the horror of the forest" nearly sapped his courage. After he and his party traveled twelve days without seeing a single soul, he noted he could not survive abandonment in the forest. Thwaites, ed., *The Jesuit Relations*, vol. 66, 269. Worse, some French behaved badly. Father Marest wrote in 1712 from Kaskaskia about additional French possibly settling there. He welcomed moral men, but cautioned "if, unhappily, some of them should come and openly practice libertinage and perhaps irreligion, as is to be feared, all would be over with our Mission. Their pernicious example would make more impression on the minds of the Savages than all that we could say to preserve them from the same dissolute conduct." Thwaites, ed., *The Jesuit Relations*, vol. 66, 293. Sometimes collisions of world views triggered trouble between French and Indians. After Father Jacques Gravier's arrival at Peoria in early 1694, one Indian elder feared priests' ability to change Indians society, and "full of zeal for the ancient customs" he

told followers what he had learned from his grandfather about "what we should believe" and urged them to "cling to our own traditions." Thwaites, ed., *The Jesuit Relations*, vol. 64, 183. Despite individuals' fine intentions, cultural differences sparked trouble, often over mundane matters.

8. Richard White discusses the middle ground in *The Middle Ground: Indians, Empires, and Republics in the Great Lakes Region, 1650–1815*. Intermarriage's influences in producing middle ground are discussed in Virgil J. Vogel, "Indian-White Intermarriage on the Frontier: The Role of Mixed-Bloods in Indian-White Relations," *Transactions: Selected Papers from the Seventh Annual History Symposium and the Eighth Annual Illinois History Symposium, 1986–1987*. Archaeologists from the Illinois State Museum note that Indians living in northeastern Illinois in the early 1800s acquired much from advancing white culture, even before settlers moved near them. For example, Potawatomi Indians lived in log cabins, enjoyed glass windows, and used firearms and European and American china and glass. They did, however, preserve ceremonies, diets, and other aspects of an older culture, but transformation of Indian life by the 1830s was so complete that Indian villages closely resembled Lincoln's New Salem. Doug Pogorski, "Study Shows Illinois' Indians Lived a Lot Like Setters in the Early 1800s," *The State Journal-Register*, August 17, 1992, 6. This heavy borrowing by Potawatomi suggests massive acculturation rather than creation of middle ground culture, but nearby whites probably borrowed from Indians. In any case, during the 1700s and early 1800s, a shifting, evolving middle ground flourished in Illinois. French colonists, especially, borrowed from Indians, create an evolving hybrid culture. However, some French borrowed little, not even language. For example, when a jurisdictional dispute arose between priests of the Seminary of Foreign Missions and the Jesuits over establishing missions in the American Bottom, one Jesuit huffed, "Those gentlemen do not even take the trouble to learn the Savage Tongues," which he implied contributed to mission failure. Thwaites, ed., *The Jesuit Relations*, vol. 66, 41. Even so, compared to the English, French colonists borrowed heavily from Indians.

9. Thwaites, ed., *The Jesuit Relations*, vol. 55, 207, 209, 211.

10. Thwaites, ed., *The Jesuit Relations*, vol. 59, 147, 149, 159, 163.

11. Bonnie L. Gums, William R. Iseminger, Molly E. McKenzie, and Dennis D. Nichols, "The French Colonial Villages of Cahokia and Prairie du Pont, Illinois," in John A. Walthall, ed., *French Colonial Archaeology: The Illinois Country and the Western Great Lakes*, 85.

12. Belting, "The Native American as Myth and Fact," 126, and Raymond E. Hauser, "The Illinois Indian Tribe: From Autonomy and Self-Sufficiency to Dependency and Depopulation," *JISHS*, May 1976,

134–135. Captain Philip Pittman spent several years in Illinois, noting of the Illinois Indians, "They are a poor, debauched, and dastardly people. They count about three hundred and fifty warriors." Pittman, *The Present State of the European Settlements on the Mississippi*, 51. These various estimates, whatever their differences, indicate a people in dire circumstances. For fine insight into material pertaining to Illinois Indians, their decline and removal, and white attitudes toward Indians, see Ellen M. Whitney, "Indian History and the Indians of Illinois," *JISHS*, May 1976, 139–146.

3. Ties South and War for Empire

1. David Keene, "Fort de Chartres: Archaeology in the Illinois Country," in John Walthall, ed., *French Colonial Archaeology: The Illinois Country and the Western Great Lakes*, 30. Captain Harry Gordon, a British Army officer, arrived at Fort de Chartres in 1766 and was impressed by much of what he saw. After commenting favorably on grain fields, French houses, and the quality of French life, he noted, "The French have large boats of 20 tons, rowed with 10 oars, which will go in *seventy odd days* from New Orleans to the Illinois." The vessels rode floodwaters in May and June from Illinois to New Orleans in just two weeks or so. Lois Mulkearn, ed., *A Topographical Description of the Dominion of the United States of America by T. Pownall*, 163–165.

2. Margaret Kimball Brown and Lawrie Cena Dean, eds., *The Village of Chartres in Colonial Illinois, 1720–1765*, preface. Brown also stresses extensive trade via pirogues and bateaux during the 1730s between the French settlements in Illinois and the lower Mississippi. However, attempts to drive oxen and horses from these settlements overland to French posts down the river ended in failure, many animals straying or dying. Margaret Kimball Brown, "*Allons*, Cowboys!," *JISHS*, Winter 1983, 273–282. One person reported in the spring of 1753: "This country . . . supplies flour to the southern part of the colony and deals in furs, lead, and salt. Buffalo and deer are particularly fond of the grazing lands surrounding the great number of salt licks in the area. The salted meat and tongues of these animals are sold to New Orleans. The hams are every bit as good as those of Bayonne. The local fruit is as good as that grown in France." Feiler, *Jean-Bernard Bossu's Travels*, 76–77. Less than two decades later a British Army officer, who served several years in Illinois after Britain gained control in 1765, reiterated the idea that Illinois was a supplier to southern Louisiana. He wrote, "In the late wars, New Orleans and the lower parts of Louisiana were supplied with flour, beer, wines, hams and other provisions from this country: at present its commerce is mostly confined to the peltry and furs, which are got in traffic from the Indians." Pittman, *The Present*

State of the European Settlements, 52. For more on trade in the lower reaches of the Mississippi, see Daniel H. Usner, Jr., "The Frontier Exchange Economy of the Lower Mississippi Valley in the Eighteenth Century," *W&MQ*, April 1987, 165–192.

3. Clarence Alvord, *The Illinois Country, 1673–1818*, 157. Winstanley Briggs, "Le Pays des Illinois," *W&MQ*, January 1990, 30–31. An early and limited version of this significant finding appeared in Alvord, *The Illinois Country, 1673–1818*, 202–204: social distinctions were weak, social lines easily crossed, the seigniorial system absent, and land was ceded *en franc alleu*, "equivalent roughly to fee simple and the opposite of feudal." And "many of the Frenchmen lived exceedingly comfortably." Alvord, *The Illinois Country, 1673–1818*, 203, 215. On the other hand, Captain Pittman, who was stationed in Illinois following the British takeover, saw much servile deference by *habitants* to the major-commandant, the senior official during the French era. He wrote of him, "He was absolute in his authority, except in matters of life and death; capital offences were tried by the council at New Orleans: the whole Indian trade was so much in the power of the commandant, that nobody was permitted to be concerned in it, but on condition of giving him part of the profits." The people, he wrote, "were happy if by the most servile and submissive behavior they could gain his confidence and favour." Pittman, *The Present State of the European Settlements*, 53, 54. Two facts qualify Pittman's account. First, he did not admire the French, being prone to parade their flaws and defects. Second, he wrote after France had lost the war, French military and civil authorities had withdrawn, and British occupation forces had arrived. In other words, the French he encountered were a defeated people, which probably accounts for submissive behavior he observed. French residents before defeat and occupation were spirited, energetic, and even raucous.

4. Susan C. Boyle, "Did She Generally Decide? Women in Ste. Genevieve, 1750–1805," *W&MQ*, October 1987, 776, 785, 789.

5. Peyser, *Letters from New France*, especially 156 and 160.

6. Details of this episode are related skillfully in Raymond E. Hauser, "The Fox Raid of 1752: Defensive Warfare and the Decline of the Illinois Indian Tribe," *IHJ*, Winter 1993.

7. A recent fine treatment of the slide into war is found in Joseph L Peyser, trans. and ed., *Jacques Legardeur de Saint-Pierre: Officer, Gentleman, Entrepreneur*, 201–222. Because Saint-Pierre commanded the French forces in the Ohio River Valley, the view presented is valuable, the work brimming with French and British documents. Vast distances between posts, limited French resources, and tug-of-war for Indian loyalty are apparent in this account. At the title suggests, French officers often played key economic roles in New France.

8. Population figures come from several sources. Alvord, *The Illinois Country, 1673–1818*, 202, 244. Daniel H. Usner, Jr., "The Frontier Exchange Economy of the Lower Mississippi Valley in the Eighteenth Century," *W&MQ*, April 1987, 167. Carl J. Ekberg, "Black Slavery in Illinois, 1720–1765," *WIRS*, Spring 1989, 6, 8, 9. By 1699 Illinois Indians received guns, hatchets, and other weapons from French in Wisconsin. Gaining a technological edge over Indians west of the Mississippi, Illinois Indians ranged west and south in search of slaves. They traded slaves to French and to Iroquois, wishing to placate the latter. By 1709 the slave population in Illinois spurted. Shortly thereafter, French arrived from Michilimackinac to trade in enslaved Indians. The British, upon displacing French power in North America, allowed the French and Indians to keep slaves. Russell M. Magnaghi, "Red Slavery in the Great Lakes Country during the French and British Regime," *TON*, Summer 1986, 201–203, 207, 211–212. Slaves in French Illinois were treated relatively well, and some of the reasons are found in Ekberg, "Black Slavery in Illinois, 1720–1765," 16–17.

9. Margaret Kimball Brown, "Documents and Archaeology in French Illinois," in John A. Walthall, ed., *French Colonial Archaeology: The Illinois Country and the Western Great Lakes*, 83.

4. Light British Rule

1. At least one British subject understood this fact. In 1766 Captain Harry Gordon of the British Army reached Fort de Chartres after a voyage down the Ohio. After noting that British possession of Illinois underscored for the Indians British superiority over the French, he observed, "Cooped up at Fort de Chartres only, we make a foolish figure; hardly have the dominion of the country." Lois Mulkearn, ed., *A Topographical Description of the Dominions of the United States of America by T. Pownall*, 165. For American colonists, opportunity did lie in the West, but three threats loomed. First, Britain had plans for the entire region, plans which precluded those of English colonists. Second, Indians believed they, not English colonists, should have the land. Third, some French riled up Indians, telling them the English intended to take the land, give it to Cherokees, and enslave the region's Indians, making them dread the arriving English. George Croghan warned, "All the French residing here are a lazy, indolent people, fond of breeding mischief, and spiriting up the Indians against the English." Croghan was an Indian agent for Britain in various places north of the Ohio. When he reached Illinois in mid-1765, he encountered sullen, fearful Indians and had to work to alleviate their concerns. George Croghan, in Thwaites, ed., *Early Western Travels, 1748–1846*, vol. 1, 148, 150. The

high costs, uncertainties, and risks involved in administering and provisioning Illinois and other lands north of the Ohio are abundantly
evident in the business activities of the Philadelphia mercantile house
of Baynton, Wharton and Morgan in Robert M. Sutton, "George Morgan, Early Illinois Businessman: A Case of Premature Enterprise,"
JISHS, August 1976.

2. The region lying between the Appalachians and the Mississippi
was crucial in negotiations to end the war. English settlers assumed,
incorrectly, that they now had free access to the region. London had
other ideas. Norman A. Graebner, "The Illinois Country and the Treaty
of Paris of 1783," *IHJ*, Spring 1985, 2. Keen American interest in this
land is discussed in Emory G. Evans, "The Colonial View of the West,"
JISHS, May 1976, 89.

3. Donald Chaput, "Treason or Loyalty? Frontier French in the
American Revolution," *JISHS*, November 1978, 243. Analysis of Captain Stirling's magnanimous proclamation is found in Alexander
Davidson and Bernard Stuve, *A Complete History of Illinois from 1673
to 1873*, 164.

4. One authority noted, "in times of political or military crisis affluent Frenchmen had a habit of moving across the Mississippi River with
their slaves into friendly Spanish Louisiana. Almost as regularly they
would move back into the Illinois country once conditions had returned
to normal." Robert M. Sutton, "Edward Coles and the Constitutional
Crisis in Illinois, 1822–1824," *IHJ*, Spring 1989, 37. The predictable return of the affluent and their slaves is significant. For ordinary people,
perhaps especially heads of young families, such bouncing back and
forth was costly and risky, so many left for good. Poorer folk simply
stayed put. Observations by Captain Philip Pittman in the late 1760s
lend credence to this idea: in 1764 some forty families lived in a village
near the fort, and he noted, "In the following year, when the English
took possession of the country, they abandoned their houses, except
three or four poor families, and settled at the villages on the west side
of the Mississippi." He also reported that in 1765 nearly every inhabitant of Saint Philippe, a community of some sixteen houses some five
miles from the fort, crossed the Mississippi. The sole exception was the
captain of militia, who had a water mill and other local assets. Captain
Pittman learned that French in St. Louis had been encouraged to leave
Illinois. Pittman, *The Present State of the European Settlements*, 46,
47, 49. Evidently, some French moved across the Mississippi after hearing
a rumor that France retained control of the west bank. Andre Michaux,
in Thwaites, ed., *Early Western Travels*, vol. 3, 72n. For more on this
movement, see Alvord, *The Illinois Country 1673–1818*, 202, and Keene,
"Fort de Chartres: Archaeology in the Illinois Country," 32.

5. John Francis Bannon, S.J., "The Spaniards and the Illinois Country, 1762–1800," *JISHS*, May 1976, 115. This anti-British resentment helped George Rogers Clark to dislodge British power in Illinois.

6. Reginald Horsman, "Great Britain and the Illinois Country in the Era of the American Revolution," *JISHS*, May 1976, 101.

7. Various facets of British policy and actions in the trans-Appalachian region are discussed in several sources: Evans, "The Colonial View of the West," 87; Graebner, "The Illinois Country and the Treaty of Paris of 1783," 2; Horsman, "Great Britain and the Illinois Country in the Era of the American Revolution," 101.

5. A Tenuous Conquest

1. Matters of French loyalty, the roles played by Thomas Bentley and Rocheblave, and related topics are discussed in several sources: Chaput, "Treason or Loyalty? Frontier French in the American Revolution," 242–252; David G. Thompson, "Thomas Bentley and the American Revolution in Illinois," *IHJ*, Spring 1990, 4; Horsman, "Great Britain and the Illinois Country in the Era of the American Revolution," 102–103.

2. Kathrine Wagner Seineke, *The George Rogers Clark Adventure in the Illinois*, 261. Most of the narrative of Clark's overland march is found in James Alton James, ed., *George Rogers Clark Papers, 1771–1781*.

3. Chaput, "Treason or Loyalty? Frontier French in the American Revolution," 248. The scope and significance of the American successes and the brisk response by British authorities are found in Horsman, "Great Britain and the Illinois Country in the Era of the American Revolution," 102–109.

4. This and the rest of the narrative of Clark's exploits and accompanying quotations are from James, ed., *George Rogers Clark Papers, 1771–1781*, 138, 139, 140, 144, 148, 149, and 607. Clark understood nature's obstacles in the line of march. This portion of Illinois, he wrote, was "one of the most beautiful Country in the world, but at this time in many parts flowing with water and exceeding bad marching." He also knew that small parties of resourceful people had accomplished great deeds against daunting odds, and he realized this desperate expedition required all his fabled confidence and talent. James, ed., *George Rogers Clark Papers, 1771–1781*, 139.

5. Techniques of threshing divided French and Anglos from the South. French farmers tilled small fields, stored grain in vertical post barns, and threshed with flails. Recent American arrivals had bigger fields, stacked grain, and threshed using horses. J. Sanford Rikoon, *Threshing in the Midwest, 1820–1940: A Study of Traditional Culture and*

Technological Change, 2. This minor difference probably caused no friction, but it underscored overall differences between the two people. In reality, however, some farmers flailed one grain and tramped another, and people probably learned beneficial lessons from each other.

6. Some French stayed in the region, but formed a cluster away from Anglos, at Prairie du Rocher. A census taken in 1787 showed that as other French villages lost population Prairie du Rocher grew. Perhaps French flocking to Prairie du Rocher wanted to put as much distance between themselves and occupying forces at the former Fort de Chartres. Edward T. Safiran, "The Louvier Site at Prairie du Rocher," in John A. Walthall, ed., *French Colonial Archaeology*, 124. One governor of New France suggested French residents in Illinois became indolent because they owned slaves. Keene, "Fort de Chartres: Archaeology in the Illinois Country," 38.

7. James, ed., *George Rogers Clark Papers, 1771–1781*, 154. Although Clark saw meadows "covered with Buffaloes," the days of buffalo in Illinois were numbered. Buffalo in Illinois suffered greatly during the winter of 1790, when they froze or starved in deep snow, died at the hands of Indians, and fell victim to roving predators. Perhaps they never recovered from these severe losses. Alfred H. Meyer, "Circulation and Settlement Patterns of the Calumet Region of Northwest Indiana and Northeast Illinois," *AAAG*, September 1954, 268.

8. Raymond H. Hammes, "Land Transactions in Illinois Prior to the Sale of Public Domain," *JISHS*, Summer 1984, 106. Some American settlers were "troubled by deep ethnic and religious convictions" about living among the French. On the other hand, some settled in clusters not far from the French settlements, seeking protection from Indian attack. Raymond Hammes, "Squatters in Territorial Illinois," *Illinois Libraries*, May 1977, 320.

9. For discussion of the theory and dynamics of migration, see Everett S. Lee, "A Theory of Migration," *Demography*, March 1966, especially 50–52 and 56–57. Differences between mere mobility and migration are explored in Ralph R. Sell, "Analyzing Migration Decisions: The First Step—Whose Decisions?" *Demography*, August 1983. Sell notes that in recent years Americans migrated in response to employment factors. The nature of those who return home after migrating is examined by Peter A. Morrison and Julie DaVanzo, "The Prism of Migration: Dissimilarities between Return and Onward Movers," *Social Science Quarterly*, September 1986. They note that migrants who are recently unemployed, less educated, less skilled, and make few plans are likely to return home quickly. These returnees, "turnbackers," were not common in the early years of the Illinois frontier, but they may have become more common as transportation improved. Another factor may have operated. An "advantage for successful adaptation to the

conditions of the frontier was the memory of a relatively low standard of living before emigration." *When* people migrated influenced the degree to which they were contented. "This may be one reason why English immigrants who arrived in Edwards County, Illinois, during the early days of its settlement, when England was in the grip of a postwar depression, seemed more content than those who came five or ten years later." Charlotte Erickson, *Invisible Immigrants*, 5.

10. Graebner, "The Illinois Country and the Treaty of Paris of 1783," 12.

11. Alvord, *The Illinois Country, 1763–1818*, 357.

6. Firm Foundations

1. Evans, "The Colonial View of the West," 89.

2. Concern over Virginia's claims is analyzed in Robert M. Sutton, "George Morgan, Early Illinois Businessman: A Case of Premature Enterprise," 37. A superb source for understanding Virginia's roles in ceding claims to northwestern lands and influencing western land policy is Peter Onuf, "Toward Federalism: Virginia, Congress, and the Western Lands," *W&MQ*, July 1977. The Revolutionary generation wallowed in suspicions. People suspected mighty Virginia of grand designs in the West, and Virginians saw conspiracy to curtail Virginia's power and even obliterate the state altogether. Against this backdrop and inadequate government under the Articles of Confederation, the cession accomplished much for Virginia, other states, the federal government, and the West. Questions of governance in the region loomed large. Thomas Jefferson's optimistic view of humankind's ability to govern itself and the transformation of these ideas into the less optimistic Northwest Ordinance are discussed in Reginald Horsman, "Thomas Jefferson and the Ordinance of 1784," *IHJ*, Summer 1986, 99–112. Another authority concludes that Jefferson never really drafted an Ordinance of 1784, and he views the Northwest Ordinance's national impact in very positive terms. Robert M. Sutton, "The Northwest Ordinance: A Bicentennial Souvenir," *IHJ*, Spring 1988, 18–20.

3. For more on this subject, see Robert M. Sutton, "Edward Coles and the Constitutional Crisis in Illinois, 1822–1824," *IHJ*, Spring 1989, 37–38.

4. One source notes, "The most important feature of Congress's new land policy was the requirement of survey before settlement, with property lines following a grid system that made clear title possible, thus permitting easy sale and resale. Together with the triumph of the fee simple principle over feudal survivals such as primogeniture and entail, the grid helped transform landed property into a marketable commodity." Peter S. Onuf, "Liberty, Development, and Union: Visions of

the West in the 1780s," *W&MQ*, April 1986, 210. Onuf also notes great concern about western anarchy, barbarism, and even disunion of the young Republic. Many regarded the West as a threat, a disrupter of order, Onuf observing, "The success of the American experiment in republican government thus seemed to depend on establishing law and order on the frontier." Although the Ordinance of 1785 worked slowly and somewhat imperfectly, it was hugely successful, and the country's well-being and unity were assured. Ibid., 179, 212–213. One source claims the region's checkerboard grid pattern of townships promoted order and authority: The townships north of the Ohio were "regular, easily replicated one-mile-square" and "symbolized order as much as openness and opportunity." Furthermore, "To compensate for their indolent inclinations, common people needed the control imposed by an ordered social space," the space provided by the orderly, regular, checkerboard system of survey. Gregory H. Nobles, "Straight Lines and Stability: Mapping the Political Order of the Anglo-American Frontier," *JAH*, June 1993, 34, and see 28, 32, 33, and 35.

5. Squatters and squatter life are discussed in Robert W. McCluggage, "The Pioneer Squatter," *IHJ*, Spring 1989. McCluggage believes squatter culture was markedly and deliberately different from the larger culture. Squatters faded in Illinois, he claims, when by the 1830s they acquired the means to buy land.

6. The meaning of Article 6 of the Ordinance, the article promising "neither slavery nor involuntary servitude" in the Northwest, is discussed in Robert M. Sutton, "Edward Coles and the Constitutional Crisis in Illinois, 1822–1824," 38. He notes that Governor Arthur St. Clair claimed Article 6 was prospective only, preventing *future* importation of slaves into the Northwest, not sweeping away existing slavery. Others were certain the article was retrospective. Essentially, St. Clair's view prevailed, but Article 6 did put slavery in the Northwest on the road to extinction. Paul Finkelman concurs. He notes, "In the long run, of course, Article 6 helped set the stage for the emergence of five free states in the region" by discouraging slave owners from bringing their slaves across the Ohio. Illinois never attracted large numbers of zealous slaveholders, so relatively few Illinoisans eagerly promoted the institution. This became very significant by 1822, when a concerted drive sought to amend the state constitution to allow slavery. The effort failed. Finkelman, "Slavery and the Northwest Ordinance: A Study in Ambiguity," *JER*, Winter 1986, 346.

7. Horsman, "Thomas Jefferson and the Ordinance of 1784," 112. For analysis of pre-statehood political conditions, see James A. Edstrom, "'With . . . candour and good faith': Nathaniel Pope and the Admission Enabling Act of 1818," *IHJ*, Winter 1995, especially 241–243.

8. Bannon, "The Spaniards and the Illinois Country, 1762–1800,"

117. Actually, three factors affected the French, not just two. Andre Michaux, a French scientist recruited by the French government to secure intelligence about the West, visited Kaskaskia in mid-1795. Some French men in Kaskaskia had adopted aspects of Indian life—had entered the middle ground—and this displeased Michaux greatly. He reported the number of inhabitants had diminished, and then wrote, "The French of the Illinois country, having always been brought up in and accustomed to the Fur trade with the savages, have become the laziest and most ignorant of all men." Andre Michaux, in Thwaites, ed., *Early Western Travels*, vol. 3, 70. On the eve of statehood visitors to the American Bottom cast aspersions about the persisting French population. For example, Elias Pym Fordham sniffed, "In the Illinois Country, Society is yet unborn,—but it will be soon. The western parts toward St. Louis are thickest settled, and with very dissipated characters. French and Indian traders, Canadians, &c, gamblers, horsestealers, and bankrupts." Fordham, in Ogg, ed., *Personal Narrative*, 181. Almost certainly, Fordham's views were too extreme and harsh, but they do reflect perceptions that French living in the American Bottom had few redeeming qualities. As late as 1825, the prim Timothy Flint, stalwart exponent of New England, observed assortments of French, French-Indians, and Indians living along the Illinois River. He saw Potawatomi Indian cabins, in which a "French woman of unmixed blood" lived with a Potawatomi man. Flint pronounced these people "the intermediate link between the social and savage state," indicating that they lived in the middle ground. Timothy Flint, *Recollections of the Last Ten Years Passed in Occasional Residences and Journeyings in the Valley of the Mississippi*, 130–131.

9. In 1818 dozens of men, mostly of French extraction, petitioned Congress. After claiming to have marched with Clark on Vincennes, they lamented their present poverty and requested "a small donation of land" for each petitioner. They noted, "The Treaty of 1783 which gave Independence, wealth and happiness to the United States had a Contrary effect upon the Inhabitants of this County." With control of the St. Lawrence and the Mississippi in foreign hands, they added, "This trade was destroyed, and the People thereby reduced to indigence. They have drained the Cup of penury to the dregs." Clarence Edwin Carter, comp. and ed., *The Territorial Papers of the United States, Volume XVII: The Territory of Illinois, 1814–1818, Continued*, 567–569. Some French found the prospect of living under the third government in nineteen years too much to take, especially with the additional burden of boisterous Americans. Raymond Hammes, "Squatters in Territorial Illinois," 320.

10. Bannon, "The Spaniards and the Illinois Country, 1762–1800," 117.

11. A voyage down the Ohio River in 1789–90 generated a fine ac-

count of planters, sawyers, and other hazards. Shortly before it entered the Mississippi, the keelboat on which Major Samuel S. Forman and his party rode became stuck on a planter, "that is, the body of a tree firmly embedded in the river bottom." Some of the men boarded the planter with saws, removed some of the offending tree, and thereby released the vessel. Forman went on to note, "Another dangerous obstruction is a tree becoming undermined and falling into the river, and the roots fastening themselves in the muddy bottom, while, by the constant action of the current, the limbs wear off, and the body keeps sawing up and down with great force, rising frequently several feet above the water, and then sinking as much below." Because they made this sawing motion, they were called "sawyers," and they imperiled unsuspecting vessels. Samuel S. Forman, *Narrative of a Journey Down the Ohio and Mississippi in 1789–90*, 44. For an instance of a concealed tree trunk damaging a boat, see Stephen Harriman Long, in Thwaites, ed., *Early Western Travels*, vol. 14, 100. To enhance security, especially at night, flatboats were lashed together. Thomas Nuttall drifted down the Ohio the year after statehood with his flatboat lashed to three others. Thomas Nuttall, in Thwaites, ed., *Early Western Travels*, vol. 13, 71. For more on planters, sawyers, and other river obstructions, see John Bradbury, in Thwaites, ed., *Early Western Travels*, vol. 5, 57, 200–201. A superb account of river life and society is Michael Allen, *Western Rivermen, 1763–1861: Ohio and Mississippi Boatmen and the Myth of the Alligator Horse*. Allen notes a qualitative change occurred in boatmen society during the 1820s, and he demonstrates the abiding importance of flatboats decades after steamboats first coursed western waters.

12. For example, in 1817 Henry Bradshaw Fearon observed, "Here, no man is either thought or called 'master;' neither, on the other hand, is there found any coarse vulgarity." Henry Bradshaw Fearon, *Sketches of America: A Narrative of a Journey of Five Thousand Miles through the Eastern and Western States of America*, 264. The breezy attitude employees showed to employers was matched by the attitude of voters toward political office holders, their elected servants. Elected officials, probably believing in republican ideas and taking cues from a vigilant public, usually behaved accordingly. They often followed George Washington's example, voluntarily surrendered their offices, stepped away from centers of political power, and returned home to pursue relatively mundane matters. Fearon sensed this republican spirit and wrote, "A senator, a secretary of state, or a president, is commonly a lawyer, who has risen by his talents or perseverance; and, in addition, he is not unfrequently a farmer: and when his official duties have terminated, he returns from Washington to his home, and resumes his former occupations." Fearon, *Sketches of America*, 381.

13. This law and those that follow are taken from Theodore Calvin

Pease, ed., *The Laws of the Northwest Territory, 1788–1800*, 26–27, 206, 286, 359, 410, 417.

14. Malcolm J. Rohrbough, *The Trans-Appalachian Frontier*, 80–81.

15. Andre Michaux, in Thwaites, ed., *Early Western Travels*, vol. 3, 70–71.

16. This colony's history is ably depicted in Edward P. Brand, *Illinois Baptists, a History*, 17–29. The name "New Design" indicates a desire for the society to be free from slave labor. See Malcolm E. Haughey, "Challenge and Response: The Role of Early Frontier Leaders," *American Baptist Quarterly*, September 1984, 199. See also Lamire Holden Moore, *Southern Baptists in Illinois*, 8–9.

7. Rumblings across the Land

1. Leland R. Johnson, "The Doyle Mission to Massac, 1794," *JISHS*, Spring 1980, especially 3, 8, 16.

2. Fortescue Cuming, in Thwaites, ed., *Early Western Travels*, vol. 4, 273–274, 279.

3. Robert P. Howard, *Illinois: A History of the Prairie State*, 81.

4. The development of the "indentured" system is discussed in Paul Finkelman, "Slavery, the 'More Perfect Union,' and the Prairie State," *IHJ*, Winter 1987, 251–253. The work also discusses complex and protracted fights over slavery, including free blacks' changing roles in Illinois and efforts to protect runaways from slave trackers.

5. Prior to the early 1800s, Illinoisans obtained salt from Ste. Genevieve, virtually the sole major producer in the West until Kentucky's salt licks began operating in the late 1700s. The Illinois Saline west of Shawneetown began functioning after leases were let in 1803, servicing Illinois, Indiana, and Kentucky, Tennessee, and Missouri. See John A. Jakle, "Salt on the Ohio Valley Frontier, 1770–1820," *AAAG*, December 1969. Political maneuvering over statehood banned further introduction of slaves into Illinois, but allowed slaves to work salines near Shawneetown until 1825. Hundreds of slaves evaporated saline water from springs, packed the salt into barrels made locally, and hauled the barrels to flatboats at Shawneetown. Meat preservation, especially for meat shipped south, required great quantities of salt. Evaporation processes and the making of barrels devoured local timber supplies, crimping operations. Coal was later used as a substitute. The Shawneetown salines functioned into the 1870s. Major saline operations opened in 1819 near Danville.

6. John Moses, *Illinois: Historical and Statistical*, vol. 1, 229.

7. Alvord, *The Illinois Frontier, 1673–1818*, 420. For an account of subterfuge employed to secure titles to land across the Mississippi from Illinois, see Long, in Thwaites, ed., *Early Western Travels*, vol. 14, 102–

103. Similar trickery was employed in Illinois. Raymond Hammes ably analyzes problems confronting potential land buyers and sellers before 1814 and attempts to solve the problems. Poor record keeping, partly a product of turbulent political and diplomatic events during the late 1700s, created confusion concerning land transactions. Cultural differences among Indians, French, British, and Americans, Hammes notes, worsened matters. Raymond H. Hammes, "Land Transactions in Illinois Prior to the Sale of Public Domain," *JISHS*, Summer 1984, 101.

8. Thomas, sensing anger back home, undertook a prudent career move and started life afresh in Illinois, the land he served so well, becoming a federal judge in the Territory of Illinois. Nine years later he presided over the State Constitutional Convention, and became a U.S. Senator when Illinois entered the Union. For more on the career of the agile Thomas, see Jo Tice Bloom, "The Territorial Delegates of Indiana Territory, 1801–1816," *TON*, Spring 1986, 12–15.

9. Reynolds, *The Pioneer History of Illinois*, 355, 362–364. Chain migration sometimes furthered specific cultural and social goals. For example, in Edwards County around the time of statehood an English colony took root. It was a sustained, organized undertaking to bring discontented English folk to Illinois for a new life. Morris Birkbeck was a co-leader of this project, and in 1817 he and nine others visited America to lay the groundwork for the colony. Elias Pym Fordham, one of the nine, wrote, "Mr. Birkbeck does not mean to introduce more American customs in our Colony than will be necessary. English ideas and manners will be preserved as much as possible." Fordham, *Personal Narrative*, 205. Efforts to maintain English culture, however, foundered on reality's shoals. The colony's basic purpose was to enable English people escape oppressive conditions. Once people came to America, however, they soaked up ideas, manners, and other traits from the larger society.

10. James E. Davis, *Frontier America, 1800–1840: A Comparative Demographic Analysis of the Settlement Process*, 75, 76, 101–110, 168–170.

11. As late as mid-century cooperative butchering brought neighbors together. See Frederic Trautmann, "Eight Weeks on a St. Clair Farm in 1851: Letters by a Young German," *JISHS*, Autumn 1982, 173–174. In late 1819, William Faux reported another community-building custom: "Log heaving, that is, rolling trees together for burning, is done by the neighbours in a body, invited for the purpose, as if to a feast or frolic. This custom is beneficial and fraternal, and none refuse their laborious attentions. Nine tenths of the adult population here own and cultivate land." William Faux, in Thwaites, ed., *Early Western Travels*, vol. II, 179. Perhaps the fact that most adults cultivated land explains why "none refuse their laborious attentions." They had received voluntary

assistance, or expected to receive it, and they understood their obligations to voluntarily pitch in and help others. House-building "frolics" gave newcomers a new house in three days, and husking "frolics" produced mounds of corn. Fearon, *Sketches of America*, 222. Although such activities were informal and voluntary, they wove a complex fabric of social debts, credits, obligations, and duties, which were broadly understood and rarely ignored.

12. Alvord, *The Illinois Frontier, 1673–1818*, 442, 446.

13. Jo Tice Bloom, "Peaceful Politics: The Delegates from Illinois Territory, 1809–1818," *TON*, Fall 1980, 207, 208. Underlying reasons for conflict between Indians and encroaching Americans were deep-seated and perhaps irreconcilable. But some friction occurred simply because the two peoples were so dissimilar, and some tension sprang from mundane misunderstandings, sometimes escalating to trouble. For example, in 1811 on the Mississippi River, John Bradbury and his party ran low on provisions on their boat, so they looked for Indians along the shore from whom to buy food. They saw five or six Indians on one side of the river, and heard a howling dog on the other side. Upon seeing Bradbury and his party, the Indians held up some venison, indicating it was for sale. Bradbury and a Indian-speaking Frenchman climbed into a canoe, paddled toward the Indians, and began negotiating with the Indians. At that moment someone in the boat fired a gun and the dog ceased howling. Furious about the dog, the Indians brandished their weapons and debated whether to kill Bradbury and his French partner, or keep them hostage until restitution was made for the dog. At this critical moment, the dog made a dramatic reappearance, anger subsided, negotiations over food went forward, and then Bradbury and his companion hurriedly paddled away. Some Indians, however, insisted that maybe the dog was wounded. In any case, when Bradbury and the Frenchman returned to the boat, they learned that someone on the boat had, indeed, fired a gun—at a bird—which apparently had startled the dog into silence. Lives were nearly lost over differing perceptions and misunderstanding, a fact probably produced by underlying tension between Indians and whites. Bradbury, in Thwaites, ed., *Early Western Travels*, vol. 5, 201–203. In this instance, the story ended peacefully, but on other occasions faulty perceptions and differing versions of reality produced conflict and even death. Alcohol sometimes clouded perceptions and judgment. Elias Pym Fordham, for example, claimed whiskey was "the fertile source of disorders" and caused frontiersmen to fight "most furiously." Fordham, *Personal Narrative*, 129.

14. Demand for a preemption law went back to 1807. At that time in the Kaskaskia land district, the register noted that hundreds of people were already squatting and that efforts to enforce laws against them

would be futile. Realizing by 1812 that Congress was about to sell the land, squatters sought the right to buy lands they had improved. They claimed their occupation of lands was a socially useful service to society. Specifically, their presence defended the frontier, their labors increased the value of unoccupied lands, and their work improved the region in general. Moreover, they argued that unless they got the right of preemption speculators would dominate land sales. Hammes, "Squatters in Territorial Illinois," 321.

15. The two major provisions of the February, 1813, law were reasonable. One required squatters to make preemption requests in writing, citing evidence of occupation and improvement prior to February 5, 1813. The second allowed applicants to buy a quarter-section at private sales before the public land was offered to the general public. Applicants had to make a down payment of $2.00, which was one-twentieth of the purchase price. Hammes, "Squatters in Territorial Illinois," 321. For contemporary perceptions of squatters' characteristics, see McCluggage, "The Pioneer Squatter."

16. Captain Wells's life, his actions on this fateful day, and his grisly death are depicted in Walter Havighurst, "The Way to Future City," *JISHS*, August 1976, 235–236.

17. Making matters worse, trouble erupted between French residents and Americans over Cahokia. By mid-1813 Americans outnumbered French residents in St. Clair County and many had moved into the American Bottom. For years French had left other villages and had flocked to Cahokia, which was the county seat and close to St. Louis, but it was inconveniently far for Americans, which caused some to petition the territorial legislature to transfer the county seat. A commission, consisting of Anglophones, was appointed to recommend a new site. George Blair owned land on the American Bottom's bluffs, and he donated land for a proposed seat, suggesting the town be named Belleville. Belleville became the county seat, undercutting Cahokia's economic and social dominance and somewhat counterbalancing booming St. Louis. For additional information on Belleville's success, see Kay J. Carr, *Belleville, Ottawa, and Galesburg: Community and Democracy on the Illinois Frontier*, 14.

8. Shaping a State

1. *Counties of Cumberland, Jasper and Richland, Illinois*, 605.
2. C. Edward Skeen, "'The Year Without a Summer: A Historical View," *JER*, Spring 1981, 51–67.
3. A recent fine treatment of tensions between southern yeomen and planters is Stephanie McCurry, "The Politics of Yeoman Households in South Carolina," in Catherine Clinton and Nina Silber, ed.,

Divided Houses: Gender and the Civil War. Such tensions in the early 1800s were probably strongest in cotton and tobacco producing regions.

4. Buck, *Illinois in 1818*, 93–95.

5. Several weaknesses of territorial government are highlighted by James A. Edstrom, "'With . . . candour and good faith': Nathaniel Pope and the Admission Enabling Act of 1818," *IHJ*, Winter 1995, 242–243. Edstrom ably discusses in detail Illinois' journey to statehood.

6. Howard, *Illinois: A History of the Prairie State*, 98.

7. Quoted in Edstrom, "'With . . . candor and good faith': Nathaniel Pope and the Admission Enabling Act of 1818," 254. Pope's insistence on securing for Illinois the northern counties, including Cook County and Chicago, is depicted in Thomas Ford, *A History of Illinois, from Its Commencement as a State in 1818 to 1847*, 20. The region is home to well over 62 percent of Illinois' population.

8. But political activities during the territorial era were peaceful, especially when compared to the turbulent politics of neighboring territories. For the pacific nature of politics in the Illinois Territory and features of disputes that did arise, see Bloom, "Peaceful Politics: The Delegates from Illinois Territory, 1809–1818."

9. Sutton, "Edward Coles and the Constitutional Crisis in Illinois, 1822–1824," 39, and Kurt E. Leichtle, "The Rise of Jacksonian Politics in Illinois," *IHJ*, Summer 1989, 94–98. For details of Coles's manumission, his public hostility to kidnaping and Black Codes, his efforts to block efforts to turn Illinois into a slave state, and the price he paid for such stands, see Adhere Ramsay Richardson, "The Virginian Who Made Illinois a Free State," *JISHS*, Spring 1952.

10. Nichole Etcheson, *The Emerging Midwest: Upland Southerners and the Political Culture of the Old Northwest, 1787–1861*, 70.

11. Arthur Clinton Boggess, *The Settlement of Illinois, 1778–1830*, 184. One historian noted, "At least half the anti-convention votes came from men of southern birth. Two of the most aggressive anti-slavery leaders, Coles and Cook, were born in slave-holding states. Clearly, then the great decision which finally closed the door to slave importation was largely due to the leadership and the votes of southern men." Evarts B. Greene, "Sectional Forces in the History of Illinois," *Transactions*, 1903, 76–77. In addition, few Illinoisans owned slaves or had a stake in slavery, the economy required no slave labor, and influential clergy solidly opposed slavery. James E. Herget, "Democracy Revisited: The Law and School Districts in Illinois," *JISHS*, May 1979. Skirmishing over this referendum is told in Leichtle, "The Rise of Jacksonian Politics in Illinois," 98–106.

12. The following counties favored calling a convention: Alexander, Fayette, Franklin, Gallatin, Hamilton, Jackson, Jefferson, Madison, Pope, Randolph, Wayne, and White. The following opposed: Bond,

Clark, Crawford, Edgar, Edwards, Fulton, Greene, Lawrence, Marion,
Montgomery, Monroe, Morgan, Pike, Sangamon, St. Clair, Union, and
Washington. Johnson County had a tie vote.

13. The serious threat the referendum posed to Illinois' future and the role Governor Coles played in defeating the threat are discussed in Robert M. Sutton, "Edward Coles and the Constitutional Crisis in Illinois, 1822–1824," *IHJ*, Spring 1989. Sutton indicates that Coles lacked traits necessary for long-term political success in the Jacksonian era's political wrangling. His formal, aristocratic bearing was a severe handicap in the era's frontier politics.

14. Emerson Davis, *The Half Century*, 202. For the impact of steamboats see Patricia Mooney Melvin, "Steamboats West: The Legacy of Transportation Revolution," *TON*, Winter 1981–1982. For more on the roles on western waters of flatboats and other forms of pre-steamboat transportation, see Michael Allen, *Western Rivermen, 1763–1861*.

15. Much of this discussion about steamboats and their impact on transportation and river towns comes from Allen, *Western Rivermen, 1763–1861*, especially 144, 149, 154, and 192–193.

16. For one thing, the sharp growth in steamboat activity on western waters allowed passengers to travel at ever-decreasing fares. Before the 1820s to travel upstream via steamboat from New Orleans to Louisville cost cabin passengers an average of $125 and deck passengers an average of $25. Downstream fares prior to 1820 were $75 and $18, respectively. During the 1840s the average fare for passengers either upstream or down was just $20 (cabin) and $4 (deck), which reflects the fact that steamboats had overcome the problems of upstream movement and were looking for passengers. Accompanying the greatly reduced fares were improvements in comfort and safety and reductions in time required for the trips. Haites, Mak, and Walton, *Western River Transportation*, 162. Flatboats continued to play important roles in trade and society, and they and supporting craft became specialized and sophisticated over time. For example, in the mid-1820s Timothy Flint observed vast assemblages of flatboats and other vessels at certain points on the river. These fleets proceeded downstream in much the manner that wagon caravans later made their way across the continent to Oregon and California. These fleets coalesced, drifted downstream, broke into parts, some of the parts rejoined and added newcomers, and again headed downstream, only to break into parts again, here and there some craft again coalescing with others. Flint observed a flotilla of eight flatboats, one of which was the scene of the slaughtering of hogs. Another flatboat was a dram and retail shop. He also discovered a tinner's establishment in one vessel, a blacksmith shop (which manufactured axes, scythes, and other tools) on another, and a dry goods store on still another. He concluded by noting one influence steamboats had on

flatboats: "It is now common to see flatboats worked by a bucket wheel, and a horse power, after the fashion of steam-boat movement." Timothy Flint, *Recollections of the Last Ten Years*, 104–105.

17. James E. Herget, "Democracy Revisited: The Law and School Districts in Illinois," 130–136.

18. Everett W. Kindig, "Journalist Hooper Warren Survives the Illinois Frontier," *IHJ*, Autumn 1986, 186. About 100 lead mines operated around Galena by 1825, and a year later some 453 operated. Roald D. Tweet, "Taming the Rapids of the Upper Mississippi," *WIRS*, Fall 1984, 49.

19. A fine account of Vandalia's rise and measured boosting associated with its success is Paul E. Stroble, Jr., *High on the Okaw's Western Bank: Vandalia, Illinois, 1819–39*.

20. Settlers in Illinois and surrounding states knew the advantages of wooded sites, and not until the mid-1820s and even later did settlers pass up timber to settle on prairie. Even when they settled on prairie, however, they often settled as close to timber as possible. For a detailed discussion of edge-of-woods settlement, Leslie Hewes, "Some Features of Early Woodland and Prairie Settlement in a Central Iowa County," *AAAG*, March 1950. For examples of edge-of-timber settlement in Illinois in 1821, see George W. Ogden, in Thwaites, ed., *Early Western Travels*, vol. 19, 56. He said the lack of timber on prairies would retard settlement for "some time," but he suggested the use of prairie coal could overcome the scarcity of fuel. He also believed that grasslands were devoid of trees because of the autumnal fires, suggesting that blocking these annual fires via settlement would spur timber growth on the prairies. See also Siyoung Park, "Perception of Land Quality and the Settlement of Northern Pike County 1821–1836," *WIRS*, Spring 1980.

21. General Thomas A. Smith's experiment in 1826 in plowing Illinois prairie grass was impressive, and helped to overcome prejudices against settling on prairies. Walter Havighurst, "The Way to Future City," *JISHS*, August 1976, 232–233.

22. One of the few accounts of scofflaws and other miscreants in frontier Illinois is by Richard Mason. He referred to "cut throats and murderers" infesting the Illinois countryside, a large region of southern Illinois "where these bandits have taken possession," and claimed, "Illinois is the hiding place for villains from every part of the United States and indeed, from every quarter of the globe. A majority of the settlers have been discharged from penitentiaries, and gaols or have been the victims of misfortune or imprudence. Many of those will reform, but many, very many are made fit for robbery and murder." Richard Lee Mason, *Narrative of Richard Lee Mason in the Pioneer West, 1819*, 20, 22, 29. Most people who wrote about crime in frontier Illinois avoided such hyperbole.

9. Migration, Trials, and Tragedy

1. Richard Powel, *Journey*, 6. Richard Lee Mason maintained, "A living is so easily obtained in the rich country that the most industrious of the inhabitants soon grow indolent." Mason, *Narrative*, 21.

2. British settlers placed great emphasis on being free from tithes and other encumbrances and on their ability to make it on their own. One source notes of British immigrants, "They placed a high premium on independence, and were able to support a relatively isolated existence by drawing comfort and companionship from family life and a circle of immigrant friends, and from their religious faith." Erickson, *Invisible Immigrants*, 78. On July 25, 1840, Charles Watts urged his brother to leave England for Illinois, arguing, "If you wish to live happy and independent, be a farmer. Why waste your strength in the service of a stranger when you might find it here under the shadow of your own vine, and enjoying the fruits of your labour, with a sure prospect of something to support you in old age." For more on high wages and feelings of independence, see Solomon Freeman, November 20, 1836.

3. *New Englander*, January 1846, 37–38. This publication, dedicated to spreading the Gospel in the West, lamented those feelings of independence which inhibited evangelization. Innumerable sources emphasized obvious signs of independence among yeoman farmers in Illinois and elsewhere. A British visitor in 1822–1823 observed, "In the United States a man, instead of renting a farm, can, for a small sum of money become a respectable landholder. He will no longer be pestered every quarter-day for rent, and tithes, and poor-rates. There is indeed a land-tax, but it is so trifling that it may be left out of any calculation, not being annually more than one farthing per acre." And then he added, "The emigrant becomes here independent: he is even considered as a member of the great political body; for, as is the case in the State of Illinois, after residing six months he is entitled to vote." Blane, *An Excursion through the United States and Canada during the Years 1822–23*, 167. See also James Caird, *Prairie Farming in America*, 57.

4. Strong feelings of independence and self-worth impressed numerous travelers to the United States. For example, in 1851 Carl Köhler, a young and perceptive visiting German, observed conditions in St. Clair County and elsewhere. After commenting on subscription school students, he wrote, "As soon as these young Americans have learned to spell, they reach fearlessly for their fathers' newspapers and begin at once to form political opinions. I have heard twelve-year-olds express themselves about politics and religion with a maturity that amazed me." He added, "At the age of sixteen, the young American male has more independence and greater masculinity than our German twenty-year-olds. Very early he hears the American motto, 'Be independent,'

and tries to acquire the skills and sharpen the capacities necessary for daily life." He then commented that "his mind grows uncommonly fast and bespeaks a sagacity common to all Americans." Frederic Trautmann, ed. and trans., "Eight Weeks on a St. Clair County Farm in 1851: Letters by a Young German," *JISHS*, Autumn 1982, 176.

5. Perhaps feelings of worth and voluntary political activity are what one observer meant when he wrote about settlers having "been compelled to settle themselves across these beautiful prairies and woodlands, and resort to measures from which are to spring, not only the wealth and physical power of this vast creation, but the moral impulses which are to guide her republican councils." A. D. Jones, *Illinois and the West*, 67. Belief in generative and regenerative qualities of western lands is a recurrent theme in literature about Illinois and the West.

6. Oscar B. Hamilton, ed., *History of Jersey County, Illinois*, 82, 84, 330.

7. For more on mortality and sickness, see M. Guy Bishop, Vincent Lacey, Richard Wixon, "Death at Mormon Nauvoo, 1843–1845," *WIRS*, Fall 1986, especially 71, 73, 77. And see R. Carlyle Buley, *The Old Northwest: Pioneer Period, 1815–1840*.

8. Legions of New Englanders plunged into the wilds of Illinois by the 1820s, girded up by their religious or social missions. One contemporary observer noted, "The western states are supplied from the northeastern with their merchants, doctors, schoolmasters, lawyers, and . . . New England is a *school*, a sort of manufactory of various professions fitted for all purposes—a talent bazaar, where you have anything at choice." Frederick Marryat, *A Diary in America*, 401. If a study of colonial Guilford, Connecticut, is any indication, many who left New England for western lands came from large families. Furthermore, most were unmarried and of modest means. People of means generally stayed in Guilford, married relatively early, and started families. John J. Waters, "Family, Inheritance, and Migration in Colonial New England: The Evidence from Guilford, Connecticut," *W&MQ*, January 1982, 82, 85, 86.

9. John F. Brooks helped found Illinois College, a product of clergy and lay people in Jacksonville and students in Yale College Theological Department, who formed the Illinois Association (later the "Yale Band") to establish the college. A student in Yale College Theological Department at New Haven, Connecticut, Brooks warned of Roman Catholicism's growing influence in the Mississippi Valley, urging counter measures by New Englanders. John F. Brooks, July 4, 1829. George W. Ogden, a Massachusetts merchant, traveled in the West for two years, visiting the American Bottom. Carrying New England predilections with him, he observed Kaskaskia "appears to be rapidly going to decay," and claimed to have found just one French person "who appeared to have

any just idea of the advantages of improvement." He then wrote, "The men here appear to know hardly any thing about agriculture, but follow, for a living, hunting and fishing." Finally, after noting the French were Roman Catholic and had a cathedral, he lamented, "it is not likely that they will very soon be brought out of that indolence and superstition, to which, at present, they are so rigidly attached." These views were common among New Englanders. Ogden, in Thwaites, ed., *Early Western Travels*, vol. 19, 60–61.

10. For analysis of the hybrid society in western Illinois produced by different streams of migration, see Susan S. Rugh, "Creating a Farm Community: Fountain Green Township, 1825–1840," *WIRS*, Fall 1990, 6–12.

11. The first steamboats, one source indicates, astonished people who saw one for the first time. Some river merchants were reluctant to entrust cargo to the new contraptions. James T. Lloyd, *Lloyd's Steamboat Directory*, 42.

12. For some indication of the ties between Indians and British and the extent to which Indians truly hoped for British support, see Anthony F. C. Wallace's introduction, 38, 45–46, 49–50, in Ellen M. Whitney, ed., *The Black Hawk War*, vol. 1. The nature of these ties was a matter of discussion not only in Illinois but as far away as Massachusetts. On August 3, 1831, the *Hampshire Gazette*, of Northampton, Massachusetts, claimed the visits of Indians to British posts in Canada "kept alive and cherished" a "rancorous hostility" by the Indians against the United States since the conclusion of the War of 1812. The article also refers to "the British Band of the Sac and Fox tribes, who have obstinately refused to quit the lands on which they have no claim whatever." The idea of "the British Band" was particularly odious to people north of the Ohio, many of whom still nursed stark memories of British-backed Indians launching raids during the War of 1812.

13. Not everyone panicked, however. Interestingly, perhaps women were less prone to panic than men. For example, Harriet Buckmaster wrote to her husband on May 27, 1832, "if one would [be] foolish enough to believe one half we hear we would be frightened every day."

14. Michael Clodfelter, *Warfare and Armed Conflicts: A Statistical Reference*, vol. 1, 447.

10. Excitement in the Land

1. For the dip in Chicago's population, see *A Guide to the City of Chicago*, 61. Albert Larson and Siim Soot, "Population and Social Geography," in Nelson, Ronald E., ed., *Illinois: Land and Life in the Prairie State*, 142. A contemporary source indicated how the Black Hawk War and two severe winters did "much towards improving the coun-

try" as far south as central Illinois by driving off "the lazy, dissipated N. & S. Carolinians, Georgians, Tennesseans. The Almighty . . . has admonished them to seek some more congenial climate—where winter is a pleasant holiday." Their abandoned farms were bought at bargain prices. Simeon Francis, May 4, 1832.

2. Patrick Shirreff, *A Tour through North America; Together with a Comprehensive View of the Canadas and the United States*, 226.

3. M. H. Tilden, *The History of Stephenson County*, 225.

4. Susan S. Rugh, "Creating a Farm Community," 8.

5. As one source put it, "Whether denigrated as ignoble savages or idealized as Native Americans living in perfect equilibrium and harmony with the environment, the Indians are given no credit for opening up the Eastern Woodlands, for creating much of America's grasslands, and for transforming hardwoods to piney woods with their "woods-burning habit." M. J. Bowden, "The Invention of American Tradition," *JHG*, January 1992, 20.

6. James Hall, *Notes on the Western States*, 252, 253, 257, 262. For more adulation of Indians during the 1830s, see, for example, "Uncle Gregory," October 19, 1839. But a Unitarian publication in 1837 commented on the recent Indian removal from Illinois, "The Pottowottomies were a savage and treacherous race—cruel to foe and faithless to friend; and we must rejoice that they are removed from lands they can no longer subsist upon, to those endless Hunting grounds beyond the Mississippi." W. S., "Prairie Voyage," *The Western Messenger; Devoted to Religion and Literature*, vol. 4, no. II, October 1837, 106.

7. John E. Hallwas, "Eliza Farnham's *Life in Prairie Land*," *TON*, Winter 1981–1982, 317–318.

8. Derived from Pease, *The Frontier State, 1818–1848*, 176–177.

9. Malcolm J. Rohrbough, *The Land Office Business*, 234.

10. Siyoung Park, "Land Speculation in Western Illinois: Pike County, 1821–1835," *JISHS*, Summer 1984, especially 117, 119, 126. Factors contributing to the surge in settlement in the Military Tract are noted in Rugh, "Creating a Farm Community," 9. Yankee settlement in western Illinois is discussed in John Leighly, "Town Names of Colonial New England in the West," *AAAG*, June 1978, 238–239.

11. Patrick E. McLear, "Land Speculators and Urban and Regional Development: Chicago in the 1830's," *TON*, Summer 1980, 137, 139.

12. David J. Baxter, "William Cullen Bryant: Illinois Landowner," *WIRS*, Spring 1978, 6, 9.

13. A. W. French, "Men and Manners of the Early Days in Illinois," *Transactions*, 1903, 71.

14. McLear, "Land Speculators and Urban and Regional Development," 145. On January 1, 1837, Daniel Goodnough wrote from the Des

Plaines River to his brother in Rutland County, Vermont, predicting, "I think that you & Bela might do well on your money here. The law allows twelve persent [*sic*] and none expect to get it less." Charles Watts, writing on July 25, 1840, claimed that in emergencies the 12 percent was abandoned and 20 percent was earned. Despite high interest rates, which reflected uncertainties and high risks, Illinoisans thrived on capital loaned to them by countless ordinary Easterners, Britons, and others.

15. Burton, "James Semple, Prairie Entrepreneur," 69.

16. *New England Farmer and Gardener's Journal*, vol. 17, No. 3, July 25, 1838, 19.

17. Charles Joseph Latrobe, *The Rambler in North America*, 206.

18. One "paper town" consisted of just one house, but lots there sold for $2,500 each. So wild was the speculation in urban lots and in the founding of towns that one serious Chicago observer proposed reserving one or two sections per township for farming. Ray A. Billington, "The Frontier in Illinois History," *JISHS*, Spring 1950, 39, 41. Even as late as the sluggish early 1840s, maps of paper towns festooned inns and taverns across Illinois. William Oliver, for example, visited Kaskaskia, where he saw in the barroom of the hotel "a splendid plan of an extensive city of the name of Downingville, with churches, public buildings, squares, etc." Upon inquiring about it, he learned it "was no other than an imaginary city of that wretched place, Kaskaskia Landing. This is one of the schemes of the speculator in town lots." Oliver, *Eight Months in Illinois*, 54.

19. Low thresholds and jacks-of-all-trades abound in the Jenkins family's activities. Helen Walker Linsenmeyer, "Three Generations of River Commerce: The Jenkins Family of Grand Tower," *JISHS*, Spring 1980, especially 55, 56, 60. John Wright, a major player in Chicago's early growth, tried his hand as a "store keeper, real estate investor, manufacturer, editor, writer, educational reformer, lobbyist, park planner, railroad promoter, and researcher in the techniques of the new agriculture." Edward W. Wolner, "The City Builder in Chicago: 1834–1871," *TON*, Spring 1987, 17. Low threshold requirements, in general, and the absence of professional standards and means of enforcing standards encouraged many people to dabble in varied undertakings.

20. Friends and relatives often speculated modestly for others, using money entrusted to them for that purpose. Ray Billington identified four kinds of speculators: ordinary farmers who took up more land than needed in order to sell the excess acreage at a profit; individual Easterners with enough capital to acquire a sizeable estate; ordinary entrepreneurs and bankers engaging in speculation for extra profit; and, large scale capitalists who controlled huge holdings of land

and served as a brokers by arranging to sell parcels to individual settlers. In William L. Burton, "James Semple, Prairie Entrepreneur," *IHJ*, Summer 1987, 68. These four models have merit, but each had variations.

21. A. D. Jones, *Illinois and the West*, 227.

22. Struggles between squatters and large-scale speculators in eighteenth-century America and difficulties in ousting squatters are discussed in Gregory H. Nobles, " Breaking into the Backcountry: New Approaches to the Early American Frontier, 1750–1800," *W&MQ*, October 1989, 654–656. In some ways these struggles pitted outside, dynamic, impersonal forces of change and modernity against rural folk, who had local values and who strove to maintain traditional arrangements and modes of production.

23. A. D. Jones, *Illinois and the West*, 229. Addressing the question of the quality and location of land obtained by nonresident speculators is Gordana Rezab, "Land Speculation in Fulton County 1817–1832," *WIRS*, Spring 1980.

24. Oliver, *Eight Months in Illinois*, 190.

25. Siyoung Park, "Land Speculation in Western Illinois: Pike County, 1821–1835," 117, 119, 126, 127.

11. Transportation, Towns, Institutions

1. Walter Havighurst's account of the construction, operation, and significance of the National Road abides. Havighurst, *Land of Promise: The Story of the Northwest Territory*, chapter 19. See also Karl Raitz, ed., *A Guide to the National Road*. Although the National Road arrived belatedly in Illinois, it impressed most who traveled on it. Nevertheless, some found it unimpressive. William Oliver, a Briton traveling in the early 1840s, struck the National Road at Vandalia. Noting that several miles of the road east of Vandalia had been completed through a swamp, he admitted that the road made it possible to traverse the swamp, and he pronounced it "a tolerably direct line from Wheeling, on the Ohio." He then complained, "Most of this road is nothing more than a track," and he implied the quality of its construction was questionable. He suggested the relatively dry climate would enable the road to withstand "a great deal of passage." Oliver, *Eight Months in Illinois*, 187–188.

2. Oliver, *Eight Months in Illinois*, 226.

3. See, for example, William L. Burton, "The Life and Death of Bloody Island: A Ferry Tale," *WIRS*, Spring 1988, 9.

4. Ronald E. Shaw, *Erie Water West: A History of the Erie Canal, 1792–1854*, 276. Shaw also notes that the wheat belt, which had been

solidly established in New York, moved westward between 1833 and 1843, resulting in a 30-percent decrease in wheat grown in New York between the early 1830s and the early 1840s. It moved to Ohio and later to Illinois.

5. Emerson Davis, *The Half Century*, 203. For details on facets of travel on Great Lakes steamers and on the Erie Canal, see Oliver, *Eight Months in Illinois*, 226–228.

6. Grenville Mellen, ed., *A Book of the United States*, 461. Flatboats and keelboats diminished in importance with the surge of steamboats, but flatboats still played a vital role. From 1823 to 1861, flatboats still commanded "20 percent of the total inland river commerce," and they "remained profitable and competitive vis-a-vis steamboats and canal boats for many reasons." Flatboat crews became more efficient, reduced overhead, relied on steamboats for a speedy and safe return home, and made several trips a year. Eventually, steamboats towed some flatboats back upstream for reuse. Keelboats were less able to adapt, and suffered irreparable decline. Allen, *Western Rivermen, 1763–1861*, 144, 154, 227.

7. Hall, *Notes on the Western States*, 263. For the speeds at which steamboats chugged up and down rivers, see W. G. Lyford, *The Western Address Directory*, 460.

8. In 1820 at least forty-three steam engines operated in the country, most of them west of the Appalachians. Although Indiana had two engines in 1820, Illinois had none. Jeremy Atack and Fred Bateman, "The Development of Industrial Steam Power in the Midwest with Special Reference to Indiana," *TON*, Winter 1982–1983, 330. Illinois got its first steam mills during the 1820s.

9. Helen Walker Linsenmeyer, "Three Generations of River Commerce," 56–58.

10. The diffusion and significance of New England place names in the West are discussed in John Leighly, "Town Names of Colonial New England in the West," *AAAG*, June 1978. Of twelve states comprising the Old Northwest and portions of the Great Plains, Illinois led in total number of town names of colonial New England, boasting 2,544. Interestingly, Missouri's 2,328 placed it in second place. The mean was 1,957. Leighly, "Town Names of Colonial New England in the West," 237.

11. Quoted in Mark Wyman, *Immigrants in the Valley: Irish, Germans and Americans in the Upper Mississippi Country, 1830–1860*, 95. Sickness was only one problem slowing construction of the canal. Even so, one observer in 1842 speculated the canal would be finished in 1844, four years before actual completion. Oliver, *Eight Months in Illinois*, 228.

12. In 1839 a committee of the House of Representatives projected great benefits for state-sponsored railroads. A Senate committee was

somewhat less sanguine, tempering the advantages of rail transportation light articles and general travel with the observation that canals were preferable for "cumbrous articles." A. W. French, "Men and Manners of the Early Days in Illinois," *Transactions*, *1903*, 66–67. A fine analysis of transportation options available in 1842, their advantages and disadvantages, and such supporting facilities as inns is found in Oliver, *Eight Months in Illinois*, 224–230.

13. For example, on January 12, 1838, months before the railroad began operating, the proposed route alarmed residents of Mt. Sterling, and because it excluded Mt. Sterling, "a perfect astonishment pervades all classes of the people in as much as the law expressly provides for its passing through Mt. Sterling." If the transient Northern Cross railway triggered such alarm, the surging and permanent railways of the 1850s often caused outright panic by bypassing towns. James W. Stephenson, January 12, 1838.

14. A. W. French, "Men and Manners of the Early Days in Illinois," 66–67. The report, furthermore, indicated an early underlying idea concerning the use of railroads, an idea that was especially prominent among people in the South and, perhaps, people in Illinois from the South. These people believed that railroads should, first and foremost, serve steamboats, not serve as an entirely separate form of transportation. The report observed that if plans for railroads in Illinois were carried out the railroads would "bring most portions of the State within 70 or 80 miles of a navigable stream." Railroads were used to connect people to navigable streams in much of the South, but this practice was less common in the North. As early as 1833, Charles Butler, an eastern financier, and his brother-in-law, William B. Ogden, saw the geographic advantages afforded Chicago by its location, and they realized that Chicago's hinterland could someday reach into the Great Plains. Ogden in 1835 advocated railroads for his adopted town of Chicago, foreseeing a time when Chicago would be part of a rail network stretching from the East Coast to Illinois and then down to New Orleans. Edward W. Wolner, "The City Builder in Chicago," 9–12.

15. Political and constitutional changes triggered by anger and frustration over legislative ineptness are ably analyzed in Rodney O. Davis, "'The People in Miniature': The Illinois General Assembly, 1818–1848," *IHJ*, Summer 1988.

16. Beneficial and detrimental effects of decisions are discussed at length in Robert P. Sutton, "Illinois River Towns: Economic Units or Melting Pots," *WIRS*, Fall 1990, 21–31.

17. Residents of Illinois understood relationships between wet ground and disease. One observer also understood the roles winds play in sickness: "On rivers, and marshes, the western side is esteemed healthier than the eastern side; as the prevailing winds during the summer and

autumn months are from the west, or some of the neighbouring points." Oliver, *Eight Months in Illinois*, 234.

18. William D. Walters, Jr., "The Fanciful Geography of 1836," *TON*, Winter 1983–84, 333–339.

19. William D. Walters, Jr., "Early Western Illinois Town Advertisements: A Geographical Inquiry," *WIRS*, Spring 1985. Additional features of towns, town size, and distance between towns in frontier Illinois and nearby states are noted in Thomas R. Mahoney, *River Towns in the Great West*, chapter 7, and 282–284. In general, the larger the town, the greater the distance between it and other towns.

20. The meteoric rise of tavern theater in Chicago during the 1830s is discussed in Arthur W. Bloom, "Tavern Theater in Early Chicago," *JISHS*, Autumn 1981. Tavern theater's success in Chicago probably sprang from its polyglot, bustling, and open nature, which contrasted starkly with communities founded by dedicated, focused colonies. It also suggests that powerful Yankee influence in Chicago was not omnipotent. Yankees heavily influenced Chicago's economics and politics, but their social influence was channeled and muted.

21. Easterners who never came to Illinois influenced the development of the state. Businessmen and bankers, for example, in New York, Philadelphia, and elsewhere maintained commercial ties with partners and clients in Illinois. Some prominent people observed Illinois from afar, and made suggestions concerning its development. For example, the talented and influential Philip Hone, sometime mayor of New York City, wrote in his diary on January 15, 1832, "I attended a meeting of a few gentlemen this afternoon at Mr. Bucknor's office to confer with Mr. Pugh, one of the canal commissioners of the State of Illinois who has been appointed to visit New York in relation to the raising of funds to construct a railroad from the head of navigation on the Illinois River, a distance of 90 miles, to Chicago, near the southern outlet of Lake Michigan." He then added an idea that guided the actions of many people in the East and in northern Illinois: "This project would be a great advantage to the State of New York, as it would divert the trade of the new Western States bordering on the lakes from New Orleans to our seaport." Philip Hone, in Allan Nevins, *The Diary of Philip Hone, 1828–1851*, 55. Although the canal was not completed for another sixteen years and the suggested railroad for another two decades and more, the basic idea was sound; improved transportation between the Illinois River and Chicago rerouted trade from a north-south axis, from the upper Mississippi to New Orleans, to an east-west axis, from the upper Mississippi region to New York.

22. Wolner, "The City Builder in Chicago," especially 11–19.

23. Advocating railroad construction, he gazed into the future and saw "continuous railways from New York to Lake Erie, and south of

Lake Erie, through Ohio, Indiana, and Illinois, to the waters of the Mississippi, and connecting with railroads running to Cincinnati, and Louisville in Kentucky, and Nashville in Tennessee, and to New Orleans," which he believed would be "the most splendid system of internal communication ever yet devised by man." Quoted in Wolner, "The City Builder in Chicago," 12. For more on Ogden see William L. Downard, "William Butler Ogden and the Growth of Chicago," *JISHS*, Spring 1982, and Wolner, "The City Builder in Chicago," especially 4–18.

24. For some factors that inhibited education in Illinois and elsewhere, see Edward W. Stevens, Jr., "Structural and Ideological Dimensions of Literacy and Education in the Old Northwest," in David C. Klingaman and Richard K. Vedder, eds., *Essays on the Economy of the Old Northwest*, especially 158–159, 167–170, 174–180.

25. *The Past and Present of Woodford County, Illinois*, 285–286. One source claimed that in Illinois in 1848 there were "two hundred and fifty-five thousand children of a proper age for school, only eighty-five thousand of whom attend school at all—that is one in three." *New Englander*, vol. 7 (New Series, vol. 1), 1849, 599. Perhaps school attendance slumped as waves of immigrants poured into Illinois in the late 1840s, possibly overwhelming existing schools. The figures for the state are in S. Augustus Mitchell, *A General View of the United States*, 82–83.

26. For more on Lincoln and the lyceum movement, see Thomas F. Schwartz, "The Springfield Lyceums and Lincoln's 1838 Speech," *IHJ*, Spring 1990, especially 45–49.

27. Juliet E. K. Walker, "Entrepreneurial Ventures in the Origin of Nineteenth-Century Agricultural Towns, Pike County, 1823–1880," *IHJ*, Spring 1985, 47–48.

28. The Deep Snow and the Sudden Freeze curbed tobacco and cotton production in Illinois, virtually wiping it out in many places. Nevertheless, both were still grown here and there. For example, in St. Clair County the chief crop was corn by the 1850s, but even then a visitor noted, "Tobacco and cotton are grown only for household use, though tobacco thrives and could become a major crop." Trautmann, ed. and trans., "Eight Weeks on a St. Clair County Farm in 1851."

29. John Carroll Power, *History of the Early Settlers, Sangamon County, Illinois*, 67.

12. Social Clashes and Economic Collapse

1. To cite just one example, German Catholic immigrants stopped at Cincinnati to learn about the West before pushing on. There they formed a colony and chose three men to scout for a place to locate. The men ventured westward in April 1837, examined numerous potential

sites, selected land about three miles east of Effingham, and arranged to buy 10,000 acres, mostly public land. The colonists left Cincinnati, established themselves at the site, and soon built a town, aptly named Teutopolis.

2. One study demonstrates the southern sense of place is "the hallmark of their regional identity." This sense focused on the "the orderly linking of names and places." Barbara Allen and Thomas J. Schlereth, eds., *Sense of Place: American Regional Cultures*, 152, 160.

3. Not only did Puritans look upon many French and Spanish residents of Illinois as slothful and lacking in other qualities, but some cousins of the Puritans, the British, regarded this residual population in much the same way. For example, in 1842 one Briton noted general decay in Kaskaskia and then observed the population was "largely mixed with half-breed French, a race of people remarkable for little besides indolence." Oliver, *Eight Months in Illinois*, 54. Of course Oliver did not see the French and mixed population at their prime energetic state, the early and middle years of the eighteen century. Charles Carter Langdon, who grew up in New England, visited Meredosia in 1842, where on Sunday morning he found "a half dozen cross-eyed Dutchmen" standing in the door of a bar, "luxuriating over a bottle of whiskey." John E. Hallwas, "Quincy and Meredosia in 1842: Charles Carter Langdon's Travel Letters," *WIRS*, Fall 1979, 134.

4. D. W. Meinig, *The Shaping of America: A Geographical Perspective on 500 years of History, Volume 2, Continental America, 1800–1867*, 266. For more on the work of Dwight and his fellow Yankees, see M. J. Bowden, "The Invention of American Tradition," *JHG*, 18, 1 (1992), 18–20.

5. Perhaps by way of projection, worried Yankees and their allies assailed Southerners for numerous alleged shortcomings: idleness, wife swapping, excessive resting, being dirty, having lice, exploding in passion, and eagerness to shed social restraints. Robert W. McCluggage, "The Pioneer Squatter," *IHJ*, Spring 1989, 48–49.

6. Mason, *Narrative*, 31.

7. After observing emotionally laden, physically exhausting worship, Dr. Horatio Newhall, a native of Massachusetts, heaped scorn on Methodists: "I attended one of their meetings on the Sabbath, but the wild, superstitious & frantic actions of these poor deluded people excited in my breast the strongest emotions of pity and disgust." Some people, he claimed, suffered "genuine hysteria," while others "were thrown into convulsions or affected with what is here called 'the jerks,' involuntarily throwing their head backwards & forwards with so much rapidity that no feature of their countenance, not even the figure of the head could be distinguished, and they are often so much 'exercised by the Spirit' on these occasions, as to labor under bodily indisposition for a

considerable length of time." Some danced, leaped, whirled on their heads, and engaged in uncontrolled laughter. Newhall added, "With respect to Politics, we [in Illinois] are but little more advanced than in the great subject of religion." Newhall, October 1821.

8. *The Past and Present in Woodford County, Illinois*, 230. A defective item with flaws deliberately obscured for sale was "yankeed over." Oliver, *Eight Months in Illinois*, 68.

9. In fact, they even organized the New England Society of Chicago. A native of the Northeast, Asa Fitch arrived in Greenville and on February 18, 1831, reflected on friction between Yankees and others, quoting someone as saying Yankees were "'the most despicable folks in the country'" because they "'always club together on every occasion." Northerners' cohesiveness frequently annoyed Southerners and others, who often founded few institutions and combined efforts largely on an *ad hoc* basis.

10. Christiana Holmes Tillson, *A Woman's Story of Pioneer Illinois*, 122–123. In 1820 Mary Norwood Leggett, a settler from the northeastern part of the country received rude treatment from residents of Illinois of southern origin, noting in 1820, "They called us Yankees, a term of great reproach in this state . . . and expressed great contempt for us." This pejorative use of the term "Yankee" occurred in the context of heated rhetoric over the Missouri Compromise.

11. Charles Church, *Past and Present of the City of Rockford and Winnebago County, Illinois*, 56.

12. Ronald E. Nelson, "The Bishop Hill Colony: What They Found," *WIRS*, Fall 1989, 44.

13. Trautmann, ed. and trans., "Eight Weeks on a St. Clair County Farm in 1851," 176–177.

14. Oliver, *Eight Months in Illinois*, 177–178. One source notes, "To some extent, the adage appears true that Yankee and Southerner avoided one another and did not settle in the same place." Timothy Frazer, "Language Variation in the Military Tract," *WIRS*, Spring 1982, 55.

15. Paul Finkelman, "Slavery, the 'More Perfect Union,' and the Prairie State," *IHJ*, Winter 1987, 259–260. For more on proposed colonization and black resistance to the idea, see Roger D. Bridges, "Dark Faces on the Antebellum West Central Illinois Landscape," *WIRS*, Fall 1983, especially 70–71.

16. Meinig, *The Shaping of America*, 268–269. Lucy Jayne Botscharow-Kamau, "Neighbors: Harmony and Conflict on the Indiana Frontier," *JER*, Winter 1991, 525–26. For precise differences in speech patterns, see Frazer, "Language Variation in the Military Tract," *WIRS*, Spring 1982.

17. For an example of culture that stood in sharp opposition to New England culture, see Robert Bray, "Beating the Devil: Life and Art in

Peter Cartwright's Autobiography," *IHJ*, Autumn 1985. Cartwright berated seminary-trained clergy who *read* sermons without passion. On the other hand, he had a true compassion for fallen humans, interceding on behalf of women of "ill-fame" and insisting that if repentant they had the same claim to salvation as many of the hypocritical men in the audience. He did, however, call upon fallen women to redirect their efforts. Most New Englanders in Illinois adhered to the Whig Party, and later the Republican Party, which contrasted with Cartwright's stark loyalty to the Democratic Party.

18. John D. Haeger, "The Abandoned Townsite on the Midwestern Frontier: A Case Study of Rockwell, Illinois." *JER*, Summer 1983, 165, and 167, 171, 174, 178, 179, 180, 183.

19. Ronald E. Nelson, "The Bishop Hill Colony: What They Found," 42.

20. Pease, *The Frontier State, 1818–1848*, 29.

21. For more on this Maryland-Kentucky-Illinois Catholic connection, see Rugh, "Creating a Farm Community," 14–15.

22. Ronald E. Nelson, "The Bishop Hill Colony: What They Found," 42. Frances Landon Willard, who sniffed at uncultured residents of the Illinois frontier, snorted at the prospects of Roman Catholics succeeding in frontier Illinois. Arriving in backwoods Illinois in 1836, by 1850 she lived in Peoria, where there was keen competition between denominations and religious schools. Using characteristically strong language for the day, she lamented, "The Catholics have edged out a Protestant in the purchase of a House for a school and now perhaps the place 'will be devoted to the Worship of the Beast.'" Jack Nortrup, "The Troubles of an Itinerant Teacher in the Early Nineteenth Century," *JISHS*, November 1978, 286–287.

23. Nelson, "The Bishop Hill Colony: What They Found," 44.

24. Although he had once owned slaves, Governor Duncan denounced Lovejoy's killing, but he also pinned the blame on radical abolitionists. Further, as a trustee of Illinois College he came to believe the college was infested with abolitionists, so he offered to resign this office.

25. McLear, "Land Speculators and Urban and Regional Development," 149.

26. *A Guide to the City of Chicago*, 61.

27. Patrick E. McLear, "The Galena and Chicago Union Railroad: A Symbol of Chicago's Economic Maturity," *JISHS*, Spring 1980, 18–19. Hog prices were so low that producers drove them to Chicago themselves, where they learned hog raising was unprofitable. E. Duis, *The Good Old Times in McLean County, Illinois*, 15.

28. This incident is recounted in Lois A. Carrier, *Illinois: Crossroads of a Continent*, 86.

29. In reality, founding a town required several steps: the speculator,

or proprietor as he was legally known, hired the county surveyor, or a deputy surveyor, to survey the site at a cost of twenty-five cents per lot, the surveyor drafted a town plat, one showing numbered lots, streets, reserved public grounds such as the lot for a court and other significant features; the surveyor then planted a rock or another substantial object, from which additional surveys were made; finally, the surveyor filed the plat with the county recorder, paying four cents per lot, and the recorder entered the transaction in the deed record book. Speed, efficiency, and reasonable cost usually attended these steps.

30. Ray Billington referred to "starry-eyed speculators" of all classes whose pragmatism and non-ideological temperament helped them obtain land. Ray A. Billington, "The Frontier in Illinois History," *JISHS*, Spring 1950, 39–40.

31. Laura Smith Porter, "'The Last, Best Hope of Earth': Abraham Lincoln's Perception of America, 1834–1854," *IHJ*, Autumn 1985, 209.

32. John Bailhache, *Brief Sketch of the Life and Editorial Career of John Bailhache*, 23–24.

33. *New England Farmer and Gardener's Journal*, July 15, 1838, 19.

34. This huge step prompted in 1846 congressional consideration of a homestead bill, which sought to bestow free public land on resident settlers who improved the land. This recurring idea finally became law in 1862, overcoming opposition from Middle Atlantic states and New England.

35. Stephen Aron, "Pioneers and Profiteers: Land Speculation and the Homestead Ethic in Frontier Kentucky," *WHQ*, May 1992, 198.

36. Some people believed that social problems stemmed from the diverse nature of the population. For instance, Mrs. R. N. Wright wrote on January 11, 1847, "Wickedness increases here as the country is filling up with every variety of people and character."

37. Wolner, "The City Builder in Chicago," 9.

13. Race, Ethnicity, and Class

1. Hamilton, ed., *History of Jersey County, Illinois*, 258–259.

2. J. C. McBride, *Past and Present of Christian County, Illinois*, 75. In fights in nearby Macon County, "it was seldom the parties resorted to knives or pistols; that was gross cowardice." Disputes, especially those involving honor, were "settled in the fisticuff style, and the fellow that was beaten said so, and they quit, shook hands and were friends again." Spectators who knew the fighters did not take part, even to separate the fighters. Rather, they made sure it was a "fair fight." Smith, *History of Macon County, Illinois*, 156. Often fights were followed by a "friendly drink." See, for example, S. J. Clark, *History of McDonough County, Illinois*, 46.

3. Mellen, ed., *A Book of the United States*, 461.

4. Richard Maxwell Brown, *Strain of Violence: Historical Studies of*
American Violence and Vigilantism, 309. Significantly, Brown indicates
that well over twenty of the slain died in the southern third of the state.
Most of those, moreover, died in the late 1840s, long after the frontier
had faded there. Varieties of Regulator activity, degrees of severity, and
diverse results are analyzed in Patrick B. Nolan, *Vigilantes on the Middle
Border: A Study of Self-Appointed Law Enforcement in the States of
the Upper Mississippi from 1840 to 1880.*

5. J. D. B. De Bow, comp., *Mortality Statistics of the Seventh Census
of the United States, 1850*, 79–85, 88–89. Some frontier counties experienced murders in their very early days, before settlers swarmed across
the land, or in later years, when the frontier was fading. Others had a
few scattered over the years. In Clark County just two murders marred
the first twelve years. William Henry Perrin, ed., *History of Crawford
and Clark Counties, Illinois*, 252. Hancock County, formed in January
of 1825, suffered its first murder in mid-1832. T. Gregg, *History of
Hancock County, Illinois*, 506. Schuyler County, also formed in January of 1825, saw its first murderer indicted in May 1831, and Brown
County, organized in early 1839, saw no murder until late 1852. *Combined History of Schuyler and Brown Counties, Illinois*, 14, 132. In Boone
County, as was true of many counties, the first court business was nearly
entirely of a civil nature. The county was formed in 1837, and as late as
1877 only forty-nine convictions for criminal offenses marred the county's
history of tranquility. Larceny accounted for thirty-two of them, burglary for seven, rape for two, counterfeiting for two, and manslaughter
for three. Moreover, some of these crimes were caused by transients.
The Past and Present of Boone County, Illinois, 244.

6. *The History of Will County, Illinois*, 261–262.

7. Mark E. Steiner, ed., "Abolitionists and Escaped Slaves in Jacksonville. Samuel Willard's 'My First Adventure with a Fugitive Slave:
The story of it and how it failed,'" *IHJ*, Winter 1996, 213–232. Helping
slaves gain freedom was nothing new for the Willard family. Religion
motivated them to get involved. For another runaway case in 1843 involving Judge Lockwood and religious motivation—a case won by a
slave owner from Randolph County, Andrew Borders—see Carol Pirtle, *"Andrew Borders v. William Hayes: Indentured Servitude and the
Underground Railroad in Illinois,"* *IHJ*, Autumn 1996. This case again
produced no serious violence. Both sides cut legal corners in this struggle,
but not enough to provoke mayhem. For antislavery activity in Bureau
County, see Karen Berfield, "Three Antislavery Leaders of Bureau
County," *WIRS*, Spring 1980.

8. Juliet E. K. Walker, *Free Frank McWhorter*. Free Frank's energy
and his other fine qualities probably went far in overcoming prejudice.
Many people north of the Ohio feared that Southerners would dump
their old, incapacitated, and feeble blacks on them. Nicole Etcheson,

The Emerging Midwest, 100. This fear produced efforts to restrict migration of blacks to Illinois and elsewhere.

9. Don Harrison Doyle, *The Social Order of a Frontier Community: Jacksonville, Illinois, 1825–70*, 57.

10. Roger D. Bridges, ed., "John Mason Peck on Illinois Slavery," *JISHS*, Autumn 1982, 181–205. Mason favored confining slavery to the South. Very likely, Missouri's entry to the Union as a slave state prompted Mason's move from Missouri to Illinois. Frances Landon Willard also ardently opposed both slavery and abolitionists. She favored gradual emancipation. Nortrup, "The Troubles of an Itinerant Teacher in the Early Nineteenth Century," 284. Many complexities and apparent contradiction in views concerning slavery, blacks, fugitives, kidnaping, and related matters are found in Paul Finkelman, "Slavery, the 'More Perfect Union,' and the Prairie State," *IHJ*, Winter 1987, 258–262, 266–267.

11. "Proceedings of the Illinois State Anti-Slavery Convention Held at Upper Alton on the Twenty-Sixth, Twenty-Seventh & Twenty-Eighth of Oct. 1837."

12. As political parties buckled under the weight of the national crisis over slavery and as abolitionism became increasingly strident, some Upland Southerners in the Midwest "resurrected their distrust of sneaky and conniving Yankees and aligned themselves in sympathy with the South." Etcheson, *The Emerging Midwest*, 118. People of good will felt shoved and pulled in various directions. Moral confusion among Illinoisans over the slave crisis is depicted in a work of fiction from the 1850s, Francis Grierson's *The Valley of the Shadows*. See also Robert Bray, "The Mystical Landscape: Francis Grierson's *The Valley of the Shadows*," *TON*, Winter 1979–1980, especially 367–368.

13. "Collegiate Education in the Western States," *New Englander*, vol. 4, 1846, 276, 278–279.

14. Jim Redd, *The Illinois and Michigan Canal*, 55, 56.

15. Mary Neth, "Gender and the Family Labor System: Defining Work in the Rural Midwest," *JSH*, Spring 1994, 563. Although even British immigrants in America often never became full members of the larger society, they were not in conflict with it. Erickson, *Invisible Immigrants*, 76.

16. Nortrup, "The Troubles of an Itinerant Teacher in the Early Nineteenth Century," 281.

17. Not coincidentally, the September 1996 issue of *American Heritage* focused on violence in America, and it put on its cover a photo of two shooting victims from the 1870s lying on a boardwalk in Hays, Kansas. To its credit, the article stresses that fact that even the trans-Mississippian frontier saw less sociopathic, wanton violence than occurs today. Further, the article correctly associates frontier violence

467

with relatively large numbers of single males, a social condition often present in trans-Mississippian frontiers but not in frontier Illinois.

18. Our frontier heritage, Michael A. Bellesîles points out, is blamed for producing our relatively violent culture. Virtually all settlers, he notes, allegedly toted firearms and sought regeneration through violence. But Bellesîles argues that evidence from the late eighteenth and nineteenth centuries demonstrates that "we have it all backwards." He demonstrates a dearth of firearms on the frontier until the mid-1800s, just when frontier Illinois was fading rapidly. Until 1849–1850, in fact, gun ownership rates among settlers were always slightly below national rates and far below rates among Southerners. Surprisingly, firearm ownership rates among northeastern urban dwellers were higher than ownership rates among pioneers until 1849–1850. Samuel Colt's ingenuity in the 1840s democratized firearm ownership. Markedly increased weapon production and falling prices encouraged widespread ownership. Even so, Union Army officers during the Civil War were appalled at their men's lack of familiarity with firearms, and two veterans formed the NRA to maintain familiarity with firearms in time of peace. Michael A. Bellesîles, "The Origins of Gun Culture in the United States, 1760–1865," *JAH*, September 1996.

19. William Oliver, *Eight Months in Illinois*, 68. This shoulder rubbing sometimes softened or removed objectionable qualities as Northerners met Southerners: In Richland County, for example, "the social customs of each section modified the other, and while the amusements and incidents of public occasions took on much of that boisterous character common to southern Illinois, they lost much of the most objectionable features earlier than many surrounding communities." *Counties of Cumberland, Jasper and Richland, Illinois*, 641.

20. Charles Augustus Murray, *Travels in North America*, vol. 2, 105.

21. Latrobe, *The Rambler in North America*, 206.

22. Robert Baird, *View of the Valley of the Mississippi: or the Emigrant's and Traveller's Guide to the West*, 87–89.

23. Buck, *Illinois in 1818*, 93–95.

24. Thomas J. Wood, "'Blood in the moon': The War for the Seat of Edwards County, 1821–1824," *IHJ*, Autumn 1992. *Combined History of Edwards, Lawrence and Wabash Counties, Illinois*, 238–239. Significantly, in post-frontier regions county-seat squabbles heated up, forcible removal of records occurring in Cass County in 1847 and Gallatin in 1849. In fact, long after frontier conditions died in DuPage County, in 1868, a county-seat fight killed one person and injured others. Wood, 159n. This may have been the only person killed in all of the bitter county-seat battles.

25. William Blane, *An Excursion through the United States and Canada during the Years 1822–23*, 158–159, 305. Blane also accused Am-

ericans of unfair, unmanly fighting and engaging in biting and gouging. Their predilection for gouging, he opined, was the greatest flaw in
the character of backwoodsmen. But this flaw soon faded in all but the
most degenerate of Illinoisans. Ibid., 161.

26. For more on this topic see Mary Ann Salter, "Quarreling in the
English Settlement: The Flowers in Court," *JISHS*, Summer 1982. For
the feuds among the Lutherans, see E. Duane Elbert, "The American
Roots of German Lutheranism in Illinois," *IHJ*, Summer 1985, 110, 112.

27. Nobles, "Breaking into the Backcountry," 645–646.

28. Selling the same parcel of land to several different purchasers
was nothing new for Indians, but there never appears to have been a
shortage of gullible settlers. Nobles, "Breaking into the Backcountry,"
646–647. On the other hand, again and again Americans maintained
Indians were savage, barely human, and unworthy of retaining land.
This justified prying land from Indians. M. J. Bowden, "The Invention
of American Tradition," *JHG*, 18 (1992), 20.

29. Martin Zanger, "Conflicting Concepts of Justice: A Winnebago
Murder Trial on the Illinois Frontier," *JISHS*, Winter 1980, 269–270,
272.

30. Oscar B. Hamilton, ed., *History of Jersey County, Illinois*, 79.

31. Susan S. Rugh, "Creating a Farm Community," 6.

32. Hildegard Binder Johnson, "The Location of German Immigrants
in the Middle West," *AAAG*, March 1951, 40.

33. Paul E. Stroble, Jr., "Ferdinand Ernst and the German Colony
at Vandalia," *IHJ*, Summer 1987, 108.

34. Timothy Flint, "National Character of the Western People,"
Western Monthly Review, vol. 1, May 1827-April 1828, 133–134.

35. Timothy Flint, *The History and Geography of the Mississippi
Valley*, I, 184.

36. Oliver, *Eight Months in Illinois*, 126.

37. Marcia Noe, "The Heathen Priestess on the Prairie: Margaret
Fuller Constructs the Midwest," *TON*, Spring 1992, especially 5–9. Major
players in accelerating technological development in Chicago and Illinois created so much power as to dominate and even alter nature, placing themselves between God and the mob. Wolner, "The City Builder
in Chicago," 18–20.

38. Stroble, "Ferdinand Ernst and the German Colony at Vandalia,"
104.

39. Abraham Lincoln expressed fear of extremism, mob action, chaos,
and disunity, fearing they would lead to despotism. He sternly warned
"against the spirit of mob violence prevalent in the Jacksonian era."
Laura Smith Porter, "'The Last, Best Hope of Earth': Abraham Lincoln's
Perception of the Mission of America, 1834–1854," *IHJ*, Autumn 1985,
211–212. Observers saw in the West politeness among ordinary people

and an absence of class distinction among the populace. Oliver, *Eight Months in Illinois*, 120. Harriet Goodnough wrote from Des Plaines on January 1, 1837 to relatives in Vermont, noting, "There is not so much distinction made between the rich and the poor but people are valued more according to their merit or demerit than by their property."

14. Conflicts and Community

1. The history, varieties, and mechanics of county formation and organization are found in Michael D. Sublett, *Paper Counties: The Illinois Experience, 1825–1867*, especially chapter 2.

2. For instance, Shelby County's residents voted on the proposed county of Okaw, but Macon County's residents did not, despite each county's standing to lose approximately the same area to the proposed county. Sublett, *Paper Counties*, 14.

3. *History of Pike County, Illinois*, 248, 251–252, 260–269. For more on county-seat struggles in Pike County and on the evolution of early courthouses there, see Carol McCartney, "The Pike County Courthouse," *WIRS*, Spring 1991, 17–22.

4. Bizarre twists and turns and compromise efforts graced county-seat squabbles in Washington County. The concept of *relative* location caused the existing county seat, Covington, to lose appeal. The seat bypassed Georgetown, a paper town, and two enterprising villages, Elkton and Beaucoup, and eventually alighted at Nashville. Over time transportation improvements—bridges, better roads, and other advances—steadily reduced time and expense required to reach county seats. But the problem was *relative* distance, the time required to reach the seat *compared to* the time it took others. *Relative* distance ignited these fights.

5. Everett W. Kindig, "'I am in purgatory now': Journalist Hooper Warren Survives the Illinois Frontier," *IHJ*, Autumn 1986, 186. Achille [Napoleon] Murat, *The United States of America*, 53.

6. *History of Bond and Montgomery Counties, Illinois*, 39–40. Some settlers drank socially, and others drank to get drunk. But still others consumed great quantities of whiskey to suppress pain caused by arthritis, sore gums, bad teeth, earaches, and other infirmities, and others sincerely believed that drinking could ward off illness. Even school children took a nip or two of whiskey before trundling off to school, and many treated their teachers to a bottle at Christmas. Moreover, teachers were fully expected by their students to provide whiskey, toddy, and other alcoholic beverages around Christmas. See, for example, *Combined History of Schuyler and Brown Counties, Illinois*, 196–197. Jasper Douthit wrote that he grew up in Shelby County, where "I began life with one dreadfully dangerous habit; namely, the custom of taking

a dram of whiskey every morning before breakfast for the sake of health. It was claimed that it would prevent the ague and milk sickness." He added, "The habit grew, of course, so that we must take a dram before each meal and then one between meals, and still oftener on stormy days and in very cold or very hot weather." Unlike many others, Douthit kicked the habit. Jasper Douthit, *Jasper Douthit's Story*, 18–19.

7. Murat, *The United States of America*, 67. In 1837 Charles Kneeland echoed Murat's sentiments, writing from Griggsville about participants in open air court "leaning against trees and lying on the ground with their hats off and listening with profound interest to a young lawyer who was laying the law down in grand style." Such "profound interest" was typical in those who took "ownership" of local judicial proceedings.

8. Wilson, "The Business of a Midwestern Trial Court," 265, 267.

9. Fordham, *Personal Narrative*, 128. These sentiments were echoed years later by David Davis, after his service on the United States Supreme Court. An attorney in early Bloomington, Davis was keenly interested in frontier legal conditions. He stressed three facts: compared to eastern lawyers, lawyers around Bloomington were every bit as efficient; the lawyer who was regarded as the "leading light of the Bar in Illinois," Stephen Logan, dressed very informally; because of the quality of pioneers, who favored "good order and the restraints of law," and the high quality of justice administered in central Illinois, "there was no portion of the United States [during the frontier years of the 1830s] in which there was less crime than in the central counties of Illinois." Harry Edward Pratt, *David Davis, 1815–1886*, 34, 25.

10. John Palmer, *Journals of Travels in the United States of North America, and in Lower Canada, Performed in the Year 1817 . . .*, 91. Flower's comments are found in Richard Flower, *Letters from the Illinois, 1820–1821*, in Reuben Gold Thwaites, ed., *Early Western Travels, 1748–1846*, vol. 10, 131.

11. Wilson, "The Business of a Midwestern Trial Court," 253, 260–262, 266–267.

12. Richard Lee Mason wrote about frontier Illinois in 1819, "But who could have believed . . . when the red men of the forest had retired from this beautiful country their place would have been supplied by persons whose characters would be softened by the appellation of savage, penitentiary outcasts, and murderers." Mason, *Narrative*, 22.

13. Spontaneous and accidental killings were certainly far more common than premeditated murder. For example, Charles Rich wrote from Metamora, Woodford County, on December 3, 1848, "There has been four young men shot by accident within fifteen miles of this place this fall, two of them within three miles. Three were shot by their own guns. The other was shot by another. The two were out hunting to-

gether, it rained, they started to run for the house, one directly behind the other. The one that was behind hit the breech of his gun and the ball went though the man before him, killing him instantly." *The Woodford County History*, 200.

14. Some existed for many years, and members sought legitimacy as quasi-legal bodies and believed Regulator organizations were voluntary, parallel institutions to existing legal institutions. See, for example, Patrick B. Nolan, *Vigilantes on the Middle Border: A Study of Self-Appointed Law Enforcement in the States of the Upper Mississippi from 1840 to 1880*.

15. Bloom, "Peaceful Politics: The Delegates from Illinois Territory, 1809–1818," 213.

16. Nobles, "Breaking into the Backcountry," 668–669.

17. Power, *History of the Early Settlers, Sangamon County, Illinois*, 69–70.

18. For a fine analysis of the tangled conditions, see Rohrbough, *Land Office Business*, 200–220, 298.

19. Burlend, *A True Picture of Emigration*, 68–69. Some historiography of silent suffering and concealed rising anger is found in James Marshall, "An Unheard Voice: The Autobiography of a Dispossessed Homesteader and a Nineteenth-Century Cultural Theme of Dispossession," *TON*, Winter 1980–81, especially 310–312.

20. Settlers' letters and diaries contain relatively little finger pointing, blame shifting, or self-pitying. County histories and memoirs certainly do—sometime to an extreme—but primary sources rarely do.

21. Oliver, *Eight Months in Illinois*, 120–121.

22. Trautmann, ed. and trans., "Eight Weeks on a St. Clair County Farm in 1851," 177.

23. *The History of Winnebago County, Illinois*, 252–253.

24. Charles A. Partridge, ed., in Newton Bateman and Paul Selby, ed., *Historical Encyclopedia of Illinois and History of Lake County*, 627, 631.

25. Ralph Mann, "Frontier Opportunity and the New Social History," *Pacific Historical Review*, November 1984, 487. In Will County violence bubbled near the stand where officials took bids on land. One person wrote, "Many moneyed speculator were present, threatening to bid against the claims of settlers. Hundreds of the latter, with sleeves rolled up and faces frowning defiance dark as a thunder-cloud, surrounded the officers' stand on all sides, ready to visit summary vengeance upon any presumptuous speculators." The account added, "All of these were intimidated save one. A powerful, gigantic Scotchman, about seven feet high, dared to bid against a settler, when in an instant *lightning* struck him in at least twenty places, and he gladly escaped with his life." *The History of Will County, Illinois*, 309–310. For popu-

list troubles in Kentucky and Indiana, see Stephen Aaron, "Pioneers and Profiteers: Land Speculation and the Homestead Ethic in Frontier Kentucky," *WHQ*, May 1992, especially 197–198.

26. William A. White, "Tradition and Urban Development: A Contrast of Chicago and Toronto in the Nineteenth Century," *TON*, Fall 1982, 264.

27. Oliver, *Eight Months in Illinois*, 120.

28. After descending the Ohio River, William Oliver faced uncertainties and fears as he waited to ascend the Mississippi. Waiting with him were four acquaintances he had made on the Ohio, and their presence buoyed him. Oliver, *Eight Months in Illinois*, 42. In 1817 at Cincinnati, to cite another example, two brothers met an assorted group including a grandmother and children from the East and helped them get to Madison County. Nathaniel B. Curran, "Anna Durkee Tauzin Young, 1753–1839: Connecticut Lady, Illinois Pioneer," *JISHS*, Summer 1984, 99.

29. Timothy Flint, "National Character of the Western People," *Western Monthly Review*, vol. 1, May 1827-April 1828, 137–139.

30. Oliver, *Eight Months in Illinois*, 183–184.

31. *Counties of Cumberland, Jasper and Richland, Illinois*, 430. Botscharow-Kamau, "Neighbors: Harmony and Conflict on the Indiana Frontier," 516, 518. Setters who butchered gave surplus parts to neighbors, and families having to go on extended visits rested assured that neighbors attended their livestock. Oscar B. Hamilton, ed., *History of Jersey County, Illinois*, 83. In Macon County, "To have refused to lend a tool would have aroused resentment of the whole neighborhood." And residents traveled far to freely assist others. Banton, ed., *History of Macon County*, 43.

32. Botscharow-Kamau, "Neighbors: Harmony and Conflict on the Indiana Frontier," 521.

33. *Combined History of Schuyler and Brown Counties, Illinois*, 367–368.

34. Bell Harlan, "'In the Early Days,' a Historical Sketch Written by Miss Belle Harlan," in *Early History of Washington, Illinois and Vicinity*, 49.

35. Stanley Elkins and Eric McKitrick, "A Meaning for Turner's Frontier. Part I: Democracy in the Old Northwest," *Political Science Quarterly*, September 1954, 331.

36. Trautmann, ed. and trans., "Eight Weeks on a St. Clair County Farm in 1851," 171.

15. Ties That Bind

1. Richard K. Vedder and Lowell E. Gallaway, "Migration and the Old Northwest," in David C. Klingaman and Richard K. Vedder, eds.,

Essays in Nineteenth Century Economic History: The Old Northwest, 163–165.

2. Emerson Davis, *The Half Century,* 202. Passage between New Orleans and Pittsburgh was $160 before the steamboat era; by the middle 1850s, just $30. James T. Lloyd, *Lloyd's Steamboat Directory,* 40.

3. Although officers and cabin crew serving western steamboats changed little during the nineteenth century, the same cannot be said for deck hands, commonly known as roustabouts, who constituted about half the employees on western steamboats. Originally, most roustabouts were veteran keelboat or flatboat crewmen. This changed by the 1840s, however, more coming from pools of unskilled labor in Ohio River ports, including recent immigrants and men from nearby farms. Masters sometimes rented out slaves as roustabouts. Patricia Mooney Melvin, "Steamboats West: The Legacy of a Transportation Revolution," *TON,* Winter 1981–1982, 348–349. One observer, however, in the late 1820s, claimed, "To become acquainted with the younger representative of the yeomanry, [a visitor] must acquaint himself with the crews of the descending flatboats." Timothy Flint, "National Character of the Western People," *Western Monthly Review,* vol. 1, May 1827-April 1828, 135.

4. Shaw, *Erie Water West,* 272. For the grain shipments, see Caird, *Prairie Farming in America,* 32. Powerful links to the East, particularly for northern Illinois, quickly tied most new settlers to a national economy. "The days of self-sufficiency and a long, drawn-out transition to a market economy had passed." Moreover, efficient transportation meant that corn replaced various subsistence crops. Rohrbough, *The Trans-Appalachian Frontier,* 294. Although during the 1850s wheat replaced corn in certain locales as the dominant cash crop, corn continued to speed to distant—even European—markets and to the region's livestock.

5. Donald L. Miller, *City of the Century: The Epic of Chicago and the Making of America,* 89.

6. Wyman, *Immigrants in the Valley,* 6.

7. Into the mid-1840s eastern shops manufactured virtually all of America's threshing machines. Poor transportation inhibited midwestern adoption of the machines, the first adopters being farmers close to urban areas. This typified Illinois, where threshing machines caught on in northern counties. One agricultural writer in 1848 noted that a day's ride in northern counties brought twenty threshers into view, but between Vandalia and St. Louis only one thresher was spotted. Even as late as the 1850s in Illinois horses tramped much grain. A wide variety of factors influenced adoption. Rikoon, *Threshing in the Midwest, 1820–1940,* 20, 21, 23–25.

8. In 1856 William Ogden obtained over 200,000 acres of pine along the Peshtigo River in northern Wisconsin. At the river's mouth, he built

a loggers' village, sawmills, and other facilities, from which he shipped huge quantities of lumber of standard dimensions to Chicago. Soon Chicago boasted the largest lumber fleet, lumberyard, and lumber market in the world. Miller, *City of the Century,* 112–113. Ironically, the very day Chicago burned in 1871, devastating fires in pine forests around Peshtigo killed hundreds of loggers and others, and consumed Peshtigo.

9. Oliver, *Eight Months in Illinois,* 195. A German visitor to St. Clair County in 1851 noted that in lieu of paying taxes residents had the opportunity to work on roads and build bridges. The township surveyor invited farmers to appear at a certain place and a specific time, and then "ordered bridges build here, holes filled there, and earth moved elsewhere. Bridge-building is very simple and soon finished, " he observed. "Six men pair off on the three nearest oaks and cut them down. It must take no longer than ten minutes, on penalty of being laughed at. Then another group splits the downed logs, which have been cut into 12-foot lengths. A third group moves this building material with oxen to the site, where the assembled crew lays the split logs side by side and covers them with small branches and then earth." The German visitor concluded, "A bridge takes an hour in all, where thirty to forty strong hands participate." Trautmann, ed. and trans., "Eight Weeks on a St. Clair County Farm in 1851," 171.

10. Trautmann, ed. and trans., "Eight Weeks on a St. Clair County Farm in 1851," 170. Livestock being walked to market was in accordance with the agricultural theories propounded by Johann Heinrich von Thunen in *The Isolated State,* 1826. He theorized different crops would be raised at different distances around a market town, based upon their ability to withstand transportation costs to market. Livestock, he wrote, would be raised furthest from town, because they could walk to market, costing the raiser relatively little. Perhaps Köhler knew of von Thunen's agricultural theories, or perhaps his observation in Illinois was independent of any agricultural theory.

11. Frontier McLean County had just one buggy. Pratt, *David Davis, 1815–1886,* 30. The appearance of buggies with a maturing frontier indicated increasing discretionary income and improving roads.

12. George Rogers Taylor, *The Transportation Revolution, 1815–1860,* 28–31. For plank road developments in Illinois, see Arthur Charles Cole, *The Era of the Civil War, 1848–1870,* 28.

13. Wolner, "The City Builder in Chicago," 12. The crucial roles of William B. Ogden in Illinois' frontier railroad development are discussed in William L. Downard, "William Butler Ogden and the Growth of Chicago," *JISHS,* Spring 1982, and in McLear, "The Galena and Chicago Union Railroad."

14. McLear, "The Galena and Chicago Union Railroad," 24. Track was laid from Chicago to Cicero in 1848 and in 1849 the railroad, "had

a few cars and a clumsy locomotive running on 'strap rails.' The schedule called for two trips daily to the city, with the fare at forty cents." For more on railroad developments, see Walter Bishop Spelman, *The Town* *of Cicero: History, Advantages, and Government,* 5.

15. See, for example, David Haney, "John Scripps: Circuit Rider and Newspaperman," *WIRS,* Fall 1986, 26. Early development and roles of telegraphs in the United States are found in Robert Luther Thompson, *Wiring a Continent: The History of the Telegraph Industry in the United States, 1832–1866.*

16. In regions far from navigable waterways, towns that sprang up in response to railroads were called "inland" towns. On May 2, 1855, Milan S. Beckwith wrote from the neonate town of Pana, which was not on navigable water and which was fathered by railroads that crossed there. Beckwith was pleased with the community and wrote, "Taking everything into consideration I have every reason to believe we shall in a few years have quite an inland town."

17. With the advent of automobiles, many right angle turns reverted to sweeping curves, again ruffling landowners.

18. Disappearing public lands are reflected in military bounty land warrant locations for veterans. Starting in 1848, each year the commissioner of the General Land Office reported the previous year's land warrant locations. Beginning in 1849 and continuing through 1853, Illinois led seventeen states and territories in land warrant acreage, peaking in 1852 with some 1,792,000 acres. (Illinois was second in 1848 and 1854.) But in 1855 Illinois contained only 16,000 acres, a tiny fraction of Iowa's 2,224,000 acres, and by 1859 Illinois ceased to have bounty land. James W. Oberly, *Sixty Million Acres: American Veterans and the Public Lands before the Civil War,* 82, 86–87.

19. *The Illinois Land Company,* 1, 8.

20. Wyman, *Immigrants in the Valley,* 90, 97.

21. White, "Tradition and Urban Development: A Contrast of Chicago and Toronto in the Nineteenth Century," 262–263.

22. Caird, *Prairie Farming in America,* 33. For details of successful efforts to overcome the wetlands, see Roger A. Winsor, "Environmental Imagery of the Wet Prairie of East Central Illinois, 1820–1920," *JHG,* 13 (1987), 380–381.

23. *A Guide to the Illinois Central Railroad Lands* (Chicago: Illinois Central Railroad Office, 1859), 58.

24. John Regan, *The Western Wilds of America,* 107.

25. William Cronon, *Nature's Metropolis: Chicago and the Great West,* 9. Railroads expanded regional and national markets, sharply reduced frontier isolation, proved a boon to people exporting from Illinois, encouraged importation from other regions, and brought swarms of settlers, who devoured the last chunks of public land. Edward K. Muller,

"Regional Urbanization and the Selective Growth of Towns in North American Regions," *JHG*, 3 (1977), 25–27. Railroads' impact on Chicago's collar communities is depicted in Carl Abbott, "'Necessary Adjuncts to Its Growth': The Railroad Suburbs of Chicago, 1854–1875," *JISHS*, Summer 1980, 17–18. By 1861 eleven separate rail lines served the center of Chicago.

26. Chicago's booming role as rail hub is found in Cole, *The Era of the Civil War, 1848–1870*, 51, and White, "Tradition and Urban Development: A Contrast of Chicago and Toronto in the Nineteenth Century," 262–263. Bustle shaped Chicago's self-definition and symbolized its being. Dense rail traffic was important to Chicagoans and other Americans. The revolution on rails symbolized successful today rushing headlong toward a better tomorrow. Residents of Toronto, Canada, viewed things differently. Toronto had defined itself before rails arrived, and railroads were seen at best as supplements to existing technologies and at worst as jarring threats to tradition and stability. Easy access to new rail transportation from Pana to the state of Vermont prompted Milan S. Beckwith, writing to his lady friend on May 2, 1855, to rather casually note, "I am tempted to visit home . . . If I should this summer again visit the State of my nativity I shall probably spend a couple of months." His comments imply the fact that travel to Vermont from central Illinois was not daunting, unlike just a few years previously.

27. Caird, *Prairie Farming in America*, 71.

28. Allan Pred, *Urban Growth and City-Systems in the United States, 1840–1860*, 103. Chicago's footwear dominance and Chicago's roles in grain, along with Chicago's growing ties to the East, are discussed in Pred, *Urban Growth*, 69–70, and White, "Tradition and Urban Development: A Contrast of Chicago and Toronto in the Nineteenth Century," 264–265.

29. Severe weather in early 1855 challenged Illinois' developing rail network. On February 4, Charles Benedict wrote about his efforts to reach St. Louis from Chicago. After being delayed by heavy snow, the train left Chicago: "Well, we started, and arrived at a small village by the name of Joliet, and there the conductor received a telegraph dispatch, telling him to remain there, for the snow was so deep that the cars could not run. Well, there we was, about three hundred of us in one little town. The Hotels were filled to overflowing." Benedict slept in the train, as did many others, and the next morning the train resumed its journey. "We started, and went about forty-five miles, and runn into a snow bank about four o'clock in the afternoon. All the passengers got out of the cars and helped push the cars through. But that time it was nearly dark. We runn on about two miles and ran into another snow drift . . . and we could neither back up or go ahead, and

fifteen miles from any place." Soon the stranded train ran out of food and fuel. Two "emigrant cars attached to the train" were especially vulnerable to the cold, "and the passengers appointed four young men as a committee to do something about getting some wood, and I was one of that committee. We went into one of the emigrant cars and drove all of them into one car, and went to cutting up the seats in the other [for fuel]. In that way we managed to keep from perishing until morning, and then was no better off than before." He and another man walked through bitter cold to Pontiac, fifteen miles further, and then returned to lead the passengers to Pontiac. Suffering frozen faces and limbs, the passengers made it to Pontiac, where residents took advantage of the situation, charging exorbitant prices for board, "and we are obliged to pay or starve."

30. Davis, *The Half Century*, 214–215.

31. Robert P. Sutton, "Illinois River Towns: Economic Units or Melting Pots," *WIRS*, Fall 1990, 22. For more on Quincy's roles in manufacturing and shipping, see Thomas J. Brown, "The Age of Ambition in Quincy, Illinois," *JISHS*, Winter 1982. According to Oren W. Fisk, a resident of Galena, in mid-1848 fifty to sixty steamboats stopped daily at Galena, most staying overnight. But even then Galena did not have regularly scheduled steamboat service with Quincy or any other town, the vessels coming and going "by chance." Fisk, July 16, 1848.

32. Edward K. Muller, "Selective Urban Growth in the Middle Ohio Valley, 1800–1860," *Geographical Review*, April 1976, 193.

33. *A Guide to the Illinois Central Railroad Lands*, 19.

34. For some objections raised against railroads and for levels of support for them, see Downard, "William Butler Ogden and the Growth of Chicago," 54. Jasper County's loss of reputation is discussed in *Counties of Cumberland, Jasper, and Richland*, 431.

35. Canadians and others were horrified by American railroads' shoddy construction and inadequate safety features. White, "Tradition and Urban Development: A Contrast of Chicago and Toronto in the Nineteenth Century," 263. For more on the "technology of haste" in the West and the ramshackle nature of American trains, track, and bridges, see Daniel Boorstin, *The American: The National Experience*, 97 and 102–107. Since "Getting There First" and "Go Ahead Anyhow" defined American movement, Boorstin argues that Americans valued rickety transportation, something that amazed foreigners.

36. Edward R. Kantowicz, "A Fragment of French Canada on the Illinois Prairies," *JISHS*, Winter 1982.

37. Wyman, *Immigrants in the Valley*, 78. For the fierce competition among towns to obtain railroads, see Muller, "Regional urbanization and the selective growth of towns in North American regions," 29. As a rule, in Indiana and Ohio "the towns that failed to obtain rail serv-

ice performed poorly." Much the same was true in Illinois. Muller, "Selective Urban Growth in the Middle Ohio Valley, 1800–1860," 194.

38. The above discussion of the pork industry is from Margaret Walsh, "The Spatial Evolution of the Mid-western Pork Industry, 1835–75," *JHG*, 4 (1978), especially 2, 3, 11, 14.

39. Railroads some distance from buildings affected the buildings' architecture. In 1858, for example, Eureka College completed a three-story classroom building, with identical north and south sides. The south side faced toward the church related to the college. A mile to the north, however, a railroad had been completed. Many assumed the new railroad would draw the town northward as the town grew, and should this happen college authorities wanted the "front" of the building to face the bulk of the town. Harold Adams, *History of Eureka College*, 45–46.

40. Trautmann, ed. and trans., "Eight Weeks on a St. Clair County Farm in 1851," 173.

41. *A Guide to the Illinois Central Railroad Lands*, 37.

16. Changing Ecology, Evolving Society

1. William B. Ogden and John S. Wright in Chicago affirmed the idea of the "middle landscape," in which preservation and cultivation of nature's world reconciled with demands of technological developments. This middle landscape—a reconciled landscape—in Thomas Jefferson's mind was essentially a rural landscape in which yeomen operated, but the middle landscape devised by Ogden and Wright included cities and supporting technologies. Wolner, "The City Builder in Chicago," 14.

2. See, for example, Bradsby, ed., *History of Bureau County, Illinois*, 227–230.

3. David Schob, *Hired Hands and Plowboys*, 131.

4. Winsor, "Environmental Imagery of the Wet Prairie of East Central Illinois, 1820–1920," 388–389. In a region bounded by a line running from the point where Wisconsin's southern border meets Lake Michigan to Springfield to Litchfield to a point about twenty miles east of Charleston, over one-third of the land was poorly drained. See Leslie Hewes, "The Northern Wet Prairie of the United States: Nature, Sources of Information, and Extent," *AAAG*, December 1951, 315–317. P. R. Bryant wrote to his brother in 1830, commenting on the infestation in July, August, and September of such flies in marshy eastern Illinois. He claimed they attacked like bees and tormented horses, forcing travelers to cross wet prairies at night. Cultivation, some noted, reduced their numbers. *Hampshire Gazette* [Northampton, Massachusetts], April 13, 1831, and *Southampton Courier* [Southampton, Massachusetts], April

20, 1831. Horatio Newhall, wrote on August 9, 1823: "A horse in crossing a prairy will be covered with blood. If exposed a whole day in the prairy, he must inevitably die." When he had to travel during the day, Newhall added, his horse dashed at full speed from grove to grove. The flies did not frequent wooded places.

5. Gordana Rezab, "The Memoir of William T. Brooking, McDonough County Pioneer," *WIRS*, Fall 1981, 147. For more on marsh-draining settlers and railroads, see Winsor, "Environmental Imagery of the Wet Prairie of East Central Illinois, 1820–1920," 381.

6. Oliver, *Eight Months in Illinois*, 63.

7. See, for example, *History of Pike County, Illinois*, 192.

8. *Illinois Annual Register, and Western Business Directory, No. 1—1847*, 19. For settlers engaged in struggles with pests new to the region, see Belle Harlan, "'In the Early Days,' a Historical Sketch Written by Miss Belle Harlan," in *Early History of Washington, Illinois, and Vicinity*, 46.

9. Nelson, "The Bishop Hill Colony: What They Found," 44–45.

10. *Hampshire Gazette* [Northampton, Massachusetts], April 13, 1831. As late as 1846, according to one visitor, Illinoisans had "a very disgusting practice of drinking from the rivers and running streams, into which every unclean thing enters." This source noted that even the purest stream "is not without its share of decaying vegetation and other matters injurious to health." Dependency on flowing water, the visitor noted, was unnecessary because, "it is known that a pure spring may generally be struck at twenty or thirty feet from the surface." Wm. J. A. Bradford, *Notes on the Northwest, or Valley of the Upper Mississippi*, 161–162.

11. Trautmann, ed. and trans., "Eight Weeks on a St. Clair County Farm in 1851," 169.

12. *Illinois Annual Register, and Western Business Directory, No. 1—1847*, 19. Although forests still blanketed much of St. Clair County as late as 1851, American settlers were "crack shots" and the forests were largely devoid of deer, so "hunters must travel a day from settlements to hunt deer." Cultural traits, however, influenced which animals were hunted to near extinction. For example, Americans in St. Clair County at this time did not hunt rabbit, partridge, prairie chicken, turkey, woodcock, or grey squirrel, so German settlers made them "welcome additions to our simple diet." Trautmann, ed. and trans., "Eight Weeks on a St. Clair County Farm in 1851," 175.

13. Oliver, *Eight Months in Illinois*, 135–137, 146, and see John T. Flanagan, "Hunting in Early Illinois," *JISHS*, February 1979, 8, 10. For evidence concerning the abundance of game, see Trautmann, ed. and trans., "Eight Weeks on a St. Clair County Farm in 1851," 175. William S. Brown found in northern Illinois abundant deer, rabbits,

squirrels, ducks, partridges, prairie chickens, and various kinds of fish, including pickerel, catfish, suckers, and bass. January 3, 1856, and May 20, 1856.

14. Hallwas, "Eliza Farnham's *Life in Prairie Land*," 309.

15. Oliver, *Eight Months in America*, 100–101.

16. Anne F. Hyde, "Cultural Filters: The Significance of Perception in the History of the American West," *WHQ*, August 1993, 364.

17. William L. Talbot, "The Warsaw Boat Yard," *WIRS*, Fall 1984.

18. Wolner, "The City Builder in Chicago," 11. For the roles of New England in fostering agricultural fairs and for the numbers of fairs operating, see Fred Kniffen, "The American Agricultural Fair: Time and Place," *AAAG*, March 1951, 43–46, 57.

19. John E. Hallwas, "John Regan's Emigrant Guide: A Neglected Literary Achievement," *IHJ*, Winter 1984, 274.

20. Creativity has marked settlement in the Old Northwest from the earliest years. See, for example, James E. Davis, "'New Aspects of Men and New Forms of Society': The Old Northwest, 1790–1820," *JISHS*, August 1976. By the 1850s inventing had become a profession, one tapped by leading manufacturers. Nader, "The Rise of an Inventive Profession," especially 399, 401, 407.

21. Oliver, *Eight Months in Illinois*, 100.

22. For more on the Manny brothers and their inventive work on harvesters and reapers during the 1850s, see John Nader, "The Rise of an Inventive Profession: Learning Effects in the Midwestern Harvester Industry, 1850–1890," *Journal of Economic History*, June 1994, 400. For information on McCormick's role in producing reapers and on Illinois' leading role in producing agricultural machinery, see Miller, *City of the Century*, 104.

23. *Hampshire Gazette* [Northampton, Massachusetts], April 13, 1831.

24. Despite its modest title, many problems, legal developments, costs, and other aspects of fencing over decades in America and Europe are ably discussed in Clarence H. Danhof, "The Fencing Problem in the Eighteen Fifties," *Agricultural History*, October 1944. Danhof notes that clashes erupted between livestock owners and cultivators of crops over who had the responsibility to fence. Common law placed the responsibility on livestock owners, but Illinois by statute lifted this responsibility, encouraging grazing on the prairies.

25. In 1850 census figures indicated about 79 percent of the country's fences were worm fences, a figure that fell to 73 percent by the 1860 census. Post and rail fences constituted 9 percent in both years. During this decade, however, board fences shot from just 5 percent to 8 percent. Stone fences, used primarily in the Northeast, fell from 7 percent to 6 percent, reflecting the Northeast's diminishing role in America's agriculture. Significantly, in 1850 the census listed no hedge fencing or

wire fencing, but by 1860 hedge fencing and wire fencing constituted 2 percent and 3 percent, respectively, of the nation's fencing, reflecting lack of wood and keen experimentation. Wire fencing surged, and by 1900 it constituted 67 percent of the country's fencing, but this was too late for frontier Illinois. Martin L. Primack, "Farm Fencing in the Nineteenth Century," *Journal of Economic History*, June 1969, 287–289.

26. In the same year, Charles M. Dupuy, Jr., land agent for the Illinois Central Railroad Company, advertised "Ready-framed Farm Dwellings, which can be set up in a few Days" and which were twelve by twenty feet, divided into a living room and three bed rooms, and cost $150, exclusive of rail transportation costs, which were eleven cents per mile. Larger houses were also available at higher prices.

27. Caird, *Prairie Farming in America*, 63.

28. One livestock owner near Springfield improved his sheep by importing pure merino rams from Germany and Spain. Caird, *Prairie Farming in America*, 58.

29. Robert G. Day, Sr., "The Peoria Party," *WIRS*, Spring 1990, 19, 24, 25.

30. Rebecca Looney, "Migration and Separation: Divorce in Kane County, 1837–1869," *IHJ*, Summer 1996, 80 and 80n. The wives left behind in Illinois were commonly called "California widows," and the separation sometimes produced divorce. Over 1,000 steamboat arrivals at St. Paul in 1856–1857 helped some 90,000 people enter Minnesota, including many Illinoisans. Tweet, "Taming the Rapids of the Upper Mississippi," 53.

31. *The History of Will County, Illinois*, 319–320. Other examples abound. For a superb account of women from Pike County who trekked overland in 1853, see Jeanne Hamilton Watson, ed., *To the Land of Gold and Wickedness: The 1848–59 Diary of Lorena L. Hays*.

32. Charles Colby, *Hand-Book of Illinois*, 18.

33. Schob, *Hired Hands and Plowboys*, 4, 131, 251.

34. Michael P. Conzen, "Local Migration Systems in Nineteenth-Century Iowa," *Geographical Review*, July 1974, 340.

35. Craig Buettinger, "Economic Inequality in Early Chicago, 1849–1850," *JSH*, Spring 1978, 413–417.

36. John Mack Faragher, *Sugar Creek: Life on the Illinois Prairie*, 190.

37. H. Roger Grant, "Utopias That Failed: The Antebellum Years," *WIRS*, Spring 1979.

38. Twice, in 1824 and in 1842, voters in Illinois had rejected efforts to call a constitutional convention to remedy perceived defects in the existing constitution. By 1847, however, the state legislature's spendthrift ways and the public's desire to control more offices via popular elections convinced voters to call a convention, which drafted the docu-

ment that in 1848 became the state's second constitution. Fifty-nine counties approved the call for the convention, while only fourteen rejected it. For fine insight into calls for constitutions and Illinois' constitutions, see Janet Cornelius, "Popular Sovereignty and Constitutional Change in the United States and Illinois Constitutions," *IHJ*, Winter 1987. Cornelius highlights widespread frustrations, anger, and fears that accompanied the creation of the Constitution of 1848.

39. The constitution was debated and adopted during a time which saw huge numbers of immigrants arrive from Ireland and the German states. This surge of immigration soon tipped the state's demographic scales. In 1850 about one in eight Illinoisans was of foreign birth, but by 1860 about one in five was foreign-born. This growth in foreign-born, moreover, was accompanied by virulent nativism during the 1850s. For severe shortcomings of the 1848 constitution, see Rodney O. Davis, "'The People in Miniature': The Illinois General Assembly, 1818–1848," *IHJ*, Summer 1988, 108. Davis refers to the new constitution as "an anachronism that could stand only a limited test of time." Despite the flawed constitution, state politics improved during the 1840s and later as appropriate structural and procedural changes within government and within parties occurred.

40. Despite increases in hired hands and tenants, people believed republicanism was still vigorous in the 1850s. For example, one eastern woman visiting Illinois in 1853 wrote about "the difficulty in obtaining 'help' in domestic service," observing, "The Irish and Germans who emigrate to the country can obtain land on easy terms, and . . . most of them are too much in love with the independence they see in all around them, to be willing to remain long in a subordinate condition." She added, "They have learned, too, to be jealous to a degree of any assumption of superiority on the part of their employers; for example, the indignity of not being invited to the family table is deeply resented," and employers lived "in continual fear of giving offence to those employed, and thereby provoking them to go away." Finally, she observed, "It was curious to observe the predominant and peculiar *Western* aspect of the multitude, a sturdy, labor-hardened look of self-reliance, an air of independent strength and will appropriate to lords of the soil, indebted to themselves alone for their right. . . . This was observable even in the women, many of whom had infants in their arms, and were followed by two or three little ones." Elizabeth Fries Ellet, *Summer Rambles in the West*, 220, 222. Carl Köhler observed that planting of oats was done at five different times with a few days between each planting, "so that all would not ripen simultaneously, for we would not have enough hands if mowing had to be done at once." Trautmann, ed. and trans., "Eight Weeks on a St. Clair County Farm in 1851," 172–173.

41. Yankee and New Yorker influence in creating townships and

adopting township government is evident in Evarts B. Greene, "Sectional Forces in the History of Illinois," *Transactions*, 1903.

42. Article XIV was submitted to a popular vote. The efforts of John Jones, an influential black Chicagoan, to repeal the Black Laws, gain black suffrage, and block passage of anti-migration provisions are discussed in Charles A. Gliozzo, "John Jones, a Study of a Black Chicagoan," *IHJ*, Autumn 1987, especially 180. This work also details blacks' resistance to such threats as the Fugitive Slave Law of 1850.

43. College foundings are discussed in John V. Bergen, "College Towns and Campus Sites in Western Illinois," *WIRS*, Fall 1990. Bergen explains problems associated with determining what constituted a college, its founding date, and other aspects of early college developments. See also Lois A. Carrier, *Illinois: Crossroads of a Continent*, 89.

44. Cole, *The Era of the Civil War, 1848–1870*, 25–26. Robert P. Sutton provides solid information about German cultural and political influences in Quincy and the founding of the Turner associations there in "Illinois River Towns: Economic Units or Melting Pots," 22–23.

45. Linda K. Kerber, "Women and Individualism in American History," *Massachusetts Review*, Winter 1989, 592.

46. Lucy Eldersveld Murphy, "Her Own Boss: Businesswomen and Separate Spheres in the Midwest, 1850–1880," *IHJ*, Autumn 1987, 157–58, 162, 165, 169.

47. White, "Traditions of Urban Development: A Contrast of Chicago and Toronto in the Nineteenth Century," 252.

48. Looney, "Migration and Separation: Divorce in Kane County, 1837–1869," especially 70–79.

49. The information in this paragraph came from papers presented by Stacy Pratt McDermott, Daniel W. Stowell, and Dennis E. Suttles at the annual Symposium of the Illinois State Historical Society, December 1997.

50. *New Englander*, vol. 7 (New Series, vol. 1), 1849, 602. The same publication contained a letter from a teacher in Illinois who lamented, "The Sabbath here is universally regarded as a holiday. Ministers and people make it a day of visiting. The grocery is open and as much frequented as on any day." Ibid., 607. Ethnic and religious dimensions of drinking in Jacksonville are ably discussed by Don Harrison Doyle, *The Social Order of a Frontier Community: Jacksonville, Illinois, 1825–1870*.

51. These and other traits of Regulators from Maine to Georgia and across the Appalachians are discussed in Nobles, "Breaking into the Backcountry."

52. Social cohesion, social discipline, and common purpose began to fade with prosperity. Colonies planted on prairie soil often flourished until perceived threats subsided and prosperity reared its head. Bick-

ering, individual secession, and finally disintegration of colonial undertakings often followed worldly success. Just four years before the Bishop Hill colony of Janssonists experienced dissension, murder, and then in 1860 dissolution, a visitor to the colony observed the material wealth the colony had piled up and concluded, "The fact is they are rich." Nelson, "The Bishop Hill Colony: What They Found," 45. This was nothing new, however, and abundance and opportunity sundered social ties among New England's Puritans. See, for example, David S. Lovejoy, "Plain Englishmen at Plymouth," *New England Quarterly*, June 1990, especially 238–239 and 247–248. Again and again, settler undertakings had difficulty withstanding for long the insidious threat of success.

53. Perhaps the respite from crime was only temporary. On December 9, 1893, the *Virginia Enquirer* complained of "an alarming increase of crime all over Illinois." It ranged from swindling and thievery to "frequent murderous assaults." For the Greenbush Vigilantes, see John Lee Allaman, "Greenbush Vigilantes: An Organizational Document," *WIRS*, Spring 1987, especially 38–39.

54. White, "Tradition and Urban Development: A Contrast of Chicago and Toronto in the Nineteenth Century," 255.

55. Ibid., 253.

56. Some observers in the early 1850s waxed nostalgic about the waning Garden. For example, one lamented the prairies' general appearance, and then added, "Cultivation, too, has sadly marred the effect of these; one can scarcely conceive how much the sight of a distant corn patch, or field of wheat, or even a fence, or inclosure round a dwelling, takes away from the aspect of romantic wilderness." Ellet, *Summer Rambles in the West*, 37–38. See also Robert Bray, "The Mystical Landscape: Francis Grierson's *The Valley of Shadows*," *TON*, Winter 1979–1980, especially 367, 381–382.

57. One visitor from Britain in Illinois in 1858, James Caird, found that some frontier traits that had long bothered Britons had not changed. After admitting that state officials were readily accessible to average Illinoisans, Caird wrote, "If there is not much ceremony, there is a total absence of it in the manners of the bulk of the people. The nasty habit of chewing tobacco, and spitting, not only gives them a dirty look, but makes them disagreeable companions." Americans' eating habits also impressed Caird: "They eat so fast, and are so silent, and run off so soon when they have finished their meals, that really eating in this country is more like the feeding of a parcel of brutes than men." Caird, *Prairie Farming in America*, 60–61.

58. Oliver, *Eight Months in Illinois*, 132–133.

59. Milan S. Beckwith, May 2, 1855.

60. Anne Ehrenpreis, ed., *Happy Country*, 246–247.

Works Cited

Collection Abbreviations

AAS: American Antiquarian Society
CHS: Chicago Historical Society
ISHL: Illinois State Historical Library
Sterling: Sterling Memorial Library, Yale University

Manuscript Sources

Sarah Aiken Papers, ISHL
John Bailhache Papers, AAS
John Barker (in David Ports Papers), ISHL
Hiram W. Beckwith Papers, ISHL
Milan S. Beckwith Papers, ISHL
Charles Benedict Papers, ISHL
John Brees Papers, ISHL
John F. Brooks Papers, ISHL
James Brown (in Daniel Weed Papers), ISHL
William S. Brown Papers, ISHL
J. Buchanan Papers, ISHL
Harriet Buckmaster (in Buckmaster-Curran Papers), ISHL
N. Burton Papers, ISHL
David Carpenter Papers, CHS
J. Carpenter Papers, CHS
Alfred Chadwick Papers, ISHL
George Churchill Papers, ISHL
G. R. Clark Papers, CHS
Adam Davis (in Daniel Weed Papers), ISHL
John Dickson Papers, CHS
Albert Dodd Papers, Sterling
William Drury Papers, ISHL
Asher Edgerton Papers, ISHL
Edward Eno Papers, CHS

John Estabrooks Papers, CHS
Rufus Everett Papers, CHS
Oren W. Fisk Papers, CHS
Asa Fitch Papers, Sterling
Andrew Fitz (in Daniel Weed Papers), ISHL
Simeon Francis Papers, ISHL
Solomon Freeman Papers, ISHL
John Garner Papers, ISHL
Daniel Goodnough Papers, ISHL
Harriet Goodnough Papers, ISHL
William Irving Papers, CHS
Joseph King (in King Papers), ISHL
Charles W. Kneeland Papers, ISHL
Samuel Knox (in Daniel Weed Papers), ISHL
Mary Norwood Leggett Papers, ISHL
Robert Leslie (in James and John Dunlop Papers), ISHL
John R. Lewis Papers, CHS
Edward McConnell (in Henry Enoch Dummer Papers), ISHL
Lucy Maynard Papers, ISHL
George E. More Papers, CHS
Griswold C. Morgan Papers, CHS
Morganian Society Constitution, ISHL
Horatio Newhall Papers, ISHL
Albert Parker Papers, ISHL
J. N. Parker (in Albert Parker Papers), ISHL
Mary Boone Perry Papers, ISHL
David Ports Papers, ISHL
Richard L. Powel, "Transcript of a Journey from Philadelphia to Illinois and Return, July–August, 1988." IHSL
Eleanor Robbins Papers, ISHL
Amelia Roberts Papers, ISHL
David Robson (in James and John Dunlop Papers), ISHL
M. W. Ross Papers, ISHL
Samary S. Sherman Papers, CHS
Lucretia Sibley Papers, AAS
Morris Slight Papers, CHS
James H. Smith and Sarah Smith (in James H. Smith Papers, Transcript Copy), ISHL
James W. Stephenson Papers, ISHL
Alma Stevens Papers, ISHL
Levi Stillman (in George Churchill Papers), ISHL
Caroline Strong Papers, CHS
Roland Tinkham Papers, CHS
Hannah Turner Papers, ISHL

"Uncle Gregory" Papers, CHS
Henry Warren Papers, CHS
William Waterman Papers, ISHL
Charles Watts Papers, ISHL
Daniel Weed Papers, ISHL
Ebenezer Welch Papers, CHS
Vienna Winslow Papers, CHS
R. N. Wright Papers, ISHL

Newspapers and Other Periodicals

Chicago Tribune
Hampshire Gazette [Northampton, Massachusetts]
Illinoian
Illinois Herald
Illinois Intelligencer
Illinois State Gazette and *Jacksonville News*
Illinoisan
The New England Farmer and Gardener's Journal
The New Englander
Pittsfield Sun [Pittsfield, Massachusetts]
Prairie Democrat
Prairie Farmer
Southampton Courier [Southampton, Massachusetts]
State-Journal Register [Springfield, Illinois]
Telegraph [Lockport, Illinois]
The Union Agriculturalist and Western Prairie Farmer [later the *Prairie Farmer*]
Virginia Enquirer [Virginia, Illinois]
Western Messenger
Western Monthly Review

Contemporary and Secondary Publications

Abbott, Carl, "'Necessary Adjuncts to Its Growth': The Railroad Suburbs of Chicago, 1854–1875," *JISHS*, Summer 1980.
Adams, Harold, *History of Eureka College*. Eureka, Illinois: Board of Trustees of Eureka College, 1982.
Allaman, John Lee, "Greenbush Vigilantes: An Organizational Document," *WIRS*, Spring 1987.
———, "The Patterson Family of Oquawka," *WIRS*, Spring 1988.
———, "Uniforms and Equipment of the Black Hawk War and the Mormon War," *WIRS*, Spring 1990.

Allen, Barbara, "The Genealogical Landscape and the Southern Sense of Place," in Allen and Schlereth, eds., *Sense of Place: American Regional Cultures*. Lexington: University of Kentucky Press, 1990.

———, and Thomas J. Schlereth, eds., *Sense of Place: American Regional Cultures*. Lexington: University of Kentucky Press, 1990.

Allen, Michael, *Western Rivermen, 1763–1861: Ohio and Mississippi Boatmen and the Myth of the Alligator Horse*. Baton Rouge: Louisiana State University Press, 1990.

Alvord, Clarence Walworth, *The Illinois Country 1673–1818*. Chicago: A. C. McClurg, 1922.

Aron, Stephen, "Pioneers and Profiteers: Land Speculation and the Household Ethic in Frontier Kentucky," *WHQ*, May 1992.

The Articles of Association of the Rockwell Land Company, La Salle County, Illinois. Cleveland: F. B. Penniman, 1836.

Atack, Jeremy and Fred Bateman, "The Development of Industrial Steam Power in the Midwest with Special Reference to Indiana," *TON*, Winter 1982–1983.

Bailhache, John, "Brief Sketch of the Life and Editorial Career of John Bailhache. Written by himself. n.p., 1855.

Baird, Robert, *View of the Valley of the Mississippi: or the Emigrant's and Traveller's Guide to the West*. Philadelphia: H. S. Tanner, 1832.

Bannon, John Francis, S. J., "The Spaniards and the Illinois Country, 1762–1800," *JISHS*, May 1976.

Banton, O[liver] T[errill], ed., *History of Macon County*. n.p.: Macon County Historical Society, 1976.

Baxter, David, "William Cullen Bryant: Illinois Landowner," *WIRS*, Spring 1978.

Bellesîles, Michael A., "The Origins of Gun Culture in the United States, 1760–1865," *JAH*, September 1996.

Belting, Natalia Maree, "The Native American as Myth and Fact," *JISHS*, May 1976.

Berfield, Karen, "Three Antislavery Leaders of Bureau County," *WIRS*, Spring 1980.

Bergen, John V., "College Towns and Campus Sites in Western Towns," *WIRS*, Fall 1990.

Billington, Ray A., "The Frontier in Illinois History," *JISHS*, Spring 1950.

Birkbeck, Morris, *Letters From Illinois*. London: Taylor and Hessey, 1818.

———, *Notes on a Journey in America, from the Coast of Virginia to the Territory of Illinois*. Dublin: Thomas Courtney, 1818.

Bishop, M. Guy, Vincent Lacey, and Richard Wixon, "Death at Mormon Nauvoo, 1843–1845," *WIRS*, Fall 1986.

Blane, William Newnham, *An Excursion through the United States and*

Canada during the Years 1822–23. London: Baldwin, Cradock, and Works Cited Joy, 1824.

Bloom, Arthur W., "Tavern Theater in Early Chicago," *JISHS*, Autumn 1981.

Bloom, Jo Tice, "Peaceful Politics: The Delegates from Illinois Territory, 1809–1818," *TON*, Fall 1980.

——, "The Territorial Delegates of Indiana Territory, 1801–1816," *TON*, Spring 1986.

Boggess, Arthur Clinton, *The Settlement of Illinois, 1778–1830.* Chicago: Chicago Historical Society, 1908.

Booher, Edwin, "The Garden Myth in 'The Prairies,'" *WIRS*, Spring 1978.

Boorstin, Daniel J., *The Americans: The National Experience.* New York: Vintage Books, 1965.

Botscharow-Kamau, Lucy Jayne, "Neighbors: Harmony and Conflict on the Indiana Frontier," *JER*, Winter 1991.

Bowden, M. J., "The Invention of American Tradition," *JHG*, January 1992.

Boyle, Susan C., "Did She Generally Decide? Women in Ste. Genevieve, 1750–1805," *W&MQ*, October 1987.

Bracken, James, "Sarah Fenn Burton's Diary of a Journey to Illinois," *WIRS*, Fall 1981.

Bradbury, John, *Bradbury's Travels in the Interior of America, 1809–1811.* In Reuben Gold Thwaites, ed., *Early Western Travels, 1748–1846, Vol. 5.* Cleveland: Arthur H. Clark, 1904.

Bradford, Wm. J. A., *Notes on the Northwest, or Valley of the Upper Mississippi.* New York: Wiley and Putnam, 1846.

Bradsby, H. C., ed., *History of Bureau County, Illinois.* Chicago: World, 1885.

Brand, Edward P., *Illinois Baptists, A History.* Bloomington: Pantagraph Printing & Sta. Co., 1930.

Bray, Robert, "Beating the Devil: Life and Art in Peter Cartwright's Autobiography," *IHJ*, Autumn 1985.

——, "The Mystical Landscape: Francis Grierson's *The Valley of the Shadows,*" *TON*, Winter 1979–1980.m

Bridges, Roger D., "Dark Faces on the Antebellum West Central Illinois Landscape," *WIRS*, Fall 1983.

——, "John Mason Peck on Illinois Slavery," *JISHS*, Autumn 1982.

Briggs, Winstanley, "Le Pays des Illinois," *W&MQ*, January 1990.

Brown, Margaret Kimball, "*Allons,* Cowboys!" *JISHS*, Winter 1983.

——, "Documents and Archaeology in French Illinois," in John A. Walthall, ed., *French Colonial Archaeology: The Illinois Country and the Western Great Lakes.* Urbana: University of Illinois Press, 1991.

————, and Lawrie Cena Dean, eds., *The Village of Chartres in Colonial Illinois, 1720–1765.* New Orleans: Polyanthos, 1977.

Brown, Richard Maxwell, *Strains of Violence: Historical Studies of American Violence and Vigilantism.* New York: Oxford University Press, 1975.

Brown, Thomas J., "The Age of Ambition in Quincy, Illinois," *JISHS*, Winter 1982.

Buck, Solon Justus. *Illinois in 1818.* Springfield: Illinois Centennial Commission, 1917.

Buettinger, Craig, "Economic Inequality in Early Chicago, 1849- 1850," *JSH*, Spring 1978.

Buley, R. Carlyle, *The Old Northwest: Pioneer Period, 1815–1840.* 2 vols. Indianapolis: Indiana Historical Society, 1950.

Burton, William L., "James Semple, Prairie Entrepreneur," *IHJ*, Summer 1987.

————, "The Life and Death of Bloody Island: A Ferry Tale," *WIRS*, Spring 1988.

Bushnell, Horace, *Barbarism, the First Danger. A Discourse for Home Missions.* New York: American Home Missionary Society, 1847.

Caird, James, *Prairie Farming in America.* London: Longman, Brown, Green, Longman, & Roberts, 1859.

Carr, Kay J., *Belleville, Ottawa, and Galesburg: Community and Democracy on the Illinois Frontier.* Carbondale: Southern Illinois University Press, 1996.

Carrier, Lois A., *Illinois: Crossroads of a Continent.* Urbana: University of Illinois Press, 1993.

Carter, Clarence Edwin, comp. and ed., *The Territorial Papers of the United States, Volume XVII. The Territory of Illinois, 1814–1818, Continued.* Washington, D.C.: U.S. Government Printing Office, 1950.

Chaput, Donald, "Treason or Loyalty? Frontier French in the American Revolution," *JISHS*, November 1978.

Church, Charles, *Past and Present of the City of Rockford and Winnebago County, Illinois.* Chicago: S. J. Clarke, 1905.

Clark, S. J., *History of McDonough County, Illinois.* Springfield: D. W. Lusk, 1878.

Clinton, Catherine and Nina Silber, eds., *Divided Houses: Gender and the Civil War.* New York: Oxford University Press, 1992.

Clodfelter, Michael, *Warfare and Armed Conflicts: A Statistical Reference, Vol. 1.* Jefferson: North Carolina: McFarland, 1992.

Colby, Charles, *Hand-Book of Illinois, Accompanying Morse's New Map of the State.* New York: Rufus Blanchard, 1855.

Cole, Arthur Charles, *The Era of the Civil War, 1848–1870.* Springfield: Illinois Centennial Commission, 1919.

Combined History of Edwards, Lawrence, and Wabash Counties, Illinois. Philadelphia: J. L. McDonough, 1883.

Combined History of Schuyler and Brown Counties, Illinois. Philadelphia: W. R. Brink, 1882.

Conzen, Michael P., "Local Migration Systems in Nineteenth-Century Iowa," *Geographical Review,* July 1974.

Cornelius, Janet, "Popular Sovereignty and Constitutional Change in the United States and Illinois Constitutions," *IHJ,* Winter 1987.

Counties of Cumberland, Jasper and Richland, Illinois. Chicago: F. A. Battey, 1884.

Courtwright, David T., "Violence in America," *American Heritage,* September 1996.

Croghan, George, *A Selection of Letters and Journals Relating to Tours in the Western Country.* In Reuben Gold Thwaites, ed., *Early Western Travels, 1748–1846, Vol. 1.* Cleveland: Arthur H. Clark, 1904.

Cronon, William, *Nature's Metropolis: Chicago and the Great West.* New York: W. W. Norton, 1991.

Cuming, Fortesque, *Sketch of a Tour to the Western Country, through the States of Ohio and Kentucky.* In Reuben Gold Thwaites, ed., *Early Western Travels, 1748–1846, Vol. 4.* Cleveland: Arthur H. Clark, 1904.

Cunningham, Eileen and Mabel Schneider, "A Slave's Autobiography Retold," *WIRS,* Fall 1979.

Curran, Nathaniel B., "Anna Durkee Tauzin Young, 1753–1839: Connecticut Lady, Illinois Pioneer," *JISHS,* Summer 1984.

Danhof, Clarence H. "The Fencing Problem in the Eighteen-Fifties," *Agricultural History,* October 1944.

Davidson, Alexander and Bernard Stuvé, *A Complete History of Illinois from 1673 to 1873.* Springfield: Illinois Journal, 1874.

Davis, Emerson, *The Half Century,* Boston: Tappan & Whittemore, 1851.

Davis, James E., *Frontier America, 1800–1840: A Comparative Demographic Analysis of the Settlement Process.* Glendale, California: Arthur H. Clark, 1977.

———, "'New Aspects of Men and New Forms of Society': The Old Northwest, 1790–1820," *JISHS,* August 1976.

———, "Settlers in Frontier Illinois: Primary Evidence, Persistent Problems, and the Historian's Craft," in Bruce D. Cody, ed., *Selected Papers in Illinois History, 1981.* Springfield: Illinois State Historical Society, 1982.

Davis, James M., in *The Illinois Land Company.* n.p.: State of Illinois, 1855.

Davis, Rodney O., "'The People in Miniature': The Illinois General Assembly, 1818–1848," *IHJ,* Summer 1988.

Day, Robert G., Sr., "The Peoria Party," *WIRS*, Spring 1990.

De Bow, J. D. B., *Mortality Statistics of the Seventh Census of the United States, 1850.* Washington, D.C.: A. O. P. Nicholson, 1855.

Douthit, Jasper, *Jasper Douthit's Story: The Autobiography of a Pioneer.* Boston: American Unitarian Association, n.d.

Downard, William L., "William Butler Ogden and the Growth of Chicago," *JISHS*, Spring 1982.

Doyle, Don Harrison, *The Social Order of a Frontier Community: Jacksonville, Illinois, 1825–70.* Urbana: University of Illinois Press, 1978.

Duis, E., *The Good Old Times in McLean County, Illinois.* Bloomington, Illinois: Leader, 1874.

Edmunds, R. David and Joseph L. Peyser, *The Fox Wars: The Mesquakie Challenge to New France.* Norman: University of Oklahoma Press, 1993.

Edstrom, James A., "'With . . . candour and good faith': Nathaniel Pope and the Admission Enabling Act of 1818," *IHJ*, Winter 1995.

Ehrenpreis, Anne, ed., *Happy Country This America: The Travel Diary of Henry Arthur Bright.* Columbus: Ohio State University Press, 1978.

Ekberg, Carl J., "Black Slavery in Illinois, 1720–1765," *WIRS*, Spring 1989.

———, "Marie Rouensa–8cate8a and the Foundations of French Illinois," *IHJ*, Autumn 1991.

Elbert, E. Duane, "The American Roots of German Lutheranism in Illinois," *IHJ*, Summer 1985.

Elkins, Stanley and Eric McKitrick, "A Meaning for Turner's Frontier. Part I: Democracy in the Old Northwest," *Political Science Quarterly*, September 1954.

Ellet, Elizabeth Fries, *Summer Rambles in the West.* New York: J. C. Riker, 1853.

Erickson, Charlotte. *Invisible Immigrants: The Adaptation of English and Scottish Immigrants in Nineteenth-Century America.* Coral Gables, Florida: University of Miami Press, [1972].

Etcheson, Nichole, *The Emerging Midwest: Upland Southerners and the Political Culture of the Old Northwest, 1787–1861.* Bloomington: Indiana University Press, 1996.

Evans, Emory G., "The Colonial View of the West," *JISHS*, May 1976.

Faragher, John Mack, *Daniel Boone: The Life and Legend of an American Pioneer.* New York: Henry Holt, 1992.

———, *Sugar Creek: Life on the Illinois Prairie.* New Haven: Yale University Press, 1986.

Faux, William, *Memorable Days in America.* In Reuben Gold Thwaites, ed., *Early Western Travels, 1748–1846, Vol. 11.* Cleveland: Arthur H. Clark, 1905.

Fearon, Henry Bradshaw, *Sketches of America.* London: Longman, Hurst, Rees, Orme, and Brown, 1818.

Feiler, Seymour, trans. and ed., *Jean-Bernard Bossu's Travels in the Interior of North America, 1751–1762.* Norman: University of Oklahoma Press, 1962.

Finkleman, Paul, "Slavery, the More Perfect Union, and the Prairie State," *IHJ,* Winter 1987.

———, "Slavery and the Northwest Ordinance: A Study in Ambiguity," *JER,* Winter 1986.

Flanagan, John T., "Hunting in Early Illinois," *JISHS,* February 1979.

Flint, Timothy, *The History and Geography of the Mississippi Valley, Vol. 1.* Cincinnati: E. H. Flint and L. R. Lincoln, 1832.

———, "National Character of the Western People," *Western Monthly Review, Vol. 1,* May 1827-April 1828.

———, *Recollections of the Last Ten Years Passed in Occasional Residences and Journeyings in the Valley of the Mississippi.* Boston: Cummings, Hilliard, 1826.

Flower, Richard, *Letters from the Illinois, 1820–1821.* In Reuben Gold Thwaites, ed., *Early Western Travels, 1748–1846, Vol. 10.* Cleveland: Arthur H. Clark, 1904.

Fogde, Myron, "Primitivism and Paternalism: Early Denominational Approaches in Western Illinois," *WIRS,* Fall 1980.

Ford, Thomas, *A History of Illinois, from Its Commencement as a State in 1818 to 1847.* Chicago: S. C. Griggs, 1854.

Fordham, Elias Pym, *Personal Narrative of Travels in Virginia, Maryland, Pennsylvania, Ohio, Indiana, Kentucky; and of a Residence in the Illinois Territory, 1817–1818.* Frederic Austin Ogg, ed. Cleveland: Arthur H. Clark, 1906.

Forman, Samuel S., *Narrative of a Journey Down the Ohio and Mississippi in 1789–90.* Cincinnati: R. Clarke, 1888.

Franke, Judith A., *French Peoria and the Illinois Country, 1673- 1846.* Illinois State Museum, Popular Science Series, Vol. XII. Springfield: Illinois State Museum Society, 1995.

Frazer, Timothy, "Language Variation in the Military Tract," *WIRS,* Spring 1982.

French, A. W., "Men and Manners of the Early Days in Illinois," *Transactions of the Illinois State Historical Society for the Year 1903.* Springfield: Phillips Bros., 1904

Frizell, Robert W., "Reticent Germans: The East Frisians of Illinois," *IHJ,* Autumn 1992.

Gliozzo, Charles A., "John Jones, A Study of a Black Chicagoan," *IHJ,* Autumn 1987.

Graebner, Norman A., "The Illinois Country and the Treaty of Paris of 1783," *IHJ*, Spring 1985.

Grant, H. Roger, "Utopias That Failed: The Antebellum Years," *WIRS*, Spring 1979.

Greeg, T., *History of Hancock County, Illinois.* Chicago: Chas. C. Chapman, 1880.

Greene, Evarts B., "Sectional Forces in the History of Illinois, *Transactions of the Illinois State Historical Society for the Year 1903*: Springfield: Phillips Bros., 1904.

A Guide to the City of Chicago. Chicago: T. E. Zell, 1868.

A Guide to the Illinois Central Railroad Lands. Chicago: Illinois Central Railroad Office, 1859.

Gums, Bonnie L., William R. Iseminger, Molly E. McKenzie, and Dennis D. Nichols, "The French Colonial Villages of Cahokia and Prairie de Pont, Illinois," in John A. Walthall, ed., *French Colonial Archaeology: The Illinois Country and the Western Great Lakes.* Urbana: University of Illinois Press, 1991.

Haeger, John D., "The Abandoned Townsite on the Midwestern Frontier: A Case Study of Rockwell, Illinois," *JER*, Summer 1983.

Haites, Erik F., James Mak, and Gary Walton, *Western River Transportation: The Era of Early Internal Development, 1810–1860*," Baltimore: Johns Hopkins University Press, [1975].

Hall, James, *Notes on the Western States.* Philadelphia: H. Hall, 1838.

Hallwas, John E., "Eliza Farnham's *Life in Prairie Land,*" *TON*, Winter 1981–1982.

———, "Quincy and Meredosia in 1842: Charles Carter Langdon's Travel Letters," *WIRS*, Fall 1979.

Halsey, John J., *A History of Lake County, Illinois.* n.p.: Roy S. Bates, 1912.

Hamilton, Oscar B., ed., *History of Jersey County, Illinois.* Chicago: Munsell, 1919.

Hamlin, Griffith A., *Monticello: The Biography of a College.* Fulton, Missouri: William Woods College, 1976.

Hammes, Raymond H., "Land Transactions in Illinois Prior to the Sale of Public Domain," *JISHS*, Summer 1984.

———, "Squatters in Territorial Illinois," *Illinois Libraries*, May 1977.

Haney, David, "John Scripps: Circuit Rider and Newspaperman," *WIRS*, Fall 1986.

Harlan, Bell, "'In the Early Days,' a Historical Sketch Written by Miss Bell Harlan," in *Early History of Washington, Illinois and Vicinity.* Washington, Illinois: Tazewell County Reporter, n.d.

Haughey, Malcolm E., "Challenge and Response: The Role of Early Frontier Leaders," *American Baptist Quarterly*, September 1984.

Hauser, Raymond E., "The Illinois Indian Tribe: From Autonomy and Self-Sufficiency to Dependency and Depopulation," *JISHS*, May 1976.

——, "The Fox Raid of 1752: Defensive Warfare and the Decline of the Illinois Indian Tribe." *IHJ*, Winter 1993.

——, "Warfare and the Illinois Indian Tribe during the Seventeenth Century: An Exercise in Ethnohistory," *TON*, Winter 1984–1985.

Havighurst, Walter, *Land of Promise: The Story of the Northwest Territory*. New York: Macmillan, 1947.

——, "The Way to Future City," *JISHS*, August 1976.

Hayter, Earl W., "Barbed Wire Fencing—A Prairie Invention: Its Rise and Influence in the Western States," *Agricultural History*, October 1939.

Herget, James E., "Democracy Revisited: The Law and School Districts in Illinois," *JISHS*, May 1979.

Hewes, Leslie, "The Northern Wet Prairie of the United States: Nature, Sources of Information, and Extent," *AAAG*, December 1951.

——, "Some Features of Early Woodland and Prairie Settlement in a Central Iowa County." *AAAG*, March 1950.

The History of Carroll County, Illinois. Chicago: H. F. Kett, 1878.

History of Henderson County. Chicago: H. H. Hill, 1882.

History of Logan County, Illinois. Chicago: Inter-state, 1886.

History of Pike County, Illinois. Chicago: Chas. C. Chapman, 1880.

History of Tazewell County, Illinois. Chicago: Chas. C. Chapman, 1879.

History of Wabash County, Illinois, New and Updated 1976. A Bicentennial Project of the Heritage Committee of the Wabash County Bicentennial Commission, the Wabash County Historical Society, and the Mt. Carmel Public Library. Evansville: Unigraphic, 1977.

History of Will County, Illinois. Chicago: Wm. Le Baron, Jr., 1878.

The History of Winnebago County, Illinois. Chicago: H. F. Kett, 1877.

Horsman, Reginald, "Great Britain and the Illinois Country in the Era of the American Revolution," *JISHS*, May 1976.

——, "Thomas Jefferson and the Ordinance of 1784," *IHJ*, Summer 1986.

Howard, Robert P., *Illinois: A History of the Prairie State*. Grand Rapids, Michigan: William B. Eerdmans, 1972.

Howe, Philip, *The Diary of Philip Hone, 1828–1851*. Allan Nevins, ed. New York: Dodd, Mead, 1927.

Hudson, John C., *Making the Corn Belt: A Geographical History of Middle-Western Agriculture*. Bloomington: Indiana University Press, 1994.

Hyde, Anne F., "Cultural Filters: The Significance of Perception in the History of the American West," *WHQ*, August 1993.

Illinois Annual Register, and Western Business Directory. No. 1— 1847. Chicago: Geer & Wilson, 1847.

The Illinois Land Company. n.p.: State of Illinois, 1855.

Jakle, John A., "Salt on the Ohio Valley Frontier, 1770–1820," *AAAG*, December 1969.

Johnson, Hildegard Binder, "The Location of German Immigrants in the Middle West," *AAAG*, March 1951.

Johnson, Leland R., "The Doyle Mission to Massac, 1794," *JISJS*, Spring 1980.

Jones, A. D., *Illinois and the West.* Boston: Weeks, Jordan, 1838.

Kantowicz, Edward R., "A Fragment of French Canada on the Illinois Prairies," *JISHS*, Winter 1982.

Keene, David, "Fort de Chartres: Archaeology in the Illinois Country," in John Walthall, ed., *French Colonial Archaeology: The Illinois Country and the Western Great Lakes.* Urbana: University of Illinois Press, 1991.

Kellogg, Louise Phelps, ed., *Early Narratives of the Northwest, 1634–1699.* New York: C. Scribner's Sons, 1917.

Kerber, Linda K., "Women and Individualism in American History," *Massachusetts Review*, Winter 1989.

Kindig, Everett, "Journalist Hooper Warren Survives the Illinois Frontier," *IHJ*, Autumn 1986.

Klingaman, David C. and Richard K. Vedder, eds., *Essays on the Economy of the Old Northwest.* Athens: Ohio University Press, 1987.

Kniffen, Fred, "The American Agricultural Fair: Time and Place," *AAAG*, March 1951.

Larson, Albert, and Siim Soot, "Population and Social History," in Ronald E. Nelson, ed., *Illinois: Land and Life in the Prairie State.* Dubuque, Iowa: Kendall-Hunt, 1978.

Latrobe, Charles Joseph. *The Rambler in North America.* New York: Harper & Brothers, 1835.

Lee, Everett S., "A Theory of Migration," *Demography*, 3, 1966.

Leichtle, Kurt E., "The Rise of Jacksonian Politics in Illinois," *IHJ*, Summer 1989.

Leighly, John. "Town Names of Colonial New England in the West," *AAAG*, June 1978.

Limerick, Patricia Nelson, Clyde A. Milner II, and Charles E. Rankin, eds., *Trails: Toward a New Western History.* Lawrence: University of Kansas Press, 1991.

Linsenmeyer, Helen Walker, "Three Generations of River Commerce: The Jenkins Family of Grand Tower," *JISHS*, Spring 1980.

Lloyd, James T., *Lloyd's Steamboats Directory.* Philadelphia: Jas. T. Lloyd, 1856.

Long, Stephen Harriman, *S. H. Long's Expedition.* In Reuben Gold Thwaites, ed., *Early Western Travels, 1748–1846, Vol. 14.* Arthur H. Clark, 1905.

Looney, Rebecca, "Migration and Separation: Divorce in Kane County,
1837–1869," *IHJ*, Summer 1996.
Lopinot, Neal H. and William L. Woods, "Wood Overexploitation and
the Collapse of Cahokia," in *Cahokia Mounds and the American
Bottom*. Southern Illinois University at Edwardsville: National Geo-
graphic Society Committed for Research and Exploration by the
Department of Geography and Office of Contract Archaeology, May
1996.
Lovejoy, David S., "Plain Englishmen at Plymouth," *New England
Quarterly*, June 1990.
Lyford, W. G., *The Western Address Directory*. Baltimore: Jos. Robin-
son, 1837.
McBride, J. C., *Past and Present of Christian County, Illinois*. Chica-
go: S. J. Clarke, 1904.
McCartney, Carol, "The Pike Country Courthouse," *WIRS*, Spring 1991.
McCluggage, Robert W., "The Pioneer Squatter," *IHJ*, Spring 1989.
McCurry, Stephanie, "The Politics of Yeoman Households in South Caro-
lina," in Catherine Clinton and Nina Silber, eds., *Divided Houses:
Gender and the Civil War*. New York: Oxford University Press, 1992.
McDermott, John Francis, "The French Impress on Place Names in the
Mississippi Valley," *JISHS*, August 1979.
McLear, Patrick E., "The Galena and Chicago Union Railroad: A Sym-
bol of Chicago's Economic Maturity," *JISHS*, Spring 1980.
———, "Land Speculators and Urban and Regional Development:
Chicago in the 1830's," *TON*, Summer 1980.
McManis, Douglas R., *The Initial Evaluation and Utilization of the Il-
linois Prairies, 1815–1840*. Chicago: Department of Geography, Uni-
versity of Chicago, 1964.
Magnaghi, Russell M., "Red Slavery in the Great Lakes Country dur-
ing the French and British Regime," *TON*, Summer 1986.
Mahoney, Timothy R. *River Towns in the Great West: The Structure of
Provincial Urbanization in the American Midwest, 1820–1870*. New
York: Cambridge University Press, 1990.
Mann, Ralph, "Frontier Opportunity and the New Social History,"
Pacific Historical Review, November 1984.
Marryat, Frederick, *A Diary in American, with Remarks on Its Institu-
tions*. 3 vols. London: Longman, Orme, Brown, Green & Longmans,
1839.
Marshall, James, "An Unheard Voice: The Autobiography of a Dispos-
sessed Homesteader and a Nineteenth-Century Cultural Theme of
Dispossession," *TON*, Winter 1980–1981.
Mason, Richard Lee, *Narrative of Richard Lee Mason in the Pioneer
West, 1819*. New York: Heartman, 1915.
Meinig, D. W., *The Shaping of America: A Geographical Perspective on*

500 Years of History, Vol. 2. Continental America, 1800–1867. New Haven: Yale University Press, 1993.

Mellen, Grenville, ed., *A Book of the United States.* Hartford [Connecticut]: H. F. Sumner, 1839.

Melvin, Patricia Mooney, "Steamboat West: The Legacy of a Transportation Revolution," *TON*, Winter, 1981–1982.

Meyer, Alfred H., "Circulation and Settlement Patterns of the Calumet Region of Northwest Indiana and Northeast Illinois," *AAAG*, September 1954.

Michaux, André, *Travels into Kentucky, 1793–1796.* In Reuben Gold Thwaites, ed., *Early Western Travels, 1748–1846,* vol. 3. Cleveland: Arthur H. Clark, 1904.

Miller, Donald L., *City of the Century: The Epic of Chicago and the Making of America.* New York: Simon & Schuster, 1996.

Mink, Claudia Gellman, *Cahokia, City of the Sun: Prehistoric Urban Center in the American Bottom.* Collinsville, Illinois: Cahokia Mounds Museum Society, 1992.

Mitchell, S. Augustus, *A General View of the United States.* Philadelphia: S. Augustus Mitchell, 1846.

Morrison, Peter A. and Julie DaVanzo, "The Prism of Migration: Dissimilarities between Return and Onward Movers," *Social Science Quarterly*, September 1986.

Moses, John, *Illinois, Historical and Statistical, Comprising the Essential Facts of Its Planting and Growth as a Province, County, Territory, and State.* Chicago: Fergus Printing, 1895.

Mulkearn, Lois, ed., *A Topographical Description of the Dominions of the United States of America by T. Pownall.* Pittsburgh: University of Pittsburgh Press, 1949.

Muller, Edward K., "Regional Urbanization and Selective Growth of Towns in the North American Regions," *JHG*, January 1977.

———, "Selective Urban Growth in the Middle Ohio Valley, 1800- 1860," *Geographical Review*, April 1976.

Murat, Achille [Napoleon], *The United States of America.* London: Effingham Wilson, 1833.

Murphy, Lucy Eldersveld, "Her Own Boss: Businessmen and Separate Spheres in the Midwest, 1850–1880," *IHJ*, Autumn 1987.

Murray, Charles Augustus, *Travels in North America during the Years 1834, 1835, & 1836, Vol. II.* London: R. Bentley, 1839.

Nabokov, Peter, and Robert Easton, *Native American Architecture.* New York: Oxford University Press, 1989.

Nader, John. "The Rise of an Inventive Profession: Learning Effects in the Midwestern Harvester Industry, 1850–1890," *Journal of Economic History*, June 1994.

Nelson, Ronald E., ed., "The Bishop Hill Colony: What They Found," *WIRS*, Fall 1989.

————, *Illinois: Land and Life in the Prairie State*. Dubuque, Iowa: Kendall-Hunt Pub. Co., 1978.

Neth, Mary. "Gender and the Family Labor System: Defining work in the Rural Midwest," *JSH*, Spring 1994.

Nobles, Gregory H., "Breaking into the Backcountry: New Approaches to the Early American Frontier, 1750–1800," *W&MQ*, October 1989.

————, "Straight Lines and Stability: Mapping the Political Order of the Anglo-American Frontier," *JAH*, June 1993.

Noe, Marcia, "The Heathen Priestess on the Prairie: Margaret Fuller Constructs the Midwest," *TON*, Spring 1992.

Nolan, Patrick B., *Vigilantes on the Middle Border: A Study of the Self-Appointed Law Enforcement in the States of the Upper Mississippi from 1840–1880*. New York: Garland, 1987.

Nortrup, Jack, "The Troubles of an Itinerant Teacher in the Early Nineteenth Century, *JISHS*, November 1978.

Nugent, Walter, "Frontiers and Empires in the Late Nineteenth Century," in Patricia Nelson Limerick, Clyde A. Milner II, and Charles E. Rankin, ed., *Trails: Toward a New Western History*. Lawrence: University of Kansas Press, 1991.

Nuttall, Thomas, *A Journal of Travels into the Arkansa Territory, during the Year 1819, with Occasional Observations on the Manners of the Aborigines*. In Reuben Gold Thwaites, ed., *Early Western Travels, 1748–1846, Vol. 13*. Arthur H. Clark, 1905.

Oakwood, J. H., "Recollections of J. H. Oakwood," in *Proceedings of the Old Settlers Meeting Held at Catlin, Illinois, Saturday, September 20th, 1885*. Danville: Illinois Printing, 1886.

Oberly, James W., *Sixty Million Acres: American Veterans and the Public Lands before the Civil War*. Kent, Ohio: Kent State University Press, 1990.

Ogden, George W., *Letters from the West, Comprising a Tour through the Western States of Ohio and Kentucky*. In Reuben Gold Thwaites, ed., *Early Western Travels, 1748–1846, Vol. 19*. Cleveland: Arthur H. Clark, 1905.

Oliver, William, *Eight Months in Illinois*. Chicago: Walter M. Hill, 1924.

Onuf, Peter S., "Liberty, Development, and Union: Visions of the West in the 1780s," *W&MQ*, April 1986.

————, "Toward Federalism: Virginia, Congress, and the Western Lands," *W&MQ*, July 1977.

Palmer, John, *Journals of Travels in the United States of North America, and in Lower Canada, Performed in the Year 1817*. London: Sherwood, Neely, and Jones, 1818.

Park, Siyoung, "Land Speculation in Western Illinois: Pike County, 1821–1835," *JISHS*, Summer 1984.

————, "Perception of Land Quality and the Settlement of Northern Pike County, 1821–1836," *WIRS*, Spring 1980.

Partridge, Charles A., ed. In Newton Bateman and Paul Selby, eds., *Historical Encyclopedia of Illinois and History of Lake County*. Chicago: Munsell, 1902.

The Past and Present of Boone County, Illinois. Chicago: S. J. Clarke, 1904.

The Past and Present of Warren County, Illinois. Chicago: H. F. Kett, 1877.

The Past and Present of Woodford County, Illinois. Chicago: Wm. Le Baron, Jr., 1878.

Pease, Theodore Calvin, *The Frontier State, 1818–1848. The Centennial History of Illinois, Volume Two*. Springfield: Illinois Centennial Commission, 1918.

————, ed., *The Laws of the Northwest Territory, 1788–1800*. Springfield: Trustees of the Illinois State Historical Library, [1925].

Perrin, William Henry, ed., *History of Bond and Montgomery Counties, Illinois*. Chicago: O. L. Baskin, 1882.

————, *History of Crawford and Clark Counties, Illinois*. Chicago: O. L. Baskin, 1883.

Peyser, Joseph L., trans. and ed., *Jacques Legardeur de Saint-Pierre: Officer, Gentleman, Entrepreneur*. East Lansing: Michigan State University Press, 1996.

————, trans. and ed., *Letters from New France: The Upper Country, 1686–1783*. Urbana and Chicago: University of Illinois Press, 1992.

Pirtle, Carol, "Andrew Borders v. William Hayes: Indentured Servitude and the Underground Railroad in Illinois," *IHJ*, Autumn 1996.

Pittman, Philip, *The Present State of the European Settlements on the Mississippi*. London: J. Nourse, 1770.

Pogorski, Doug, "Study Shows Illinois' Indians Lived a Lot like Settlers in the Early 1800s," *State Journal Register*, Springfield, Illinois, August 17, 1992.

Porter, Laura Smith, "'The Last, Best Hope of Earth': Abraham Lincoln's Perceptions of America, 1834–1854," *IHJ*, Autumn 1985.

Power, John Carroll, *History of the Early Settlers, Sangamon County, Illinois*. Springfield: E. A. Wilson, 1876.

Pratt, Harry Edward, "David Davis, 1815–1886." Thesis, University of Illinois, 1930.

Pred, Allan, *Urban Growth and City-Systems in the United States, 1840–1860*. Cambridge: Harvard University Press, 1980.

Primack, Martin L., "Farm Fencing in the Nineteenth Century," *Journal of Economic History*, June 1969.

Proceedings of the Illinois State Anti-Slavery Convention Held at Upper Alton on the Twenty-Seventh & Twenty-Eighth of Oct. 1837.

Raitz, Karl, ed., *A Guide to the National Road*. Baltimore: Johns Hop-
kins University Press, 1996.
Redd, Jim, *The Illinois and Michigan Canal: A Contemporary Perspective in Essays and Photographs*. Carbondale: Southern Illinois University Press, 1993.
Regan, John, *The Western Wilds of America*, 2d ed. Edinburgh: John Menzies and W. P. Nimmo, 1859.
Reynolds, *The Pioneer History of Illinois*, 2d ed. Chicago: Fergus, 1887.
Rezab, Gordana, "Land Speculation in Fulton County, 1817–1832," *WIRS*, Spring 1980.
———, "The Memoir of William T. Brooking, McDonough County Pioneer, Part 1," *WIRS*, Fall 1981.
Richardson, Adhere Ramsay, "The Virginian Who Made Illinois a Free State," *JISHS*, Spring 1952.
Richmond, Volney P., "The Wood River Massacre," *Transactions of the Illinois State Historical Society for the Year 1901*. Springfield: Phillips Bros., 1901.
Rikoon, J. Sanford, *Threshing in the Midwest, 1820–1940: A Study of Traditional Culture and Technological Change*. Bloomington: Indiana University Press, 1988.
Rohrbough, Malcolm J., *The Land Office Business: The Settlement and Administration of American Public Lands, 1789–1837*. London: Oxford University Press, 1968.
Rugh, Susan S., "Creating a Farm Community: Fountain Green Township, 1825–1840," *WIRS*, Fall 1990.
Safiran, Edward T., "The Louvier Site at Prairie du Rocher," in John A. Walthall, ed., *French Colonial Archaeology*. Urbana: University of Illinois Press, 1991.
Salter, Mary Ann, "Quarreling in the English Settlement: The Flowers in Court," *JISHS*, Summer 1982.
Schob, David, *Hired Hands and Plowboys: Farm Labor in the Midwest, 1815–1860*. Urbana: University of Illinois Press, [1975]
Schoolcraft, Henry R., *Travels in the Central Portions of the Mississippi Valley*. New York: Collins and Hannay, 1825.
Schwartz, Thomas F., "The Springfield Lyceums and Lincoln's 1838 Speech," *IHJ*, Spring 1990.
Seineke, Katherine Wagner, *The George Rogers Clark Adventure in the Illinois and Selected Documents of the American Revolution at the Frontier Posts*. New Orleans: Polyanthos, 1981.
Sell, Ralph R., "Analyzing Migration Decisions: The First Step—Whose Decisions," *Demography*, August 1983.
Shaw, Ronald E., *Erie Water West: A History of the Erie Canal, 1792–1854*. Lexington: University of Kentucky Press, 1966.
Shirreff, Patrick, *A Tour through North America: Together with a*

Comprehensive View of the Canadas and the United States. Edinburgh: Oliver & Boyd, 1835.

Skeen, C. Edward, "The Year without a Summer: A Historical View," *JER*, Spring 1981.

Smith, John W., *History of Macon County, Illinois.*

Spelman, Walter Bishop, *The Town of Cicero: History, Advantages, and Government.* [Cicero, IL: n.p., 1923.]

Steiner, Mark E., ed., "Abolitionists and Escaped Slaves in Jacksonville. Samuel Willard's 'My First Adventure with a Fugitive Slave: The Story of How It Failed,'" *IHJ*, Winter 1996.

Stevens, Edward W., Jr., "Structural and Ideological Dimensions of Literacy and Education in the Old Northwest." In David C. Klingaman and Richard K. Vedder, eds., *Essays on the Economy of the Old Northwest.* Athens: Ohio University Press, 1987.

Stover, John, *History of the Illinois Central Railroad.* New York: Macmillan, 1975.

Stroble, Paul E., Jr., "Ferdinand Ernst and the German Colony at Vandalia," *IHJ*, Summer 1987.

———*High on the Okaw's Western Bank: Vandalia, Illinois, 1819–39.* Urbana: University of Illinois Press, 1992.

Sublett, Michael D., *Paper Counties: The Illinois Experience, 1825–1867.* American Universities Studies, Series XXV. Geography, Vol. 4. New York: P. Lang, 1990.

Sutton, Robert M., "Edward Coles and the Constitutional Crisis in Illinois, 1822–1824," *IHJ*, Spring 1989.

———, "George Morgan, Early Illinois Businessman: A Case of Premature Enterprise," *JISHS*, August 1976.

———, "The Northwest Ordinance: A Bicentennial Souvenir." *IHJ*, Spring 1988.

Sutton, Robert P., "Illinois River Towns: Economic Units or Melting Pots," *WIRS*, Fall 1990.

Swenson, Russell, "Wind Engines in Western Illinois," *WIRS*, Spring 1984.

Talbot, William L., "The Warsaw Boat Yard," *WIRS*, Fall 1984.

Taylor, George Rogers, *The Transportation Revolution, 1815–1860.* New York: Harper & Row, 1951.

Thompson, David G., "Thomas Bentley and the American Revolution in Illinois," *IHJ*, Spring 1990.

Thompson, Robert Luther, *Wiring a Continent: The History of the Telegraph Industry in the United States, 1832–1866.* Princeton: Princeton University Press, 1947.

Thwaites, Reuben Gold, ed., *Early Western Travels, 1748–1846,* 32 vols. Cleveland: Arthur H. Clark, 1904–1907.

——, ed., *The Jesuit Relations and Allied Documents.* Cleveland: Burrows Brothers, 1896–1901.

Tilden, M. H., *The History of Stephenson County.*

Tillson, Christiana Holmes, *A Woman's Story of Pioneer Illinois.* Milo Milton Quaife, ed. Chicago: R. R. Donnelley & Sons, 1919.

Trautmann, Frederic, trans. and ed., "Eight Weeks on a St. Clair Farm in 1851: Letters by a Young German," *JISHS*, Autumn 1982.

Tweet, Roald D., "Taming the Rapids of the Upper Mississippi," *WIRS*, Fall 1984.

Usner, Daniel H., Jr., "The Frontier Exchange Economy of the Lower Mississippi Valley in the Eighteenth Century," *W&MQ*, April 1987.

Vedder, Richard K. and Lowell E. Gallaway, "Migration and the Old Northwest." In David C. Klingaman and Richard K. Vedder, eds., *Essays on the Economy of the Old Northwest.* Athens: Ohio University Press, 1987.

Vogel, Virgil J., "Indian-White Intermarriage on the Frontier: The Role of Mixed-Bloods in Indian-White Relations," *Transactions: Selected Papers from the Seventh Annual History Symposium and the Eighth Annual Illinois History Symposium*, 1986–1987.

Walker, Juliet E. K., "Entrepreneurial Ventures in the Origin of Nineteenth-Century Agricultural Towns: Pike County, 1823–1880," *IHJ*, Spring 1985.

——, *Free Frank: A Black Pioneer on the Antebellum Frontier.* Lexington: University of Kentucky Press, 1983.

——, "Legal Processes and Judicial Challenges: Black Land Ownership in Western Illinois," *WIRS*, Fall 1983.

Wall, John A., *Wall's History of Jefferson County, Illinois.* Indianapolis: B. F. Bowen, 1909.

Wallace, Anthony F. C., "Introduction." In Ellen M. Whitney, comp. and ed., *The Black Hawk War, Vol. 1, Illinois Volunteers.* Springfield: Illinois State Historical Library, 1970.

Walsh, Margaret, "The Spatial Evolution of the Mid-western Pork Industry, 1835–75," *JHG*, January 1978.

Walters, William, Jr., "Early Western Illinois Town Advertisements: A Geographical Inquiry," *WIRS*, Spring 1985.

——, "The Fanciful Geography of 1836," *TON*, Winter 1983–1984.

Walthall, John A., "Aboriginal Pottery and the Eighteenth-Century Illini." In John A. Walthall and Thomas E. Emerson, eds., *Calumet Fleur-de-Lys: Archaeology of Indian and French Contact in the Midcontinent.* Washington, D.C.: Smithsonian Institution Press, 1992.

——, and Thomas E. Emerson, eds., *Calumet Fleur-de-Lys: Archae-*

ology of Indian and French Contact in the Midcontinent. Washington, D.C.: Smithsonian Institution Press, 1992.

———, *French Colonial Archaeology: The Illinois Country and the Western Great Lakes.* Urbana: University of Illinois Press, 1991.

Waters, John J., "Family, Inheritance, and Migration in Colonial New England; the Evidence from Guilford, Connecticut," *W&MQ*, January 1982.

Watson, Jeanne Hamilton, ed., *To the Land of God and Wickedness: The 1848–59 Diary of Lorena L. Hays.* St. Louis: Patrice Press, 1988.

White, Richard, *The Middle Ground: Indians, Empires, and Republics in the Great Lakes Region, 1650–1815.* Cambridge: Cambridge University Press, 1991.

White, William A., "Tradition and Urban Development: A Contrast of Chicago and Toronto in the Nineteenth Century," *TON*, Fall 1982.

Whitney, Ellen M., comp. and ed., *The Black Hawk War, Vol. 1, Illinois Volunteers.* Springfield: Illinois State Historical Library, 1970.

———, "Indian History and the Indians of Illinois," *JISHS*, May 1976.

Wilson, Terry, "The Business of a Midwestern Trial Court: Knox County, Illinois, 1841–1850," *IHJ*, Winter 1991.

Winsor, Roger A., "Environmental imagery of the wet prairie of east central Illinois, 1820–1920," *JHG*, October 1987.

Wolner, Edward W., "The City Builder in Chicago: 1834–1871," *TON*, Spring 1987.

Wood, Thomas J., "'Blood in the Moon': The War for the Seat of Edwards County, 1821–1824," *IHJ*, Autumn 1992.

Wyman, Mark, *Immigrants in the Valley: Irish, Germans, and Americans in the Upper Mississippi Country, 1830–1860.* Chicago: Nelson-Hall, 1984.

Zanger, Martin, "Conflicting Concepts of Justice: A Winnebago Murder Trial on the Illinois Frontier," *JISHS*, Winter 1980.

Zelinsky, Wilbur, "Classical Town Names in the United States: The Historical Geography of an American Idea," *Geographical Review*, October 1967.

Index

Note: Many places, individuals, and events mentioned only once have been omitted.

first to reach the Mississippi, 371; Chicago and Aurora line, 364; Chicago & Burlington, impact on Warren Co., 369; Chicago, Burlington & Quincy, 370, 378; Chicago and Milwaukee, 370; Chicago and Rock Island, 371, 377; Galena & Chicago Union RR., 240, 269, 364, 380; Hannibal and St. Joseph RR., impact on Chicago and St. Louis, 371; Illinois Central, 363, 366, 368, 371, 375, 377, 381, 392; Michigan Central, 371; Mississippi and Chicago, 368; New York and Erie, 240; Northern Cross, 230, 231, 232, 239, 269, 364; Ohio and Wabash, 382; Sangamon and Moran, 364; Terre Haute & Alton, 376, 381
Randolph Co., 104, 115, 116, 117, 140, 163, 171, 304, 362, 395
Randolph Co. Agricultural Society, 395–96
Rangers (War of 1812), 135–36
Reagan family: killed, 150
Red Bird: Chief in "Winnebago War," 193
Referendum: by proslavery forces (1824), 167–68, 268, 296
Regan, John, 276, 177, 394
Regulators, activities, 177, 287, 336, 422–23
Religion, 4, 25, 28, 31–32, 33, 34, 40–44, 47, 49, 54, 59, 60, 63, 64, 78, 79, 80, 98, 100–1, 111, 112, 159, 176, 179, 183, 185, 187, 191, 192, 196, 242–43, 249, 258–60, 262–67, 293, 300–2, 303, 304, 307–8, 311, 318; see also specific denominations
Republicanism, 7, 49–50, 70, 75, 78, 80, 91–92, 95, 96, 97, 106, 107, 139–40, 164, 167, 181–82, 183, 258, 259, 324, 329, 332, 333, 334, 412
Reynolds, John, 147, 155, 194, 229
Richard, a slave with great latitude, 292, 293, 294
Richland Co., 278; agricultural society, 395
Richland Co. Agricultural Society, 395
Roads, 17, 18, 76, 105, 108, 169, 174, 201, 220, 221, 230, 358, 360–62, 365–66, 377, 379, 393
Robbins, Eleanor, 179; opinion of Southerners, 314
Roberts, Amelia: sees men do "women's" work, 106
Rock Island, 86; fighting at in War of 1812; 149 Fort Armstrong erected, 156
Rock Island Co., 234, 326
Rock River, 14, 75, 222, 231, 305
Rock Run (Will Co.): railroad accident, 377
Rockford, 162, 193, 221, 241, 256, 326, 243, 364, 373, 397, 416, 421

Rockwell, John A.: founds town, 260–61
Rockwell (La Salle Co.), 260–61, 263
Rockwell Land Co., 260
Roman Catholics, 20, 26, 27, 28, 29, 30, 31, 32–34, 36, 37, 38, 40–41, 45, 47, 49, 54, 59, 60, 64, 78, 79, 80, 98, 100–1, 112, 183, 185–86, 248, 251–52, 260, 262, 264–67, 301, 302, 311, 421
Rouensa, Marie: Indian woman who attains status in French society, 30
Rushville, 179, 335; Masonic lodge, 416
Russell, Colonel William, 135
Rutherford, Larkin, 82

St. Clair, Gov. Arthur, 99, 101, 102, 103, 104, 110, 115, 145
St. Clair Co., 82, 101, 103, 112, 115, 116, 117, 140, 163, 191, 264, 298, 362
St. Clair Society for the Prevention of Slavery (1823), 298
St. Cyr, Father Irenaeus Mary, 265
Ste. Genevieve (Mo.), 50, 53, 59, 61, 69, 85; women "decided," 50
St. Joseph (Mich.), 52, 86, 221
St. Louis, Mo., 59, 62, 71, 85, 86, 119, 125, 130, 148 149, 156, 168, 213, 220–21, 238, 245, 265, 270, 313, 324, 345, 347, 359, 365, 371, 375, 378
St. Philippe, 48, 54, 111
Saline Co., 321; founded late (1847), 411
Sangamon Co., 167, 257, 263, 337, 424; divorces, 419; lyceums, 243; phalanxes, 409
Sangamon Co. Lyceum, 243
Sangamon River, 14, 147, 175
Sauk Indians, 26, 28, 86, 135, 149, 193, 198
Saunders, John: guides Clark's forces, 70
Savanna, 325, 326, 362
Scherer, Rev. Daniel, 307, 308
Scholl, Abraham, antislavery Southerner, 294
Scott, Gen. Winfield, 203
Scully, William: debilitating tenant system (1850s), 406, 407
Schuyler Co., 217, 225, 335, 339, 341, 403, 407; population peaks, 402
Second Party System, 201, 227–29, 232–33, 252, 279, 295, 301, 302, 424
Semple, James: runs prairie steam-car, 361
Settlement on the "edge"; see "Edge" settlement
Shawnee Indians, 26, 50, 57
Shawneetown, 119, 142, 148, 165, 166, 171, 173, 174, 205, 231, 332
Shelbyville, 231
Sherman, Samary S., 373, 374, 398, 403
Ships and boats: *Black Hawk*, 204; *Choctaw*, 204; *Griffon*, first ship of sail on

JAMES E. DAVIS

is William and Charlotte Gardner Professor of History and Professor of Geography at Illinois College. He is the author of *Frontier America, 1800–1840: A Comparative Demographic Analysis of the Settlement Process* (1977), *Dreams to Dust* (1989), and a number of articles, monographs, edited works, and reviews. Professor Davis is recipient of the Harry J. Dunbaugh Distinguished Professor Award for outstanding teaching (1981 and 1993) and was an NEH Fellow in St. Petersburg and Moscow, where he studied Russian architecture and art. He currently serves as a member of the Board of Directors of the Illinois State Historical Society and as a member of the Editorial Advisory Board of the *Journal of Illinois History.*